MEADE

CIVIL WAR SOLDIERS AND STRATEGIES
Brian S. Wills, Series Editor

MEADE

The Price of Command,

1863–1865

JOHN G. SELBY

The Kent State University Press

Kent, Ohio

© 2018 by The Kent State University Press, Kent, Ohio 44242
All rights reserved
First paperback edition, 2024

Library of Congress Catalog Number 2018008752
ISBN 978-1-60635-475-9 (paper)
ISBN 978-1-60635-348-6 (cloth)
Manufactured in the United States of America

Library of Congress Cataloging-in-Publication Data
Names: Selby, John Gregory, 1955-
Title: Meade : the price of command, 1863-1865 / John G. Selby.
Description: Kent, Ohio : The Kent State University Press, 2018. | Series: Civil war soldiers
        and strategies | Includes bibliographical references and index.
Identifiers: LCCN 2018008752 | ISBN 9781606353486 (hardcover : alk. paper)
Subjects: LCSH: Meade, George Gordon, 1815-1872. | Generals--United States--Biography.
        | United States. Army--Biography. | United States--History--Civil War,
        1861-1865--Campaigns.
Classification: LCC E467.1.M38 S45 2018 | DDC 355.0092 [B] --dc23
LC record available at https://lccn.loc.gov/2018008752

28 27 26 25 24   5 4 3 2

To Hampton Newsome—friend, collaborator, and a true scholar

Contents

Acknowledgments

Much help has been received in this six-year journey to understand the leadership of George G. Meade. Librarians and archivists at the following institutions greatly facilitated my primary source materials research: the Historical Society of Pennsylvania, the New York State Library Manuscripts and Special Collections, the Library of Congress, the National Archives, the Heritage Center of the Union League of Philadelphia, the U. S. Army Military History Institute, and the Gettysburg National Military Park Archival Collection. The interlibrary loan coordinator at Roanoke College, Jeffrey Martin, promptly and efficiently procured dozens of books for me, often on short demand. The department secretary, Karen Harris, helped me with Word and Dropbox at some crucial moments in the creation of this book. Departmental student assistants Emma Clemente, Sydney Brennert, Mady Palmer, and Taylor Thompson helped with typing and cataloguing at various stages of the project. Special thanks goes out to former student assistant John Stang, who copied hundreds of pages from the Meade collection on microfilm and prepared extensive lists of the letters found in those pages; and to another former student departmental assistant, Kassie Wines, who took a brief "postgraduation" post as a chief typist for me for two drafts.

Colleagues and friends provided support and encouragement throughout the process. Holding the John R. Turbyfill Chair in History at Roanoke College for six years gave me considerable time and some financial support to work on the project. The college dean, Richard Smith, has shown interest in the work from the day I first described it to him. My colleagues in the History Department have provided steady encouragement over the years, and my former department chair, Mark Miller, has been a champion of the "Meade manuscript" from start to finish. About halfway through my work I discovered the George G. Meade Society of Pennsylvania, and the enthusiasm of the society's chair, Dr. Andy Waskie, has lifted me every time I felt like the project would never be finished. I especially thank Andy for squiring me around the historic Union League of Philadelphia. My long-time friend John Bierlein has never ceased asking how the work was going, and my former student Andy Blair has been a cheerleader for the project from the day it began.

Special thanks goes out to several people. Laura Dewey took on the daunting job of preparing an index for this long manuscript, and did an outstanding job. The well-known Civil War cartographer, Dr. Bradley Gottfried, took time out from his own busy research schedule to prepare thirteen maps for me; I only wish we could have doubled that number. The team at Kent State University Press shepherded this manuscript into a book: Mary Young, managing editor; Chris Brooks, design and production; and Susan Cash, marketing. Will Underwood, acquisitions editor, has been a steadying influence throughout the long process. Laura Dewey, copy editor, brought consistency, clarity, and prose variety to a lengthy manuscript. The two readers for the press offered numerous recommendations that improved the work; any shortcomings are now solely my responsibility. My good friend and fellow collaborator on an earlier work of Civil War history, Hampton Newsome, read every word of a sprawling draft of this book and made many suggestions for strengthening the book.

Family members bolstered me throughout the long period of reading and writing. Cousins, siblings, and in-laws asked what I was working on, and my family—Deb, Meg, and Jack—patiently bore with my long hours in the office cranking away on the manuscript. They even tolerated some "vacations" to places like Philadelphia and Albany so I could dig into archival materials while they toured the cities. Though they heard more about the Civil War and George G. Meade than they ever wanted, I hope that they see in this book the story of a professional struggling to do the best he could under his circumstances.

Introduction

George Gordon Meade has not been treated kindly by history. Victor of the Battle of Gettysburg, longest-serving commander of the Army of the Potomac, and the fourth highest-ranked general at the end of the Civil War, Meade is largely known today for his crucial role at Gettysburg. After that battle his eight-month stint as commander of the largest army in the Civil War is glossed over as the war narrative speeds to the appointment of Ulysses S. Grant as general-in-chief in March 1864. From that moment until the end of the war, Meade is sometimes mentioned as the commander of the Army of the Potomac, but convenient shorthand usually summarizes the fighting in the East for the last thirteen months of the war as Grant versus Lee.

Meade has always had his defenders, though their names and influence pale compared to that of his critics. His nephew, Richard Bache, wrote a long and flattering biography of him published in 1897. Isaac R. Pennypacker added support for Meade in the short biography of him written for the Great Commanders series. The strongest contemporary case made for Meade came from the labor of love produced by his son, George Meade, and brought to publication by his grandson, George Gordon Meade. The two-volume *Life and Letters of George Meade* is the standard primary source on Meade, encompassing hundreds of private letters, official documents, newspaper articles, maps, and a narrative of his life and accomplishments. Given its authorship, and the knowledge that the private letters were edited by both Meades, the source has always been used cautiously. The last important source from a contemporary was the publication of some of the letters his aide and friend, Theodore Lyman, sent home while on Meade's staff from 1863 to 1865. Lyman was a first-rate writer with unusual powers of observation and expression, and his letters home—although not in their original form due to thorough editing—have been a useful source frequently consulted by students of the last two years of the war in the East.[1]

Meade has found a few new defenders in the modern era of Civil War scholar-
ship. Edward Coddington began the reappraisal with an essay on Meade's reputation published in *The Historian* in 1962 and continued his balanced assessment of
Meade in his now classic *The Gettysburg Campaign: A Study in Command.* Meade's
most ardent champion in the 1960s was the amateur historian Freeman Cleaves,
who wrote a laudatory biography entitled *Meade of Gettysburg.* Archer Jones aided
in the rehabilitation of Meade's military reputation in his award-winning book,
Civil War Command and Strategy. More recently, Richard A. Sauers has written
two books and an article dealing with Meade, striving to land somewhere between
the unremitting hostility of his critics and the glossy sheen of his admirers. Ethan
Rafuse analyzes the factors that restricted Meade's decisions in *George Gordon
Meade and the War in the East,* and in an essay on the Grant-Meade relationship
in *Grant's Lieutenants: From Chattanooga to Appomattox.* Christopher Stowe has
written extensively on Meade's prewar life in his 2005 dissertation, and he produced three essays that examine Meade's fight to preserve his military reputation
after the Battle of Gettysburg, his performance as a corps commander, and the
gendered restraints in his life that limn the "boundaries of nineteenth century
military masculinity." Herman Hattaway boosts Meade in the American National
Biography series, writing that Meade's "reputation has not achieved the high level
it deserves." Lastly, Tom Huntington's wry, boisterous biography-within-a-travel-
journal, *Searching for George Gordon Meade,* strives to remake the reputation of
Meade and offers a compelling new way to approach biography.[2]

Whether these recent books or a smattering of favorable reviews of Meade's
leadership buried in campaign monographs can refashion an interpretation of
Meade forged over 150 years ago remains to be seen. The goal of this study is to reassess Meade's leadership through a close analysis of his two years as commander
of the Army of the Potomac. Given this focus, the first chapter is a brief account of
Meade's life and work up until he assumed command of the Army of the Potomac
on June 28, 1863. The last chapter is even shorter, as it covers Meade's postwar
career (1865–72). As overviews, they rely heavily on secondary sources. The ten
chapters devoted to his tenure as commander of the Army of the Potomac are
largely based on official documents, contemporary letters and journals, and, to a
limited extent, memoirs. One of the major problems in studying Meade's generalship is getting past the 150 years of interpretation, whose foundations were laid
during the war. Historians have relied on a number of colorfully written memoirs
to reinforce views that Meade was a thin-skinned leader of limited imagination,
nerve, and drive.[3] Such a general needed the determination and vision of Grant,
and the reckless aggressiveness of Sheridan, to defeat Lee.

What this study will show is that this well-established view of Meade is wrong.
Operating under political and strategic constraints from June 1863 to March 1864,
Meade was hobbled by restricted options in his efforts to fight and defeat Lee. His

"team" of corps commanders worked together pretty well at Gettysburg (except for Daniel Sickles) but would never work as harmoniously again. The appointment of Grant as commander-in-chief helped Meade because he and Grant shared a similar vision of the strategy for defeating Lee; where they differed was on the tactics that should be used. Grant had the unyielding support of President Lincoln and Secretary of War Edwin Stanton that former commander-in-chief Henry Halleck lacked, plus vital political support from some members of Congress and most of the public (when his armies were winning). That support allowed Grant to pursue Lee in a manner Meade had wanted but not been permitted to try. At the same time, Meade had one of the most unenviable positions in American military history: command of a large army when his immediate superior was always nearby. Grant would swing from hands-off to hands-on without any warning, and over time it became easier for a good soldier like Meade to simply run all major decisions by Grant, rather than argue or act independently. Their relationship evolved slowly, though, and throughout their time together Meade and Grant shared more operational and tactical decision making than is generally known. Consequently, a close examination of official correspondence, sometimes tracked down to the minute, is needed to produce a fuller picture of Meade's leadership.

Underlying the examination of Meade's leadership will be a central question: what price did Meade pay to command the Army of the Potomac for two years? He wanted the job in 1863, though he had doubts about his capacity to effectively manage such a large army. Once he had it, he mainly wanted to keep it, except when he felt he had been snubbed or neglected, and then he offered to resign. What mattered most to Meade was not whether he held the position but how his performance affected his military reputation. Though it is not known if Meade ever read Professor Francis Lieber's published commencement address at Miami University entitled *The Character of the Gentleman,* he would have agreed with Lieber's definition of the term: a person "distinguished by strict honor, self-possession, forbearance . . . essential truthfulness, courage, both moral and physical, self-respect, a studious avoidance of giving offense to others . . . and loftiness of conduct to the rigid dictates of morality." Meade regarded himself as a gentleman and expected to be treated with the respect due to a gentleman. As historian Lorien Foote argues, honor served as a foundation of identity for nineteenth-century males in the North. She writes, "Honor, simply put, is when a man's self-worth is based on public reputation and the respect of others." Time and again in Meade's correspondence to his wife and others he refers to his honor and reputation. As his close friend and confidant John Cortlandt Parker wrote of Meade many years after his death, "No man loved appreciation more; no man longed for it more ardently; no man, in his heart, more demanded it as a right; no man more carefully forbore to complain where he found himself comparatively forgotten. He was one of those who make the mistake of believing that fame, promotion, and fortune followed desert."[4] As criticism of him intensified after Gettysburg and then waxed and waned over the next two years, Meade did not develop a thicker hide or a dense network of political and social allies. Instead, he grew more defensive, angry, and isolated. Before he took command, he had few enemies in the army, the government, or the press; by the end of the war, he had accumulated a small legion of enemies.

Meade's story as commander of the Army of the Potomac does not rise to the level of Greek tragedy, nor is it as facile as invoking the Peter Principle to describe his performance. Meade could handle the logistics and personalities of a high command in a large army; Meade could fight a sound defensive battle and conduct offensive operations as well. But he never learned how to maneuver politically as well as militarily—nor did he want to. Instead, he expected his "just deserts" for his leadership, and he often failed to hear or receive them. He had his share of faults as a leader, which will be discussed in the chapters on his command of the Army of the Potomac. Furthermore, in some battles on the Overland Campaign and the Petersburg siege, he had more authority than usually noted, which makes him more responsible for the successes and failures of those battles. As a general he was much more than the "victor of Gettysburg." He commanded the largest Union army that fought the best Confederate army for two long years. That story deserves a full and fair analysis. In telling that story, however, one will see the enormous price that Meade paid for his two years of command.

From Cadiz to Gettysburg

Meade's Life and Career up to the Battle of Gettysburg

George Gordon Meade's life began under a financial cloud. His father, Richard, a native of Philadelphia, had moved to Spain in 1806 to better manage his family's growing mercantile business. He served as the United States naval agent to Spain during its long struggle against the forces of Napoleon, and he prospered as a merchant while keeping the Loyalists alive. Richard also acquired enormous debt, and, following Napoleon's defeat in 1815, he petitioned the government of Spain for $800,000 in compensation. The petition quickly made him enemies in the government, and he was imprisoned twice in the following three years. During this dangerous and uncertain time for the family, George was born in Cadiz on December 31, 1815. Two years later, he left Spain for America with his mother, never to return.[1]

Richard Meade's claim consumed him for the next decade. He stayed in Spain until 1820, relentlessly pushing his claim. Unsuccessful, he returned to the United States to begin his quest against a new government—his own. Under the terms of the recently signed Florida Treaty (1819), the United States assumed claims against Spain by American citizens up to a total of $5 million (in return for Florida and a new boundary line with the United States). The Spanish government whittled Meade's claim down to $375,000, and he pressed for that amount for eight years. When the United States Claims Commission denied his claim because of lack of original contracts from Spanish authorities, he appealed to Henry Clay, the secretary of state, and other friends in Washington. No effort proved successful, despite his constant presence in Washington (his family joined him there in 1825) and his persistent badgering of some individuals, including the president, John Quincy Adams. All he managed to do was work himself to an early death and imperil his family's precarious finances.[2]

As a widow struggling to raise eleven children, Margaret Meade stayed in Washington for a few years after her husband's death to continue to fight for the family claim. Four of her daughters married in the 1820s, and her oldest son, Richard Worsam, entered the Navy in 1826. But she had more children at home to raise and educate, so young George attended several schools in the following order: a day school in Philadelphia, a boarding school near Philadelphia, a private school in Washington headed by the young Ohio lawyer Salmon P. Chase, and then another boarding school, the Mount Hope Institution of Baltimore. George excelled at his studies and told adults he was interested in law. But with limited funds, that choice would not be his. His mother had him apply to the United States Military Academy in 1830—at the age of fourteen. He was not appointed, but he reapplied and earned appointment in 1831 (to enter that fall with the class of 1835).[3]

Meade did not distinguish himself at West Point. Homesick, lonely, and buffeted by bouts of illness, Meade accumulated demerits year after year for minor mistakes, usually concerning his dress. Despite his great intellectual promise, especially in math, he settled into the top third of his class in most of his subjects and stayed there for his entire four years. He may have found the subject matter easy and boring, and after his first two years, his desire to do his required one year of service and then resign for "civil pursuits" only seemed to "grow in strength." A classmate of Meade's, Herman Haupt, later characterized young Meade as "dignified, courteous and gentlemanly, though lacking personal magnetism." Regardless of illness or temperament, Meade graduated on time in 1835, ranked nineteenth in a class of fifty-six. His most notable classmates included Haupt, Montgomery Blair (future politician in Maryland), and Marsena Patrick, his provost general during his tenure as commander of the Army of the Potomac.[4]

Lacking the grades required to be assigned to the elite Corps of Engineers, Meade soon acted on his earlier desire to enter into "civil pursuits." After putting in his requisite year of service in Florida (chasing Seminoles) and the Ordnance Department in Watertown, Massachusetts, he resigned from the Army in 1836 (as a 2nd lieutenant). Over the next six years he held a variety of jobs, usually as a surveyor for railroads or of boundaries between nations. The pay exceeded his Army salary, but the contracts were always terminal. He also married well during this period. He met Margaretta Sergeant (called Margaret by her family), one of the charming daughters of the prominent Philadelphia lawyer and Whig politician John Sergeant, and they held a beautiful wedding amidst a major snowstorm on Meade's birthday, December 31, 1840. The next year, Margaret's sister Sarah married a young Whig congressman from Virginia, Henry Wise, thus entwining the fates of those two families for generations. In 1841 the Meades celebrated the birth of their first child, John Sergeant (nicknamed "Sergie" by the family).[5]

When Congress decided to save money by using its own Corps of Topographical Engineers to do surveys instead of contracting with civilians, Meade chose to rejoin the United States Army. With the help of his new brother-in-law, Henry Wise, Meade not only obtained his reappointment to the Army but also found a position in the Corps of Topographical Engineers as a 2nd lieutenant.[6] For the next three years, he supervised the construction of lighthouses on Delaware Bay. Though Meade complained throughout the Civil War that he lacked political influence, it was his family's political connections that had aided his appointment to West Point, procured his first jobs, and allowed him to rejoin the Army in 1842. How much his connections helped him during the war will be examined later.

Meade's brief yet enjoyable sojourn as a lighthouse surveyor and builder came to an abrupt end when he suddenly received orders to report to Gen. Zachary Taylor at Aransas Bay, Texas, in August 1845.[7] It was the beginning of his formative Mexican War experience.

Meade's time on the "Mexican front" fell into three phases. The first phase, September 1845 to March 1846, was a time of waiting and preparation for war. The second phase, active fighting, began in April 1846, after Taylor had marched his small army into the disputed region of Texas between the Nueces and Rio Grande Rivers. When the Mexican Army attacked and killed some American cavalrymen, Taylor and his army girded for combat. In two sharp battles in May at Palo Alto and Resaca de la Palma, Meade ably served as a courier for Taylor, often coming under fire. This service was a prelude to a more critical role for Lieutenant Meade when Taylor's army assaulted the well-guarded city of Monterrey. Meade was a lead scout for Gen. William Jenkins Worth's division, and several times he led attacking columns up treacherous mountain paths—once even in the dark. The result was attack and victory, and a brevet promotion the next year for his service at Monterrey.[8]

The third phase, limited staff work, under Gen. Winfield Scott, lasted only a brief time, from January to March 1847. Consequently, he missed participating in Taylor's greatest victory at Buena Vista in February 1847. He also had little to do with the successful capture of Vera Cruz in March 1847 because of the surfeit of engineers on Scott's staff. That same month, he was ordered back to Washington, his short stint in the Mexican War officially over.[9]

War service firmly established Meade as a military professional. He also developed some strong views on several subjects that would undergird his years of command in the Civil War. Meade felt satisfied he had properly answered the basic question every soldier asks: can I handle combat? Although he had "no stomach" for war, he felt he had done his "duty" well. He also believed many of the soldiers had performed admirably, though initially he had grave reservations about the volunteers, who were "perfectly ignorant of discipline, and most restive under restraint." After six months of watching and commanding them, Meade had a more tempered view. He wrote to his wife, "The volunteers have in this war, on the whole, behaved better than I believed they would." Still, lack of discipline always led to problems, and the key was leadership: they needed regular officers

and sergeants to command them. Of course, simply being a regular officer did
not make a man a good officer, and he criticized his much-admired senior commander, Zachary Taylor, for the "entire and utter ignorance of the use to which
the staff department can be put." For Meade, matters of supply, logistics, and topography were as essential to command as courage and executive decision making. But Meade saved his sharpest criticisms for those officers who curried favor
with the press and politicians in general. Some had sent embellished accounts of
their actions or the actions of fellow officers to newspapers. Meade wrote in the
strongest terms, "If there is anything I do dislike, it is newspaper notoriety. I think
it is the curse of our country, and fear it is seriously injuring our little army." As for
politicians, Meade fully shared the viewpoint of most West Point graduates described by historian Ethan Rafuse: politicians were "meddlesome figures, wholly
ignorant of military affairs." Meade wrote of the government's decision to take
much of Taylor's victorious army from him to staff the invasion of Tampico, "It is
well understood how this is done, by the mighty engine of political influence, that
curse of our country, which forces party politics into everything."[10]

Despite his condemnation of the "politicization" of war, Meade was not above
using political influence when needed, as he did when asking his father-in-law to
put in a good word for his brevet. He thanked him for his help and undoubtedly
felt genuine joy when a group of fellow citizens of Philadelphia presented him
with a ceremonial sword for his steady service in the war. Meade had worried
about his next assignment when recalled to Washington, but he was simply ordered to report to Maj. Hartman Bache for assistance in constructing the Brandywine Lighthouse in Delaware Bay.[11] By age thirty-two, 1st Lt. George Gordon
Meade had earned respect for his peacetime and military service, gained financial
security for his growing family, and reinstated the honor of the family name again
after the long travails of his father.

With his reassignment to Bache, Meade entered one of the busiest periods of
his antebellum military career. Over the next nine years, he surveyed for, built,
or supervised construction of lighthouses in Delaware, New Jersey, and Florida,
including Sand Key in Florida and Cross Ledge in the Delaware Bay. Promotions
came steadily in this period: to first lieutenant in 1851 and to captain in 1856. From
1854 to 1856, he supervised the Fourth (New Jersey and Delaware) and Seventh
(Florida) Lighthouse Districts. He even invented a special lamp for the lighthouse
at Sand Key. During these same years, four more children were born to George
and Margaret Meade, and in 1856 Meade made the acquaintance of a young scientist fresh from the Lawrence Scientific School at Harvard, Theodore Lyman.
Meade provided assistance for Lyman's specimen-collecting crew, and the two
men struck up a friendship.[12]

Later in 1856, Meade received a new assignment: assistant to the officer in
charge of the survey of the Great Lakes. The survey was a labor-intensive, long-

operating project, begun in 1841 and not concluded until 1881. Meade became head of the operation in 1857, and in four years he and his growing crew surveyed the entire shores of Lake Huron and Saginaw Bay, and began examining the eastern coast of Lake Michigan and even a few harbors in Lake Superior. Meade improved upon the method of determining longitude and showed "that comprehensive mental grasp of the country which makes the born surveyor, to perfect which practice alone is needed, and without which no amount of practice is of any avail." Meade moved his family to the burgeoning city of Detroit, and everyone seemed to enjoy the bustle of the largest city in Michigan.[13]

As removed as the family was from the daily ferment of the East Coast, no one could avoid the coming political storm. As a strong believer in the Union, Meade could not tolerate the extreme elements in the Republican and Democratic parties, and in the election of 1860 he cast his vote for the Constitutional Union ticket led by John Bell (with no fanfare—officers often kept their votes private at the time). His vote made little difference, as Lincoln and the Republican Party swept to victory in Michigan and other Northern states. When Southern states began seceding that winter, Meade strongly opposed it and fully intended to do his soldierly duty to uphold the Constitution of the United States.[14]

It would prove hard for anyone to quietly stand by in those tense days, and after the firing on Fort Sumter, a large public gathering in Detroit demanded that "all civilian officials and military officers with their uniformed commands" publicly renew their vows of allegiance on April 20. Meade believed that army officers should take a public oath of allegiance only if ordered by the War Department, not by local officials or a crowd. All but one of his subordinates agreed with him, and when the meeting occurred, his absence was duly noted. When Sen. Zachariah Chandler (a Republican—considered radical) learned of Meade's stand, he was furious—and would have opportunity to punish Meade for his stance later in his career. For the time being, the tempest passed and seemed not to faze Gov. Austin Blair, who offered Meade a colonelcy in a Michigan volunteer infantry regiment.[15]

Meade did not immediately accept the offer. Instead he asked his wife to return to Philadelphia to press his case for a higher appointment. Family friend William Morris Meredith, the attorney general of Pennsylvania, lobbied Sen. David Wilmot, among others. In June Meade went to Washington to talk directly to Secretary of War Simon Cameron (another Pennsylvanian). Cameron promised him that a positive action would be taken, but when not done instantly, a dejected Meade returned to Detroit to mull over Governor Blair's offer. He seriously contemplated resigning to take the colonel's position, when welcome news reached him on the banks of Lake Superior in August: he had been appointed brigadier general of volunteers, to be assigned to command the Second Brigade of the newly raised Pennsylvania Reserves, a division under the command of Brig. Gen. George A. McCall. On August 31, 1861, George G. Meade's Civil War career officially began.[16]

In his first command, Meade insisted on discipline and drill, much to the disgust of his "citizen-soldiers." He enjoyed sharing his experiences with Brig. Gen. John F. Reynolds of the First Brigade (West Point class of 1841, an old friend and fellow Pennsylvanian) and Brig. Gen. Edward O. C. Ord (West Point class of 1839) of the Third Brigade. Together, they chafed under the lackluster leadership of McCall (West Point class of 1822) and itched for action. Except for a small fight by Ord's brigade at Dranesville, Virginia, in December 1861, the winter passed uneventfully. When the Army of the Potomac was organized into four corps in March 1862, the Pennsylvania Reserves were assigned to the First Corps, led by Brig. Gen. Irvin McDowell of Bull Run notoriety. Meade's position was unchanged by this reorganization.[17]

McDowell's corps was left behind to protect Washington (from Maj. Gen. Thomas Jackson operating in the Shenandoah Valley) when Maj. Gen. George McClellan began moving the bulk of the Army of the Potomac to Yorktown by boats in late March of 1862. Chafing under this restriction, Meade and his fellow generals felt they had missed the key campaign of the war, until the Pennsylvania Reserves were released from duty in Washington and sent (through attachment to Brig. Gen. Fitz-John Porter's Fifth Corps) to augment McClellan's large force.[18]

Meade showed his resolution and bravery under fire in the Seven Days battles outside Richmond in June 1862. On June 27 the Second Brigade found itself nearly overwhelmed by fleeing Union soldiers at the Battle of Gaines Mill. Stunned, the Pennsylvania Reserves trudged south with the rest of the army toward the James River. By June 30 they were positioned in the center of the Union line that hugged the west side of Charles City Road to Glendale, then farther south along Quaker Road. Meade's brigade straddled Long Bridge Road. With just six guns under Lt. Alanson M. Randol to protect them, the reduced ranks of Meade's brigade found itself under fierce attack by Brig. Gen. Cadmus Wilcox's Alabama Brigade. As fighting raged around the guns, Meade seemed to be everywhere, encouraging the men to either hold their positions or advance, as the circumstances allowed. During the heat of battle, one of Meade's aides was killed and another wounded. Then, at sunset, Meade was hit by two bullets, one in the left arm, the other in his side. Sore, with blood visible on his saddle, Meade ordered Randol to hold onto his guns as long as he could. He then rode back to see a surgeon after turning over his command to Col. Horatio G. Sickel of the Third Pennsylvania. Attended by the division physician, Dr. Stocker, Meade dashed off a quick letter to his wife, telling her the wounds were not "dangerous, though they require immediate and constant medical attendance."[19]

Back home in Philadelphia, Meade mended quickly under the care of the family physician, Dr. Addinell Hewson. The wound in the forearm healed first, but the hole from the bullet that had gone in his side (and barely missed his spine) healed far more slowly. His physician asked the War Department for a leave of fifty days, but Meade left a week earlier, eager to return to the field.[20]

A number of important personnel changes had occurred during his absence. John Pope had been summoned from the West to command a new army, the Army of Virginia. McClellan was supposed to coordinate with Pope as he withdrew his army from Harrison's Landing. George McCall had been captured at Glendale, paroled, and then exchanged in August. Placed on sick leave, he resigned the following year. John Reynolds replaced him as division commander. Meade took command of Reynolds's old brigade, the First. Governor Andrew Curtin of Pennsylvania recommended Meade for promotion to major general, but it did not happen. Reynolds's division now returned to McDowell's Third Corps, which guarded Washington.[21]

Meade took these changes in stride, writing to his wife that McClellan had "lost the greatest chance any man ever had on this continent." He was uplifted by the cheers he received from his old brigade when he returned to the ranks, and by other officers telling him that the stand of the Pennsylvania Reserves at Glendale on June 30 saved the army. He eagerly awaited orders on August 21 "to hurry up to Pope's rescue or fall back upon Washington" (they were camped at Fredericksburg).[22]

Meade's prediction of a rush to rescue Pope proved true. The Pennsylvania Reserves marched out past Groveton by August 28, and for the next two days skirmished and maneuvered against Jackson's troops. On August 30, the climactic day of the Second Battle of Bull Run, the Pennsylvania Reserves played a critical role in stopping the last Confederate push of the day under Brig. Gen. D. R. Jones. With Reynolds leading the charge, the Reserves slammed into the troops near Sudley Road. Outnumbered, they held to their new position precariously, until Meade's request for reinforcements reached McDowell. Referring later to Meade as that "intelligent as well as gallant officer," McDowell sent in five regiments. They bolstered the sagging spirits of the exhausted Pennsylvanians, and the Confederates soon pulled back. Meade could safely report to his wife that he was "just as well as ever," though his staff and "most of the command are completely knocked up."[23]

There would be little time to recuperate, though, with Lee's victorious army on the move somewhere in northern Virginia. Lincoln and Halleck believed changes were necessary, and over his cabinet's objections, Lincoln expanded McClellan's authority to include all the soldiers in the field. Pope was transferred out west and McDowell was relieved of immediate field command. The Pennsylvania Reserves were placed in Maj. Gen. Joseph Hooker's First Corps, with division commanders retained (as was Meade as brigade commander). Asst. Adj. Gen. Seth Williams told Meade that McClellan wanted him to have a division at the next reorganization, though Meade did not consider himself part of McClellan's circle of "old friends." As the Army of the Potomac soon followed Lee's army into Maryland, Meade told his wife, "[I am not] very sanguine of our power. The morale of the army is very much impaired by recent events."[24]

Lee's steady movement north produced a sudden and dramatic change in Meade's career. John Reynolds was ordered to Harrisburg to train volunteers to fight the impending "invasion" of Pennsylvania, and Meade was given command

of Reynolds's First Division. Meade experienced quick success as a division commander in the battle at Turner's Gap on September 14. Assigned to the right flank
of Hooker's First Corps, Meade's division made its way to the top of the ridge,
which the Confederates finally abandoned after dark. Meade felt justifiably proud
of his achievement as a new division commander, writing to his wife, "Their
movements were the admiration of the whole army, and I gained great credit."[25]

There was no time to rest or celebrate as the Army of the Potomac pursued Lee's
retreating army to the little town of Sharpsburg, Maryland. In the early evening
of September 16, Meade's division skirmished with Brig. Gen. John Bell Hood's
division for control of the East Woods. The firing ended at dark, and the First
Corps rested uneasily around the farm of J. Poffenberger on the eve of the Battle
of Antietam. Meade's men resumed the fighting the next morning before daylight, and for the next four hours, Meade's division and the First Corps engaged in
some of the heaviest fighting of the war in places now regarded as slaughter fields,
the Cornfield and the East Woods. Meade calmly led his men that morning, even
after a spent grape shot hit his thigh and left him with a bruise. His favorite horse,
Old Baldy, was not as lucky; he was hit in the neck and initially presumed dead.
Hooker was also hit and had to leave the field. He turned over the command of
the First Corps to Meade, who immediately went to Brig. Gen. James B. Ricketts
(Second Division), who was his senior in rank, and turned the command over
to him. McClellan countermanded this move, saying in his second message to
Meade that the order was "given without regard to rank, and all officers of the
Corps will obey your orders." The same orders instructed Meade to "reorganize it
[First Corps] and make it serviceable." His task in the afternoon was to hold the
right, not advance. Meade felt comfortable with this decision, as his ammunition
was exhausted. He also felt that the much-criticized day of rest after the battle
was necessary, as the "army was a good deal broken and somewhat demoralized."
Finally, his temporary promotion had answered his "wishes in regard to my desire
to have my services appreciated."[26]

The promotion was short lived. When Reynolds returned to the Army of the
Potomac, he was given command of the First Corps while Hooker recuperated,
and Meade returned to division command. He fretted in Sharpsburg with the
rest of the army while they waited on resupply and McClellan decided what to do
next. Meade accompanied Lincoln when he visited the battlefield in early October, and then he watched as the political intrigue concerning McClellan played
out over the next month. Even Meade felt that McClellan erred on "the side of
prudence and caution," and his "failure to immediately pursue Lee" would cost
him his job. It did: on November 8 McClellan was relieved from duty with the
Army of the Potomac. Meade joined Reynolds, Brig. Gen. John Gibbon, and Brig.
Gen. Abner Doubleday on a visit to McClellan to wish him well and express their
sorrow. McClellan came close to crying. He was not the only one saddened by this

decision; Meade heard that Maj. Gen. Ambrose Burnside—appointed as McClellan's replacement—had cried when he heard the news and said he was not "fit for command." Meade believed the decision to be entirely "political" and found the army to be "filled with gloom and greatly depressed."[27]

Meade stuck it out, regardless of changes at the top, though he wondered how long he would have to wait for his promotion when he heard of Reynolds's promotion on December 1. The wait was brief: on December 6 he told his wife that he had received a telegram noting his promotion to major general. He wrote, "I am truly glad, for your sake as well as my own." With this promotion Meade had achieved one of the "tangible rewards," in Chris Stowe's phrasing, "in an era noted for producing and celebrating unpretentious civic heroes." Meade retained command of his old division when Burnside shuffled structure by creating three Grand Divisions of two corps each. The First and Sixth Corps became part of Maj. Gen. William B. Franklin's left Grand Division (Reynolds in command of the First Corps). Burnside proceeded to move the entire army south to Fredericksburg.[28]

Though Meade initially doubted that the Confederates would pitch a battle in Fredericksburg, "at such a distance from Richmond," he had an even deeper problem with the political need to simultaneously defend Washington and take Richmond. Expressing the point of view of a man at war in the East, on November 22 Meade wrote a letter to his wife outlining in operational terms how the war should be prosecuted, previewing the approach that would ultimately win the war. He wrote, "I have always maintained that Richmond need not and should not be attacked at all; that the proper mode to reduce it is to take possession of the great lines of railroad leading to it from the south and southwest; cut these and stop any supplies going there, and their army will be compelled to evacuate it and meet us on the ground we can select ourselves." To get to Richmond one needed to go via the James River, "the true and only practicable line of approach to Richmond." As historian Ethan Rafuse argues, "Using the James River, Meade recognized—as did Grant and Lee—played to the Union's strength and negated those of the Confederacy."[29]

It was Burnside who decided to give Lee a fight in Fredericksburg, and on December 12 he ordered Maj. Gen. William B. Franklin to send a division to seize the heights south of town near Hamilton's Crossing. Franklin selected Meade's division, which marched out with flags flying on the bright, cold morning of December 13. When Confederate artillery opened fire on Meade's five thousand men, the Battle of Fredericksburg commenced.[30]

After raking the Confederate position with artillery fire, Meade sent in his infantry. They were temporarily stopped by Confederate artillery, until Union artillery neutralized them. His men then found a gap in the Confederate lines and poured through, capturing hundreds of Confederates. Then Confederate reinforcements arrived, and with insufficient support from Brig. Gen. David B. Birney's Third Corps, Meade's division had to retreat. Though he emerged unscathed (except for two bullet holes in his hat), eighteen hundred of his men were killed, wounded, captured, or missing. He reportedly said to John Reynolds, "Did they think my division could whip Lee's whole Army!"[31]

Fredericksburg was a disaster for the Army of the Potomac. High casualties crippled a number of brigades that day, as the Army of the Potomac vainly attempted to capture Marye's Heights in Fredericksburg. The staggering losses depressed the Northern public, and an intense period of fault finding followed.

While Burnside and Franklin came under heavy criticism, Meade's star rose, and on December 23 he learned that he had been given command of Fitz-John Porter's old corps, the Fifth Corps. That corps had been temporarily commanded by Brig. Gen. Daniel Butterfield, a top executive in the American Express company before the war who had extensive political connections. Meade had complained privately to Burnside when Butterfield had been appointed (Porter had been relieved from command in November under charge of misconduct at the Second Battle of Bull Run). Senior to Butterfield in the army, Meade felt that his seniority should have given him preference. Burnside told him he was ignorant of that fact and that he would appoint him to the command, unless an officer with greater seniority (like Maj. Gen. John Sedgwick) was put forth instead. Burnside reiterated his support for Meade in another private meeting held after the Battle of Fredericksburg. On December 23 Meade learned of his promotion, and he celebrated by drinking champagne with generals Franklin, Smith, Reynolds, and Brooks. Meade even shared a rare moment of humor, writing to his wife that the generals all agreed that Congress should create the grade of lieutenant general and appoint Meade, as long as he provided his friends "with such good wine!" Two days later, Meade took command of the Fifth Corps, and in a gesture of goodwill, outgoing commander Butterfield invited him to stay for Christmas dinner. After dinner they discussed the reassignment, and Meade told him "he was fully justified in being disappointed and put out." Butterfield admitted he was just that because Burnside had assured him "positively and distinctly that it [his appointment] was permanent." Meade pleaded with Butterfield not to hold him responsible and felt that Butterfield indeed did not, writing that "the affair appears to be definitely and satisfactorily settled."[32] Little did he know that, quite to the contrary, his replacement of Butterfield was but the beginning of a poisonous relationship.

Few affairs were completely settled during the acrimonious winter of 1862–63. Burnside tried to salvage his job and reputation by embarking on another offensive, this time in January. Winter weather did not cooperate, and Burnside's offensive ground to a halt on impassable roads, earning the derisive nickname "Mud March." An angry Burnside dismissed four generals and relieved five more. When he insisted that Lincoln support his decisions, Lincoln did not. Instead he transferred Burnside to the Department of the Ohio, replacing him with Joseph Hooker.[33]

Burnside's removal surprised Meade, but he also believed that Burnside "was not equal to the command of so large an army." He lacked "knowledge and judgment, and was deficient in that enlarged mental capacity which is essential in a commander." As for Hooker, Meade thought him to be a "good soldier," though too much enthralled by "bad influences, such as Dan Butterfield and Dan Sickles," who were more "intellectually clever" than Hooker. As for himself, he had heard rumors that his name came up for the job, though he doubted he would get it. He believed he could do the job, but the position was "anything but enviable. This army is in a false position, both as regards the enemy and the public." The army needed more men to defeat Lee's army, and the public shifted from "exaggerated praise" before an operation to condemnation when a campaign failed or fell short of expectations.[34]

Meade did not get a new position but remained in command of the Fifth Corps. He became enmeshed in the battle over "who lost Fredericksburg" between Burnside and Franklin, testifying in March for the first time before the group that would become the bane of his existence, the Joint Committee on the Conduct of the War. He read his official report to the committee (only Sen. Benjamin Wade was present that afternoon of March 16), then answered two questions. First, did he know of Burnside's order to Franklin to attack with his whole force? He had not. Second, would Meade's attack have succeeded if Franklin had sent in his whole force? Meade believed it would have. From his questions Meade surmised that Franklin would be blamed for the failure at Fredericksburg, and the committee did just that. Throughout this period, Meade saw and communicated with Burnside and Franklin, and as he told his wife, "My position, with my friendly feelings for both, is not only peculiar but embarrassing."[35]

For a man who continually professed no interest in politics, Meade kept wading into deeper political waters. When Lincoln visited the army in April, Meade dined with the president's party, and over the next few days he gently lobbied Lincoln for the vacant brigadier general slot and defended Franklin for misunderstanding Burnside's order at Fredericksburg.[36]

Meade also got his men ready for the next movement, which everyone knew was coming, but not when or where. Meade closely observed Hooker's management style—exuding confidence but wrapped in secrecy. At one point he heard Hooker say that "not a human being knew his plans either in the army or at Washington."[37] Whether this approach worked would soon be settled in the woods west of Fredericksburg known by locals as "the Wilderness."

Hooker launched the first offensive against Lee's army in late April. On April 27 the Fifth Corps led the Army of the Potomac toward the pontoon bridge at Kelly's Ford on the Rappahannock River. The plan was for the bulk of the army to come in behind Lee's army in Fredericksburg while two other corps attacked over the same ground as in December. Together, they would either defeat Lee's army or force its retreat from Fredericksburg. On April 29 the Fifth Corps crossed the Rappahannock, then marched on to the rain-swollen Rapidan River, which they crossed with water lapping up to their chests at Ely's Ford. When Meade appeared at the ford, the men cheered, and he doffed his cap. He then crossed the river and that evening let his men light small fires to dry out damp clothes, despite prior orders to not attract attention by lighting fires.[38]

The difficult yet successful river crossing may have been the highlight of the Battle of Chancellorsville for Meade. The next six days proved to be one of the most frustrating periods of his tenure as corps commander. On April 30 Meade's lead divisions reached the Chancellor house, and Brig. Gen. Charles Griffin's division skirmished with Confederate troops as they marched east on the Orange Turnpike for Fredericksburg. Then his men were ordered to stop their advance and pull back to the Chancellor House, to await the arrival of three more corps. A similar movement occurred the following day, with Meade taking two divisions to Banks's Ford on the Rappahannock and Sykes's division marching eastward on the Orange Turnpike. All three divisions were recalled to Chancellorsville by Hooker. His plan was to dig in and wait for Lee to spend his army on a futile attack (a "Fredericksburg in reverse"). Meade's Fifth Corps occupied the left of Hooker's line on May 2. It was the right side of the Union line, however, manned by the Eleventh Corps that proved vulnerable to Stonewall Jackson's attack. Jackson's force pushed the Union right back nearly a mile, but the center of the line held.[39]

The next day (May 3) the Confederates, now under Maj. Gen. J. E. B. Stuart (Jackson had been wounded), resumed the attack, and Hooker himself was knocked out by a wooden column split off from the Chancellor House by a cannon shell. He quickly recovered, but as his army's position crumbled, he still would not authorize Meade to attack Stuart's left and rebuked Meade for sending a brigade to support Reynolds on the right side of the Union line. Hooker called his corps commanders to his tent in the late morning and ordered a withdrawal of the entire army, supervised by Maj. Gen. Darius Couch, the senior corps commander who would temporarily command the army while Hooker recovered. Though fierce fighting continued that morning and into the afternoon, as Union forces under Major General Sedgwick captured Marye's Heights and pushed westward, the moment of possibility had passed for Joseph Hooker.[40]

The next day saw some tough fighting at Salem Church but no decisive repositioning of the armies, and Hooker ordered Sedgwick to evacuate via Banks's Ford over the Rappahannock. The day, and the battle, culminated in an odd midnight meeting on May 5 that would be remembered and "re-remembered" differently in the following weeks and even years. Hooker summoned his corps commanders to his headquarters to discuss whether the army should stay and fight or retreat. To allow for frank discussion, Hooker and his chief of staff, Daniel Butterfield, excused themselves from the meeting. Hooker framed the discussion, however, by telling his generals that he had to protect Washington, save the army, and rebuild morale among now-skittish troops. Despite his warnings, Meade, Reynolds, and

Maj. Gen. Oliver O. Howard voted to attack the Confederates (Meade, in particular, worried that the guns would be captured in a retreat). Maj. Gen. Daniel E. Sickles, the only non–West Pointer, argued that the political cost of further losses outweighed the cost of immediate retreat. Couch ended the discussion by saying he favored attacking, but not with Hooker in command. Hooker returned and told his generals he planned to retreat. Though Reynolds fumed over holding a meeting with no purpose, Hooker had telegraphed his view before the meeting, so his final decision should not have been a surprise.[41]

The next day, the withdrawal began in a pouring rain that swelled rivers and made the recrossing of the Rappahannock extremely difficult. By May 6 the entire army had gotten across the river, and the shock of the defeat had just begun to reach the Northern public.[42]

The first sign of serious trouble for Hooker came with a visit from Lincoln and Halleck to Hooker's camp on May 7. Lincoln wanted to talk to all the corps commanders, and Meade reported to his wife that "nothing was said of our recent operations, or any references made to the future, nor was any corps commanders called on for an option." But in his oblique way, Lincoln showed his hand, as "he thought its [Chancellorsville's] effect, both at home and abroad, would be more serious and injurious than any previous act of the war." Someone would have to pay for the loss, and this time no corps commander was the easy choice.[43]

The fall-out from Chancellorsville and the northern march of Lee's army created six weeks of turmoil within the ranks of the Union high command and genuine fear among the citizens of Maryland and Pennsylvania. Meade was flattered when fellow corps commanders told him they wished he would take command of the army, with three of his seniors in rank—Couch, Sedgwick, and Maj. Gen. Henry W. Slocum—informing him that they would be "willing to serve" under him. Hooker himself, in an unguarded moment, had told Meade after the midnight meeting that "he was ready to turn over to me the Army of the Potomac."[44]

Hooker's momentary lack of self-confidence soon passed, and within two weeks he confronted Meade about a private conversation Meade had had with Gov. Andrew Curtin (when Meade was critical of Hooker) and his interpretation of the meaning of Meade's and Reynolds's votes on May 5. Hooker said that Meade's argument for keeping the army in place—that it was "impracticable to withdraw the army"—actually convinced him that he should withdraw the army. Meade's argument gave Hooker an opening: withdrawal was impracticable but not impossible. And since Hooker knew it could be done, he later used Meade's argument as cover for having done so. Meade found Hooker's argument "ingenious" but completely contrary to his proposition on May 5, and that Meade would "deny" ever advocating withdrawal if asked. Meade considered himself at "open war" with Hooker, seeing that Hooker now believed he should not have retreated, but rather than admit a "grave error," sought "to cast it off on the shoulders of others."[45]

The row between commanders continued in June. Meade refused to join Couch in a special visit to Lincoln and to aid Slocum's nascent efforts to have Hooker removed. He did, however, send a circular letter to his fellow corps commanders, asking for their recollections of the May 5 meeting. Meade continued to believe that "Hooker would be allowed another chance," knowing that Secretary of Treasury Chase and others supported him. He also still had some faith in Hooker, writing his wife that he thought "he will do better next time, and [I] still think there is a great deal of merit in him." However, Hooker continued his secretive ways, and as the Army of the Potomac followed Lee, Meade wrote his wife on June 11 that he "was removed from Hooker's headquarters and know[s] nothing of what is going on, either of plans or surmises." He found out that John Reynolds had visited with Lincoln, and while critical of Hooker, Reynolds refused to take Hooker's job. Lincoln replied that "he was not disposed to throw away a gun because it missed fire once; that he would pick the lock and try again." But Lincoln had second thoughts on the subject, as what historian Stephen Sears calls the "revolt of the generals" weighed on him. Most of the generals who visited Lincoln that spring "announced their loyalty to their own candidate, George Meade," according to Sears.[46]

By the end of June, Meade's corps was at Aldie, Virginia, and he assured his wife that the "visions" of his being placed in command of the entire army "had all blown over." In the same letter, he listed his accomplishments in the war, commended himself for refraining from intrigue among fellow officers, and remarked that he had no "friends, political or others, who press or advance my claims or pretensions." Consequently, he did not believe he would get the job if Hooker were removed, though he thought the only fair argument against him was that it remained "to be seen whether I have the capacity to handle successfully a large army."[47]

Unbeknownst to Meade, however, an angry Hooker had asked to be relieved after seeing an order from Halleck to Maj. Gen. William French at Harper's Ferry telling him to ignore orders from Hooker (who wanted to abandon the vulnerable outpost at Harper's Ferry). Lincoln accepted the resignation, then quickly cast about for a replacement on June 27. Opposed to McClellan, the next obvious choices were Couch and Reynolds, who both declined to accept the job. Tentative inquiries to Maj. Gen. Winfield Scott Hancock and Maj. Gen. John Sedgwick had not received positive responses. Stanton and Halleck favored Meade, as did the corps commanders in the Army of the Potomac. When Lincoln heard that Meade was a Pennsylvanian, Lincoln replied that he might "fight well on his own dunghill." With this colorful but tepid endorsement, machinery was set in motion to appoint George G. Meade as commanding general of the Army of the Potomac.[48]

To his credit, Meade had grown as a commander in his two years as a general. He demonstrated clear thinking, even under fire; a good eye for terrain and its use; steady control of his men; bravery; obedience to orders (even those he questioned); a minimal interest in Army politics compared to some fellow generals;

and a weak connection to politics in Washington. Ironically, as argued by Chris Stowe, Meade's devotion to a "military culture that subordinated outward self-promotion and political displays in favor of the national interest," and his willingness to seek battle rather than inaction, pushed Meade to the top of Lincoln and Halleck's list.[49] He had proven to be a good soldier and officer, but whether he could handle a large army against a wily opponent and please the politicians, press, and public remained to be seen.

He also displayed some of his defects as a leader. He almost always erred on the side of caution in military operations, especially if an aggressive move carried great risk. He supported the inclination of McClellan to rest after a major battle, rather than push on in a risky attempt to strike a death blow to the enemy. He truly believed in the importance of division and corps commanders working in synch, thus opening him to the charge that he relied too heavily on the concurrence of others to make a decision. His constant complaints to his wife about the ignorance of politicians and the fickle nature of public support for the war did not bode well for someone expected to handle the stresses of battlefield as well as public opinion.

Finally, he had become an integral part of a cadre of generals who could not defeat the Army of Northern Virginia, except at the Battle of Antietam. Crippled by commanders that proved to be either too fearful (McClellan and Hooker) or too rash (Pope, Burnside, and Hooker) to fight Lee's army to a standstill at critical moments, the top leadership of the Army of the Potomac gradually developed an inferiority complex toward Lee. As historian Bruce Catton succinctly stated, "Lee was the one soldier in whom most of the higher officers of the Army of the Potomac had complete, undiluted confidence."[50] The Union soldiers fought as well as their opponents, but their commanders continually squandered their valor. The top Union generals became obsessed with divining Lee's next movements, which meant that their actions would be consistently reactive, not proactive. Meade shared the history of this hard-luck army, imbibed some of the fears of his fellow generals, and definitely embraced the beliefs and values of the professional military officer. Whether he could help the army rise above its past and conquer some of its fears would be his first major test.

That "test" would begin at 3 A.M. on June 28, when Col. James A. Hardie of Stanton's staff shook Meade awake in his tent and told him he had come to give Meade "trouble." Startled by the appearance and comment of Hardie, Meade replied that his "conscience was clear, void of offense towards any man." Few transfers of command of large standing armies in American history have begun as inauspiciously as Meade's.[51]

Hardie was not there to "relieve or arrest" him as he feared but to offer him the job he had wanted yet dreaded: command of the Army of the Potomac. One dramatic postwar account by Charles Benjamin (of Hardie's staff) has Meade vigorously objecting to the offer, insisting that Reynolds should get the job, that his information about the army's placement was too limited for him to take command at that moment, and that he was opposed to the request that he accompany Hardie to Hooker's headquarters to convey the message of relief of command. Some or all or even none of this may be true, but the terse summary of the decision he sent his wife explained why Meade accepted the offer: "You know how reluctant we both have been to see me placed in this position, and it appears to be God's will for some purpose—at any rate, as a soldier I had nothing to do but accept and exert my utmost abilities to command success."[52] As a soldier, he had to carry out the order. As a religious man, he wanted to believe that God willed his acceptance. And yet harking back to earlier letters to his wife, it is clear that, as an ambitious officer, Meade wanted to test himself at the highest level of command.

So he took the offer, then rode off with Hardie and Capt. George Meade, his son and an aide-de-camp, to find Hooker and discuss the situation with him. According to his son, "the little party rode silently along," with Meade apparently buried in thought.[53] Someone had told Hooker the party was coming, as he did not appear surprised to see the group. He ushered them into his tent, and the two talked privately for a short time. Hooker's chief of staff, Daniel Butterfield, soon joined the two generals as they discussed the location of the various Union corps and the information that Hooker had on the movements and positions of Lee's army. Benjamin wrote that the conference was "trying to the whole party," but what exactly transpired is not known. Hooker plainly accepted the fact that his resignation offered earlier had been accepted, and he made plans to depart from camp by the evening. When Meade emerged from the meeting, he told his son, "Well, George, I am in command of the Army of the Potomac," and a new era in the eastern theater had begun.[54]

Meade was at that moment at the height of his physical and professional powers. An officer at Gettysburg, Lt. Col. Frank Haskell, described Meade as a "tall spare man, with full beard, which with his hair, originally brown, is quite thickly sprinkled with gray—has a Romanish face, very large nose, and a white large forehead, prominent and wide over the eyes, which are full and large, and quick in their movements, and he wears spectacles." Another observer, journalist Whitelaw Reid, used similar terms to describe Meade in action at Gettysburg, "quick and nervous in his movements, but calm, and as it seemed to me, lit up with the glow of the occasion." Others referred to his "scholarly" appearance, though with his ever-present glasses and heavy eyelids, a less kind description was "a damned old goggle-eyed snapping turtle!"[55]

The latter description encompassed a well-noted and oft-cited aspect of his personality, his temper. Few commentators failed to mention it, and in time it became a touchstone to understanding Meade. The comments by contemporaries and historians are too numerous to be listed here, but Grant's aide Horace Porter had a mild description of his temper: "He had much to try him upon this occasion, and if he was severe in his reprimands and showed faults of temper, he certainly displayed no faults as a commander." He also captured another aspect of Meade's anger that was usually noted: it flashed quickly, followed by an apology, with no lingering traces of a grudge. In the same discussion of Meade in mid-May 1864, Porter wrote, "When the battle was over no one was more ready to make amends for the instances in which he felt that he might have done injustice to his subordinates." Meade was also acutely aware that his flashes of anger reflected poorly on the gentlemanly qualities he sought to display. As Lorien Foote writes, "Anger particularly revealed a loss of control and thus a gentleman controlled his temper, no matter how provoking the circumstances."[56]

His temper or, rather, lack of control of his temper, was a personal handicap and a hindrance to command—some of the time. Many Civil War generals were known to have quick, sharp tempers, among them William T. Sherman and Philip Sheridan. Other famous generals in American military history have been known for their sharp tempers: Andrew Jackson, George Patton, Dwight Eisenhower, and Norman Schwartzkopf, to name a few. The key question is not, did the person have a quick temper? Rather, the question is: did that temper help or hinder his command? That question is always up for debate, though anger, when used discriminatingly, can be an effective tool of command. The problem with Meade, as even some friends noted, was proportionality. He sometimes berated low-level officers for annoying but uncritical mistakes, which not only wounded the recipient of his wrath but led others to question his self-control and live in fear of his "moods." As will be seen, his angry outbursts did not serve him well over the course of the war.

But flashes of anger hardly captured the full personality of George G. Meade. A journalist close to Grant, Sylvanus Cadwallader, wrote that Meade was "uniformly dignified, polite, attentive and generally quite affable in demeanor, under all the conditions I ever saw surrounding him. . . . In all our after meetings for years, he proved to be an accomplished gentleman." Meade never saw this description by Cadwallader but would have been pleased to read it. Charles Devens, attorney general of the United States, said of Meade in his speech before the Society of the Army of the Potomac in 1873, "[He was the] embodiment of the scholar, the soldier, and the gentleman." Meade had been well schooled in the manners and courtesies of the elite in the nineteenth century, and his biographer Pennypacker wrote, "In the city where a century and a half of assembly balls have not left opinion untrained in such matters, General Meade's manner in a ballroom is still said by competent judges to have been superior to that of the most celebrated locally of the assembly leaders."[57] *Well-educated, curious, polite,* and *friendly* are not the usual adjectives used to describe Meade—but they were key parts of his personality. These aspects of his personality, as well as all his leadership skills, would be thoroughly tested in the days to come.

As one of the busiest weeks of his life began, Meade carried out a critical task. He met with Hooker again, and they decided upon the wording of the general orders that transferred command. Those straightforward commands were issued later in the day. Meade had a refreshing meeting with his good friend and ally, John Reynolds, who pledged to give him "the best support he could." Meade also met with Hancock and John Gibbon that evening, and though Gibbon wrote his wife that Meade appeared "very anxious" at the assumption of his new command, Gibbon added that he could "feel his confidence restored and I believe we shall whip these fellows." Sometime that night, Hooker bid farewell to his staff; just before he left, Meade approached him alone, took his hand, and spoke briefly to him. Hooker then rode off with Hardie in a spring wagon.[58]

Meade had been given direction and latitude by Halleck, Stanton, and Lincoln in a separate letter that accompanied General Orders 194 giving him command of the army. In terms of latitude, Halleck was both specific and generous in ways that Hooker had not enjoyed. Halleck wrote, "You will not be hampered by any minute instructions from these headquarters." Furthermore, "all forces within the sphere" of his operations, including the garrison at Harper's Ferry (a point of contention between Hooker and Halleck), would be "subject" to Meade's orders. He was also given an authority last granted to McClellan; he was "authorized to remove from command, and to send from your army, any officer or others person you may deem proper, and to appoint to command as you may deem expedient." Finally, he had "all the power and authority which the President, the Secretary of War, or the General-in-Chief can confer on you, and you may rely on our full support."

At the same time, Halleck was quite clear on Meade's charge: "The Army of the Potomac is the covering army of Washington as well as the army of operation against the invading forces of the rebel." Meade must "maneuver and fight" to protect Washington and even Baltimore (added to the responsibility of the commander of the Army of the Potomac for the first time).[59]

So Meade had to continue to interpose his army between Lee's army and Washington, figure out where Lee's divided forces were headed, and attack them, if possible. But an army of over 100,000 men could not be quickly turned to face one direction or the other, so Meade had to decide how to chase, catch, and fight Lee's army, while leaving enough troops in the proper position to thwart any sudden thrusts toward Washington or Baltimore by Lee.

Meade spent the first day of his new command doing that, establishing the location of his scattered forces, attempting to discover the whereabouts of Lee's men and their destinations, and putting his corps in motion to find Lee and prevent him from attacking Washington and Baltimore. By the evening of June 28, he knew that the bulk of Lee's army was north of Hagerstown, headed toward Pennsylvania. He also knew that Maj. Gen. Jubal Early's division marched toward York or Hanover Junction (and had passed through Gettysburg). Finally, he knew that a body of Confederate cavalry was between his army and Washington. With this information, Meade sent each corps out on June 29, most departing at 4 A.M. along separate roads, some headed north, others northeast, to catch Lee's army. The First Corps under his good friend Reynolds would march to Emmitsburg; the Eleventh Corps, still under the command of Maj. Gen. Oliver Howard, would also march to Emmitsburg; the Second Corps, led by another friend, Winfield Scott Hancock, would head toward Frizellburg; the Third Corps, commanded by Daniel Sickles, was ordered to Taneytown; Slocum's Twelfth Corps would also head toward Taneytown; the Sixth Corps, led by John Sedgwick, marched to New Windsor; the Fifth Corps, now led by the redoubtable Maj. Gen. George Sykes, would begin moving at 8 A.M., following the Second Corps, yet camping at Union; and the Reserve Artillery would precede the Twelfth Corps, stopping for the night between Middleburg and Taneytown. The engineers and bridge train would follow the Fifth Corps, the headquarters staff would start at 8 A.M. for Middleburg, and the cavalry would "guard the right and left flanks and the rear," as well as perform reconnaissance.[60]

Once the corps began moving in the morning, Meade had the time to write Halleck a lengthy letter describing his decisions, rationale, and goals. The letter revealed not only a tactician's mind at work but also a cautious general, one careful to note his objectives and show his precautions. He began the letter by detailing the movement of each corps, then explained his goals: "If Lee is moving for Baltimore, I expect to get between his main army and that place." If Lee planned instead to cross the Susquehanna River, Meade would "rely upon General Couch, with his force, holding him until I can fall upon his rear and give him battle, which I shall endeavor to do." (Couch had command of about sixteen thousand men in Pennsylvania, mainly militia.) As for Harper's Ferry, he had ordered it abandoned, and three thousand soldiers of its force moved to Washington. He was well aware of Stuart's cavalry ride and the panic it caused in Washington; he would send his own cavalry to find and fight Stuart's men. But he remained fixed on the primary mission that some in his previous post had forgotten: "While I move forward, I shall incline to the right, toward the Baltimore and Harrisburg road, to cover that . . . my main objective point being, of course, Lee's army." Lincoln and Halleck must have been reassured to read that objective because some of his predecessors had focused on capturing Richmond instead. He concluded, "My endeavor will be in my movements to hold my force well together, with the hope of falling upon some portion of Lee's army in detail."[61] Although Meade did not know exactly where Lee's main force was or where it was headed, he had pulled together his army and planned a march to the north to either block Lee and give battle or fall on his rear.

Despite inevitable mistakes and delays, the bulk of the soldiers marched down muddy roads toward their destinations, with almost every corps in its assigned position by nightfall of June 29. In general, the entire army had moved twenty miles to the north or northeast, with the Second Corps marching the most, some thirty-two miles in one day, and the Third Corps the least, not making sixteen miles let alone reaching its destination. Meade reprimanded Sickles in a letter; his assistant adjutant general, Brig. Gen. Seth Williams wrote, "The commanding general noticed with regret the very slow movement of your corps yesterday." Commenting on the fact that the corps had marched only twelve miles by 6 P.M., the letter stated that such progress "was far from meeting the expectations of the commanding general, and delayed to a very late hour the arrival of troops and trains in your rear." Williams compared the slow pace of the Third Corps to the quickness of the Second Corps, which "made a march nearly double your own." He concluded with a thinly veiled warning, "the commanding general looks for rapid movement of the troops."[62] A small matter in a big march, it was nonetheless a rebuke that stung and later contributed to deteriorating relations between Meade and Sickles.

Other impediments to the marches included the clerk's failure to get Meade's first order to Hancock, which meant the Second Corps started out three hours later (the clerk was punished); the delay of the departure of the Fifth Corps because of the slowness of the Second Corps; the Twelfth Corps' waiting on the plodding Third Corps; and, potentially most troublesome, the drunken shenanigans of some soldiers in Frederick on June 28 and 29, when they freely cavorted around town while the provost marshall, Brig. Gen. Marsena R. Patrick, suffered from lack of troops. When Slocum told Meade of the problems, Meade assigned two squadrons of the Second Pennsylvania Cavalry to Patrick, who promptly rounded up stragglers and brought them to their units.[63]

During the day, Meade received disturbing news from Couch, who wrote that he had fortified his defenses along the Susquehanna River as best he could, considering that it would take only "five thousand regulars" to "whip" his ragtag army of sixteen thousand. His men had burned the Columbia Bridge and now stood ready to defend their side of the river. His messages to Meade and Secretary of War Stanton sent shock waves through Pennsylvania and prompted former Secretary of War Simon Cameron to write President Lincoln from Harrisburg that Meade must strike Lee before he crossed the Susquehanna. His fears were echoed by Governor Joel Parker of New Jersey, who urged Lincoln to reappoint McClellan as commander of the Army of the Potomac or, failing that, at least make him head of all troops from "New Jersey, New York, and Pennsylvania" now in Pennsylvania.[64] Thankfully for Meade, Lincoln and Stanton did not flinch: they continued to leave military affairs in the hands of Meade and his fellow generals. By giving Meade just a little time, the movements of Lee's army the following day rendered the panic baseless.

By the evening of June 29, Meade could be relatively satisfied after two full days in command. He had pretty good information on the whereabouts of Lee's scattered corps, and he put his vast army into motion to simultaneously find Lee's army and keep Washington protected. He would march up through Manchester and Hanover toward Harrisburg, compelling Lee to pull back his advanced units from Harrisburg. He made plans for each corps to continue marching the next day, though with the exception of the Sixth Corps, they would march considerably less than on the twenty-ninth. The Sixth Corps would form the right flank of Meade's army, camping at Manchester on the thirtieth. Meade's headquarters would be at Taneytown by the evening of June 30. All the infantry corps (except the Sixth) and the Artillery Reserve would be within ten miles of Taneytown by nightfall on June 30, thus allowing Meade to move units with alacrity if needed.[65]

The troops started marching the next morning, but reports of the movements of Lee's cavalry and infantry streamed into Meade's headquarters, prompting him to reassess his plans. Some of the clearest reports came from the reliable Brig. Gen. John Buford, commander of the First Division of the Cavalry Corps. Described by one observer as a "man of middle height with a yellow mustache, and a small triangular grey eye," with a "sinister" expression to his face, he was also known for his "cool daring."[66] As early as 5:30 A.M., he wrote to Reynolds that "the enemy has increased his forces considerably. His strong position is just behind Cashtown." His men also "met a superior force" near Mummasburg, while another group heard that "either General Gregg or Kilpatrick had fought with General Stuart near Littlestown." Buford's men entered Gettysburg at 11 A.M. on June 30, where he found "everybody in a terrible state of excitement on account of the enemy's advance upon this place." Fortunately for the citizens of Gettysburg, the arrival of the cavalry halted the march of the Confederates on the town, and Buford's men pushed back the skirmishers of what would be Maj. Gen. William Dorsey Pender's division under Lt. Gen. A. P. Hill. Buford then ordered his men to fan out from the town, looking for Confederates and provisions for the horses. While the men found no sizeable number of troops north of town, they did procure some valuable information from a captured courier of Lee's: Lt. Gen. Richard C. Ewell's corps was marching to the south, away from Carlisle, and Lt. Gen. James A. Longstreet's corps was behind Hill's. There were constant reports of Confederate advances from York toward Gettysburg, but none had proved true. Making matters worse was the fact that he could "get no forage or rations"; his men had to buy food and forage from the citizens. He waited on his wagons, although he told his commanding officer, Maj. Gen. Alfred Pleasonton, that he had "no need of them, as I can find no forage."[67]

Though Buford had encountered elements of Hill's corps at Gettysburg, it was still not clear to Meade where Lee's army was headed. Additional reports trickled in that clarified the picture for Meade. Couch sent a telegram to Meade that gave his opinion that "the enemy's operations on the Susquehanna are more to prevent cooperation with this army than offensive." A message from Brig. Gen. Herman Haupt late in the day confirmed this view; he wrote, "Lee is falling back suddenly from the vicinity of Harrisburg, and, concentrating all his forces. York has been evacuated. Carlisle is being evacuated. The concentration of forces seems to be at or near Chambersburg."[68]

So whether the concentration was going to be at Gettysburg or Chambersburg, the quick reversal of Ewell's and Early's marches from their original destination of Harrisburg meant that one part of Meade's charge could be considered done: the immediate protection of Philadelphia, Baltimore, and Washington. As Williams wrote in a letter to Major General Howard, "The general [Meade] believes he has relieved Harrisburg and Philadelphia, and now desires to look to his own army." But what did that mean? Williams explained that Meade planned to "assume position for offensive or defensive, as occasion requires, or rest to the troops."[69] So a battle loomed, but where, and on whose terms, had yet to be decided.

In the context of imperfect information, Meade decided to be ready for either attack or defense. He sent the "Third Corps to Emmitsburg; Second Corps to Taneytown; Fifth Corps to Hanover; 12th Corps to Two Taverns; First Corps to Gettysburg; Eleventh Corps to Gettysburg (or supporting distance); Sixth Corps to Manchester." The cavalry would ride to the "front and flanks, well out in all directions, giving timely notice of positions and movements of the enemy." Equally important was to lighten the load for each corps, indeed each soldier. "All empty wagons, surplus baggage, useless animals, and impediments of every sort to Union Bridge." Each soldier would have "three days' rations in haversacks, and with 60 rounds of ammunition in the boxes and upon the person." Only "ammunition wagons and ambulances" would be allowed to accompany the troops.[70]

Looking at a map, Meade had set up a thrust toward Gettysburg led by his most trusted general, John Reynolds, using the reliable First Corps and the checkered Eleventh Corps. The Third Corps was close by, at Emmitsburg, less than a day's march from Gettysburg if needed. Meade had given Reynolds temporary command of these three corps, the left wing of the army. The Twelfth Corps under the steady hand of Slocum was even closer to Gettysburg, at Two Taverns. The Fifth Corps would cover the flank of the army at Hanover, in a perfect blocking position should some of the Confederate troops turn away from Gettysburg and head southeast. The Second Corps would be near headquarters in Taneytown, just thirteen miles from Gettysburg. Only the Sixth Corps back in Manchester seemed underused, but it provided a deep reserve at seventeen thousand men and a ready bulwark in case of a rapid retreat. Buford's cavalry were in and around Gettysburg, watching all Confederate movements.

This moment of Meade's career is the earliest that has drawn criticism of him as an indecisive leader. Allen Guelzo, for example, argues that rather than risk battle in Gettysburg, Meade wanted "withdrawal" from the area (though Meade told Reynolds on June 30 that his "present position was given more with a view to an advance on Gettysburg."). Meade's critics argue that he should have lunged at Lee's most exposed forces and brought on a battle. He had numerous advantages:

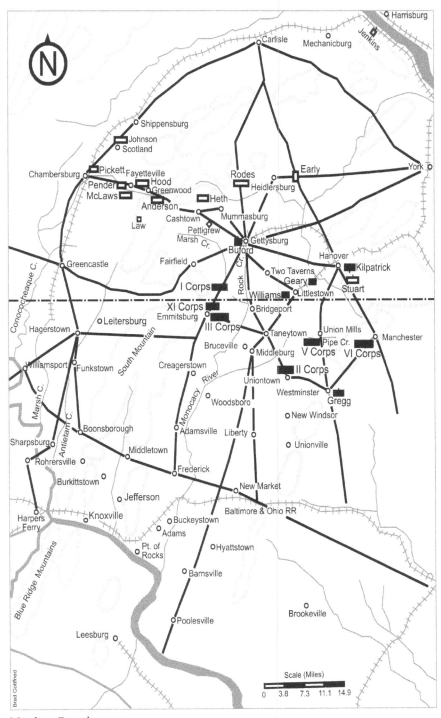

March to Gettysburg

more troops, more supplies, interior lines, and the zeal of fighting on one's home soil.[71] Yet Meade had always been regarded as thorough, methodical, and practical: he would not attack (unless ordered to) until he knew what he faced and that he had the means to win the battle. This level-headed steadiness is one key reason he got the job, and it would have been highly unlikely for him to suddenly change when given a large command. So he planned to be ready to give battle in several places, as needed.

Nor was he the only general groping in the dark of Pennsylvania. Troubled by the information he got from a spy on June 28, Lee recalled all of his troops to Cashtown, including his leading elements under Early at the outskirts of Harrisburg. In his official battle report, Lee stated that the purpose of the concentration of force was to "deter him [the enemy] from advancing further west, and intercepting our communication with Virginia." He later wrote that even after the first day's fighting, "it had not been intended to deliver a general battle so far away from our base unless attacked."[72] So like many Civil War battles, this one would begin with a collision of armies on unchosen ground, and defense and offense would have to be improvised. One can criticize Meade for not aggressively seeking to start a battle with an invading army, but he was also doing nothing less than what winning generals had done time and again in the war: gather as much information as possible on the enemy's whereabouts and intentions before giving battle.

Without knowing Lee's intentions, Meade had set in motion a limited offense with reinforcements nearby. Sometime during the evening of the thirtieth or very early in the morning on July 1, he formulated another plan, which he issued as a circular to his generals. A defensive plan, it came to be called the "Pipe Creek circular," for the natural landmark that would form its outline. Its language was conditional throughout, and it did not supersede any orders given on the thirtieth or on the first. Yet it has blemished Meade's reputation as a general ever since it was circulated.

The Pipe Creek circular opened with a description of success through rapid movement: "the relief of Harrisburg, and the prevention of the enemy's intended invasion of Philadelphia, &c beyond the Susquehanna." This left Meade in a new position, as "it is no longer his intention to assume the offensive until the enemy's movements or position should render such an operation certain of success." So why move two entire corps to Gettysburg? "If the enemy assume the offensive, and attack, it is his intention, after holding them in check sufficiently long, to withdraw the trains and other *impedimenta*; to withdraw the army from its present position, and form line of battle with the left resting in the neighborhood of Middleburg, and the right at Manchester, the general direction being that of Pipe Creek." He then issued precise instructions for the repositioning of each corps, the cavalry, the artillery, and the trains.[73]

Had Meade composed a plan to retreat to a position of strong defense, and there await Confederate attacks (the reverse of Fredericksburg)? No, not exactly.

And this is where the critics of Meade fail to dig deeply into the circular. Three paragraphs in the middle are crucial:

> The commanders of corps are requested to communicate at once the nature of their present positions, and their ability to hold them in case of any sudden attack at any point by the enemy.
>
> This order is communicated, that a general plan, perfectly understood by all, may be had for receiving attack, if made in strong force, upon any portion of our present condition.
>
> Developments may cause the commanding general to assume the offensive from his present positions.[74]

Meade had made a plan to retreat to a defensive line, but only if needed. He also kept open the option of going on the offense. Did he prefer to take the defensive line? Perhaps—that would be the import of the long circular. But he remained committed to a reconnaissance in force by the First and Eleventh Corps, and to the possibility of assuming the offensive if the conditions warranted.

Further insight into Meade's thinking late on June 30 comes from his long message to Reynolds sent on July 1 (and probably never received by him). In the words of Williams, "The commanding general cannot decide whether it is his best policy to move to attack until he learns something more definite of the point at which the enemy is concentrating." If the enemy were amassing around the Union right near Gettysburg, he wrote, "that point would not at first glance seem to be a proper strategic point of concentration for this army." If the concentration were "in front of Gettysburg or to the left of it," Williams continued, "the general is not sufficiently well informed of the nature of the country to judge of its character for either an offensive or defensive position." He had estimates of the size of Lee's army: 92,000 infantry, 6,000–8,000 cavalry, and 270 artillery pieces. With the addition of French's Eighth Corps (due to connect with the army on July 2), his own numbers exceeded these estimates. What he wanted, then, was Reynolds's "views upon the subject, at least so far as concerns [Reynolds's] position." He also wanted to learn the "*morale* and proportionate strength [of the army] compared with its last return." Trusting Reynolds to know "more of the conditions of the troops in [his] vicinity and the country" than he did, Meade genuinely wanted a discussion: "You have all the information which the general has received, and the general would like to have your views." As historian Brian Holden Reid argues, "If Reynolds decided to fight, Meade would be content in the knowledge that Reynolds thought it was the right place for a battle, and one where the Army of the Potomac had a strong chance of winning."[75]

There is one more bit of evidence to consider when evaluating Meade's plans on the evening of June 30, a letter to his wife. The exact timing of the letter is not known, except for the date. He wrote, "All is going on well. I think I have relieved

Harrisburg and Philadelphia, and that Lee has now come to the conclusion that he must attend to other matters." So far this news was in keeping with what he communicated to others. He added, "I continue well, but much oppressed with a sense of responsibility and the magnitude of the great interests entrusted to me. Of course, in time I will become accustomed to this." He ended with a request for even greater assistance, "Pray for me and beseech our heavenly Father to permit me to be an instrument to save my country and advance a just cause."[76]

Meade evidently felt the weight of command pressing on him and had not completely settled on his next step. But this is neither surprising nor a real issue, unless one is trying to weave a tapestry of failure using many strands of thought and action. His uncertainty about what to do is clear in his letters to Reynolds and his wife. His predilection for precise planning, detailed instructions, and alternate approaches should one fail is seen throughout the orders and letters he sent on June 30 and July 1. Did he plan to find, fix, and attack Lee's army? Only if he felt he could defeat or hold it in check. Did he prefer to draw Lee into a trap and fight Lee's army defensively on ground of his own choosing? Absolutely. Does that make him an indecisive general, afraid to make a plan and stick by it? Not at all. It demonstrates his preference for information, order, advantage, and yes, caution, before engaging the enemy. In the Pipe Creek circular, Meade had created a contingency plan. With partial information he had pressed his subordinates to find and engage Lee's army. At the same time, he created a fall-back plan. Under the circumstances, that was entirely reasonable. Lee had entered Meade's home state with a large, dangerous force. The exact location of all the elements of his force was unknown, as were his intentions. Meade showed vigor in pushing out some of his corps and prudence by keeping them close enough to move to the aid of each other. He could fight in a number of places if necessary, though the easiest place to secure was along Pipe Creek.

As the sun rose on July 1, Meade could feel his army was ready for several contingencies. The true test at Gettysburg would be his nerve.

❧TWO❧

Gettysburg

Test of Command

On July 1 Meade sent his first message of the day from his headquarters in Taney-town to Halleck in Washington. He apprised him of the location of his army and the minimal knowledge he had on the location of Lee's corps. Lee was up too, after spending a night in Greenwood. The night before, he had heard of the presence of Union cavalry in Gettysburg, but it did not faze him because he believed that the bulk of the Union army was still in Middleburg. Given Lee's lack of concern, A. P. Hill authorized Maj. Gen. Henry Heth to take his division into Gettysburg to search for shoes on July 1. Still, Lee had been careful to tell his corps commanders *not* to bring on an engagement until all the army was together.[1] So without knowing the number of Union cavalry in Gettysburg or the whereabouts of several Union corps, the four brigades under Heth marched blindly down the Chambersburg Pike into immortality.

The story of that morning clash is well known. Buford's cavalry slowed the advance of Brig. Gen. James C. Archer's brigade while he waited for infantry under Reynolds to come to his aid. Buford had sent a messenger to find Reynolds, and as soon as the messenger found the general, Reynolds galloped off to find Buford. Once he found him, he made the critical decision to bring up as many troops as fast as he could to hold Gettysburg. He dispatched Capt. Stephen Weld to ride to Meade's headquarters at Taneytown and tell him the fight was there. He also wrote to Maj. Gen. Oliver O. Howard to bring up the Eleventh Corps as fast as he could. Reynolds then returned to the advance division of the First Corps, under Brig. Gen. James C. Wadsworth, to hurry it along and guide it toward McPherson's Ridge. As he guided units into position ranging from the Chambersburg Pike in the north to Fairfield Road in the south, he perilously exposed himself to enemy fire. He encouraged the Second Wisconsin to rush into the McPherson

Woods to check the advance of Archer's men. While looking backward toward the seminary, he was struck and killed by a single minie ball.[2]

While Reynolds's aides began the sad task of removing his body from the field (and eventually carrying him all the way back to his hometown of Lancaster), the fighting raged on McPherson's Ridge. Maj. Gen. Abner Doubleday had command of the First Corps, and his men fought a desperate battle with Heth's men for the remainder of the morning. During the battle, Maj. Gen. Oliver O. Howard, commander of the Eleventh Corps, rode into Gettysburg ahead of his lead divisions looking for Reynolds (Reynolds had ordered Howard to march his corps to Gettysburg at 8 A.M. that morning). He soon learned that Reynolds had been killed. As the ranking general on the field, Howard "assumed command of the left wing, instructing General Schurz to take command of the Eleventh Corps." Howard surveyed the entire terrain and decided to put his headquarters on the "highest point" of Cemetery Ridge, the "only tenable position" for his force, as he saw it. When Maj. Gen. Carl Schurz arrived at noon, he ordered him to send the First and Third divisions of the First Corps north of town, hoping to ensure that Doubleday's right flank was not turned.[3]

Meanwhile, Meade had first received news from Gettysburg around 11 A.M. when Captain Weld of Reynolds's staff delivered the message that the Confederates were moving toward Gettysburg in force, and that Reynolds would strive to hold the enemy in place in Gettysburg, even if it meant barricading the streets. Weld also claimed that Meade replied, "Good, that is just like Reynolds."

With fighting underway at Gettysburg, Meade sent new orders to his corps commanders. He ordered his aides to "hurry up Hancock and all the other commands." To Sedgwick went the order to be ready to move his Sixth Corps from Manchester "in such direction as may be required in a moment's notice." He ordered Slocum to send his "trains" to Westminster immediately, and to be prepared to follow through on the Pipe Creek circular plan if necessary (this order went out before Meade learned of Reynolds's death). Slocum was also to stay in contact with Sykes and his Fifth Corps, coordinating their movements when new orders were issued. Meade ordered Maj. Gen. William French, commander of the troops at Frederick, to hold that town and guard the bridges over the Monocacy. In case of retreat of the Army of the Potomac, French's army was to move to Washington to defend it. Not long after this, Hancock arrived in town and paid Meade a courtesy visit; the two generals talked for some time about the evolving situation. After Hancock left the tent, Meade sent a message to Couch in Harrisburg: "The enemy are advancing on Gettysburg—Hill, from Cashtown; Ewell, from Heidlersburg. Can you throw a force in Ewell's rear, to threaten him and at the same time keep your line of retreat open? If you can, do so." It was, of course, a long shot, but another option Meade felt compelled to utilize (Couch did not attack). Meade then issued an order for Hancock to march the Second Corps to

Gettysburg to see if Reynolds was either in a severe battle or unable to cover the road leading from Gettysburg to Taneytown. If he could cover the road, the Second Corps was to withdraw to Frizellburg.[4]

Once again, Meade hedged his bets. He hurried certain elements to the brewing fight but still maintained the possibility of falling back under the contingency set out in the Pipe Creek circular.

Then news arrived that changed the entire course of events: the fighting had intensified in Gettysburg, and Reynolds had been killed. Undoubtedly stunned by the sad news, Meade did not have the luxury of time to consider the tragedy. He asked Hancock to ride to Gettysburg and take command of all the forces there, thus holding the same position that Reynolds had. Hancock would turn over command of the Second Corps to Brig. Gen. John Gibbon, ride to Gettysburg to take control, and determine whether the "ground" and "circumstances" made it sensible "to establish the line of battle at Gettysburg." Hancock raised a few objections: he was junior in rank to Sickles and Howard, and Gibbon was not the senior brigadier general in the Second Corps. Meade told him he would give him the authority over Sickles and Howard, and that Secretary of War Stanton had given him the power to move his commanders as he saw fit. Hancock may have asked for the authorization in writing, for a letter to Hancock from Maj. Gen. Daniel Butterfield, Meade's chief of staff, gave him that power explicitly: "By virtue of this order, in case of the truth of General Reynolds' death, you assume command of the corps assembled there, viz, the Eleventh, First, and Third, at Emmitsburg. If you think the ground and position there a better one to fight a battle under existing circumstances, you will so advise the general, and he will order all the troops up. You know the general's views." The order was written at 1:10 P.M.[5]

There now began one of the great working partnerships of the war, perhaps exceeded only by that of Grant and Sherman. Winfield Scott Hancock was a West Point graduate, an Army veteran, and a renowned fighter and leader, earning accolades for his performances at Williamsburg, Antietam, Fredericksburg, and Chancellorsville. Another Pennsylvanian like Reynolds and Meade, Hancock told his wife in late May that he had "been approached again in connection with the command of the Army of the Potomac." Though lifting a division commander at the time above seven corps commanders was unlikely, it did not matter anyway because, as he wrote his wife, "under no conditions would I accept the command. I do not belong to that class of generals whom the Republicans care to bolster up. I should be sacrificed." He was, however, happy to accept the promotion to commander of the Second Corps, a position that Couch resigned from in June.[6]

Hancock possessed some of the features Meade lacked. To begin with, he was a handsome man, who looked like a general. Theodore Lyman described him as a "tall, soldierly man, with light brown hair and a military heavy jaw; and [he] has the massive features and the heavy folds around the eye that often mark a man of ability." Quick in response, though "meticulous" and "thorough" in preparation for battle, he exuded confidence and command. His booming voice was well known to men under his command, as was his creative use of profanity to emphasize his points. He placed high demands on his subordinates but also praised them for their work. Over time, he and Meade would become friends as well as colleagues, with Lyman describing an afternoon meeting between the two in July 1864 as a time when Meade was "fixed for an hour at least. When he gets down with Hancock they talk, and talk, and talk, being great friends. Hancock is a very great and vehement talker but always says something worth hearing." The roots of that friendship were already seen in their meeting on July 1, and according to Lt. Col. C. H. Morgan, Hancock's chief of staff, Meade wanted Hancock to take command of the left wing of the army because he had the latest information, and "at this crisis he must have a man he knew and could trust" in charge (he also told Hancock he did not know Howard as well).[7]

Where Hancock fell short, as did so many others generals in the Army of the Potomac, was his visceral dislike of the politics that went with supreme command. Meade may have had an equal degree of disgust for politics, but either out of a sense of duty or ambition, he thought he could handle the job despite the politics.

All that, of course, lay in the future. As Hancock rode off toward Gettysburg on the hot, sultry day, Meade was busy preparing orders for his other corps commanders. The Second Corps had already been ordered to march on Gettysburg from Taneytown. After receiving word that Howard had ordered the Third Corps to march to Gettysburg, Meade sent a message to Sickles: "Hold on until you shall hear from General Hancock, leaving a division at Emmitsburg, as it is a point not to be abandoned excepting in an extremity." Fortunately, Sickles had already put his divisions into motion upon receiving Howard's first order, while leaving two brigades behind to defend the roads leading into Emmitsburg.[8]

Meanwhile, Hancock rode in an ambulance to Gettysburg, hunkered down with maps to get a picture of the field he was about to command. As he drew close to town, he left the ambulance for his horse and rode swiftly up to Howard's headquarters on Cemetery Hill. Arriving around 4 P.M., what he initially saw must have worried him: hundreds, perhaps thousands of Union troops were streaming toward hastily erected defenses on Cemetery Hill. Some soldiers were fleeing in disorder, others were marching in formation, but all were headed for the safety of the Union lines on the hill. He approached Howard, and there ensued a conversation with several versions passed down through history. The two men finally agreed that Howard would retain command, and Hancock rode off to position some of the troops.[9]

As usual, Hancock gave orders crisply and authoritatively. He sent Brig. Gen. James F. Wadsworth's First Division of the First Corps to occupy Culp's Hill; ordered artillery there to support Wadsworth's division; and when Brig. Gen. John W. Geary's Second division of the Twelfth Corps arrived on the field sent them toward the left of the line, at a place called Little Round Top. One sergeant who observed Hancock later recalled that he was "all excitement—not nervous—looking in a thousand ways every minute and giving directions as carefully and precisely as though he was preparing for a great parade." Hancock then ordered the trains to the rear.

Next, he sent two notes to Meade, updating him on the situation. In the first note he told him he would hold the position until night. In the second note he offered the view that the position at Gettysburg "appears not unfavorable with good troops." When Slocum arrived on the field around 6 P.M., Hancock transferred command to him, then rode off to Taneytown to find Meade. After giving Meade a full report, he rested for a few hours before riding out to catch up to his corps.[10]

As Hancock managed the fight at Gettysburg, Meade concluded that the Confederate thrust would be in that town, and that he needed to rearrange his troops to meet the new reality. At 4:30 P.M. he sent an order to Sedgwick to "move your command up to Taneytown tonight," sending the trains to Westminster (except ambulances and ammunition), and keeping the Fifth Corps and the cavalry apprised of his movements. Later he sent another order to Sedgwick, telling him he had appointed Maj. Gen. John Newton to command the First Corps (thus replacing Abner Doubleday, whose performance at Gettysburg had been criticized by Howard, and Howard's comments passed on unfiltered to Meade). Fifteen minutes later, he sent a letter to Sickles telling him to "hold on" until he had further communication with Hancock and to leave a division in Emmitsburg to guard the army's "left and rear." By 6 P.M., after hearing Hancock's first report, Meade wrote to Hancock and Doubleday, giving Slocum command at Gettysburg upon his arrival and informing them that Sedgwick was moving up there and would be "pushed forward in the night, if required."

Then followed the key sentence in the note to Hancock, which undermines all the arguments made that Meade sought to avoid or postpone fighting until his army could be on the defensive. Meade wrote, "It seems to me we have so concentrated that a battle at Gettysburg is now forced on us, and that, if we get up all our people, *and attack with our whole force tomorrow,* we ought to defeat the force the enemy has" (author's italics). Any caution or equivocation had ended. With more complete information, Meade set a firm course: he would take the fight to Lee.[11]

Meade modified his plans a bit after talking to Hancock's aide Capt. I. B. Parker sometime after 6:00 P.M. At 7:00 P.M. he wrote to Sykes, "Move up to Gettysburg at once upon receipt of this order, if not already ordered to do so by General Slocum. The present prospect is that our general engagement must be there." A half an hour later, a new order went out to Sickles to move all his forces, including the division held at Emmitsburg, up to Gettysburg by daylight. He then sent a new order to Sedgwick: "It is of the utmost importance that your command should be up" at Gettysburg by the next morning because a "general battle seems to be impending." Sedgwick should stop or turn out all trains that hindered his "progress" and make a "forced" march to the town. Without the Sixth Corps on the ground, "we shall probably be outnumbered." Furthermore, Meade wanted to see his old and trusted friend that evening, writing, "[I will be] waiting to see you here before going to the front."[12]

Meade never saw Sedgwick that night. He waited until midnight, then set off for Gettysburg, leaving Butterfield to wait for Sedgwick. Butterfield gave up at 5:30 A.M. on July 2, when he sent a message and memorandum to Sedgwick. Not wanting to accuse Sedgwick of failure, Butterfield wrote, "Your non-arrival, prob-ably owing to the failure of orders to reach you, causes me to submit the following memorandum of the views of the general as far as your forces are concerned." The memorandum, dated July 1, 10 P.M., repeated the message Meade had sent earlier: "The general proposes to make a vigorous attack upon the enemy tomorrow." Knowing that the Sixth Corps would be too tired to fight on July 2 after a long night march, Meade thought that the Sixth Corps should "move forward as far as possible, and take up position in line of battle at some strong point, so that in the event of the general's being compelled to withdraw, you can cover his withdrawal. If he is successful, you can push forward to aid him." Of course, the memorandum supposed that the Sixth Corps would march through Taneytown, and if instead he chose to march through Two Taverns, that would of course change his ar-rival point in Gettysburg. Whatever the case, the memorandum continued, "[You should] communicate sufficiently in advance of your column, wherever it may be, to get orders direct from General Meade."[13]

On the evening of July 1, Meade and his staff saddled up and headed to Get-tysburg. Meade had much time to think about his situation and the contingencies of a looming battle. To start, he had no clear estimate of the total number of ca-sualties. Meade knew that the First and Eleventh Corps had fought hard, suffered high losses, yet were intact in a good defensive position on Cemetery Ridge. The Twelfth Corps had arrived in Gettysburg, and the Second, Third, and Fifth Corps would be en route or at Gettysburg no later than dawn. The exact location of the Sixth Corps was not known, but the orders to Sedgwick to join the army in Get-tysburg were explicit, and Meade had complete trust in Sedgwick to carry them out. The cavalry would have the flanks covered, the artillery reserve would be in place in Gettysburg, and Meade had even had Butterfield send orders to Capt. George H. Mendell of the battalion of engineers to guard the trains at Westmin-ster and Union Bridge from Confederate cavalry attacks.[14]

As for generals, Meade's inclination to allow his generals to run their own corps was about to be fully tested. So far, he had to make few changes, except to send Newton to command the First Corps (superseding the angry Doubleday) and to place Hancock in temporary command of the now-defunct "left wing" of the Army of the Potomac. Undoubtedly shocked and troubled by the death of his friend John Reynolds, he had acted promptly, giving the vigorous Hancock the same authority as Reynolds for a few crucial hours. By early evening, however, he had restored order to the high command by passing the mantle of field command to the ranking general at Gettysburg, Henry Slocum.

So far, Meade had fulfilled the vision of those who promoted him to be the commanding general: he had handled his new army well, let the generals run their corps, and ruffled few feathers. He had set the dispersed corps into motion upon taking command, but when he received sufficient information to know where Lee's army was headed, he responded by issuing new orders that channeled a large part of his army to attack Lee in Gettysburg, while keeping his wings solidly protected. He had lost a strong leader in Reynolds but quickly tried to fill that void by empowering Hancock. He had a contingency plan should the battle go against him, and he had kept his subordinates and superiors aware of his plans and decisions.

When he looked across his ledger of corps commanders, though, he must have had some lingering concerns. He had more faith in John Newton, West Point class of 1842, than his classmate of the same year, Abner Doubleday, though it was not a faith shared by all. Newton had a fine career in the prewar Corps of Engineers, but his most distinguished moment to date in battle had been at Marye's Heights during the Battle of Chancellorsville. At the head of the Second Corps he had Hancock, a friend, and perhaps his most dependable fighter since the death of Reynolds. He had a strong belief in John Sedgwick, his old friend and early supporter, and depended on him to lead the largest corps in a predictable manner. His loyalty to another early supporter, Henry Slocum, was undergoing a test, as information drifted in on Slocum's apparent slowness to arrive at Gettysburg and hesitancy to help others fight there. The head of the Fifth Corps, George Sykes, still rode on his reputation from his valiant leadership at the Battle of Bull Run. A graduate of the same West Point class as Newton, Doubleday, and Seth Williams, Sykes was new to corps command, having assumed that position upon Meade's promotion. No wonder Meade wanted Sykes to stay in close contact with the ranking officer on the field, Henry Slocum.[15]

As for the pious, one-armed abolitionist at the head of the ill-starred Eleventh Corps, Oliver O. Howard, a "well-dressed little gentleman," Meade's only known assessment from this time was that he did not "know" Howard as well as he did Hancock (the source is a staff officer of Hancock's). However, three messages sent by Howard on July 1 had been troubling. He did not acknowledge Hancock's authority over him until he received a written order at 7 P.M. Once he received that order, he turned over command to Slocum, the ranking general on the field. Referring to Hancock's role that afternoon, he simply noted that "General H. assisted me in carrying out orders I had already issued." As for the general retreat of the two corps under his command, Howard blamed lack of reinforcements and poor positioning, not his leadership. Reaching for the dramatic that the generals of the

Army of the Potomac often used, he appealed to Meade, "The above [retreat] has mortified me and will disgrace me. Please inform me frankly if you disapprove of my conduct today, that I may know what to do." In his final message from Gettysburg, written at 10 P.M., he assessed the day's casualties: "3,000 killed, wounded, and missing" from the Eleventh Corps, and one piece of artillery lost.[16] Meade definitely needed to talk to this corps commander when he arrived in Gettysburg.

Meade's greatest concerns, however, had to be the commander of the Third Corps, Daniel Sickles, and his own chief of staff, Daniel Butterfield. As early as January 1863, he had called these men "bad influences" in a letter he sent to his wife. His prediction of their power over Hooker had proven true: Hooker had overplayed his political hand after the Battle of Chancellorsville, and now these very same individuals were in vital positions under Meade. Of course he had been warned about retaining Butterfield as chief of staff on June 28, but then again, no one else had wanted the job.[17] So he was stuck with two men who he must have known would knife him in the back, if they felt threatened.

Other key positions were held by trustworthy generals. The strong-willed Henry J. Hunt commanded the artillery for the army, with the equally firm-minded Charles S. Wainwright as his top lieutenant. Gouverneur K. Warren had the ear of Meade and, with his good eye for topography, had been appointed chief engineer of the Army of the Potomac. Meade had already used him to scout out the Pipe Creek defensive position, and he had arrived in Gettysburg just after Hancock on July 1, assisting in the placement of the troops in their new defensive positions. Seth Williams, the adjutant general of the army, had retained that position upon Meade's assumption of command and would remain in that post until the next year, when he became inspector general of the army. The provost marshal, Marsena Patrick, was irascible but dependable. The quartermaster, Rufus Ingalls, and the head of railroads, Herman Haupt, were also reliable. The commander of cavalry, Alfred Pleasonton, had made his reputation at the Battle of Brandy Station, but Haskell hinted at other views of him in his thumbnail sketch, describing him as "a nice little dandy, with brown hair and beard—a straw hat with a little jockey rim, which he cocks upon one side of his head, with an unsteady eye, that looks slyly at you, then dodges."[18]

Taken together, these men would be part of the leadership team Meade would depend on over the three-day battle. Whether his more inclusive style of leadership would work best with this group remained to be seen.

Sometime after midnight, Meade and his staff arrived at Gettysburg. They rode through the cemetery, then stopped at the lodge at the entrance on the Baltimore Pike. Here Meade found his main generals: Slocum, Howard, Sickles, and Warren. They updated him on the positions and conditions of their troops, and he told them that the entire Army of the Potomac would be in Gettysburg by early morning, except the Sixth Corps, which would arrive later. After Howard remarked how strong the Union position was, Meade replied that he was "glad" because it was "too late to leave it." After hearing the updates, Meade walked over to the guns posted at the top of Cemetery Hill, squinting through the darkness at the campfires of the Confederate soldiers on Seminary Ridge. What he thought at that particular moment was not recorded, but surely he had to wonder if all of Lee's forces were up and ready to do battle, perhaps attacking before the Army of Potomac had assembled. He had not sought a battle here, but now he was in one. So Meade walked back to the lodge, got on his horse, called Howard and Hunt to join him, and together they rode off accompanied by Capt. William H. Paine (an engineer) to examine the current lines.[19] The longest and most momentous day of George Meade's life has just begun.

The men rode the length of the line for several hours, while Captain Paine drew a map of the field (no easy feat in the dark while sitting on a horse), marking the spots where Meade planned to send each corps. They found the Eleventh Corps holding on to Cemetery Hill, the First Corps stretched out along Cemetery Ridge, the Third Corps just south of the First Corps, winding back toward Little Round Top, the First Division of the First Corps holding Culp's Hill, and part of the Twelfth Corps camped where Rock Creek intersected with the Baltimore Pike. Noting the fact that the First and Twelfth Corps did not connect, Slocum asked for help in plugging that gap. Hunt first sent three artillery batteries to cover the gap, and later in the morning they were joined by Brig. Gen. John Geary's Second Division and Brig. Gen. Alpheus S. Williams's First Division of the Twelfth Corps, which effectively closed the gap. Meade ordered Slocum and Warren to study the terrain in front of the Twelfth Corps to see if it would be conducive for an attack. The attack might occur once the Second and Fifth Corps arrived on the field.[20]

Around 6 A.M. Meade decided to make his headquarters at the small frame house owned by "Widow" Lydia Leister, which sat on the west side of Taneytown Road, close to the cemetery keeper's lodge. The house's main room was not more than "ten or twelve feet square," with one bed, one table, and "five or six straight-backed rushed-bottom chairs." Its lack of size did not matter, however, for Meade would be spending the bulk of his time outside. It was there that he met Brig. Gen. John Gibbon, who was in the van of the Second Corps as it marched into Gettysburg.[21]

Meade spent the next few hours gathering information and placing the corps in position to attack or defend, as conditions warranted. He told Gibbon to put his troops near the Granite Schoolhouse Lane, awaiting further orders. Next to arrive were two divisions of the Fifth Corps, which came to Wolf Hill around 7 A.M. They too awaited further orders.

By mid-morning Meade had information that persuaded him to prepare to defend, not attack. Slocum and Warren reported to Meade that the terrain to their front was not suitable for a Union assault. With this information, Meade temporarily abandoned thoughts of attack and instead dwelled on repositioning units for defense. He sent the Second Corps to replace the tired-out First Corps on Cemetery Ridge. The First Corps became the reserve behind the Eleventh Corps on Cemetery Hill. The Fifth Corps was brought in to be the reserve force in the Union center, essentially taking the place just held by the Second Corps. The Twelfth Corps was pulled back, setting up a continuous line between Culp's Hill and Rock Creek. That morning also saw the arrival of three more of the five brigades in the Artillery Reserve, thus adding a total of 108 pieces of artillery to the corps batteries. Equally vital was the 23,883 rounds of artillery ammunition brought by the three artillery brigades, which replaced the rounds fired on July 1. The cavalry were assigned to the flanks of the tightening Union position, and by 3 P.M. the first of thirteen thousand men of Sedgwick's Sixth Corps had trudged into Gettysburg.[22]

Meade could feel comfortable that he had concentrated his forces quickly and efficiently in a tight "fishhook" with good interior lines and a headquarters positioned in the middle of the field. Though the Artillery Reserve and the Sixth Corps had not arrived by 9 A.M., with all the men converging on Gettysburg, and no strong attack yet from the Confederates, it was not surprising that he called out to his new aide and son, Capt. George Meade, and talked to him for a few minutes. Captain Meade recalled that "he seemed in excellent spirits, as if well pleased with affairs as far as they had proceeded."[23] Little could either man know that in issuing his next order, which was no more or less technical than any he had given so far that morning, he would be setting into motion a string of events and charges that would nearly cost him his job, and cast aspersions on his performance as commander that would haunt his reputation for generations.

Meade sent his son to see if Sickles had finished carrying out the order sent to relieve Geary's division, link up with the southern end of the Second Corps, and stretch his line to Little Round Top. Meade needed the Third Corps in this position to guard the high ground of Little Round Top and connect to the Second Corps. Captain Meade did not get to speak to Sickles; he was resting in a tent. Instead, artillery Capt. George E. Randolph talked to Sickles, who told him to tell Meade that the Third Corps was not in position, and he was not sure what that position was supposed to be. Captain Meade dutifully rode back to his father with this reply, and Maj. Gen. Meade made it clear that his earlier orders were unambiguous: connect with the left of the Second Corps and extend his line to Little Round Top. Meade sent his son back to Sickles with his message, and Captain Meade found Sickles on his horse outside his headquarters. Meade conveyed his father's orders to him, and Sickles replied that he would put his troops in place soon, but in his view, Geary's troops had been "massed," not positioned. He then asked if Major General Meade could send Major General Hunt to look over the battery positions of the Third Corps.[24]

When Hunt did not quickly appear, Sickles sent his top aide, Major Henry E. Tremain, to discuss the situation with Meade. Sickles's primary concerns were his

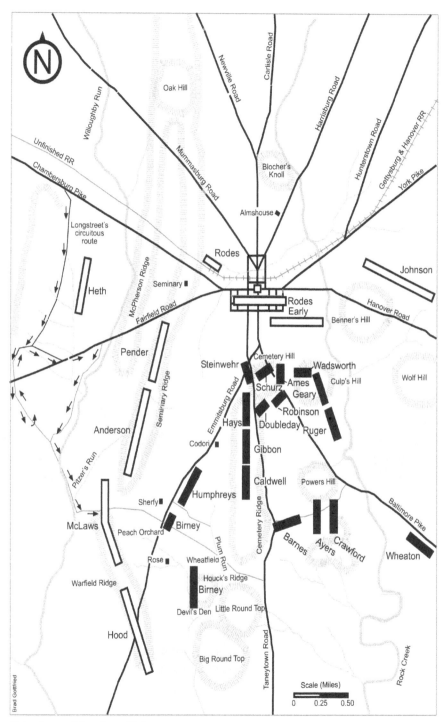

Gettysburg—Morning of July 2

left flank, and the low position he had been assigned. His troops could not see over Houck's Ridge, and Sickles wanted his men further west, along the Emmittsburg Road, so they could see the enemy coming. Tremain told Meade these concerns, and according to his recollections, Meade appeared unfazed, only remarking that cavalry were in position to protect the left flank of the Third Corps. When Sickles heard these remarks, he decided to visit Meade himself to press his case. The fullest account of their conversation comes from *Historicus,* which most historians believe came from Sickles himself, writing several months after the battle. Sickles proposed he occupy the higher ground up at the Peach Orchard, instead of the lower ground between Little Round Top and Cemetery Ridge assigned to him. Sickles feared that he was vulnerable to a frontal attack; Meade supposedly replied, "O, generals are all apt to look for the attack to be made where they are." Meade reiterated his earlier commands for the placing of the Third Corps. He declined to accompany Sickles on a ride to the Peach Orchard, but he did agree to send Hunt in his stead. Before leaving Sickles asked if he could post the troops as he saw fit, and according to *Historicus,* Meade answered, "Certainly, within the limits of the general instructions I have given you; any ground within those limits you choose to occupy, I leave to you."[25]

So Hunt rode off with Sickles, and they examined his current position and the position proposed by Sickles. Though Hunt recognized that the Peach Orchard provided high ground and more generous fields of fire, his major concerns were connecting to the Second Corps and finding enough men to staff Sickles's preferred line. Sickles's proposal would leave a gap between the Second and Third Corps, and to hold the new line he would need the Fifth Corps, which at that moment was the only reserve the army had. Meade's preferred position was half the length of Sickles's proposed line, and could be adequately held with the troops on hand (without using the reserve). After discussing the proposal, Hunt prepared to leave. Sickles asked if he should move the Third Corps into his preferred position. Hunt replied, "Not on my authority. I will report to General Meade for his instructions." Hunt then rode off to see Meade.[26]

Hunt told Meade that Sickles's proposed line had merits, but its faults outweighed its advantages, and that he should examine it himself before he re-positioned troops. Meade "nodded assent," and Hunt rode off to Cemetery Hill.[27]

During the next two hours three separate events occurred that would be woven into a single narrative later by Sickles. First, a shuffling of units left Sickles without cavalry support, causing him some anxiety. Pleasonton had ordered Buford's two cavalry brigades to Westminster to refit and guard the army's trains. Meade had authorized this departure, believing that Pleasonton would replace the brigades with others. But he did not, and it took two messages from Meade just after noon to prompt Pleasonton to order Brigadier General David McM. Gregg to send a "regiment" to patrol the Emmitsburg Road, when "practicable." Secondly, as Buford's cavalry withdrew under the new orders from Pleasonton, Sickles naturally grew edgy. He sent Colonel Hiram Berdan with four companies of his sharpshooters, supported by the Third Maine, to recon the Pitzer Woods. As they did so, they came under fire, heavy enough to drive them back before long. Thirdly, while this small operation occurred, Butterfield was busy working on a contingency plan for retreat from Gettysburg, should that prove necessary. Meade had sent a circular to his corps commanders at 11 A.M., instructing them to prepare sketches of their positions and those of the enemy in front of them. He apparently asked the newly arrived Butterfield to gather these reports and produce a contingency plan, though no such document was found in his or anyone else's papers, nor did Meade specifically remember assigning Butterfield this task. But Butterfield remembered preparing it, and Adj. Gen. Seth Williams either saw it or knew of it, as did John Gibbon. But what did it *mean*?[28]

Long after the battle Sickles used the missing document as a cudgel to pound Meade for his alleged fear of battle at Gettysburg. Butterfield hedged in his view, telling the Joint Committee on the Conduct of the War that Meade "may have desired it prepared for an emergency, without any view of executing it then, or he may have had it prepared with a full view of its execution." Gibbon did not see it this way at all, nor did Hunt.[29] In fact, no order given by Meade in the morning or the afternoon suggested retreat from Gettysburg. He consistently arranged men and artillery for a defensive battle, to be sure, but not for a retreat. In the spring of 1864, however, when another long season of fighting lay ahead, and politicians in Washington were looking for scapegoats for the inability of the Army of the Potomac to destroy the Army of Northern Virginia after Gettysburg, this missing memo would be one more patch to add to the quilt of condemnation prepared to remove Meade from command.

Sometime during this sequence of events, Major Tremain reappeared at Meade's headquarters. He conveyed three concerns of Sickles to Meade: the threat of an attack, the news of the arrival of his last two brigades from Emmitsburg, and the possibility of the Third Corps using Emmitsburg Road for its trains, provided that cavalry protected the road. Meade appeared distracted to Tremain, replying only that the cavalry would protect the road and his earlier orders on the trains remained the same. Disappointed, Tremain rode back to Sickles to tell him the story. This was the last straw for Sickles: he ordered Maj. Gen. David Birney to use his division to occupy the forward position he had recommended to Hunt. When asked about this decision by the Joint Committee on the Conduct of the War, Sickles answered unequivocally: "It was not through any misinterpretation of orders. It was either a good line or a bad one, and whichever it was, I took it on my own responsibility."[30]

So Sickles had ignored—or deliberately defied—a direct order from his commanding officer, and at least eight months after the battle, owned his decision. Sickles thrust his entire corps well ahead of Meade's main line, rendering his men and the right flank of the Second Corps highly vulnerable to attack from the Confederates. Just after the battle, Meade and Halleck generously offered that there could have been misinterpretation of orders, but in his own testimony, Sickles would have none of that.[31]

While Meade had been busy moving his troops and preparing for defense, his counterpart, Gen. Robert E. Lee, had been equally busy preparing his troops to attack. Therein lies a principal difference between the two commanders. After the first day's hard fighting, before all his troops were up, Lee had discussed the army's options with his key subordinate, Lt. Gen. James Longstreet. Historians have drawn heavily on Longstreet's writings for accounts of their discussion, but within hours, most generals heard whiffs of the basic disagreement: Longstreet wanted to withdraw the army to the southeast, find a good defensive position, and let the Army of the Potomac attack. Lee found flaws in this argument: no cavalry was present to screen the march to the southeast, the Confederate trains were stretched for miles all the way back to Chambersburg and could not easily be rerouted, the routes of travel were not known, and the countermeasures of the Army of the Potomac were completely unknown (indeed, the exact whereabouts of each Union corps was not known). The Confederates had the initiative and should keep it. Lee sent Col. Armistead L. Long to reconnoiter the Union positions in the late afternoon of July 1; when Long returned, he told them what they suspected: the Union held the high ground along Cemetery Hill, Culp's Hill, and Cemetery Ridge. That did not deter Lee: he turned to generals Longstreet and Hill and said, "Gentlemen, we will attack the enemy in the morning as early as practicable."[32] So Lee had analyzed a difficult challenge and decided to attack, while Meade had assessed an evolving situation and decided to *prepare* for an attack. Two generals, two different temperaments, two different strategic assignments, and two different responses. One was a gambler, the other was cautious. Which course was appropriate was about to be tested.

That evening (July 1), Lee rode over to Lieutenant General Ewell to discuss the possibility of an attack by his corps in the morning. When Ewell did not attack the next morning (July 2), Lee rode over to him and told him to launch an attack once he heard Longstreet's guns. That plan settled, Lee rode back to his headquarters for another discussion with Longstreet, who implored him to wait to attack until Maj. Gen. George E. Pickett's division and Brig. Gen. Evander M. Law's brigade were in Gettysburg. Lee only gave him permission to wait until Law's brigade arrived (around noon, as it turned out). Lee's plan was to seize the high ground along Emmitsburg Road, with Maj. Gen. John Bell Hood's and Maj. Gen. Lafayette McLaw's divisions leading the attack on the Union left, and Hill's corps attacking the Union center (and Ewell joining in, perhaps for the final envelopment). When Law's brigade finally arrived, Longstreet put his corps into motion.[33]

As Longstreet's corps began its long and tiring march and countermarch, the hum of activity at Meade's headquarters grew louder. Unfortunately, most of the messages sent by Meade were not preserved, as he himself noted in an interview several months after the battle. There are a few official documents that note orders, a mention of a meeting, and an air of expectancy and urgency. But there are not enough official documents to create a time line of actions between noon and 3 P.M. on July 2 for Meade. Official records do note the several orders sent to Pleasonton in the early afternoon, the mixed messages received from signalmen atop Round Top (the Confederates are coming; no, they are not), and an order from Meade to the commander of the Artillery Reserve to send a battery to Sickles. Just after 2 P.M., the lead elements of the Sixth Corps came swinging into view on the Baltimore Pike, after an exhausting and historic forced night march of thirty-two miles.[34]

With the arrival of his last major corps, Meade felt ready to face Lee. Consequently, he called his corps commanders to his headquarters for a brief meeting and sent off a message to Halleck summarizing the situation. To begin with, he had a "strong position for the defensive." He had not attacked yet because he wanted the Sixth Corps and other divisions to arrive, and he wanted Lee's position to be "more developed." He still did not know what Lee intended to do, only that he had been "moving on both my flanks." If Lee chose not to attack, and if Meade could find "positive information on the position of the enemy," he would attack—unless he found it "hazardous" to attack, or that Lee was actually trying to get between Meade and Washington. If the latter case, he would move back to his supply base at Westminster. While Meade's critics could hardly find a commander preparing to retreat in this letter, his proponents could not find a bold general on the verge of a major strike. Meade's closing sentence captures his feelings after less than a week in command of the Army of the Potomac: "I feel fully the responsibility resting upon me, but will endeavor to act with caution."[35]

Surprisingly, no complete account of the meeting of the corps commanders at 3 P.M. exists. Before Sickles arrived, however, Warren told Meade that the Third Corps was not in position. According to Warren, this was news to Meade. Consequently, Meade ordered Sykes to take his Fifth Corps out of its reserve position and hold the left flank of the Union line "at all hazards." The meeting then ended, and as the generals rode off, Sickles and his staff finally appeared. With the sound of artillery fire coming from the position of the Third Corps, Meade sharply told Sickles to return to the line he had been "instructed to take." He then told Sickles he would soon join him at the Third Corps position.[36]

Meade then mounted a horse on loan from Pleasonton (Old Baldy had been wounded) and began riding toward Sickles's position. On the way, he told Warren to investigate the sound of artillery firing near Little Round Top or, as one of Warren's aides recalled the conversation, "Warren, I hear a little peppering going on in the direction of the little hill off yonder. I wish that you would ride over and if anything serious is going on . . . attend to it." So Warren rode off to Little Round Top and his moment of greatest fame in the Civil War. When Meade arrived at Sickles's headquarters near the Peach Orchard, he was astonished. This was not the line he had ordered Sickles to establish, and now the Third Corps was overextended, which rendered the rest of the Union line vulnerable as well. Meade called for Sickles and pointed out the ridge behind him that he had wanted Sickles to occupy. Sickles apologized and offered to reset his line. Meade replied, "Yes, you may as well, at once. The enemy will not let you withdraw without taking advantage of your position, but you have to come back, and you may well do it at once as at any other time." Sickles turned to give the orders, but it was too late. Confederate cannon opened fire on the Peach Orchard, and Meade said to Sickles, "I wish to God you could [withdraw], but the enemy won't let you!"[37]

Some shells hit near the generals, and one round frightened Meade's new horse. The horse jumped around, but Meade managed to stay on. What might have happened if Meade had been thrown and injured? We shall never know. Thankfully, he was not, and he rode off toward headquarters.[38]

On the way, he received word from Warren that men were desperately needed to hold Little Round Top. Meade immediately ordered Brig. Gen. Andrew Humphreys's Second Division (Third Corps) to the hill, not knowing when the Fifth Corps would be up. In fine fashion, Humphreys turned his division on its march toward Emmitsburg Road to the left flank, in a well-executed marching maneuver. No sooner had the men begun marching toward Little Round Top when Meade received a second message from Warren, telling him that men from the Fifth Corps were arriving on the hill to defend it. Meade cancelled his original order, and Humphreys's division turned again, marching back toward it original destination.[39]

As the lead regiments of Hood's division set off toward Devil's Den and Little Round Top at approximately 4 P.M., the fiercest sustained fighting of the three-day battle was about to begin. Longstreet would later call the performance of his First Corps to be the "best three hours fighting ever done by any troops on any battlefield."[40] While that may well be true, the Union fighting was pretty outstanding too, as the combined efforts of the Third, Fifth, and Sixth Corps could attest.

After the brief meeting of the generals, Hancock returned to Brig. Gen. John Gibbon's position on Cemetery Ridge. There they watched Humphreys's division march toward Emmitsburg Road. Hancock remarked to Gibbon and the staffers nearby, "Gentlemen, that is a splendid advance. But, those troops will be coming back again very soon." Before that occurred, however, Hancock received orders from Meade to send a division to aid Sykes's Fifth Corps, which had begun its desperate defense of the Union left flank. Hancock ordered Brig. Gen. John C. Caldwell to lead his First Division (Second Corps) to Sykes's aid, and off the four brigades marched into the maelstrom known as "the Wheatfield." By now the fighting ranged from Little Round Top to the Peach Orchard, and while the Fifth Corps barely held on to Little Round Top, the exposed Third Corps was being pushed back from its salient. Suddenly, a shot struck Sickles in the right knee, and as aides helped him off his horse, shells fell around them as they huddled near the Trostle house. Propping Sickles up on a large boulder, the aides waited for an ambulance. Sickles remained alert enough to give orders to Maj. Gen. Birney to take command of the Third Corps, then with lit cigar in hand, Sickles raised up on the stretcher bearing him away and exhorted his men to stand firm. As the Confederate advance continued and only artillery defended the area around the Trostle house, Birney made the difficult decision to have Humphreys pull back his division to Plum Run, in an effort to establish a new line from Cemetery Ridge to Little Round Top (Meade's original line).[41]

Hearing of the wounding of Maj. Gen. Sickles, Meade ordered Hancock to assume command of the entire left wing of the army. At nearly the same time, Union reserves were sent into action, with Fifth Corps troops under Brig. Gen. Samuel W. Crawford charging down into the Wheatfield just as Confederate troops were withdrawing. Crawford's men were supported by a brigade of the Sixth Corps, which had just arrived on the battlefield and been sent immediately to the right of Crawford's division.

With the Union left finally secure, Meade turned his attention to the center of his line, ordering Slocum to send him all available reinforcements from the Twelfth Corps. Meade also sent orders to Hancock to reinforce the Third Corps with another brigade from the Second Corps, so Hancock told Col. George Willard of Brig. Gen. Alexander Hays's Third Division to follow him to the field. Willard's brigade slammed into Brig. Gen. William Barksdale's charging Mississippians and stopped their advance. Yet trouble still lurked in the wide gap between the Third and Second Corps. Seeing Confederate troops under Brig. Gen. Cadmus Wilcox heading straight for the crest of Cemetery Ridge, Hancock saw another regiment just coming up to the field, the First Minnesota, and exclaimed to Col. William Colville, "Advance, Colonel, and take those colors!" Off the First Minnesota charged, bayonets in front, 262 men versus 1,600, suffering 80 percent casualties as their shock attack halted Wilcox's charge.[42]

As Hancock sent units to defend the gap, Meade temporarily returned to his headquarters and sent an order to Newton to send two divisions to plug the last hole in the Union line. Then Meade rode to the gap in the line, watching as Confederate soldiers approached the crowd of aides around him. Would this small band of men, led by the commander of the entire Army of the Potomac have to stop this attack? His son, describing the moment in dramatic language, wrote, "He straightens himself in his stirrups, as do also the aides who now ride closer to him, bracing themselves to meet the crisis." Will he "throw himself into the breach?" As shots flew and shells struck around the group, someone yelled, "There they come, general!" It was Newton himself, leading the van of Doubleday's division down Taneytown Road. The soldiers swung to their right and charged toward the advancing Confederates. Caught up in the thrill of the battle, Meade rode up with the skirmishers, shouting, "Come on, gentlemen!" One aide remarked how desperate the situation had just been, and Meade replied, "Yes, but it is all right now, it all right now." Receiving word that the Confederates were massing a large body of troops just over the ridge, Meade ordered the First Corps to halt at the crest of the ridge. As the light began to fade, it was prudent to hold up in a strong defensive position.[43]

As dusk descended on the battlefield and the last units fought to recover artillery from the field, attention turned toward the north and east, where Maj. Gen. Edward Johnson's three brigades were making a determined attack on the 1,350 men of Brig. Gen. George Sears Greene's brigade, now holding the entirety of Culp's Hill after the departure of the rest of the Twelfth Corps to other portions of the battlefield. Slocum's divisions had not yet returned to the hill at the time of Johnson's attack, and only the quick support from other generals helped to hold the vital hill. When the firing started, Greene asked Howard and Wadsworth to send help, and each general sent four regiments to support him. Even Hancock joined in the fight; when he heard the sound of gunfire from Culp's Hill, he ordered Gibbon to send two regiments to aid Greene. This was in addition to the brigade under Col. Samuel S. Carroll and the two regiments sent by Brig. Gen. Alexander S. Webb to help Howard stop a fierce attack by two brigades under Maj. Gen. Jubal Early on Cemetery Hill. Also coming to their aid was the Second Division of the First Corps under the command of Brig. Gen. John C. Robinson.

Meade had ordered Newton to send a division to help the Eleventh Corps when he heard the sounds of the firing (though by the time they got there, the fighting had ended). Meade watched the battle from McKnight's Hill, sending word to the troops on Cemetery Hill that help was on its way. The Confederates got to the crest of the hill and swarmed around two Union artillery batteries, but they were soon driven off. Without an accompanying attack by the three brigades under Maj. Gen. Robert E. Rodes, the two Confederate brigades had no choice but to retreat from the hill back into town. By mid-evening, the nighttime assault had been thwarted, and Cemetery Hill and Culp's Hill rested securely in Union hands.[44]

Once assured that the Cemetery hill remained in Union hands, Meade returned to his headquarters and updated Halleck. His opening sentence summarizing the day's events read, "The enemy attacked me about 4 pm, this day, and, after one of the severest contests of the war, was repulsed at all points." He noted the high number of Union casualties, then listed the two generals killed and the four generals wounded. He closed his brief paragraph with his plan, "I shall remain in my present position tomorrow, but am not prepared to say, until better advised of the condition of the army, whether my operations will be of an offensive or defensive character."[45]

With a day of hard fighting over, Meade sought to gauge the "condition" of the army and the spirit of his generals. He called for his generals to meet him at his headquarters in the Leister house. Unfortunately for Meade, the meeting came to be called a "council," which in some military circles implies a democracy of generals, instead of a hierarchy. Yet Meade himself did not seem troubled by the designation, for he later referred to the group meeting as a council. The meeting began sometime after 9 P.M. and broke up at midnight, even as the sound of firing on Cemetery Hill could be heard. Twelve men were in the small front room, just over ten square feet, with only a bed, a table, and six chairs for furniture.[46] Whether the meeting took so long because each general had to give a report as he arrived or because of lively discussion, the historical record does not say. *Some* of what was said was recorded by Daniel Butterfield, acting as secretary for the group. What it meant or even implied became fodder for future debates over the leadership of Meade.

All that would lie in the future, however. That hot July evening, as thousands of men lay dead and wounded on the battlefield, the generals described their commands and discussed the options facing the army. The first order of business was to establish the number of able-bodied men available to fight. Though no official returns had been tallied yet, Butterfield used the rough numbers supplied by each general to arrive at a figure of fifty-eight thousand infantrymen. Of course, the fighting condition of the men could not be quantified, nor did the generals have any reliable information on Lee's number of able-bodied troops. The question of adequate supplies came up, with only one day's rations on hand and the bulk of the army's wagon trains twenty miles away near Westminster. The generals felt they could get by through additional purchases from local farmers, so that concern was addressed. The only major debate point became the army's line. John Newton, the newly designated commander of the First Corps, a "muscular, well-dressed man" with "swagger," argued that "this was no place to fight a battle in." Surprised by the firmness of this opinion, John Gibbon, the junior officer in the group, boldly asked him to explain why. Newton feared that Lee might shift an entire corps that night and attack the Union left in the morning. Meade then expressed a different concern: the current line was too irregular. This topic appeared to be going nowhere, so Butterfield proposed to ask the generals three questions, a procedure Meade agreed to. Suddenly, and probably without complete intention, a freewheeling discussion turned into a vote, with a record.[47]

Butterfield's first question was "Under existing circumstance, is it advisable for this army to remain in its present position, or to retire to another nearer its base of supplies?" By convention the junior officer votes first in such a council, and Gibbon, not wanting to upset a superior (Newton), answered, "Correct position of the army, but would not retreat." Each general then concurred, with Hancock insisting that any changes in position should not force the army to "give up [the] field."[48]

Then Butterfield posed his second question: "It being determined to remain in present position, shall the army attack or wait the attack of the enemy?" Gibbon began again with the view that the army was "in no condition to attack." Each general fundamentally agreed with Gibbon, with only Howard hinting at some offensive response by saying, "Wait [to] attack until 4 P.M. tomorrow."[49]

The final question got to the matter of timing. Butterfield asked, "If we wait [to] attack, how long?" Gibbon said to wait until the enemy "moved"; Williams, Birney, Sykes, and Sedgwick said to wait one day. Newton had no time line, just a worry: "If we wait, it will give them a chance to cut our line." Hancock was also worried but did not advocate attack. He said, "Can't wait long, can't be idle." Slocum was clear on all three questions: "Stay and fight it out." Only Howard suggested offensive operations, though hedged by time and Lee's actions. He argued that if Lee did not attack, the Union army should "attack them."[50]

With the voting finished, Meade spoke up: "Such then is the decision." Although critics such as Sickles and Butterfield later said that this remark proved that he followed the advice of his generals rather than heed his own counsel, that is not how Sykes, Newton, Sedgwick, and Gibbon saw it, as they explained in letters written in March 1864 in reply to a circular from Meade asking them to comment on "what transpired at the council" and whether Meade "at any time insisted on the withdrawal of the army from before Gettysburg." Gibbon was particularly detailed about the evening, stating unequivocally, "I never heard General Meade say one word in favor of a retreat, nor do I believe that he did so, being confident I should have heard it, the council meeting in a room not to exceed 10 feet square." Furthermore, he remembered, "There was great good feeling amongst the corps commanders at their agreeing so unanimously." Certainly, Meade did not remember advocating retreat nor needing the advice of his generals to make his decision. As he told the Joint Committee on the Conduct of the War in March 1864, "The opinion of the council was unanimous, which agreed fully with my own views, that we should maintain our lines as they were then held, and that we should wait the movements of the enemy and see whether he made any further attack before we assumed the offensive. I felt satisfied that the enemy would attack again." In fact, Gibbon later recalled, Meade spoke to him as the meeting broke up, saying, "If Lee attacks tomorrow, it will be in *your front*." Why, asked Gibbon? Meade replied, "Because he has made attacks on both our flanks and failed, and if he concludes to try it again it will be on our center."[51]

Before trying to catch a few hours' sleep before the next day's fight began, Meade had one more military matter to attend to. When Slocum and Williams returned to the Twelfth Corps, they found that part of their line had been occupied by Confederate troops. Williams asked permission to attack the entrenched Confederate troops at daybreak, and Slocum granted him permission, passing on the request to Meade, who also approved the attack.[52] With that decision made, Meade settled in for a brief rest before morning.

Though his mind was probably focused on the challenges of the next day, Meade surely knew he had held firm in one of the sharpest attacks of the war by the best Confederate army in the field. The exact numbers were not recorded yet, but later estimates would place Union losses at ten thousand and Confederate losses at sixty-eight hundred.[53] The day's fighting inverted the normal ratio of casualties, with defensive casualties nearly twice as high as offensive casualties. Why? It could have been first-rate Southern marksmanship, but the fairly well-organized echelon assault under Longstreet's command versus the piecemeal insertion of Union brigades and regiments into the fight probably played a bigger role. Longstreet sent eleven brigades to attack twenty-two Union brigades, and the Confederates had nearly broken through the thin Union line several times. Longstreet's men had damaged or shattered the better part of thirteen Union brigades. How? By exploiting the weak and exposed Third Corps line before it had time to dig into its new position. The Third Corps paid dearly for Sickles's bold and insubordinate decision to occupy a line of his choosing; it would be so decimated after the battle that it would be broken up the next year and divided up among some remaining corps. The Fifth Corps had lost heavily, but it would survive intact as a corps. The Second Corps suffered as well, though not as severely as the Third or Fifth Corps. On Culp's Hill some brigades of the underappreciated Twelfth Corps fought hard and took heavy casualties, as did a few regiments of the Eleventh Corps on Cemetery Hill. Various artillery batteries had fought with distinction and valor on July 2, losing many men and horses.

Throughout the battle, Meade had been an active and engaged leader. He had shuffled brigades, even divisions from one section of the battlefield to another, and assigned his most trusted and capable lieutenant, Hancock, to manage the fighting of the entire left wing, a job Hancock had performed magnificently. His other corps commanders had been allowed to manage their own troops, with almost no interference from Meade. The one blemish on the day was the insubordination of Daniel Sickles. Sickles's dangerous maneuver had put Meade's entire army in jeopardy, though once the firing began, Sickles led his corps valiantly until his wounding. But it was Meade and Hancock who directed the brigades that filled the gaps, thus saving the Union army. When the firing died down, Meade assembled his generals in a meeting, and there he learned the condition of his army and the resolution of his generals. To a man they wanted to stay and fight—and they did.

By comparison, Lee had managed his attack in his usual way. After giving orders to his corps commanders, he let them do their work, not overseeing their decisions in any deliberate way all day. He stayed near his headquarters on Seminary Ridge, watching the battle proceed through his binoculars. Though his hard-fighting troops would not let him down that day, his corps commanders did, but he did not admonish them in his official report.[54] Historian Russell Weigley, not as gentle in his assessments of Lee and his corps commanders in this battle, writes, "Lee's failure to obtain the actions he expected from Stuart, Ewell, and Longstreet could serve as an object lesson in how not to command an army and how not to deal with subordinates." Blame and what-ifs have been argued for generations about that fateful day and will continue to be argued as long as the battle is studied. But in truth, Lee's hands-off approach to battle once orders had been given had already been established in other battles, and it would continue after Gettysburg. Would better reconnaissance, clearer orders, and more aggressive responses from his corps commanders made a difference? Without a doubt. But the quick and firm responses of the generals facing his army must be considered as well, not to mention the stubborn fighting spirit of the hard-luck Army of the Potomac. Weigley gives considerable credit for the victory to Meade's leadership, saying that Meade had "thoroughly outgeneraled Lee."[55]

At the end of the day, the Union line held. The Army of the Potomac had withstood an attack as great as that at Chancellorsville, and this time the commander had not buckled. By the rapid and effective repositioning of the troops, the interposition of his army between Lee's army and Washington, the acceptance of battle on a field not of his choosing, and the full use of all his forces, Meade had led the Army of the Potomac to its greatest victory.

Meade had a short sleep in the early morning hours of July 3. Though it is unclear when his day started, he hardly could have slept through the noise of the twenty-six guns of the Union Twelfth Corps that fired toward Culp's Hill at 4:30 A.M. Once up, he sent out a flurry of orders that morning.

He remained concerned about the roads leading to Gettysburg, the possibilities of assuming either offense or defense after another day of battle, and the protection of Washington. The first official notice of Meade's activity appeared in a 6 A.M. message from Pleasanton to Gregg. Pleasanton wrote, "The general commanding [Meade] is fearful of the enemy obtaining possession of the ridge on the Baltimore turnpike, behind the bridge, which is the right of General Slocum's position, and wishes you to place a force of cavalry and battery, to hold that position, to the right of the road facing Gettysburg. This point is so important that it must be held at all hazards." The next message went out at 7 A.M. to French in Frederick, Maryland. Meade expected the attack to be "renewed today," and if that happened, and the Confederates fell back toward the Potomac River after the fighting, French was to march his army to Harper's Ferry and "annoy and harass" the Confederates' retreat. If the Union army had to withdraw, he was to "look to Washington, and throw your force there for its protection." As always, Meade never lost sight of one of his primary responsibilities: protect Washington. To Couch in Harrisburg he wrote at 8:30 A.M., "The sound of my guns for these three days, it is taken for granted, is all the additional notice you need to come on. Should the enemy withdraw, by prompt cooperation we might destroy him." However, should Meade's army be defeated, "your return and defense of Harrisburg and the Susquehanna is not at all endangered."[56]

Meade also shuffled troops to help with the fighting at Culp's Hill and to reinforce Howard in case Lee attacked his position. Meade ordered Sedgwick to
send Brig. Gen. Alexander Shaler's First Brigade to help out the Twelfth Corps on
Culp's Hill. At 8 A.M. Meade sent another message to Sedgwick; this time he asked
him to send two brigades "to be massed in a central position" near Howard in case
the attack came there.[57]

Then before riding out to inspect his lines, Meade dashed off a short letter to his
wife, summarizing the great battle and reassuring her of his safety: "We had a great
fight yesterday, the enemy attacking and we completely repulsing them; both armies
shattered. Today at it again, with what result remains to be seem. Army in fine spirits and every one determined to do or die. George and myself well. Reynolds killed
the first day. No other of your friends or acquaintances hurt."[58]

To prepare for the upcoming battle, Meade strove to bring every available able-
bodied man to the front lines. He issued two circulars around 9 A.M. to effect that
desire. The first instructed corps commanders to "keep their troops under arms
and in all respects equipped to move at a moment's notice." The second circular
ordered corps commanders to find and bring to the front "all their stragglers and
men absent from the ranks." Furthermore, "the ordnance officers should be required to see that all the arms and equipments scattered over the field are picked
up and sent to the rear in ammunition wagons."[59]

Meade's hands-on management bred confidence in his subordinates. Lt. Frank
Haskell saw Meade checking his lines and surveying the enemy's position that
morning. He wrote, "His manner was calm and serious, but earnest. There was no
arrogance of hope, or timidity of fear discernible in his face; but you would have
supposed he would do his duty conscientiously and well, and would be willing
to abide the result. You would have seen this in his face." Haskell heard Meade
discuss the relative strengths of his left, center, and right with Hancock when
Meade visited with the commanders of the Second Corps. Meade felt that his
left and right would hold strong, and if the attack came on his center, it would be
well guarded by artillery. Essentially, Meade reinforced the view he had expressed
to Gibbon the night before. He also told Hancock that the Fifth and Sixth Corps
could be used to attack the Confederates' flank, should the main fighting occur
along Cemetery Ridge.[60]

Meade returned to his headquarters, where reporter Whitelaw Reid glimpsed
him later that morning. An earlier critic of Meade's, Reid now wrote, "Quick and
nervous in his movements, but calm, and it seemed to me, lit up with the glow of
the occasion, he looked more the General, less the student." Reid also noted that
"Warren, calm, absorbed, earnest as ever, was constantly in consultation with the
commander." He saw Pleasonton there as well, "polished" and "fashionable looking," occasionally adding "some earnest remark." The Leister house was a hive of

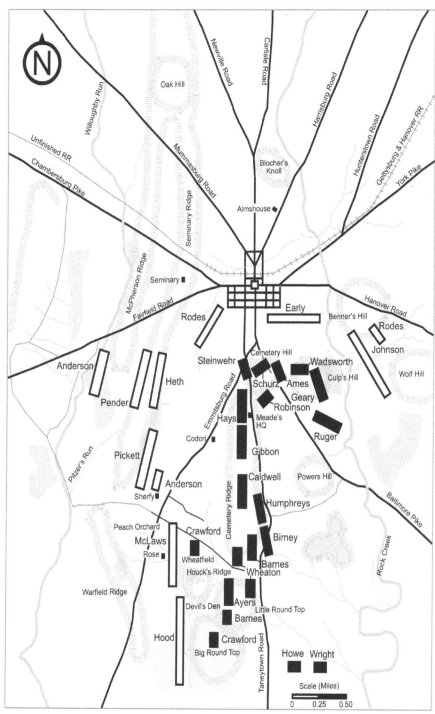

Gettysburg—Morning of July 3

activity, with "orderlies and aides" "dashing up with reports and off with orders," and signal officers "bringing in the reports telegraphed by the signal flags from the different crests that overlooked the fight."[61]

Sometime later that morning, perhaps around noon, Meade had a meal with Gibbon and some other officers. Meade's grandson, George, mentioned a "hasty breakfast" with the men, while Gibbon much later recalled that he had gone to the Leister house to convince Meade to eat something with them (and he did). After the battle, Haskell recounted a rambling tale of a "huge loaf of bread" wrenched from the jaws of a hog, water drawn from "near a barn," and chickens of "good *running* order." Regardless of the origins of the food, the steward, "John," made an "enormous pan of stewed chickens" with fixings, and the generals and their staffs commenced eating. Meade rode by and was invited to join the group by Gibbon. An "empty cracker box" served as his seat, with blankets or the ground sufficing for the others. Haskell wrote, "The generals ate, and after, lighted cigars, and under the flickering shade of a very small tree, discoursed of the incidents of yesterday's battle, and of the probabilities of today." Hancock thought the coming attack would hit the Second Corps hardest, but Meade felt the army was "ready for them." Meade also thought that the provost guards were better used in the ranks than in the rear and ordered them to rejoin their regiments. Around 12:30, the generals began leaving, with Meade heading out first.[62]

Meade then rode the entire line he expected would be attacked, stopping to talk with some of his generals as he rode. He began with Gen. Alexander Hays's Third Division of the Second Corps, which held the right of the Union line on Cemetery Ridge. Then it was on to the headquarters of Newton and Sedgwick. He finished the tour with a visit with Warren on Little Round Top, where they discussed the enemy buildup of artillery and infantry. After talking with Warren, he returned to his headquarters.[63]

While many officers napped or rested in the noontime heat, the ever-vigilant Hunt rode from battery to battery along the length of the Union line, instructing his gunners to hold their fire for fifteen or twenty minutes after "cannonade commenced, then to concentrate their fire with all possible accuracy on those batteries which were most destructive to us—but slowly, so that when the enemy's ammunition was exhausted, we should have sufficient left to meet the assault." Hunt had come to this decision after watching the slow buildup of Confederate artillery along a two-mile front, from the Peach Orchard to Oak Ridge northwest of town. At exactly 1:07 (according to Professor Michael Jacobs of Gettysburg College), the largest single cannon bombardment in the Civil War began. One hundred sixty-three Confederate guns opened fire at the Union lines, and the sound was so deafening it could be heard in Washington.[64]

The fear invoked by this massive shelling was indescribable, though many would try. Gibbon gave as good as a description as anyone, writing years later that "the whole air above and around us was filled with bursting and screaming projectiles, and the continuous thunder of guns." Unable to procure his horse, Gibbon ran to his line to see what was happening: "At last I reached the brow of the hill, to find myself in the most infernal pandemonium it has ever been my fortune to look upon." As the men of the Second Corps hunted for whatever cover could be found under rock, wall, or tree, the hard-hit artillery batteries of the Second Corps did not wait their full fifteen minutes: they began to fire back. What Gibbon and Hunt (watching as he rode back from Little Round Top) and others could plainly see, however, was that the bulk of the Confederate shells were passing over the infantry lines. The eighty-seven-degree air was still, and with the smoke generated by both sides' cannon fire, it was very difficult for the Confederates to pinpoint their proper range. Meanwhile, thousands of shells fell just behind the lines, sweeping the area of "camp followers and the unordered attendants of an army," in the words of Second Corps historian Francis Walker.

Meade remained calm throughout the shelling, even trying to relax his staffers by telling a story from the Mexican War. Hundreds of shells landed directly around Meade's headquarters at the Leister house, killing and wounding sixteen staff horses, hitting the house in several spots, and even flying through the open door. Though staffers implored Meade to leave this dangerous post, he refused because he wanted to be in a central place for messengers to reach him. He did move outside, where he paced back and forth in the backyard as shots fell around him. When he noticed staffers joining him in larger numbers than before, he asked, "Gentlemen, are you trying to find a safe place?" He then told a story from the Mexican War: "You remind me of the man who drove the ox-team which took ammunition for the heavy guns to the field of Palo Alto. Finding himself with range, he tilted up his cart and got behind it. Just then General Taylor came along, and seeing this attempt at shelter, shouted, 'You damn fool, don't you know you are no safer here than anywhere else?' The driver replied, 'I don't suppose I am, general, but it kind o' feels so.'"

No one recorded whether this story drew a laugh from his listeners or assuaged their fears. The general then moved the staff to a large barn several hundred yards away, but it too suffered from heavy bombardment. One shell fragment clipped Butterfield in the side, who then left the field in an ambulance.[65]

Somehow during this frightful bombardment Meade continued to manage his large command. He prepared for the assault he knew was coming by shifting troops to reinforce parts of his long line. He ordered Slocum (Twelfth Corps) "to send all the troops he could possibly spare to reinforce and strengthen that part of the line extending to the left of Cemetery Hill." He moved Robinson's Second Division of the First Corps from reserve to the "line on the right of the Second Corps." He reassigned the busy First brigade of Shaler's Third Division, Sixth Corps (which had been sent to help the Twelfth Corps at Culp's Hill in the morning), to the "rear and left of the Second Corps" to be held in reserve. He ordered

Col. Eliakim Sherrill's Third brigade (Third Division, Second Corps) to move into the line of the Second Corps. The remnants of the Third Corps were also shuffled quite a bit: two brigades were placed in reserve of the Second Corps, and three brigades were placed in reserve of the First Corps. Meade moved Col. Henry L. Eustis's brigade (Third Division, Sixth Corps) from Little Round Top to the "rear of the Second Corps, in reserve." Another brigade of the Sixth Corps was placed in the rear of the Fifth Corps. Meade also ordered Brig. Gen. Joseph J. Bartlett's two brigades from the Sixth Corps to the Wheatfield.[66]

Just as on the Second of July, Meade carefully deepened his numbers in strategic places, gambling that the main attack would be on the Second Corps. Though the men moved into position under artillery fire, Meade had more breathing room than on the previous day, when he and Hancock had to push units into intense firefights throughout the afternoon just to keep the line from buckling.

To find some protection from the hailstorm of shot and shell, Meade rode down to Powers Hill, the site of Slocum's headquarters. He found a signal officer there, but when that officer attempted to communicate with the signal officer at the Leister house, there was no reply. Exasperated, Meade rode back along Cemetery Ridge toward his previous headquarters.[67]

When the shells began falling, another general, Winfield Scott Hancock, had his own response: he slowly rode the length of the Second Corps line, with a staffer carrying the flag of the corps behind him, to the unbridled cheers of the embattled foot soldiers of the Second Corps. Only once did he pause: when his horse became unmanageable under the fire and he had to switch horses.[68] There were compelling reasons for the men under his command to be inspired by his bravery.

As Hancock rode the line, he found that some artillery batteries were not firing back. When he asked why, he was told that they had orders from Hunt to conserve their ammunition. Hancock said his authority was supreme in that section of the line and directly ordered some batteries to open fire. Some did, and in some instances, some did not. Hancock wanted the batteries to return fire mainly as a morale boost to his infantrymen.

However, it was Meade, not Hunt, who had decided to cease return fire so as to fool the Confederates into thinking its batteries had been suppressed, and he sent his order to Hunt. Of course, this dovetailed with Hunt's earlier commands and actually worked to perfection: not long after Union batteries ceased firing, the lead line of Lee's troops could be spotted marching over Seminary Ridge.[69]

Though Meade was at that precise moment riding somewhere between his two headquarters, the men of the Second Corps saw a sight they would never forget: thirteen thousand men moving in steady formation toward them. As Haskell wrote of the moment, "More than a half a mile their front extends; more than a thousand yards the dull gray masses deploy, man touching man, rank pressing rank, and line supporting line. The red flags wave, their horsemen gallop up and down." Though the perfect order would soon be shattered by the precise firing of Union cannons, "in spite of shells, and shrapnel and canister, without wavering or halt, the hardy lines of the enemy continue to move on." Gibbon sent Haskell to find Meade and tell him of the attack, but Haskell could not find him at the Leister house and instead had a message sent to him by signal: "The enemy is advancing his infantry in force upon my front."[70]

Meade did not need to receive this message to know that an attack had begun; the sound of Union artillery firing again, followed by heavy musketry, was all the noise he needed to know where the fighting would be. He rode to the crest of the ridge to see the action, and when his son and aide Capt. George Meade caught up with him, he found him striving to see through the smoke of the battlefield. He turned to his son and said, "Hello, George, is that you? I am glad you are here, you must stick by me now, you are the only officer left." Telling George it was a "lively" place, Meade started riding toward the right of his line, initially looking for Brig. Gen. William Hays (Second Corps). They did not find Hays but an artillery officer that Captain Meade knew, Lt. John Egan. Egan said he had seen Hays lead some men over the wall in a counterattack on the Confederates. Meade asked if the enemy had retreated, and Egan replied, "Yes. See General Hays has one of their flags." Meade testily replied, "I don't care for their flag. Have they turned?" Egan said they had, and with that bit of reassurance, Meade turned to his left and headed south down the line. The massive assault, which would be known as Pickett's Charge, was over.[71]

Meade soon ran into a group of Confederate prisoners from the charge, who asked him where they should go. Bemused, Meade pointed toward the rear of the line and said, "Go along that way and you will be well taken care of." He had not gone much farther when he met the ubiquitous Haskell, who had just been in the thick of the fighting in the Angle. Meade asked, "How is it going here?" Haskell replied, "I believe, general, the enemy's attack is repulsed." Surprised and pleased as he began to look over the scene of battle, Meade pursued his inquiry, "What! Is the assault already repulsed?" Haskell answered, "It is, sir." His face lighting up, Meade simply responded, "Thank God." The Army of the Potomac had just stopped the largest infantry assault of the war. Meade started to reach for his hat, but checked himself, and merely raised his right hand and shouted, "Hurrah." His son George was not afraid to show his full emotion, doffing his hat and shouting "hurrah" three times.[72]

At this, the greatest moment in his military career, Meade presented a humble picture. Haskell described him as he saw him that afternoon on the battlefield: "He was a plain man, dressed in serviceable summer suit of dark blue cloth, without badge or ornament, save the shoulder-straps of his grade, and a light, straight sword of a General or General staff officer. He wore heavy, high-top boots and buff gauntlets, and his soft black felt hat was slouched down over his eyes." He continued, "His face was very white, not pale, and the lines were marked and earnest and full of care."[73]

Though cognizant of the victory, Meade had unfinished business to attend to. After looking silently over the field, he asked Haskell who was in command (he had already heard that Hancock and Gibbon had been wounded). Haskell told him that Brig. Gen. John Caldwell was now the ranking officer of the corps, then without waiting for more, Meade spoke up, "No matter; I will give my orders to you and you will see them executed." He instructed Haskell to re-form the troops and stay in place, in case the Confederates attacked again. He added that he would be sending up some reinforcements, told Haskell where they should be placed, then left with his last order to Haskell, "If the enemy does attack, charge him in the flank and sweep him from the field; do you understand?" After this, Meade rode off to check on the firing on Cemetery Hill.[74]

After examining the Union position at Cemetery Hill, Meade decided to ride the entire length of the Union line, this time accompanied by his staff. As he rode the line in the hot summer sun, he was cheered all the way down to Little Round Top. For a very brief moment, the victor of Gettysburg could enjoy his triumph over Lee's Army of Northern Virginia. Then it was back to the business of fighting. When he got to Sykes's Fifth Corps stretched out around Little Round Top, he gave the order to send the "pickets and skirmishers in front to be thrown forward to feel the enemy, and for all preparations to be made for the assault." But with the Fifth Corps scattered about, it took time to organize a significant advance, and only one brigade of the Fifth Corps (supported by some men from the Sixth Corps) actually marched into the Wheatfield and briefly fought with some Confederate troops, who retreated quickly, thus surrendering the blood-soaked wheat field to the men of the Pennsylvania Reserves (First brigade, Third Division, Fifth Corps). Thus ended the infantry fighting on the third day of battle at Gettysburg.[75]

That evening at 8:35, Meade sent a message to Halleck. He described the day's fighting, which involved "150 guns" firing for three hours, two assaults on Meade's "left center," both "handsomely repulsed," "with severe loss to him, leaving in our hands nearly 3,000 prisoners." But the cost had been high: "The loss upon our side has been considerable." He noted the wounding of Hancock and Gibbon. Then he discussed the brief follow-up to the assault: "An armed reconnaissance was pushed forward from the left, and the enemy found to be in force." His cavalry had been engaged as well, "harassing and vigorously attacking him with great success." (Over six thousand cavalry had fought a brief but fierce battle on John Rummel's farm east of town, with no tactical advantage to either side after incurring over five hundred casualties.) Meade had suspended all operations for the day. With victory, however, the "army was in fine spirits."[76]

No one recorded what the general thought as he tried to catch a few hours of sleep that night. There could be no time for celebration, with Lee's wounded yet

defiant army hunkered down for the evening along Seminary Ridge. He could not
have any real idea of the extent of his casualties, though he would know the toll was
enormous. He would have heard some of the cries of the thousands of wounded
men and perhaps seen comrades moving quietly through the night in search of
lost friends. He would acutely feel the loss of the two generals he counted on the
most, Reynolds and Hancock, with gaps in command left by the wounding and
removal of Gibbon and Sickles. Thankfully, his son George was unhurt, but that
would be no consolation to the families of the almost twenty-three thousand men
killed, wounded, captured, or missing from the Army of the Potomac. Nor could
he know that the Confederacy had been hurt in almost equal measure, eventually counting nearly twenty-three thousand casualties of its own.[77] He could not
even rest in his temporary headquarters at the Leister house, which had been
converted into a hospital to treat the wounded. Instead, he and his staff had to lie
down by some rocks within a quarter of a mile of the house, where they slept as
the rain poured down in torrents throughout the night.[78]

Though Meade could not rest easy that night, with Lee's mighty army lurking
less than a mile away, he could not have any idea how important his first battle as
commander of the Army of the Potomac had been, or how his performance would
be scrutinized, criticized, and judged for generations to come. Because he would
not assault Lee the next day, nor the day after, nor the entire way back to the Potomac, his failure to catch and trap the Army of Northern Virginia would forever
blemish his outstanding victory at Gettysburg. He would survive the criticism of his
pursuit of Lee, and even hold on during the vituperative campaign of Sickles and his
friends to discredit him. Much later, after the internecine rivalries of the generation
that fought the war faded into history, historians and students of the battle would
study the battle and its leadership, focusing more attention on why Lee lost instead
of why Meade won. Though he had his defenders in his lifetime and in the years
immediately following his death, he would not find a modern sympathetic review
until Freeman Cleaves, Edwin Coddington, Richard Sauers, Herman Hattaway, Archer Jones, and Russell Weigley completely reexamined his role in the battle and
offered more favorable interpretations of Meade's leadership at Gettysburg. In his
sweeping treatment of command before, during, and after the battle, *The Gettysburg
Campaign*, Coddington argued that "the men knew what they could do under an
extremely competent general; one of lesser ability and courage could well have lost
the battle. . . . The mistakes of the Confederates which in another battle would have
been mere slips of the tongue, so to speak, became fatal at Gettysburg." Writing
three decades later, Meade biographer Richard Sauers analyzed the leadership of
Meade on the third day of the battle, cautiously complimenting his actions: "Although his detractors, and historians relying upon their writings, have denigrated
Meade's performance, the general did rather well. His work on July 3 continued his
steady, if unspectacular, guidance of the first two days."[79]

Though these judgments, supported by carefully marshaled facts, are more balanced and positive than most Meade has received, a few modern historians are even more generous. Herman Hattaway and Archer Jones write that the "Union high command had played its role . . . [in] giving command of the Army of the Potomac to the steady and capable Meade." Archer Jones in his work *Civil War Command and Strategy* lavishes a higher compliment on Meade, "The Army of the Potomac had at last found its general." And Russell Weigley provides even more detail on why Meade succeeded. He put the "right subordinates in the right place with the right understanding of the mission throughout the battle, with almost uncanny consistency."[80]

Assuming command of an army scattered throughout Maryland, Meade had quickly focused all his attention on his two goals: to protect Washington and Baltimore, and pursue Lee to a point where a battle could commence. Though neither commander chose Gettysburg as a battle site, once fighting erupted there, both generals committed their men to a battle in that town. Meade used every single corps he had at Gettysburg, and he kept French's army in Maryland and Couch's army in Harrisburg on alert. The first day began with the Union fighting defensively, remaining so for the next two days. Once Meade got to Gettysburg and saw just how strong his defensive line could be, he naturally reinforced that line and waited for Lee to attack, much as Lee had waited for Burnside to attack at Fredericksburg. During his two days on the field, Meade shuffled brigades as needed; used his cavalry effectively as screens and reconnaissance; let his artillery do much of his work (under the leadership of the highly capable Henry Hunt); communicated often and freely with his corps commanders (unlike Hooker); relied on his corps commanders to do their jobs; empowered his best general, Winfield Scott Hancock, to be in tactical command of parts of the battlefield at crucial times; stayed in touch with his superiors in Washington as best he could; kept careful watch on the field and his men; never lost his nerve nor made a hasty, costly decision; and, most importantly, let Lee do the attacking, which gave Lee the initiative but Meade the advantage, given his better defensive position, greater number of troops, and superior effectiveness of his artillery.

Meade did a first-rate job at Gettysburg, and to him belongs the title "victor." What undoubtedly pleased him was the letter he received from Halleck two weeks after the battle. Halleck wrote: "Your fight at Gettysburg met with universal approbation of all military men here. You handled your troops in that battle as well, if not better, than any general has handled his army during the war. You brought all your forces into action at the right time and place, which no commander of the Army of the Potomac has done before. You may well be proud of that battle." Meade's artillery commander at Gettysburg, Henry Hunt, offered a more detailed assessment of Meade's leadership at Gettysburg in a letter he wrote in 1888. He told Alexander Webb that Meade "rarely consulted" him "as a chief of artillery is consulted." Moreover, "there was no close personal relations between us . . . that could or would in any respect whatsoever sway my judgment. We differed on some points; sometimes I was vexed; once I demanded to be relieved, so I could be impartial, I think." As Hunt studied and wrote about the battle, he found that "Meade has grown and grown upon me." Though he did not know Meade's "views and determination about the different phases of the campaign and battles," he was assured that Meade preferred the very strong Pipe Creek line to all others, but that once the troops were committed to battle in Gettysburg, Meade abandoned his first wish to set up a defensive line there. Hunt made a list of what he thought Meade had done correctly: "He was right in his order as to Pipe Creek; right in his determination under certain circumstances to fall back to it; right in pushing up to Gettysburg after the battle commenced; right in remaining there; right in making his battle a purely defensive one; right, therefore, in taking the line he did; right in not attempting a counterattack at any stage of the battle; right as to his pursuit of Lee." Hunt concluded, "Rarely has more skill, vigor, or wisdom been shown under such circumstances as he was placed in."[81]

Hunt's analysis is sound. Meade had made all the right decisions and provided that intangible resolve that infused confidence into his officers and men. As Francis Walker felicitously wrote over one hundred years ago, "At Gettysburg the Army of the Potomac had a commander in every sense. . . . His presence and watchful care, his moral courage and tenacity of purpose, contributed largely to the result."[82]

Maj. Gen. George Gordon Meade had just led the largest army in the biggest battle of the Civil War, and won. Now he had the even harder job of pursuing, fighting, and subduing the best army in the Civil War. It would take him almost two years to do it.

The Pursuit of Lee

July 5–14, 1863

When Meade got up from his rock the morning of July 4, he simply could not know what the next day, let alone the next week, would bring. Nor could he have any inkling of the extent to which his career would be judged by what he did and did not do during July 4–14. By the time he got up, the reserve trains of the Army of Northern Virginia had already begun their long march of forty-five miles to the Potomac River crossing at Williamsport. The next ten days would be a race between two large armies, as Lee pushed his army and its vast number of wagons through the South Mountain range pass at Monterey and on to Williamsport. Meade pursued him for ten days, always striving to find, flank, and fight Lee's army. It would turn out to be one of the most frustrating command experiences of Meade's tenure.

Meade took stock of the situation on the rainy day of July 4, 1863. First, his tired army, short on rations and ammunition, had just suffered thousands of casualties. Secondly, it had withstood three days of attacks from Lee's formidable Army of Northern Virginia, but did that mean Lee was done attacking? No one knew. While Meade did not expect Lee to attack on the fourth, he could not have known that would be the case, until he woke up to the good news that no attack had occurred that morning. Was Lee expecting Meade to attack? If so, Meade would not give him the opportunity to slaughter his men as the Union army had done to Lee's on July 3. Meade had already written to Couch the previous evening that if Lee withdrew his army from Gettysburg, he would then "move down on this side of the mountain," while Couch should chase him as "rapidly as possible down the Valley." Meade feared following Lee directly because he had heard that Lee had "fortified" the "mountain passes."[1]

So Meade set about to learn the enemy's position and communicate with his superiors. His first official message of the day was sent to Newton at 6 A.M. News had reached him from the wounded Brig. Gen. Francis Channing Barlow (convalescing in the town) that a movement of the "enemy [was] to be a mere feint." His orders to Newton were as clear as possible: "The general only wishes to know where the enemy are, and not by any means to bring on an action." Meade's next message went to Halleck at 7 A.M. Meade noted that Confederates had "withdrawn" their pickets from the positions of the third, but as to why, his information was not "sufficient . . . to decide its character yet—whether a retreat or maneuver for other purposes." His next task was to reply to a request from Lee to exchange prisoners. In his refusal, Meade cited a lack of authority, writing, "It is not in my power to accede to the proposed arrangement." Whether or not that was true, Meade simply did not want to ease Lee's possible retreat by exchanging prisoners. Meade soon issued two circulars, one ordering his commanders to collect all weapons and material from the Confederate dead, then count and bury the dead enemy soldiers. The other circular ordered commanders to report on the number of men present, the supplies on hand, and the condition of both. He then made his plans for the day completely clear: "The intention of the major general commanding is not to make any present move, but to refit and rest for today." But Meade did want Major General French's army to set into motion, ordering him to send part of his army to hold the South Mountain passes, while using the other portion of his army to "reoccupy Maryland Heights." Shortly after sending this order, Meade rescinded it because he had new information "that the enemy may have retired to take a new position and await an attack from us." He then ordered French to stick with the instructions of the day before, "making your movements contingent upon those of the enemy."[2]

By all his actions that morning, it is plain to see that Meade had no intention of attacking Lee on July 4. He might attack him later, but only after he had a clear sense of Lee's plans. There is nothing surprising here: Meade had shown his preference for defense and his reluctance to go on the offensive until he felt assured of success. Also, like McClellan, he saw nothing wrong with resting and resupplying a large army after a major battle, as McClellan had done after Antietam. So Meade was no Lee—but then, neither were any of his predecessors in command of the Army of the Potomac.

His cautiousness was hardly misplaced on July 4. Not only was Meade's huge army shattered and worn, with supply wagons not yet arrived from Westminster, but as the rain continued to fall, Lee was simultaneously preparing to retreat and erect defensive works. Confederates hungered for the Union troops to get a taste of their own medicine on the fourth, but Meade had no wish to get caught in a Fredericksburg-style slaughter again. So the Army of the Potomac gathered up its dead, treated its wounded, and waited in the rain for their rations to arrive.[3]

Meade had plenty to do regardless of whether or not his men stayed put. He ordered Pleasonton to have his cavalry "harass and annoy" the Confederates as much as possible in their rear and their lines of communication. Pleasonton promptly sent seven of his eight brigades into the countryside, most to the south of Gettysburg, where they were to turn west and then north, cutting into the Confederate retreat if it occurred. Meade updated Halleck at noon, telling him that the "position of affairs is not materially changed from my last dispatch at 7 a.m." He informed Halleck that Lee's army had pulled out of Gettysburg, which the Union army now held. He added that he had no plans to attack that day, noting, "I shall require some time to get up supplies, ammunition, etc., rest the army worn out by long marches and three days' hard fighting."

For his troops he prepared a General Order, in which he thanked the men for their fighting. He exclaimed, "An enemy, superior in numbers, and flushed with the pride of a successful invasion, attempted to overcome and destroy this army. Utterly baffled and defeated, he has now withdrawn from the contest." His thrilling compliment would echo down the ages: "The privations and fatigue the army has endured, and the heroic courage and gallantry it has displayed, will be matters of history, to be ever remembered." Then he added a line of inspiration that would get him into trouble with President Lincoln: "Our task is not yet accomplished, and the commanding general looks to the army for greater efforts to drive from our soil every vestige of the presence of the invader."[4]

The phrase "drive from our soil" particularly rankled Lincoln, as it was almost the exact line McClellan had used the previous year. It implied that the Confederates had "invaded" the North, when in reality, as Lincoln said to his secretary John Hay, "the whole country is our soil." Undoubtedly, Meade had no idea the impact his single phrase would have on some in Washington; it was a classic rallying cry used by commanders to embolden their troops. (And no complaint had come from Washington when Meade used similar language in a circular issued on June 30 to inspire his army, "The enemy are on our soil; the whole country now looks anxiously to this army to deliver it from the presence of the foe.") For the record, he also thanked the "Almighty Dispenser of events," who had "thought fit to give victory to the cause of the just."[5]

As the rain came down in torrents, Meade called another meeting of his top generals for the evening of July 4 (or as he preferred to view them, "consultations"). They met in Brig. Gen. Thomas Neill's headquarters, which offered more shelter than Meade's tent. The meeting began with Meade asking his senior commanders, Slocum, Sedgwick, and Howard, for their advice on what steps should be taken next. Howard and Sedgwick said to wait and see what Lee would do, while Slocum suggested moving the entire army to Emmitsburg and, if necessary, intercepting Lee before he crossed the Potomac. Meade then proposed that all the generals address four questions. Butterfield's minutes read:

1. Shall the army remain here?
2. If we remain here, shall we assume the offensive?

3. Do you deem it expedient to move towards Williamsport, through Emmitsburg?
4. Shall we pursue the enemy if he is retreating on his direct line of retreat?

The generals agreed unanimously on only one of the four questions: no one
thought the Army of the Potomac should "assume the offensive." On the question
of whether to wait and see what Lee did, or move out toward Williamsport without waiting on Lee, Slocum had Newton and Pleasonton on his side. The six other
generals—Sedgwick, Howard, Sykes, Birney, Hays, and Warren—wanted to see
what Lee did before moving. Not everyone answered the third question, though
Slocum picked up another vote when Hays agreed it was the right direction to
take. As for pursuit of Lee, only Birney opposed it: the others thought it should be
done by either cavalry alone or cavalry and infantry combined. Meade did not record his view of their advice, except to tell the Joint Committee on the Conduct of
the War the next year that these "consultations . . . were probably more numerous
and more constant in my case, from the fact that I had just assumed command of
the army, and felt that it was due to myself to have the opinions of high officers
before I took action on matters which involved such momentous issues."[6]

The meeting broke up, and Meade ordered Major General Sedgwick to support Warren in a reconnaissance of Lee's position to begin at 4:30 A.M. on the next
day. Meade also wrote a brief note to Halleck informing him that there had been
"no change of affairs since dispatch of 12 noon," that he planned a reconnaissance
in the morning, and that the cavalry was "moving toward the South Mountain
Pass, and should the enemy retreat, [Meade would] pursue him on his flanks."[7]

As the generals grabbed a few hours of fitful sleep, the rain came down relentlessly, and Lee's army continued the retreat begun in the early hours of July 4. One
column of Lee's large army, the seventeen-mile-long train under the protection of
Brig. Gen. John Imboden's Northwest Brigade of cavalry, rolled relentlessly toward
Williamsport on the Chambersburg Pike, reaching New Franklin, Pennsylvania,
in the early morning hours of July 5. The much longer supply column, the forty-
mile-long reserve train under the command of Ewell's chief quartermaster, Maj.
John Alexander Harman, had been the first supply units to leave Gettysburg, and
by dawn on July 5 its lead wagons were rolling into Hagerstown, Maryland. But
even a four-mile train was vulnerable in many places, and in the driving rain, cavalry troops under Brig. Gen. Judson Kilpatrick struck and captured a number of
Maj. Gen. Robert E. Rodes's ambulance trains at Monterey Pass. Though Kilpatrick would make exaggerated claims about the number of men he captured, he had
fulfilled the orders of his commanding general to "harass and annoy" the enemy.[8]

Meade was up and active by 4:30 A.M. on July 5, issuing orders that put his army
in pursuit of Lee's retreating force. He first ordered Sykes to march the Fifth Corps
four to five miles out on the Emmitsburg Road and await further orders. The next

order displayed some confusion between Butterfield, Meade, and Sedgwick. But-terfield wrote to Sedgwick (Sixth Corps), "Indications on our right indicate the withdrawal of the enemy via Cashtown and Fairfield." However, Meade specifically forbade Sedgwick to open fire: "It is not the intention of the general to bring on an engagement. . . . The orders for the reconnaissance were with a view to as-certaining the position and movement of the enemy, not for a battle." Sedgwick's reconnaissance in force soon confirmed what signalmen were telling Meade that morning: Lee's whole army was in retreat, split into two columns, one traveling on the Chambersburg Pike, the other on the Fairfield Road. To augment his forces for the next possible battle, Meade sent a message to Brig. Gen. William F. Smith, commander of seventy-six hundred soldiers at Waynesboro: "Your reenforcement to this army would be a valuable one and appreciated." Next he turned to his own army's march, deciding to divide his army into three wings, each marching down different roads to a convergence at Middletown, Maryland. The First, Third, and Sixth Corps would march on the Emmitsburg Road; the Fifth and Eleventh Corps would march on the Taneytown Road; and the Second and Twelfth Corps were to march via Taneytown, Middleburg, and Woodsborough. The trains would ac-company their corps, the Artillery Reserve would follow the Second and Twelfth Corps, the quartermaster's supplies would be moved from Westminster to Freder-ick, and the headquarters would strive to be at Creagerstown by nightfall. The plan was to rendezvous at Middletown on July 7. The corps began marching out.[9]

By 12:30 P.M. Meade had enough information to initiate a more aggressive pur-suit. He ordered Sedgwick: "Push forward your column in a westerly direction. Fire on his force. If rear guard, it will [be] compelled to return; if not, you will find out." He added urgently, "Time is of great importance, as I cannot give order for a movement without explicit information from you." Sedgwick did as ordered, firing upon Lee's wagon trains again, and using infantry to probe his defenses. His men captured 250 Confederates. These actions confirmed Meade's view that a Confederate retreat was occurring on the Cashtown and Fairfield roads, and that his original plan to march southwest and cut off Lee's retreat before it crossed the Potomac River was the best course. Still, he waited to hear what Warren (leading Sedgwick's reconnaissance force) had seen and thought.[10]

While Meade confirmed the information on Lee's retreat and set his army into motion to catch Lee, others began to wonder if Meade had missed an extraordi-nary opportunity to destroy Lee's army entirely. On July 4, railroad chief Her-mann Haupt wrote to Halleck, "I fear that while Meade rests to refresh his men and collect supplies, Lee will [be] off so far that he cannot intercept him. A good force on the line of the Potomac to prevent Lee from crossing would, I think, in-sure his destruction." He voiced these same ideas to Meade and Pleasonton when they chatted on July 5 and came away with the impression that Meade was not suf-ficiently concerned about Lee's retreat. He carried these views directly to Halleck and Lincoln, whom he saw in Washington the next day. With Haupt's misgivings, and the fragmentary news emanating from Meade and his generals on July 4–6, it is not surprising that Lincoln would send his strong message of July 6 to Halleck, in which he criticized the "drive the invaders from our soil" line in Meade's Order No. 68 and Meade's halting of the army on July 5 to ascertain what Lee's next move would be. Lincoln's fear was simple: "These things all appear to me to be connected with a purpose to cover Baltimore and Washington, and to get the enemy across the river again without a further collision, and they do not appear connected with a purpose to prevent his crossing and to destroy him." Lincoln and some others in Washington were convinced that if the Army of the Potomac pounced on the Army of Northern Virginia before it crossed the Potomac River, it could be destroyed. That belief undergirded his growing frustration with Meade in the aftermath of the Battle of Gettysburg. Historian Donald Stoker pushes this interpretation even further, writing that Meade seemed to "have been the only important figure in the Union high command that did not sense the immense opportunity before him."[11]

However, contrary to these emerging opinions in Washington, Meade saw danger in pushing too hard against Lee. In the morning, he had heard a report that the "rebels are fortifying themselves in Newman's Cut, South Mountain." Warren visited Meade in the evening of July 5 with an update from Sedgwick's reconnaissance. Sedgwick and Warren believed that Lee intended to wait at Fairfield to fight the Sixth Corps, which made Meade decide to temporarily suspend his march south. What Meade wanted to avoid on July 4 and the days after was to attack a "strong position" of Lee's, "in consequence of the bad example he had set [Meade] in ruining himself attacking a strong position."[12]

Meade then turned his attention to some crucial personnel matters. Abner Doubleday had been so incensed that John Newton, a junior in seniority, had been placed in command of the First Corps that he refused to take orders from him or Meade. Meade had no choice but to relieve him from duty and order him to Washington. Meade also had to relieve Butterfield from his duties because his wound rendered him unable to do his tasks. For the next few days, Warren and Pleasonton served as acting chiefs of staff, until Meade convinced Brig. Gen. Andrew A. Humphreys to take the job. Meade also found time to write a brief but frank letter to his wife, assuring her that he and their son George were fine, though two of George's horses had been killed, and Meade's horse Old Baldy "was shot again." Still reveling in his well-deserved victory, Meade summed up the import of what had happened in one sentence, "It was a grand battle, and is in my judgment a most decided victory, though I did not annihilate or bag the Confederate Army." He also explained why he had not attacked them when they were recovering: "They awaited one day, expecting that, flushed with success, I would attack them when they would play their old game of shooting us from behind breastworks—a game we played this time to their entire satisfaction." His greatest praise he gave to his soldiers, when he wrote, "The men behaved splendidly; I really think they are becoming soldiers." He closed by revealing the biggest command problem he faced, "The most difficult part of my work is acting without correct information on which to predicate action."[13]

What Meade did the rest of the night is not clear, though as early as 2 A.M. on July 6 he sent out a message ordering Sedgwick to "push [his] reconnaissance, so as to ascertain, if practicable, how far the enemy has retreated." Essentially, Meade asked Sedgwick to use a corps to find the intelligence he needed to make his next move. He asked him to determine the "character of the gap and practicability of carrying the line same," should Meade "determine to advance on that line." He implored Sedgwick, "Keep me fully advised of what occurs" and "report at least every two or three hours." Sedgwick maintained command of the First and Third Corps as well, which could be called upon for support if required, wrote Meade. He closed the message with an indication of his leading plan: "I shall not move the army from its present position until I am better satisfied the enemy are evacuating the Cumberland Valley."[14]

The July 6 dispatch to Sedgwick reveals that caution remained Meade's watchword. However, Meade also showed that he was not afraid to engage Lee's army; he just wanted to do it on his terms. Not knowing exactly where the bulk of Lee's army was, or where it was headed, he hesitated between two choices: to march his large army to the southwest, hoping to prevent Lee's army from crossing the Potomac River, or give Lee's army a vigorous chase and fight its rearguard. He also relied on his corps commanders, especially the senior commanders such as Sedgwick, whom he empowered to control several corps and give him solid intelligence and advice. Furthermore, he preferred to let them fight as they saw fit, just as he had done at Gettysburg. But that could lead to problems, as ultra-cautious corps commanders tended to see small difficulties as insurmountable. Meade wrote of this tendency to his wife on July 18: "Another great trouble with me is the want of active and energetic subordinate officers, men upon whom I can depend and rely upon taking care of themselves and their commands. The loss of Reynolds and Hancock is most serious; their places are not to be supplied."[15] Sedgwick was respected by his fellow officers, beloved by his men, and quite brave—but he was no Reynolds or Hancock. Meade can be criticized for not boldly—and blindly—pushing forward the Sixth Corps (and others) to give battle to Lee's rearguard on July 4 and 5, but that would have been a gamble that could have failed spectacularly. In retrospect, Meade could have sent several brigades of cavalry riding around Lee's lines on July 4, hoping to cut off the retreating infantry at Monterey Pass. But Meade never seriously entertained that idea, nor did it have a chance of being realized once Pleasonton sent his three divisions on widely divergent paths to find and interdict Lee's army. As historian Russell Weigley points out, the popular and theoretical vision of a vigorous pursuit of a weakened foe climaxing in a coup de grace against a retreating army "practically never occurred" in the Civil War—or earlier wars. Weigley continues, "Napoleon himself almost never contrived the relentless pursuit favored by military theory." As historians Herman Hattaway and Archer Jones note, "Save for a few instances—Richmond, Kentucky, or Nashville—none of them at all similar to the situation at Gettysburg and in no way arguable parallel, always the defeated Civil War army could find safety in retreat and still thereafter offer resistance."[16]

In the end, a commander who seeks the advice of his subordinates will undoubtedly rise and fall within the parameters of that advice. The "consultation" of the corps commanders on July 4 is a perfect example: not a single general wanted to attack Lee. Given this mindset, even if Meade had been a far more aggressive general, he had to work with and through a cautious group of corps commanders. This same caution also extended to Meade's immediate superior, Halleck, who wrote him on July 5, "Your movements are perfectly satisfactory. Your call for re-enforcements to Frederick has been anticipated. Call to you all of Couch's force." By July 6, however, the feeling among some in Washington—most importantly Lincoln—was that Meade was not moving quickly and decisively to stop Lee before he crossed the Potomac. Historian T. Harry Williams writes that Lincoln feared that Meade, "unless urged on from Washington, would let Lee escape." Lincoln held the belief, "like so many Americans," according to historian Gabor Boritt, that "one great Clausewitzian battle (though he had never read the Prussian theorist)" could "bring the terrible war to an end." Meade did not react quickly and vigorously enough for some of his superiors, and he would pay a steep price.[17]

July 6 would turn out to be another day of delay for Meade. All morning, Sedgwick gave excuses for not pushing his troops forward, and all Meade desired was reliable information that Lee's army was "retiring from the mountains." Meade confirmed this probe in a dispatch to Major General Couch written at 9:50 A.M., complaining that he could not get "reliable intelligence of the enemy's movements." However, he believed that they were in "retreat for the Potomac." He would delay his "flank movement," however, until he had solid information. A similar letter went to Major General French at Frederick. That afternoon, Meade finally got some solid information, when Col. John B. McIntosh's First Brigade of cavalry (Second Division) reported that it had fought the "enemy's rear guard" on the Waynesborough Pike. McIntosh wrote, "Lee's whole army passed through Fountain Dale and Monterey yesterday. . . . I think they are making for Hagerstown." This information confirmed Meade's supposition, and he now felt comfortable in ordering Sedgwick to pull back all his forces from Fairfield, except the brigade under Brigadier General Neill, and "execute the order of march of July 5" (Sixth, First, and Third Corps would march to Emmitsburg, then head toward Middletown via Lewistown).[18]

While Meade finally set his army into motion, other government officials were doing all they could to aid and augment Meade's shrunken and depleted army. Five thousand horses were shipped to Meade from all parts of the Union, 750,000 pounds of grain and 250,000 pounds of hay were ordered to be shipped daily to Frederick, and thirty-nine hundred additional soldiers were sent from Baltimore to French in Frederick (to increase his number to ten thousand). Meade also wanted an honest assessment of the quality of the troops under Couch, and Couch replied with complete frankness. Of the ten thousand men under Brig. Gen. William Smith, "one-half are very worthless, and 2,000 cavalry, with a battery, can capture the whole party in an open country. That is why I put them in or near the mountains; there they could do service." The soldiers under his direct command in Harrisburg were not much better: "I have 2,000 men here; 500 that ran so rapidly from Gettysburg, much demoralized, and one regiment New York troops that won't march." More troops were being readied, "3,000 nearly equipped and probably 5,000 at Reading are being equipped." Another group at Mercersburg numbered four thousand, though fifteen hundred were considered "utterly worthless." There were even one thousand men that Couch "did not march, having been demoralized at York." Given this candid and depressing appraisal, Meade simply ordered Smith to bring his men to Gettysburg and guard the hospital, until he received further orders.[19]

Late in the day of July 6, sharp fighting occurred between Union cavalry and Confederate cavalry and infantry at Williamsport and Hagerstown. Despite bold attacks by the Union cavalry, the Confederate forces held their ground, and both towns remained in Confederate hands. By evening, the Union cavalry retreated to its temporary base at Boonsborough, sending out patrols to guard the South Mountain passes while the Army of the Potomac marched south toward Middleton. At the same time, Lee's sprawled-out army continued its slow march toward Williamsport.[20]

With his far-flung command attended to, Meade settled in for some much-needed rest at his headquarters in Gettysburg on the evening of July 6. His acting chief of staff, Governeur Warren, even took it upon himself to not wake Meade when a message from Smith came in around 10 P.M. Smith reported that he was at Newman's Cut, and Warren updated him with the current situation (the army would march toward Middleton the next day, McIntosh and Neill were left behind to follow the Confederate retreat down the Fairfield Road, and Smith should occupy Gettysburg with his men). Warren closed with a bit of solicitude, "As your note requires no special action, I do not awake General Meade to reply, as he is now refreshing himself with the first quiet sleep he has had since he came into command, if not for many nights before."[21]

The next several days would be largely a story of movement for both armies. Starting before dawn on July 7, Meade's army made phenomenal time, marching on muddy roads and through soggy fields, averaging fifteen to twenty-five miles, with the Eleventh Corps marching the farthest, over thirty miles (Emmitsburg to Middletown). Meade's headquarters went even farther, marching thirty-three miles to Frederick (instead of setting up in Creagerstown). Confederate forces continued their steady advance toward the Potomac River, with the bulk of the infantry in Hagerstown by July 7. The two commanders were in a race. Lee wanted to get his vast stores, wounded men, and active soldiers across the Potomac River without a fight. Meade wanted to stop the crossing, by moving his army to Middletown and Frederick and, from there, marching through the South Mountain passes to attack Lee's army at Williamsport.[22]

On July 7 Lee rode into Hagerstown, rested briefly, then helped position the divisions as they came marching into the area. Meanwhile, the sole ferry in Williamsport continued to transport the wounded across the river and bring back ammunition for the impending battle. On the next day, Lee, his generals, and his engineers began riding throughout the countryside, examining the terrain to determine the best places to build breastworks and set gun emplacements for the defensive line they wanted to construct from Hagerstown to the Potomac.[23]

As for Meade, once he established headquarters in Frederick on July 7, he received some very welcome news from Halleck: he had been appointed a brigadier general in the Regular Army, "to rank from July 3, the date of your brilliant victory at Gettysburg." That made Meade one of only a handful of brigadier generals in the Regular Army. Meade gave an update on the progress of the march to Halleck, informing him that the army would be "assembling today and tomorrow at Middletown." He reported that Williamsport was guarded by the Confederates, who were growing in number, and that they were crossing the river in flatboats because French had destroyed the pontoon bridges on July 4. Though Meade planned to move on Williamsport, he asked Halleck a key question: "Should the enemy succeed in crossing the river before I can reach him, I should like to have your views of the subsequent operations—whether to follow up the army in the Valley, or cross below and nearer Washington." This was not a question Halleck wanted to hear. He replied: "You have given the enemy a stunning blow at Gettysburg. Follow it up, and give him another before he can reach the Potomac. When he crosses, circumstances will determine whether it will be best to pursue him by the Shenandoah Valley, or this side of Blue Ridge. There is strong evidence that he is short of artillery ammunition; and, if vigorously pressed, he must suffer." Halleck added to the weight of his request by enclosing a note from Lincoln in a later dispatch that read: "We have certain information that Vicksburg surrendered to General Grant on the 4th of July. Now, if General Meade can complete his work, so gloriously prosecuted thus far, by the literal or substantial destruction of Lee's army, the rebellion will over."[24]

Now Meade knew that Lincoln and Halleck were largely focused on the destruction of Lee's army, and not worried as much about the defense of Washington. Though he might gripe about the change in strategic concern, he could not say his

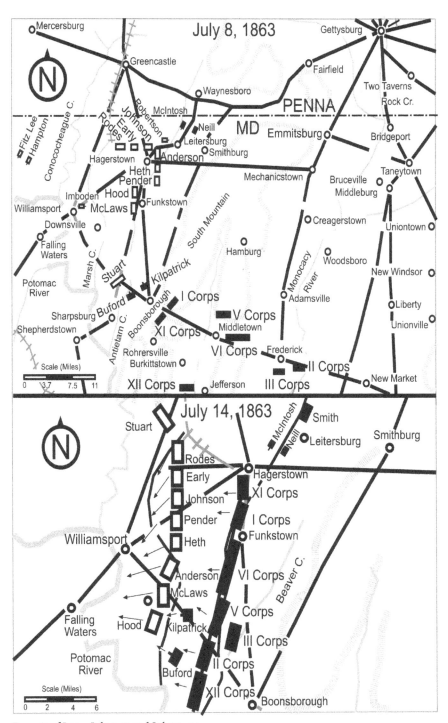

Pursuit of Lee—July 7–8 and July 13–14

new instructions were vague. His challenge would be putting the pieces together to do the job.

But much stood in Meade's way. Specifically, he had four distinct issues to deal with. The first two were logistical. His tired men had to climb muddy roads to get through the South Mountain passes, and it took almost two days to get his entire army and artillery through the passes. The second logistical issue was lack of supplies. Many of his men were hungry, without shoes and socks, and using worn-out horses as transportation. Even with the vast supplies of the North and the best railway lines in the country, there were problems supplying the army. For example, Howard wrote to Warren on July 8, "I have not yet gotten shoes and stockings. About one-half of my command are now destitute, or have shoes too poor to march. . . . The moment I get supplied with provisions, as the rations in the haversacks are out, I will push forward as ordered." Howard got his rations, pushed his men to the top of the mountain, then stopped. He wrote to Brig. Gen. Seth Williams: "My men are suffering for want of shoes. I want 3,000 pairs. I shall make every exertion to get them before morning. Cannot a load be sent me tonight." This lack of supplies was felt by the entire army, with railroad snafus and ordering bottlenecks partly to blame.[25] Meade's other two challenges were Stuart's cavalry, which performed some excellent screening on July 7–9, and the sheer ability of Lee and his men to erect a defensive line, build a bridge, and methodically transport thousands of animals, wagons, and men across the Potomac River in a matter of a few days.

Perhaps the greatest challenge of all was the pursuit itself with the leadership Meade had after the battle of Gettysburg. Russell Weigley writes that Meade's "command structure was shattered" by the battle, and that "pursuit is an offensive action and one likely to demand rapid and even intricate maneuver under adverse circumstances; it requires more from commanders even than a fighting retreat, one of the most difficult activities in war."[26] As Meade would write to his wife later that month, his new commanders lacked the fighting spirit of some of his generals lost at Gettysburg.

As Meade pushed his army, so his superiors pushed him. Though Halleck had dutifully passed on the president's wishes for Meade's army to destroy Lee's, Meade could not move fast enough to please Lincoln, especially after Halleck had heard on July 8 that Lee's army was crossing at Williamsport. Halleck wrote a forceful message to Meade: "The opportunity to attack his divided forces should not be lost. The President is urgent and anxious that your army should move against him by forced marches." Meade had to take the time to respond with *his* information: "My information as to the crossing of the enemy does not agree with that just received in your dispatch. His whole force is in position between Funkstown and Williamsport." Furthermore, "my army is and has been making forced marches, short of rations and barefooted." Despite this situation, he would "use his utmost effort to push forward this army." Halleck quickly replied, trying to mollify Meade and simultaneously show he was a messenger for Lincoln: "Do not understand me as expressing any dissatisfaction; on the contrary, your army has done most nobly. I only wish to give you opinions formed from information received here." He stressed the importance of attacking before Lee crossed the Potomac River, but he also understood that if Lee has "massed his whole force on the Antietam, time must be taken to also concentrate your forces." To help Meade with the upcoming battle, Halleck was sending him more troops, some directly to Harper's Ferry, others under Brig. Gen. Benjamin F. Kelley to attack from the west.[27]

Despite the demands of his job, Meade found time on July 8 to write to his wife, giving her a glimpse of the physical and mental toll command placed on him. He wrote, "From the time I took command till today, now over ten days, I have not changed my clothes, have not had a regular's night rest, and many nights not a wink of sleep, and for several days did not even wash my face and hands, no regular food, and all the time in a great state of mental anxiety." Giving an assessment of this intense period, Meade wrote, "I think I have lived as much in this time as in the last thirty years." On the bright side, he and their son George were well, his horse, Old Baldy, had survived a bullet wound to his stomach, and the citizens of Frederick had treated him royally upon his arrival. He continued, "A few moments after my arrival I was visited by a deputation of ladies, and showers of wreaths and bouquets presented to me, in most complimentary terms." Though moved by the attention, he admitted, "I cannot say I appreciated all this honor, because I feel certain it is undeserved, and would like people to wait a little while." He also revealed a bit of his strategy to her: "I think we shall have another battle before Lee can cross the river. . . . For my part, as I have to follow and fight him, I would rather do it at once and in Maryland, than to follow into Virginia."[28]

In his next letter to his wife, written on July 10, he shared some of his frustration with his superiors and the "people": "I also see that my success at Gettysburg has deluded the people and the Government with the idea that I must always be victorious, that Lee is demoralized and disorganized, etc., and other delusions which will not only be dissipated by any reverse that I should meet with, but would react in proportion against me." This assessment of the perils of command showed Meade's astute reading of his evanescent popularity. He explained that he and Halleck had a "decided correspondence" on this subject and on the speed at which Meade had moved his army. However, "the firm stand I took had the result to induce General Halleck to tell me to act according to my judgment." He firmly believed that Lee had a "strong position" and was "determined to fight before he crosses the river"; in fact, without bridges he had to stand and fight, even if he did not want to. Meade felt confidence in his army, which was "in fine spirits." If battle came, he hoped he could "manage to keep them together, and not be required to attack a position too strong." Overall, it was all in "God's hands."[29] Once again, Meade was displaying his cautiousness, though simultaneously speaking of upcoming combat.

Meade continued to push his tired troops into position to attack Lee's newly built defensive line near Williamsport. On July 9 Meade wrote to Halleck with his plans, "I propose to move on a line from Boonsborough toward the center of the line from Hagerstown to Williamsport, my left flank looking to the river and my right toward the mountains, keeping the road to Frederick in my rear and center." He was bringing all his scattered forces to bear, too, as he noted that Brigadier General Smith and Brigadier General Neill had joined up in Waynesborough, and "if the forces under them are of any practical value, they could join my right flank and assist in the attack." His cavalry would be out in front, hoping to obtain information. Despite the problems of fatigue and lack of supplies ("two corps will march without their artillery, the animals being completely exhausted"), Meade believed that he was steadily getting his men into position for the "decisive battle of the war." He then asked for some patience and latitude, adding, "In view of its momentous consequences, I desire to adopt such measures as in my judgment will tend to insure success, even though these may be deemed tardy."[30]

Halleck seemed content with this report. He wrote back that afternoon, "The evidence that Lee's army will fight north of the Potomac seems reliable. . . . Everything I can get here will be pushed on to Harper's Ferry, from which place you can call them in to your left." Then he offered Meade the latitude he had been demanding: "Do not be influenced by any dispatch from here against your own judgment. Regard them as suggestions only. Our information here is not always correct." Later that afternoon, Halleck followed up with news that he was sending three brigades, two full regiments, and two complete batteries to Harper's Ferry.[31]

But Lee was preparing to meet whatever Meade threw at him. On July 10 he rode the entire length of the nine-mile line at Williamsport, checking for weak spots. He knew that with the river still too high to cross he needed a new pontoon bridge built, so he ordered his staff engineers and pioneer corps to begin building that bridge. What Lee needed was some time for his defenses to be strengthened and his escape constructed, and it fell to Major General Stuart to give him that time. Stuart's cavalry, with assistance from infantry and artillery units, fought a sharp engagement with Brigadier General Buford's cavalry and a brigade of soldiers from the Sixth Corps for the possession of Funkstown. By the end of the day, the superior weight of the Union forces forced Stuart to withdraw from Funkstown, but he bought twelve crucial hours for Lee.[32]

Ironically, Meade had also "bought" some time on July 10 and July 11 when he got his first very cautious message from Halleck. In the evening of July 10, Halleck wrote to Meade, "I think it will be best for you to postpone a general battle till you can concentrate all your forces and get up your reserves and reinforcements." Moreover, he should "beware of partial combats." Instead, he gave his familiar advice, "Bring up and hurl upon the enemy all your forces, good and bad." Meade may also have gotten conditional support from a secret message from Lincoln, perhaps delivered in person by Vice-President Hannibal Hamlin on July 10. The story originated with Robert Todd Lincoln, the longest-surviving son of Abraham Lincoln, who first told the story in 1872 of a discussion he had with his father on July 14. According to Robert's recollections, President Lincoln sent Meade a confidential message ordering him to attack Lee as soon as possible, and if the attack failed, Lincoln would take full responsibility for the failure. Meade never mentioned this secret message, but the story was repeated by Robert Lincoln throughout his life and has been investigated most recently by Gabor Boritt. Whether he received the message or not, Meade did not promptly attack Lee's army.[33]

Instead, Meade pushed his corps forward, even sending advance units of the Eleventh Corps into Hagerstown on July 12 to secure possession of that town. Meanwhile, Lee's pioneer corps worked feverishly to build a pontoon bridge at Falling Waters while his infantry reinforced their defensive works. By late afternoon of July 12, the two huge armies had settled into their final positions before what most assumed would be a major battle. The Confederate line stretched from Downsville in the south (with its far right resting near the Potomac River) to just northwest of Hagerstown. Some of the soldiers referred to it as the "Downsville Line," in reference to the road that ran nearly half the length of the line. Union forces began close to Tilghmantown in the south, then ran all the way up to Hagerstown. From north to south the order of the corps was Eleventh, First, Sixth, Fifth, Second, and Twelfth. With the capture of Hagerstown, Meade could finally bring the men under Generals Smith and Neill into his army, adding a mix of veterans and militia to his slowly swelling army.[34]

At midday on the twelfth, Meade received some troubling news from one of his engineers: the Potomac River had fallen eighteen inches in the past twenty-four hours, and continued to fall. Giving yet more bad news, the officer, Lt. Ranald S. Mackenzie, wrote, "A citizen states . . . that the fords near Shepherdstown and Williamsport are now practicable for infantry." So Meade had to strike soon, or else Lee might be able to get away. To that end, he ordered all corps commanders to send their pickets out as far as they could "and report the condition of the country in front."[35]

He also sent a message to Halleck that would haunt him for the rest of his career. He reported on the extent of his line and that of Lee's, then finished, "It is my intention to attack them tomorrow, unless something intervenes to prevent it, for the reason that delay would strengthen the enemy and will not increase my force." Little did he know that the "thing" that would intervene would be the timidity of his corps commanders.[36]

To assess the condition of troops and line, and ascertain the viability of an attack, Meade called together another "council" of his corps commanders for the evening of July 12. They met in Meade's small tent near Beaver Creek five miles behind the front at 8:00 in the evening. Eleven generals attended the meeting (including

Meade): Slocum of the Twelfth Corps, Sedgwick of the Sixth Corps, Sykes of the Fifth Corps, Howard of the Eleventh Corps, James Wadsworth of the First Corps (filling in for Newton, who was ill), William Hays of the Second Corps (temporary commander), William French of the Third Corps (recently named commander of the Third corps), Pleasonton, Warren (still chief engineer of the Army of the Potomac), and Meade's new chief of staff, Andrew Humphreys. The several accounts of the meeting do not suggest a long session with extensive discussion. Meade began by presenting what information he had, including his view that Lee's position was a strong one. Still, even though he had not had the time to determine the "precise mode of attack or any precise point of attack," he "was in favor of moving forward and attacking the enemy and taking the consequences." However, and this was the critical qualifier in the minds of his critics, he "left it to their judgment, and would not attack unless it met with their approval." He quickly found out it did not: five opposed it, including his four senior generals (Slocum, Sykes, Sedgwick, and French). In fact, Gouverneur Warren would later tell the Joint Committee on the Conduct of the War that he had never seen "the principal corps commanders so unanimous in favor of not fighting as on that occasion." But why? Wadsworth later recalled that there was not much discussion on that question until he asked the opposing generals to state their views. Sedgwick thought that Meade risked jeopardizing the great victory at Gettysburg by a rash attack; Sykes and French worried that if the attack failed, there was no blocking army between Lee and Washington.[37]

These arguments were unpersuasive to those in favor of the attack. Warren argued strongly for an attack, Humphreys agreed, especially if done as a "reconnaissance in force" initially, and Pleasonton, Wadsworth, and Howard were eager to attack. But Humphreys did not consider himself part of the council, just an adviser. Though he did not say it, he implied in his testimony to the Joint Committee on the Conduct of the War that he did not feel that Pleasonton's and Warren's votes "counted," either. As for Howard and Wadsworth, Warren shared a confidence with the committee that did not endear him to the commander of the Eleventh Corps: "General Howard's opinion did not carry much weight with the rest, because his troops did not behave well. The conduct of his troops at Gettysburg was not such as to restore them to the confidence of the army." Wadsworth was handicapped because he was seen as a temporary replacement for Newton (and was a political general, without West Point training).[38]

Without the support of his senior commanders, Meade decided to delay an attack for a day until he had time to examine the enemy's line closely. This sole decision, taken at great risk to his job and his reputation, would be the decision that received the most criticism. He explained his decision to delay in a telegram to Halleck sent on July 13: "Upon calling my corps commanders together [on July 12] and submitting the question to them, five out of six were unqualifiedly opposed to it. Under these circumstances, in view of the momentous consequences attendant upon a failure to succeed, I did not feel myself authorized to attack until I had made more careful examination of the enemy's position, strength, and defensive works." He had spent the better part of July 13 making that inspection, with Humphreys at his side, and found the enemy "strongly intrenched on a ridge running from the rear of Hagerstown past Downsville to the Potomac." He also received intelligence that a bridge was nearly finished at Falling Waters, which meant that Lee had built his escape route. Knowing his window of opportunity to attack Lee before he crossed the river was rapidly shrinking, he continued to check out the enemy's defenses in the rain and mist, hoping to find a "weak point" where he could "hazard an attack."[39]

Meade and Humphreys had seen a forbidding line. Guns were emplaced deeply, with six-feet-wide parapets, and positioned precisely to "get a perfect cross fire" according to the artillery officer Lt. Col. Charles Wainwright when he rode past them a day later. Infantrymen were protected by parallel lines of works, with the second, closest to Williamsport, actually built up with "fences rails, rocks, and packed earth." The lines were constructed along Salisbury Ridge, and the heavy rains for four days during the pursuit of Lee had turned the "lowlands along Marsh Run into lakes," according to Kent Brown, the leading historian of Lee's retreat. Union soldiers would have to cross these temporary ponds before reaching the fortified ridge. Brown argues that "no position ever held by Lee's army, save for Marye's Heights at Fredericksburg, was more formidable."[40]

None of this satisfied Halleck. He wrote back on the evening of July 13: "You are strong enough to attack and defeat the enemy before he can effect a crossing. Act upon your own judgment and make your generals execute your orders." As for Meade's penchant to ask for his generals' advice, Halleck had grown tired of that practice: "Call no council of war. It is proverbial that councils of war never fight." His final order: "Do not let the enemy escape."[41]

Meade undoubtedly assumed Halleck would send such a preemptory command because even before he received Halleck's telegram that evening, he had ordered four of his corps commanders to make a reconnaissance in force beginning at 7 A.M. on July 14. So now he was acting, despite the objections of his senior corps commanders. Meade also ordered Pleasonton to send a cavalry division to Harper's Ferry and, when the new bridge was finished, have the division "annoy . . . trains and communication" of the enemy between Williamsport and Winchester. As the possibility of Lee's escape grew more imminent, Meade prepared to attack—and to give chase to Lee's army should it manage to slip away.[42]

What Meade could not know was that the benefits of an attack had already been lost. Lee had ordered all the supply and hospital wagons to march to the newly constructed bridge at Falling Waters, and they began crossing the Potomac River in the early hours of July 13. When gunfire erupted along the long picket lines on the morning of July 13, the Confederates braced behind their fortifications for an attack. But it never came, and when Lee saw that it would not, he made his second critical decision: he ordered the retreat of his infantry, to begin after dusk on July 13. Ewell's corps would march to Williamsport and cross at the ford (followed by Stuart's cavalry). Longstreet's and Hill's corps would march out after dark, but they would go to Falling Waters and cross over the Potomac on the bridge. Heth's division would serve as the rearguard for these infantrymen. Ewell's men left their positions first that evening, keeping one regiment from each brigade in the breast-works to act as a rearguard, until finally relieved by cavalry. They left behind hun-dreds of burning campfires, logs cut to the shape of artillery barrels, and flags with cloth painted red. As historian Kent Brown eloquently describes the evacuation, "Lee would withdraw under cover of darkness, rain, and heavy smoke just as he had done at Gettysburg on the night of July 4 and in the wee hours of July 5."[43]

Unfortunately for Meade and the Army of the Potomac, this retreat in the dark was as successful as that of July 4. Over muddy roads so thick a man could hardly make steps, infantrymen, artillery caissons, and cavalry slowly made their way toward their crossing—and freedom. As early as 6:35 A.M. on July 14, Major Gen-eral Howard sent a message to Meade, "My brigade commander in Hagerstown reports the works in his front evacuated." By 8 A.M. he had confirmation of the retreat: "No enemy on the Williamsport road. Enemy's work very strong. Com-menced moving at dusk; last left about midnight." Meade pushed his other corps forward that morning, and one by one they came back with the same report: Lee's army had retreated. Brig. Gen. Judson Kilpatrick led his cavalry brigade in an impetuous attack on Heth's rearguard at Falling Waters, but after stiff fighting, the Confederates ran across the bridge, protected by some of their artillery guns resting on the south shore of the Potomac River. When the last men over cut the pontoon bridge loose, the long pursuit of Lee's army was over. Now the recrimi-nations and finger pointing would begin.[44]

The criticisms came quickly. Meade reported to Halleck at 11 A.M. on July 14 that the enemy had "evacuated" his lines. Halleck wrote back at 1 P.M., "The enemy should be pursued and cut up, wherever he may have gone. . . . I need hardly say to you that the escape of Lee's army without another battle has created great dissat-isfaction in the mind of the President, and it will require an active and energetic pursuit on your part to remove the impression that it has not been sufficiently ac-tive heretofore." These words stung Meade to the quick, and he promptly offered his resignation: "Having performed my duty conscientiously and to the best of my ability, the censure of the President conveyed in your dispatch of 1 p.m. this day, is, in my judgment, so undeserved that I feel compelled most respectfully to ask to be immediately relieved from the command of this army." Halleck acted quickly to pacify Meade (and retain him in command). He replied, "My telegram, stating the disappointment of the President at the escape of Lee's army, was not intended as a censure, but as a stimulus to an active pursuit. It is not deemed a sufficient cause for your application to be relieved."[45]

Halleck had only hinted at Lincoln's frustration. In a long letter Lincoln wrote but never sent, the president completely vented his feelings: "I had been oppressed nearly every day since the battles at Gettysburg, by what appeared to be evidences that yourself, and Gen. Couch, and Gen. Smith, were not seeking a collision with the enemy, but were trying to get him across the river without another battle. . . . You had at least twenty thousand veteran troops directly with you, and as many more raw ones within your supporting distance, all in addition to those who fought with you at Gettysburg; while it is not possible that he had received a single recruit; and yet you stood and let the flood run down, bridges be built, and enemy move away at his leisure, without attacking him." In sum, "he was within your easy grasp, and to have closed upon him would, in connection with our other late successes, have ended the war. . . . Your golden opportunity is gone." His secretary, John Hay, wrote of similar feelings Lincoln expressed on July 14 and 15.[46]

First newspapers, then generals soon echoed Lincoln's criticisms. For example, on July 17, the *New York Herald* opined that "the rebel army of Virginia has slipped through the fingers of General Meade." As for generals, Pleasonton later told the Joint Committee on the Conduct of the War exactly what it wanted to hear: "It was my opinion that our army should have attacked the rebel army at Falling Waters. . . . I believed that we should have captured—if not captured, at least dispersed—three fourths of that army, at least taken all their artillery." (To his credit, at the July 12 council, Pleasonton had advocated attack).[47]

Of course, the generals who did not want to attack had their day as well. For example, Sedgwick told the Joint Committee on the Conduct of the War the next spring, "They occupied a very strong position there. . . . My subsequent intimation confirmed me in the opinion that I was right in so voting: that the enemy occupied too strong a position for General Meade to attack."[48]

More nuanced views came from Warren and Humphreys. Warren plainly stated before the Joint Committee that he believed that the army "should have fought the enemy" on the morning of July 12 (before the council met that day). After the council met, however, he felt the weight of the senior commanders' opinion that the attack should not occur, haunted as they were by what occurred at Malvern Hill, Fredericksburg, and Gettysburg when the "enemy's positions and intrenchments were too strong to carry." He reminded the congressmen that Meade did decide to fight, over the objections of his advisers, on July 13 (to begin on July 14). He added, "General Meade has always been anxious to fight the enemy when he could." Humphreys maintained that Meade had done the right thing by delaying for a day to allow for future inspection, then ordering a reconnaissance in force to be made: "Subsequent information showed that the enemy had a very strong position, and indicated that had we made an attack we should have suffered very severely." Still, the move would have been worthwhile. He lectured the men, "I think that the public, and probably a great many officers, confound attacking field-works or intrenchments, where there is a small body of men posted, with attacking a whole army that has thrown up

intrenchments.... When you have to attack a whole, that is intrenched, you will suffer terribly in getting up to them." He added that he believed that even if the Union
had suffered losses, it would have held its ground. But it could not hope to break or
capture the entire Army of Northern Virginia, as "an army of 60,000 to 80,000 is
not to be knocked to pieces by any such battle as we have found yet." The criticisms
and defenses of Meade's decisions during the pursuit would persist through the end
of the war, and long after it, even down until today (though recent histories of Lee's
retreat argue that Meade made the right decision on July 12).[49]

It is revealing to read what Meade himself explained about his decisions in his
confidential letters to his wife. In his letter of July 14, he noted the "censure" he had
received from Lincoln and Halleck for his decision, complaining, "This is exactly
what I expected; unless I did impracticable things, fault would be found with me."
One of the key ideas here is that of impracticality; Meade strongly believed that
Lee's defenses were too strong at Williamsport to be breached successfully. In his
letter of July 16, he added more reasons for his anger and his special hatred of the
term *active pursuit:* "[They] insist on my continuing to try to do what I know in
advance it is impossible to do. My army (men and animals) is exhausted; it wants
rest and reorganization; it has been greatly reduced and weakened by recent operations, and no reinforcements of any practical value have been sent." Still, he was
told to pursue and fight Lee's army: "This has been the history of all my predecessors, and I clearly saw that in time their fate would be mine. This was the reason I
was disinclined to take the command, and it is for this reason I would gladly give it
up." So now the strength of the opposition, the unanimity of the corps commanders, the condition of the army, and the politics of the time had all been used as
evidence. It was the next letter, however, that offered a slightly different view, and
a real insight into Meade's strategic thinking. He wrote, "The proper policy for the
Government would have been to be contented with driving Lee out of Maryland,
and not to have advanced till this army was largely reinforced and reorganized, and
put on such a footing that its advance was sure to be successful."[50]

This last point is critical. Though Meade did want to fight Lee's army, he only
wanted to attack on a ground and time of his choosing. Pressured by Washington
to attack at Williamsport, he went outside his comfort zone by going against his
corps commanders with his order of the thirteenth (to attack the next day). That
it fizzled was a "disappointment" to Meade, as it was to many others, but it was not
a "dissatisfaction" (the term he used in a letter to Halleck sent later that month).[51]
For Meade, if the conditions favored an attack while Lee's army was in Maryland,
he would attack. But if they did not, then he was more than content to wait until
another time and place to attack.

What Meade truly miscalculated (as he did on a number of occasions), was the
political purpose of attacking Lee at Williamsport, and the enormous repercussions if he did not. While he properly worried about the unknown strengths of

Lee's defenses and the ramifications of failure to capture or seriously damage Lee's army, his superiors in Washington were anxiously awaiting another complete victory as was just achieved by Grant in Vicksburg, with an end to the war in sight. Although that view was unrealistic at the time, it was a view and a hope that never truly died. For Lincoln and members of Congress, the morale of the Northern public was always on their minds. They needed military victories to sustain morale and justify the costs of war. They could push their case without military victories, but at the very least there had to be demonstrable efforts to achieve military victory, even at a high cost in lives. Politically, Meade should have attacked, even if Lee's army ultimately escaped. As journalist William Swinton wrote just after the war of Meade's decision, "even had the army attacked and been repulsed, General Meade would have been forgiven; for in war it is often better to have fought and lost, than never to have fought at all."[52]

But George G. Meade was not the general to attack solely for political reasons, nor if he did not believe that he would succeed. Though brave and unafraid of battle, he was also calculating and precise, preferring to maneuver and defend unless he felt confident that an attack would produce victory. Most of his corps commanders had similar attitudes, so in any group meeting, their views and fears tended to reinforce each other. Looking back at every "council" or "consultation" Meade held with his corps commanders during the Gettysburg campaign, not once did a majority favor an attack. While they did counsel defensive fighting at Gettysburg on July 2, they never as a group advocated an offensive posture. Meade could have safely predicted what his generals would say on the night of July 12, though perhaps the intensity of their aversion to attack was different, if Warren's recollections are accurate. Of course, he could have followed French's advice: "It does not make any difference what our opinions are; if you give the order to attack, we will fight just as well under it as if our opinions were not against it."[53] While that is obviously a plea for a decisive general, it is disingenuous. Meade had seen how slowly his generals sometimes responded—Slocum at Gettysburg, Sedgwick in the pursuit—and these were the leaders he had to rely on to carry out an attack. Meade knew some of his corps commanders well, especially their strengths and limitations. The senior generals were good managers, but, as he wrote to his wife, they did not possess the energy and fighting spirit of a Hancock or a Reynolds.[54] Meade was an Army officer through and through, who gave and obeyed orders and believed in working with his team to achieve a team success. That approach had worked well at Gettysburg when the army was on the defensive; it could also stifle rapid and hard-hitting movement, especially on the offensive. Without his corps commanders behind him, Meade was reluctant to attack.

For Meade, war was primarily a military matter best left in the hands of trained professionals. Intellectually, he knew that his view was not shared by Lincoln and many others in Washington, but emotionally and as a matter of conduct, he would not change his basic approaches to managing an army to suit the demands of politicians in Washington. Ironically, one of the primary reasons he got the job was his lack of political connections and unwillingness to engage in political intrigue. It would also be the same reason he would never garner the hearty support of Abraham Lincoln and most leaders of the Republican Party. Without that strong support, every decision would be scrutinized, every mistake magnified, and every accomplishment minimized. The failure to fight and destroy Lee's Army of Northern Virginia in Maryland after the Battle of Gettysburg would tarnish his reputation and limit his possibilities for the remainder of the war.

⚜FOUR⚜

Fall Frustration

Meade and Lee Spar in Virginia, July–November 1863

Though many felt that an opportunity to catch Lee and end the war had been squandered in Maryland, Meade did not. He saw the pursuit and eventual fight with Lee as one long sparring match, as each general tried to discover the where-abouts and weaknesses of the other's position, then strike. Meade would plan a total of four attacks on Lee that fall, and with some degree of success in two of them, his star appeared on the rise again. But that success proved temporary, as a failed attack in late November left him right where he was when he found that Lee's army had escaped across the Potomac River: surprised, angry, disappointed, frustrated, and uncertain whether he would retain command.

Following the stand-off at Williamsport, Meade needed to get his huge army across the Potomac River. He accomplished that major logistical effort in record time, with pontoon bridges being built at Berlin and Harper's Ferry. Meade or-dered four corps to cross at Berlin, and three to cross at Harper's Ferry. By July 18 Meade reported that "four infantry corps, the Reserve Artillery, and two divi-sions of cavalry have crossed the Potomac." The remainder of his army crossed the Potomac the next day. Meade also sent forward a division of cavalry to occupy Snicker's Gap and ordered another division of cavalry to take "possession of the gaps as far as Chester Gap." He left four thousand soldiers to guard Harper's Ferry and pushed two brigades of cavalry to "protect the Orange and Alexandria Rail-road." Though intelligence was sparse, it appeared that Lee's army had marched to Winchester, then on to Front Royal, with Culpeper as its destination. Meade had once again pursued what he saw as his strategic imperatives: to follow Lee, strike him when possible, and keep his army between Lee's army and Washington.[1]

As Meade marched his army toward Warrenton, he felt he had an opportunity to strike part of Lee's army when he received a message from his Signal Corps officer at Ashby's Gap on July 21: "The enemy are moving up the Valley in considerable force this am. Their train is immense." With cavalry under Brigadier General Merritt watching for the retreating Confederates, Meade sent his corps into motion, ordering the Third Corps to Piedmont, "looking to Manassas Gap, with a view to supporting the cavalry now in that Gap"; the First Corps to White Plains; the Second Corps to Paris; the Sixth Corps to the Rectortown Cross Roads; and headquarters to Upperville. As Meade's infantry marched to their designated positions, reports of Confederate movement south toward Culpeper poured in from several cavalry units.[2] It looked as if it might be possible to cut, if not sever, the Confederate forces marching south. To the critical job of probing this possibility Meade mysteriously assigned the new commander of the Third Corps, the untried William "Blinky" French. Why Meade gave this job to the Third Corps is not known, but it would prove to be a costly decision.

Meade ordered the Third Corps to "move up through Manassas Gap at 4 am and, if practical, attack the enemy now moving through Front Royal and Chester Gap." The movement began auspiciously, with the First Division under Brig. Gen. Hobart Ward joining Buford's cavalry to occupy the gap by 11 P.M. on July 22. The next morning, the First Division was deployed as skirmishers along a long front, and they waited for the Second and Third Divisions to join them at the gap. Once they did, they were "deployed in line of battle," and the First Division set forth to drive out the skirmishers and punch through the new line of battle set up by the Confederates. Though French's report spoke of the "brilliant" performance of the Excelsior Brigade in driving the last Confederates out of the Gap, Meade had viewed French's leadership differently. At 2:45 P.M. he urged French to "continue pushing them, and when the cavalry joins you, to do so with more rapidity." His exhortations fell on deaf ears. Warren reported back to Meade from a signal station at 5:45 P.M.: "French's skirmishers only have been engaged. The enemy shows about 5,000 men and eight guns in line about a mile in front of General French's main body. . . . General French's troops are not advancing." French himself had noted that "continuous columns of cavalry, infantry, artillery, and baggage-wagons were seen during the day moving from the direction of Winchester toward Strasburg, Luray, and Front Royal, the force in front of us being evidently a large flank guard to delay our advance." But he could not break through that "advance guard," and he "permitted" his men to lie on their arms at nightfall. So with one corps under his direct command and two more waiting to assist him, French could secure only a few more yards than Buford had with his cavalry. The next day, Second Division pickets found that the "enemy had withdrawn in the night."[3] Once again, the Confederates had eluded the grasp of Meade.

Though disappointed with what could be called the "Manassas Gap Reconnaissance in Force," Meade did not criticize French in his telegraph to Halleck. On July 24 he reported that he had pushed nearly all five corps through the pass, only to find that the "enemy had again disappeared." Troops were sent to Front Royal, but they found only some wounded soldiers left behind. They could see a rearguard heading south. Now Meade had more information: the bulk of Lee's army had retreated through Strasburg and Luray, and it was a small force that had been sent to Chester Gap to "cover his flank." So even if French had moved with great speed, he might not have caught the main body of the Confederate army, but that did not erase the fact that he had dithered. Meade's new chief of staff, Andrew Humphreys, wrote his wife that if the army could have moved faster, then "six hours earlier would have made the operation the most brilliant ever accomplished in this country." But Lee had moved too fast for the army, and Meade then decided to withdraw from the gaps and march to Warrenton and Warrenton Junction.[4]

As the corps quickly marched to the area around Warrenton, Meade sought advice on his next steps. His first suggestion, the "reoccupation of the Shenandoah Valley," was quickly rejected by Halleck. To goad Meade, he added, "Lee's army is the objective point." Meade did not give up, arguing that his goal would be "to prevent the enemy from having the benefit of the incoming crops, which last year, I understand, he employed his army in gathering, and sent to the rear for winter use." Halleck still rejected the argument, replying that "the occupation of the Shenandoah is now a matter of very little importance."

Meade's next suggestion was to prepare his army "for an advancement." He had to wait until the Rappahannock became fordable, and he needed fresh horses for his cavalry and artillery. He would "advance on the railroad to Culpeper," then hold and guard the entire railroad from Manassas Junction to Culpeper, thus testing "the capacity of the Orange and Alexandria Railroad to supply the army and the practicability of maintaining open such a long line of communication." His biggest handicap was information: "No reliable intelligence of the position of the enemy has been obtained."[5]

The next day, he received Halleck's reply, in the form of a note from President Lincoln to Halleck. Lincoln wrote, "[Meade] supposes the Government here is demanding of him to bring on a general engagement with Lee as soon as possible. I am claiming no such thing of him." His reasoning must have cut Meade to the quick: "If he [Meade] could not safely engage Lee at Williamsport, it seems absurd to suppose he can safely engage him now, when he has scarcely more than two-thirds of the force he had at Williamsport, while it must be that Lee has been re-enforced." He left the ultimate decision in Halleck's hands, writing, "I shall be glad for you to so inform him, unless your own judgment is against it." Halleck was not one to stand up to Lincoln, nor did he like to make independent decisions. So he had simply included Lincoln's note to him in a message to Meade, then added his own weight to Lincoln's view, "I think it would be best to hold for the present the upper line of the Rappahannock without further pursuit of Lee."[6]

Meade did not submit meekly to the new directions. He wrote back that he had thought he was supposed to "pursue Lee and bring him to a general engagement, if practicable." He then challenged the President's arguments: "I did not fail to attack Lee at Williamsport because I could not do so *safely;* I simply delayed the attack until, by examination of his position, I could do so with some reason degree of probability that the attack would be successful" (author's italics). Also, "my army at this moment is about equal in strength to what it was at Williamsport" (he had been sent a division of men to replace the nine months' men). Meade continued with his own ideas, to find a spot to build pontoon bridges to cross the Rapidan River, then to "advance," as long as Lee was "not found in a very strong position." His plan was based on maintaining his current number of troops, which Halleck had already hinted might be reduced to help quell the draft riots in New York City. Finally, if he had to hold, he preferred not to remain on the Upper Rappahannock because it was a line Lee could easily breach or flank.[7]

The next day, Halleck responded to Meade's proposal, ordering him to send him four regiments of infantry to New York City. He also said he could not send him any reinforcements because "every place has been stripped to the bare poles." As for the critical questions about advances and lines, he simply said, "Keep up a threatening attitude, but do not advance."[8]

With these sparse orders, Meade settled into a long period of relative inactivity. He sent his cavalry out to reconnoiter the enemy's position and reported to Halleck on August 4 that he would "make no further movements without your instructions, except to occupy as much of the ground between the Rappahannock and Rapidan by my cavalry as I can without requiring too great and unnecessary loss on my part."[9] Meade had resigned himself to the new operating orders from his superior.

During the next two months, Meade was busy with many things, but not with chasing Lee. On August 14 he went to Washington for his first meeting with the Cabinet and Lincoln. Meade wrote very little about the meetings to his wife, but what he said was unfailingly positive: "The manner in which I was received and treated in Washington by all with whom I came in contact was certainly most gratifying to me. I really believe I have the confidence of all parties and will continue to retain it, unless some great disaster should overtake me, which I ought not to anticipate." No detailed account of his conversation with Lincoln exists, though likely topics included his performance at Gettysburg, Williamsport, and the necessity to remain in place while some of his men were transferred to New York City to restore order. Meade had already learned of Lincoln's kind words about him contained in a letter to Major General Howard: "I am now profoundly grateful for what was done, without criticism of what was not done. General Meade has my confidence as a brave and skillful officer and a true man."[10]

In a similar vein, Halleck's unofficial letter of July 28, praising Meade for his performance at Gettysburg, had bolstered his confidence. Halleck wrote, "You handled your troops in that battle as well, if not better, than any general has handled his army during the war." Still, he felt that Lincoln's "disappointment" at the escape of Lee's army was understandable. Meade stubbornly clung to his earlier argument in his reply to Halleck: he did not want to make a "blind attack" at Williamsport and expose his army to "all the risks attending such a venture." He averred that he could have "erred in judgment" and reiterated his request to be relieved if "found wanting." Halleck did not feel the need to respond to Meade's second offer to resign.[11]

Meade quickly got to work in assigning units to go to New York City. By August 16 he had sent nearly ten thousand men to Alexandria, those whom he considered to be "my best troops and some of my best officers." They would not return until early October.[12]

Meade also had some key personnel matters to attend to. On July 19 he recommended his reliable subordinate, Gouverneur Warren, for promotion to major general, with temporary command of the Second Corps while Hancock recovered from his Gettysburg wound. He also recommended colonels Kenner Garrard and Sidney Burbank for promotion to brigadier general. When he did not get a response from Halleck, he prodded him on July 25, asking "whether any action has been had." Halleck responded bluntly: "It is impossible to promote General Warren at present. There is no vacancy." Then he vaguely added, "I have recommended the discharge of certain useless major-generals, but it has not been acted on." When Major General Humphreys shared this message with Warren, he was undoubtedly depressed, but Stanton and Halleck quickly had a change of heart, meeting with Warren in early August, then promoting him to major general and giving him command of the Second Corps. At age thirty-three, Warren became one of the youngest major generals in the Union armies. A jubilant Warren looked forward to his new responsibilities. Garrard was promoted to brigadier general, but not Burbank.[13]

Meade seemed to have a special fondness for Warren. With a strong background in engineering and topography, Warren and Meade inclined to look at terrain and operations in complementary terms. Theodore Lyman described him as an "original officer . . . with a restless black eye, like a weasel. . . . His mind is extremely ready and sure, on all points." His modern biographer, David Jordan, put a sharper edge on that view of Warren, writing, "Conscious of his own talents, all too intolerant of shortcomings in others, and aware of the prerogatives of rank, Warren at times was arrogant and overbearing."[14]

When not dealing with administrative matters, Meade had time to take a delightful trip to Philadelphia at the end of August to receive a ceremonial sword given to him by his former unit, the Pennsylvania Reserves. Governor Andrew Curtin and other Pennsylvania dignitaries attended the ceremony, and Meade's speech was covered by several major newspapers. Of course, the man who abhorred politics and never played them well was once again outmaneuvered by politicians. Just before his speech, he had been asked to say something in favor of Curtin, and he did, mentioning his support for the volunteers of Pennsylvania and the Union cause, "I hope that the citizens of Pennsylvania have appreciated and will remember his services in promoting the interest of our country and suppressing this Rebellion." When one editorial turned this into an endorsement of Curtin for reelection, Meade could only fume in a letter to his wife, "I said nothing of the kind, and made no allusions to elections."[15] It would not be the last time the politically tone-deaf Meade ran afoul of journalists.

In September, a new aide joined Meade's staff, his friend the scientist, Theodore Lyman of Massachusetts. Meade greeted him with a friendly "Hullo, how are you Lyman?" and asked Lyman to mess with him. Lyman found Meade to look a "little thinner but otherwise the same." Lyman would soon be traveling with his commander to far-flung posts of the army and entertaining a constant stream of foreign visitors to the camp.[16] In one week in September, headquarters received an Austrian officer (who could not "speak a word of English"), Queen Victoria's seventy-five-year-old physician Sir Henry Holland, and three officers from Mexico, including General Jose Cortez. In October, Lyman got a Swedish officer as a temporary tent mate, and in November he entertained four English officers, including Lord Castle Guff, a sixteen-year-old officer in the Grenadier Guards. Lyman led them over much of the army's position and pleased them by setting up a charging exercise from Warren's Second Corps.[17] Throughout Meade's tenure as commander of the Army of the Potomac, he would play host to foreign and domestic visitors, a task he handled well, though it must have been wearing for him at times (and Grant, who also had a steady stream of guests).

A good description of Meade emerges from this time, written by another one of his aides, Morris Schaff: "His face was spare and strong, of the Romanish type, its complexion pallid. His blue eyes were prominent, coldly penetrating and underhung by sweeping lobes that when cares were great and health not good had a rim of purplish hue. . . . He wore a full, but inconspicuous beard, and his originally deep chestnut, but now frosted hair, was soft and inclined to wave on good, easy terms with a conspicuous and speaking forehead." He had a "rich, cultivated voice," manners that were "native and high-bred," and "easy and suggestive speech" when relaxing among friends. His uniform was regulation casual, with an open coat, "displaying his well-ordered line, vest, and necktie," and when riding a horse, he usually wore a "drooping army hat and yellow gauntlets." His greatest fault was his temper; even his loyal aide Schaff had to admit that he had seen him "so cross and ugly that no one dared to speak to him."[18]

Though almost every account of Meade mentions his temper, few mention another side: his ability to admit fault in himself, and even make jokes about it. When a blistering critique of Meade appeared in the *Spirit of the Times* on August 29, 1863, accusing him of timidity and sheer fortune of position at Gettysburg, he read it in its entirety to his staff, offering "running comments, with that close sense of justice, for which he is very remarkable." For example, he said, "Well, that's true, I did think so, and was quite mistaken." As Lyman astutely noted about Meade, his critical eye caught everyone, himself included. He wrote, "I never saw a man in my life who was so characterized by straightforward truthfulness as he is. He will pitch into himself in a moment, if he thinks he has done wrong; and woe to those, no matter who they, who do not do it right!"[19]

It is important to recognize this side of Meade, for it is not mentioned by his critics, nor does it appear as often in his many letters to his wife and in some of his official communications with his superiors. To his wife, he complained more and critiqued himself less (though he did admit failings at some critical moments). To his superiors, he could be extremely touchy and sensitive to every perceived slight, whether real or not. An overwrought sensitivity to criticism permeates his correspondence, but he was hardly alone: the official and unofficial correspondence of most of the generals in the Army of the Potomac (and their staff officers, who often wrote the history of the war) overflows with charges, recriminations, grievances, tortured explanations, and, occasionally, apologies.

A clear test of the respect and support Meade had in Washington came in mid-September. Around September 6, the first inkling that Lee might transfer troops to Bragg in Tennessee arrived in Washington, and Meade was ordered to find out more information. Meade sent spies to gather information and the cavalry to probe the Confederate positions, and in less than a week he knew that Longstreet's entire corps was to be transferred to east Tennessee. With Lee's army reduced by one-third, Meade felt he had the opportunity to begin his own strategic plan: to move his army (once his detached troops returned) to either the Fredericksburg Railroad or the James River. He knew the latter would be unpopular because it left Washington unguarded and would remind politicians of McClellan's failed campaign of 1862. But he had high hopes for basing his army in Fredericksburg and moving south, given that his supply lines could be shorter, easier, and well guarded.[20]

He asked Halleck for his views and waited a day to hear them in full. In a long letter, Halleck explained the entire picture of the war and stressed the importance of the government knowing just how many troops Lee had sent to Tennessee. As for Meade's army, the plans were quite clear: "The main objects are to threaten Lee's position, to ascertain more certainly the actual conditions of affairs in his army, and, if possible, to cut off some portion of it by a sudden raid, if that be practicable." He could not send any reinforcements to Meade at the time, so Meade should not try any "rash measures." Still, "if Lee's force has been very considerably reduced, something may be done to weaken him or force him still farther back." The government now expected William Rosecrans to receive the "shock" of a new Confederate attack. Halleck enclosed a letter from Lincoln to him, in which he stated of Meade, "He should move upon Lee at once in manner of a general attack, leaving to developments whether he will make it a real attack. I think this would develop Lee's real condition and purposes better than the cavalry alone can do. Of course, my opinion is not to control you and General Meade."[21]

For someone of Meade's temperament and inclination, these responses were completely inadequate. Meade always wanted clear and precise orders, and he would faithfully carry them out, regardless of what he thought of them. Halleck practically had an aversion to giving orders with powerful consequences, so he relied on Lincoln to give the orders. But Lincoln wanted his generals to make bold decisions while keeping larger strategic and political considerations in mind. So the two men wanted Meade to "threaten" Lee's army but not bring on a general engagement, unless he felt he could win. Either the superiors had lost faith in Meade, or they had changed their strategic concerns for Washington and Lee's army.

Though puzzled by the lack of direction from Halleck and Lincoln, Meade acted promptly. He sent his infantry across the Rappahannock, headed toward the Rapidan. When they neared the Rapidan, they immediately observed the strength of Lee's defenses. In a long letter to Halleck written on September 18, Meade shared his thoughts and asked for more direction. Though he felt he might be able to get his army across the river at a "considerable sacrifice," he would gain almost nothing except a "longer line of communication."[22]

Meade heard back from Halleck and Lincoln the next day. Halleck lectured Meade on the need to make his own decisions: "I never attempt to direct a general when, where, or how to give battle. He must decide such matters for himself. No one else can do it for him. I have no idea of playing the Austrian ruler." Reiterating the view that Lee's army was the objective, not Richmond, he continued, "The object to be obtained is to do it as much harm as possible with as little injury as possible to yourself." Essentially, Halleck wrote, order raids on Lee's outposts or "withdraw your army to some point nearer Washington." Lincoln, of course, set a milder tone, arguing in his best attorney style that there was no merit to attack, if nothing could be gained from the attack except casualties. He then came to his central point: "To avoid misunderstanding, let me say that to attempt to fight the enemy slowly back into his intrenchments at Richmond, and there to capture him, is an idea I have been trying to repudiate for a quite a year. My judgment is so clear against it that I would scarcely allow the attempt to be made, if the general in command should desire to make it."[23] What Meade probably guessed, but would not know until two days later, was that he was being softened for the decision to take part of his army away from him.

Knowing that Lincoln and Halleck wanted to see more information and action from his army, Meade sent cavalry divisions on a long ride to the west of Lee's positions, to ascertain if Lee's left was vulnerable. The cavalry under Buford left on September 21, rode as far south as Liberty Mills, skirmished a bit with Stuart's cavalry, then returned by September 23, reporting that Lee's left did appear vulnerable. Officers began to anticipate a movement of the entire army soon.[24]

But it would not happen. The long-awaited battle between Rosecrans and General Braxton Bragg out West had begun along the banks of Chickamauga Creek in northwestern Georgia on September 19. As the telegraphic reports dribbled in during September 19–21, Abraham Lincoln fretted over the battle and the future of the war. After spending a sleepless night in the telegraph room of the War Department, he had a frank, pessimistic, and private conversation with Secretary of the Navy Gideon Welles (who has the only record of the conversation). Admitting to Welles that he was "feeling badly" about the news from Chickamauga, the talk drifted to Meade and his army. Lincoln said, "It is the same old story of this Army of the Potomac. Imbecility, inefficiency—don't want to do—defending the Capital." Welles added his own list of criticisms of Meade and his army, then asked the president directly why he did not simply remove Meade. Lincoln replied: "What can I do with such generals as we have? Who among them is better than Meade? To sweep away the whole of them from the chief command and substitute a new man would cause a shock, and be likely to lead to combinations and troubles greater than we have now have. I see all the difficulties you do. They oppress me."[25]

This was a harsh assessment of Meade and his team. Even if enhanced by Welles (no fan of Halleck, Meade, and most of the Eastern generals), it most likely conveyed Lincoln's raw feelings at this low point in the war. Defeat in the West, Meade stalled near Washington, and Democrats sensing victory in the upcoming fall elections—nothing was going his way that morning. Still, he would never speak this harshly or frankly to Meade (or Halleck, for that matter). Instead, he told Halleck to summon Meade to Washington for a conference. He was, of course, formulating his arguments for sending some of Meade's army to Tennessee.

Meade was called to Washington for a critical meeting with his superiors on Tuesday, September 22. He arrived there toward midnight and immediately went to the War Department to meet with Halleck. The next morning, he met at the White House with Lincoln, Stanton, and Halleck. They discussed the situation in Tennessee and Meade's plans. Lincoln, Stanton, and Halleck felt that Rosecrans needed immediate and massive reinforcements to his army in Chattanooga to survive. While Meade understood their arguments, he believed that a temporary reduction in the size of his army indicted his leadership. For the *third* time, Meade offered his resignation, writing, "I told the president and General Halleck that if they thought I was too slow or prudent, to put some else in my place." The response of Halleck was telling: "Halleck smiled very significantly, and said he had no doubt I would be rejoiced to be relieved, but there was no such good luck for me." He did not record Lincoln's exact response. Once again the proud Meade played what he felt to be his trump card—his offer to resign. But just as before, he found that its use had little effect on a political decision. Showing either a very poor reading of his superiors or else being deceived by superb acting, Meade left Washington "with the belief that the President was satisfied" with his current level of troops and plans.[26]

He could not have been more wrong. At 2:30 A.M. on September 24, Halleck sent him a brief but full telegram: "Please answer if you have positively determined to make an immediate movement. If not, prepare the Eleventh and Twelfth Corps to be sent to Washington, as soon as cars can be sent to you. The troops should have five days cooked provisions." Knowing full well that Meade did not have a plan for an immediate movement, Halleck safely knew his answer.[27]

But Meade had one more round of fight in him. He wrote back, "I contemplate no immediate movement, though until your telegraph the decision was not positive—awaiting information to be obtained today." Halleck and Lincoln would have none of that. Halleck wrote back later that morning: "Your telegram of this morning has been shown to the President. He directs that the Eleventh and Twelfth Corps be immediately prepared to be sent to Washington, as conditionally ordered before." At last Meade and Halleck had the direct order they preferred. Meade offered no more protests or counterproposals. He ordered the sixteen thousand men of the Twelfth Corps and the fifty-seven hundred men of the Eleventh Corps to be prepared to be transported the next day.[28]

The next major move would be Lee's. He soon learned that Meade's army would be reduced by two corps. When the news became verified, Lee made a decision that showed why his daring kept Meade and all the other Union generals off guard: he decided to flank Meade's army, hoping to draw him into a battle he could not win. Lee knew he was still outnumbered, that his army needed new horses and supplies of all kinds, but still he wanted to move and fight, if necessary. With his forty-five thousand men he planned to do a virtual repeat of his successful Second Manassas campaign; he would keep some cavalry positioned along the Rapidan River to fool Meade, while his two infantry corps would march north, attempting to flank the Union right. His soldiers began marching on October 8.[29]

But Meade was not caught by surprise. As Ethan Rafuse states, "Unlike Pope, Meade would give the Rebel commander no opening for a decisive stroke." With improved intelligence gathering from the interrogation of deserters and code breaking among signalmen, he knew when Lee's army had begun moving, and the only uncertainty he had was its purpose. He wrote Halleck on the evening of October 9: "A movement on the part of the enemy has taken place today. . . . What his intentions are is as yet uncertain. Whether falling back from the Rapidan, or making a flank movement against me by way of Madison Court House and Weaverville, I cannot say." To be ready to meet any contingency, he sent one division of cavalry to cross the Rapidan and see if the army had retreated, sent another division of cavalry to watch from Madison Court House, and ordered the infantry to be ready to move at a moment's notice.[30] As usual, Meade prepared for several possibilities at once, demonstrating a strength of his leadership.

The next two days saw a succession of fierce cavalry skirmishes as Union cavalry first crossed the Rapidan River, then recrossed when further intelligence confirmed that Lee was intent on a flanking maneuver, not a retreat to Richmond. On the afternoon of October 10, Meade decided to move his army back behind the Rappahannock, writing Halleck of his plans: "I shall, tonight, withdraw to the north side of the Rappahannock, and endeavor, by means of the cavalry, to find out what the enemy propose. My belief now is that his movements are offensive."[31]

Both commanding generals now entered a foot race, in which neither knew exactly where the other's army was, or where it was headed. Lee continued to push his army northward, striving to get in Meade's rear. Meade marched his men quickly northward to prevent this from happening, though at midday on October 12, he sent Major General Sedgwick and two corps back across the river and toward Brandy Station, to ascertain Lee's movements. Later in the day, Meade learned that Lee's army had crossed the Rappahannock at Fauquier White Sulphur Springs, so he immediately sent word to Sedgwick to reverse his course and march his men back toward Warrenton Junction. Though Meade told Halleck on October 12, "If Lee will give me battle between the Rappahannock and the Rapidan I will fight him," by late evening he reported news of a different sort to Halleck, "There is no doubt that the whole of Lee's army is crossing on my immediate right." He added, "If I am not attacked tomorrow, I shall move forward and attack him." Meade moved promptly to order all his corps to march toward and assemble at Three Mile Station and Warrenton Junction the next day, marching with "the utmost vigilance, promptitude, and celerity."[32] Though startled by the turn of events, Meade kept his cool and acted decisively to meet this new and growing threat.

Meade had to remain flexible because, even as the weary soldiers marched in the dark to their new positions, more bits of intelligence came to his headquarters. First came information from a private in the Tenth New York Cavalry, who had been stranded for hours behind enemy lines but escaped in the early hours of the morning and found his way to Meade. He had watched Ewell's corps march over the bridge at Fauquier White Sulphur Springs, which confirmed the information Meade had acted on the day before. Everything changed, however, when Major Brown of the First Maine Cavalry rode up to headquarters late in the morning of October 13. He described how his men had barely escaped from the grip of Hill's hard-marching corps as they marched through Amissville (almost due west of Warrenton) the previous evening. That meant that part of Lee's army was practically behind Meade.[33]

This news prompted Meade to rethink his entire estimate of Lee's intentions. He now believed that Lee intended to split his army, sending Hill on a long march up to Salem, then turning east to hit the Union rear at Manassas Junction (just as Stonewall Jackson had in August 1862), while Ewell's corps would head for the same place down the Warrenton Pike. Though criticized in the most current analysis of the Bristoe campaign for his "false conclusion" that led him to abandon his earlier pledge to fight Lee, there is an alternate explanation. Meade, like most of the senior generals in the Army of the Potomac, was haunted by Lee's stunning successes in 1862 and 1863. Meade had written his wife earlier in the fall: "I have now got as far as Pope was last year when he fought the battle of Cedar Mountain. I trust I will have better luck than he had." Also, despite the repeated insistence of Halleck and Lincoln that "Lee's army" was to be his primary object, Meade felt that he must always protect Washington and *his* army. If Lee got in his rear, as he had done to Pope in 1862, it could be Second Manassas all over again. With that fear in mind, Meade issued new orders: the army would make haste for Centreville Heights, with an interim defense line set up between Greenwich and Bristoe Station for the night of October 13. The orders went out by 1:00 P.M. on October 13, and the men began marching toward their destinations that afternoon.[34]

The foot race was initially one-sided because, unbeknownst to Meade, Lee had Ewell's corps wait at Warrenton while Hill's corps marched up. Lee did send Stuart out toward Catlett's Station to determine where Meade's forces were. There was a brief cavalry skirmish at Auburn on October 13, then Stuart's brigades had to hide out in a forest near the town to avoid a bigger battle and potential capture. The cavalry skirmish at Auburn did not alter Meade's plan to march his army to Centreville; late in the evening of October 13, he sent a circular to all the commanders outlining the route of their march the following day.[35]

Many men had a sleepless night. French's Third Corps had resumed its march to Greenwich, with its last troops exiting Auburn past midnight. Meanwhile, Warren's Second Corps started toward Auburn at 4 A.M. on October 14, having no idea that three thousand Confederate cavalry hid in the woods near Auburn, nor that an entire Confederate corps under Ewell was marching at the same time toward Auburn.[36]

The Battle of Auburn on October 14 began with Union cavalry firing on Ewell's lead division (under Rodes). For the next five hours, Warren would be everywhere, striving to get the Second Corps and its long ammunition train of 100 wagons and 125 ambulances safely through Auburn and then southeast to its next destination, Catlett's Station. Through skillful use of cavalry and artillery, Warren got the job done, with his last troops arriving at Catlett's Station by early afternoon. Meanwhile, Stuart came out of hiding, fired upon Warren's van, then led his brigades away to safety. Ewell's corps marched steadily toward Auburn. The Battle of Auburn ended before noon on October 14.[37]

Though the morning's skirmishing had occurred only five miles from Meade's headquarters at Catlett's Station, the commanding general was nonplussed. With mid-morning reports showing that each corps—including the hard-pressed Second Corps—was carrying out the marching orders from the day before, Meade felt comfortable enough to move his headquarters up to Bristoe Station by noon (eight miles from Catlett's Station). He telegraphed Halleck that all was well and proceeding as planned: "My movement thus far is successful. . . . The enemy are advancing from Warrenton, but will hardly be able to arrest my movement." He then sent a message to Warren instructing him to march his corps quickly to Bristoe Station, though vigilantly watching for an attack coming from the west. To aid him, Sykes's Fifth Corps was to remain at Bristoe Station until he arrived, and stay in communication throughout the march of the Second Corps.[38]

Meade's intelligence had been correct: Hill had pushed his corps all that morning, hoping to catch some Union troops as they pulled up the rear of Meade's army. For most of the morning, they had been at the heels of French's Third Corps, though by late morning, French's men moved out of their immediate reach. By early afternoon, the van of Hill's corps, Maj. Gen. Henry Heth's division, was within one and one quarter miles of Bristoe Station (actually north of the station). Hill rode up and saw Union soldiers crossing Broad Run near Bristoe Station. He assumed these men were from the Third Corps. What he actually saw was Sykes's Fifth Corps rearguard.[39]

Hill then showed the initiative and aggressiveness for which the generals of the Army of Northern Virginia were famed and feared: he decided to attack. Though handicapped by lack of cavalry, insufficient troops (two divisions trailed far behind Heth), and lack of knowledge of where Ewell and Lee were, A. P. Hill saw an opportunity, and he took it. As he wrote in his report after the battle, "I am convinced that I made the attack too hastily, and at the same time that a delay of half an hour, and there would have been no enemy to attack. In that event I believe I should equally have blamed myself for not attacking at once." Hill ordered Heth to form a line of battle and attack the Union troops visible at Bristoe Station. Heth sent three brigades forward, leaving one in reserve.[40]

There then occurred one of the most fortuitous moments in Warren's checkered military career. The Third and Fifth Corps had exited Bristoe Station, and now the lead division of the Second Corps (under Brig. Gen. Alexander Webb) approached Bristoe Station from the southwest. Most importantly, Webb's route (parallel to the railroad tracks) led to a ridge south of the tracks. From the ridge Webb could see the last of Sykes's Fifth Corps marching off to the northeast (Sykes mistakenly thought Warren's troops were closer) and Confederate infantry moving toward the railroad. He immediately ordered his men to occupy the railroad embankment, which provided excellent cover. Soon after issuing these orders, Webb was joined by Warren, who ordered him not to attempt to link up with the Fifth Corps but to set up a stronger defensive line along the embanked railroad tracks. Artillery batteries were brought up to support Webb, and heavy firing between the two sides began. The Battle of Bristoe Station had commenced.[41]

The arrival of more Union troops did not deter the oncoming Confederate brigades. They marched steadily toward the railroad track, unaware that the last section of land they had to traverse was completely open, offering superb lines of fire for the Union soldiers. As Warren described the moment: "A more inspiring scene

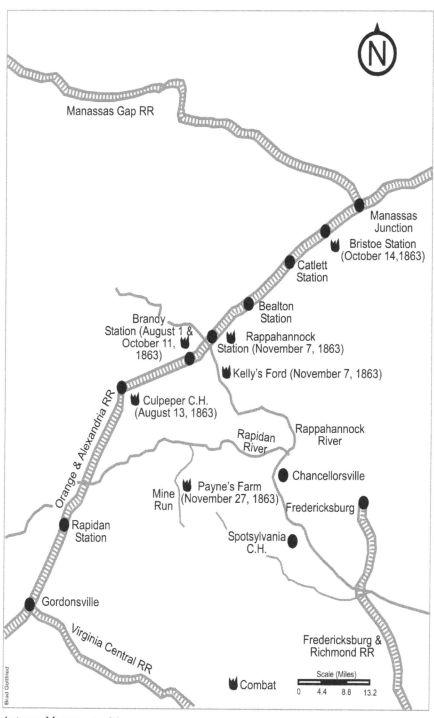

Manassas Gap RR

N

Manassas
Junction

Bristoe Station
(October 14, 1863)

Catlett
Station

Bealton
Station

Brandy
Station (August 1 &
October 11,
1863)

Rappahannock
Station (November 7, 1863)

Kelly's Ford (November 7, 1863)

Culpeper C.H.
(August 13, 1863)

Orange & Alexandria RR

Rapidan
River

Rappahannock
River

Chancellorsville

Payne's Farm
(November 27, 1863)

Mine
Run

Fredericksburg

Rapidan
Station

Spotsylvania
C.H.

Gordonsville

Virginia Central RR

Fredericksburg &
Richmond RR

Scale (Miles)
0   4.4   8.8   13.2

Combat

Brad Gottfried

Autumn Maneuvers, 1863

could not be imagined. The enemy's line of battle boldly moving forward, one part of our own steadily awaiting it and another moving against it at double-quick, while the artillery was taking up position at a gallop and going into action." Soon they charged the Union lines, in some places three deep, and met with a withering barrage of rifle fire. By 3:30 the ninety-minute battle was over, and the surviving troops of the two Confederate brigades attempted to retreat under withering fire. Warren reported capturing "450 prisoners, 2 stands of colors, and 5 field pieces." Hill's rash attack gained no tactical advantage or ground, but it brought him over 1,300 casualties (Warren reported 546 casualties for the Bristoe Station and Auburn battles).[42] Two Confederate brigades had been shattered for naught.

The Confederates were not finished, however. When General Lee and the lead division of Ewell's corps arrived around 4 P.M., Lee ordered Ewell's men to extend Hill's line to the east in an effort to turn the Union left. Confederate troops seized the bridge over Kettle Run (southwest of Bristoe Station), but darkness stopped them from advancing farther. It rained for a while, then became overcast and moonless. In that Stygian darkness, Warren's men quietly marched east toward the safety of Manassas Junction.[43]

The next morning, Confederate skirmishers probing Union lines found the exact opposite of Williamsport: this time it was Union troops that had slipped away in the night. While officers and men scoured the field for friends and left-behind supplies, Lee received word that Meade's army had made it to Centreville, where it was digging in. Realizing he had lost the "foot race" with Meade and would have no more opportunities to cut off a corps or two from the main army, Lee decided he could neither turn nor overwhelm Meade in his new location. Bereft of a real connection to the south (Meade had burned the Orange and Alexandria bridge over the Rappahannock River on October 12), short on rations and forage, and temporarily camped in a stripped-over countryside, Lee thought he should destroy the twenty miles of the Orange and Alexandria Railroad between Manassas and Rappahannock. Meanwhile, he would send out Stuart to do a reconnaissance of Meade's lines.[44]

Stuart found Meade's army dug in from Frying Pan Church in the north to Union Mills in the south. As the rain poured down, Stuart surveyed most of the line; the rain began falling on October 15 and did not let up until October 18. While Stuart's men rode the line, Lee's infantry did not let the torrential rain divert it from its primary task; they methodically tore apart the railroad and burned the ties and rails.[45]

Meade did not get immediate credit for the victory at Bristoe Station. Instead, he found himself under criticism for three decisions: retreating from his earlier position, overestimating Lee's reinforced strength, and hoping that Lee would attack him on grounds favorable to Meade. Halleck told him bluntly that he should give Lee battle: "Is he not trying to bully you, while the mass of the rebel armies are concentrating against Rosecrans? I cannot see it in any other light. Instead of retreating, I think you ought to give him battle." Even Lincoln urged him to fight Lee, writing Halleck on October 16, "I do not believe Lee can have over 60,000 effective men. . . . If General Meade can now attack him on a field no more than equal for us, and will do so with all the skill and courage which he, his officers, and men possess, the honor will be his if he succeeds, and the blame may be mine if he fails."[46]

Meade did not budge. If Lincoln had indeed used such an approach to goad Meade at Williamsport, it had not worked then, and did not work now. Meade wrote back to Halleck, "It has been my intention to attack the enemy, if I can find him on a field no more than equal for us, and that I have only delayed doing so from the difficulty of ascertaining his exact position, and the fear that in endeavoring to do so my communications might be jeopardized."[47]

The pressure to act mounted quickly, however, and on October 18 Meade gave orders to prepare to advance. The tipping point was not the letter from Lincoln but news that Brig. Gen. John Imboden had attacked Charles Town, West Virginia. Afraid that Lee might be preparing to send more troops to Tennessee, Meade wanted to arrest that potential movement by probing Lee's defenses. He sent cavalry to find the Confederates, while ordering the infantry to be ready to follow.[48]

On October 19, the Union cavalry under Brig. Gen. Judson Kilpatrick found and fought Confederate cavalry near Buckland, and the men under Kilpatrick barely made it out of a growing Confederate trap (Confederates called the retreat "the Buckland Races"). The next day, Stuart was ordered to evacuate Warrenton. Union troops entered the town later in the day, thus ending the Bristoe Station campaign.[49]

For the next four days, Meade strengthened his defenses in anticipation of an attack that never came. His failure to go on the offensive irked Lincoln and Halleck, and on October 18, a flurry of messages between Halleck and Meade started the same old round of rebuke, defensiveness, and apology. As usual, Halleck kicked off the cycle. He wrote Meade on October 18: "Lee is unquestionably bullying you. If you cannot ascertain his movement, I certainly cannot. If you pursue and fight him, I think you will find out where he is. I know of no other way." Incensed, Meade wrote back quickly, complaining of opinions disguised as "truisms," lack of orders, and offering once again to resign. Now Halleck felt the need to apologize, or at least smooth things over, so the next day he wrote Meade that he felt "regret" for his words. But punctilious as ever on matters of responsibility, he wanted Meade to know that the demands for fighting ultimately came from Lincoln. He wrote, "I have repeated the suggestion made to me of the necessity of giving battle." Still, Meade understood the wishes of Lincoln and Halleck, so he analyzed the possibility of attack, especially in light of the thorough destruction of the Orange and Alexandria Railroad from Bristoe Station to Culpeper Court House by Lee's retreating army. Fearful of repeating Burnside's ill-fated "Mud March," Meade suggested to

Halleck that campaigning be suspended for the winter: "It would be better to withdraw the army to some position in front of Washington."[50]

Alarm bells went off in Washington. Lincoln asked Meade to come to Washington to discuss his plans, and he went immediately on October 22. Meade wrote his wife that the "President was, as he always is, very considerate and kind. He found no fault with my operations, although it was very evident he was disappointed that I had not got a battle out of Lee. He coincided with me that there was not much to be gained by any farther advance; but General Halleck was very urgent that something be done, but what that something was he did not define." No decision was made, as Lincoln and Halleck were awaiting the return of Secretary of War Stanton from Tennessee. After Stanton's return, Halleck sent a direct order to Meade on October 24 that read, "The President desires that you will prepare to attack Lee's army." Meade, the ever-faithful soldier, began preparations to carry it out.[51]

It was in this context of indecision and critical review that Meade wrote a tough critique of his performance to his wife. On October 21, he wrote that Lee had "retired across the Rappahannock." He added some analysis: "His object is to prevent my advance, and in the meantime send more troops to Bragg. This was a deep game, and I am free to admit that in the playing of it he has got the advantage of it." The authors of the most recent study of the Mine Run campaign, Martin F. Graham and George F. Skoch, quote that sentence of Meade's to argue that Meade knew he was no match for Lee.[52] This judgment is unfair to Meade because it fails to contextualize his self-appraisal. If one looks at the sentence that preceded the "deep game" comment and reviews the story of the Bristoe Campaign, the appraisal becomes case specific. Meade never could know or even guess Lee's next move throughout October 1863, and he always closely evaluated intelligence about alleged troop movement to try to decipher whether Lee was growing or shrinking his army. By frequent and surprise troop movements, Lee had been able to keep a larger army at bay while the Confederates fought in Tennessee. Also, unlike Meade, Lee enjoyed the support of his president and the freedom to leave Richmond somewhat undefended. Meade knew he had to protect Washington at all times, and to do that, he needed to have a direct, high-functioning communications and supply line to Washington. That knowledge constricted his movements, and when he sought to break out of this strategic box, he was slapped down. So his "deep game" comment gave Lee credit for keeping him off balance in the fall, but it pertained only to that one campaign.

With Lincoln's order on his mind, Meade created a plan to march on Lee's army. He proposed to march his entire army on Lee's right flank (toward Fredericksburg). He explained his reasoning in a long letter carried directly by an aide to Halleck on November 2: "The success of this movement will depend on its celerity, and its being kept from the enemy. From my latest information, he had no force below the junction of the two rivers." Meade had considered a flanking on Lee's left but discarded that possibility because he would have had to "abandon" his own communications lines and travel over terrain "broken and rough, deficient in roads." Meade believed that fighting Lee's army along the Orange and Alexandria Railroad favored the defender, while moving first to Fredericksburg, then south, would allow his army to use the Richmond, Fredericksburg, and Potomac Railroad, and later the Tidewater rivers, to keep his army supplied (a foreshadowing of what Grant would do the next spring).[53]

Lincoln and Halleck saw the plan differently, highlighting the confines under which Meade operated. Halleck replied to Meade's plan, using Lincoln's views as his authority: "He [Lincoln] does not see that the proposed change of base is likely to produce any favorable result, while its disadvantages are manifest. I have fully conferred in the views he has heretofore communicated on the subject. Any tactical movement to turn a flank or threaten a communication is left to your own judgment; but an entire change of base under existing circumstance, I can neither advise nor approve." Ironically, the very phrase of McClellan's, "change of base," that had so haunted him after Seven Days was now used against Meade's proposal. Meade dutifully abandoned his plan and returned to watching Lee and sending his cavalry to check any movements by the Confederate cavalry.[54]

Once again, Meade complained of his treatment in a letter to his wife: "Now I have clearly indicated what I thought feasible and practicable and my plan is disapproved. I think under these circumstances justice to me and the true interests of the country justify their selecting someone else to command."[55] Though a bit self-indulgent, Meade did have a point: his superiors wanted a plan of action, and when he offered one, they rejected it. To be fair, they may have felt that the plan offered nothing more than movement and, without a battle, was meaningless. Also, they had lost faith in Meade to achieve a quick surprise attack. Regardless, it placed Meade in an unwinnable position, so it is not surprising that he continually asked for his one way out: replacement.

Despite this rejection, Meade made a new plan. He would split his army into two wings and march across the Rappahannock. Sedgwick would lead the "right column," composed of the Fifth and Sixth Corps, to attack the Confederate bridgehead at Rappahannock Station. French would lead the "left column," consisting of the Third, Second, and First Corps, across the river at the lightly defended Kelly's Ford. French would cross the river, then march up behind the Confederate lines to assist Sedgwick's crossing of the river. Once reunited, the two wings were to march to Brandy Station. If Sedgwick could not cross the bridge at Rappahannock Station, he was to march instead to Kelly's Ford, cross the river, then link up with French for the march to Brandy Station. The soldiers were ordered to begin marching at daylight on November 7.[56]

By early afternoon, the van of French's Third Corps had reached the northern bank of the Rappahannock River. Using a combination of artillery fire and sharpshooters' accuracy, Union troops quickly pushed aside the two Confederate regiments guarding Kelly's Ford. By 3 P.M. French had an entire division across the river, with a loss of only 42 men (compared to 359 for the Confederates).[57]

Meanwhile, Sedgwick had marched to the crossing at Rappahannock Station and found an entirely different situation. Lee had constructed two redoubts on the north bank of the river, with a pontoon bridge connecting the men on that bank with reinforcements on the south bank. Though formidable, Sedgwick saw a chance, if his infantry grabbed enough ground near the redoubts, to move up their artillery. They did this quickly, and the artillery began firing upon the redoubts. The shelling went on for three hours, but the Confederates neither surrendered nor fled. Infantry would have to dislodge them.[58]

Though no general appeared eager to attack, Sedgwick ordered it done. Two brigades were chosen. After another round of artillery fire, the Union soldiers plunged across a ditch, then ran straight toward the redoubts in the gathering darkness. Struck by volleys of rifle fire, the men surged on, and as regiment after regiment charged through the smoke and darkness, eventually the Confederate regiments gave way. Through hand-to-hand fighting, the Union soldiers gained control of the redoubts and the rifle pits, forcing the remaining troops to flee across the bridge to safety. In less than an hour, Union forces had caused nearly seventeen hundred casualties, at a loss of a little over four hundred.[59]

All this had happened unbeknownst to Lee and Major General Early. Lee, in fact, had retired to his headquarters to plan his attack the next day. Early got the bad news of the attack from some of his staff. He quickly brought up artillery to guard the southern bank, gathered the refugees together, and burned the south end of the bridge.[60]

Meade had been equally in the dark. At 4 P.M. he sent a message to Sedgwick asking him his situation and, if unfavorable, to prepare to be sent to Kelly's Ford (to cross there). He had not heard from Sedgwick by 6:30 P.M., so he sent another message, asking what had happened and how many men he would need to "prevent the enemy from crossing to this side." By 8 P.M., though, Sedgwick had sent three messages, describing his capture of two redoubts and plenty of Confederate soldiers. The news thrilled Meade. He told Humphreys to write to Sedgwick, "The major general commanding is highly gratified as to the brilliant manner in which your operations have been commenced."[61]

It was a demoralizing day for the Confederates. In two brief battles they had lost over two thousand men, many of them veterans, compared to fewer than five hundred casualties for the Union. Furthermore, some men from French's Third Corps were safely across the Rappahannock River at Kelly's Ford. Meade's offensive, late as it was, had gotten off to a rousing start.[62]

The next few days brought something to Meade and the Army of the Potomac not seen since the victory at Gettysburg: unadulterated praise. From newspapers to Congress, the accolades flowed in. The *Washington Evening Star* noted Meade's "masterly movements," while the *New York Herald* claimed that the Confederates were "forced to retreat precipitately." In a letter full of rare good news and some uncharacteristic bragging, Meade wrote his wife, "The operation being successful, the army is in fine spirits, and of course I am more popular than ever, having been greeted yesterday as I rode through the ranks with great cheering." Most heartening of all might have been the message received from President Lincoln, "I wish to say, 'Well done.'" Meade even allowed himself to get carried away in his private analysis, writing his wife that he hoped his victory would "convince the intelligent public that my retreat to Centreville was not to avoid battles, and that Lee, who was not outflanked, or had his communications threatened, but was attacked in front, and yet withdrew, is really the one who has avoided battle." Eight battle flags and nineteen hundred men captured all made for good press, but the best appraisal of all may have come from his friend and aide, Theodore Lyman. He wrote, "I think it no small praise to General Meade to say that his plans were so well laid out that our loss in all is but about 400. No useless slaughter, you see."[63]

But the euphoria was short lived. Minimal marching occurred on the "smoky and hazy" morning of November 8, and when the fog lifted, Union troops discovered that the Confederates had evacuated their positions south of the river. Meade immediately ordered a pursuit, but the Confederates had the jump on them, safely withdrawing to Brandy Station. Disappointment grew to dissatisfaction when the Confederates continued their withdrawal on the bitter cold night of November 8, eventually returning to their camps along the Rapidan River.[64] Once again the fast-moving Confederates had slipped out of the ponderous Union grasp, and Meade could expect another torrent of criticism.

This time the criticism dripped in steadily, epitomized by the cold decision of Stanton not to receive the honor guard holding the captured battle flags of Rappahannock Station (led by the hero of the battle, Brig. Gen. David Russell). Meade knew he must do something, so he asked Halleck if he could come to Washington to meet with him and Stanton. Though no one recorded what was said at the meeting, the inference is that Meade was told to pursue Lee as soon as possible. Though Meade did not discuss the meeting with his subordinates, he ordered stepped-up cavalry patrols. When Meade wrote to Halleck on November 20, he made it clear that once the recently rebuilt railroad to Brandy Station was fully functioning and his men resupplied, Meade would be ready to move. Of course, the Confederates had not been idle during this time; they improved their winter camps and erected stronger breastworks along the eighteen-mile-long line they built on the north side of the Rapidan River, stretching from Liberty Mills in the north to Morton's Ford in the south.[65]

In late November, Meade decided to conduct the fourth and final operation against Lee since Gettysburg. He would split his army into three columns. Each column would cross the Rapidan River at different fords—Germanna, Jacob's, and Culpeper Mine—that were south of Hill's strong defenses at Mine Run (the end of Lee's eighteen-mile-long line). The troops would hit Lee's right flank by surprise, then roll down the unobstructed Orange Plank Road and Orange Turnpike, either splitting Lee's army or trapping it completely against the Rapidan River. One reason for Meade's sudden aggressiveness may have been strong evidence that his original estimate of Lee's strength, eighty thousand, had been woefully exaggerated. Based on the reports from his cavalry officers, he revised his estimates downward to fifty-five thousand, which was actually quite accurate for once. With an aggregate strength of over eighty thousand men equipped and present for duty, that gave Meade quite an advantage. Overall, Meade's plan was bold for him, though modeled somewhat after Hooker's plan of the previous May. Meade could only hope he would have better success than Hooker.[66]

The plan depended on two vital elements often lacking in the Army of the Potomac's execution of orders: surprise and speed. To achieve surprise, Meade did not tell his corps commanders his plans until the evening of November 23, showing more confidence in himself as commander than he had exhibited since Gettysburg. This time Meade did not ask for their input; he simply told them where they would march and to bring only essential wagons.[67]

Just as orders were being sent to all the men and the generals attended nervously to the myriad details surrounding a big march, the weather intervened—again. A strong nor'easter blew in just after midnight on November 24, quickly swelling rivers and streams, and turning roads into mud pits. Meade felt that he had no choice but to postpone the march for two days. All he could do was hope for the rain to end, and for Lee's intelligence to fail.[68]

He got only one of these wishes. The rain did end, allowing him to put the Army of the Potomac into motion on November 26. But Lee's scouts reported that rations had been issued and a movement prepared, so Lee put his troops on alert. Though he could not be sure exactly *when* Meade would send his troops, he had predicted two weeks earlier that any crossing would take place by the "lower fords, Germanna and Ely's, as if with the intention of striking for the Richmond and Fredericksburg Railroad." To raise the stakes even higher, Meade received a telegram from Washington informing him of Grant's great victory at Chattanooga. Dutifully, Meade ordered that it be read to the troops before they began their march on the morning of November 26.[69]

When the Army of the Potomac finally moved out, the progress of its three columns fell into now familiar patterns. French's Third Corps got stalled by high water, slow marching on muddy roads, and an engineering oversight: they were one pontoon short of crossing the river, now swollen due to recent rains. So engineers had to build a trestle to complete the bridge. It was not until 4 P.M. that French had his first division across the Rapidan at Jacob's Ford. Meanwhile, Warren's Second

Corps and Sykes's Fifth Corps got to their fords well before noon, where they had to wait for hours until French got his corps across the river and into position to protect the westward advance of the other wings of the army. It was not until late afternoon that the first three corps crossed the Rapidan, leaving the First and Sixth Corps on the northern bank. Meade halted all his men for the night, frustrated by the unforeseen delays.[70]

Meade put his army into motion early the next morning, insisting that they march through a heavy fog. Warren's Second Corps marched to the Orange Turnpike, then headed west for its destination, Robertson's Tavern. Lee, of course, had not been idle. Unsure of Meade's intentions, he prepared for two possibilities: an "advance toward Richmond or move up the Rapidan upon his right flank." He sent Early's Second Corps east on the Orange turnpike, where its skirmishers began exchanging fire with Warren's skirmishers near Robertson's Tavern. Each commanding general then decided to postpone a major attack until more troops could be brought up.[71]

As the Second Corps of each side marched toward Robertson's Tavern, cavalry collided on the Orange Plank road, three miles south of Robertson's Tavern, near New Hope Church. Here the cavalry commanders waited for infantry to arrive: Hill's Third Corps for the Confederates and Sykes's Fifth Corps for the Union. The Fifth Corps stopped near New Hope Church around 4 P.M., and Meade told Sykes to wait until he knew that the Third Corps had connected with the flank of Warren's Second Corps.

Once again, Meade's detailed instructions had not been followed. He had ordered his corps commanders to gather at Robertson's Tavern, then march six miles west on Orange Turnpike to Old Verdiersville (hoping to either split Lee's army or induce Lee to attack him). Now, as daylight ebbed on November 27, he found his army stalled far short of his goals. Warren waited for help from French at Robertson's Tavern, while Sykes was held up at New Hope Church. Most problematic of all, again, was the dilatory marching of French. Led by the Second Division (under the command of the slow and indecisive Brig. Gen. Henry Prince), French's corps had not only failed to connect with Warren's right flank by midday but also advanced only two miles to the "Widow Morris's" farm by noon, almost two miles short of Warren's right flank. An angry Meade sent multiple messages to French in the morning, climaxing with the one he sent at 11:30 A.M.: "What are you waiting for? . . . The commanding general directs that you move forward as rapidly as possible to Robertson's Tavern, where your corps is wanted."[72]

Unfortunately for Prince and French, the Confederate general rushing troops to face the Third Corps was neither timid nor cautious. Showing the dash and initiative that many senior officers of the Army of Northern Virginia were known for, Maj. Gen. Edward Johnson (nicknamed "Clubby") surveyed the enemy troops in front of him, stretched his division of fifty-three hundred men along a short line, then ordered an attack on Brig. Gen. Joseph B. Carr's Third Division on French's left flank. In gathering darkness the men fought on, with French throwing two more divisions into the battle at Payne's Farm. Utter darkness finally halted the fighting, with no ground lost by the Union. Still, Johnson had only 545 casualties to French's 952, defying the normal math of higher casualties when on the offensive. More importantly, Johnson's fierce attack had stopped the two corps from linking up, thus preventing Meade from orchestrating any combined, coordinated attack on November 27. The praise heaped upon French for his quick attack at Kelly's Ford was now forgotten in his poor performance at Payne's Farm. He would soon pay a price for his dilatory movements—but so would Meade.[73]

That evening, a disappointed and frustrated Meade made fresh plans for attack on the next morning. The First, Second, and Sixth Corps would attack along a broad front, with the Third and Fifth Corps held in reserve. It was a sensible plan, but Lee anticipated and prepared for such an attack, as he had at Falling Waters. He had his entire army retreat to higher ground west of Mine Run and build breast-works all through the early hours of November 28. When Meade's skirmishers set out at dawn to probe the Confederate position, they found the original line de-serted. Once again Lee had refused to wait idly for an attack, and all Meade could do was to send his army off in pursuit. In a driving rain the men set out, the Second Corps leading the way.[74]

They stopped short of the breastworks now crowning the west bank of Mine Run, waiting for orders to attack that never came. At one point in the morning, Meade left his staff and "rode alone to reconnoiter." What he saw worried him deeply: an extraordinarily strong defensive position, with "infantry parapets, aba-tis, and epaulements for batteries" arranged on the slope of the western bank. The run itself was swampy, with almost one thousand cleared yards on a gradual rise to assault. A modern student of field fortifications in the East, Earl Hess, found the Mine Run line to be "the strongest fieldwork built to date by the Army of Northern Virginia." Meade studied that line all day, searching vainly for a weak spot. He also waited for his soldiers to march into position, itself a difficult task on "narrow wood-roads, deep with mud," as Lee reinforced his defensive works.[75]

That evening, Warren came to Meade with a new plan: he would lead the Sec-ond Corps and elements of the Union left on a march to hit the Confederates' right flank (to the south). It would involve a long march of eleven miles over muddy roads, but it was the only feasible plan the generals could see. Meade accepted the proposal and gave Warren an additional division (from the Sixth Corps), three artillery batteries, and three hundred cavalrymen, bringing his total to eighteen thousand men.[76]

Warren set his soldiers into motion before dawn on November 29. They marched unimpeded for almost the entire distance, with the exception of the cav-alry, which fought a brief skirmish with Stuart's cavalry at Parker's Store on the

Orange Plank Road. Later that day, a captured prisoner informed the Confederates of Warren's march, and Stuart sent Lee the news. The Second Corps continued its steady march westward, brushing aside vedettes encountered at New Hope Church. At last they crossed Mine Run and did not see any infantry or breastworks in front of them. Warren's plan had worked! Or had it? The march consumed all the daylight hours, and now the Second Corps had to camp for the night. Though disappointed he had not gotten farther, a fairly contented Warren rode back to Meade to tell him of his progress. He found that Meade's staff was preparing an assault for the following day, though French did not feel his Third Corps could reasonably attack the center of Lee's defenses. Based on Warren's positive report, Meade adjusted his battle plan for the next morning: artillery fire would begin on Lee's center and left at 8 A.M., accompanied by an attack of the Second Corps on Lee's right. At 9 A.M. the Fifth and Sixth Corps would attack Lee's left. Meade later wrote, "When these attacks proved successful, the three divisions of the Third and First Corps left to hold the center would assault, in conjunction with the others." Here, at last, was the double envelopment with a center coup de grace that Meade had been seeking.[77]

Warned by Stuart and confirmed by their own observations, Lee and Hill knew of Warren's advance and what they must do. All through the bitter cold night of November 29–30, the men of Hill's corps dug entrenchments, using axes, shovels, and planks to dig and move dirt. Just six hundred yards away, the anxious men of the Second Corps could hear the scraping of dirt and the crack of axes, and they knew that the Confederates were erecting breastworks. To stay on full alert, the men were forbidden to light fires or set up tents, so they lay on the cold, wet ground, shivering in the below-freezing temperatures. At 3 A.M. the order came to fall in and prepare for an attack at 8 A.M. They were not to fire until ordered. When light finally dawned, the front row of troops could see the result of a night's work: "strong and high works of timber and each with abatis in front of use and stretching far to the right," recalled Chaplain H. S. Stevens of the Fourteenth Connecticut Infantry. Veterans were reminded of the defenses at Fredericksburg, and they attached paper nameplates to their coats or shirts.[78]

Warren had been busy through the night as well, putting his now twenty-eight thousand men (Meade had given him two more divisions from the Third Corps) into two lines along a one-mile front. At dawn he rode out to look at what his men faced, and it nearly took his breath away; Warren later reported, "The line had been reinforced with all the troops and artillery that could be put into position; the breastworks, epaulements, and abatis perfected, and that a run for eight minutes was the least time our line could have to close the space between us, during which we would be exposed to every species of fire." Seeing the depth and extent of the Confederate defenses, and being too far to ride to Meade immediately with a report, Warren faced the most important decision of his short stint as a corps commander: to attack, or wait. As one of his staffers, Capt. Thomas Livermore wrote shortly after the war, "When to do nothing was almost as bad as a defeat; with such orders that the responsibility of defeat would have rested wholly or in great measure on General Meade; with a command full of courage, and believing that he would be the greatest man in in the army if he succeeded . . . [Warren then] thought of the wounded who were frozen at Fredericksburg." That final thought, combined with the strength of the Confederate defenses, helped Warren to make his decision: he would call off the attack.[79]

At 8 A.M. the Union guns opened as planned. Meade and his staff waited to hear the sound of rifle fire on their left, but it never came. At last, an aide to Warren, Capt. Washington Roebling, rode up with the bad news: Warren had suspended the attack. Shocked, Meade handed the note to Humphreys and said, "Read that." Then he turned to Roebling and exclaimed, "My God! General Warren has half my army!" He looked to Roebling for more information, but Roebling only "shrugged his shoulders." He must have felt that Warren's terse note offered sufficient explanation: "His [the enemy's] position and strength seem so formidable in my present front that I advise against making the attack here. The full light of the sun show me that I cannot succeed." Meade immediately ordered all firing to cease, then he began a long conversation with Humphreys and Sedgwick about the next steps. He suspended Sedgwick's attack, and at 9:45 A.M. saddled up and rode off to find Warren. Captain Livermore recalled passing by Meade on his way to Warren, and found him "looking as savage as anyone could." But Lyman, who knew Meade's moods as well as anyone, felt that Meade was remarkably restrained, writing, "General Meade and General Humphreys . . . really took it admirably, for both of them have excellent tempers of their own, which, on occasions, burst forth, like twelve-pounder spherical case." When Meade met up with Warren, they had a long talk, and neither one ever recorded the substance of the conversation. The outcome was that Warren clung to his decision, and Meade did not reexamine his front, nor countermand the order. Col. Francis A. Walker would later write, "Since General Warren had taken it upon himself to say that the position could not be carried, and had assumed the responsibility of arresting the attack, it was proper that General Warren, and not himself, should carry that responsibility." So Meade held to his suspension order.[80]

That night, Meade held one of his "councils of war." He asked his corps commanders to determine "the practicability of carrying the enemy's intrenchments, so far as they are known to you, within the limited of the front of your command." Only French felt it was possible, but with his small force and reduced credibility, his opinion would not carry much weight with Meade. Meade considered moving the entire army around Lee's right flank but rejected that idea because it would leave Washington unguarded. Another choice was to occupy Fredericksburg, but that proposal had been consistently vetoed by Halleck and Lincoln. So that left Meade with one disappointing option: abandon his new line and return to the camps north of the Rapidan. He stoutly defended his decision in his after-battle report, writing, "After mature deliberation, I decided to withdraw the army." He knew this decision would be widely condemned in Washington, so he countered with what he felt was his strongest argument: "Considering how sacred is the trust of the lives of the brave men under my command, but willing as I am to shed their blood and my own when duty requires, and my judgment dictates that the sacrifice will not be in vain, I cannot be a party to a wanton slaughter of my troops for any mere personal end." He ordered the withdrawal to begin on December 1. That he made the withdrawal quickly and quietly is little noted, though it did surprise Lee's advancing troops on December 2.[81]

The Mine Run campaign had ended, and though Meade had two small victories to claim, the overall position of the armies had not fundamentally changed. Combining the casualties of Rappahannock Station, Kelly's Ford, and Mine Run, Meade had fewer losses than Lee, 2,094 to 2,826. Furthermore, most of Lee's losses had come from two veteran brigades hammered at Rappahannock Station, where 1,631 men were captured or missing. But these small advantages meant little to Meade's superiors, critics, and many men in the Army of the Potomac (a "general feeling of disappointment and despondency had, on Monday night, taken possession of the whole Army," according to Provost General Patrick). With superior numbers, adequate supplies, and efficient lines of supply and communication, Meade had been unable to force Lee's army into a major battle, let alone trap or capture all or a big chunk of that army. Once again Meade had been thwarted by weather and crippled by the poor performance of some of his corps commanders, especially William French. Meade himself would not gamely shoulder all the blame this time. In his report, he cited two primary causes for his "failure" that were "beyond my control." One was French's laggard advance, the other the "unfortunate error of judgment of Major-General Warren." Such criticisms, although valid, did not reflect well on Meade's leadership. In fact, it showed his worst side: rigidity, anger, defensiveness, and petulance. In time, Warren's decision would be partially vindicated; recently, the historian Earl Hess studied the hastily built Confederate line at Mine Run and declared it to be "one of the strongest defensive positions of the war."[82] Those views would not be the leading ones in the winter of 1863–64, however, and Meade would have to face the fall-out from the aborted attack at Mine Run.

Overall, where Grant had ended his fall campaign with a stunning success in Chattanooga, Meade had no similar victory to show. Still, his decision to support Warren had shown his soldiers a "moral courage they had not often seen in their top leaders," according to historian John J. Hennessy. Indeed, Hennessy regards the decision as "probably the most important nonevent in the army's history," which would make it second in importance to Meade's victory at Gettysburg in his short tenure of command thus far.[83] That interpretation of Mine Run was not shared by all, however, and as December began, Meade would find himself in almost the same situation he was in back in August: scrutinized, criticized, micromanaged, and insecure in his appointment.

George G. Meade standing in front of a tent (Library of Congress)

Meade's headquarters at Gettysburg (Library of Congress)

Winfield Scott Hancock (Library of Congress).

Daniel Sickles (Library of Congress)

Oliver O. Howard (Library of Congress)

Henry Slocum (Library of Congress).

Henry Halleck (Library of Congress)

John Sedgwick (Library of Congress).

Gouverneur Warren (Library of Congress)

Daniel Butterfield (Library of Congress).

Generals of the Army of the Potomac, September 1863 (Library of Congress)

Meade and his staff, 1863 (Library of Congress)

Above: Marsena Patrick (seated) and his staff, 1863 (Library of Congress)

Left: Ulysses S. Grant (Library of Congress)

Above: Philip Sheridan
(Library of Congress)

Right: Ambrose Burnside
(Library of Congress)

Winfield Scott Hancock (seated) with his division commanders, Francis Channing Barlow, David Birney, and John Gibbon, May 1864 (Library of Congress)

Council of War, May 1864 (Library of Congress)

George G. Meade sitting for a formal photo (Library of Congress)

Meade's horse, Old Baldy (Library of Congress)

FIVE

Winter's Worries

Meade Fights for His Job, December 1863–April 1864

From the moment he made the decision to postpone the attack on November 30, Meade knew he put his job in even greater jeopardy than before. Keeping his job, and defending his decisions on that day and others before it, would consume much of his attention throughout the winter. At the same time, he had a large army to manage, a family back home he missed, and his own health issues to contend with. For one month he remained in limbo about his future, only to find that once he had survived this latest scare, his critics soon mounted their fiercest, most sustained attack on him yet, waged in the newspapers, halls of Congress, and drawing rooms of Washington. He survived this attack as well, but his core concern—his reputation—would take a beating from which it has yet to recover.

As Meade quietly withdrew his large army from Mine Run, he also shuffled some of his corps to different spots. He waited to see Lee's response, and on the evening of December 3 told his corps commanders to be "in readiness for immediate movement," as it appeared that Lee's army was moving in force at "Raccoon Ford and Morton's Ford." But Lee's troops were quickly driven back across the Rapidan River, and Meade then ordered corps commanders to put their men to the task of improving the roads "leading from their corps to the depots at Brandy Station and those connecting with the adjoining corps." Meade would not let his men remain idle while he waited for Lee's next move and further orders from Washington. He even asked for permission to come to Washington on December 4, and Halleck curtly replied, "You have my permission to visit Washington whenever you deem proper, reporting to the Adjutant-General at the War Department."[1]

Interpreting this pro forma reply to mean he had no need to visit Washington unless called, Meade spent part of his time the next few days preparing his formal report of the Mine Run campaign and fretting over his future. He first laid out the essence of his report in a long letter written to his wife on December 2. He explained his plan to have his army attack in three columns and how, "owing to the failure of others to whom its execution was necessarily intrusted, it failed." He then detailed how the slowness of "one corps" interrupted the timetable for the rest of the operation, and how "one corps commander" had been given twenty-eight thousand men to use in an attack but found the enemy's breastworks so formidable that he called off the attack. Meade had no choice but to call off the other attacks that were dependent on the first attack, thus giving Lee a day to beef up his defenses even more. When Meade surveyed the field and his options the following day, he came "to the conclusion that an attack could not be successful, [and so] determined to, and did, withdraw the army."

Meade was not naïve about the ramifications of his decision. Beginning a letter to his wife with a prediction, he wrote, "I expect your wish will now soon be gratified, and that I shall be relieved from the Army of the Potomac." He blamed this forthcoming decision on "political considerations . . . and the failure of the Army of the Potomac to do anything, at this moment, will be considered of vital consequence, and if I can be held responsible for this failure, I will be removed to prove that I am." Using his own brand of sarcastic wit to characterize his impending removal, Meade wrote, "It will be proved as clear as the light of day, that an attack was perfectly practicable, and that everyone, except myself, in the army, particularly the soldiers, was dying for it, and that I had some mysterious object in view, either in connection with politics, or stock-jobbing, or something else about as foreign to my thoughts, and finally the Administration will be obliged to yield to popular clamor and discard me." Still defensive of his decisions and his reputation, he continued: "My conscience is clear. I did the best I could. If I had thought there was any reasonable degree of probability of success, I would have attacked. I did not think so; on the contrary, believed it would result in useless and criminal slaughter of brave men, and might result in serious disaster to the army." To give him a little cover once the deluge of criticisms began, he asked Margaret to show the letter "confidentially" to "Courtland Parker, W. Harding, and other friends, whose good opinion I am anxious to preserve."[2]

Meade's anxiety continued for the next week, intensified by the lack of communication from his superiors in Washington. Rightly or wrongly, Meade perceived that the army was behind his decision: "My course has met the full approbation of the army and increased the confidence they had before in me." Four days later, he was still "on the anxious bench" though feeling better because he had sent his official report to Washington and received supportive letters from his old friend Courtland Parker and Brig. Gen. John Gibbon. His aide, Theodore Lyman, sensed the change in Meade, writing in his diary, "The General has been rather sad, of late, but is cheering up now [that the report had been sent]." Meade even showed flashes of his biting humor in a letter to his wife: "[The] *Herald,* inspired by my *friend,* Dan Sickles, is constantly harping on the assertion that Gettysburg was fought by the corps commanders (i.e. D. S.) and the common soldiers, and that no generalship was displayed. I suppose after a while it will be discovered, I was not at Gettysburg at all." But the fundamental issue, his loss of his reputation, remained the outstanding fear. He wrote Margaret, "I am only concerned with my reputation as a soldier—if I can preserve that they are at liberty to deprive me of command."[3]

In his report to Halleck, Meade criticized his subordinates more than he had ever done before in a formal report. Perhaps still simmering from the collapse of his plans in late November, or profoundly worried about retaining his position, Meade unequivocally laid the blame for the failure of the operation on the shoulders of William French. In ten finely detailed paragraphs, which even Meade called "minute," he proceeded to describe every order and French's responses. He reasoned that "the unnecessary delay in the progress of this corps, and the failure to attack the enemy as soon as he was encountered, deploying to the left, and allowing the Sixth Corps to pass and continue to line to Warren, was the cause that a junction of the center and right columns was not made early on the morning of the 27th, and was one of the primary causes of the failure of the whole movement." The problems with French continued, and new problems with Warren developed (both promoted to their commands by Meade). On November 29, Warren had marched his corps to Lee's right flank, and by evening he reported to Meade, in person, that he could "carry everything before him as to induce him to give the opinion that he did not believe the enemy would remain overnight, so completely did he command him." Furthermore, French had told Meade he did not think his Third Corps could assault the enemy's center with any good results, which convinced Meade to change his plan "so far as to abandon the center attack, and reenforce Warren's column with two divisions of the Third Corps, which would give him six divisions, nearly half the infantry force" in Meade's army. When morning came, however, Meade was shocked to receive a dispatch from Warren at 8:50 A.M. telling him that he had suspended his attack because the enemy's defenses were too strong. Meade immediately called off Sedgwick's attack, then rode four miles to Warren's position, where he found "his views unchangeable, and that it was his decided opinion it was hopeless to make any attack." Meade then ordered the two divisions of the Third Corps to return to the center, and the Sixth Corps to stand down. Knowing that Lee would only extend and deepen his defenses overnight, Meade reached the conclusion that an attack would be "hopeless," so he ordered a withdrawal to the south bank of the Rapidan River.

He could not resist some final digs at those with whom he found fault. To the general-in-chief he complained again about being forced to operate away from his strong base at Fredericksburg, writing, "I cannot but think that substantial advantages would have resulted from such a disposition of the army." He even turned on his friend and protégé Warren, placing the lion's share of the blame for the failure to attack on November 30 on him: "I have reason to believe, but for the unfortunate error of judgment of Major-General Warren, my original plan of attack in three columns would have been successful, or at least, under the view I took of it, would certainly have been tried." Finally, though he left out any references to politicians and newspapers, he argued that he saw no reason to attack just to show that "victory was impossible." As he put it more dramatically, "Considering how sacred is the trust of the lives of the brave men under my command, but willing as I am to shed their blood and my own where duty requires, and my judgment dictates that the sacrifice will not be in vain, I cannot be a party to wanton slaughter of my troops for any mere personal end."[4]

Though generals French and Warren could not have been pleased to read the report (though they had inklings of what would be written), it did not have an immediate impact in Washington. On December 11, Meade wrote to Margaret: "[I have] not heard a word from Washington, but from what I see in the papers and what I hear from officers returning from Washington, I take it my supersedure is decided upon, and the only question is who is to succeed me. I understand that the President and Secretary Chase are very anxious to bring Hooker back but Halleck and Stanton will undoubtedly oppose this. A compromise may perhaps be made by bringing Thomas here, and giving Hooker Thomas's army." He was heartened by letters of support from Gibbon and Hancock, "each saying they had not lost a particle of confidence" in him. He added, "Many officers in the Army have expressed the same feeling, and I really believe the will of the army will sustain me." Still, such support counted "for nothing in Washington." He returned, as always, to the matter of reputation: "The only point I am concerned about is my reputation as a soldier; I do not want to lose this entirely."[5]

While Meade struggled to retain his position, his daily demands as commander of the Army of the Potomac continued without pause. There were reports of Confederate movement across the Rapidan River, which caused Meade to put his entire army on alert. When those reports proved to be nothing more than skirmishers testing the Union cavalry, Meade had another matter to attend to: continuing complaints from Provost Marshal Patrick that Union soldiers, especially in the Third Corps, were committing "all sorts of depredations and vandalism." Patrick implored Meade to do something about this wanton behavior, and Meade told him he would soon issue a "stringent" order banning the "destruction of private property" (although he did not). Of greater concern to Meade was the reenlistment of veterans. He begged Halleck to allow him to grant furloughs of thirty days to reenlistees, as authorized under General Orders No. 376, as soon as possible. It would mean that as many as fifteen thousand men would be furloughed, which equaled the largest corps he had. He did not want to release that many men unless Halleck agreed to it and also allowed Meade to remove his army to the "line of the Warrenton Railroad, holding in force the covering of the Rappahannock at the railroad bridge."[6]

While Meade waited to hear Halleck's response, surprisingly positive news arrived in the mail via the *Washington Chronicle,* a newspaper published by John W. Forney. Meade wrote to his wife, "[It] announces that I am *not* to be relieved. As this paper is edited by Forney who is supposed to have confidential relations with the Administration, I presume this announcement may be considered semi-official." Meade countered the good news by writing in the same letter, "I cannot say I am delighted, for the hope and yearning I have to return to you and the children, had quite reconciled me to being relieved." But his protests may have been pro forma; Lyman noted in his diary for December 13 that, upon reading the news in the *Chronicle,* "the General is in much better spirits thereat." What he could not know, however, was that any relief was premature.[7]

Even as Meade read the news, Asst. Sec. of War Charles A. Dana was visiting with Maj. Gen. Ulysses S. Grant in Chattanooga, and among the many topics they discussed was the replacement of Meade with either Maj. Gen. William T. Sherman or Maj. Gen. William "Baldy" Smith. Dana floated this idea by Lincoln, Halleck, and Stanton; all three seemed to favor the appointment of Smith (keeping Sherman in the West) as late as December 21. Apparently, no one, especially Grant, lobbied particularly hard for Baldy Smith, and he did not get the job. Meade's fate, therefore, was still up in the air at Christmas. When his good friend Hancock finally returned to the Army on December 27, they talked about this subject at length. Hancock told him that the plan had been to relieve Meade, and that it was "intimated to him that he would be placed in command." But the thinking of the three principals changed in mid-December after reading Meade's report of Mine Run and listening to the "unanimous opinion of all returning officers" (that Meade had acted properly during the campaign). So for the first time in nearly a month, Meade could relax—except that the newspaper *Spirit of the Times* reported that Hooker had planned Gettysburg and Butterfield wrote the orders, while Sickles did all the fighting. As Meade sarcastically summed it up, "Before long it will be clearly proved that my presence on the field was rather an injury than otherwise." So new storm clouds were gathering, even as Meade prepared to go to Washington to talk with Lincoln about his policy of "executing deserters."[8]

Meade had a busy week in Washington and at his headquarters in Virginia. He met with Lincoln on December 31, 1863, and the two leaders moved closer to a middle ground on the Army policy of executing deserters. They ultimately decided to ship deserters to the prison on the Dry Tortugas islands (off the coast of Florida). The next day, Meade attended a New Year's reception at the White House, made most enjoyable because of the presence of his wife, Margaret. Though he had to return to Army headquarters rather quickly, he fondly recalled the evening in a letter to Margaret sent on January 5, remarking how "affable the Secretary" (Stanton) was to her, "I told him the next day I saw he was a quiet diplomat and that he had completely won your heart." Upon returning to his headquarters, Meade was in a "constant state of excitement . . . by a raid the rebels are making on the Baltimore and Ohio Railroad." Still, Meade found time to watch over the reenlistment of veterans (over sixteen thousand), which pleased the general because he found that a "good many of the old volunteers have re-enlisted, more than I expected." When it became apparent that the Confederates were too constricted by high waters on the Shenandoah to perform any serious attacks, Meade was finally able to go home to Philadelphia, leaving Sedgwick in temporary command of the army.[9]

Meade's celebrated return home soon turned into a dismal month, as a cold led to a bout of pneumonia. He rallied enough to address a group of wounded soldiers who came by his house, saying, "We want you all to return and bring all you can with you; and may you all live to see, what we all want to see, this struggle brought to a speedy and glorious end." On February 9, 1864, he was the guest of honor at a reception held at Independence Hall, where he was told he would soon receive a $1,000 sword as a token of appreciation from the citizens of Philadel-phia. Later that month, as the effects of pneumonia finally waned, he learned that the Senate had confirmed his appointment to brigadier general in the Regular Army, to date from July 3, 1863.[10]

By mid-February, Meade felt sufficiently well to return to the winter camp of the army. On his way there, he had two meetings with Stanton, where they dis-cussed reorganizing the Army of the Potomac and shuffling out some generals. Though Meade would not reveal the contents of the conversation for some time, the rumor mills were rife with ideas on who would stay, and who would go. Mean-while, as Meade waited for the Department of War to finalize the decisions, he had the joy of attending a well-organized "ball" held at camp headquarters on February 22 (Washington's birthday). Tickets for the ball were hot commodities in Washington, especially with three hundred women on the guest list. Meade himself stayed until 4 A.M. and was not the last to retire. The next day, he was up for a seven-mile ride to Stevensburg, where he and a number of the guests from the night before (including V.P. Hannibal Hamlin and Sen. Morton Wilkinson of Minnesota) watched a review of the Second Corps and a portion of the cavalry, led that day by Brig. Gen. Hugh Judson Kilpatrick. Kilpatrick, West Point class of 1861, was in high spirits that day, fond as he was of women, partying, and per-formance (in no particular order). Described by Lyman as a man with "colorless eyes, big nose, and narrow forehead," the slender, intense, and ambitious cavalry-man had already made a name for himself as a reckless leader, whose checkered reputation as an officer was matched by his admitted abilities as a speaker, self-promoter, and political operator. Seeking an outlet for his energy and ambition in the dull winter months, he had proposed to President Lincoln a daring raid on Richmond to free all the Union prisoners there. Desperate for some good news, Lincoln authorized such a raid, to be led by Kilpatrick and supported—not directed—by Kilpatrick's own superiors, Pleasonton and Meade. Reluctantly yet dutifully, both Pleasonton and Meade offered their support for the operation, and one of the worst-kept secrets in the Army was about to commence a few days after the ball on Washington's birthday.[11]

As Meade's vigor returned ("I have quite recovered my strength," he wrote to his wife), his friend and aide Theodore Lyman got to see a side of the man he had not glimpsed since he first met him in the 1850s. He wrote to his wife Mimi: "General Meade is in excellent spirits and cracks a great many jokes and tells stories. You can't tell how different he is when has no movement on his mind, for then he is like a firework, always going bang at someone, and nobody ever knows who is going to catch it next." In a note in his diary two months later, he expanded on some of this characterization of Meade: "He is a slasher, is the General, and cuts up people without much mercy. His family is celebrated for fierceness of temper and a sardonic sort of way that makes them uncomfortable people; but the General is the best of them, and exhausts his temper in saying sharp things. When it comes to practice he is full of kindness and often lets off men that should be summarily dealt with." Meade would have to struggle to control his temper and sarcasm over the next eight weeks, as a new command relationship came into being that completely shaped the rest of his military career, and he had to fight what he called "the last Battle of Gettysburg" to keep his job and reputation as the Joint Committee on the Conduct of War began its investigation of him.[12]

The spring of 1864 brought a huge change to the Union war effort. Lincoln appointed Grant to hold a new rank created by Congress, lieutenant general, and to be in charge of all the Union armies. The modest and unassuming Grant had won a string of victories in the West—Fort Henry, Fort Donelson, Shiloh, Vicksburg, and Chattanooga—that made him the most successful general in the Union army. Lincoln wanted a "winner" he could work with, and Grant filled the bill perfectly. Grant came to Washington in March, and after a brief round of formal visits to politicians and a trip to Meade's headquarters, decided he would make his headquarters in the field, next to Meade. That decision would influence not only his reputation but Meade's as well.[13]

For thirteen months, these men of opposite temperaments worked closely together, and the usual narrative of their relationship places the touchy, explosive, and cautious Meade under the steadying hand, relentless drive, and grand vision of Grant. As in all such narratives, there are elements of truth to that characterization. Grant had a natural reticence and preternatural calm that tamped down fears and excitement for those who worked closely with him. He also developed a strategy for the Union military that hammered the Confederacy into submission. Meade had the personality traits noted above, plus a thin skin and almost tone deafness to politics. But he proved useful to Grant, not just because he handled the bureaucratic demands, logistical challenges, and battlefield tactics of running the largest army in the Union against its toughest opponent. He primarily aided Grant because he knew and was respected by the generals of the Army of the Potomac; historian Mark Grimsley goes so far as to argue that "Meade, not Grant, . . . remained the principal influence on the Army's organizational culture." Historian Wayne Wei-siang Hsieh gives Meade credit for holding the Army of the Potomac together by virtue of not being a "disruptive intriguer." Stephen R. Taaffe strengthens that praise of Meade's conduct, writing that Meade had "performed a service for the Union effort second only to his victory at Gettysburg" by "quieting" the "troubled waters" of the army's high command in 1863–64.[14] By the time Grant arrived in the field, Meade had demonstrated the executive ability to successfully manage a large army in the field, and he would soon show that he could be a loyal soldier to Grant by following his orders, seeking his counsel, and not scheming to replace him or advance a political career. Though Meade had a sharp tongue that he was unafraid to use, he also knew when to bite it, as he had shown when he worked with McClellan, Burnside, and Hooker.

Instead of viewing Meade as a timid, unimaginative general with no drive or ambition who needed Grant to push him to bring Lee's army to its knees, it is more instructive to ask: who else in the Union high command would have worked as effectively *under* Grant for thirteen crucial months, barely squawking as a solid relationship became frayed by insults of design or neglect? The simple facts are these: Grant kept Meade on as commander because he was useful *and* effective. Together they defeated Lee's Army of Northern Virginia, although in the succinct narrative of the war, the last thirteen months of fighting in Virginia is reduced to a war of wills between Grant and Lee. But it was the Army of the Potomac that ultimately defeated the Army of Northern Virginia, and George Meade was commander of that army. How he and Grant managed that feat together is one of the most important stories of the war.

The first time Meade mentioned Grant in any serious context was in the hectic weeks after the Battle of Gettysburg. In late July, Meade wrote to his wife, "I hear from officers who have been in Washington that the president offered the command of this army to Grant, who declined it, but recommended Sherman." When passions cooled and Meade was retained in command, he wrote nothing more about Grant until December, when Rep. Elihu Washburne introduced a bill in the House of Representatives to revive the rank of lieutenant general, recommending Ulysses S. Grant to hold the position. Naturally, this aroused the interests of the Army officers, and in reply to his wife's questions about Grant, Meade wrote: "You ask me about Grant. It is difficult for me to reply. I knew him as a young man in the Mexican War, at which time he was considered a clever young officer, but nothing extraordinary. . . . I think his great characteristic is indomitable energy and great tenacity of purpose. He certainly has been very successful, and that is nowadays the measure of reputation." Analyzing, as only an Easterner might, the differences in the challenges they faced, he continued, "The enemy, however, have never had in any of their Western armies either the generals or the troops they have had in Virginia; nor has the country been so favorable for them as here." Still, he concluded with compliments for Grant, "[He] has undoubtedly shown very superior abilities, and is I think justly entitled to all the honors they propose to bestow upon him."[15]

The next time Meade put his thoughts down about the rise of Grant, he previewed his belief that he would finally be removed from his post. In late February 1864, he wrote his wife, "I see Congress has passed the Lieutenant General bill. This will make Grant Commander-in-chief; what will become of Halleck I can't tell, and possibly when Grant is responsible for all military operations, he may want someone else whom he knows better in command of this army." He continued this line of reasoning a little over a week later, after the first of several interviews by the Joint Committee on the Conduct of the War, writing to his wife that Grant "may desire to have his own man in command, particularly as . . . he is indoctrinated with the notion of the superiority of the Western armies, and that the failure of the Army of the Potomac to accomplish anything is due to their commanders."[16]

When Grant received his appointment and then showed up at the Army of the Potomac headquarters on March 10, 1864, Meade attempted to spare himself and Grant any awkwardness by offering his resignation. Grant refused the offer, writing years later in his *Memoirs:* "This incident gave me even a more favorable opinion of Meade than did his great victory at Gettysburg the July before. It is men who wait to be selected, and not those who seek, from whom we may always expect the most efficient service." Meade's interpretation of the discussion largely followed Grant's. He wrote to his wife on March 14: "I think I told you I was very much pleased with General Grant. In the views he expressed to me he showed much more capacity and character than I had expected. I spoke to him very plainly about my position, offered to vacate the command of the Army of the Potomac, in case he had a preference for any other. This he declined in a complimentary speech, but indicated to me his intention, when in this part of the country, of being with my army. So that you may look now for the Army of the Potomac putting laurels on the brows of another rather than your husband."[17]

Meade had hit the nail on the head: as long as Grant headquartered near him, the army would be regarded as Grant's, not Meade's. Grant himself admitted one version of this issue; in his *Memoirs* he wrote, "Meade's position afterwards proved embarrassing to me if not to him. . . . All other general officers occupying similar positions were independent in their commands so far as any one present with them was concerned." Grant protested a bit too much, emphasizing as much the cost to him as to Meade. In reality, it was Meade's authority and reputation that would suffer, not Grant's. As Meade astutely wrote his wife a month later: "It is undoubtedly true he will go with it [the army] when it moves, and will in a measure control its movements, and should success attend its operations, that my share of the credit will be less than if he were not present. Moreover, whilst I have no doubt he will give me all the credit I am entitled to, the press, and perhaps the public, will lose sight of me in *him*." Even so, at this early stage in the new relationship, Meade preferred Grant to his predecessor, writing, "He is so much more active than his predecessor, and agrees so well with me in his views, I cannot but be rejoiced at his arrival, because I believe success to be the more probable from the above facts." As historian Ethan Rafuse points out, "they had a meeting of the minds on operational matters, which would help explain why Meade found Grant so agreeable and was so enthusiastic at the prospect of working under him." However, Meade still complained that his role thus far had been untenable, writing his wife, "My position before, with inadequate means, no power myself to increase them, and no effort made by others do so, placed me in a false position, causing me to be held responsible, when in fact I could do nothing." What he saw, above all else, was his way forward: "My duty is plain, to continue quietly to discharge my duties, heartily co-operating with him and under him."[18]

Coming to terms with Grant, however, would prove far more manageable than fighting for his job and reputation before Congress and the press. His latest round of trouble began in late February when the Joint Committee on the Conduct of the War began interviewing generals involved in Gettysburg. The committee had been created by Congress in December 1861 and, according to historian Bruce Tap, "committee members, largely ignorant of military science, attempted constantly to direct and influence military science." Moreover, "the result of their interference spawned distrust and jealousies among the top Union military commanders . . . and contributed to the politicization of military appointments." Dominated by radical Republicans like Benjamin Wade, Zachariah Chandler, and George Julian, the majority of committee members thought little of most professional Army officers. They believed that military science was simple "common sense," and that West Point was an incubator of conservative Democrats. They would have little faith in a prewar Whig and Constitutional Unionist like Meade who had identified with the cadre of generals beholden to McClellan at the start of the war. Historian Christopher Stowe, in an even stronger condemnation of the work of the committee, writes, "The committee was the prime agent of Radical Republicanism in the North and worked to destroy Meade's reputation and oust him as commander of the Army of the Potomac."[19]

In March 1864, the committee interviewed three generals—Sickles, Doubleday, and Howe—with axes to grind against Meade. Sickles, still smarting over the reports on Gettysburg that found fault with him, had the greatest influence. They were so moved by Sickles's arguments that on March 4 they (Wade, Chandler, and Benjamin Loan) had a special meeting with Lincoln in which they urged him to remove Meade and appoint someone "more competent to command." When asked who they suggested as a replacement, their only proposal was the discredited Joseph

Hooker (who was sufficiently radical on race and vigorous in his support of a hard war), though they left the door open by arguing that they were not "advocates of any particular general," but if there were "any general whom the President considered more competent for the command, then let him be appointed." They tried to exert further leverage by threatening "to make the testimony public," but that had no effect on Lincoln because they had already played that hand by leaking testimony to Sen. Morton Wilkinson of Minnesota, who heartily condemned Meade on the floor of the Senate on March 2. It may have been Lincoln, in fact, who encouraged the members of the committee to talk to Meade before going any further, knowing that he was going to be in town for military business on March 5.[20]

Meade dutifully reported to the committee meeting in the basement of the Capitol building (in the Committee on Territories room). His only interviewer was Senator Wade of Ohio, the chairman of the committee. According to Meade, Wade was "very civil," "denied there were any charges against me," then explained that the committee was merely compiling a "sort of history of the war." Knowing of Wilkinson's attack on him on the floor of the Senate, and hearing that Sickles and Doubleday had made "grave charges" against him, Meade had to know that the interview held much more importance. Whether he knew of the visit to Lincoln to demand his removal is not known, but even if he had, it would not have changed his obligation to attend. Without official papers, notes, or even time to prepare, Meade spoke for three hours, giving what he called a "succinct narrative of events." He gave an account of his entire command history up through Mine Run, prompting only a few questions from Wade. One exchange offered insight into Meade's offensive strategy:

> Question: When you retired on that retreat to Centreville, it was not with any view to avoid a battle?
>
> Meade: Not at all. Why should I avoid a battle, when it was my business to fight? This matter must be settled by fighting.
>
> Question: Your constant object was to bring on a battle on advantageous terms?
>
> Meade: My object was to maneuver so as to bring my army into such a position that, when giving battle to the enemy, I would have a reasonable probability of success; and in the event of a disaster, I would have line or retreat of communication open.

Though Wade did not press him on this subject, this exchange did offer insight into Meade's strategic thinking: fight when you can win; avoid fighting when you cannot.

Despite knowing of Sickles's criticism of him at Gettysburg, Meade did not feel the need to respond in kind. Instead, he offered a neutral view of Sickles's decisions at Gettysburg. "I am of the opinion that General Sickles did what he thought was for the best; but I differed with him in judgment. And I maintain that subsequent events proved that my judgment was correct, and his judgment was wrong."[21]

Meade went on to recap all the major events the army had been engaged in since Gettysburg, ending with Mine Run. At the conclusion of the Mine Run accounting, Wade asked, "Is there anything further you desire to say?" Meade answered bluntly, "I would probably have a great deal to say if I know what other people have said." Wade obliquely replied, "I have briefly called your attention to the point upon which I have heard criticisms." With that evasive answer, Meade's first interview in 1864 by the Joint Committee on the Conduct of the War ended.[22]

Although Meade felt he had acquitted himself well, the storm was far from over. On March 7, an anonymous article in the *New York Tribune* attacked Meade on several points: demonstrating passivity at Gettysburg, "weakly and ignorantly" missing the opportunity to capture or destroy the "entire Rebel army" after Gettysburg, deliberately disbanding the Third Corps because Sickles failed "to subscribe to the McClellan testimonial," and, most painful of all, "expressing the opinion that we cannot subdue the Rebels." Some of these ideas came from the testimony of generals Birney and Pleasonton, who were interviewed by the committee after Meade. Most galling to Meade was the testimony of Pleasonton; as Meade told his wife, "[Pleasonton's] course is the meanest and blackest ingratitude; for I can prove, but for my intercession he would have been relieved long since."[23]

Matters seemed quiet for a few days, giving Meade time to prepare for the arrival of General Grant on March 10. But the quiet had been a mere lull in a storm, as Sickles prepared his next, most extensive round of attacks yet. On March 12, the *New York Herald* published an extraordinarily long article from "Historicus," giving the full Sickles version of the Battle of Gettysburg. It was quickly challenged by letters from a "staff officer of the 5th Corps" and Brig. Gen. James Barnes of the same corps. Historicus could not let the challenges rest, writing a long rebuttal published by the same newspaper on April 4, 1864. Though the identity of Historicus has never been uncovered, students of this controversy have agreed with Meade that Sickles either wrote it or approved it. Meade himself did not want to let this attack rest; he asked Halleck to form a "court of inquiry" to investigate Sickles's role in the creation and publication of the document. The request went all the way to Lincoln, who denied the request, telling Meade, "[It was] quite natural that you should feel some sensibility on the subject; yet I am not impressed, nor do I think the country is impressed, with the belief that your honor demands, or the public interest demands, such an Inquiry." Softening his response with praise, he added, "The country knows that, at all events, you have done good service; and I believe it agrees with me that is much better for you to be engaged in trying to do, than to be diverted, as you necessarily would be, by a Court of Inquiry."[24]

While the dust raised by Historicus clouded the air of Washington, Meade found himself in the cross-hairs of another political fight. He had sent a private letter to Sen. Reverdy Johnson of Maryland (a Democrat), outlining in detail the errors present in Wilkinson's testimony against him in the Senate. Displaying the political naivete he exhibited too often, Meade seemed genuinely surprised to find that Johnson had shared the letter with friends, and Forney's *Washington Chronicle* mentioned its existence. He was further stung by Stanton's criticism of his action. Stanton attempted to explain his objection in a meeting with Meade, telling him that Johnson's "political status was such that any identification with him could not fail to damage" Meade and his cause. Though Stanton could hardly be considered impartial on this subject (he was a friend and supporter of Sickles), Meade followed his advice and asked Johnson to keep the letter private.[25]

Belatedly, Meade tried to work his few political channels, asking his brother-in-law Henry Cram of New York to explain to his friends Meade's actual decisions at Gettysburg, and to get some favorable accounts of Meade republished in other newspapers, if possible. He also discovered that he had allies on the Joint Committee. Though they played smaller roles than Chandler and Wade, they could serve to thwart the dominant members on occasion. The men were Daniel Gooch of Massachusetts, Benjamin Harding of Oregon, and Moses Odell of New York (the sole Democrat on the committee). Odell, in particular, began attending the hearings and questioning witnesses, determined to give Meade a fair audience. Lastly, he found an ally in Grant, who supported Meade as new attacks appeared, even commenting on newspaper publisher's Horace Greeley's demand for his removal, "If he saw Greeley, he should tell him that when he wanted the advice of a political editor in selecting generals, he would call on him."[26]

As heartening as Grant's support must have been, Meade spent the last two weeks of March fighting the "last battle of Gettysburg" tooth-and-nail with a new adversary, none other than his former chief of staff, Daniel Butterfield. As early as March 20, he heard from Gibbon that Butterfield was scheduled to come to Washington and tell the committee that he had prepared, per Meade's orders, an order to withdraw the Army of the Potomac from Gettysburg on July 2. Given the chain of command and Butterfield's responsibilities, Meade knew this could be the most damning charge of all. He also felt they were likely to be completely false. As he wrote to his wife, "God knows that my conscience is clear that I never for a moment thought of retreating." He had admitted, however, in a letter to Henry Cram, "[As a] prudent general, whilst my orders were always looking to fighting, I did at times, in discussions, councils, preparatory orders, etc., hold in view the contingency of a reverse and endeavor to be prepared for it." Even worse than the charge, however, was the knowledge that "Butterfield commenced deliberately, from the time I assumed command, to treasure up incidents, remarks and papers to pervert and distort in the future to my injury."[27]

Butterfield played his part to perfection. He told the committee that not only had *he* been the person who convinced Meade to fight at Gettysburg on July 1 (against Meade's wishes), but Meade had ordered him to draft an order to retreat on July 2, an order that he did not have in his possession but assumed was in the hands of Seth Williams, assistant adjutant general of the Army of the Potomac.[28]

To combat these charges, Meade appeared before the committee for a third time in four weeks, denying all of Butterfield's allegations. He then gave the committee a list of corroborating witnesses, and in quick succession the committee interviewed John Gibbon, Henry Hunt, John Sedgwick, and Seth Williams (Gouverneur Warren and Winfield Hancock had been interviewed earlier in March). Each one supported Meade. As for the critical missing order, Williams believed he might have "prepared" such an order, but he was sure that the order had never been "distributed." Furthermore, "no vestige" of it was found by him. Also, he had "very good reason to suppose that General Meade knew nothing of the existence of such an order." Pressed on this view, he took a line of reasoning similar to most of the generals interviewed before him, testifying, "I think all his actions that day lead irresistibly to the conclusion that he intended to fight at Gettysburg, because the 6th Corps, some distance to the rear, was hurried up, orders were repeatedly sent to the commanders of corps to move up as rapidly as possible, and all of General Meade's arrangements looked to fighting the battle in the position in which it was finally fought." Williams had seen no "preparations" for retreat and would have naturally been made aware of "instructions issued for such a movement." Williams's testimony—along with the letter from Lincoln explaining why he would not approve a court of inquiry against Sickles—signaled the change in Washington, emanating from the top: Lincoln and Stanton were no longer going to play along with the committee; instead they would follow Grant's desires to move forward on the planning for the spring campaign.[29]

Even as Meade defended his decisions before the committee, he and Stanton were planning significant changes in command, which Stanton approved in early March. Grant offered no objections to the changes proposed by Stanton and Meade, but they would have repercussions for years afterward. With the great loss of life in the First and Third Corps, Meade felt it necessary to consolidate the remaining brigades into the Second, Fifth, and Sixth Corps, though allowing members of the two extinguished corps "to retain their badges and distinctive marks." With the dissolution of these two corps, major generals Sykes and French lost their commands and their appointments in the Army of the Potomac (Sykes went to the Department of Kansas, and French went home to Philadelphia, to await further orders). Maj. Gen. John Newton was sent to Sherman, and generals Kenly and Meredith were also sent elsewhere. Another casualty of the reorganization was Pleasonton, who was sent west to the Department of the Missouri. Meade felt the worst about Sykes, writing his wife, "I join with you in the regret expressed at the relief of Sykes." He had also tried to "retain Newton, and even French, as division commanders, but without avail." He proclaimed a passive role in the removal of Pleasonton by withdrawing his "objections," but it is unlikely he had much use for Pleasonton after his testimony against Meade before the Joint Committee. Little known is the fact that Meade "had very hard work to retain Sedgwick." As a portent of the future, Grant brought not only his staff to the field but also his new favorite, Maj. Gen. Philip Sheridan, to command the cavalry of the Army of the Potomac in place of Pleasonton.[30]

Meade now had three of his most trusted generals, Hancock, Sedgwick, and Warren, in command of three expanded corps. Though his chief of staff Andrew Humphreys would later write that he felt the expanded corps (up to twenty-five thousand men in some) were too large and unwieldy for one man to command, especially in the tangled undergrowth of the Wilderness, Meade felt comfortable with the new structure, and Humphreys made plans for movement with it in mind. Francis Walker, Hancock's chief of staff, would write after the war that Meade "believed he could find three first-class commanders for the army assembled around Brandy Station; he did not feel sure of a fourth, much less of a fifth." This postwar recollection must be taken with a grain of salt because Meade had tried to keep two of his appointees, French and Newton, and kept a third, Warren, in position, despite pointedly blaming French and Warren for the failure at Mine Run. Lyman, for instance, who seemed quite close to Meade, never mentioned having such a discussion with Meade about these generals, though he did note Humphreys's strong dislike of French and "implied that 'Johnny' Newton" was not much of a fighter. Fortunately for Meade, the arrival of Grant and the scheduling of corps' reviews for the new commander in April kept officers busy for a good deal of the time, thus allowing him to take a very favorable view of the changes by mid-April. He wrote his wife Margaret, "The reorganization, now that it is over, meets with universal approbation, and I believe I have gained great credit for the manner in which so disagreeable an operation was made acceptable to those concerned."[31]

Another source of anxiety for Meade that winter was the risky operation to liberate the Union soldiers held in Richmond. Concocted by the confident and ambitious Brig. Gen. Hugh Judson Kilpatrick, it was proposed to Lincoln in February—without the consultation or permission of his superiors—and approved the very evening it was presented. Kilpatrick got to work directly with the War Department, thus bypassing his incensed commander, Pleasonton. Though Meade did not have confidence in the feasibility of the operation, he gamely went along, knowing how much it meant to Lincoln and Stanton. Kilpatrick was given four thousand cavalrymen, fresh horses, and the benefit of three diversions sponsored by Meade. The keys to the operation were secrecy and speed, but few seemed in the dark, except most of the troopers involved. Joining Kilpatrick would be one of the wounded luminaries in the cavalry, Col. Uric Dahlgren, son of Adm. John Dahlgren, a personal favorite of Lincoln's. Knowing Dahlgren's popularity among the press and public, Kilpatrick gave him a special task: he and his five hundred men would separate from the main column, ride south of Richmond, then charge into the city while the main force distracted the Home Guard, thus allowing them to free the Union prisoners.[32]

The troopers departed on a clear winter night, February 28, and rode on un-opposed through the night and most of the next day. Meade allowed himself to be cautiously optimistic, writing his wife that if the mission succeeded, it would be the "greatest feat of the war . . . and will immortalize them all." Alas, when the forces reached the outskirts of Richmond, the hastily planned operation began falling apart. Dahlgren could not find the proper place to cross the James River, and when the hard-driving Kilpatrick reached the lightly defended outer works of Richmond, he lost his nerve, ordering cautious reconnaissance when a lightning strike was needed. He then decided that retreat was his best option, and he led his force off on a long ride to the safety of Major General Butler's lines. Meanwhile, Dahlgren learned that Kilpatrick had called off the attack and retreated, but he decided to attack regardless. His fierce attack soon faltered, and he too attempted to lead his men safely away from Richmond. With fewer soldiers and every mili-tiaman from the James River to the Mattaponi alerted to their presence, Dahlgren had an exhausting ride, finally ending in a hail of bullets as his tiny band was ambushed at Mantapike Hill. Kilpatrick, on the other hand, made it to safety, eventually returning by steamer to the protection of the Army of the Potomac. Meade wrote his wife: "You have doubtless seen that Kilpatrick raid was an utter failure. I did not expect much from it. Poor Dahlgren I am sorry for."[33]

But the repercussions from the failed operation lingered for a month for Meade, and for years for some of the principals. According to Confederate authorities, doc-uments found on Dahlgren's possession called for his men to "destroy and burn the hateful city" of Richmond and "not allow the rebel leader Davis and his traitorous crew to escape." The publication of this purported address inflamed the citizens of the Confederacy, and the Richmond press fanned the outrage and anger for weeks. General Lee finally had to respond, and on April 1 he sent a formal letter to Meade asking him if the "designs and instructions of Colonel Dahlgren . . . were authorized by the United State Government or by his superior officers, and also whether they have the sanction and approval of those authorities." The receipt of the letter was de-layed for two weeks because of spring flooding, but when the letter reached Meade, he asked Kilpatrick for another copy of his report. Kilpatrick categorically denied giving such orders to Dahlgren, as did Meade, who said as much in a formal reply to Lee. Meade did not trust Kilpatrick (his "reputation, and collateral evidence in my possession, rather go against this theory"), but no one, from Lincoln to Stanton to Kilpatrick, wanted to take responsibility for such an order or exhortation, whether it happened or not. Honestly labeling it "a pretty ugly piece of business," Meade, like everyone else, wanted nothing to do with it. He candidly admitted to his wife, "I was determined my skirts should be clear."[34]

With the critical question of the Dahlgren raid resolved (at least to the Union's satisfaction), Meade could now turn his full attention to the upcoming spring offensive. On April 9, Grant sent Meade a long letter, explaining his plans for the "armies to move together" and for the Army of the Potomac to make the Army of Northern Virginia its "objective point." He added for emphasis, "Wherever Lee goes, there you will go also." Nothing new here, it was the same message preached by Lincoln and Stanton for two years. But Grant's simple statement of the plan reflected his strategic desires *and* his political instincts because he knew this was exactly what the administration wanted to read. Lincoln and Halleck had already rejected two initial proposals from Grant: one to move the bulk of the Army of the Potomac to North Carolina to force Lee to fight there, and the other to move the Army of the Potomac down the Chesapeake and up the James (à la McClellan in 1862). Given these rejections, Grant proposed to move on Lee from the old base of operations in northern Virginia. Writing much later in his memoirs, he justified his change in view because he believed it "better to fight him [Lee] outside of his stronghold than in it." So that left two land options. One option, to march toward Lee's left flank between Culpeper and Orange, had the advantage of open terrain but the acute disadvantage of just one supply line, the Orange and Alexandria Railroad, which could be attacked anywhere by Col. John Mosby or other Confederate cavalry. The other option was to march around Lee's right flank, using the same fords utilized in the Chancellorsville and Mine Run campaigns. At best the army might surprise Lee and wedge itself between Lee and Richmond. At worst, Lee would attack, and the Union would lose men in the Wilderness in a costly battle of attrition. The Union would have the advantage of short supply lines reinforced by easy access provided by the Potomac River and Chesapeake Bay, as well as the nearly twenty-thousand-strong Ninth Corps to use as reinforcement or guards of the supply line. Ironically, this was a version of the very plan proposed by Meade in the fall of 1863 and rejected by his superiors. But now its impetus came from Grant, the general Lincoln and Congress had chosen to lead the Union to victory. At some level, they felt compelled to support the general they had appointed. Grant and Meade discussed both options and decided to march around Lee's right flank. Overall, Grant's "operational blueprint shrewdly incorporated elements of both the Lincoln-Halleck doctrine and Meade's views on operations," according to Ethan Rafuse. He continues, "Making Lee's army the objective point corresponded with the Lincoln-Halleck doctrine, but having Butler's and Meade's armies operate on separate lines violated Lincoln and Halleck's obsession with the concentration of force and the danger of operating on exterior lines." But Grant expected "great things from an operation under Benjamin F. Butler along the James River in 1864."[35]

Meade and Grant ordered Humphreys to work out the details of the plan for the Army of the Potomac while they continued their reviews of the corps, concluding with the Second Corps review on April 22. After Grant reviewed the Sixth

Corps, he told Meade that he "was highly pleased, and is quite astonished at our system and organization." Yet despite the excitement attendant upon an upcoming campaign, Meade's apparent survival of his inquisition, and his positive and deepening relationship with Grant, Meade wrote to his wife on April 24, "[I feel] very sad and dispirited, and yearn more than ever for the quiet happiness of home and the society of my dear children." Meade was quite attached to his family, and the continuing health problems of his oldest son, Sergeant (he suffered from tuberculosis), worried him immensely.[36]

To make matters worse, Margaret had urged him to resign, and in a long private letter written on April 26, he gave free rein to his feelings on the matter. He felt that the time to resign had already passed; it had to be done before Grant was appointed lieutenant general in command of all the armies. The full weight of an earlier insight, that the press and the public would "lose sight of me in him," was now sinking in, as reporters, visitors, and officers flocked to Grant's headquarters when they visited the Army of the Potomac. Besides, to resign now would be "fatal" to his reputation, especially just as the army was "going into battle." Moreover, "disappointing as my position may be, it is better than being an idler with some nominal duty like Couch at Chambersburg or Cadwalader in Philadelphia, or McClellan, Fremont, McDowell, and Pope." No, he "was in the service and must remain in it." Though he might be "deprived of the credit [he] could under other circumstances gain," Meade was "in command of a large army, in the field and about to meet the enemy." He then attempted to move to a higher level, beyond the "selfish and self-interested," by saying, "I am working for Grant . . . and for the cause and for the country, and that it is my duty to do all I can to advance that cause." Overall, his "personal interests" were in "remaining and not retiring." He hoped that if he did his duty to the best of his ability, "all will turn out right in the end."[37] Once again, Meade had hit on the essential realities of his situation: it was better for his reputation to be in Grant's shadow than an "idler" back home, but any achievements of the army would redound to Grant, not Meade.

Meade's forced optimism was an apt reflection of the toll the winter had taken on him, and his prospects for the future. For four months he had been buffeted by attacks, accusations, innuendoes, rumors, partial truths, courtlike examinations, and shifting political alliances. He had seen a younger officer raised in rank to command all the armies and that same taciturn individual make his headquarters next to Meade's. His closest friends had stood by him, though his wife on more than one occasion encouraged him to resign. That he somehow survived one of the sternest trials suffered by an American Army commander in the field was a testimony to his sense of duty and his sense of righteousness. He knew what he had done, and what he had not done. He had wanted the army to attack at Mine Run, though it did not; he had wanted to make the stand at Gettysburg, though he had not chosen the place nor the time to fight; and he had wanted to attack at Williamsport, though again Lee managed to elude him. That knowledge fortified him through the trials of March, but as he well knew, his actions did not protect him from his critics, nor salvage what to him was as dear as his family, his reputation. By the spring of 1864, he sadly knew all that would haunt him: different interpretations of his actions at Gettysburg, persistent criticism of his failure to catch Lee's army in its retreat from Gettysburg, and constant carping at his inability to bring Lee's entire army into battle in the fall of 1863. A simple comparison would govern all future analyses: Grant had routed the largest armies in the West, and Meade had not done the same in the East. Grant had been acclaimed as the best general in the Union army and been given a new rank and the responsibility of commanding all the armies to bring the war to a close. With Grant coming east and lurking virtually next to Meade for the following year, the last chapter of the story of the war in the East would always be reduced to "Grant v. Lee," not "Meade v. Lee."

For his honor, his sense of duty, his pride, and his earnest desire to see the Union win the war, Meade elected to fight to keep his job, and to stay in it as the spring campaign commenced. Whether he could pay the price that this decision demanded would be tested time and time again over the next twelve months.

New Commander, Same Foe

The Battle of the Wilderness, May 1864

As the spring leaves filled out the trees and the reviews of troops came to an end, Meade held discussions with Grant concerning the upcoming campaign against Lee. They decided to march the entire Army of the Potomac's ninety-nine thousand men around Lee's right, crossing the very same fords of the Rapidan River that had been bridged back in November during the Mine Run campaign. Marching behind and in support of Meade would be the nineteen thousand men of Burnside's independent Ninth Corps. Plans to move to Lee's left or take the army south by ship again had been discussed and rejected. As Grant had written to Meade on April 9, "Lee's army will be your objective point." By moving to Lee's right— quickly—the Union high command hoped to avoid fighting in the difficult terrain of the Wilderness, draw Lee farther south into more open ground (advantageous to the Union), and by edging closer to Richmond, force Lee to fight or rapidly retreat. Meade's chief of staff Andrew Humphreys was ordered to draw up the plan of movement, a complex task involving not only 119,000 soldiers but also over four thousand supply wagons, the largest supply train ever assembled in North America. With intense concentration, Humphreys set to work, and by early May had a well-developed plan approved by Meade and Grant. Thoroughly detailed yet flexible, it had one glaring weakness that did not seem to bother its author or his superiors: it assumed a slow response by Lee (the same pace he had showed during the Mine Run campaign). Neither principal saw this as a major problem then, or afterward. It would, however, prove costly to the more than seventeen thousand Union soldiers who lost their lives during the upcoming three-day battle.[1]

A big part of the problem was overconfidence. From Lieutenant General Grant to the newest recruit, expectations rode high. Late in the evening of May 3, Grant talked expansively to his aides about his grand plan to put all his armies into motion, and the particular move against Lee that was already underway. One of his top aides, Horace Porter, later wrote, "Grant rose from his seat, stepped up to a map hanging upon the wall, and with a sweep of the forefinger indicated a line around Richmond and Petersburg, and remarked, 'When my troops are there, Richmond is mine. Lee must retreat or surrender.'" That same day, Meade had taken the time to write to his wife Margaret: "I hope and trust we will be successful, and so decidedly successful as to bring about a termination of this war. If hard fighting will do, I am sure I can rely on my men. They are in fine condition and in most excellent spirits, and will do all that men can do to accomplish the object." In a more poetic vein, Capt. Morris Schaff of Warren's staff wrote of the soldiers on the forthcoming march, "The troops were very light-hearted, almost as joyous as schoolboys; and over and over again as we rode by them, it was observed by members of the staff that they had never seen them so happy or buoyant."[2]

The first major campaign in Virginia in 1864 fittingly began with the Second Division of cavalry under the reliable Brig. Gen. David McM. Gregg riding out before dawn on May 3 for Ely's Ford. They hauled pontoons and canvass boats to erect the bridge for the infantry to use to cross the ford. They proceeded without incident, and near midnight on May 3 the infantry set off, led by the vaunted Second Corps under the command of their seasoned commander, Maj. Gen. Winfield Scott Hancock. At nearly the same time they were departing, the Third Cavalry Division, led by a favorite of Sheridan's, Brig. Gen. James H. Wilson, began riding toward Germanna Ford. Before long, they were followed by the Fifth Corps, with the Sixth Corps bringing up the rear of the infantry columns before dawn on May 4. And rumbling behind the two wings were the thousands of wagons carrying ten days of supplies for the largest army ever assembled on the continent. As Grant would later write, "[It was] a wagon train that would have extended from the Rapidan to Richmond, if stretched along in single file."[3]

The troops marched on without skirmishing, and before dawn on May 4 Meade and his staff mounted their horses and rode south from Brandy Station. They crossed Germanna Ford at 9:30 A.M., and headquarters was set up close to the river so he could observe the crossing of the troops. Meade ordered his new "magenta-colored swallow-tailed flag, with an eagle in gold, surrounded by a silver wreath for an emblem," to be raised by his tents. When Grant saw that later in the day, he remarked to his aides, "What's this? Is Imperial Caesar anywhere around here?" (Near the end of the month, Meade quietly had the flag removed and replaced with a small American flag, the same as Grant flew.) Grant rode down later in the morning and established his headquarters in a house near Meade's headquarters. Though Meade had stationed himself along the route of Warren's and Sedgwick's corps, he stayed in close communication with his left wing under Hancock.[4]

So far, the movement had gone resoundingly well, with no fighting or serious obstructions. The Confederates finally started in motion, but whether they were sending men to fight the oncoming Union army or to reinforce the Mine Run defenses could not be determined. Grant felt relaxed enough to order Burnside to "make forced marches until you reach this place." He no longer worried that Lee might use this march as his time to launch a countermovement toward Washington. While some soldiers continued to march to their destinations, others reached them and began setting up camps for the night. By early evening, orders went out to the corps commanders for the marches of the following day, with the Fifth and Second Corps ordered to connect their wings at Parker's Store. Sometime in that long day of marching, Meade sent out a circular—flavored by several stirring sentences—exhorting his army to fight: "Soldiers! The eyes of the whole country are looking with anxious hope to the blow you are about to strike in the most sacred cause that ever called me to arms." Adding words of support, he continued, "Bear with patience the hardships and sacrifices you will be called upon to endure." He concluded with a soaring cry for victory, "With clear consciences and strong arms, actuated by a high sense of duty, fighting to preserve the Government and the institutions handed down to us by our forefathers—if true to ourselves—victory, under God's blessing, must and will attend our efforts."[5]

When night began to fall, most of the infantry had gotten to their assigned positions, and men were setting up camp among the trees and bushes where some had fought less than a year ago. The supply wagons slowly rolled to their destinations, and the cavalry settled in for some uneasy slumber around the outskirts of the vast army. The generals were quite satisfied with the day's march; Humphreys later wrote, "It was a good day's work in such a country for so large an army with its artillery and fighting trains to march twenty miles, crossing a river on five bridges of its own building, without a single mishap, interruption, or delay." Grant was pleased as well, later writing, "[The march] removed from my mind the most serious apprehensions I had entertained, that of crossing the river in the face of an active, large, well-appointed, and ably-commanded army, and how so large a train was to be carried through a hostile country and protected."[6]

Meade, however, with his long experience in the East with Lee, felt apprehensive. Over cigars with Grant, they discussed his modifications to the original plan of movement, based on information received during the day. He now believed—and Grant concurred—that Lee was shifting his army to the Mine Run defenses. To prepare for an assault by Lee or, barring that, a provocation by him to bring on a Union attack, Meade made the following changes: the three corps would connect in a long line, with Hancock stretching the Second Corps the farthest south, to Shady Grove Church, linking his right up with Warren's Fifth Corps at Parker's Store. Warren, in turn, would link his right with Sedgwick's left at Old Wilderness Tavern. Upon arrival, all would wait to move forward (Grant had ordered Burnside to make a forced march, including through the night, to catch up to the Army of the Potomac). Sheridan's Third Cavalry Division would screen these movements. Sheridan's two remaining cavalry divisions would ride back to Hamilton's Crossing (outside Fredericksburg) to protect the supply wagons from possible attacks from Stuart's cavalry.[7]

Although Grant and Meade did not know the disposition of Lee's troops or his intentions, they did know that some of his men were on the move. What was surprising, especially from Meade, was that they retained the belief that Lee would move to his Mine Run line, awaiting a Union attack. Lee had almost always done the opposite of conventional thinking, and shown an inclination to attack. Why would he hunker down behind his breastworks when he could catch the Army of the Potomac in the tangled woods? Union artillery fire would be curtailed, the immense supply train would have to be protected, and Union cavalry appeared taxed by its dual mission of screening the infantry and protecting the lifelines to the rear. Granted, he had fewer troops than Grant, and an entire corps under Longstreet was not yet up to the Wilderness. Moreover, the safety of the Mine Run defenses could also be a trap, if the Union army moved quickly enough on either flank. Yet just as Meade expected Lee to attack in the fall—and he did not—he now thought he would set up defenses. Perhaps Bruce Catton analyzed this thinking best when he wrote, "Its [the Army of the Potomac's] own plans never seemed to matter, because sooner or later both the armies moved by Lee's plan."[8]

Instead of anticipating the unconventional, Meade, and surprisingly, Grant, preferred to watch Lee's moves before making their own. It was in character for Meade to take a cautious course—moving his corps slowly into position and waiting to react once he was sure of Lee's plans. But Grant was known as a risk taker who wanted the initiative, so for him to take a watch-and-wait approach was more unusual. He may have decided to give some latitude to Meade, who knew Lee better, but based on subsequent actions, that theory does not carry much weight. Whatever the reasons for their cautious approach, it played into Lee's hands: on May 4 he ordered Ewell's Second Corps to march east on the Orange Turnpike, Hill's Third Corps to march east on Orange Plank Road until they reached New Verdiersville, and two divisions of Longstreet's First Corps to march from Gordonsville to Richard's Shop. Lee himself rode out near New Verdiersville, and that evening he sent orders to Ewell for the next day, to bring the Union army "to battle as soon now as possible." As usual, Lee was willing to do the unpredictable—attack a much superior force—to retain the initiative.[9]

Lee's aggressive move forced Meade to change his plans on the morning of May 5. After Warren's men saw Confederate soldiers digging a line of breastworks along Orange Turnpike, Warren sent a message to Meade with the information. Warren then rode to meet Meade at the Wilderness Tavern, and Meade decided to shift from marching to offense. He told Warren "to attack them at once with his whole force." Furthermore, until he saw what this force of troops was up to, he "suspended" the march of the rest of the corps. Hancock was ordered not to "advance beyond Todd's

Tavern." Meade speculated, "I think the enemy is trying to delay our movement, and will not give battle, but of this we shall soon see." Grant quickly responded, "If any opportunity presents itself for pitching into a part of Lee's army, do so without giving time for disposition."[10]

With Confederates headed straight into the heart of the long column of the Army of the Potomac, Meade rushed troops from the Sixth Corps to link up with Warren's right flank. Attempting to spur him into fighting, he ordered Warren, "Attack as soon as you can, and communicate, if possible, with Wright." He updated Grant, adding a touch of bellicosity for good measure: "Warren is making his disposition to attack, and Sedgwick to support him. Nothing immediate from the front. I think, still, Lee is simply making a demonstration to gain time. I shall, if such is the case, punish him." Meanwhile, news of a cavalry fight near Parker's Store soon reached Meade. Though it did not immediately worry him, it did trigger a new question: where was Wilson? He was supposed to be scouting south of the advancing army and simultaneously screening the troops. Meade added a brief note to his message to Warren, "I have sent to Wilson, who, I hope, will himself find out the movement of the enemy."[11]

Meade's problems with Wilson were just beginning. Meade had sent Wilson's cavalry division south to Craig's Meeting House on the Catharpin Road. Wilson's two tasks were to scout for Confederate forces and guard the intersection at Parker's Store. Unfortunately for Wilson, he soon faced Confederate cavalry under Brig. Gen. Thomas Rosser on Catharpin Road and the van of Hill's Third Corps marching east down the Orange Plank Road. After some brief fighting, Wilson pulled his cavalry back from Craig's Meeting House and Parker's Store, sending urgent messages for help.[12]

The situation for Meade unraveled even more as the morning wore on. By noon, nearly ten thousand men in the Second Corps under Maj. Gen. Hancock had marched up the Orange Turnpike and dug a rough line of breastworks on the west and north sides of Saunder's Field, with lead elements of the corps sliding up Spotswood Road. Heth's division, the van of Hill's Third Corps, had marched down the Orange Plank Road and nearly reached its objective of Brock Road. When the division met some Union resistance, it set up infantry and artillery on the east side of "Widow" Tapp's farm (the farm where Lee soon established his field headquarters).

As Warren moved his men into defensive lines (he did not attack as ordered) to prepare for the Confederate assault, Grant rode south from Germanna Ford, finally reaching Meade at the Lacy House at 10 A.M. The generals discussed the evolving battle, and they decided to rush a division of the Sixth Corps to the vital junction of Brock and Orange Plank Roads. Brig. Gen. George W. Getty's Second Division managed to reach the crossroads just in time to set up defensive lines, thus halting the rapid progress of Hill's Third Corps. Now it was up to Hancock to bring his Second Corps back to reinforce Getty.[13]

Unfortunately for history, the substance, let alone the exact words, of the mid-morning meeting between Grant and Meade were not recorded. Gordon Rhea argues that, based on the flurry of activity that occurred soon after Grant arrived, he most likely was behind the new orders, as "it was only upon Grant's appearance that a unified, aggressive Federal plan began to take shape."[14] A close inspection of the events, however, calls into question this interpretation. When Warren first ran into Confederate troops coming along the Orange Turnpike in the early morning, Meade told him to give battle, an order later backed by Grant. But Warren's brigadiers hesitated, and Warren was seeking explanations for that reluctance throughout the morning. Warren also despaired over the absence of Sedgwick from his right. An alternate explanation is that Meade simply reacted to Lee's initiatives and did so in a defensive mode, as was his pattern. His 7:30 A.M. order to Warren had been to attack "as soon as you can," and he had to know that with Warren that meant when he was ready, and not a moment sooner. As for the surprise advance of Hill's corps to the south on the Orange Plank Road, that problem stemmed from the dearth of information from Wilson. Once it became apparent that Wilson was not available to guard any intersection, Meade ordered Getty's division to secure the Brock–Orange Plank intersection. So far, Meade responded in a defensive manner, which was typical. That Grant was frustrated and perplexed is a safe assumption, and much of the fierce and futile attacking of the afternoon could likely be attributed to his prompting or, at the very least, an expectation that he wanted the attacks to occur.

The first futile attacks occurred in the early afternoon. Warren sent two divisions across Saunder's Field, and they were chewed to bits by accurate rifle fire. After ninety minutes of fighting, they retreated to their original positions.[15]

The Fifth Corps brigadier generals, Charles Griffin and James Wadsworth, were furious. Griffin rode back to headquarters, and in a loud voice excoriated Horatio Wright (Sixth Corps, First Division) for leaving him alone out there and Wadsworth for falling back. Grant was so surprised by the outburst that he said to Meade, "Who is this General Gregg? You ought to arrest him." But Meade did not. Instead he turned to Grant, whose coat was open, and calmly replied as he fastened it for him, "It's Griffin, not Gregg, and it's only his way of talking." Warren was equally upset, but he held his views in private until a decade after the war, when he wrote to Charles Porter that this attack was the "most fatal blunder of the campaign."[16]

The real mystery is why the attack at Saunder's Field occurred at all. To begin with, it was uncharacteristic of Warren and Meade. Warren did not want to attack until at least a division from the Sixth Corps was up and aligned on his right flank. The fullest account of the disagreement among the generals comes from Lt. Col. William Swan, an aide to one of Griffin's brigade commanders, Brig. Gen. Romeyn B. Ayres. According to Swan—who told the story fifteen years after the event—neither Ayres nor Griffin wanted to attack, and both conveyed their objections in unequivocal terms to Warren. Their views supported Warren's reluctance, but he ordered them to attack anyway. Why? Swan wrote, "It was afterwards a common report in the Army that Warren had just had unpleasant things said to him by General Meade, and that General Meade had heard the bravery of his army questioned." When Warren still refused to budge from his position, Meade told him flatly, "We are waiting on you."[17]

These are colorful stories, but are they accurate? Sadly, the contemporary record is silent. Officially, Warren ordered the attack. The assumption has to be that Meade gave him the order. But did Grant tell Meade to tell Warren to attack? There is no record of such an order. Perhaps Meade had reached the end of his rope with Warren; once again, as at Mine Run, Warren had been slow and refused to attack when ordered. Meade had supported his subordinate at Mine Run at a high cost to his reputation. Perhaps he was tired of wasting his political capital on Gouverneur Warren. Or maybe Grant told Meade to begin an attack. Surely he was frustrated by the lack of speed and aggressiveness shown by some Union generals that morning. Or maybe Meade just wanted to probe Lee's defenses, after five hours of waiting.

Whatever the precise chain of comment, insinuation, denunciation, remonstration, and, finally, order, the attack commenced—and failed. As hundreds of wounded and frightened men retreated to their defensive works, Grant cast about for other tools he could use to attack. Much like Lee, Grant was not stymied by a failed attack; he merely saw it as a sign to try something else.

That something else came in the form of four brigades of the Sixth Corps under the command of Brig. Gen. Horatio Wright. They finally linked with up with Warren's battered right flank around 3 P.M., after struggling through underbrush over uneven terrain while Confederates shot at them and even set the fields ablaze. They began their assault, which, like the Fifth Corps' earlier, sputtered out in vain attempts to pierce stiff Confederate defenses concealed by woods. They stopped after an hour of futile fighting, as no headway could be made. Once again, an unsupported attack by brigades attacking almost alone had ground to a halt in the thick woods and dense undergrowth of the Wilderness.[18]

Again, the precise chain of command was not recorded. It can be assumed that Meade gave the order to attack, but was it his impetus or Grant's? Or was he merely trying to please his new boss by acting aggressively? Either way, it was not his style to attack without full reconnaissance—that was Grant's. In the end, it was the men at the tip of the Union spear that paid the price for the tactical difference between two strong-willed generals.

And what of the corps directly under Grant's command, the huge (nineteen thousand men) Ninth Corps led by Burnside? Grant had ordered Burnside to march quickly to catch up to the Army of the Potomac on May 4. Burnside had followed orders, pushing his men through a forced night march to cross the Rapidan River by the morning of the fifth (some marched more than thirty miles). By early afternoon, nearly all of Burnside's men had crossed the river, and many had stacked arms to catch a well-deserved breather. At 3 P.M. Grant sent a message to Burnside, "If General Sedgwick calls on you, you will give him a division." But either Sedgwick did not call for troops, or the requested troops were sent elsewhere by Grant—there is only one account, and that is by regimental surgeon and historian of the Sixth Corps, George T. Stevens (he stated the latter explanation). Whatever the reason—or lack thereof—Burnside's nineteen thousand men sat idle while brigades of the Sixth Corps vainly tried to break through stout Confederate defenses. This was one failure of the Wilderness that could not be laid at Meade's feet.[19]

Almost nothing went right for the Army of the Potomac on the southern end of the advance on May 5, either. Around 10:30 A.M. Meade sent a message to Hancock to reverse his direction and march to Orange Plank Road, and perhaps Parker's Store. This message did not reach Hancock until 11:40 A.M.. Hancock reacted immediately, but he could not move his vast corps and wagons strung out on narrow country roads quickly. At noon Meade sent another message to Hancock: "Move out the plank road toward Parker's Store, and, supporting Getty, drive the enemy beyond Parker's Store, and occupy that place and unite with Warren on the right of it." More orders were sent to Hancock through early afternoon, as he struggled to get his large corps into position to attack in coordination with Getty's Second Division of the Sixth Corps.[20]

At 4:15 P.M. the Orange Plank Road assault began. Getty sent three brigades forward, and the Second Corps divisions under Maj. Gen. David Birney and Brig. Gen. Gershom Mott soon joined in the assault. One brigade after another charged toward the woods and thickets, only to be met by a murderous wall of musket fire. Lyman updated Meade at 5:05 P.M.: "There is a general attack as per diagram. It holds in some places, but is forced back to the Brock road on the left. Gibbon is just coming up to go in, and Barlow is to try a diversion on the left." Lyman ended his dispatch ominously, "A prisoner of Archer's [Tennessee] division says he was told that Longstreet was today on their right."[21] Perhaps the arrival of Longstreet was imminent, thus rendering Hancock's exposed left flank vulnerable.

For the moment, though, the immediate issue was breaking through Lee's thin line. To shore up his defenses, Lee ordered Maj. Gen. Cadmus Wilcox's division to leave its breastworks along the Chewning Farm and go to Heth's (under Hill) aid. Leaving one part of his long line virtually open to stop an attack on his right was an enormous gamble, but Lee had made a career out of such gambles. The two brigades marched quickly to their spots, counterattacked the Second Corps, and bought a few minutes' time for Hill's exhausted men. Later attacks by Union troops also got stopped in the woods, and as darkness settled over the smoky woods, both sides abruptly stopped fighting. There would be no breakthrough on the southern end of the line that day.[22]

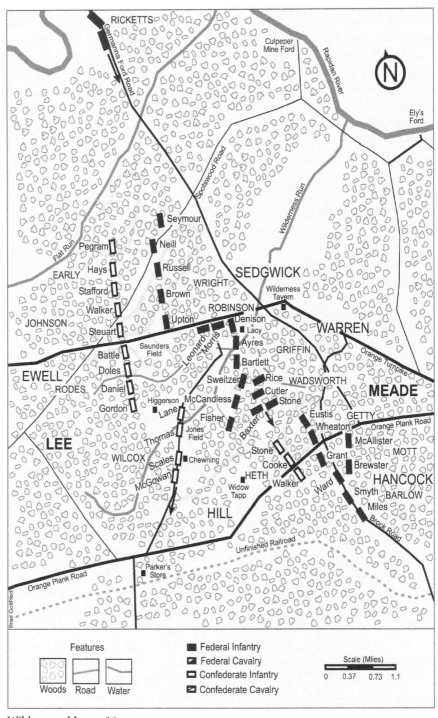

RICKETTS

Culpeper
Mine Ford

Rapidan River

Germanna Ford Road

Ely's
Ford

Spotswood Road

Wilderness Run

N

Seymour

Neill

Pegram

Flat Run

Hays

Russell

EARLY

WRIGHT

SEDGWICK

Stafford

Brown

Wilderness
Tavern

Walker

Upton

ROBINSON

JOHNSON

Steuart

Denison

Lacy

WARREN

Battle

Saunders
Field

Morris

Ayres

GRIFFIN

Leonard

Doles

Bartlett

EWELL

RODES

Daniel

Sweitzer

Rice

WADSWORTH

MEADE

Gordon

Higgerson

McCandless

Cutler

Stone

Orange Turnpike

Lane

Fisher

Baxter

Eustis

GETTY

Jones'
Field

Wheaton

Orange Plank Road

LEE

Thomas

WILCOX

Scales

Chewning

Stone

McAllister

MOTT

Grant

Brewster

McGowan

Cooke

HETH

Walker

HANCOCK

Widow
Tapp

Ward

Smyth

BARLOW

HILL

Miles

Brock Road

Unfinished Railroad

Parker's
Store

Orange Plank Road

Brad Gottfried

Features

Woods   Road   Water

■ Federal Infantry
◪ Federal Cavalry
▢ Confederate Infantry
◪ Confederate Cavalry

Scale (Miles)

0   0.37   0.73   1.1

Wilderness, May 5, 1864

While the fighting raged along Orange Plank Road on the afternoon of May 5, Meade prodded Warren and Sedgwick to look anew for possibilities for attack. After the Ninth Corps crossed the Rapidan, Brig. Gen. James B. Ricketts's Third Division, Sixth Corps, was ordered to the front, thus giving new men for Warren and Sedgwick to use in an attack (one brigade each). Sedgwick sent the brigade under Brig. Gen. Truman Seymour to the end of his right flank, to see if Ewell's left was exposed. After a short march, the men turned west, only to find Confederate troops dug in. Though Seymour and his subordinates did not want to attack, they received direct orders to do so from Meade (who did not know what they had found). They attacked, and were severely repulsed. Warren, on the other hand, refused to attack, even with an additional fresh brigade. Reporter Charles A. Page of the *New York Herald* insinuated that Warren and Meade discussed the stiffness of the Confederate defenses, and Meade gave Warren permission to stand down. Whether or not this story is true, Warren did not attack, leaving two of Sedgwick's regiments under the command of Col. J. Warren Keifer to fight it out alone. At 10 P.M. Seymour finally called off the futile attack. No ground had been gained in these evening attacks.[23]

Little had been gained by the cavalry that day either. Wilson's division had not performed adequate reconnaissance, and then had to be rescued in the early afternoon. Brig. Gen. Alfred Torbert's First Division spent almost half the day just wending its way through the vast train of supply wagons on the roads below Ely's Ford. As for the large force of Confederate cavalry supposedly seen at Fredericksburg, two Union cavalry regiments found them gone by the time they got there. Only Gregg's division got to partake in that aggressive style of cavalry fighting that Sheridan preferred; it was sent to find and extricate Wilson's division in the afternoon, and not only did that but also led a counterattack against Rosser's cavalry. By nightfall cavalry skirmishing had ended, and Meade ordered Sheridan, "Cover our left flank and protect the trains as much as possible. . . . If you gain any information that leads you to conclude that you can take the offensive and harass the enemy without endangering the trains, you are at liberty to do so." This order was highly unsatisfactory to Sheridan, though circumstances and chain of command forced him to accept it. He wrote back later that evening, "I cannot do anything with the cavalry, except to act on the defensive, on account of the immense amount of material and trains here and on the road to Ely's Ford. . . . Why cannot infantry be sent to guard the trains and let me take the offensive?" Meade did not respond to his question, which spoke volumes about his view of the role of cavalry: it should act as a guard for supplies and reconnaissance for the army, not as a semiautonomous command constantly seeking the offensive. This philosophical disagreement about the role of cavalry would soon come to a head, and it would be an early test of Grant's leadership as to whom he would favor in the argument.[24]

In the evening of May 5, the generals and their staffs gathered to discuss the day's events and prepare for the fighting the next day. The Fifth and Sixth Corps straddled the Orange Turnpike, facing Ewell's Second Corps. The Second Corps and part of the Sixth Corps covered the Orange Plank Road, with Hill's Third Corps behind their breastworks to the west. Grant and Meade made plans for assaults the following morning. Hancock's Second Corps and Wadsworth's Fourth Division of the Fifth Corps would attack Hill's battered corps at 4:30 A.M., while the rest of Warren's Fifth Corps and Sedgwick's Sixth Corps would attack at the same time to keep the Confederates off balance. Burnside would bring his three divisions to the battle, sending Brig. Gen. Thomas Stevenson's division to aid Hancock, and the other two divisions to attack between Wadsworth and Warren. Orders had gone out from Meade's headquarters for "every man," including "train guards," to join the "troops at the front before daylight tomorrow morning." (That is why Sheridan's cavalry was needed to guard the trains, though that reality is rarely noted in discussions of the battle.) After Grant and Meade broke up the meeting, Meade met with his corps commanders and Burnside, who had arrived that evening. Though Burnside promised that his men would begin marching at 2:30 A.M. (one half hour later than Grant ordered), most of the men in the meeting doubted his word. After Burnside left, the generals implored Meade to ask Grant for a later starting time, afraid that Burnside would not be in position in time. At 10:30 P.M. Meade wrote to Grant asking for a starting time of 6 A.M., owing to the "dense thickets," "fatigued condition of the men," and "the necessity of some daylight to properly put in reinforcements." Although he judiciously left out Burnside by name, Grant could not fail to see the implications from his reasoning. He wrote back to Meade that the attack could commence at 5 A.M. instead of 4:30 A.M.[25]

Preparations for the next day's battle were underway on the opposite of the field as well. Ewell spent the night shifting some troops and reinforcing his earthworks, intending to begin his attack at 4:30 A.M. Lee had called for Longstreet's First Corps to make a forced march to join his battered army. They covered thirty-two miles in twenty-four hours on May 4–5 (but with another ten miles to go before they reached Hill's line). They temporarily stopped in the evening of May 5 to catch a few hours of sleep, then resumed their march at 1 A.M. The real mystery of the evening's preparations for battle revolved around Hill's disjointed line. His men were in clumps across a wide area, and most rested that evening, instead of straightening their lines or fortifying their positions. Some officers noticed this and shared their concerns with Lee, but apparently his complete faith in Longstreet's anticipated prompt arrival before dawn allowed him to let it pass. It would be one of the few times in the war that A. P. Hill—and Robert E. Lee—would be caught unprepared by the Army of the Potomac.[26]

One wonders how Meade and Grant assessed the first day of fighting. Over a quarter century after the battle, Horace Porter recalled that Grant told his staff he was "pretty well satisfied with the result of the engagement."[27] No similar record of Meade's evaluation of the day's fighting survives. The day had not been one that fit his style, with repeated attacks against entrenched positions, despite opposition from corps commanders and their subordinates. The entire day had been one of improvisation, as he and Grant both responded to attacks and initiated some of their own. Meade was accustomed to improvisation on the battlefield—he had been fighting against Lee for two years now. But his comfort zone was defensive improvisation—with considerable latitude given to his corps commanders—and it had served him well, especially at Gettysburg. He had never shown the same capacity with offensive improvisation, especially when his subordinates argued against it. Meade always wanted to have each element in position, with a fall-back option, before he made an attack.

Equally unsettling to Meade would have been the challenges of having his superior officer, with a history of active and decisive leadership as a commander of an army, in the tent virtually next to his. No contemporaneous record of each conversation exists, but there are accounts of times when the two men and their staffs were together. It is logical to assume that a dutiful soldier like Meade would inform his superior whenever he moved men or planned to move men. To what degree certain movements were initiated by Grant instead of Meade is not clear from the record, though historical interpretation has favored giving credit for offense to Grant (with sensible reasoning behind it). As mentioned earlier, this subject is important to evaluating Meade's leadership, but it cannot be done with certainty in the absence of written evidence. Direct orders to Burnside, however, can be attributed to Grant because the Ninth Corps was an independent command. What *can* be examined are moments when Grant bypassed Meade, thus raising the fundamental question of Meade's true role in the evolving relationship. For example, during the morning, Grant sent an order to Ricketts (Third Division, Sixth Corps) to rejoin his command after Burnside's Ninth Corps reached the Rapidan crossings. Unbeknownst to Grant, Meade also sent an order to Ricketts, to "hold the roads leading from the enemy's line to our right flank." Seeking clarification, he wrote Grant, "Ricketts having received my order after yours in awaiting your action on this suggestion." Grant solved the issue by ordering Burnside to indeed replace Ricketts's men at the crossings. Meade's advice to the courier, Henry Hyde, to ride back to Ricketts and tell him "to obey General Grant's order" had been wise—and deferential to Grant.[28] This small incident revealed that Grant was going to have a hard time letting Meade run a big army under his very nose. Meade had wanted a more supportive and aggressive superior than Halleck but had feared that Grant would soon be viewed as *the* leader of the Army of the Potomac. That Grant would take a direct role in the handling of the army must have been anticipated by Meade—and dreaded. Another day of fighting would demonstrate whether Grant would continue to expand his control or retract it.

The vast majority of officers and men caught a few precious hours of sleep on a warm, moonless night, with the pungent odor of freshly burnt wood wafting across the field and through the forest in the still night air. The surgeons had kept up their fearsome duty all night, while comrades had moved cautiously among bodies looking for survivors. Some men spent the night improving breastworks or carrying ammunition to the front, while others marched steadily toward the blood-soaked woods. It is not recorded how Meade slept, or if he slept at all. As for Grant, Porter has another amusing story, this time with Grant retiring at 11 P.M. with a comment to the staff on the "restorative qualities of sleep," adding, "[I] always like to get at least seven hours of it."[29]

But he and his staff did not get the full sleep because Burnside's divisions began marching by his tent at 4 A.M. At 4:45 A.M. the Confederates started the second day of fierce fighting in the Wilderness when Ewell's corps attacked Sedgwick's defenses. At 5 A.M. Hancock began *his* assault across the lightly defended line held by Hill's men. By 5:30 A.M. the battle was raging in earnest in two spots, with Warren's corps the only one not fully engaged because he and his subordinates believed that Confederate defenses were just too strong. But that was not the case where Hancock attacked, and as early as 5:40 A.M. Meade's aide Lyman wrote to him, "General Hancock went in punctually, and is driving the enemy handsomely." At the same time, Hancock briefly wrote, "We have driven the enemy from their position, and are keeping up the plank road, connected with Wadsworth, taking quite a number of prisoners." The exultant troopers of the Second Corps continued to roll over regiment after regiment of Hill's corps for the next half hour or so, until the advance that was "over 2 miles out" hit the brick wall of Longstreet's advancing First Corps, which came hustling down the Orange Plank Road at double time. They hit the tired and disorganized Second Corps with all the force and fury a Confederate corps could muster, and Hancock's men began to fall back. By 6:30 A.M. Lyman wrote Meade: "General Hancock requests that Burnside may go in as soon as possible. As General Birney reports, we about hold our own against Longstreet, and many regiments are tired and shattered."[30]

But Burnside was nowhere near Hancock at that time. As predicted, his march had been slow, almost glacial. One problem was not of his making: the artillery and wagons of the Sixth Corps clogged the Germanna Plank Road, the main artery for the Ninth Corps. This obstacle should have been removed by Grant or Meade, but when confronted with the opportunity to remove the artillery from the road before 5 A.M., Meade said, according to Lyman, "No Sir, I have no command over General Burnside." It is impossible to tell whether Meade interpreted his authority so literally as to really mean what he said, or if he were playing out some passive-aggressive role with Grant on the second day of battle. Regardless of the motivation, without removal, the artillery and wagons slowed Burnside's progress, and ordering a break for breakfast around 7:00 A.M. promptly brought the entire march to a halt.

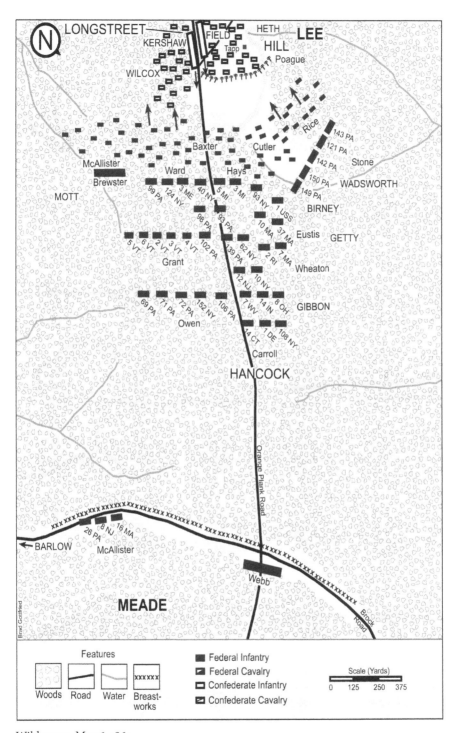

Wilderness, May 6, 1864

Two results of Burnside's "genius of slowness" (Lyman's inimitable phrase) were the isolation of Hancock's men, and the need for a reserve to be created from the Ninth Corps. Stevenson's First Division was ordered to remain at Wilderness Tavern, while Brig. Gen. Robert Potter's Second Division and Brig. Gen. Orlando Willcox's Third Division continued rumbling toward Chewning Farm (and the sound of Hancock's men fighting). The divisions were soon halted by some fierce fire from Brig. Gen. Stephen D. Ramseur's brigade at the farm, and while Burnside consulted with his staff and one of Grant's aides, Hill sent reinforcements to Ramseur. Though Meade had written Hancock at 8 A.M. to expect Burnside to join him in a fresh attack, that message was based on a wish more than a fact. With Burnside stymied in front of Chewning's Farm, there would be neither help for Hancock nor a coordinated assault, a reality that finally set in at headquarters by 9 A.M. when a new order reached Hancock: "Colonel Comstock has gone out to General Burnside to point out to him where to attack the enemy or near the plank road. He directs that you attack at the same time with Burnside." Undoubtedly pleased to know that Burnside's divisions would finally be sent into the mix, Hancock would have been puzzled by the last sentence because he had yet to see Burnside.[31]

Burnside was not the only corps commander giving Meade and Grant problems that morning. Sedgwick had followed through with orders to attack Ewell's northern section of line, but well-entrenched Confederates stopped every advance cold. Warren had exhibited his normal cautiousness, writing to Meade at 6:25 A.M., "I think it best to not make the final assault until the preparations are made." He updated Meade a half hour later, "Matters are much as they have been for the last half hour." That was too much for Meade. At 7:15 A.M. he sent a direct order to Warren: "The major-general commanding considers it of the utmost importance that your attack should be pressed with the utmost vigor. Spare ammunition and use the bayonet." But even that order did not spur Warren into action. His division commanders advised against assault, and after the disastrous losses of the day before, he feared similar results would occur that morning. So he did not attack. Recognizing the futility of demanding attacks when none would be forthcoming, at 10:35 A.M. Meade sent a new order to Warren: "Under existing circumstances your attack and that of General Sedgwick be suspended. You will at once throw up defensive works to enable you to hold your position with the fewest possible number of men." Ewell's thin line had held, and there would be no further attempts at grand assaults against him that day.[32]

The rest of the morning did not go well in Hancock's sector either, with one dangerous moment involving Meade's headquarters. Hancock did not wait for Burnside's arrival to attack because he spent the second half of the morning moving regiments and brigades from one sector of his area to the other to counter Confederate attacks. The low point of the mid-morning occurred with the sharp attack on Brig. Gen. Lysander Cutler's Iron Brigade, which had to retreat in disorder, with some men streaming past Meade's headquarters. Schaff believed he saw "seven or eight hundred" men retreating, and he told Meade there was a "serious break in Wadsworth's lines." Showing considerable aplomb, Meade remained unrattled, though initially he and his staff could not "believe it." After seeing the wounded men, he wrote to Warren: "Send some force to prevent the enemy from pushing past your left, near your headquarters. They have driven in Cutler in disorder and are following him." Warren ordered his artillery to open fire, and that alone stopped the Confederate advance in that sector. As a precaution, Meade ordered Hancock to help seal the gap as well: "Make immediate disposition to check this movement of the enemy across and through General Warren's left." Hancock ordered Birney to send some troops to the area, and by 10:30 A.M. the Union line finally connected without gaps from the Orange Plank Road to the Orange Turnpike.[33]

With the Confederate counterattack spent, the gaps in the Union line plugged, and Burnside's divisions not yet in position to attack, fighting ceased for a few hours in Hancock's sector. A small but critical cavalry battle occurred just south of Hancock's line in the late morning, and though Brig. Gen. George A. Custer's brigade held to its position at the intersection of Furnace and Brock Roads, the brief battle had one enormous impact: it kept headquarters, and Hancock, preoccupied with protecting Hancock's left flank from a surprise attack by Longstreet's missing Third Division. Proof of their concern that Longstreet might attack came as early as 8:45 A.M., when Meade wrote to Hancock that "General Sheridan has been directed to make an attack with a division of cavalry on Longstreet's flank and rear by the Brock road." That concern was still very much alive later in the morning, when Sheridan updated Humphreys, "It is reported that there is infantry in their [Custer's] front. . . . Every attack made upon the cavalry so far has been handsomely repulsed." At noon he sent another message with a report from Custer, who wrote, "The enemy retired rapidly to my left, and are now in front of Gregg." He said nothing about spotting infantry, which probably relieved headquarters.[34]

The lull in fighting in Hancock's sector was short lived. In one of the most effective flanking maneuvers of the entire "forty days" of continuous fighting between the two huge armies, Lieutenant General Longstreet sent three brigades under the leadership of a close staff officer, Col. Moxley Sorrel, down an unfinished railroad cut. After marching for about a half mile largely undetected, they turned to the north and began a fierce attack on the unsuspecting left flank of Hancock's corps. They rolled them up so quickly that the units retreated all the way to the Orange Plank Road. They did not tarry there long, however, because Longstreet added to his assault by sending four brigades under the command of Maj. Gen. Charles W. Field and Brig. Gen. George T. Anderson straight at the Union lines on the north side of the Orange Plank Road. Though a number of Union regiments either held to their position or even counterattacked, all were eventually swept backward by the momentum of the attacking Confederates. Leading one counterattack was

Brigadier General Wadsworth, who was felled by a bullet to the back of the head. Despite frantic efforts by officers to stop the flight of the men—including even the volunteer staffer Theodore Lyman, who drew his "sword and tried to stop them, but with small success"—the men fell back all the way to the safety of the defenses erected along Brock Road.[35]

At 11:30 A.M. Lyman updated Meade on this deteriorating situation: "The rebels have broken through Barlow's right, and are now pushing us back along the plank road. General Gibbon has been sent for to close the gap. Sharp firing along the plank road." When Hancock's aide brought the news of the reassembling of the troops back to where they had been at the start of the day, Meade knew he had to shore up that sector. He sent a message to Warren: "General Hancock is very heavily pressed and has had to retire. It may perhaps be necessary to either to make an advance from your left, or send troops to him from your command. Have some in readiness." He sent a similar request to Sedgwick, who wrote back, "It is my opinion to hold this [line] securely not a regiment should be withdrawn. . . . If absolutely necessary I can send Russell's brigade, which has suffered the least." While Meade undoubtedly fretted over the inability of his two corps commanders to release any regiments, Hancock's line stabilized, and by 1:30 P.M. the momentary crisis had passed. Meade told Warren to "send the other brigade of Robinson's to report to Hancock immediately. Some regiments of reserve [heavy] artillery that were to have been sent to Hancock will be retained here."[36]

Before he knew that the crisis had passed, however, Meade had received some disquieting news from Sheridan regarding the safety of his supply trains. At 11:40 A.M. Sheridan wrote, "I think it is best not to follow up any advantage gained, as the cavalry is now very far from this place and I do not wish to give them any chance at getting at our trains." Even the later news of Custer's minor victory did not alter Meade's new thinking: he wanted to protect the trains. He sent a message to Sheridan at 1:00 P.M.: "General Hancock has been heavily pressed and his left turned. The major general commanding thinks you had better draw in your cavalry so as to secure the protection of the trains." Sheridan promptly obeyed the orders, sending thirteen hundred men to guard Ely's Ford and calling back his men from Todd's Tavern and Brock Road. After the war, Sheridan would complain that because of Meade's order the enemy regained valuable sites, which "cost much fighting on the 6th and 7th, and many gallant officers and men." But the official records show no questioning of his orders.[37]

What truly saved the Union army from greater disaster that day was one of those momentous events upon which Civil War battles hinged. As Union troops retreated to the safety of their dirt-and-log breastworks along the Brock Road and Confederate officers rode the field trying to organize their disparate units, Longstreet prepared for his coup de grace: an attack right down the Orange Plank Road by Brig. Gen. Micah Jenkins's fresh brigade. Meanwhile, he sent Maj. Gen. Martin

Smith, the engineer who had discovered the railroad cut earlier in the morning, to lead another regiment of troops farther along the cut, to ideally hit Hancock's extreme left. As he and Jenkins rode at the head of the column marching down the Orange Plank Road, shots rang out from both sides of the road, as the breathless and disorganized Confederate troops could not distinguish the officers because of their dark gray uniforms. Jenkins was shot in the head and Longstreet in the neck. Jenkins's wound proved mortal, but Longstreet's bleeding was stopped to the point where he could be safely withdrawn from the field, conscious and speaking the entire time. He left orders for Field to organize the attack, but when Richard Anderson arrived soon after, he took command of the troops (he outranked Field), and both generals worked patiently to reassemble the units for an attack.[38]

While the Confederate generals reorganized for attack and Hancock's exhausted troopers rested behind their breastworks, Burnside's three brigades finally arrived on the battlefield. They briefly engaged some Confederate troops sent out to meet them, then returned to the safety of the Second Corps line. Burnside and Meade's aide Lyman urged Hancock to aid Burnside's attack, but Hancock said, "With much regret that it would be to hazard too much." One wonders how much this refusal was due to exhaustion and disorganization versus payback for a day's fighting without Burnside's assistance, but neither general commented on this possibility. Meade heard from Burnside during these crucial minutes and wrote to Hancock, "Help him if you can." He gave him a way out, however, adding, "[If] the enemy leave you undisturbed, I would let the men rest till 6 pm, at which time a vigorous attack made by you, in conjunction with Burnside, will, I think, overthrow the enemy." Hancock's unusual state of depression became manifest in his reply: "The present partially disorganized condition of this command render it extremely difficult to obtain a sufficiently reliable body to make a really powerful attack. I will, however, do my best and make an attack at that hour in conjunction with General Burnside."[39]

While examining the possibility of attack, Hancock's exhausted men faced one more attack from Lee's men. Across a cleared expanse the Confederates surged, only to be met by a wall of gunfire. Just when it looked as if the attack had stopped, brush in one section of the line caught fire, and the wind sent the smoke straight at the Union line. In the confusion of the moment, Confederate troops climbed over the breastworks, and only the rapid response of some infantry regiments and the continuous fire of twelve Union artillery pieces kept the gap from breaking wide open.[40]

During this brief and furious attack, messages to Meade's headquarters overestimated the threat. When Lyman heard the firing around 4:30 P.M., he quickly rode to Meade and "asked if he could not get Burnside ordered in to attack and help Hancock." A surprised Lyman wrote that "Meade seemed skeptical of the severity of the attack." Meade sent Lyman back to Hancock to assess the situation, and as he approached he met an aide who told him that the "enemy had broken through at the plank, and there was no communication with the left wing!" He then rode up to Birney, who gave him the same news. Worried, Lyman dashed off a note to Meade at 5:15 P.M.: "I cannot get to Hancock and am on the crossroad. General Stevenson says he has no order to move down to General Hancock. . . . I hear musketry as if Burnside were attacking, but not heavy." This urgent note arrived after a messenger from Birney had come to Meade's headquarters with the same news, prompting Humphreys to write to Lyman, "What are the facts?" Not waiting for Lyman's update, Meade ordered Warren to "send what men you can spare to General Hancock's assistance. The enemy has broken through his line, and communication between the two parts is cut off." But almost as soon as the message went out, a fuller update arrived from Hancock: "The attack was strongest from the left up to the plank road. The enemy was finally and completely repulsed at 5 o'clock." As for the breach in his line, "toward the close one brigade of the enemy [Anderson's] took my first line of rifle-pits from a portion of the Excelsior Brigade, but it was finally retaken by Colonel Carroll." That news prompted Meade to rescind his earlier order to Warren, whom he then ordered to "recall the troops just sent to Hancock as soon as they have rested." He explained that Hancock's line had not been broken, nor was Hancock in trouble anymore.[41]

Still, Hancock did not feel his men were up for an attack at 6:00 P.M. as ordered earlier by Meade. He wrote, "Owing to the fact that I cannot supply my command with ammunition, my wagons being so far to the rear. . . . I do not think it advisable to attack this evening, as the troops I would select are the ones whose ammunition is exhausted, and I would have not time to prepare a formidable attack, the troops are so mixed up, owing to occurrences of today." Reading this, and knowing that the Second Corps had been fighting since before dawn, Meade replied, "Do not attack today. Remain as you are for the present."[42]

A similar order to halt offensive action did not reach Burnside in time, so around 5:30 P.M. he sent two divisions directly at the same Confederate lines attacked earlier in the afternoon. The Confederates reeled back but then stiffened their defenses, and by 6:00 P.M. the attack was spent. Burnside soon received an order from Grant that reflected the new thinking of headquarters: "Orders have been sent to Hancock suspending the order to attack at 6 pm. In your movements for the balance of the day, or until you receive further orders, hold your own and be governed entirely by circumstances. Should the enemy attack Hancock, give such aid as you can." As for the late attack by Burnside, Meade privately told Lyman that it was "the best thing old Burn' did during the day."[43]

Just as the firing had died down on the southern edge of the Union line, the Confederates showed they had more fight left in their ranks; near dusk, Brig. Gen. John B. Gordon led a three-brigade assault on the northern point of the Union line, lightly held by two Union brigades. With only minor exaggeration, Brig. Gen.

Alexander Shaler wrote in his diary, "The most extraordinary fact was seen that an army of 100,000 men had its right flank in the air with a single line of battle without entrenchments." Though entrenchments were being constructed that evening, Shaler was correct that his ranks had been thinned by the constant draining of troops to plug gaps in the Sixth Corps line. Gordon had observed this weakness, and by dusk finally was given the men to exploit it. His brigades surged out of the woods and quickly rolled back most of Shaler's Fourth Brigade and Seymour's Second Brigade. Responding to the sudden attack, John Sedgwick rode directly down the Germanna Plank Road to see the extent of the disaster. When he reached the fighting, Sedgwick was nearly shot, and Shaler and Seymour were captured while trying to rally their men. Only a handful of regiments stood their ground, but they were immediately joined by Brig. Gen. Thomas H. Neill's Third Brigade, which he split in order to stop the Confederate assaults from his front (facing west) and the north (where the other brigades had been routed).[44]

Messengers quickly reached Meade's headquarters and told Humphreys that the Confederates were "advancing down the Germanna Plank Road on our right and rear, following the fugitives from Shaler's and Seymour's brigades; and . . . that probably both Sedgwick and Wright were captured." Displaying the coolness for which he was known, Humphreys sent word to Meade of this attack (Meade was at Grant's headquarters) and ordered the provost guard, some troops from Warren, and some reserve artillery to go forward to meet the advance. Meade and Grant soon arrived at Meade's headquarters. Almost immediately, Meade was besieged by two aides, whom Lyman described as "quite out of their heads." Meade asked them, "And where are Upton and Shaler's brigades, that Sedgwick said he could spare me, this morning?" Lt. Col. Jacob F. Kent answered, "I don't know Sir." Meade got sarcastic, "Do you mean to tell me that the 6th Corps is not to do any more fighting this campaign?" Kent replied, "I am fearful not, Sir!"[45]

Though largely nonplussed by the news from the frightened aides, Meade ordered Warren, "Withdraw General Griffin to your second line, or rifle-pits, and put the Pennsylvania Reserves on your right." In a second order to Warren, he asked: "Can you send me some infantry to put across the plank road? Stragglers of the Sixth Corps are coming down the road, followed by a column of the enemy. I have directed the infantry [Baxter's] you sent me to form across the plank road, but we want more." By this time, Grant had returned to his camp, so Meade sent Lyman to update Grant, who Lyman felt "seemed more disturbed than Meade" about the situation. Meade went to Grant to discuss their next steps.[46]

Even as they talked, the crisis ended. Two of the Confederate brigades had not been able to punch through the Union breastworks, and Gordon's brigade was stopped by a combination of disorientation in the Wilderness and fierce fighting by Neill's brigade.[47] By nightfall the fighting largely subsided along the entire line, and though no one knew it then, the carnage of the last two days was coming to an end.

With the latest crisis passed, the generals talked for a while, then returned to their respective tents. No contemporary recorded his impressions of Meade that evening, though several did of Grant. Porter told a colorful story: Grant offered Hancock a cigar when he came by headquarters around 8 P.M., only to find that he had just one left after smoking twenty cigars that day ("he never afterward equaled that record in the use of tobacco"). He also related the great line that Grant supposedly said when an unnamed general breathlessly described Lee's next daring steps: "Oh, I am heartily tired of hearing about what Lee is going to do. Some of you always seem to think he is suddenly going to turn a double somersault, and land in our rear on both of our flanks at the same time. Go back to your command, try to think what we are going to do ourselves, instead of what Lee is going to do." It is a great story, to be sure, and one that is often cited in histories as proof of Grant's fearlessness in the face of the audacious Lee (and by insinuation, his fortitude versus the fear of the generals in the Army of the Potomac). But Porter was not only a friend and aide to Grant, he also was promoted to the rank of brevet major by Grant for his role in the battle, so his stories may be taken with a grain of salt. Little wonder, then, that when Porter had to wake Grant to tell him of yet another attack by Gordon's men after 10 P.M., he did nothing but listen, then "turned over in his bed, and immediately went to sleep again."[48]

A very different picture of Grant emerges from the recollections of his closest aide, John Rawlins, who much later in his life told James H. Wilson that Grant "withdrew to his tent and, throwing himself downward on his cot, instead of going to sleep, gave vent to his feelings in a way which left no room to doubt that he was deeply moved." This completely uncharacteristic response unnerved his staff. Another man in his retinue, journalist Sylvanus Cadwallader, wrote after the war that Grant came out from his tent and gazed at the fire for half an hour, saying nothing. The only observation of that late evening that does not come from one in Grant's circle was Lyman's, who wrote in his journal that "Grant told Meade that Joe Johnston would have retreated after two such days' punishment. He recognized the difference of the Western rebel fighting."[49]

The reason these stories need to be conveyed and analyzed is that they indirectly address three questions critical to assessing the leadership of the top Union generals in the battle. What was Meade's role in the battle? What was Grant's role in the battle? And is it fair to say, as Gordon Rhea argues (and many others before him have argued similarly), "Grant had a degree of dogged persistence unknown in his predecessors"?[50]

To answer the first question, Meade's leadership is present in all the major official decisions, except those involving Burnside's Ninth Corps. As noted in several places in the chapter, the contemporary record almost never reveals who conceived of an order, though the overwhelming trend of historians has been to attribute most decisions to Grant. In the absence of written proof, however, the battle must be judged as Meade's. On that ground, several decisions stand out. First, and most importantly, was the complete misreading of Lee's response to the movement of the Army of the Potomac. Why Humphreys and Meade in particular, and Grant in general, did not expect Lee to attack them in the Wilderness will always be a mystery. Secondly, Meade continued to underuse or misuse his cavalry. Torn between his consuming desire to protect his trains and the need for reconnaissance, he split the cavalry to achieve both ends, much to the continuing consternation of the new commander of the cavalry, Philip Sheridan. But Sheridan was not yet the general he would become, as he allowed a junior commander, James H. Wilson, to take the smallest division on the most important task of all: finding Lee's army and tracking its movements. Meade believed his orders to Wilson were clear enough, and upon reading them, one finds that there is nothing vague about them. However, Wilson added his own interpretation of the orders, and it proved to be a costly mistake. The biggest personnel problem that Meade faced was Gouverneur Warren. On three separate occasions, Warren was directly ordered to attack—the morning of May 5, afternoon of May 5, and morning of May 6—and each time Warren hesitated or refused. Meade sputtered, but in each instance he backed down when faced with the reality of Warren's reluctance. When Warren did attack on May 5, he was proven right: his men were mowed down. Still, in an army, orders must be obeyed, and each of Warren's refusals directly affected the attack of other divisions in other corps.

Overall, Meade was stymied by the Wilderness and the quick fortifications the Confederates erected. Not a single time did a corps move at the pace he expected, and in the confusion of the battle, misinformation reached him as often as correct information. Lyman captured the sentiment of most when he wrote in his journal, "Macy told me that though he lost ¼ of his men killed and wounded he *never saw a rebel*. In truth this whole Battle of the Wilderness was a scientific 'bushwhack' of over 200,000 men!" (italics in the original). Other writers used the term *Indian fighting* to convey the challenges of fighting a foe in dense vegetation. The quickly built breastworks proved to be a severe obstacle as well. Lyman said it was a "rule that, when the Rebels halt, the first day gives them a good rifle pit; the second, a regular infantry parapet with artillery in position; and the third a parapet with an abattis in front and entrenched batteries behind. Sometimes they put this three days' work into the first twenty-four hours." Of course, "our men can, and do the same; but remember, our object is offense." Historian Earl Hess has subjected these interpretations of Lyman's and others to the critical test, arguing that "neither army used field fortifications uniformly during the fighting of May 5 and 6." He points out how Ewell made solid fortifications, and Hill did not. Similarly, Sedgwick, Warren, and Hancock all ordered fortifications to be built, and some proved essential to Union survival. Hess advances the thesis that, overall, "trench warfare—the reliance on field fortification as a matter of course—pivoted on the experience of battle in the Wilderness and settled in during the Spotsylvania phase of the Overland campaign."[51]

The Wilderness not only slowed Union marching progress; it created the same problems for the Confederates. Lee depended on rapid movement and quick attacks for his successes, both of which proved almost impossible to achieve in the Wilderness. The Wilderness also restricted the use of artillery, which undoubtedly weighed heaviest on the Union side, which had come to depend on their superior number of cannons and accuracy to win or at least not lose a battle (as they had been used so effectively at Gettysburg). Artillery fire helped the Union at some critical moments, but it could only be used sparingly in a battle amidst thick woods.

For Meade the battle must have been another moment of frustration in ten months of the same. He had developed a good plan to get around Lee, only to have Lee spoil it by attacking early, and hard, for two days. He had gone on the offensive, just as Grant wanted, on May 5 and May 6, only to be thwarted by Warren's refusal on May 5 and Longstreet's timely appearance on the morning of May 6. Outnumbering his foe by nearly two to one, his army had been fought to a standstill in the tangled thickets, stubborn scrub trees, and undulating ridges of the Wilderness, the exact place he did not want to get tied down in. Complicating his usual issues of misreading Lee and the slow, cautious corps commanders was the odd situation of Burnside's corps. Meade had to coordinate with Grant and Burnside to get the Ninth Corps into a position to help, and the ineffectiveness of Burnside and the two-layer command was apparent to all by the failure of Burnside to arrive on the battlefield in time to help Hancock on May 6. If Lyman is a reliable witness, Meade's frustration showed in the early hours of May 6, when Meade failed to give orders to the Sixth Corps to move its wagons and artillery. That refusal shows Meade at his most petty, but it also reveals his anger at Burnside, whom he had helped the night before by urging Grant to delay the time of attack.

Meade had struggled, as he always did, to keep his infamous temper in check. When yelled at by Charles Griffin, he let it pass, reassuring Grant that it was Griffin's "way of talking." And he lost neither his temper nor his cool when early reports of a Union rout reached him on the morning of May 6, or when panicked staffers approached him in the late afternoon and evening of May 6. But he had already made plenty of enemies with his sharp tongue. Morris Schaff later recalled that on the evening of May 6, "the rumor was started . . . that Meade was ready to take the back track [retreat across the Rapidan]." Unfortunately, after Cold Harbor, "unscrupulous staff officers and newspaper correspondents whom he had offended declared the rumor to be a fact." Measuring Meade's temper differently, Schaff wrote, "His chief trouble was that he always made ill-breeding, shrewdness, and presuming mediocrity, uncomfortable."[52]

Adding to Meade's stress was his evolving professional relationship with Ulysses S. Grant. Meade had planned his army's movement and managed the responses to Lee's attacks, careful to consult Grant on every step. Grant had largely left Meade alone, except for command of Burnside, who was not under Meade, and for a moment or two in the battle. Meade had even adopted a more aggressive posture, which was not in his nature. Yet the results had been much the same: an inconclusive battle with Lee, far higher casualties for the Union (17,600) than for the Confederates (11,000), and little to show for the battle, except the dislodgment of Lee from his winter defenses and a position closer to Richmond. Grant was suitably modest in his first appraisal of the battle to Halleck on May 7; he wrote that "at present we can claim no victory over the enemy, neither have they gained a single advantage." He put a much more positive spin on the battle in a dispatch the following day: "The results of the three days' fight at Old Wilderness was decidedly in our favor. The enemy having a strong intrenched position to fall back on when hard pressed, and the extensive train we had to cover, rendered it impossible to inflict the heavy blow on Lee's army I had hoped." Still, he had moved Lee out of position and moved closer to Richmond, and even hoped to "form a junction with General Butler as soon as possible." Many years later in his memoirs, he returned to his first assessment: "As we stood at the close, the two armies were relatively in about the same condition to meet each other as when the river divided them. But the fact of having safely crossed was a victory."[53]

Sometime during that evening of May 6, Grant and Meade, or Grant alone, decided that the next step would be to stealthily move the huge army to Spotsylvania. Historians have given Grant the sole credit for the decision, though no official written record confirms that interpretation. Meanwhile, Meade had to live with the rumors noted by Schaff. Yet it was Schaff who also wrote in his book on the Wilderness, "But as for his taking the back track, on the contrary he [Meade] is reported to have exclaimed, 'By God! The army is across now, and it has got to stay across.'" Few must have heard this remark, if indeed it was even said. But nothing Meade had done in the past few weeks suggested that he would consider a different course, though what he thought at that time would become less and less important in the coming days, as Grant steadily took command of Meade's army. Unfortunately, his earlier prediction of his fate serving under Grant while Grant traveled with the Army of the Potomac was already coming true: "Whilst I have no doubt he will give me all the credit I am entitled to, the press, and perhaps the public, will lose sight of me in him."[54] The creation of an image that has endured for 150 years had already begun.

Grant Takes Command

The Battles for Spotsylvania Court House, May 1864

Something changed in Ulysses S. Grant by the end of the Battle of the Wilderness. Gordon Rhea argues that he had decided to "assume an active role in the Army of the Potomac's daily affairs."[1] Meade refined that view in an assessment written to his wife later that month, although Grant never wrote that he had assumed direct command. But in a very clear manner he did directly order and supervise the Army of the Potomac over the next week *at times*. Yet it was not complete command and control, as discussion of the next week of fighting will show.

The exact moment when the decision was made to move the army south rather than attack Lee or wait to receive an attack from Lee is not clear from the record. Humphreys wrote that "on the morning of the 7th, reconnaissances were made of the enemy's position, which was found to be well entrenched. . . . To attack a position of such character, situated as this was, covered by a tangled forest that inevitably disordered the attacking forces as they advanced was not judicious; it promised no success" (though much the same could be said of the attacks of the sixth of May). Horace Porter would write in his memoir that after breakfast that morning Grant summarized the battle for his staff, then stated that his order to march away from the battlefield would, in Grant's words, "enable me to carry out my intention of moving to the left, and compelling the enemy to fight in a more open country and outside of their breastworks."[2]

Whenever Grant made a decision, it was not issued until after some tension in the early hours of the morning as the Union high command tried to discern what Lee was doing. The day began before 4:30 A.M. for Winfield Scott Hancock, who wrote to Meade around that time, "The enemy commenced moving to the extreme left of my line about 6 last evening." Unable to discern Lee's plans, Hancock asked for more troops. After a flurry of messages between Meade and his generals as Meade looked for reinforcements, no Confederate attack transpired, and Hancock told Meade at 6:10 A.M., "I shall do my best with what I have without asking for reinforcement, except in case I can advantageously use them. I do not know that I shall require any."[3]

Upon hearing that good news, Grant would send the order that showed he would take direct supervision over the Army of the Potomac (at least for the next movement). He wrote to Meade at 6:30 A.M., "Make all preparations for a night march, to take position at Spotsylvania Court House with one army corps; at Todd's Tavern with one, and another near the intersection of Piney Branch and Spotsylvania Railroad with the road from Alsop's to Old Court House." The order even burrowed down to which corps would take the assigned positions: "I think it would be advisable in making this change to leave Hancock where he is until Warren passes him. He could then follow and become the right of the new line. Burnside will move to Piney Branch Church. Sedgwick can move along the pike to Chancellorsville, thence to Piney Branch Church and on to his destination." Quiet would be a goal: "All vehicles should be got out of hearing of the enemy before the troops move, and then move off quietly."[4]

As Meade's staff began further refining Grant's orders, both generals waited to hear more information about Lee's position, to be sure he was not preparing for another attack. Meade ordered Sedgwick, Warren, and Hancock to send units to probe the Confederate defenses. While Warren and Hancock found little evidence of a pending attack (though Warren had initially worried about one around 7:30 A.M.), Sedgwick sent a shiver through headquarters based on an erroneous report from a green cavalry unit. The Twenty-Second New York Cavalry reported that Confederate infantry were moving on to Sedgwick's vulnerable right flank. Meade told Sedgwick to do nothing until a seasoned cavalry commander, Colonel John B. McIntosh, returned to check the situation out. When that unit found nothing, Meade turned on the negligent commander of the Twenty-Second New York cavalry, firing him on the spot.[5]

Sheridan's cavalry had a vital role to play that morning as well. Needing the Brock Road open for a march south, Sheridan sent Brig. Gen. Wesley Merritt's First Division to secure the intersection of Brock and Catharpin Roads. Skirmishing between Merritt's lead brigade (under Custer) and Maj. Gen. Fitzhugh Lee's division began as soon as the Union cavalry approached Todd's Tavern (at the intersection). Skirmishes turned into a full-fledged battle, with both sides funneling fresh cavalry troopers into the fight until darkness set in and Sheridan called off his men. Sheridan then let his weary men rest—without gaining control of Brock Road. Meade's general orders sent at 3 P.M. had been unambiguous: "Major General Sheridan, commanding Cavalry Corps, will have a sufficient force on the approaches from the right to keep the corps commanders advised in time of the appearance of the enemy." But Sheridan made no mention of the orders in the report he sent to Meade at 8 P.M., which meant either he had not received his orders—or he had ignored them. Either way, the result was the same: when the Army of the Potomac began its historic night march, the Brock Road below Todd's Tavern was still Confederate property.[6]

If Grant and Meade had spent the better part of the day divining Lee's intentions, he had been busy doing the same for them. When news of Union cavalry probing Todd's Tavern reached him, Lee decided to order Brig. Gen. William N. Pendleton, his artillery chief, to build a trail south from the right flank of the First Corps to Catharpin Road. If built quickly, he could move his troops south as fast as the Union troops moved. Later he sent cavalry to explore the territory north of the Rapidan River, and they reported it to be empty. This news confirmed Lee's growing belief that Grant and Meade would either march south toward Spotsylvania Court House or east to Fredericksburg (though that possibility seemed unlikely). That evening Lee instructed the new commander of the First Corps, Maj. Gen. Richard H. Anderson, to gradually withdraw his men from their defensive lines, then begin a night march toward Spotsylvania Court House at 3 A.M. Their mission was to "meet" the enemy at its next destination. Ewell's Second Corps would fill in when Hill's men departed, though he had to be ready to follow Anderson's command if Anderson indeed met up with the enemy or even found him "moving in that direction."[7]

While Lee investigated his defenses and contemplated his next move on the afternoon of May 7, Meade and his staff finalized the precise orders for the night march. Trains of each corps would be moved first to Chancellorsville, where they would then follow their respective corps on the night march. Warren's Fifth Corps would start marching down Brock Road toward Todd's Tavern at 8:30 P.M.; Sedgwick's Sixth Corps would leave at the same time, moving first by "pike and plank roads" to Chancellorsville, where it would turn south on the roads leading from Alrich's farm to Piney Branch Church and ultimately Spotsylvania Court House. The Second Corps would follow the Fifth Corps, and the Ninth Corps would follow the Sixth Corps. Pickets would be withdrawn beginning at 1 A.M., and the headquarters staff would travel "along the route of the Fifth and Second Corps."[8]

The slow march down a narrow forest road began at its allotted hour. The tired men, worn out from battle and the stress of three days of being on alert, marched like automatons out of the horrors of the Wilderness. Col. Charles C. Wainwright wrote in his journal, "Never before did I see such slow progress made: certainly one step at a time." Morris Schaff recalled more poetically that "up in the towering tree-tops of the thick woods beyond the entrenchments tongues of yellow flames . . . [were] pulsing from dead limbs lapping the black face of the night."[9]

Riding to the front of the long column, Grant and Meade and their staffs soon came to the intersection of Orange Plank Road and Brock Road. If they turned east, on Orange Plank Road, the men would know that the Army of the Potomac was retreating to the safety of the east—again. If the entourage headed south, it was on to Richmond. The generals turned to the south. The moment was beautifully captured by Bruce Catton: "Now there was nothing more than a bent shadow in the night, a stoop-shouldered man who was saying nothing to anyone, methodically making his way to the head of the column—and all of a moment the tired column came alive, and a wild cheer broke the night and men tossed their caps in the darkness." Of course, Catton drew on the memories of men who were there, such as Horace Porter, who wrote: "Wild cheers echoed through the forest, and glad shouts of triumph rent the air. Men swung their hats, tossed up their arms, and pressed forward to within touch of their chief, clapping their hands, and speaking to him with the familiarity of comrades. Pine knots and leaves were set on fire, and lighted the scene with their weird, flickering glare. The night march had become a triumphal procession for the new commander."[10]

A special, perhaps transcendent moment in the history of the war, to be sure, but someone is missing from these accounts: George Meade. Porter had mentioned his presence earlier in the book when he wrote, "Generals Grant and Meade, accompanied by their staffs, after having given personal supervision to the starting of the march, rode along the Brock road toward Hancock's headquarters, with the intention of waiting there till Warren's troops should reach that point." But Meade disappears when the men come forward to touch Grant. Schaff remembered to include both men in his account, however, writing, "In the dusky light, as Grant and Meade pass by, they gave them high, ringing cheers."

Is this simply an oversight, a minor omission not worth mentioning? Perhaps, except that the story gets repeated in practically every account of Grant and the Army of the Potomac, and is often used as a symbol of Grant's new approach, dogged determination, and incipient popularity among the troops.[11] The moment may well symbolize all of those things—but Meade was there with Grant as well, and the men might have been cheering for *both* generals, not just Grant.

To Grant's credit, he asked his staff to urge the men to be quiet, lest they attract the attention of Lee's army. He then rode on with Meade to Hancock's headquarters, where they stopped and talked for a while. Before long the two generals were told that their staffs were holding up the march for the Fifth Corps, so the men got back on their horses and rode south toward Todd's Tavern. At one point they went down the wrong trail, heading straight for the Confederate lines, before an alert cavalryman halted them and told them to turn back. They did, and rode on without incident to Todd's Tavern, where Grant promptly lay down next to a fire and fell asleep.[12]

Meade undoubtedly wanted to go to sleep but could not once he found that Gregg's and Merritt's cavalry were resting for the night at Todd's Tavern, unable to secure the road ahead. He promptly sent orders to the two generals: Merritt's divisions should move beyond Spotsylvania Court House, guarding the approaches to it and the supply trains, while Gregg's division would ride to Corbin's Bridge and "watch all the roads approaching from Parker's Store." To keep Sheridan in the loop (and head off an argument), he dashed off a terse note to him at the same time he sent the other orders (1 A.M.): "I find Generals Gregg and Torbert without orders. They are in the way of the infantry and there is no time to refer to you. I have given them the enclosed orders, which you can modify today after the infantry corps are in position."[13]

Unbeknownst to Meade, at the very same time, Sheridan was writing orders for Gregg, Merritt, and Wilson. Gregg was to cross the river at Corbin's Bridge, then hold Shady Grove Church; Merritt would follow Gregg until he reached Shady Grove Church, when he would head down the Block House road and take up position at the Block House; and Wilson would lead his division to Spotsylvania Court House and then on to Snell's Bridge. All movements were to begin at 5 A.M. When the orders finally reached Gregg and Merritt at Todd's Tavern, they were already gone. After the war, Sheridan correctly wrote that Gregg and Merritt had "orders to move in the morning, at daylight, for the purpose of gaining possession of Snell's Bridge." He then added that when Meade arrived at Todd's Tavern "the orders were changed . . . [and] I was not duly advised of these changes." Unless Sheridan had given some verbal orders to his cavalry chiefs, there were no orders until Meade gave them, and by the time Sheridan's alternate orders reached Todd's Tavern, his generals were gone. He also must have forgotten Meade's clear message to him of 1 A.M.—or he never saw it. So while Sheridan tried to place the blame for the next day's frustrations on Meade, it was he who had failed to clear the roadway for the infantry in the first place. In the end, though, these orders meant little; as Humphreys wrote, "Fitzhugh Lee's presence on the Brock road prevented our gaining Spotsylvania Court house. . . . [Also] Hampton's cavalry and Longstreet's corps on the Shady Grove road settled the question as to who should first hold the court House with infantry."[14] The failure of Sheridan's cavalry to secure the roads leading to Spotsylvania Court House was destined to play a much larger role in the upcoming battle than anyone could foresee.

Meade finally grabbed a few hours of sleep as the advance units of Warren's Fifth Corps marched to and then past Todd's Tavern, arriving at Merritt's battle line south of the tavern. In Warren's own words, his men would "drop to sleep as soon as halted." At 5 A.M. on May 8, Warren wrote a rather petulant message to Meade, telling him, "[Merritt] will have to clear the way or make way a little himself for me to get to the front. . . . I am aware of the importance of getting to Spotsylvania Court House as soon as may be, and should have taken the front and attacked if the cavalry had not been moving up to do it." When Merritt could not drive back Lee's men by himself, he asked Warren for help, who promptly sent forward Brig. Gen. John C. Robinson's division at 6:00 A.M. They made steady progress against Lee's horse artillery and dismounted cavalry, so much so that by 8:00 A.M. Warren felt more sanguine about his progress, as he wrote, "If there is nothing but cavalry we shall scarcely halt, if our troops can be made to move, but they are exceedingly hesitating, I think." As Henry Hyde remembered that night, "having been for three days and two nights on a constant nervous strain, and with scarcely any sleep, this night was a medley of phantasmagoria."[15]

The night was just as tiring for the Confederate soldiers, yet somehow Anderson managed to march his First Corps all night, and lead elements arrived at the Block House Bridge by 7:30 A.M. Messengers from Fitzhugh Lee and J. E. B. Stuart found Anderson and informed him that infantry and artillery were desperately needed at Laurel Hill and Spotsylvania Court House (where Wilson's cavalrymen were fighting a regiment of the Third Virginia Cavalry). Anderson sent two brigades to each location. The exhausted infantrymen quietly slid into the breastworks and woods on the south and east sides of Spindle Farm (Laurel Ridge rose to the southwest behind the farm), and there prepared to meet the attack of the Fifth Corps.[16]

For once in this tiring campaign, Warren promptly followed orders: he directed his men to charge directly at the breastworks at the base of Laurel Ridge. His assault stemmed not only from orders but also from a critical miscalculation: he assumed he was still attacking worn-out cavalrymen. So he ordered Robinson's division (under Griffin) to attack—in waves. Each regiment was successively mowed down by withering artillery and rifle fire, with only one regiment (the Eighty-Third Pennsylvania) reaching the Confederate breastworks. Despite inspirational action by several generals, including Warren who rode for a time carrying the shattered flagstaff of the Maryland brigade, the infantry made no progress. Meade understood part of what was happening, writing that "this may be some mounted infantry to strengthen" the Confederate line. Meade ordered Sedgwick to aid Warren with a division and to "attack vigorously without loss of time." Still, he operated under the same miscalculation that had cost Warren's men so severely, and noted, "I hardly think Longstreet is yet at Spotsylvania."[17]

Warren knew that Meade wanted him to advance regardless of the situation, so as soon as the divisions of Lysander Cutler and Samuel Crawford arrived, he sent them forward in a second wave of attacks. Unfortunately for those two divisions, Evander Law's brigade of Confederate troops had also arrived on the field, and they provided extra manpower and artillery for the beleaguered defenders. When the fresh Union troops marched across the fields of Spindle Farm, they met the same fate as their comrades had earlier: devastating rifle and artillery fire that mowed them down before they could reach the breastworks. As usual, there was a time lag between the attack, its results, and awareness of results at headquarters. All that Meade knew by noon on May 8 was that Warren had two divisions leading a second attack, with a division from Sedgwick with him for support. Consequently, his 12:00 order to Warren was unambiguous and completely aggressive: "Attack vigorously. Let the men know it is our interest to prevent a concentration to stop our march, and that they should drive them."[18]

But the order came too late to have any effect. At 12:30 P.M., Warren updated Meade and conveyed his exhaustion and frustration as well. He wrote, "[We] have not quite gained the junction of the Catharpin road with the one I have been moving on. . . . I have again suffered heavily, especially in stragglers." The news got worse: "I have done my best, but with the force I now have I cannot attack again unless I see very great weakness on the enemy's left flank." He continued on a personal note, "I have lost the old white horse. Colonel Ryan is killed; my staff is all tired out." He ended by asking for more ammunition and ambulances.[19]

It was fortunate that Meade did not get this message until early afternoon because he had just been in the midst of one of the more dramatic arguments between Union high commanders ever witnessed. One spark had been the plight of Wilson's cavalry division; caught off-guard by the sudden appearance of a brigade of Confederate infantry, Wilson quickly decided that retreat was the best option, so he ordered his men to abandon Spotsylvania Court House and ride back to the east. Sheridan was aware of this perilous situation and blamed Meade for it. At the same time, Meade was frustrated by Sheridan's inability to carry out his orders and summoned Sheridan to meet with him. Around noon Sheridan found Meade's tent, and the fireworks began immediately. According to Lyman, "Meade told him sharply that his cavalry was in the way, though he had sent him orders to leave the road clear. Sheridan replied that he never got the order. Meade then apologized, but Sheridan was plainly full of suppressed anger, and Meade was in an ill temper." Porter gave a more colorful description, writing that Meade "had worked himself into a towering passion regarding the delays encountered in the forward movement, and when Sheridan appeared went at him hammer and tongs." As for Sheridan, "all the hotspur in his nature was aroused." He declared with "great warmth that he would not command the cavalry under such conditions, and said if he could have matters his own way he would concentrate all the cavalry, move out in force against Stuart's command, and whip it. His language throughout was highly spiced and conspicuously italicized with expletives." Sheridan's own account many years later contained essentially the same details, though he added that since Meade "insisted on giving the cavalry orders without consulting or even notifying me, he could henceforth command the Cavalry Corps himself—that I would not give it another order." Sheridan then said that the "acrimonious interview ended with this remark." Another account, by former cavalry commander Theodore F. Rodenbough, had a different ending to the meeting. Rodenbough wrote that Meade "instantly remarked, 'No, I don't mean that,' and put his hand, in friendly fashion, on Sheridan's shoulder." Sheridan's reaction was abrupt and telling: "The cavalry general moved aside impatiently and replied with spirit, 'If I am permitted to cut loose from this army I'll draw Stuart after me, and whip him, too.'"[20] Considering that Rodenbough served under Sheridan and thought quite highly of him, there may be some truth in his recollections, though one always wonders if, after twenty years, the recollection of exact words and actions in discussions can be accurate. The characterizations of both men, however, does fit with the general impression: both had sharp tempers, though Meade's outbursts were known to blow over quickly, while Sheridan's appeared to be the building blocks of a long-simmering fire.

The final chapter of the story comes straight from Philip Sheridan (and was repeated by Horace Porter). Meade apparently went to Grant's tent to talk over the matter, and according to Sheridan, Grant's response was, "Did he say so? Then let him go and do it." Whether it played out exactly like that will never be entirely confirmed, but Sheridan did get his way: at 10:00 P.M. Meade ordered Sheridan, "Immediately concentrate your available mounted force, and with your ammunition trains and such supply trains as are filled (exclusive of ambulances) proceed against the enemy's cavalry, and when your supplies are exhausted . . . return to this army." In Sheridan's version this order was reprinted with a 1:00 P.M. time stamp, which better suited his memory that "this intimation was immediately acted upon by General Meade, and a little later the following order came in." Sheridan had been cut loose from his tether to Meade.[21]

Though this was only one moment of tension in a long, difficult day for the Army of the Potomac, it reinforced the new order of things: Grant would give orders, and Meade would carry them out. By giving Sheridan essentially an independent command, Grant demonstrated his great confidence in Sheridan, and his diminished faith in Meade. No one could fail to see the import of this decision, even if little discussed in the press of immediate demands. It would also test Grant's experiment with cavalry as a roving strike force, rather than as the eyes and ears of the slow-moving Army of the Potomac.

The morning's frustrations extended into the afternoon. After a fruitless artillery duel from noon to 1 P.M., Meade sent an order to Sedgwick: "Proceed with your whole corps to Spotsylvania Court House and join General Warren in a prompt and vigorous attack on the enemy now concentrating there. Use every exertion to move with the utmost dispatch." Sixth Corps soldiers began arriving by mid-afternoon, extending Warren's line to the east. Though Sedgwick should have assumed command by seniority, Warren knew the ground better, and a later account of Meade's wish to accommodate both generals by having them cooperate makes a colorful story. According to James Wilson (recalling a conversation he had with Warren after the war), the conversation went like this:

Meade: "Warren, I want you to cooperate with Sedgwick and see what can be done."
Warren: "General Meade, I'll be damned if I'll cooperate with Sedgwick or anybody else. You are the commander of this and can give your orders and I will obey then; or you can put Sedgwick in command and he can give the orders and I will obey them; or you can put me in command and I will give the orders and Sedgwick

will obey them; but I'll be God damned if I'll cooperate with General Sedgwick or anybody else."

A great story, and one probably with some kernel of truth in it, but equally interesting was Meade's response: he simply rode off without comment and "continued to funnel troops to the line," according to Wilson's account. Temper tantrums never fazed George Gordon Meade, whether having them or being on the receiving end of them. He also wanted his corps commanders to cooperate, not bicker.

Reflecting on the tension and frustrations experienced by the commanders, Lyman wrote: "A little below where road opens into an extensive open space found Generals Sedgwick, Warren, and Wright. Was struck by their worn and troubled aspect, more especially in Sedgwick, who showed its effect more from contrast with his usual calmness." Lyman theorized it was a combination of sudden action and exhaustion, as "never, perhaps, were officers and men more jaded and prostrated than on this very Sunday." Another active observer that day, Charles Wainwright, wrote in his diary, "I feel awfully tired tonight, now the excitement is over, having had not a wink of sleep for forty hours." (Yet Lyman saw him that afternoon and remarked that he "seemed in better spirits than the rest.")[22]

Around 4:30 Meade and Grant rode out with their staffs to see the field for themselves, surveying it for an uncomfortable length of time, as Lyman recalled: "We sat on horseback while the bullets here and there came clicking among trunks and branches and an occasional shell added its discordant tone. I almost fancy that Grant felt mad that things did not move faster, and so thought he would go and sit in an uncomfortable place. General Meade, not to be bluffed, stayed longer than Grant, but he told me to show the General the way to the new headquarters." Showing the eminent common sense he was known for, Lyman wrote, "Oh, with what intense politeness did I show the shortest road! For I had picked out the camp and knew the way."[23] Not for this staffer the frustrations of command or the need to demonstrate courage in the face of fire.

Frustrated by a long day of delays, Meade ordered a two-part attack on the Laurel Hill defenses. Two New Jersey regiments would probe the enemy's strength on Laurel Hill, while the Pennsylvania Reserves would hit the right flank of the Confederate line that stretched north from Laurel Hill. Both attacks were severely repulsed. The New Jersey regiments ran into a dense wall of fire and had to retreat. The Pennsylvania Reserves marched into the woods, only to be counterattacked by the just-arrived troops of Ewell's Second Corps. Fighting in near darkness in thick woods, the Union attack quickly turned into another retreat. The road to Spotsylvania would not be cleared that evening. Maj. James C. Duane, Meade's chief engineer, expected a tongue lashing for not ferrying more troops into the battle. Instead, Meade said to him, "I suppose you did all that you could."[24]

That same judgment also held true for his favorite corps commander, Winfield Scott Hancock. The bulk of the Second Corps had spent the entire day around Todd's Tavern, guarding the rear of the Army of the Potomac. Confederate infantry under Brig. Gen. William Mahone and a cavalry brigade under Maj. Gen. Wade Hampton probed the Second Corps line, simultaneously learning that the Second Corps firmly held the intersection at Todd's Tavern but also tying down the Union corps for the whole day. Though reporter and author William Swinton would criticize Meade's "timid generalship" for allowing an entire corps to be held back to protect the rear of the Army of the Potomac (rather than be used offensively at Laurel Hill), the biggest problems were endemic: lack of real-time intelligence on the movements of Lee's troops, and the underlying fear that Lee was up to something that no general had imagined.[25]

By nightfall the sporadic fighting of May 8 had ended. While infantrymen on both sides improved their defenses throughout the night, the generals dissected the day's events and gave orders for the following day.

It had been a long and trying day for George G. Meade. Every effort to get his corps commanders to move with alacrity, despite his "circling and swooping about as usual," had failed. After a "late dinner," Meade vented his frustrations to Theodore Lyman. Burnside had been "too late in the Wilderness to do any good." His old friend Sedgwick was "constitutionally slow." And his best protégé, Warren, "had lost his nerve." Meade told Lyman that he had said that very thing to Warren earlier in the day, and that Warren "professed to be very indignant." Meade even had to relieve Brig. Gen. J. H. Hobart Ward (First brigade, Second Corps) because "they say he was in liquor in the Wilderness and that he rode away from the fight on a caisson."[26]

At 11:05 P.M. Meade issued new orders that reflected the reality and disappointment of the day: "The army will remain quiet tomorrow, 9th instant, to give the men rest and to distribute ammunition and rations." The corps would be busy, however, strengthening "their positions by intrenchments." If the Confederates could erect solid breastworks in less than a day, so could the Union troops.[27] Conveying the same message to Burnside that evening, Grant wrote, "The enemy have made a strong resistance here; so much so that no advance will be attempted tomorrow." Consequently, Burnside was to halt his "advance beyond [south of] the Gate."[28]

The Army of the Potomac had failed to break through and seize Spotsylvania Court House. What had gone wrong? Essentially, Warren and Sedgwick had been unable to move and attack when ordered. Add to that the dust-up with Sheridan, the mystery surrounding the movements of Lee's troops, the sturdy defenses the Confederates quickly erected (especially on Laurel Hill), and the fortuitous arrival of several Confederate units, and one has a prescription for failure. For most of the day, Grant and Meade were not at the front giving direct commands, though

Meade had taken a very active role in the late afternoon, surveying lines and even ordering an evening attack that was quickly repulsed. However, neither Grant nor Meade typically rode close to the front and exercised direct command; both preferred to give orders to their corps commanders and remain at headquarters in the rear (though sometimes riding out to see things for themselves). The real problem might have been the fatigue and nervous prostration observed by Lyman, Wainwright, Warren, and many others. Few leaders moved crisply, and both sides operated in an intelligence vacuum.

Despite these handicaps, though, Robert E. Lee managed to get the jump on the Army of the Potomac, hold his positions with relatively few men, and move the bulk of his army down by the courthouse and into a defensive posture. During the night, the Confederates extended and raised their breastworks, and though no one knew what the Army of Potomac would do next, the outnumbered Confederates could feel good about their current situation. Confederates were fast learning how to quickly build solid breastworks with interlocking fields of fire. Andrew Humphreys described how the stout defenses helped even out the disparity in numbers between the two armies: "With such intrenchments as these, having artillery throughout, with flank fire along their lines wherever practicable . . . the strength of an army sustaining attack was more than quadrupled, provided they had strength enough to man the intrenchments wall."[29]

As soldiers improved their defenses that night, Meade also got little sleep as he tended to troop positioning and lines of authority. Hancock would stay at Todd's Tavern for the time being, with Gibbon's division as his reserve. As for the command of the Fifth and Sixth Corps when they had a combined operation, that person would be Sedgwick. Meade sent a similar order to Warren. After receiving Meade's order, Sedgwick showed the magnanimity for which he was known; he told Maj. Washington Roebling to tell Warren to "go on and command his own corps as usual. I have perfect confidence that he will do what is right, and know what to do with his corps as well."[30]

Grant and his staff rode out to survey the lines in the morning of May 9, stopping to talk to Sedgwick. Porter recalled that Sedgwick appeared "particularly cheerful and hopeful that morning" and "expressed every confidence in the ability of his troops to respond heroically to every demand made of them." After Grant rode off, Sedgwick checked the position of some troops near two guns, and as soldiers around him dodged bullets, Sedgwick chided them: "What! What! Men dodging this way for single bullets? What will you do when they open fire along the whole line? I am ashamed of you. They couldn't hit an elephant at this distance." Suddenly, his chief of staff Lt. Col. Martin T. McMahon heard the "shrill whistle" of a marksman's bullet, followed by a "dull, heavy stroke." He looked at Sedgwick and saw "blood spurting from his left cheek under the eye in a steady stream." Sedgwick collapsed into McMahon, and they both fell to the ground. A surgeon arrived and examined Sedgwick, but there was nothing he could do but wash the blood off his face. Brig. Gen. James Ricketts then rode up, and he refused to assume command of the corps, knowing that it was "General Sedgwick's desire, if anything should happen to him, that General Horatio G. Wright, of the Third Division, should succeed him." McMahon rode off to tell Meade the tragic news, only to find that Meade had already heard. Meade placed Wright in command of the Sixth Corps and told someone to bring Sedgwick's body to his headquarters. It lay on a "bower of evergreens" until the night, when it was removed and transported to Connecticut by some of Sedgwick's staffers.[31]

The news of Sedgwick's death traveled through the ranks of the Army of the Potomac like an electric shock. If the most beloved Union general could be suddenly killed, who was safe? And who would take his place? Theodore Lyman summarized the feelings of many in a letter he sent home the next week: "So fell 'good Uncle John,' a pure and great-hearted man, a brave and skillful soldier. From the commander to the lowest private, he had no enemy in this army."[32]

Despite the shock and sorrow from the death of Sedgwick, the Army of the Potomac had to maintain its fighting edge. Per Sedgwick's wishes, Meade appointed Horatio Wright to replace him. Though several small attacks were attempted during the day by Union troops, the Fifth and Sixth corps remained essentially static, tied down by focused Confederate sharpshooting and breastworks too strong to overcome. The Confederates on either side of Laurel Hill remained stationary as well, preferring to let the Union be the aggressor this day.[33]

Unable to discern Lee's movements because almost the entire cavalry force had ridden south with Sheridan, Grant and Meade had two infantry corps perform reconnaissance. Hancock pushed some troops south and southeast from Todd's Tavern, testing the extent and strength of Lee's western defenses. Burnside sent some men marching southeast toward the Alsop house, and from there they were to march southwest to check the eastern approaches to Lee's line on the Fredericksburg Road. Neither probe went as planned, or discovered much. Some of Burnside's units marched to the Ni River, where they were stopped by Confederate cavalry and infantry. Burnside himself rode at a leisurely pace, never pushing his corps. Hancock, meanwhile, did push forward, crossing the Po River by early evening. That left him vulnerable, though, to a surprise attack by Lee.[34]

As darkness fell on the two armies, Meade and Grant sent out orders to their corps commanders to hold their troops "in readiness to advance against the enemy" the next day. Meanwhile, Sheridan's force of ten thousand cavalrymen had reached the North Anna River, freeing some Union prisoners and destroying Confederate supplies along the way. Still, Grant's impulsive decision to set Sheridan free from reconnaissance had ensured that the Army was more blind to Lee's locations and intentions than before.[35] Overall, the two generals had another day of movement, uncertainty, and cautious negotiations of authority. Meade continued to face the specter of the wily Lee, though now burdened with the presence of Grant and his staff at his elbow. It was a trying day for all concerned.

The next day, May 10, began like the others that had preceded it, with Union scouting of Confederate lines and occasional infantry probes to assess the strength of certain positions. As the hours passed and more information trickled in, Grant and Meade altered plans several times, striving to adapt to perceived opportunities for attacks or responding to Lee's countermoves. The final plan called for a general assault across the length of Lee's line in the late afternoon. It is usually assumed by most writers that Grant developed the plans for the day (and the days that followed). Two contemporaries and supporters of Grant, Dana and Porter, gave credit to Grant. Porter wrote of Grant's thinking on May 9, "The demonstrations made by Lee, and the strengthening of his right, revived in General Grant's mind the impression that the enemy might interpose between us and Fredericksburg." Putting it much more forcefully, "Meade was in command of the Army of the Potomac, but it was Grant, the lieutenant general of the armies of the United States, who was really directing the movements." Gordon Rhea repeatedly refers to Grant as the chief planner and mover: for example, Grant "discerned possibilities" and Grant's "new scheme." Historian William Matter simply states that Grant "determined to conduct simultaneous attacks with Meade's three corps" that afternoon.[36]

But the official record is not that precise. Most of the time, Meade gave the orders for the Army of the Potomac. We know that the two generals talked often during these days, but we do not know who necessarily authored a plan or a response, or whether the two developed plans together. It is better, then, in the absence of definitive authority, to refer to Grant *and* Meade; except where it is entirely clear that only one man authored the plan (and that may still be slighting Meade's role).

Several corps were active that morning. Hancock sent out three separate probes of Mahone's and Heth's lines south of Shady Grove Road. The most promising information came from Lt. Col. John S. Hammill's Sixty-First New York, who found a place to turn the Confederate line by crossing the Po River "halfway between the bridge and the mouth of Glady Run" (the Po River formed a horseshoe around the Second Corps). Hearing of this success, Hancock began to plan to send some brigades on the same path.[37]

While Hancock's men probed Mahone's defenses, Warren did the same to Anderson's defenses at Laurel Hill. First he sent troops under Crawford and Cutler to find soft spots in the Confederate line. Crawford thought he found such a spot, and around 10:30 A.M. Warren ordered an attack of both divisions. They were met almost immediately by a wall of shell and rifle fire, and Warren had to call off his attacks.[38]

With little progress by mid-morning, Grant took the time to contact Halleck and Burnside. From Halleck he requested "all the infantry [he could] rake and scrap," plus more provisions and ammunition. He sent a strong signal to Lincoln that he was not deterred by Lee's tenacity, writing that he would take "no backward steps." Instead, he would hold fast against Lee's "very strong force . . . and in the end, beat Lee's army, I believe." To Burnside he gave clear orders: "Reconnoiter the enemy's position in the meantime, and if you have any chance of attacking their right do it with vigor and with all the force you can bring to bear."[39]

By mid-morning Grant and Meade had finalized plans for the afternoon assault. Meade began sending orders to his corps commander. He instructed Hancock, "Immediately transfer two divisions of your corps to General Warren's position, and make arrangements, in conjunction with the Fifth Corps, to make a vigorous attack on the enemy's line punctually at 5 pm." To avoid any confusion over seniority, Meade's simultaneously issued order to Warren was explicit: "Major-General Hancock will by virtue of his combined seniority have the command of the combined operations." Horatio Wright, commander of the Sixth Corps, received a similar order to attack from Meade.[40]

Though the main thrust of the assault would be at Laurel Hill, the Sixth corps had a special role: Col. Emory Upton, commander of the Second Brigade, First Division, would test his theory that a column attack could break through a strong defensive line. He had successfully used a similar tactic at Rappahannock Station in November 1863, and now he was to be given twelve regiments to attack a perceived weak spot in Ewell's large salient lines that resembled a "mule shoe" (the exact spot for the charge would be at "Doles's salient," so named for the commander in charge of that sector of the line). The first line of attackers would not stop to fire: they were to press forward at the double-quick across the clearing, not firing until they reached the Confederate breastworks. They would quickly be followed by two more lines of troops, each turning either north or south of the breached line, as needed. Upton's attack was to be supported by a simultaneous attack of Brig. Gen. Gershom Mott's Fourth Division of the Second Corps, temporarily gathered north of Ewell's line near the Brown house. Finally, Burnside was to threaten the Confederate right flank on Fredericksburg Road, even pushing through if possible.[41]

It was a workable plan on paper, but its biggest failure was blindness to the difficulty of breaching and maintaining a break in a strongly fortified defensive line. Of all the elements of the plan, the one with the most potential was Upton's column attack, but its success would depend upon speed, surprise, *and* support. The weak links were Mott's division and Burnside's Ninth Corps. Earlier in the day, Mott had been ordered to connect with Burnside and, if possible, with Wright. Then he received new orders to attack at 5 P.M. (the original time for the grand assault). As for Burnside, he had approached Lee's lines carefully, done some fighting, and was stalled by late afternoon. His potential for even distracting Lee seemed minimal.[42]

The plan fell apart before it got started. Wanting to rescue his failing reputation, Warren approached Meade in the afternoon asking if he could attack early. His motivation is easy to see—why Meade agreed to his request is less clear. Was he also frustrated by three days of failed movements and assaults? Tired of Grant's staff looking askance at every decision he made that did not result in offensive action? There is no record of his thoughts on the subject. All that is known is that Meade acceded to the request and updated Hancock on the change of plans. Meade ordered Gibbon's division to support Warren, and after Gibbon saw what he faced, he tried to talk Warren out of the attack. He later wrote, "I told General Warren no line of battle could move through such obstacles to produce any effect." Warren did not budge, but he did agree to ride over to Meade's headquarters with Gibbon and see if Meade would change his mind. He did not, and it still rankled Gibbon twenty years later when he wrote, "He, however, seemed to rely wholly upon Warren's judgment in the matter, and the latter seemed bent upon the attack with some idea that the occasion was a crisis in the battle of which advantage must be taken." The attack would go forward, despite the fears of many men besides Gibbon.[43]

Gibbon's fears were quickly realized. Around 4 P.M. the dreaded attack began, and one by one, the brigades were pinned down and raked by accurate Confederate rifle and artillery fire. Making matters worse, the pine needles and dry cedar caught fire, producing heat, flames, and smoke across Spindle's Field. The charge quickly collapsed, and for the next hour soldiers crawled, ran, or hobbled back to the safety of their lines. The Fifth Corps and part of the Second Corps was beaten before a grand assault could be made.[44]

The failure of Warren's premature assault did not alter Grant and Meade's master plan. When Hancock returned to Laurel Hill, Meade ordered him to attack at 6:30 P.M. over the same ground that Warren had. While preparing for the attack, Hancock was told to send troops to Barlow's right to meet a "heavy column" of troops; no sooner had he given the order than he was told to countermand it, as the information had been false. Hancock then ordered portions of Gibbon's and Birney's divisions, plus the Fifth Corps, to ready for an attack.[45]

As Hancock's men prepared for their suicidal charge, Upton assembled his regiments (five thousand men) for their attack against Ewell's lines around the Harrison and McCoul farms. Just before 6 P.M., three Union batteries opened fire on Brig. Gen. George Doles's salient, the vulnerable spot in Ewell's line. They continued firing for over half an hour, while Meade waited to hear if Hancock was ready to attack Laurel Hill (he was not). Unfortunately, the shelling alerted Dole and Ewell that an attack was imminent. Finally, Meade ordered Upton to attack. The first line emerged from the woods and ran across the clearing, not stopping to fire or to duck from the intense barrage of bullets fired at them. The line of men hit the breastworks and began firing and stabbing at the defenders. They were quickly followed by Upton's second line, which climbed over the breastworks and began fanning out to the left and right. While some Union soldiers raced to capture several Confederate cannons, Ewell channeled all available units to the break in his line. Upton's third line was now at the breastworks, struggling to hold on to it as Confederate reinforcements streamed in. Where was Mott's division? Unfortunately, due to lack of communication, Mott had already tried to reach Upton at 5 P.M., but the intense fire had driven his attacking force back. His regiments were actually at the Brown house during Upton's attack. Now without Mott's assistance, Upton asked if he could retreat, and his immediate superior, Brig. Gen. David Russell, gave him permission. As darkness fell over the woods, the last remnants of Upton's attacking force (several Vermont regiments), fought to get back to the safety of their lines.[46]

In an utter absurdity of the day, Hancock's attack on Laurel Hill was not called off as daylight ebbed. It started at 7 P.M., and several divisions barely budged from their positions, knowing that certain death awaited them. Only the fresh First Brigade, Third Division, Second Corps under the ill-starred J. Hobart Ward actually ran to the Confederate lines through a hail of fire, managing to jump on top of the parapets and fight hand-to-hand for a brief spell, before it needed to retreat, owing to lack of support of the nearby troops (much like Upton's men). By 8 P.M. the last assault of the day had ended.[47]

With Burnside's entire Ninth Corps stymied by a single Confederate division sprawled across Fredericksburg Road, the only good news of the day came from Sheridan. He pressed his troops south all day, heading eighteen miles below Beaver Dam Station (on the Virginia Central Railroad) to the Ground Squirrel Bridge over the South Anna River. Moving slowly and deliberately, he virtually invited Stuart's tired troopers to attack.[48]

There are no records of Meade and Grant's discussions on the night of May 10. It had been the heaviest day of fighting for the Army of the Potomac since the Wilderness, with casualties climbing over four thousand. Grant and Meade had shuffled troops all day and ordered attacks against well-fortified lines in different places, without significantly moving Lee's line or altering his overall tactical situation. In one of Charles Dana's lengthy reports to Stanton, he zeroed in on a major problem facing the Army of the Potomac: lack of adequate information on the enemy's location and plans. He wrote, "Whether Lee's entire army is here, or whether any part has been detached to Richmond, is a question concerning which we have no positive evidence."[49] Without cavalry to perform reconnaissance or a steady stream of reliable intelligence from spies or deserters, Grant and Meade could only guess at Lee's positions and intentions. Grant and Meade tried breaking Lee's lines several times during the day, learning the lessons of the Wilderness over and over again: well-constructed breastworks in a wooded area, supported by adequate firepower, were virtually impregnable. Upton's column attack had shown that with speed and high casualties such defenses could be breached, but support for such strikes needed to be perfectly coordinated, not left to chance. Also, fast-acting generals could seal the breaches by quickly moving troops from other parts of the line. Furthermore, the Union attacks had been piecemeal, when they needed to be well-coordinated grand assaults.

Military analysts would closely study May 9–10 after the war, looking for options that might have provided success. Andrew Humphreys argued that the critical moment occurred on May 9, when Hancock was ordered to cross the Po River. That movement "put Lee on his guard, and enabled him to bring troops to the threatened flank by daylight of the 10th and throw up entrenchments." Humphreys believed that Hancock should have waited to cross the river until the "daylight of the 10th" and, once across, pushed on sharply (even on the tenth after he stalled in front of the Confederate entrenchments). Others, like Francis Walker, focused on the potential of Upton's attack, finding Mott at fault for failing to "give to Upton a prompt and effective support."[50]

But Walker would not single out Mott or any division commander alone for the failure of the assaults. He wrote that such attacks should have been backed by many divisions, not just one. He argued further, "The characteristic fault of the campaign then opened was attacking at too many points." Instead, the generals should have found the one weak spot and hit it hard. He elaborated, "It is the office of the commander of the army to discover that weak point; to make careful and serious preparation for the attack, and to mass behind the assaulting column a force that shall be irresistible, if only once the line be pierced." To the credit of Grant and Meade, they were beginning to glimpse the possibility of Walker's approach after the events of May 10. Sometime that night or early the next day, the generals decided to find a weak spot in Lee's lines and use the entire Second Corps to exploit it. Several probes of Longstreet's line on the west side of the salient constructed by Ewell's men were made, and they confirmed what the generals tended to believe: the weakest spot of the salient was at the tip of the fortification, close to where Mott had been ordered to attack the day before.[51]

Just before issuing orders on May 11, Grant had breakfast with one of his chief political supporters, Representative Elihu B. Washburne of Illinois, who had been traveling with Grant for ten days. Washburne planned to return to Washington, and he asked Grant if he could bring a message from him to Lincoln and Stanton, conveying his intentions. Grant complied, writing a brief message that would soon become as well-known as his "unconditional surrender" expression at Fort Donelson. He wrote, "We have now ended the sixth day of very heavy fighting. The result to this time is much in our favor. But our losses have been heavy, as well as those of the enemy. . . . I am now sending back to Belle Plain all my wagons for a fresh supply of provisions and ammunition, and *propose to fight it out on this line if it takes all summer*" (author's italics). He also asked for reinforcements and reassured Halleck that the enemy was "very shaky" and that Lee's army was not being divided to attack Butler near Richmond.[52]

Having firmly stated his determination to continue to fight Lee, Grant then turned his complete attention to the next day's offensive. For only the third time since the beginning of the campaign, he issued orders to Meade down to the division level. He ordered Meade to send three divisions of the Second Corps "by the rear of the Fifth and Sixth Corps under cover of night so as to join the Ninth Corps in a vigorous assault on the enemy at 4 am tomorrow." Meade dutifully carried out the order, informing Hancock to use Birney's, Barlow's, and Mott's divisions to "assault the enemy's line from the left of the position now occupied by General Wright and between him and General Burnside."[53]

What Meade thought of this new level of micromanaging is not entirely clear from the written record. Marsena Patrick wrote in his diary on May 11, "He is as cross as a bear, at which I do not wonder, with such a man as Grant over him." But did that comment refer specifically to Grant's orders of May 11? Or did it refer to the relationship in general? Or even to the very specific matter that preceded it? Patrick was frustrated by the fact that no one had helped him get the prisoners of war to Washington. He wrote, "I have been talking with Grant and Dana on the subject, as I can get nothing from Meade." Maybe Meade was just tired of Patrick's pestering—there were many times in the diary when Patrick expressed his anger, resentment, and dislike of Meade. Perhaps the feeling was mutual.[54]

However Meade truly felt, he carried out his orders faithfully. That evening he met with his three corps commanders, and they discussed the role of each corps. Warren was ordered to fill in the holes in the lines left by the departure of the divisions, and to shorten his lines wherever possible. The Sixth Corps was ordered to be ready to move when needed.[55]

The other side of the attack axis rested on the alacrity and ferocity of the Ninth Corps. Grant gave specific and precise orders to Burnside. The Ninth Corps would join the Second Corps "in a vigorous attack against the enemy at 4 am of tomorrow." Grant further ordered, "Move against the enemy with your entire force promptly and with all possible vigor." It is not known whether he shared the contents of the order with Meade, but the entire sentence was meant to relieve the standard concerns about Burnside's promptness, use of his whole force, and energy when attacking. He even sent his aides, Comstock and Babcock, to be with Burnside, "to render . . . every assistance in their power." Warren and Wright would hold their corps in place and join the attack with their "whole force if any opportunity presents itself."[56]

Whether Grant's order assuaged fears of the Army of Potomac generals about Burnside is not clear from the record, but that little confidence existed among the division generals leading the attack is well documented. The fundamental issue was lack of adequate reconnaissance. After the war, Francis Barlow gave a lecture on the attack, and in his trademark sardonic tone, he vividly conveyed some disturbing "truths" about the preparation for the attack. The engineers did not know the distance, the ground to be covered, the strength of the works, or the firepower in the works. Absent any vital information, Barlow formed his division "in column of regiments, each doubled on the center." Barlow and his men then caught a few hours of sleep in the rain and the mud.[57]

Meanwhile, on the opposite side of the field, Confederate soldiers heard sounds of men moving closer to them, en masse. They conveyed their impressions to Maj.

Gen. Edward Johnson, who passed on his concerns to Ewell. Johnson felt better when he was allowed to tell his brigade commanders to expect an attack at daylight. Ewell even got Lee to send some artillery back to the salient (he had removed some earlier in the day when he received reports from Early that Union troops were moving to his right). On Lee's right, Lt. Col. Comstock was actually moving the troops Early's men had heard, striving to reorient Burnside's Ninth Corps to attack in concert with the Second Corps.[58]

As 4 A.M. on May 12 approached, Hancock and his generals decided to wait another half hour for daylight—it was just too dark to attack in that cloud-covered, fog-rising night. Barlow insisted on keeping his men in columns, arguing, "I propose to have men enough, when I reach the objective point, to charge through Hell itself and capture all the artillery they can mass in my front."[59]

At 4:35 A.M. the order "to your commands" launched the largest infantry assault of the Overland Campaign. As the lead elements made their way across a clearing, down into a ravine, then up to the Confederate defenses on a ridge, a spontaneous yell erupted from Barlow's men, drifting back to the thousands of men massed to their rear. Grant and Meade were too far away to hear the yell, but the boom of cannons and the rattle of musketry soon reached them. Grant's aide Porter had just come back from his meeting with Burnside, gulping down a hot cup of coffee as he sat by Grant's fire. Meade arrived soon after Porter, and together the two commanders tried to piece together what was happening from the reports that kept arriving. Hancock's 5 A.M. message conveyed the first bit of good news, "Our men have the works, with some hundred prisoners; impossible to say how many; whole line moving up." This was followed within an hour by a request for more troops: "It is necessary that General Wright should attack at once. All of my troops are engaged." At about the same time, Meade wrote back, "Burnside attacked at the appointed hour. Wright is ordered in at once at your right. Hold all you get and press on." Simultaneously, Grant wrote Burnside, "General Hancock is pushing forward vigorously. He has captured three generals. Push on with all possible vigor." Wright's brigades began attacking the western edge of the salient, and under heavy fire, Wright sought refuge in a "little hollow" from where he directed troops. All the good news made Grant's aide Rawlins so excited that he shouted, "By God! They are done!—Hancock will just drive them to Hell!" His boss, Grant, was more sanguine, only expressing real pleasure when he heard that Hancock had captured several thousand prisoners, "That's the kind of news I like to hear." There was even a moment of warmth and nostalgia amidst the horror and excitement of the early morning: one of the captured Confederate generals, Edward Johnson, was greeted by his old Army acquaintances, Grant and Meade, and taken to breakfast by Seth Williams. (Another general, George H. Steuart, refused to shake hands with Hancock and was sent with the rest of the prisoners to Fredericksburg—on foot).[60]

Yet at this very moment of grand triumph, the entire assault on the salient began to unravel. By 7:15 A.M. Hancock reported that his troops were "in great dis-

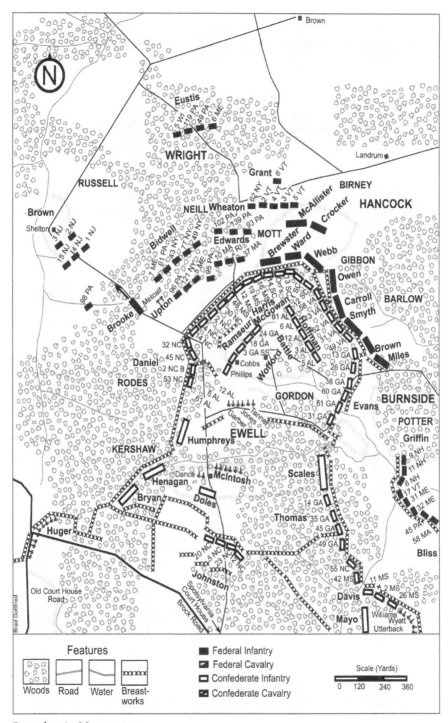

Spotsylvania, May 12, 1864

order." Burnside's attack soon became stalled, despite Grant's urging ("push the enemy with all your might"). Brig. Gen. John B. Gordon had mounted a stiff counterattack with just two brigades, and with thousands of Union troops crammed into a small plot of land, they were able to blunt Barlow's advance. Confederate troops had also stopped Wright. That left only Warren's corps in reserve.[61]

As early as 6 A.M., Meade had instructed Warren to "keep up as threatening an attitude as possible to keep the enemy in your front." He added, "Wright must attack and you may have to." By 7:30 A.M. the situation was more critical. Meade wrote that Wright's right flank had been attacked and that he "wants support." Pressing Warren to help, he wrote, "Your attack will in a measure relieve him, but you must also support him with some of your troops, or you will be turned." Once again, though, Warren failed to follow Meade's orders to attack, and Meade had to repeat his order: "Attack immediately with all the force you can, and be prepared to follow up any success with the rest of your force." Meade and Grant believed that the battle was at a tipping point, and perhaps Warren's attack would break the back of the thin Confederate defenses.[62]

But Warren would not budge. An hour later he wrote to Humphreys, "I cannot advance my men at present." He asked for another brigade of troops (Bartlett's). Humphreys denied his request. Warren responded immediately, "My left cannot advance without a most destructive enfilade fire until the Sixth Corps has cleared its front." He concluded his refusal with the French tactical language taught at West Point: "The enemy's line here appears to be strongly held. It is his *point-d'appui* if he throws back his right."[63]

That was the final straw for Meade. It was Mine Run all over again, except this time his commanding officer, that officer's staff, and Lincoln's handpicked observer, Charles A. Dana, were present. Through Humphreys he sent a stern order: "The order of the major-general is preemptory that you attack at once at all hazards with your whole force, if necessary."[64]

Humphreys, a friend and mentor of Warren's, knew that his protégé's career hung in the balance. He wrote a private, unofficial message to Warren: "Don't hesitate to attack with the bayonet. Meade has assumed the responsibility and will take the consequences." Meade even sent Brig. Gen. Joseph Bartlett's brigade to assist Warren. Reluctantly, Warren obeyed his orders. He told Griffin, "General Meade repeats in most preemptory manner the orders to attack at once with your whole force. Do it. Don't mind consequences." Warren sent the same order to Crawford. He could not, however, resist one more dig at Meade, and at 9:40 A.M. he wrote to his commander: "My lines nearest the salient of the enemy are reported constantly advancing up to the enemy's works. My orders are to attack with the bayonet without regard to consequences that may result unfavorably."[65]

Despite his objections, Warren ordered the attack. It failed miserably, just as he predicted. Griffin's and Cutler's brigades met a solid wall of fire, only finding safety in a ravine. Crawford's brigade met a similar fate. Hearing of the difficulty advancing,

Meade backpedaled a bit, writing to Warren, "Should it fail, make your dispositions to draw in your troops and send them as fast as possible to the support of General Wright and General Hancock." He also sent Humphreys to assess the situation. In the meantime, Meade wrote to Grant, sharing his exasperation: "Warren seems reluctant to assault. I have ordered him at all hazards to do so, and if his attack should be repulsed to draw in the right and send his troops as fast as possible to Wright and Hancock. Tell Hancock to hold on." Grant replied emphatically, "If Warren fails to attack promptly, send Humphreys to command his corps, and relieve him."[66]

Humphreys saved lives—and Warren's job—that morning. When he got there, he concurred with Warren's assessment and called off the attack. Meade then ordered Humphreys to send some of Warren's troops to Wright and Hancock. When Humphreys replied that it would be "some time before the pickets are drawn in from the extreme right," Meade would have none of it. He answered, "Do not wait for the pickets, but move on." Two divisions were then ordered to support Wright and Hancock, thus ending the attack on Laurel Hill that day.[67]

As fighting continued at the salient and Warren's attacks fizzled, Grant tried to breathe new life into Burnside. He wrote to Burnside mid-morning: "Move one division of your troops to the right to the assistance of Hancock, and push the attack with the balance as vigorously as possible. Warren and Wright have been attacking vigorously all day. See that your orders are executed." Burnside finally launched a fresh attack just after noon—at the same time that Early did the same. Both attacks were stopped.[68]

Meade and Grant then attempted to marshal troops for one more assault that day. Meade ordered the Fifth Corps to join the Sixth Corps. He rather optimistically wrote to Grant: "He [Warren] will organize a heavy column of assault from both corps, which I trust will break through the enemy's line. Hancock will press forward at the same time, and I trust Burnside will do the same. Everything is working well on the field by my reports." Grant dutifully informed Burnside of Meade's plan, then instructed him, "Keep your division commander on the lookout to take advantage of any weakening on your front to meet it." If there was one more attack, Burnside's Ninth Corps would definitely be playing a supportive role.[69]

But neither general had adequately considered the consequences of a full day of fierce fighting on the spirit and energy of the men to try another charge. Wright decided to use Cutler's division to relieve some of his "exhausted troops," then put Griffin's and Crawford's divisions into the new column of assault. He soon discovered, however, that the two divisions numbered no more than five thousand men and felt he could furnish only another one thousand men from the Sixth Corps. Sometime between 4:30 and 5:10 P.M., Wright told Humphreys that he could not "insure success," and that after consulting with Hancock, he would "assault, or not, according to [his] discretion and that of General Hancock, unless positively ordered." In fact, he so feared a counterattack that he and Hancock were already "intrenching" to the rear of their position.[70]

To no one's surprise, Wright "pulled a Warren" a few minutes later: he announced he would not "make the assault for the reasons given in the previous dispatch" (insufficient troops and fear of counterattack). Invoking Hancock's name to give credence to his decision, he wrote, "General Hancock desires me to say that he fully concurs in the views I have expressed."[71]

Meade and Grant bowed to this new reality. Meade wrote back to Wright, "Your dispatch abandoning attack received and approved. Rectify your lines and connect with Warren." In a similar message to Burnside, Grant wrote, "You will strengthen your position so as to hold it against any attack of the enemy, and give your men as much rest as you can consistent with your work in fortifying your position." Grant even had Burnside withdraw from the day's advances back to the works built earlier by his men on the east side of the Ni River. The last great assault simply never happened.[72]

The fighting, however, continued at the "Bloody Angle" on the west side of the salient well into the night of May 12. As exhausted soldiers continued to fire into and out of the reinforced works, some Confederates worked past midnight in the softly falling rain to build a new defensive line. Around 3 A.M. on May 13, Confederate troops quietly withdrew from the salient. The longest day of continuous fighting in the Civil War had ended.[73]

In the morning of May 13, Union skirmishers pinpointed the extent of Lee's withdrawal. While he had abandoned the salient, he now had a new fortified line stretching from just west of the Block House Road to south of the Brick Kiln. While the generals on both sides tried to divine the other side's next move, surgeons operated around the clock and Union soldiers began burying the dead. The horrors of that day's fighting at the Bloody Angle and elsewhere in the salient have been described by many, including Horace Porter: "Our own killed were scattered over a large space near the 'angle,' while in front of the captured breastworks the enemy's dead, vastly more numerous than our own, were piled upon each other in some places four layers deep, exhibiting every ghastly phase of mutilation. Below the mass of fast-decaying corpses, the convulsive twitching of limbs and the writhing of bodies showed that there were wounded men still alive and struggling to extricate themselves from their horrid entombment."[74]

Though Porter's impressions were initially confirmed by Humphreys's estimate of Union losses of 6,820 (compared to Confederate losses close to 8,000), later estimates (and modern ones) put Union losses closer to 9,000.[75] May 12 was the bloodiest day of the fighting around Spotsylvania Court House, rivaling each day of the Wilderness for casualties. And for what? The lessons of the Wilderness were either verified by the bloodbath in the fight for control of the salient or still insufficiently understood by Grant and Meade. Though Upton and Hancock had proved that stiff defensive works could be carried under just the right conditions, those perfect circumstances rarely existed, and even if they did, the successive problems of reinforcement and lack of space to maneuver fresh troops had yet to be solved.

In terms of leadership, the top Union generals had been found wanting again and again. Grant had shown quick instincts for attack, but the terrain, the troops (especially the commanders), the intelligence (gained from reconnaissance), and his opponent had not accommodated his plans. His impulsive decision to allow Sheridan to ride off with virtually his entire cavalry deprived him of critical information on Lee's positions and movements. He had largely continued to work *through* Meade, but the relationship frayed under the stress of constant combat. And neither general played an active or inspirational role for their soldiers, unlike Lee, who was often seen guiding troops to spots on the battlefield.

Meade continued to labor under an exceedingly difficult command relationship. Though his role as commander of the Army of the Potomac was in fact more active than asserted by contemporaries or most historians, he still worked in the shadow of Grant and his staff. While almost all the orders to the Army of the Potomac bear his name, at some critical moments, Grant took direct command, thus undercutting Meade's authority. To extrapolate from those instances that Grant made *all* the decisions is conjecture, but given Meade's dutiful and cautious nature, it is safe to assume he discussed important maneuvers with Grant.

Equally burdensome to Meade were the independent corps commanders, Sheridan and Burnside. Sheridan practically refused to work under Meade, and while his departure undoubtedly reduced tension at headquarters, the entire Union army paid a price for his absence. Burnside remained under Grant's direct command, which relieved Meade of supervising him but never lessened his dependence on one of the more cautious—and undependable—army commanders in the field. As for Meade's corps commanders, Wright had proven to be steady. Hancock continued to be his most reliable, aggressive corps commander, though even he had some moments of indecision in the deadly terrain around Spotsylvania. Warren's insubordination had reached new heights, and it was only a paternal fondness for his headstrong protégé that kept Warren in command—for the time being. Meade's sole rock in the storm was his chief of staff, Andrew Humphreys. He had proven to be a good choice: intelligent, analytical, attentive to details, thoughtful, good at planning, and pretty good at Army politics. Though he had the same tendencies toward self-aggrandizement and self-promotion that characterized most of the top Union generals, for now he was still loyal and helpful to Meade.

As the soldiers and officers adjusted to the new lines and took care of the wounded and dead, the commanding generals on both sides plotted their next moves. Grant had shown his determination to keep the pressure on Lee, and the test of the next month would be whether the commander of the Army of the Potomac and his troops could withstand the sacrifice that relentless pursuit would entail.

≋EIGHT≋

The "Hammering" Continues

From Spotsylvania to Cold Harbor

As the longest day of fighting in the Civil War stretched until nearly midnight, the commanding generals got what sleep they could before beginning another day of war. Once the armies sufficiently probed each other the next day, it would be time to consider the Battle of Spotsylvania Court House officially over. Twice more the armies would clash in big battles in the next three weeks, before the Overland Campaign would come to an end. The awkward command relationship of Grant and Meade at Spotsylvania would be continually tested, with a somewhat surprising twist by mid-June.

All that lay in the future on May 13. It is not known if Meade snatched any sleep that night because as early as 12:15 A.M., Humphreys wrote to Wright asking him if he planned to release Griffin's division. Other generals were up as well: Wright responding to Humphreys, Hancock replying to Humphreys, and even Grant sending orders to Burnside to send out men to determine the new position of the Confederates. At first light, Hancock sent sharpshooters into the "enemy's works," and they found that their enemy had fallen back by two miles.[1]

As Union troops gingerly probed the extent of the Confederate retreat that morning, the commanding generals were busy collecting information on the just-concluded battles and soliciting recommendations for promotion. After corresponding with each corps commander, Meade made recommendations to Grant, which he forwarded to Halleck in Washington. Wright and Gibbon would be promoted to major general, and Carroll, Upton, and William McCandless (Pennsylvania Reserves) to brigadier general. Grant added four names to this list: Grenville M. Dodge (to major general from his western army); Hancock to be promoted to brigadier general in the regular army; and Sherman and Meade be promoted to major generals in the regular army. He added some compliments for good effect: "General

Meade has more than met my most sanguine expectations. He and Sherman are the fittest officers for large commands I have come into contact with." If they were promoted, he would feel "personally gratified." And to forestall any jealousy or rancor, he closed his letter with a request: "I would not like to see one of these promotions at this time without seeing both."[2]

Grant shared his recommendations with Meade, who in turn would share them with his wife Margaret two days later. Though Meade wrote modestly of his own recognition, he had to feel pride after reading Grant's reasoning. He wrote to Margaret, "I told him I was obliged to him for his good opinion, but that I asked and expected nothing from the Government, and that I did not myself attach any importance to being in the regular army, so long as I held an equal rank in the volunteer service."[3] As usual, Meade was not being honest with his wife or himself in regard to promotions: few things wounded his pride more than being unrecognized through promotion for his services. Yet he continued to write both statements of humility and pique over slights for his service throughout his military career.

Though it is not recorded *when* Grant showed Meade his recommendation, he may have waited until he had heard back from Edwin Stanton on May 14. In his reply, Stanton discussed Grant's recommendations one by one (all but Gibbon and Dodge got the promotions—theirs depended on vacancies to open), finishing with a promise, "Your recommendations in favor of Meade and Sherman will be carried out."[4]

Grant probably did not share with Meade the substance of another conversation that occurred on May 13 among his staff. According to Horace Porter, an "animated discussion took place at headquarters that day regarding General Meade's somewhat anomalous position, and the embarrassments which were at times caused on the field by the necessity of issuing orders through him instead of direct to the corps commanders." Strong arguments were made for Grant to take command of the Army of the Potomac: too much "time was often lost" in passing orders through Meade; the transmission of orders to corps commanders "might be either so curtailed or elaborated as to change their spirit"; Meade's position was "in some measure a false one; that few responsibilities were given him, and yet he was charged with the duties of an army commander"; and finally, he had "an irascible temper, and often irritated officers who came in contact with him." Grant, as usual in Porter's descriptions of his conduct and thought processes, listened carefully and quietly to his staff, then rose above their petty complaints with his judgment: "I am fully aware that some embarrassments arise from the present organization, but there is more weight on the other side of the question. . . . Meade has served a long time with the Army of the Potomac, knows its subordinate officers thoroughly, and led it to a memorable victory at Gettysburg." He added, "General Meade and I are in close contact on the field; he is capable and perfectly subordinate, and by attending to the details he relieves me of much unnecessary work, and gives me more time to think to mature my general plans. I will always see that he gets full credit for what he does." Still, Porter noted that "after that day he [Grant] gave a closer personal direction in battle to the movements of subdivisions of the armies." He also pointed out that, to his credit, "Meade manifested an excellent spirit through all the embarrassments which his position at times entailed."[5]

Porter must have kept extensive notes of that meeting to recall all the fine details forty years later, but even if the discussion was a compilation of several discussions, it revealed the concerns of Grant and his staff about the awkward command relationship. It put Grant in a most favorable light, but that was true of all of Porter's memoir. Another contemporary of the two generals, Andrew Humphreys, described the same problem in his analysis of the Virginia campaigns of 1864 and 1865: "There were two officers commanding the same army. Such a mixed command was not calculated to produce the best results that either singly was capable of bringing about. It naturally caused some vagueness and uncertainty as to the exact nature of each, and sometimes took away from the positiveness, fullness, and earnestness of the consideration of an intended operation or tactical movement that, had there been but one commander, would have had the most earnest attention and corresponding action." Other contemporaries blamed Meade for any failures of the relationship. Charles Dana wrote, "[Meade] lacked self-confidence and tenacity of purpose, and he had not the moral authority that Grant had attained from his grand successes in other fields." Furthermore, he did not have the "boldness that was necessary to bring the war to a close." But one of Meade's aides, James C. Biddle, saw other forces at work. He wrote to his wife that Meade "has commanded the Army and has once more proved himself an able leader. I do not want to detract from General Grant, but it sickens me the way General Meade has been ignored." He explained further, "All these stories in the newspapers about Grant are disgusting. I have such a good opinion of Grant that I take it for granted they are as repugnant to his feelings. . . . Meade is equal in my opinion if not better than Grant."[6]

Though few contemporaries besides a Meade staffer would have placed Meade's leadership on the same level as Grant's, historian Mark Grimsley goes against the grain of conventional interpretation when he argues that not only did Grant find Meade useful and capable but the "two commanders worked smoothly together" as well. Grimsley finds friction not in their personal relationships but in their "contrasting command styles." He characterizes Grant's style as one of "coping," in which a leader tries to channel "any outcome toward a desired objective." Meade, on the other hand, desired "control." Under this style, a leader tries to "use resources and to manipulate variables so as to guarantee success" (or "avoid failure"). Unfortunately for the Army of the Potomac, this style produced a "cautious, half-defensive mindset" that infected the corps commanders and thwarted Grant's more flexible approach to problems. Whether this distinction accurately reflects the decisions and reasoning of Grant and Meade, it does open up a new perspective on their obvious difference in approach and reaction to battles.[7]

However one views Meade's leadership style, he had become quite despondent about his situation after Spotsylvania. On May 23 he wrote to his wife, "If there were any honorable way of retiring from my present false position I should undoubtedly adopt it, but there is none and all I can do is to patiently submit and bear with resignation the humiliation which few know."[8]

Despite his frustration and sense of hopelessness, Meade felt it was his duty to stay at his post; he had an army to run and a war to win. To those ends, he asked his corps commanders to send him detailed information on what they had captured or retrieved from the field of battle. Using this information, Meade tried to rally his tired army with stirring rhetoric in a May 13 circular. He praised them for their "heroic deeds and noble endurance of fatigue and privations" and also noted the "18 guns, 22 colors, and 8,000 prisoners" taken. He emphasized that the battles *had* accomplished an objective: "You have compelled him [the enemy] to abandon his fortifications on the Rapidan." But their work was not finished, and "the enemy must be pursued, and, if possible, overcome." He shared the praise of Edwin Stanton, who wrote Meade that the "Department congratulates you and your heroic army, and returns its cordial thanks for their gallant achievements during the last seven days, and hopes that the valor and skill thus far manifested will be crowned with the fruits of ultimate and decisive victory."[9]

To obtain that "ultimate victory," Lee's army had to be pressed. Showing some of that stronger "guiding hand," Grant ordered Meade on the morning of May 13 to "push with at least three good divisions to see beyond doubt what they are doing." Meade dutifully responded, ordering Hancock, Wright, and Warren to each "throw forward a division of their respective commands to feel the enemy's position." They did so, and found that Lee's lines held firm. With that information in hand, Grant and Meade devised a new plan.[10]

Essentially, Grant and Meade sought to turn Lee's right east of Spotsylvania Court House. There would be a night march followed by a surprise attack on Lee's right the next morning. The less-depleted Fifth Corps would be the tip of the spear, first slowly peeling away from its entrenchments, then marching behind the other corps to the extreme left of the current Union line (on Fredericksburg Road). It would be followed by the Sixth Corps. Once the two corps got into position, they would attack the weakest part of Lee's line. To increase Union firepower, Grant ordered Burnside "to support them if required."[11]

Unfortunately, despite exhortations from Warren that "officers will make every exertion to keep their men closed up regardless of the mud," problems of movement surfaced almost immediately. Warren's artillery found itself blocked by "endless trains on their way to Belle Plain," his supply wagons arrived late and were "greatly in the way," and the roads proved to be so muddy that they created a "vast amount of straggling." As for Wright, he could not even put his Sixth Corps in motion until just shy of 3 A.M. when the "rear of General Warren's column" passed him. He wrote to Meade, "It will not be possible for me to get into position at 4 o'clock." The "dense fog and drizzling rain" that started after midnight only exacerbated the problems for the marchers.[12]

Meade forwarded Warren's situation to Grant at 6 A.M. on May 14, emphasizing Warren's assessment that "he doubts the practicability of getting his command into a condition to do anything today." Admitting his failure in his next dispatch, Warren wrote, "My inability to get my men here prevented" a surprise attack at dawn. Even worse, only a few of his men had arrived at the designated position, and those were "exhausted with fatigue." He then asked, "Have you any further directions to give in view of this statement?" Meade digested this news, then replied, "The major general has no further instructions to give except that you report as soon as your force is together." Bowing to the reality of the moment, even Grant recognized the impossibility of attack at that time, writing to Halleck that the "very heavy rains of the last forty-eight hours have made it almost impossible to move trains or artillery. Two corps were moved last night . . . but owing to the difficulties of the road have not fully got into position. This with the continued bad weather may prevent offensive operations today." Within the next two hours, the two commanding generals suspended the attack planned for the day.[13]

Much of the remainder of the day was occupied with Union efforts to take, and hold, the prominent Myers Hill that loomed on the south side of the Ni River. In the morning, Meade ordered Warren and later Wright to seize the hill. Col. El-well S. Otis led two regiments for the Fifth Corps, and Col. Emory Upton led his brigade from the Sixth Corps in the spirited attack on the hill. The Confederate cavalry that held the hill retreated under bombardment, and by late morning the hill was in Union hands. In the afternoon, Meade and Wright crossed the Ni to inspect Upton's line of hastily built defenses, when suddenly a brigade of Georgia troops under Brig. Gen. Ambrose Wright assaulted the hill in force, supplemented by artillery and dismounted cavalry. Upton's brigade was forced to retreat back across the Ni, with Meade and Wright barely escaping. Meade's aide Biddle described the tense moment in a letter to his wife: "[Meade] was obliged to cross the Ni for safety; fortunately Captain Micheler was with him who knew of a ford." Now it was Meade's turn to get serious about controlling the hill, so in the early evening, troops from the Fifth and Sixth Corps assaulted the hill again, and Early ordered his men on the hill to retreat before they were captured. After two days of frustrating delays, Meade finally had something to feel good about, writing to Warren, "I thank you and Ayres for taking the hill; it was handsomely done."[14]

After the hill had been secured, Warren noticed Confederate troops moving to his left. He informed Meade of the development, and Meade shifted more of his troops south. He wrote to Grant, "Don't you think Hancock had better move around, starting before day tomorrow. I would like to get the Army of the Potomac together, and Burnside would have the right flank." Grant authorized this move, and, according to Gordon Rhea, he preferred to have Hancock's Second Corps as his potential shock troops, rather than Warren's Fifth Corps. At 10 P.M. Meade ordered Hancock to move all but one division south, along the "route taken by the 6th Corps this morning."[15]

On Sunday, May 15, the Second Corps left its position north of the infamous salient at Spotyslvania to join the bulk of the army spread out along the south side of the Ni River. Grant had hoped to attack the Confederate line that day but wrote to Halleck at 7 A.M. that "the very heavy rains of the last three days have rendered the roads so impassable that but little will be done until there is a change." But there was not a change, as the rains continued all day. Meade ordered each corps commander, "Hold your command ready at short notice to advance against the enemy in your front." But the order never came. The corps were too spread out, roads and fields a sea of mud, and the men fatigued. At 7:45 P.M. Meade sent out new orders: "The directive to be in readiness to attack is rescinded." An assault would have to wait another day.[16]

That day would not be May 16. Charles A. Dana wrote in his daily dispatches to Stanton, "The rain has continued at intervals, and the mud is as bad as ever." Those conditions pushed Grant to make a key decision: "All offensive operations [will] necessarily cease until we can have twenty-four hours of dry weather." He described the roads in a letter to Halleck as "so impassable that ambulances with wounded can no longer run between here and Fredericksburg." He assured his superiors, though, "that the elements alone have suspended hostilities and that it is in no manner due to exhaustion or weakness on our part."[17]

The lull in the movement and fighting gave Meade and Grant time to study the casualty returns and tend to other matters. In a three-way conversation with Dana, the men found that the Army of the Potomac had 31,851 men listed as killed, wounded, or missing, and the Ninth Corps 5,021 in the same categories. These staggering numbers (one-third of the men who had crossed over the Rapidan two weeks earlier) even shook Grant, who "expressed great regret at the loss of so many men," according to Dana. Dana also remembered Meade interjecting, "Well, General, we can't do these little tricks without losses," which sounds like Meade's well-known sarcasm, though out of character at this early stage in his relationship with Grant.[18]

Grant and Meade then attended to another issue: the superfluousness of the Reserve Corps of Artillery. It had not been used in the campaign so far and had even clogged roads at times. Grant and Meade thought of getting rid of all the Reserve Corps artillery, but Brig. Gen. Henry Hunt convinced them to use the reserve guns as replacements for any worn-out weapons or teams. Each infantry corps would have twelve four-gun batteries in place of the current eight six-gun batteries. Even the usually critical Colonel Wainwright found the change beneficial; as he acknowledged, "The change has at least the advantage of enabling us to put the remaining guns in complete order."[19]

The generals also had an unexpected visit from two politicians, Sen. William Sprague of Rhode Island and Sen. John Sherman of Ohio, who gave Meade some unexpected praise. Lyman comically described these two physical opposites: Sprague was a "small headed, black-eyed sparrow little man," while Sherman was "very tall, as flat as a pancake, and ornamented with a long linen duster that made him look 12 feet high." The two politicians from different parties (Sprague a war Democrat, Sherman a moderate Republican) had a lengthy conversation with Meade, and he wrote his wife that "both were very complimentary to me, and wished me to know that in Washington it was well understood these were my battles." Meade had a curious response to these compliments. He wrote Margaret, "I told them such was not the case; that at the first I had maneuvered the army, but that gradually, and from the very nature of things, Grant had taken the control; and that it would be injurious to the army to have two heads." Meade refined this view further, saying that the editor Henry Coppee "about hits the nail on the head" when he wrote in the *United States Service Magazine* that the Army of the Potomac was "'directed by Grant, commanded by Meade, and led by Hancock, Sedgwick, and Warren.'"[20]

It is Meade's own analysis that an army cannot have "two heads" that has influenced generations of historians. The standard interpretation is to see Meade as Grant's chief of staff over the Army of the Potomac, and thus make Grant the primary decision maker. Gordon Rhea, for example, argues that "Grant informally relegated the blustery army commander to the role of staff officer seeing that the Army of the Potomac did Grant's bidding."[21] Even Meade sometimes complained of this tendency in private letters. But a close reading of the original sources nudges one to look more closely at Coppee's characterization. While Grant set the operational parameters for the Army of the Potomac, Meade was its tactician ("commanded by Meade"). It is therefore analogous to Grant's direction of Butler's Army of the James, not, by contrast, Grant's direct command of the two armies at Chattanooga.

So as the two generals continued to work out their command relationship, they also had to figure out Lee's next move. So once again they ordered Warren and Wright to "push out [their] skirmishers and pickets, properly supported, to feel the enemy and ascertain whether there is any change in his position." As usual, Warren replied with his own plans. He said he had already sent out his skirmishers "to the edge of the open field, and cannot well be advanced further." Meade had grown tired of Warren's alterations of orders, so he simply wrote, "General Warren was ordered to push out and support developments." Warren would not give up, citing the help of another authority, Colonel Comstock, who had seen his position and "thought we had already developed the condition of affairs in our front." Now the "two heads" problem had reared its ugly head. Meade referred the situation to Grant, who replied, "All I wanted was to be assured that the enemy retained their old position, or if they had taken up a new one, to find out where it was." Meade soon had Comstock's report, and he rescinded his order to advance to Warren. Thankfully, there would be no useless attacks that day, and both sides continued improving their defensive lines.[22]

The next day, May 17, brought renewed vigor to both sides, as the five-day rain finally ended and roads began to dry. Lee received some good news that morning: Sigel had been stopped in the Shenandoah Valley, and Butler had been driven back to Drewry's Bluff. Lee knew he might get reinforcements from the two victorious Confederate armies, though that would take time. Lee ordered his three corps commanders—Anderson, Ewell, and Hill—to strengthen their lines, and their men went it at with gusto. Ewell's corps in particular built high dirt walls with slits for men to shoot from safely. Ewell also had twenty-nine well-protected guns with clear lines of fire.[23]

By contrast, Grant and Meade planned for an attack. The initial plan was for the Second and Sixth Corps to attack the southern end of Lee's line, charging up the Massaponax Church Road. But Wright sent out infantry probes against Anderson's defenses, and found them to be formidable. He discussed his findings with Humphreys, who brought the information to Grant. Hearing the situation, Grant and Meade changed their plan: Hancock and Wright would march to the north and attack over the old Mule Shoe grounds. They reasoned that Lee had weakened his left to strengthen his right.[24]

The day was spent preparing for the night marches. Meade wrote his wife, "I have been riding all day, getting ready for tomorrow's battle." He found some degree of hope in renewed assault, adding that "there is a determination on all sides to fight it out, and have an end put to the war; a result which I think will most certainly be accomplished if we can overcome the army before us." Colonel Wainwright was less sanguine. He wrote in his diary, "The Second and Sixth Corps are to return to the old ground on the right and pitch in there; great things are hoped from it by Grant. I fear he will not find Lee asleep."[25]

That evening and on through the night the men of the Second and Sixth Corps marched to their launch positions. For the Second Corps, some were in the same spot as on May 12. They were heartened by the arrival of eighty-eight hundred fresh troops, almost all "green" soldiers sent by Halleck to replace Hancock's losses. Seeing their condition, Hancock ordered them to hold the line and not join in the attack. The Sixth Corps also returned to familiar ground, with Brig. Gen. Thomas Neill's Second Division connecting with Hancock's right at the Bloody Angle. In many places, men found corpses that had yet to be buried.[26]

As the men marched to their designated positions, Grant updated Burnside. He told him of the change in plans and asked him to be "prepared, however, to follow

Hancock and Wright if they should succeed in breaking through, or to strengthen Warren if the enemy should move on him."²⁷

After six days of false starts and thwarted movements, the long-awaited grand assault began on the morning of May 18 with a Union artillery barrage at 4 A.M. During the night, Grant had changed his mind and ordered Burnside to have two brigades join the initial assault, and they moved out first that morning, stepping into a heavy fog. They soon were pinned down by enfilading artillery fire and could not advance. Hancock's Second Corps waited in vain for Brig. Gen. James Ricketts's Third Division (Sixth Corps) to show up and start the attack, but when it did not, Hancock ordered three of the best combat divisions to attack (Gibbon, Barlow, and Neill). They were stopped in their tracks by twenty-nine Confederate cannons that appeared to fire without ceasing. The Union troops managed to get to a place of refuge just in front of the Confederate lines, where they pressed into the earth and outer lines to protect themselves. When Ricketts's division finally got into position, the firing was too intense to advance.²⁸

After less than an hour of fighting, Hancock wrote to Humphreys (5:40 A.M.), "General Barlow thinks doubtful if our men can penetrate it." At 6:10 A.M. Brig. Gen. Robert Potter wrote Burnside that he had connected with Barlow's division, but that he could not "advance much further." At 6:15 A.M. Meade told Hancock to see if Wright had found a "practicable point of attack." Wright immediately responded, "I have not found a practicable point of attack yet." A half hour later, Hancock was even more pessimistic, writing, "The division commanders think that the point is impracticable for attack on their fronts; but I am holding them, but awaiting developments from General Wright." As Meade and Grant discussed their options, the men of the Second Corps withstood a fierce barrage of artillery fire. When Hancock's next message arrived at 8:30 A.M., "nothing has been heard from General Wright," it tipped the scales for Grant and Meade: they called off the attack and ordered the troops to withdraw and form a "defensive position."²⁹

In some ways it may have been the nadir of operations since the fighting at the Bloody Angle on May 12. Over twelve thousand men had been stopped, and mauled, by twenty-nine well-positioned cannons inflicting over fifteen hundred casualties in just three hours. Confederate losses were under one hundred. As Lyman wrote in his journal, "So far from being surprised, the rebels had spent the last days in strengthening their fronts and had rendered it impregnable." He continued, capturing the mood at headquarters, "It was a depressing day!"³⁰ Adding to the gloom at headquarters was the news that finally reached Grant that morning: Sigel's and Butler's armies had been defeated.

But Grant never brooded about failures. Instead, he made plans to swing the Army of the Potomac south, forcing Lee to abandon his defenses and either fight him or move to protect Richmond. This time there was no discussion with Meade: Grant sent detailed orders to Meade later that day, showing that for this next move, *he* was firmly in charge of the Army of the Potomac. Though Meade probably bristled at Grant's micromanaging, he expressed his sole consolation in a letter he wrote to his wife: "We found the enemy so strongly entrenched that even Grant thought it useless to knock our heads against a brick wall, and directed a suspension of the attack."[31]

The major movement of the Union army to the south took place in stages. The first stage was a night march by the Second Corps from Massaponax Church to Anderson's Mill, a distance of twenty miles. The Ninth Corps followed and by daylight of May 19 held the southern end of the Union line. Wright's Sixth Corps took over the Ninth Corps' position, setting up new lines in front of Myers Hill. The Fifth Corps remained in position, holding the northern end of the Union line at daybreak.[32]

The tiring night march led to a day of rest for most of the soldiers, except Confederate troops in Ewell's Second Corps and a heavy artillery brigade serving under Col. G. Howard Kitching in Warren's Fifth Corps. Lee knew that Grant was shifting his army south, but he wanted more information to determine whether Grant was planning a new attack, retreating to a base to the east, or beginning a major move to the south. He ordered Ewell to "find Grant's right" and "develop his purpose." Find it he did, attacking Kitching's brigade in the late afternoon at Harris's farm. When Grant and Meade heard the sounds of musket fire to their north, they sprang into action. They sent reinforcements to Kitching, and as veteran troops poured into the field it was Ewell's turn to worry. His men held on until dark, when they slipped away. Ewell suffered nine hundred casualties in his attack, but the green troops under Kitching suffered more, fifteen hundred casualties. But they had held their ground well, and the next day Meade gave them a special commendation for their valor. After that day, they were no longer teased for being "band box" soldiers.[33]

Later that evening, Grant decided not to put his army into motion after midnight. He wrote Halleck, "Not knowing their [Lee's army] exact position, and the danger our trains at Fredericksburg will be in if we move, I shall not make the move designated for tonight until their designs are fully developed."[34]

Grant's decision gave a well-needed second day of rest to the tired infantry, though some units were shuffled into new positions to prepare for another night march. At 1 P.M. on May 20 Meade instructed Hancock to march using the orders of May 19, though he did have the latitude to start at a time that would "best secure the object of the expedition." His corps would march to "Bowling Green and Milford Station, via Guiney's Station," taking "position on the right bank of the Mattaponi, if practicable." If he ran into Confederates, he was to "attack [them] vigorously." He would be accompanied by Torbert's cavalry brigade, a battery of horse artillery, an engineer, and guides. Warren was ordered to move south as well, following Hancock the next day to Massaponax Church, where he would turn south on Telegraph Road. Wright would hold the right of the Union line, and Burnside the left.[35]

For the moment, Grant and Meade had the initiative. Lee was trying to figure out how to protect Hanover Junction from Sheridan's cavalry (who were returning from Richmond), while arguing with Beauregard about the wisdom of combining their armies. In the end, Davis and his new chief military advisor, Braxton Bragg, agreed that Lee's army should be left alone to fight as he saw fit. Still, Lee received information that led him to believe that Grant would shift south, down Telegraph Road. Lee countered that move with one of his own: Ewell's Second Corps would leave its line, march behind the army, and entrench at Mud Tavern. Meanwhile, good news arrived during the day: Sheridan could not cross the swollen Pamunkey River, and four infantry brigades were being sent to him from Richmond, two already en route to Milford Station.[36]

Though Lee had a counter plan, Grant and Meade had the lead, and they used it. For once a Union army corps left earlier than expected, with the Second Corps beginning its march at 10 P.M. By 5:30 A.M. on May 21 Hancock had reached Guinea Bridge, and by 9 A.M., the van of the Second Corps reached the village of Bowling Green. Though some men had learned the art of sleepwalking that night, others were pleased to find themselves in a rich agricultural county (Caroline) that had yet to be picked clean by soldiers.[37]

But Lee had not been idle during the night. By 4 A.M. on May 21, he had Ewell's Second Corps marching behind his other corps, and by mid-morning, they had reached their objective of Mud Tavern. That effectively blocked Warren's intended march down Telegraph Road, and rather than send the men against Ewell's rapidly constructed defensive works, Meade and Grant changed their plans. At 9:45 A.M. Meade sent an order to Warren to "proceed to Guiney's Bridge by way of Massaponax Church and Guiney Station [Hancock's route], instead of taking the Telegraph Road for Massaponax Church." Wright was updated as well, being told to "follow Hancock's route." As for Burnside, Grant told him to follow Warren. Hancock's new orders were to hold Guiney's Bridge until the "head of Warren's column" reached him (unfortunately, by the time Hancock got this message at 3 P.M. he was long gone from the bridge).[38]

Once Grant and Meade were satisfied that Warren's withdrawal from his sector of the Union line was underway, they left with their staffs, riding ahead of the Fifth Corps. They stopped for a time at Massaponax Church, where Timothy O'Sullivan took a now-famous photograph of the generals and their staffs sitting on the pews dragged out in the churchyard. It may be illustrative of the relationships that had formed by then that Charles Dana sat on Grant's left and his chief aide Rawlins sat on his right, while Meade sat at the end of the pew perpendicular to Grant's pew. They stayed until 1:40 P.M., when they took off again and rode ahead of the Fifth Corps. They stopped at the home of George Motley, a "good house," according to Lyman, with "strawberries beginning to ripen and apples as big as bullets." Before the generals could rest, however, something had to be done about the Confederate cavalry seen at the Guiney Bridge. The only troops available to chase them off were the headquarters guard, the 114th Pennsylvania, under the command of the flamboyant Col. Charles T. Collis, and Maj. James Walsh's Third Pennsylvania Cavalry. Meade ordered Provost Marshal Patrick to "drive them out," and his men did just that. Collis wrote a message to Meade mimicking the famous line written by Oliver Perry after the Battle of Lake Erie in 1813, "I have met the enemy and he is mine." After that small skirmish, Meade sent a message to Hancock, who had not been heard from since 9 A.M. He admonished him, "The commanding general considers that with the cavalry force placed at your disposal, you should have kept open communication with him during the day, and he wishes you use this cavalry force in keeping up frequent communication with these headquarters." Unfortunately, the time lag in communication would continue: they would not hear from Hancock for hours.[39]

Hancock had been operating on his own all day. He had reached Bowling Green, then pushed on to Milford Station, where he ran into advance units from the Confederate brigades sent up from Richmond to help Lee's army. Not wanting to start a major engagement without knowing how many soldiers he faced or where he could find support, Hancock decided to dig in for the night just west of Milford Station.[40]

Given the dearth of information from Hancock during the day, and signs that Lee's army was on the move, Grant and Meade decided to concentrate their forces further south. Warren was ordered to head south and cross the Ta River; Burnside's orders were to take the "direct ridge road"; and Wright was told to follow Burnside. The Fifth and Ninth Corps marched to their new positions during the evening and through the night, while Wright's Sixth Corps attempted to settle in for an uneasy rest that long night.[41]

Little did the generals know as they snatched a few hours of sleep the night of May 21–22 that a superb opportunity to strike Anderson's corps presented itself. Anderson's corps had left their trenches by 8 P.M. and marched wearily down the Telegraph Road, which Ewell's corps had marched on earlier. At one point, only a mile separated Anderson's tired marchers from Warren's soldiers sleeping between Guiney Bridge and Mud Tavern (Crawford's division). But the exhausted Union troops never stirred, and General Lee had no desire to start a battle with only one corps at hand (he wanted to get to the North Anna River before Grant and Meade).[42] So an opportunity was ignored by both sides as the weary foot soldiers finally left the bloody and foreboding Wilderness for good.

There would be no time to analyze the extended battles in the Wilderness for the tired Union generals. Without sufficient cavalry to probe and harass Lee's marching columns (Sheridan had not yet returned from his Richmond raid), the Union army leadership was operating blindly. The Sixth Corps stumbled through another exhausting night march, and the Fifth Corps finally left its works at 9:30 A.M. on May 22.[43]

The effort to concentrate the corps was brought together in a general order that went out on May 22. The Second Corps would remain at Milford, the Fifth Corps would march to Harris's store (and stop there), the Sixth Corps would encamp behind the Fifth Corps, and the Ninth Corps and army headquarters would bivouac at New Bethel Church. All wagons would be moved to Bowling Green. The few remaining cavalry units were assigned to three corps. By mid-afternoon the corps had reached their assigned positions, and the exhausted infantrymen could finally get some much needed rest.[44]

The half-day of rest for the infantry would turn into a day of humiliation for George Meade. After just a little rest on the night of May 21–22, Meade said mournfully to Lyman at breakfast, "I am afraid the rebellion cannot be crushed this summer." His mood was not lightened by the inevitable traffic snarls the army wrestled with as the corps slowly made their way to their assigned positions. He and Grant rode with their staffs in the afternoon to New Bethel Church, where they stayed on the Tyler plantation. Sometime during that evening Grant and Meade discussed their next step, with Grant advocating a pursuit of Lee to the North Anna River, even if it meant more direct fighting. Meade argued for a wide sweeping move to the southeast, headed for the Pamunkey River. The army could follow the Second Corps, meet up with Sheridan's cavalry at White House, and march to the battlefields of the Seven Days campaign. But Grant overruled him, as Provost Marshal Patrick noted in his diary, "Meade was opposed to our crossing the North Anna, but Grant ordered it, *over his head*" (author's italics). Then, in the most direct sequence of command yet officially visible in the Overland Campaign, Meade sent out an order to his army *from* Grant that had detailed instructions for each corps movement on May 23. It began, "The following order has been received and is published for the guidance of all concerned." Grant detailed the time of readiness (5 A.M.), the role of the cavalry, and the precise movements each corps would make the following morning.[45] After three weeks of working through Meade, Grant had finally torn the veil off that structure and resorted to direct command.

This naked assertion of power led Meade to his strongest complaint about Grant to that date: the May 23 letter to his wife in which he lamented his "false position." He attempted to soften the implications it made of Grant by adding, "I don't think he is a very magnanimous man, but I believe he is above any littleness, and whatever injustice is done me, and it is idle to deny that my position is a very unjust one, I believe it is not intentional on his part, but arises from the force of circumstances, and from that weakness in human nature which compels a man to look to his own interests." Meade's case was also argued by his aide, James Biddle, in a letter he wrote to his wife on June 4. He insisted that Grant left "everything to General Meade—whom I consider as far superior as a general—his talents have shown out in this campaign, and I am sure Grant appreciates them."[46]

Regardless of his personal feelings toward Grant and his increasingly impotent role as commander of the Army of the Potomac, Meade still had an army to manage. All the corps marched on their designated roads the morning of May 23, while Grant and Meade left the Tyler plantation to make a new headquarters at the Moncure house. On the ride to Moncure's, Grant pulled ahead of Meade on his "black Mississippi pony," which irked Meade who, according to Lyman, "pushed on with his big trotter, beating Grant very soon, and followed by staff and orderlies as best they could." Meade's frustrations had boiled over into a mini–horse race. More adventure occurred when Meade discovered a house occupied by four single women. Concerned for their safety, Meade left a guard at the house to protect the women from "stragglers."[47]

By early afternoon, the generals had established their respective headquarters at the Moncure farm. Warren had pushed his corps to the North Anna River at Jericho Mills, where he sent his lead units to ford the river. Reflecting the new arrangement of command, Meade did not immediately send new orders to Warren. Instead, he sent on Warren's message to Grant, and asked him, "Should he go on or hold the crossing? What should Wright do; cross after Warren or go to some point higher up?" Grant quickly replied with detailed instructions: "The Fifth Corps will occupy the bank of the river to cover and hold Jericho Ford. The Sixth Corps will take place on the right of the Fifth Corps. If any bridge or ford is to their front it will be seized and held; if none in front efforts will be made to open roads to the river at points where crossings may be effected to their front." Grant also had specific plans for the other corps. The Second Corps would camp at the New Bridge on the North Anna and secure it, crossing the river "if possible." The Ninth Corps would march to the right of the Second Corps and seize Ox Ford (which crossed the North Anna River west of New Bridge). With these directions before him, Meade ordered Warren to cross the river and entrench.[48]

For once in the past few days, the Union generals had the jump on Lee. Most of his men spent the day resting after their long marches. Lee believed that Grant and Meade would move in the direction of Milford Station. Lee asked Davis if he could have the aid of Beauregard's army to take the offensive. Davis did not respond to the request immediately. Lee's main concern was to keep the Union troops from crossing the Chickahominy River.[49]

Lee's belief left two of his units sitting in the path of approaching Union infantry corps. At Henagan's Redoubt (a bridge built in 1863 to protect the Chesterfield Bridge) on the north side of the river was Kershaw's South Carolina brigade, commanded by Col. John Henagan. Up the river a few miles was Jericho Mills, with the Virginia Central Railroad tracks a mile to the southwest. The tracks were protected by the Fourteenth South Carolina of McGowan's Brigade (at Noel's Station). These were the infantry troops spotted by Warren's skirmishers after they crossed the river and marched inland a bit.[50]

These two units (and a few others) would pay the price for Lee's misreading of Grant and Meade's movements. At 2:35 P.M. Hancock wrote to Meade asking whether he should "force a crossing." In keeping with the day's pattern of communication, Meade sent the question on to Grant. He replied, "By all means."

Hancock soon discovered that his men had forded a creek, not a river, and that a redoubt guarded the Chesterfield Bridge. Hancock prepared for a much bigger undertaking, and with artillery opening at 5:30 P.M., sent Birney's division to drive out the defenders of the redoubt. With gusto and superior numbers they accomplished their mission, though they were unable to take and hold the bridge as well.[51]

Over at Jericho Mills, Confederate Maj. Gen. William H. F. "Rooney" Lee arrived after 5 P.M. with erroneous information. He told Col. Joseph N. Brown (commanding McGowan's Brigade) that two cavalry brigades had crossed the river and, if attacked, could be easily pushed back across the river. So he attacked, but it was not cavalry they assaulted but Griffin's First Division of the Fifth Corps. Catching Griffin off guard, they managed to push back some units toward the North Anna River. But not for long. With steady support from Wainwright's artillery and counterattacks by Cutler's Fourth Division, the Confederates were driven back to Noel's Station. With darkness descending, Warren decided to stop the counterattack.[52]

The two victories after so many days of frustrating marches and feints led to some gloating on the Union side. Meade praised Warren and his "gallant corps for the manner in which [they] repulsed the enemy's attack." Hancock called Birney's capture of the redoubt among the "most brilliant assaults of the war." Even Grant caught the spirit of hyperbole, writing to Halleck late that night that "everything looks favorable to us."[53]

But not everyone felt so elated. Though Wainwright was justly proud of the stand his batteries had made—"all three opened within canister range, and did not spare ammunition"—he found Warren at one point to be a "good deal scared," and noted that the "infantry were so shaken that the batteries had to keep up a steady fire. The roar of the twenty brass guns in position was continuous." Wainwright was also miffed and complained, "Warren has not given me one word of commendation for myself or my batteries."[54]

No Union general would have felt so satisfied if he had any idea of Robert E. Lee's next move. That evening Lee sat down with his generals and engineers to decide on the next step. The key question was whether to protect Hanover Junction (intersection of the Virginia Central Railroad and the Richmond, Fredericksburg, and Potomac Railroad) or fall back to the Chickahominy River. Consensus formed around guarding Hanover Junction. What Lee did, however, was one of the most daring defensive maneuvers of the war. Relying on the keen eye and all-day exploration of the terrain performed by his chief engineer, Maj. Gen. Martin Smith, Lee decided to pull together his army into an inverted V. Hill's corps would cover the Virginia Central Railroad and stretch its defenses to the North Anna River along the old stage road from Richmond. Anderson's line would begin at Ox Ford and run southeast along high bluffs to Miller's farm. There Ewell's corps would construct a small L-shaped line that straddled the Richmond, Fredericksburg, and Potomac Railroad, then turned south to cover Hanover Junction. Gordon's division would be in reserve for Ewell, while Breckinridge's and Pickett's divisions would play the same roles for Hill and Anderson. The exposed formation took advantage of the natural elevation, while forcing Union troops to either cross at Ox Ford (a vulnerable point) or cross the Chesterfield Bridge and expose themselves to enfilading fire from Anderson and Ewell. Lee expected the aggressive Grant to cross at both spots, and he planned to move his troops across the interior lines of the inverted V as needed. Moreover, if Warren and Wright marched down the Virginia Central Railroad to attack Lee's left flank, Lee could easily shift troops to reinforce Hill. With the decision made, the generals departed, and their men spent the night erecting defensive fortifications along the new lines.[55]

Not knowing Lee's plan, Grant and Meade operated under the assumption that Lee had retreated (or was retreating), most likely to the South Anna River. Consequently, each Union corps was on the move the morning of May 24, with the goal to have all of them completely across the North Anna. Meanwhile, Warren sent out skirmishers "in every direction," and by 7:30 A.M. they had "possession of the wagon road beyond the railroad." Warren also reported that two of Wright's divisions had crossed the river and were in reserve behind the Fifth Corps.[56]

Bolstered by this good news, Meade and Grant left their tents at Moncure's and rode south to Mt. Carmel Church. On his way there, Meade looked for Hancock, and together they examined his lines. Hancock had questioned two black men who had crossed the river the night before, and they said the Confederates (under Gordon) had left their rifle pits and marched toward Hanover Junction. Meade talked to the two men as well, and wrote to Grant, "From what they say the enemy has fallen back beyond the South Anna." The two men also offered up a bit of local knowledge that would be crucial to the Union troops later that day: there was a "good ford (Quarles's) between Warren and Burnside." Meade sent one of the men with an officer to Burnside to share the information, recommending that Burnside cross at this ford "if opposed at Ox Ford." Meade had also finally heard from Sheridan, who was "this side of the Pamunkey, near Dunkirk." Sheridan was out of forage and had tired horses. Reverting to his new role, Meade asked Grant, "Had he better come to the train and feed and rest?" Though Grant did not officially answer, Sheridan's men did just that. Grant updated Halleck on the situation, "The enemy have fallen back from North Anna; we are in pursuit." For the moment, he wanted Butler to remain where he was but to prepare Smith's army to move. He added, "I will probably know today if the enemy intends standing behind South Anna."[57]

It is not known whether Grant shared information from a letter sent the day before from Halleck. It hinted at the political troubles that still dogged Meade. Halleck told Grant that he had put forth Meade and Sherman for promotion to major general, but there was "some obstacle in the way and I can't remove it." He added, "I am not certain what it is but can guess." He could not help himself from revealing more: "I understand the names of Butler and Sickles have been strongly urged by politicians, in order they say to break down 'West Point influence.' It will not be difficult to draw conclusions." For the time being, then, Meade's anticipated promotion would have to wait (even though his political enemies would remain active).[58]

Meanwhile, Grant and Meade established their new headquarters in the morning of May 24 at the "mean little" Mt. Carmel church, and their staffs soon turned the nave into an office, placing some boards across the aisle to make a "table where sat Meade, Grant, General Williams, etc. writing." It was during this quiet moment that Meade wrote to his wife, telling her the Army of the Potomac had "compelled" the Army of Northern Virginia "to fall back from the North Anna River, which they tried to hold. Yesterday Warren and Hancock both had engagements with them, and were successful." He added for emphasis, "We undoubtedly have the morale over them, and will eventually, I think, compel them to go into Richmond; after *nous verrons* [we shall see]."[59]

Yet even in this moment of quiet expectancy, disappointment and frustration lurked in the background for Meade. A courier delivered a telegram to Grant from Sherman, which he then showed to Dana. Seeing another opportunity to needle Meade (whom he disliked), Dana read the telegram out loud. As summarized by Lyman, "The army of the west, having fought, could now afford to maneuver, and that, if his [Grant's] inspiration could make the Army of the Potomac do its share, success would crown our efforts." Lyman noted that Meade's "grey eyes grew like a rattlesnake's," and in a voice "like cutting an iron bar with a handsaw" Meade angrily stated: "Sir, I consider that dispatch an insult to the army I command and to me personally. The Army of the Potomac does not require General Grant's inspiration or anybody else's inspiration to make it fight!" No record of Grant's response was recorded, but Sherman's words bothered Meade all day, and at dinner that night he referred to the western army as an "armed rabble."[60]

Meade did not have the time to continue brooding because he had to get his army across the river, and he soon found himself tracking the movements of several parts of his large force. He urged Warren to send some troops down the south side of the river to help Burnside cross at Ox Ford, which he did. Meade suggested to Grant that Burnside send a "few" men across at Quarles's Mill, which Grant conveyed to Burnside in a message sent at 1 P.M. He ordered Burnside to move his "entire corps, with trains, to the south side of the North Anna this afternoon." If he could not cross at Ox Ford, he should send some troops up to Quarles's Mill, and others to Chesterfield Bridge. Burnside replied that he had already sent Maj. Gen. Thomas Crittenden's First Division to Quarles's Mill, and that he would still try to cross at Ox Ford, though it was difficult. While all this unfolded, Hancock's divisions had crossed the river and fanned out southward, finding limited opposition.[61]

By mid-afternoon, though, the Union advance came to a grinding halt. Crittenden's lead brigade, commanded by the unsteady Brig. Gen. James Ledlie, pushed down the river until it ran into thick earthworks near the apex of the inverted V.

Fueled by alcohol, Ledlie drunkenly led a charge into well-protected Confederate infantry and artillery, which shredded Ledlie's brigade. Ledlie's tattered regiments retreated. At nearly the same time Ledlie's brigade marched toward the inverted V defensive line, Hancock's lead regiments pushed out to the eastern side of the inverted V. They too were pinned down by Confederate musket and artillery fire, and then pushed back by a fierce Confederate counterattack. Only a thunderstorm, followed by darkness, ended the fighting.[62]

With the Union advance stalled, Meade sent out new orders to his corps commanders that evening. Hancock was ordered to entrench, Warren to prepare to move at 4 A.M. the next morning to determine the strength of the Confederate lines, Wright to follow and be on Warren's right, and Burnside to divide his divisions so that some would cross at Chesterfield Bridge and others at Quarles's Mill.[63]

Though stalled, the Union army had avoided a major blow because General Lee had fallen ill with dysentery and did not feel he had a corps commander capable of carrying out a strong attack across the Confederate inverted V. For years after the war, armchair critics argued about the "lost opportunity" of May 24.[64]

That evening, Grant made a crucial decision that either showed new confidence in Meade (thus contradicting his growing assumption of direct command) or perhaps showed that he was trying to determine how to get the maximal performance out of the eastern armies: he assigned Burnside and his Ninth Corps to the Army of the Potomac. Though his special orders stressed the need for the "greatest attainable efficiency in the administration of the army," one wonders if efficiency was the primary motive. Burnside had been dilatory on numerous occasions in the past three weeks, and rarely did the Ninth Corps coordinate easily with other corps. Horace Porter emphasized the time lost in communicating all instructions twice, so at least Grant's staff toed to his official line of reasoning. To Burnside's credit, he accepted the order gracefully. He wrote to Grant, "I am glad to get the order assigning the corps to the Army of the Potomac, because I think good will result from it." According to Porter, when Grant rode by Burnside's tent the next morning, Burnside strode out and said, "That order is excellent; it is a military necessity and I am glad it has been issued." Though awkward (if not humiliating) for Burnside to now serve under a man he once commanded *and* outranked, he at least initially accepted the fact of the new situation.[65]

Early the next morning (May 25), skirmishers from the Fifth Corps and Second Corps probed the Confederate defenses. Warren spent the morning riding over the area and preparing a map. By noon Warren had a sketch of the entire area and he wrote to Meade, "I feel satisfied that I should have great difficulty at best in whipping the enemy in my front." Meade sent Warren's message on to Grant, adding his own recommendation, "Unless Warren attacks, not much more can be done in his front." Agreeing with Meade, Grant replied, "I do not think any attack should be made until preparations are made to use our whole force." Hancock's skirmishers had also been busy that morning, and his chief of staff talked to Colonel Brooke, who found the enemy to be "stronger than last night."[66]

Given this situation, Grant decided it would be best to stay in place for the day, and he wrote Halleck, "[It would] probably take us two days to get in position for a general attack or to turn their position." He also ordered Halleck to send him Butler's army, which had become inactive and bottled up at Bermuda Hundred. He wanted to concentrate his forces, as Lee was doing. He also wanted Maj. Gen. David Hunter to march his army to Charlottesville and Lynchburg, destroying railroads and canals. If possible, he might join up with the Army of the Potomac after he finished his work of destruction.[67]

In the evening, Grant held his own "council" of war to discuss the next move with his top generals. Warren and Hunt proposed doing the unexpected: marching west to hit Lee's left flank. Meade and Grant's aide, Cyrus Comstock, counseled just the opposite: shifting the army east and south, crossing the Pamunkey River, then driving toward Richmond, thus forcing Lee to march south to interpose his army between the Army of the Potomac and Richmond. In the end, Grant went with Meade and Comstock's suggestion, writing to Halleck the next day that he had "determined, therefore, to turn the enemy's right by crossing at or near Hanovertown. This crosses all these streams as once, and leaves us where we can still draw supplies." The Pamunkey River became a critical factor because it could be used to ferry the army's vast provisions as it marched south.[68]

Though Meade did not write to anyone about the adoption of his plan, he must have felt vindicated for earlier suggestions and actions. He had urged this approach three days before, but Grant had rejected it. He could have written to his wife the same message he sent her on May 19, "Even Grant thought it useless to knock our heads against a brick wall." He now felt better about his widely criticized decisions in the fall; Lee had not attacked the Union defenses, Meade wrote, but had "performed the same operation which I did last fall, when I fell back from Culpepper, and for which I was ridiculed; that is to say, refusing to fight on my adversary's terms." He had even predicted Grant's decision on May 23, when he wrote to his wife, "I suppose now we will have to repeat this turning operation, and continue to do so, till Lee gets to Richmond."[69]

Of course, Comstock was pleased as well, while Meade's usually reliable supporter, Wainwright, found this approach foolhardy and blamed Grant. He wrote in his diary: "Can it be that this is the sum of our lieutenant general's abilities? Has he no other resource in tactics? Or is it sheer obstinacy? Three times he has tried this move, around Lee's right, and three times been foiled. . . . Officers and men are getting tired of it and would like a little variety on night marches and indiscriminate attacks on earthworks in the daytime."[70]

Regardless of the views, once Grant made a decision, he rarely second-guessed himself, and this time was no different. In keeping with his new policy of direct command, he sent Meade a detailed order for the movement of the troops, down to the divisional level. Warren and Wright were to move nonessential artillery and wagons to the north side of the river on May 26. The critical artillery and wagons of the Sixth Corps, guarded by Wright's "best division," would march as "far as it can go on the road to Hanovertown without attracting attention." Sheridan's cavalry was ordered to seize Littlepage's Bridge and Taylor's Ford the next day, providing safe passage for the infantry. Wright's division would begin its march to Hanovertown on the night of May 26, and when it left, the Fifth and Sixth Corps would abandon their positions on the south side of the river and cross over to the north side. The "two divisions of the Ninth Corps not now with Hancock" were ordered to cross to the north side of the river to help Hancock or follow the Fifth and Sixth Corps. Hancock's Second Corps would leave last.[71]

The next day brought rain and the inevitable muddy roads, but the troops departed on schedule in the dark. Pontoon bridges were dismantled and Chesterfield Bridge burned down. By daylight on May 27 the Army of the Potomac was back across the North Anna, heading east by southeast. As Frank Wilkeson recalled that march, "How we longed to get away from North Anna, where we had not the slightest chance of success, and how we feared that Grant would keep sending us to the slaughter." Lee monitored this departure, and by 6:45 A.M. on May 27 told authorities in Richmond the news, noting that Union cavalry and infantry had already "crossed at Hanovertown." His next move would be to send "cavalry in that direction to check the movement, and [to] move the army to Ashland."[72] Another foot race to Richmond had begun.

The urgency of a night march left the principals with no time to reflect on the events of the past five days. Much later participants would write of the "Battle of North Anna River," and commentators emphasized both the daring of Lee's inverted V and his frustrations over his "lost opportunity" to strike at one of the Union corps. Overall, Lee had misread Grant and Meade a few times, but he had improvised remarkably well under duress. Grant had succeeded in leaving the Wilderness and pushing Lee farther south, but the fighting along the North Anna might have been completely avoided if he had followed Meade's suggested route from the beginning. The Army of the Potomac had continued to be blind without the cavalry, thus resorting to the use of infantry as scouts and skirmishers. Though the relationship between Grant and Meade remained professional, it had frayed significantly during the stressful weeks of May, capped by Grant seizing direct command of the army in the waning days of May. New pressures would soon show whether this new arrangement was sustainable.

For the moment, however, all attention was focused on getting the army first across the North Anna River, then farther south to cross the Pamunkey River. Despite inevitable snarls and arguments, the entire army made it across the North Anna River by daylight on May 27, and now it was Lee's turn to play catch-up. He pushed his army hard on May 27, dividing it and sending the corps down different roads to rendezvous at Hughes Crossroads.[73] Like the exhausted men of the Army of the Potomac, Lee's tired veterans could not put some distance between themselves and the dark, bloody woods of the Wilderness behind them fast enough.

Grant and Meade rode south as well, riding between infantrymen as they tried to get in front of Wright's Sixth Corps. They followed the route that Sheridan's cavalry had been on earlier, along Ridge Road. When Lyman tried to buy beets from a household, the children of the house cried out, "We shall starve!" Meade took such pity on the family that he gave them his lunch ration and five dollars.[74]

Riding in advance of the Army of the Potomac was the hard-driving Sheridan and his cavalry. They crossed the Pamunkey River at Dabney Ferry before 9 A.M., set up two pontoon boats over the river, then proceeded to capture some Confederate cavalry in several skirmishes to the west of the river that morning. Still basking in the glow of his dramatic foray to the outskirts of Richmond (Porter wrote that when Sheridan had returned to camp he was "warmly greeted by General Grant at headquarters, and heartily congratulated on his signal success"), Sheridan may have heard the gist of Dana's report to Stanton: "Rebel cavalry is exceedingly demoralized, and flees before ours on every occasion." Regardless of the truth of that assertion, Sheridan wisely guarded the roads leading to Dabney Ferry, keeping a close eye out for the movements of Breckinridge's division near Hanover Court House (rumored to be near ten thousand men).[75]

With all the units safely in motion by mid-day, Grant and Meade felt confident enough in the progress of the armies to set up temporary headquarters at Mangohick Church by 1:00 P.M. on May 27. Grant had been administered chloroform to relieve the pain of a migraine headache, while Meade stayed busy reading reports from his corps commanders. Some marching orders were altered, but by nightfall, all the infantry were in camp at their designated areas, with the exception of the Ninth Corps, which marched into the night for a time. As Dana wrote Stanton, "Everything goes well."[76]

Lee's army had also been on the march all day, and like the Army of the Potomac, most units were in camp by nightfall. Lee could still not discern Grant's planned moves, so he decided to push his cavalry out the next day to Haw's Shop, while his infantry would march rapidly to get behind (to the west of) Totopotomoy Creek.[77]

The next morning, the Union corps were set in motion with virtually no snags as each one crossed the Pamunkey River. But Meade was concerned: where was Lee's army? He ordered Sheridan to "demonstrate" south "in the direction of Mechanicsville, in order to find out the enemy's whereabouts." With all his cavalry divisions guarding crossings or the rear of the march, only Gregg's cavalry division was available for reconnaissance. When it got to the vicinity of Haw's Shop, it found that Lee had a similar idea, except his horsemen had set up a "temporary breastwork of rails." The two cavalry groups collided at Enon Church, two miles west of Haw's Shop. A hot fight ensued, with both sides hunkered down behind any cover they could find, instead of charging each other. Sheridan fed more troops into the fight, and by late afternoon the Confederates withdrew. During this day-long battle, the top two Union generals were curiously quiet, with Grant still sick and looking "sallow," according to Frank Wilkeson. When the men saw him at Nelson's Bridge, they "did not evince the slightest enthusiasm. None cheered him, none saluted him." Meade had a similar reception, and Wilkeson recalled that Meade stood by Grant's side and "thoughtfully stroked his own face." That evening he and Grant slept in tents near Dr. Nelson's home. Meade ordered Brig. Gen. Nelson Miles to send the Second Brigade as "rapidly as possible" to Haw's Shop, but when they arrived, Sheridan ordered them to serve as his pickets so he could rest his exhausted men. The Union army was finally across the Pamunkey River.[78]

The next day, Sunday, May 29, was the coolest day since May 19, with temperatures in the sixties and seventies. The cool air lifted the men's spirits, as did the relief engendered by successfully crossing the Pamunkey without a major battle. The next order of business was to find Lee's army. Though some of Sheridan's cavalry were undoubtedly tired, Grant and Meade showed their unimaginative and ineffective use of cavalry by letting the horsemen rest on May 29. That left Union infantry to find Lee's army, and Meade dutifully sent out three divisions at noon, one from each corps, to look for the opposing army. Brig. Gen. David Russell's First division (Sixth Corps) marched northwest on Hanover River Road, heading toward Hanover Court House. Barlow's First Division (Second Corps) marched west on Atlee Station Road, headed toward Totopotomoy Creek. Griffin's First Division (Fifth Corps) marched across Totopotomy Creek to Shady Grove Road, where it would march west toward Pole Green Church and Hundley Corner. Burnside's Ninth Corps waited in reserve.[79]

Each division found something different. Russell's men brushed away some Confederate cavalry to cover Hanover Court House. Barlow's men ran into Breckinridge's small force dug in along the Totopotomoy Creek and had to stop without further support. Griffin's men found trouble near the Via house along Totopotomoy Creek, and skirmishers exchanged fire in the late afternoon. Early sent Pegram's Brigade (under Col. John S. Hoffman) to meet the new advance.[80]

Meade updated Grant about developments at 4 P.M. Grant synched with Meade's instincts, instructing him to "close up" on the troops sent out by morning, or even that evening if the troops were severely threatened. He thought Barlow should be "supported before making the attack." With Grant's backing, Meade put more troops into action, sending Hancock to support Barlow, Warren to be ready to support Griffin, and Wright to stand ready to help Russell. By midevening, Hancock and Warren had examined their fronts and moved divisions to be ready for a Confederate attack. Wright was to extend his line to Hancock's right, and Burnside to fill in on his left. Warren was to be on Burnside's left, with

Sheridan sending pickets to cover Wright's left. Meade sent orders to Burnside and Wright to move to their new positions in the morning.[81]

What all this Union activity meant was not clear to Lee, who spent the day receiving updates on Union infantry movements and meeting President Davis and General Beauregard. Lee had hoped that Davis would order Beauregard to send him some troops, but Davis would not. So Lee prepared to meet Union attacks, not launch one of his own.[82]

To be closer to what might be another battle, Meade moved his headquarters from Dr. Nelson's yard to Enon Church, behind the Second Corps. Though much closer to the front, it was also a gloomy place to camp; Lyman recorded that the "pulpit and pews were stained with blood."[83]

On May 30 the Union corps commanders sent more units to probe Confederate defenses and also finished the realignment ordered by Meade the day before. The first battle of the day was a fierce cavalry fight off to the northwest of Old Cold Harbor along Matadequin Creek. Confederate cavalry were trying to ascertain if Union infantry had marched that far and, at a cost of over one hundred casualties, found it had not. Sheridan bragged again about the role of his men, while ignoring his failure to offer more protection to Warren's left flank. He wrote to Meade that evening: "Had a sharp engagement of nearly two hours. We defeated them and drove them to Cold Harbor. It was a very handsome affair. . . . I have had troops on the left of General Warren's corps all day, and connected with him."[84]

A second battle that day, the Battle of Bethesda Church, would cause much more stress for Meade than the cavalry fight along Matedequin Creek. In the mid-afternoon, forward elements of Col. Martin D. Hardin's First Brigade, Fifth Corps (Meade's old unit, the Pennsylvania Reserves), found themselves alone on Old Church Road, suddenly under attack by hundreds of veterans under the command of Brig. Gen. Bryan Grimes. They ran or were captured, and Grimes quickly pushed east, swooping up more prisoners and scaring the men of the Pennsylvania Reserves into fleeing back north toward the Bowles farm. Wainwright had seen the attack and thought it looked "very squally for a complete turning of our left." The rest of Major General Rodes's division had also arrived at Bethesda Church and were organizing to march north. Col. G. Howard Kitching's Independent Brigade (Third Division, Fifth Corps) soon stood alone in front of the fast-moving Confederate infantry, while Warren dug a defensive line along Shady Grove Road. He hurriedly wrote Meade at 4 P.M., "The enemy may have got in force around my left flank. Any troops that can be sent to the Via house are desirable."[85]

Meade responded with alacrity. He ordered all of his corps commands to attack to their fronts, hoping to relieve the pressure on Warren's Fifth Corps. Hancock responded quickly, but Wright and Burnside got tied down.[86] But it was a massive response to a minor threat. The Confederates had stopped to reorganize, giving just enough time for Union troops to establish a strong east-west line along

Shady Grove Road, and for artillery to be brought up. When Early told Brig. Gen. Stephen Ramseur to send John Pegram's Brigade of five hundred men to test the enemy, Ramseur did just that, sending the men into a virtual hailstorm of rifle fire and canister. They were completely stopped, suffering over 450 casualties. The brief battle of Bethesda Church was over.[87]

Warren updated Meade on the battle, prompting Meade to call off the attacks by his corps commanders. For Warren it had been another success, coming on the heels of the fight at Jericho Mills on May 23, and he must have believed he was regaining favor with Meade. Sheridan also had another notch on his belt, and with sufficient cavalry now connecting to Warren, even Warren might have felt secure.[88]

As Meade settled in for a rare quiet night at Enon Church, he must have felt some degree of success, though Lee's location was still unknown. Grant was waiting for the arrival of Maj. Gen. William F. ("Baldy") Smith and his newly formed Eighteenth Corps, expected to march up from White House. With the addition of Smith's seventeen thousand men, Grant could put new pressure on Lee. He cautioned Meade to be ready for Lee to make a "dash to crush him," and he ordered Meade to tell Sheridan to "watch the enemy's movements well out toward Cold Harbor, and also on the Mechanicsville road." Showing his old willingness to micromanage, Grant drilled down to the brigade level of detail: "I want Sheridan to send a cavalry force of at least a half a brigade, if not a whole brigade, at 5 o'clock in the morning, to communicate with Smith and return with him." With these plans in place, Meade could finish the evening with a message for Warren: "It is not intended to take the offensive tomorrow unless the enemy should interpose between you and General Smith. . . . Should the cavalry report any such movement, General Wright will be moved across to the left, and in conjunction with you, the enemy attacked."[89]

Meanwhile, Lee was busy as well, processing new intelligence that Smith's corps would soon join Grant and Meade. Lee telegraphed Davis that he needed more troops from Beauregard immediately: "The result of this delay will be disaster. Butler's troops [Smith's] will be with Grant tomorrow. Hoke's division, at least, should be with me by light tomorrow." Davis ordered it done. Unknown to the Union generals, Lee had no intention of falling back or waiting to be attacked.[90]

The next morning began sultry and got hotter as the sun rose. While Grant waited for the arrival of the Eighteenth Corps, Meade decided to probe Lee's defenses along Totopotomoy Creek. At 7:30 A.M. he sent an order to all of his corps commanders to "press forward their skirmishers up against the enemy and ascertain whether any change has taken place in their front." The corps' progress fell pretty much in line with past performances. Under Barlow the First Division (Second Corps) pushed forward a bit before hitting a stiff line. Wright's Sixth Corps made similar progress, before hitting "strong entrenchments with abatis." Warren's Fifth Corps also made some advance, before it found the enemy with a "strong front." Burnside's Ninth Corps made slower progress, but after nearly a mile of forward movement, ran into entrenchments. Given this wall of resistance faced by each corps, Meade did not issue an order to attack in the evening of May 31.[91]

While the infantry was stalled, Sheridan's cavalry claimed two important prizes: it gained possession of Cold Harbor after a fight with infantry and cavalry, and Wilson's brigade captured Hanover Court House to the north of the Union army, thus protecting the army from a sudden cavalry attack at its rear. Sheridan boasted in his report about the capture of Cold Harbor, careful to emphasize the new fighting spirit of the cavalry inspired by his leadership, "The fight on the part of our officers and men was very gallant; they were now beginning to accept nothing less than victory." Even Sheridan knew better than to take on infantry, though, and he left his position that night—only to be ordered to return to it in the night. He did so without losing his position, demonstrating that he could be a recipient of luck as well as an architect of success.[92]

Lee did not react passively to Union probes. Concerned all day that Smith's army might move to attack Cold Harbor and cut off his lines to Richmond, the short battle at Cold Harbor confirmed his fears (even though it was not clear if his men were fighting infantry or dismounted cavalry). So he peeled away Anderson's First Corps from their well-built lines and sent them marching south. Warren sent word of this movement to Meade and Grant, which, combined with Sheridan's account of fighting infantry at Cold Harbor, finally alerted Meade and Grant to the importance of Cold Harbor. Meade ordered Wright to take his veteran Sixth Corps on another all-night march, this over fifteen miles to Cold Harbor, where they were to relieve the cavalry.[93]

Another corps was available, but the readiness and combat worthiness of the Eighteenth Corps were untested. Still under the direct command of Grant, Smith received orders to march at first light to New Castle Ferry. Unfortunately, Grant's aide Orville Babcock got it wrong—Grant meant for the corps to march to Cold Harbor and assemble on the right of the Sixth Corps. To compound the problem, Smith had only "three days' rations," between "40 and 60 rounds of infantry ammunition, and no artillery ammunition, save what it is in the caissons." His supply wagons lagged a day behind him.[94]

After a short night of rest, Meade was up early on June 1 monitoring his orders to Hancock, Warren, and Burnside: "Press the enemy with your skirmishers, and endeavor to develop [Lee's] line of battle and his line of works." That meant another trying morning of probes and repulses for the tired Union troops, with little easily gotten information to show for their losses. By mid-morning, Grant added another corps to Meade's command, Smith's Eighteenth Corps. Though observers expected sparks to fly—Smith had been a corps commander before Meade had, and was touted as Meade's replacement back in the winter of 1863–64—initially, the appointment made sense. Meade now commanded the largest army he would ever have (114,000 men), and he needed to have the Eighteenth Corps under his eye, just as he had the Ninth Corps. With that addition to the might of the Army of the Potomac, Grant and Meade now expected to use the combined force of the Sixth and Eighteenth Corps, some thirty thousand men, to hit Lee's right hard at Cold Harbor. By noon Meade informed Smith of the new plan, "General Wright is ordered to attack the enemy as soon as his troops are up, and I desire you should cooperate with him and join in the attack."[95]

This new plan depended on several factors, none of which looked promising. Sheridan had held on to his position, despite an ill-advised attack by Confederates in the morning. When Wright's lead units arrived around 9 A.M., Sheridan was more than eager to rest his troops near Prospect Church. Secondly, Wright's troops were exhausted and hardly desirous of rushing into attack on another steaming hot Virginia day. Furthermore, they did not arrive by noon—it took until 2:10 to get the last troops there. At that time, Wright wrote Meade that when his troops were arranged he could "press my skirmish line forward." The third factor was Smith's corps, which, according to Wright, was not there yet at 2:10 P.M. The Eighteenth Corps had gone off on the wrong road because of Babcock's error, but even with that mistake rectified by mid-morning, only the lead elements of the corps had arrived by 3 P.M., and they too were hot and tired. Smith had enough troops on hand by late afternoon to deploy north of Wright, but not enough to connect with the Fifth Corps. Lastly, another day-long wait for fatigued troops to get into position to attack meant that any attack would have just a few hours of daylight, and that the Confederates had an entire day to reinforce their lines.[96]

During this day (June 1) of marching and waiting, Grant and Meade moved their headquarters to Mrs. Via's farm. Meade found a few moments to write to his wife, telling her, "We are pegging away here, and gradually getting nearer and nearer to Richmond." He noted that the strong entrenchments of the Confederates had forced the Army of the Potomac to "move around their flank" four times since the beginning of May. He continued, "We shall have to do it once more before we get them into their defenses at Richmond, and then will begin the tedious process of a quasi-siege, like that at Sebastopol; which will last as long, unless we can get hold of their railroads and cut off their supplies, when then must come out and fight." He prophetically added, "The papers are giving Grant all the credit of what they call successes; I hope they will remember this if anything goes wrong."[97]

After a two-hour artillery barrage, Wright's Sixth Corps attacked at 6 P.M. Despite heavy fire, some regiments gained enough ground so that by 7:30 P.M. Wright wrote to Meade, "Everything is going well up to this time. . . . I think that you should get me some reinforcements tonight, if possible." Meade and Grant decided to pull Hancock off his line to have his Second Corps execute another night march to reach Wright by the morning. The two generals saw that a concentration of their forces at Cold Harbor might lead to the assault that would finally break Lee's army.[98]

Later that evening, Meade decided there would be an all-out attack the next day. Imbibing some of the aggressive spirit of his superior, Meade wrote to Grant that "as soon as Hancock is within supporting distance," the attack of three corps

(Sixth, Eighteenth, and Second) should begin. He also thought that Warren "should be ordered to attack in conjunction with the others." As for Burnside, he should "hold ready to reinforce Warren, if necessary." The offensive-minded Grant swiftly responded, "The attack should be renewed tomorrow morning by all means." He agreed with the roles given to each corps by Meade.[99]

With Grant's endorsement, Meade sent out new orders quickly. Hancock's corps was to march all night from its northern position near Polly Hundley's corner, then "take a position on the left of the Sixth Corps and at once attack the enemy, endeavoring to turn his right flank and interpose between him and the Chickahominy." Hancock also had the option upon arrival at Cold Harbor to "support" Wright's attack, if "deemed more expedient" by himself and Wright. Meade warned Wright that Hancock might not arrive until six or seven in the morning, but as soon as Hancock's corps drew "within supporting distance," he should attack. Meade ordered Smith, "Attack tomorrow morning on Major General Wright's right, and in conjunction with that attack. This attack should be made with your whole force, and as vigorously as possible." He closed with a pointed rebuke, "I have had no report of your operations this afternoon." Warren was ordered to attack with all "available force," with Burnside as his reinforcement if needed. Lastly, Meade ordered Burnside, "Hold your command in readiness tomorrow either to attack on your front or to move to the support of General Warren, if required."[100]

With all orders sent, Meade hoped to relax, until he finally heard from Smith near midnight. Smith described his thinly held lines and complained about his lack of ammunition, with "one division being almost entirely out of ammunition, and one brigade of General Brooks having but a small supply on hand." This was too much for Meade; he yelled out to no one in particular, "Then, why in Hell did he come at all for!" Lyman recorded that such profanity was "rare" for Meade, though it so shocked the sensibility of Smith's aide Lt. Francis Farquhar ("bright, active, self-sufficient" in Lyman's characterization) that he reported these words verbatim to Smith, who later included them in his official report. In defense of his action, Smith wrote, "My justification was the orders I had received from the lieutenant-general, and the fact that he knew my condition when I moved." The moment did not serve Meade well, though Lyman also wrote that Meade was angry at several corps commanders that evening, and, in Lyman's sardonic appraisal, Meade was "in one of his irascible fits tonight, which are always founded in good reason though they spread themselves over a good deal of ground that is not always in the limits of the question."[101]

With another long day ending on a sour note with twenty-two hundred casualties in a short evening's fight, the generals and their soldiers settled for another warm, uncomfortable night—except for the exhausted men of the Second Corps. They tramped all night in an air "intensely-hot and breathless" on roads "deep with dust, which rose in suffocating clouds as it was stirred by thousands of feet of men and horses and by the wheels of the artillery," according to Francis Walker (aide to Hancock).[102]

What happened next could have been predicted, based on the events of the past five weeks. Warren wrote a long dispatch at 5 A.M. on June 2, noting that his line was "5 miles long" and "too weak to attack." Hancock's night march was so difficult (it included wrong directions as well) that by early morning he sent word that only the "First Division" was up, and it would be some time "before the corps is up and in position." He admitted that "there was a good deal of straggling, owing to the extreme fatigue of the men and the dusty roads." Hancock even had to leave a division with Smith until the Eighteenth Corps got its ammunition. Without Hancock ready by early morning and Smith's and Warren's problems, Meade bowed to the inevitable limits of what tired soldiers could do: he postponed the attack until 5 P.M. in the afternoon.[103]

Even that alteration in plans proved too optimistic. At 2 P.M. Grant wrote to Meade, "In view of the want of preparation for an attack this evening, and the heat and want of energy among the men from moving during the night last night, I think it is advisable to postpone an assault until early tomorrow morning."[104]

The full day's delay offered rest to some of the weary Union troops, and an ideal opportunity for Lee to move the rest of his army south to the new defensive line stretching from Shady Grove Road to the north to Turkey Hill and Chickahominy Creek in the south. Lee even used the detected departure of Hancock's Second Corps to attack Burnside's Ninth Corps. In the late afternoon, Jubal Early's Second Corps attacked with vigor, causing one thousand Union casualties, though not altering Burnside's line. Confederate troops under Gordon had also attacked, this time against Warren's Fifth Corps. They too were stopped.[105]

While the fighting on the afternoon of June 2 went on, Grant and Meade made their plans for the major attack the next morning. Grant wrote Meade at 2:00 P.M. that "all changes of position already ordered should be completed today and a good night's rest given the men preparatory to an assault at, say, 4:30 in the morning." Meade sent a circular to his corps commanders informing them that the attack originally scheduled for 5 P.M. would instead commence at 4:30 A.M. on June 3. As usual, Meade relied on his corps commanders to perform the tactical legwork, telling them to make "examination of the ground in their fronts . . . perfecting their arrangements for the assault."[106]

Gordon Rhea faults Meade and Grant for not surveying the ground or, once the fighting began, taking direct command. These are valid criticisms, but also a statement of fact: neither Grant nor Meade typically took immediate supervision of a battle, preferring to work through their corps commanders (or in Grant's case, through his army commander). Rhea's second criticism, that Meade did "little" preparation because he had "no heart for the assignment," fits with his overall narrative of Meade's role in the Overland Campaign but does not jibe with the historical record. Not only was it typical of Meade to leave corps-level tactical details to his corps commanders, but, as he bragged in a letter to his wife sent on June 4 (concerning the battle of Cold Harbor), he had "immediate and entire command on the field all day, the Lieutenant General honoring the field with his presence only about one hour in the middle of the day." Adding his usual complaint about the press coverage to round out his point, he wrote, "The press will, however, undoubtedly inform you of all his doings, and I will therefore confine myself to mine." As shown in his numerous letters, Meade was never shy about highlighting his own role vis-à-vis Grant's in his personal correspondence to his wife; thus he was truly saying that it was he who managed the battle. Rhea's third criticism, that a general assault on a well-fortified line had rarely worked and had been executed at great cost of life, was shared by Meade's contemporaries. Lyman wrote to his wife on the day of the battle of Cold Harbor, "I can't say I heard with any great hope the order, given last night, for a general assault at 4:30 the next morning." Wainwright complained that "the order issued for the attack to the corps commanders was the same which has been given at all such times on this campaign, viz: 'to attack along the whole line.'" Or as Francis Walker later analyzed the problem, it was "attacking at too many points."[107]

But on June 2, the after-action criticisms lay in the future. That day, Meade and Grant moved their headquarters to Kelly's house. Though Lyman described the location as "Sahara intensified," it was fairly near the Second Corps line, though safely tucked behind a "pine woods." Meade could get no rest that evening, badgered by Warren's complaints until nearly midnight. Warren whined in one dispatch, "I hardly know what you would like to have us do under the circumstances." He sent his top aide Roebling ("the silent," according to Lyman) to explain his situation. Roebling even suggested that Meade come to Bethesda Church and take personal command of the Fifth and Ninth Corps. This role Meade categorically refused, telling Roebling that "at 3 am he had had ordered his coffee, at 4 he was going to mount with his staff, and at 6 he would smash the rebel army at Cold Harbor." He offered an alternative to Roebling: ask Grant what he thought of having either Burnside or Warren take command at Bethesda Church. Grant did not favor this idea, and Meade had to end the discussion by sending a detailed message to Warren stressing that both generals must attack as ordered at 4:30 A.M. on June 3, "by such combinations of the two corps as may be in both your judgements, be deemed best." He closed with a wish, "Harmony and cooperation on the part of General Burnside and yourself are earnestly enjoined." Roebling rode back to Warren after midnight to deliver the disappointing news. Lyman wrote in his journal that "the General is getting more and more discontented with Warren."[108]

As Meade and his staff settled in for a few hours of fitful sleep in a drizzling rain, many Confederate soldiers kept busy enlarging and bolstering their breastworks. By daybreak, some fortifications were eight feet high and seven feet deep. The Confederates had a line that stretched for six miles, and according to Earl Hess, "other than Edgar's Salient on Breckinridge's right, there were no longer any weak spots along the Confederate position by dawn of June 3."[109]

After a short sleep, troops of the Second, Sixth, and Eighteenth Corps marched into position in the early morning hours of June 3, aligning themselves to attack promptly at 4:30 A.M. Thousands of men stepped off into mist and fog on a rainy morning, so reminiscent of the attack on the salient at Spotsylvania. This time, however, there would be no swift initial breakthrough. Without overall coordination and planning, the envisioned "grand assault" became a series of disjointed corps attacks by just three of the five corps available. In each case, the first wave ran into incredibly stout Confederate lines, and men were mowed down by the hundreds. Though the oft-quoted numbers of seventy-five hundred or even twelve thousand Union casualties in the first hour of the assault have been discredited by Gordon Rhea and other historians, the losses were still high for barely an hour's worth of fighting. The Second Corps had twenty-five hundred casualties, the Eighteenth Corps had fifteen hundred casualties, and the Sixth Corps had six hundred casualties. Nor were casualties evenly distributed among the regiments of the respective corps; each corps had only a few brigades that saw fierce action, and throughout the morning the pattern remained the same, in which "new regiments lost heavily," according to Rhea.[110]

Of course the casualties would not be officially tallied until later in the day. The first reports from the Second Corps were good: "General Barlow reports that he has enemy's works, with colors and guns," according to Hancock at 5:20 A.M. Meade forwarded this dispatch to Smith, undoubtedly to prod him to carry on. But the news quickly turned sour as it arrived at the quiet spot behind the pine forest. At 6 A.M. Hancock wrote, "The men are very close to the enemy, under a crest, but seem unable to carry it. . . . I shall await your orders, but express the opinion that if the first dash in an assault fails, other attempts are not apt to succeed better." At 6:45 A.M. Hancock provided more details: "The result of my attack thus far is the capture of from 300 to 400 prisoners, and one color. The enemy's line was carried in one or two points, but not held." Gibbon was making "temporary entrenchments to try and hold his advanced position" but did not feel the spot was "tenable." Even worse, two colonels were killed (Orlando H. Morris and Frank Haskell) and two other senior officers wounded (John Brooke and Robert H. Tyler). As for Smith's Eighteenth Corps, Brig. Gen. John H. Martindale's Second Division had attacked the line "three times, and each time [had been] repulsed." His assessment: "My troops are very much cut up, and have no hope of being able to carry the works in my front unless a movement of the Sixth Corps on my left may relieve at least one of my flanks from this galling fire." Wright had a better report at 7:45 A.M.: "I am in advance of everything else." But he complained of lack of support from the Eighteenth Corps. Besides, he had "ordered" an attack but did not state whether it had been carried out. (It turned out that Wright had occupied a skirmish line but nothing more.) That left Warren and Burnside to force the issue. Warren insisted he could not advance "unless those on my right or

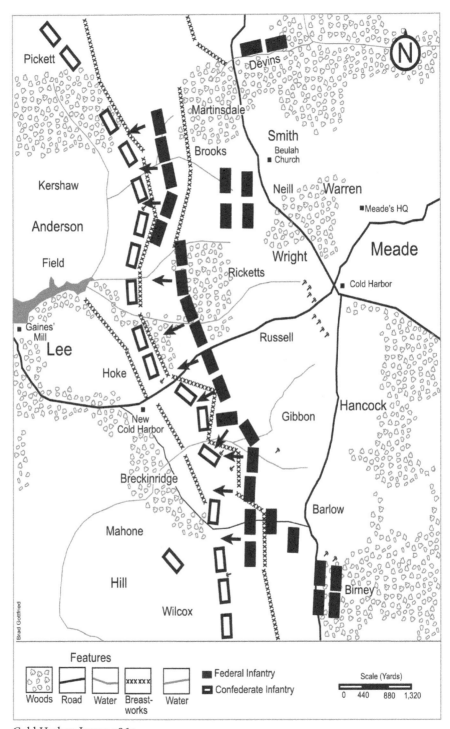

Pickett

Devins

Martinsdale

Smith

Brooks

Beulah
■ Church

Kershaw

Neill

Warren

■ Meade's HQ

Anderson

Meade

Field

Wright

Ricketts

Gaines'
■ Mill

Russell

Cold Harbor

Lee

Hoke

New
■ Cold Harbor

Hancock

Gibbon

Breckinridge

Barlow

Mahone

Birney

Hill

Wilcox

Brad Gottfried

Features

Woods	Road	Water	Breast-works	Water

■ Federal Infantry

□ Confederate Infantry

Scale (Yards)

0   440   880   1,320

Cold Harbor, June 3, 1864

left succeed in doing so." Burnside had a bit more success, reporting at 7:35 A.M. that his men had "carried the front line of the enemy's works."[111]

With the grand assault stalled, Meade wrote to Grant at 7 A.M., "I should be glad to have your views as to the continuance of these attacks, if unsuccessful." Some historians have argued that Meade attempted to shift the responsibility for the failed attack to his superior, but there is another interpretation based on the events of the previous three weeks. Meade had learned the hard way that Grant could not resist micromanaging troop selection from time to time. Although neither constant nor consistent, Grant's micromanaging occurred just often enough to make a dutiful soldier like Meade believe that all important decisions had to be vetted by Grant. So here was another stalled assault, and before Meade either called it off or tried to make it work, he wanted Grant's views and permission. This time Grant refused to accept responsibility, if that was ever Meade's intent. He replied to Meade, "The moment it becomes certain that an assault cannot succeed, suspend the offensive, but when one does succeed push it vigorously, and if necessary pile in troops at the successful point from wherever they can be taken." This was neither an order nor an answer but more a basic lesson in military tactics. Meade must have been displeased.[112]

With negative reports increasing and Grant leaving the decision in his hands, Meade tried to prod Hancock to do more: "I desire every effort be made to carry the enemy's works. Of course if this is deemed impracticable, after trial, the attack should be suspended, but the responsibility for this must be on your judgment. I cannot give more decided orders." Either Meade was trying to pass responsibility for the offensive on to Hancock, or he simply wanted his best corps commander to make further efforts or honestly tell him it was impossible to do so. Hancock soon sent his blunt assessment of the situation, writing, "If the guns on the left can be silenced, General Barlow will reassault, and I have directed General Gibbon to let me know what he requires to do the same. . . . I consider that the assault failed long since." That shot of reality braced Meade, and he quickly replied, "Wright and Smith are both going to try again, and unless you consider it hopeless I would like you to do the same."[113]

But Wright and Smith did not renew their attacks, and in a clear sign that the offensive had sputtered to a close, Meade acceded to Warren's request for additional support by ordering Birney's division of the Second Corps to march to Warren's left. Though reporter William Swinton wrote of a "mutiny" against Meade by men refusing to attack, and Baldy Smith much later stated he had directly refused a verbal order from Meade to attack again, neither story appeared in contemporaneous accounts. The truth was much simpler: the attacking brigades of the five corps had run into thick breastworks and enfilading fire, either stopping in place or retreating to avoid being slaughtered. In the late morning, Grant rode to each corps commander and asked for their views. Each spoke of the impossibility of successful attack, and by 12:30 P.M. Grant wrote to Meade, "You may direct a suspension of farther advance for the moment." He further instructed Meade, "Hold our most advanced positions, and strengthen them. . . . Reconnaissances should be made in front of every corps, and advances made to advantageous positions by regular approaches." Meade dutifully sent out orders to his corps commanders with Grant's instructions, thus ending the last major battle of the Overland Campaign.[114]

This last failed assault soon gained notoriety for being the last in a series of bloody, largely fruitless attacks conducted during the Overland Campaign. The public memory of the battle was given fresh life when Horace Porter told the often-repeated story of men pinning their names to the backs of their shirts before the attack (thoroughly disproved by Rhea), and more importantly, by Grant's rare admission of battlefield mistakes in his *Memoirs* when he wrote, "I regret that the last assault at Cold Harbor was ever made."[115]

It would have been cold comfort to the exhausted veterans of the Army of the Potomac to know that, according to Rhea, the Battle of Cold Harbor was only the "fifth bloodiest day for the Federals since crossing the Rapidan." Coming at the end of one month of continuous fighting for the army, it had simply reinforced the fact that was patently obvious to the lowliest private: strong Confederate defenses could simply not be carried, unless some measure of surprise, atmospheric condition, or luck allowed for a break. At the cost of fifty-five thousand Union casualties, this hard lesson had been learned and tested again and again by Union troops. Grant had achieved only one central strategic objective: he had pushed Lee south, almost backing him into the Confederate capital of Richmond. The steep cost of this achievement was borne particularly heavily by one critical group in the army, its natural leaders. With keen insight, Lyman wrote, "The best officers and men are liable, by their greater gallantry to be first disabled; and, of those that are left, the best become demoralized by the failures, and the loss of good leaders; so that, very soon, the men will no longer charge entrenchments and will only go forward when driven by their officers." At Cold Harbor, as at all the other battles of the horrific Overland Campaign, Lyman felt that the army "gained nothing save a knowledge of their position and the proof of the unflinching bravery of our soldiers."[116]

In his letters home, Meade did not take such a dismal view of this battle or of the Overland Campaign. As noted earlier, in his June 4 letter to his wife he boasted about having "entire command" of the field on June 3. He felt that the "battle ended without any decided results," with losses "estimated about equal on both sides." (This estimate was wrong, even if recent figures replace some older ones: the ratio was closer to four Union casualties for every one Confederate casualty.) As for the march south and the future, Meade speculated, "How long this game is to be played is impossible to tell; but in the long run, we ought to succeed, because it is in our power more promptly to fill the gaps in men and material which this constant fighting produces." In a longer letter written the next day, Meade gave full vent to

his still-simmering anger from earlier criticisms and vindication for his past decisions. He wrote: "I feel a satisfaction in knowing that my record is clear, and the
results of this campaign are the clearest indications I could wish of my sound judgment, both at Williamsport and Mine Run. In every instance that we have attacked
the enemy in an entrenched position we have failed, except in the case of Hancock's attack at Spotsylvania, which was a surprise discreditable to the enemy. So,
likewise, whenever the enemy has attacked us in position, he had been repulsed. I
think Grant has had his eyes opened, and is willing to admit now that Virginia and
Lee's army is not Tennessee and Bragg's army." He closed with his usual pessimistic
note, "Whether the people will ever recognize this fact remains to be seen.[117]

One thing the people around headquarters had noticed was Grant's occasional
direct assumption of command of the Army of the Potomac. In maneuvers on May
18, 22, and 25, Grant had told Meade where to place each corps, leading Meade to
refer to his "false position" in a May 23 letter to his wife. Simultaneous with this
command assumption was a command expansion, as Grant put the Ninth and
Eighteenth Corps under Meade's authority. A common interpretation is that Grant
"took over" for Meade, but that does not explain Meade's responsibility for much
of the Battle of Cold Harbor on June 3, or Grant's adopting the plan of Meade and
Comstock to "turn the enemy's right by crossing at or near Hanovertown." Historian Wayne Wei-siang Hsieh argues that Grant "never revealed any special interests in tactical questions," nor did he have a "real intellectual commitment . . .
[to] strategic abstraction."[118] As Grant got to know the strengths and weaknesses
of each corps in the Army of the Potomac, he developed ideas on how they should
be moved and used, and he put those into orders in late May. Once the corps were
in position at Cold Harbor, he turned over the battle to Meade. What Grant may
have seen as common sense, or simple expedience, Meade regarded as a public de-
motion, if not veiled criticism, of him as a commander. Meade's list of grievances
would, unfortunately, continue to lengthen as his time under Grant continued.

NINE

South to Petersburg

*The Army Moves South and Begins the
Siege of Petersburg-Richmond*

After a hard month of fruitless assaults on well-fortified enemy lines, even Grant had to admit a new approach was needed. Soon after the Battle of Cold Harbor, he decided to disengage the Army of the Potomac from its lines and move it south, across the Chickahominy and James Rivers, to attack Petersburg. The following six weeks would see the exhilaration of a difficult march well executed, the frustration over a failed attack at Petersburg, and the ultimate debacle at the "Crater" at the end of July. After planning the march south, Grant allowed Meade to handle most of the operational decisions for the next six weeks. Thus the results would fall more squarely on Meade's shoulders, though he would shift blame for failures to his corps commanders.

The worn-out soldiers at Cold Harbor experienced cooler temperatures than usual on June 4 as they continued strengthening their lines and digging trenches toward Confederate lines ("regular approaches" in Army language). Meade visited his corps commanders and had some units shuffled from one position to the next.[1] Though no memoirist discusses conversations that day between Meade and Grant, there must have been some, because on June 5 Grant detailed his plans in several messages.

Grant sent Halleck a long letter assessing the situation and outlining his next steps. He rejected a suggestion to hold a line that would simply "protect the Fredericksburg railroad" because it would be too long and vulnerable to defend. Instead, he intended to "hold substantially to the ground now occupied by the Army of the Potomac," while waiting for a cavalry detachment "to destroy the Virginia Central Railroad from about Beaver Dam for some 25 or 30 miles west." Once the railroad was destroyed, he would "move the army to the south side of James River."[2]

Grant wrote a note to Meade, focusing on the task of the cavalry: "The object of the cavalry expedition to Charlottesville and Gordonsville is to effectively break up the railroad connection between Richmond and the Shenandoah Valley and Lynchburg." The cavalry was instructed to ensure that every rail was destroyed and, when finished, to "should keep north of the Pamunkey River."[3]

Though Meade and Grant could make more use of Sheridan's cavalry when it was with the army rather than away, this mission was a good tactical move, and it kept Sheridan away from Meade, which was also a good move. When Warren complained about the lack of cavalry to Meade, who passed on the complaint to Sheridan, the young general tartly responded that the reason for the broken connection was the "withdrawal of some army corps without any notification to the cavalry. Infantry commanders are very quick to give the alarm when their flanks are uncovered, but manifest inexcusable stupidity about the safety of cavalry flanks." Meade could not leave the matter or the tone alone. He wrote a lengthy reply detailing the movements of Burnside and Warren, explaining how they had done nothing wrong. Then he twisted the knife, adding, "The commanders of infantry corps are instructed to keep in communication with the commanders of the cavalry on their flanks, but they have sometimes reported they have been unable" to do so. Undoubtedly it was beneficial to both generals that Sheridan departed with two divisions on June 7.[4]

Tempers calmed down on June 6, as Sheridan prepared for his mission and Meade busied himself with the plans for the impending march south. Meade toyed with the idea of another assault, asking Hancock and Smith to assess the "practicability of an assault on the enemy works in your front," and by mid-afternoon Hancock responded, "My judgment is averse to an assault." In a similar vein Smith responded, "I do not think an assault practicable from any point in my front." With these sober recommendations, Meade decided not to attack. He continued, however, to press the matter of a truce between the two combatants to allow for the retrieval of dead and wounded men. On June 5, Hancock initiated a request to pursue a truce, which Meade endorsed and forwarded to Grant. However, in asking Grant for permission, Meade had to reveal that he had been snubbed by Lee: "Any communication by flag of the truce will have to come from you, as the enemy do not recognize me as in command whilst you are present." Grant assented to Meade's request, and Colonel Lyman brought the note to the Confederate lines, waving a white flag made from a pillowcase. Lee responded that he "could not consent to the burial of the dead and the removal of the wounded between the armies in the way" Grant proposed, but he would accept a request by "flag of truce in the usual way."

It was not until early evening on June 7—four days after the end of the Battle of Cold Harbor—that troops went out from both sides to see to their fallen comrades. Fortunately, the frontline soldiers had surreptitiously snuck out to rescue their wounded comrades at night, and as Lyman said, "those not reached either died from exposure or were relieved by a friendly bullet." The armies did pull some of their dead comrades from the field for burial. Overall, it was embarrassing to both leading generals that it took so long to effect a one-hour truce.[5]

Though most of the day of June 7 proved "all quiet" in Captain Meade's journal, a slow-simmering attack on Meade had reached its boil. The episode had begun on May 6, at the end of the Battle of the Wilderness, when Grant and Meade favored a partial withdrawal (Meade wanted both wings back a little more than Grant). Somehow this episode became distorted by the soldiers' rumor mill and Frank Wilkeson, who recollected that "Meade had strongly advised Grant to turn back and recross the Rapidan." When the exiting army did not march in that direction, instead turning south to fight Lee again, Grant was cheered and Meade was painted as the timid defender. Grant's patron, Elihu Washburne, shared this story with a war correspondent for the Philadelphia *Inquirer*, Edward Cropsey.

Cropsey praised Meade in an article published in the pro-war *Inquirer* on June 2, 1864, writing, "He is as much the commander of the Army of the Potomac as he ever was." He then detailed Meade's duties but closed with jagged criticism: "History will record that on one eventful night during the present campaign Grant's presence saved the army and the nation, too. Not that General Meade was on the point of committing a great blunder unwittingly, but his devotion to his country made him loathe to lose her last army on what he deemed a last chance. Grant assumed the responsibility and we are still 'On to Richmond!'"[6]

When Meade read this article, he lost his notorious temper. He summoned Cropsey to his headquarters, demanding to know who had told him this "base and wicked" lie. Cropsey replied that it was "the truth of the camps." Meade rejected that premise and told Cropsey that he would "make an example of him." Meade issued an order to have Cropsey arrested, "paraded through the line of the army with a placard marked 'libeler of the press,' and . . . then be put without the lines and not permitted to return." Meade told the reporters that this action was a warning; he would not "hesitate to punish with the utmost rigor all instances like the above where individuals take advantage of the privileges accorded to them to circulate falsehood and thus impair the confidence the public and army should have in the generals and other officers."[7]

The next day Cropsey was mounted backward on a mule that rode along the back of the battle line, wearing a placard that read, "Libeler of the Press." Frank Wilkeson recalled that the men in his battery "howled" at Cropsey, and "the wish to tear him limb from limb and strew him over the ground was fiercely expressed." Meade had cleared matters first with Grant, who said he personally knew Cropsey and that the family was considered "respectable" in Illinois. Still, Grant approved the action, and Provost Marshal General Patrick gleefully carried it out. Meade wrote to his wife that the action was the "delight of the whole army, for the race of newspaper correspondents is universally despised by the soldiers." He was also bolstered when he heard that Stanton had said that "the lying report . . . was not even for a moment believed by the President or myself. We have the most perfect confidence in him [Meade]."[8]

But Meade's "victory" over press "lies" proved Pyrrhic, if not crippling to his reputation at the time and since. According to the reporter Sylvanus Cadwallader (writing many years later in his memoir), newspaper reporters held a meeting and agreed to henceforth give Meade the silent treatment. From that day forward, "Meade's name never appeared . . . if it could be omitted."[9] Meade had never been a darling of the press, but now he was its enemy. Furthermore, one of Meade's few friends in the press was the young publisher of the Philadelphia *Inquirer,* William Harding. Meade would have to work his few political back channels hard over the next six months to mend fences with Harding. Though Grant would survive episodic rough treatments by reporters and Sherman somehow managed to restore favorable coverage after treating a reporter more harshly than Meade had treated Cropsey, there would be no full restoration of good graces for George G. Meade.

After the drama of the drumming out of Cropsey, the bulk of the army spent the next few days reinforcing defenses and trying to survive the oppressive heat as best they could. Meade surveyed the lines and visited his corps commanders. His best time was probably the lunch he had with Hancock on June 9, when they teased each other about who would win the sword at the Philadelphia Fair (a fund-raising effort for the war that created a contest between Meade and Hancock, with the winner of the most votes receiving a ceremonial sword). According to Lyman, Meade offered to "give over his pretensions to the Philadelphia Fair sword if he [Hancock] would send him some fresh bread, which his ingenious cook makes." There was also time for a group photo of Meade and his staff taken on June 11 by Matthew Brady. And too much time for some of the generals, who squabbled over the promotions that became public (for example, Gibbon was promoted to major general, and Barlow was not).[10]

With the pace reduced to a crawl, Meade had time to learn one important fact and infer another one. First, in a conversation with Grant in which Meade "commented on some of Mr. Stanton's dispatches," he learned that Grant's dispatches were not sent to Stanton but to Halleck. Stanton's information came directly from Charles Dana, the president's special representative in the Army of the Potomac. Meade had noticed that "in all Mr. Stanton's dispatches from Grant's headquarters [his] name was never alluded to." Now he knew who was responsible for that deliberate exclusion—but of course had no political lever to pull to change it. Meade also believed that Grant's primary patron, Elihu Washburne, "started the story" that Meade wanted to recross the Rapidan after the Wilderness. Regardless of whether he could prove his supposition, Meade really had no way to counteract Washburne's influence. Meade now knew why his name was slighted in official documents, but just as with the press's hostile treatment of him, there was little he could do about the situation.[11]

During this lull in fighting, Grant sent two trusted aides, Porter and Comstock, to find the best places to ford the James River. Because both men had been on McClellan's staff in 1862, they knew the territory well. They left camp on June 7 and did not return until June 12. They recommended a pontoon bridge be built at Fort Powhatan, the "narrowest point that could be found on the river below City Point," and watched in fascination as Grant absorbed their information, showing "the only anxiety and nervousness of manner had even manifested on any occasion." It was obvious that Grant had been ready to move for days, and now he was trying to quickly gather the final details he needed before ordering a huge march.[12]

The major action during these quieter days in mid-June was Sheridan's battle against two divisions of Confederate cavalry at Trevilian Station. Sheridan attacked Confederates on June 11, pushing them back and then out of the station. The next day the Union cavalry "destroyed the railroad from this point [the station] to Louisa Courthouse." Union cavalry also moved toward Gordonsville, where it met stiff resistance from Confederate cavalry and infantry. Though Sheridan regarded the cavalry battle at Trevilian Station as "by far the most brilliant one of the present campaign," others did not share his view. As Sheridan's seven thousand cavalrymen made their way back to the army, they carried out one critical mission that had not even been in their orders: they forced Lee to divert two of his top cavalry divisions to watch them, thus depriving Lee of his needed reconnaissance.[13]

With Sheridan's cavalry drawing Lee's cavalry away and reducing his scouting abilities, Grant saw the perfect opportunity to make his next grand maneuver: a long march out of the works at Cold Harbor to the James River, which would be crossed, and then on to Petersburg. On the evening of June 12, the Fifth Corps and Wilson's cavalry gladly departed the blood-soaked fields of Cold Harbor. The next night (June 13) the other three corps departed. Though the roads were dusty and the men hated night marches, it was a relief from the sun and the heat of the day. They first crossed the Chickahominy River, then moved toward the wide James River. Meanwhile, almost five hundred men worked to build the longest pontoon bridge of the war, over two thousand feet long, comprising "92 boats braced by three schooners." They finished near midnight on June 14, just in time for the Second Corps to cross over the next day.[14]

Not only was June 14 a red-letter day for military engineering, it was also the day that Grant conveyed some, but not all, of his strategic thinking to Butler, and thus set in motion another failure for Meade. According to Grant's report, he traveled by steamer to see Butler at Bermuda Hundred and to "give the necessary orders for the immediate capture of Petersburg." Perhaps to keep the orders secret, he gave the orders verbally. Butler was to "send General Smith immediately, that night, with all the troops he could give him without sacrificing the position he had." Once the Army of the Potomac had crossed the James River, he would "throw it forward by divisions as rapidly as it could be done."[15]

After conveying these orders to Butler, Grant returned by boat to Wilcox Wharf (the site of the bridge building). He dashed off a short update to Halleck, noting that "the enemy shows no signs yet of having brought troops to the south side of Richmond." Then he optimistically predicted that his forces would "have Petersburg secured, if possible, before they get there in much force." He also praised the troops for marching "with great celerity and so far without loss or accident."[16]

Meanwhile, Meade spent the day checking on troop movement and monitoring the progress of the bridge construction. The bulk of the Second Corps (two divisions) crossed the river by boats during the day. Meade knew part of Grant's plan and told Hancock in the early evening of June 14, "You need not spend any time in taking up a line, but hold yourself ready to move, as you may receive orders to march to Petersburg." By 10 P.M. the plan had been set into motion. Meade wrote Hancock that Butler would send rations to the Second Corps at Wind-Mill Point, and once he had all of these he should move his corps "by the most direct route to Petersburg, taking up a position where the City Point railroad crosses Harrison's Creek at the cross-roads indicated on the map at this point, and extend your right toward the mouth of Harrison's Creek." Less than one hour later, Meade heard from Brig. Gen. Henry Benham that the bridge was finished (save one last boat). Meade told him to "complete the bridge." He then ordered Burnside, Wright, and Warren to "send over their trains and surplus artillery" first.[17] The great crossing of the James had begun.

The majority of the soldiers and their equipment crossed the river on June 15, with Grant and Meade watching their progress from different locations. In a lyrical description of this march, Horace Porter wrote, "Drums were beating the march, bands were playing stirring quicksteps, the distant booming of cannon on Warren's front showed that he and the enemy were still exchanging compliments; and mingled with these sounds were the cheers of the sailors, the shouting of the troops, the rumbling of wheels, and the shrieks of steam-whistles." The best news, of course, was that by the end of the day, the bulk of the Army of the Potomac had successfully crossed the James River.[18]

The Eighteenth Corps under Baldy Smith reached Petersburg first that day. Though Beauregard pulled men from Drewry's Bluff to reinforce the three thousand men he had on the "Dimmock Line," the fresh troops did not arrive before the evening assault by ten Union brigades. After capturing 250 men and one mile of entrenchments, Smith ordered his men to rest until the Second Corps arrived.[19]

The Second Corps began arriving around 5 P.M. Two divisions had made the fourteen-mile march in just over five hours, a solid achievement for men on a hot day with no food to sustain them. The men were slowed by faulty maps, and Hancock needed his staff to reconnoiter new paths. Neither Hancock nor Smith ever recorded the full substance of their conversation, but the outcome was a decision not to launch a night attack. Updating Butler at midnight, Smith wrote, "It is impossible for me to go farther tonight, but, unless I misapprehend the topography, I hold the key to Petersburg."[20]

Smith and Hancock did hold the "key" to Petersburg, more than they knew that night or the next day. But with the bulk of the cavalry of both sides away from the main armies, none of the commanders could do sufficient reconnaissance to know exactly what the other side was doing. On the Confederate side, Lee still could not

be sure that the main threat would be at Petersburg, so he ignored Beauregard's repeated demands for more troops. The troops that Beauregard had called upon earlier
finally marched through Petersburg that night to the fresh line being constructed
behind the Dimmock Line that Beauregard abandoned under cover of darkness.
On the Union side, Grant was not sure what Lee was doing with his men, or of the
strength of the Confederate defense of Petersburg. With the cautious Butler facing
Lee's army at Bermuda Hundred, and almost the entire Army of the Potomac on the
move, it was hard to make a plan. However, Grant had been bolstered by Smith's success ("carried very strongly located and well-constructed work") and a brief telegram
from Lincoln he received on June 16, which read: "Having just read your dispatch of
1 p.m. yesterday I begin to see it. You will succeed. God bless you all."[21]

Another factor that inhibited Union aggressiveness was the poor physical condition of the two corps commanders, Smith and Hancock. Smith felt sickly on June 15,
while Hancock's old wound from Gettysburg had reopened and begun to suppurate
at Cold Harbor, causing him such pain that by June 15 he had to ride in a wagon.[22]

But the leadership of the Army of the Potomac had experienced worse physical
impairment and communication lapses before. What the opportunity lost at Petersburg on June 15 particularly revealed was the perils of divided leadership. Grant
was trying to keep two armies in motion in two different areas, shifting divisions
as rapidly as possible by water and land. While amazing at tactical and logistical
levels, it led to Hancock's receiving orders from Grant through Butler (who was far
from the scene), and the commander of the army tasked with "taking" Petersburg,
Meade, being "copied" through various orders but unsure of the speed at which his
men should move, and the intensity with which they should attack.

Overall, the failure to take Petersburg on June 15, either by day or even by night,
became one of the great missed opportunities of the war. Lyman would write later:
"Oh! That they attacked at once. Petersburg would have gone like a rotten branch. In
war there is a critical instant—at night—perhaps only a half hour, when everything
culminates. He is the military genius who recognizes this instant and acts upon
it, neither precipitating nor postponing the critical moment." Hancock had shown
that genius at Gettysburg; he would not have the chance on the evening of June 15.
Smith, a cautious engineer, had never shown such dash. And Grant and Meade were
too far from the lines to order a swift attack that evening. As Frank Wilkeson recalled that moment of anticipation when the men of the Second Corps expected to
be given the order to attack and take Petersburg, "And then—and then—we went to
cooking." With sickening dread the men of the Second Corps rested in the trenches
knowing that Confederate reinforcements were on their way.[23]

Before catching a few hours of sleep himself, a tired Hancock sent out an uncharacteristic order to his division commanders (Birney and Gibbon) at 12:25 A.M.
on June 16: "If there are any points in your front, commanding your position, now
occupied by the enemy, the major-general commanding directs that they be taken

at or before daybreak, preferably before." It was unusual for Hancock to leave the full responsibility for taking positions up to his division commanders; it was even more unusual that he did not follow up on them until dawn.[24]

When the lines were attacked vigorously by Col. Thomas Egan's First Brigade after 8 A.M., the men managed to seize one battery but not break the line. Hancock then called off further assaults, awaiting the arrival of new orders and the Ninth Corps.[25]

As the bedraggled men of the Ninth Corps shuffled into line to the left of the Second Corps that morning, Grant and his staff went up to the front to visit Smith. He praised Smith for his gains, especially those secured by the black troops. He wrote Meade, "Hurry Warren up by the nearest road to reach the Jerusalem plank road . . . [and] start yourself, by steamer, and get here to take command in person." Grant and his staff then departed for his headquarters at City Point, and on the ride there met Meade and part of his staff. According to Lyman, Grant summarized Smith's success as the taking of a "line of works . . . stronger than anything we have seen this campaign." He verbally gave Meade new—though flexible—orders: "If it is a possible thing, I want an assault made at 6 o'clock this evening!"[26]

Meade rode on toward the front, stopping briefly to talk to Burnside, then reaching Hancock's headquarters at 1:45 P.M. Meade sent Comstock and Col. J. C. Barnard to find weak spots to attack; after a brief survey, they reported that the woods in front of Barlow's division looked best for the attack, though they had "no means of judging of the force . . . the enemy has to resist an assault." Despite the paucity of information, an energized Meade pressed ahead with plans for an attack after further consultations with Hancock. He decided that Barlow and Birney should attack at 6 P.M. "at such point" as either one selected. Burnside's Ninth Corps would form to the rear of Barlow, "to act as a support." Smith's Eighteenth Corps would "threaten an attack" to confuse Confederate generals.[27]

Where or why Meade suddenly found such determination to attack is unknown. Undoubtedly, he found encouragement in several developments: Smith's success the day before, the knowledge that Lee's veterans were *not* the men manning the city's defenses (though they were en route), Grant's excitement and clear decision to let Meade have command of the corps arriving at Petersburg, and the simple fact that the objective, Petersburg, could be glimpsed from many spots on the Union line (unlike the blind and foreboding forest of the Wilderness). Of course he may have been overcompensating for past failures, especially now that it appeared that Grant would actually let him command the fresh assault. Regardless of the reasons for his renewed determination to score a victory after the bloody stalemates of the previous month, "Meade would prove to be the only major Union commander not caught in the throes of lethargy," writes Sean Chick, a modern student of the Battle of Petersburg.[28]

What Meade did not know—without the full intelligence that a large and active cavalry force would have provided—was that the Confederate lines were quite redoubtable, even if manned by tired, less-experienced soldiers (though Lee's veterans in Bushrod Johnson's division had marched to the front all day). Also, the greatest weakness was not the center of the Confederate line but its far right flank. Unfortunately, Meade planned to hurl two divisions of tired veterans at the strong breastworks at the center of the Confederate lines on one of the hottest days of the summer.[29]

Despite such concerns, the attack began promptly at 6 P.M. on June 16 with an intense artillery barrage. Smith sent two brigades forward, which managed to tie down almost two Confederate brigades. To Smith's left was Gibbon's division; Birney sent in two brigades, which were repulsed with high losses. Barlow's division formed at the left of the Second Corps, and the aggressive young general took his orders seriously; he led his four brigades in the assault (one brigade followed another), and none of them breached the Confederate lines. Rounding out the assault was Burnside's Ninth Corps, which advanced only a few yards before halting. The attacks sputtered out as darkness fell, with the Second Corps reporting the heaviest losses: four brigade commanders (including the indomitable commander of the "Irish Brigade," Col. Patrick Kelly), sixteen officers, and nearly two thousand men. The durable Second Corps had taken another brutal beating.[30]

Throughout the battle, Meade sat on his horse and closely observed the action, peering through the "dust and powder smoke . . . [that] gave a copper color to the scene." At one point, the fighting found him. Lyman recorded that Meade had a "very narrow escape from a round-shot which bounded just past him and Gen. Humphreys." Horace Porter also observed Meade during the battle and found him "actively engaged in superintending the attack." He added, "His usual nervous energy was displayed in the intensity of his manner and the rapid and animated style of his conversation." But energy and focus could not win this battle, and Meade sent Lyman to see Grant after dark with a report of the attack. Lyman delivered the report in person to Grant, whom he found sitting on his cot in his shirt and drawers. Grant responded, "I think it is pretty well to get across a great river, and come up here and attack Lee in his rear before he is ready for us."[31]

Meade was not done. Despite the failures on the sixteenth, Meade decided to try again on the seventeenth. He ordered Burnside to make a night attack (in the moonlight) when he felt ready. The Second Division under the steady hand of Brig. Gen. Robert Potter was ready to attack by 3:15 A.M., when Burnside asked Meade whether it should attack or march to Smith's aid. Meade answered definitively, "I want the attack to go in as ordered, with all the force you can put in." Marching silently without pausing to load or fire weapons, the men of Brig. Gen. Simon G. Griffin's Second Brigade ran up Hickory Hill at daybreak, swiftly capturing cannons, men, and flags. Col. John Curtin's First Brigade also successfully charged up Hickory Hill, though it did exchange fire because Curtin did not plan for a bayonet-only assault. In less than two hours, Potter's two brigades captured six hundred soldiers, four guns, and five flags, at a cost of two hundred men. By 6 A.M. on June 17, they temporarily controlled a half mile of earthworks, making it one of the most successful charges of the past six weeks. A pleased Meade sent a rare official note to Burnside commending him for the attack: "It affords me great satisfaction to congratulate you and your gallant corps on the successful assault made this morning."[32]

Meade also sent Humphreys south of the Union lines to the Norfolk Railroad to scout out a place for possible attack, but after spending "some hours there," Humphreys rode back to Battery No. 14, where he met Burnside. He did not recommend attacking the Confederate far right flank (a suggestion Barlow had made on the sixteenth of June that was not followed). Meade considered Hancock's proposal that Warren attack with his corps to Burnside's left, but with Warren's exhausted men still filing in for most of the morning, Meade was content to order Warren to "make reconnaissances, so as to ascertain the position of the enemy and the character of the ground in their front, to guide us in future operations." Meade also worried about a flank attack on his left by Lee's veterans, as Lee had surprised the Army of the Potomac several times before. Consequently, he ordered Warren to "send an officer and escort to examine the Blackwater Swamp, to your left and rear."[33]

Overall, Meade dithered on the morning of June 17 after the initial success of the Ninth Corps assault. The Second Corps had advanced only a little, the Eighteenth Corps was tied down, and the Fifth Corps had yet to arrive prepared to attack. He missed the services of the Sixth Corps, which had been sent off to help Butler at Bermuda Hundred. He also missed the services of the cavalry under Sheridan and, to his own detriment, he sent Brig. Gen. August V. Kautz's cavalry division to Butler (as requested). That left Meade with only a small detachment of cavalry (the Third Pennsylvania) under Provost Marshal Patrick, which he sent to help Warren, if needed. Meade was able to watch the Confederates build a new defensive line along Baxter Road (that led into Petersburg). Meade did not have enough information on Confederate numbers or the strength of their new line, nor did he have a fresh corps to throw at the line to break it. But Meade did not appear fazed by this lull in the action, as he took the time at noon to write a letter to his wife. He updated her on the long march and the quick attacks of the sixteenth and seventeenth, deeming both to be "successful." He also took the credit for the attacks, stating that he had been "placed by General Grant in command of all the troops in front of Petersburg . . . Grant being back at City Point." He hinted at his view of the current situation: "We find the enemy, as usual, in a very strong position, defended by earthworks. . . . It looks very much as if we will have to go through a siege of Petersburg before entering on the siege of Richmond, and that Grant's words of keeping at it all summer will prove to be quite prophetic."[34]

In hindsight, Meade lost another opportunity to break through the Confederate defenses. He could have been suddenly enervated, or, if his comments to his wife were any clue to his thinking on that day, he may have believed that although the Ninth Corps had made some small gains, he needed more time to assess the new situation. He was not pushed in any direction by Grant, who briefly visited him in the afternoon at Hancock's headquarters. In fact, he may not have even known the full extent of the fighting done by Burnside's First and Third divisions in the afternoon. Revealing his lack of information, Meade wrote to Warren in the evening of June 17, "I have no report from Burnside, but only a message from Lieu-tenant-Colonel Locke, your assistant adjutant general." A half hour later, Meade asked Frederick T. Locke to send him "the prisoners who think Petersburg can be taken if we go ahead." Based on these evening dispatches, Meade not only did not know the full result of Burnside's afternoon attacks, but he also did not know how thinly held the Confederate lines were. Unfortunately, there was little he could do with the information. Warren sent Brig. Gen. Samuel Crawford's division on a reconnaissance that could have led to a nighttime assault, except they got lost and tangled in the woods and ravines. Even before he learned this fact, Meade had resigned himself to attempting a larger attack the following day. He wrote Warren, "If time is required for preparation I would prefer the attack being postponed till daylight tomorrow, and the men allowed to rest. Show this to Burnside."[35]

The message reached Col. Jacob Gould's First Brigade, First Division of the Ninth Corps too late, as it was engaged in a desperate fight to hold on to the sa-lient it had made in the Confederate lines. After enduring several fierce attacks, the remnants of the brigade fell back just before midnight. As the exhausted men collapsed, their counterparts on the Confederate side were already preparing to work all night to prepare a new, shorter defensive line, much closer to the city, but much more compact, too. Some men were tasked with keeping campfires blazing all night to hide the retreat and work of many others. The tired Confederates were preparing to defend their city again.[36]

No one at Union headquarters got much sleep that night, either. Meade spent the early hours of June 18 preparing for another assault. Hancock told him he could muster four lines for a brigade front attack. Then at 1 A.M. Hancock sent his last order of the morning: a "vigorous assault" would begin at 4 A.M., led by Birney's Third Division. Meanwhile, Hancock's pain from his old Gettysburg wound had become so intense that he had to relinquish his command to Birney one hour later. Burnside hesitated to attack. He wrote Meade at 3:15 A.M. that the "First Division is in no condition to attack . . . [and] the two other divisions are very much wearied as we made three assaults yesterday." He pleaded, "I can attack with them, but I am not confident of doing much. Shall I attack with them?" Meade tersely and emphatically replied, "I want the attack to go on as ordered with all the force you can put in."[37]

With Hancock and Burnside reluctant to attack, and Smith and Warren unreli-able to attack, why did Meade insist on attacking on June 18? Part of his thinking was revealed late in the day after a brutal period of fighting and corps leadership collapse; he told Lyman at dinner, "I had hoped all along to have entered Petersburg this day."[38] It is easy in hindsight to see what historians Thomas Howe and Sean Michael Chick have proven about the four-day battle, that, in Chick's estimate, "a general Union assault might have succeeded on June 16 or June 17."[39] Furthermore, numerous testimonies from Union soldiers strongly convey the view that the night of June 15 offered an even better chance to take Petersburg. However, by June 18 Beauregard had been amply reinforced and had been given several days to strengthen and rearrange his defenses.

So why attack on the eighteenth? To begin with, Meade was not on the field on June 15, and the two corps commanders did not take full advantage of their momentum that evening. The attacks on the sixteenth and seventeenth had been more piecemeal than coordinated, and it was not until midday on the seventeenth that Meade's full contingent of soldiers was present. So given his caution and deliberate mind-set toward assault preparations, it is logical that he hoped to strike the final blow on June 18. He also never knew the disposition of the enemy defenses or the exact location of Lee's troops, though enough men had been captured by the late hours of the seventeenth to reassure him that the majority of Lee's army had not yet reached Petersburg. Of course he always had the aggressive Grant looming behind him, and that awareness undoubtedly fueled his desire to attack the Confederates again. Finally, his sensitivity about his reputation may have played a role. When describing to his wife why he dealt so severely with Cropsey even though some newspaper editors urged him to ignore such camp gossip, he argued, "Neither of the papers can appreciate the particular force of this libel which served to confirm the charges brought at Williamsport, Centreville, and Mine Run, being that I was always on the defensive and prepared to run away in the plea of saving the army."[40] George G. Meade did not need Grant's staff whispering about his unwillingness to go on the offensive—he had his own demons goading him. For all these reasons, Meade forged ahead with his plan to attack—only to face one of the most frustrating and ultimately mismanaged operations of his entire tenure as commander of the Army of the Potomac.

Despite the hesitancy of his corps commanders, the assault commenced at 4 A.M. with cannon fire. Skirmishers moved silently through the fog at first light only to find nothing. In a moment eerily reminiscent of Meade's bitter experience at Williamsport, the first group of men found Confederate lines deserted. Finally at 5:30 A.M., the first wave of Gibbon's Second Division of the Second Corps ran into the fire from the new, hastily built Confederate line. Fearful of what lay ahead that they could not see, the lead units stopped and entrenched.[41]

That story would be repeated by lead units of the other corps throughout the morning. Units would advance through woods or ravines, only to emerge onto open fields where Confederate gunners and marksmen had a clear line of fire. Making matters both worse and infuriating, Meade learned shortly after 7 A.M. that Baldy Smith had departed from the area with one division (without informing

Meade) to join Butler at Bermuda Hundred. He left behind two divisions under the senior commander, Brig. Gen. John H. Martindale, and the newly arrived Second Attached Division of the Sixth Corps, led by Brig. Gen. Thomas H. Neill. Showing again the problems with a divided command, Meade now had to rely on two inexperienced corps commanders (Martindale and Birney) and two slow, timid, and obstinate corps commanders (Burnside and Warren). The slow progress of the Second Corps that morning was emblematic of the problems of each corps. At 7 A.M. Meade wrote Birney, "It is of great importance the enemy should be pressed, and if possible, forced across the Appomattox." Knowing he had numerical superiority, Meade added: "They cannot be over 30,000, and we have 55,000. If we can engage them before they are fortified we ought to whip them." (As usual, Union estimates of Confederate numbers were wildly exaggerated; Beauregard had only eleven thousand men present before Lee's army began arriving in mid-morning.) But Birney found the line too strong to attack, and by 10 A.M. Meade plaintively asked him, "What progress are you making? . . . I think there is too much time taken in preparations, and I fear the enemy will make more of the delay than we can." Meade's fears were well founded: Lee had finally ordered five divisions (Joseph Kershaw's, Charles Field's, and three divisions under A. P. Hill) to march to Petersburg, and they were filling in the line as the morning wore on. Meanwhile, Beauregard's exhausted men pushed themselves to build their defenses higher and stronger. Not until just before noon did the Second Corps hit the new Confederate line with force, and they were stopped cold.[42]

Meade still believed that a simultaneous, strong attack from all corps could break the strong yet thin Confederate lines. At 11:34 A.M. he sent an order to all four corps commanders: "The attack ordered will be made by your command punctually at 12 m. Please telegraph to these headquarters for the time, in order that the attack may be as simultaneous as possible." Having learned from Upton's and Hancock's assaults at Spotsylvania, he told the commanders to attack in columns, not lines, so the defenses could be broken in vulnerable spots. He exhorted his commanders to "push them vigorously, endeavoring to have them advance rapidly over the ground without firing till they have penetrated the enemy's line."[43]

Then, as so often happened, no sooner had the orders been issued than Warren found reasons not to carry them out. At 11:36 A.M. he wired Meade, "I am gradually forcing the enemy's skirmishers back and getting batteries forward. I cannot be ready to attack in line or column before 1 p.m." An exasperated Meade promptly replied, "I cannot change the hour of attack just issued. Everyone else is ready. You will attack as soon as possible after the hour designated, and endeavor to be ready at that hour." With these sharp words staring at him, Warren advanced some units at noon, yet even by 12:45 P.M. progress was slow, as Lyman (sent to be with Warren) wrote to Meade, "The line is advancing. No assault yet on the entrenchments." Some units did eventually attack, as did brigades from the other three corps. One by one, however, they were stopped by murderous fire. As the assault sputtered, Meade received a strange and infuriating message from Warren, endorsed by Burnside. Warren had not attacked in full yet (by 2 P.M.) because Barlow's division (on Burnside's right) could not advance owing to enfilading fire. He suggested a new plan, "a rush at, say, 3 p.m." Burnside's accompanying note said, "I fully concur with the statement of General Warren." Meade's frustration with his corps commanders reached new heights. He wrote back: "I am greatly astonished at your dispatch of 2 p.m. What additional orders you require I cannot imagine. My orders have been explicit and are now repeated, that you each immediately assault the enemy with all your force, and if there is any further delay the responsibility and the consequences will rest with you."[44]

Still seething, Meade soon demonstrated he had reached a low point in his tenure as commander of the Army of the Potomac. Frustrated for more than ten hours by corps commanders who appeared unable if not unwilling to carry out his orders, he sent a new order to Birney at 2:30 P.M. that displayed every shade of his frustration: "I have sent a positive order to Generals Burnside and Warren to attack at all hazards with their whole force. I find it useless to appoint an hour to effect cooperation, and I am therefore compelled to give you the same order." He concluded with a plea, "You have a large corps, powerful and numerous, and I beg you will at once, as soon as possible, assault in a strong column."[45]

At last the urgency got through to Meade's corps commanders. One by one they sent some (but not all) of their brigades toward ever-stronger Confederate lines, and everywhere they were stopped. When the fresh and relatively unscarred First Maine Heavy Artillery of the Third Brigade, Third Division of the Second Corps charged by the Hare House and lost over six hundred men in ten minutes, Birney, and soon Meade, bowed to the truth of the situation: the lines could not be breached that day. At 5 P.M. Meade wrote to Birney: "Sorry to hear you could not carry the works. Get the best line you can and be prepared to hold it. I suppose you cannot make any more attacks, and I feel satisfied all has been done." An hour and a half later, he sent a similar message to Warren and Burnside: "Birney has made a strong attack and been repulsed. Exercise your judgment as to further operations. . . . When you conclude that nothing further is practicable straighten your lines and make your connections secure." Meade sent almost the same message to Martindale. When Warren suddenly and strangely found a willingness to attack at 7 P.M. ("we want to make another effort at dark"), Meade stopped him cold, writing, "It is useless to make another attack, because I doubt your or my ability to follow it up." On that sad and sour note, the four-day battle of Petersburg came to a close.[46]

Nothing remained for Meade to do but monitor the safety of the Union lines and report to Grant. When he wrote Grant at 6:30 P.M. on June 18, Warren and Burnside were still advancing, but Meade was not hopeful of success, given "indications that Beauregard has been re-enforced by Lee." Grant promptly replied, "I think that after

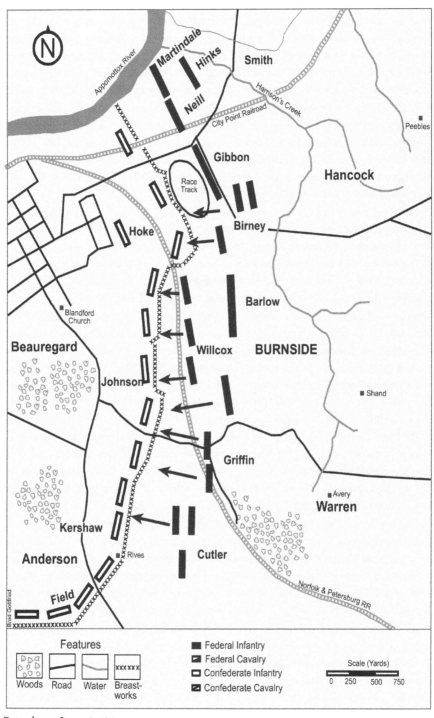

Petersburg, June 18, 1864

the present assault, unless a decided advantage presents itself, our men should have rest, protecting themselves as well as possible." Later in the night, Meade sent Grant a full report of the day's fighting, generously giving only light criticism of Warren's and Burnside's actions in the early afternoon: "Warren was not quite ready, and Burnside, whose movements were somewhat connected with Warren, delayed also." But then he mentioned the fighting that each of the corps did later in the day, declaring they had "no better success than others." He plainly admitted that "losses . . . have been severe," though not more "than would be expected from the numbers engaged." Finishing with an apology of sorts, he wrote, "It is a source of great regret that I am not able to report more success, but I believe every effort to command it has been made."[47]

Apparently Grant felt the same. He quickly replied to Meade, "I am perfectly satisfied that all has been done that could be done, and that the assaults today were called for by all the appearances and information that could be obtained." He then suggested a new tactic that unofficially ended the longest, bloodiest campaign of the war: "Now we will rest the men and use the spade for their protection until a new vein can be struck."[48]

Other contemporaries' views of the Battle of Petersburg were not as generous as Grant. Colonel Wainwright took a dim and bitter line when evaluating the Fifth Corps' attack on June 18: "The attack this afternoon was a fiasco of the worst kind; I trust it will be the last attempt at this most absurd way of attacking entrenchments by a general advance in the line. It has been tried so often now and with such fearful losses that even the stupidest private now knows it cannot succeed." Lyman held a similar view, though expressed in his less pessimistic, pithy style. He wrote, "It was as I expected—forty-five days of constant marching, assaulting and trenching are a poor preparation for a rush!"[49]

It was good that Grant had finally seen the benefit of rest, for the army was nearing its breaking point. Several observers, including Frank Wilkeson, noted that some Union regiments refused to charge. After talking to men of the Excelsior Brigade (Second Corps), he summarized their feelings, "I spoke to many of these men, and all I spoke to were resolute in their purpose not to make a determined charge of the Confederate entrenchments. And they did not." Wainwright witnessed the same behavior among men of the Fifth Corps and noted, "The very sight of a bank of fresh earth now brings them to a dead halt." The day after the fighting, his view of the state of the army was even lower; he wrote in his diary, "As to getting the men up to assaulting point, I do not believe it is possible; never has the Army of the Potomac been so demoralized as at this time."[50]

Finally recognizing the physical and emotional state of his soldiers, on June 21 Meade wrote to his wife, "The army is exhausted with forty-nine days of continued marching and fighting, and absolutely requires rest to prevent its *morale* being impaired." Three days later, he took even more responsibility for the failure at Petersburg but offered reasons for it as well. He wrote to his wife, "On the 18th I assaulted several times the enemy's positions . . . [but] I failed, and met with serious loss." He elaborated, "Principally owing to the moral condition of the army; for I am satisfied, had these assaults been made on the 5th and 6th of May, we should have succeeded with half the loss we met." Reinforcing the depressing results of continual losses of men were the deaths and wounding of "superior and other officers." In the Second Corps alone, "twenty brigade commanders" had fallen, and "the rest of the army [was] . . . similarly situated." Still, Meade was optimistic that the Union, with its reservoir of men and resources, would prevail, "but it is a question of tenacity and nerve, and it won't do to look behind, or to calculate the cost in blood and treasure; if we do we are lost and our enemies succeed."[51]

It was necessary for Meade and Grant to put the best light possible on this disappointing battle. As Sean Michael Chick says of the last battle of the Civil War in which combined losses totaled over fifteen thousand men, "Making the defeat more bitter was the fact that few Civil War battles could have been as decisive as the Battle of Petersburg." Though Meade, Grant, Hancock, and other top Union commanders in the East might have disputed the potential of a win at Petersburg, what was not up for dispute was the main reason for the loss, summed up best by Lyman. He wrote, "You cannot strike a full blow with a wounded hand."[52]

The next day, Sunday, June 19, found both the "wounded hand" that was the Union army and its exhausted yet defiant counterpart beginning the grimy work of building or strengthening breastworks around Petersburg. Lyman was sent out again to meet with Confederate officers to "get an armistice for burial of the dead and removal of the wounded." (Beauregard refused the offer.) Sharpshooters stayed busy all day and the next, occasionally joined by artillery fire. Wright and the remaining division of the Sixth Corps were ordered to return to Meade, replacing Martindale's division of the Eighteenth Corps on the far right of the Union line (it would go to Butler).[53]

On the following hot, sunny Monday, Meade rode off to meet with Grant and on the way had a conversation with Warren. It turned into a shouting match whose effects lingered for months.[54]

The conversation occurred in Warren's tent, but it was not held in private: Brig. Gen. Samuel Crawford was present, and "several officers" were just outside the tent. Meade never recorded the exact words that were spoken, but he later wrote to Warren in an official letter, "[I was] much irritated, and felt deeply wounded by the tone and tenor of your conversation . . . [and was] fully determined, on leaving you, to apply to have you relieved."[55]

Warren wrote of the same conversation to his wife Emily on the day it occurred, but his interpretation of its impact differed completely from Meade's. He wrote, "A rupture is probable between me and General Meade who has become very irritable and unreasonable of late, and with whom I had a square understanding today, to the effect that I was no creature of his." Displaying that supreme confidence and self-vindication he was known for, he added, "[I am] so well satisfied with my efforts and integrity—that I would not fear to run against General Grant if necessary."[56] Warren came very close to running that gauntlet because Meade discussed the situation with Grant when they met later that day, and Grant gave his permission for Meade to relieve Warren, if he felt it necessary. Meade chewed on the subject for a day and, on June 21, wrote a long letter to Grant's top aide, Brig. Gen. John Rawlins, in which he explained his reasons for asking for Warren's dismissal.[57]

But he never sent the letter. Showing again his extreme reluctance to remove his corps commanders (especially Warren), he "withheld" the letter "in the hope the causes of disagreement would not occur in the future." Instead, the argument he had with Warren became an important subject of camp gossip, finally boiling over a month later when the *Pittsburg Commercial* published a story referring to it. In a letter to Meade, Warren asked him if one part in particular, that Meade had "threatened" him with a court-martial if he did not resign, had been stated by Meade to the newspaper reporter. Meade replied at length, describing the angry exchange of June 20 and his subsequent actions. As for the major concerns of Warren, that Meade had "preferred charges against . . . [him] for disobedience and tardy execution of orders," Meade categorically denied such an action; it was "entirely without foundation in fact." His denial partially satisfied Warren, though in private he still fumed.[58] For the time being, the generals would continue their working relationship, but the wound would take months to heal (if it ever did).

Although Meade never sent his letter to Rawlins, its existence was well known among top-level staffers, and it provides valuable insight into Meade's views of his protégé in the summer of 1864. Meade began his analysis with praise: "No officer in the Army exceeds General Warren in personal gallantry, in activity, in zeal and sleepless energy, nor in devotion to his duties." Getting to the heart of the problem, he wrote, "The defect with General Warren consists in too great reliance on his own judgment—and in an apparent impossibility to yield his judgment so as to promptly execute orders, where these orders should happen not to receive his sanction or be in accordance with his views." Meade then gave three cardinal examples of Warren's "defect" on display. At Mine Run, Warren's decision to suspend the attack caused "such delay and loss of time as virtually produced an entire suspension of operations and the withdrawal of the Army." At Spotsylvania Court House on May 12, Warren's delay and then refusal to attack, despite saying earlier he would, left Hancock's Second Corps alone and stranded. He did not blame Warren for the result of the battle, or even question his judgment on the wisdom of an attack. His main complaint in that instance was that Warren "had no right to delay executing his orders under any circumstances." He hedged his complaint by stating that if Warren had told him "promptly" of his views—but still followed his orders—he actually might have "yielded" his own judgment on the wisdom of an attack, given his high "opinion of General Warren's judgment."

The third incident occurred on June 18 at Petersburg, when, in the process of advancing and probing the enemy's position, all the corps commanders communicated to Meade the time they would be ready to attack, except Warren, "who said he could not tell when he would be ready." Meade then issued "a positive and preemptory order" to attack at noon, and Warren replied he could not be ready until 1 P.M. In response, Meade authorized Warren to commence his attack at 1 P.M., but Warren did not order an attack at 1 P.M., or even 2 P.M. Warren asked Meade for further orders, and Meade said this dispatch "produced astonishment." He was then sternly ordered to attack—and he did (but it was probably too late). Meade carefully noted that he did not believe Warren had exercised a "willful disobedience of orders," but because he was not ready to attack at 1 P.M., the original order lost its standing. Meade concluded by saying he had hoped Warren would "correct" his defect, and that was why he did not dismiss him after Spotsylvania, though Grant had authorized him to do so. But after Warren's outburst on June 20, in which he forgot "the respect due to me as his superior officer," Meade finally admitted his "inability" to reform Warren. Therefore, he asked that Warren be relieved of command.[59]

Several things are revealed in this long letter. First, the embarrassment of Mine Run and the disappointment of Spotsylvania and Petersburg were fresh on Meade's mind. Secondly, he had enormous respect, if not fondness, for G. K. Warren. Next to Hancock he had been Meade's most trusted corps commander, but also his biggest headache. Yet even now, after Warren had challenged an order or refused to carry it out, Meade's unwillingness to fire subordinates, not his famed temper, may have been his greatest failure as a general. A window into this vulnerability was partly opened in his letter to Warren on July 22, 1864, when he wrote, "It is my earnest desire to have harmony and cooperation with my subordinate officers, but I cannot always yield my judgment to theirs."[60] Yet at crucial moments in his career he had yielded to "their" judgments—and paid a stiff professional price for this loyalty.

Despite his frustrations with Warren and other generals, Meade still had a war to win. The principal subject of his meeting with Grant at City Point on June 20 was not Warren's insubordination but the development of a plan to pressure the Confederates. Grant and Meade decided to put three groups into motion. Wilson's Third Cavalry Division would ride as far west as the Danville Road, damaging as much of the railroads they crossed as possible. Meanwhile, the Second and Sixth Corps would be used to extend the Union line to the Appomattox River. Grant would order Butler to destroy the railroad bridge over the Appomattox River north of Petersburg.[61]

The plans were set in motion the following day, June 21. The Second Corps moved to the left of the Fifth Corps, and Wilson's division was augmented with four regiments of cavalry under Kautz. Meade and Grant expected Sheridan to keep Hampton's cavalry busy at White House. They also hoped that Wilson might ride so far east he would link up with Hunter's army near Lynchburg.[62]

While thousands of men trudged to new positions, Grant and Meade had a visit with President Lincoln on June 21. Though Lincoln spent most of the day with Grant and his staff riding among troops, he came to Meade's headquarters where they had a good conversation. Meade recounted to his wife how Lincoln "was so gracious as to say he had seen you in Philadelphia." That evening, Lincoln regaled Grant's staff with some of his fabled storytelling, and the next day went to see the Union gunboats, traveling on a steamer chugging upriver.[63]

On the day Lincoln left Grant's headquarters (June 22), the Second Corps suffered a stinging defeat southeast of Petersburg. As the Second Corps began probing the Confederate defenses, the Confederates found and exploited a seam in the Union assault. The plan was for the First and Third Divisions of the Second Corps to move forward, with the Sixth Corps moving simultaneously on the left of the First Division under Barlow. Unfortunately, Wright's Sixth Corps could not advance through the woods and thickets, leaving the First Division of the Second Corps vulnerable to attack, though it was able to connect with Mott's Third Division on its right. Barlow sought guidance on the matter, and at 10 A.M. he received a new order that reflected the reality of the situation, which greatly worried him. Birney's chief of staff, Lt. Col. Charles H. Morgan, told Barlow, "[Continue] moving forward . . . until your whole line is in close proximity to that of the enemy." Furthermore, his division would not "be dependent on any movement of the 6th Corps." This order was also conveyed in person by Meade, who said to him, "You cannot connect with both; keep your connection to the right; each corps must look out for itself."[64]

But Confederates were not idle that morning. In addition to the heavy skirmishing with Wright's Sixth Corps that had already begun, the possibility of an attack on the exposed left flank of Barlow's division presented itself to Confederate officers, especially Petersburg prewar railroad executive Brig. Gen. William Mahone. Lee gave him permission to use three brigades. Mahone led them into position through a hollow, and around 2 P.M. they attacked on the "left and rear" of Barlow's division. The fast-moving Confederates quickly overwhelmed three Union brigades, which retreated in panic to the breastworks they had left that morning. The frightened Union troops imperiled Mott's left, which also collapsed. When the excited Confederates pressed on, they were finally stopped by Gibbon's Second Division of the Second Corps.[65]

Counterattacks were undertaken by the Second Corps that afternoon and evening, but little ground was regained. By 9 P.M. Meade had already ordered the Second and Sixth Corps to attack the next morning at 3:30 A.M. Based on very fragmentary reports, Meade sent a highly positive message to Grant at 9 P.M. While acknowledging the loss of four guns, he declared that "the effect of the advance has been good." In terms of human losses, he wrote, "We have taken about 100 prisoners; probably lost as many. Our casualties are, I think, light."[66]

He could not have been more wrong about the casualties. By the end of the day, Confederates had captured 1,742 men, 2,000 rifles, and 8 battle flags. It was one of the worst losses of the entire war for the Second Corps, for which Barlow blamed not only the separation from the Sixth Corps but also his own men, writing, "The troops did not meet the attack with vigor and courage and determination." The loss was yet another result of over fifty days of fighting, with Barlow's Second and Third Brigades becoming "too unsteady, from loss of commanding and other officers and other causes."[67]

Somehow Barlow and other divisional commanders managed to steady their units because early the next morning the First division of the Second Corps advanced as ordered, covering over a mile by 6 A.M. By 8:30 A.M. Meade was so satisfied with the advance that he instructed them not to "attack" the "enemy's works." He further ordered, "As soon as you can advance your line in connection with Wright to envelop the enemy's line, I desire it done, and that you entrench yourself in the strongest manner possible." The order must have been music to the ears of the Second Corps infantrymen. Meade's immediate concern, however, was the puzzle of Wright's apparent lack of progress. At noon he reiterated earlier orders: "Advance until you meet the enemy and press them back into their works." Barlow's skirmishers were out one and a half miles—where were Wright's? Meade also wanted Wright's small cavalry detachment to "feel for the enemy" and "destroy the railroad" to the left of the advancing Sixth Corps.[68]

But while Wright had been tentative in his movements that morning, Lee and A. P. Hill had not. The two Confederate generals had seen another possibility for attack, and they ordered the reliable Mahone to use six brigades and two batteries to hit the exposed left flank of the Sixth Corps. The attack began shortly after 3 P.M. and moved quickly along the Weldon Railroad. Wright notified Meade of the attack, and Meade asked Warren to send two brigades to support Wright. He also told Birney to prepare to pull back his line and defend, if necessary. Sensing some panic in Wright's dispatches, Meade sent a full and clear order at 4 P.M.: "Take the initiative and attack the enemy if, in your judgment, this course is advisable." If not advisable and a withdrawal were necessary, Meade added, "Notify General Barlow, who will be directed to withdraw his left as you do your right." He informed him that reinforcements from Warren were on their way and finished with a strong plea: "The enemy must be resisted with all your force, and, if practicable, forced back."[69]

Yet no matter how much Meade urged, Wright would not attack. In a series of dispatches between 6:30 P.M. and 7:35 P.M., Meade respectfully instructed Wright to attack, as in the 6:55 dispatch: "I would attack at once wherever the enemy has shown himself in force." Meade did not want to lose ground, the railroad, or, especially, large numbers of men in the Sixth Corps should the Confederates get behind them. But Wright just as persistently preferred to defend. At 7 P.M. he wrote to Meade, "So far it has been as much as I could do to prevent my flank being turned and quite impossible to form a column of attack." He added, "It seems to me that till everything is quiet our role is the defensive. In this opinion I am fully sustained by two division commanders; the other is not here." Exasperated, Meade wrote back, "Your line of battle is the formation to attack in. I know there is no time to form columns." When there was no word of an attack, Meade lectured Wright, "Your delay has been fatal. . . . I will not blindly order you to do what you seem reluctant as a matter of judgment, but as I stated in my last you must be responsible for the consequences." At 8:40 P.M. Wright reported that he had withdrawn his troops to the position of the day before. Given the darkness, Meade accepted the inevitable, authorizing a withdrawal, though he told Wright to be ready to "take the offensive tomorrow at early daylight" and to report to his headquarters. Once again, Meade's plans had been thwarted by the timidity of one of his corps commanders.[70]

Before Wright arrived at Meade's headquarters, Lyman returned from a long, frustrating day by Wright's side and found his commander "in a tearing passion at Wright and at everybody else. . . . He undertook to pitch into me." But Lyman stood his ground and proved to Meade that the Confederates had indeed got into the "rear" and not just the "flank" of the Sixth Corps. Lyman's journal entry included a withering judgment from the usually objective observer who strived to find some good in most actions: "I look on June 22 and 23 as the two most discreditable days to this army that I ever saw! There was everywhere, high and low, feebleness, confusion, poor judgment. The only person who kept his plans and judgment clear was General Meade himself." Lyman was especially critical of Wright, who "on this particular occasion . . . showed himself totally unfit to command a corps."[71]

It was fortunate for Wright that Meade had time to "let off steam," and that Lyman was not his commanding officer. Lyman recorded that Wright and Meade talked that evening and "parted on good terms." He added, "The General respects him, though grievously disappointed this time." It was also fortunate that Wright did not yet know the extent of his losses that day: six hundred men and officers had been captured.[72]

After a few hours of sleep for men and officers, Sixth Corps skirmishers cautiously pushed out in the early hours of June 24, encountering only stragglers. Unbeknownst to them, Mahone and Hill had withdrawn the troops the night before. By mid-morning the Sixth Corps skirmishers had "advanced to the position" it held the day before, two and a half miles beyond the breastworks. Wright asked Meade what he should do next. Meade told him to send his pickets forward; once they "secured sufficient ground," he further ordered, "[move] your line of battle . . . forward, connecting with General Birney's, whose left will be moved to correspond with your right." In other words, both the Second and Sixth Corps would return to their forward locations of the day before. Meanwhile, Meade waited for Grant to join him at the front.[73]

When Grant showed up at Meade's headquarters, he had with him two French officers who came to observe the Union army. After lunch Grant left the officers with Meade's staff, and Lyman had to play host to them for the next *three* months. Grant joked to the group about his unfamiliarity with French, telling them that if his West Point class ranking had been turned to the "other end" he would have "graduated high in French." At some point during the lunch Meade and Grant huddled alone to discuss their next steps. Shaken by the losses of the Second Corps and the shaky performance of the Sixth Corps, they decided to rest the men and improve their breastworks while they considered options for their next move. As Grant wrote to Halleck the next day, "I shall try to give the army a few days' rest, which they now stand much in need of."[74]

The "few days of rest" would stretch to over a month, at least for the generals and some of the men. During that month breastworks would be strengthened, corps and divisions occasionally moved from one place to another, and Wilson's battered cavalry division would return (on July 1) after near capture at Ream's Station. Grant and Lee used the month to rest and refit their men, while constantly evaluating options for attack and looking for weaknesses on the other side. Lee ordered Early to move his small army up the Shenandoah Valley, then across Maryland and Virginia to the very outskirts of Washington by July 14. That bold move so rattled the authorities in Washington that Grant was forced to send the Sixth Corps to reinforce the city and then chase the Confederates to the west (with a promise to send the Nineteenth Corps from Louisiana to its aid if needed). The loss of one corps and the delay in adding another confined the scope of Grant's possibilities for attack. By late July he would be finalizing plans for a two-pronged offensive against the Confederate lines: one near Richmond at Deep Bottom, and the other a direct attack on Pegram's Salient just outside Petersburg. Meade would be at the center of most of the deliberations during that month, except when he was preoccupied by rumors about his job security and performance.

One of Meade's constant aggravations was his continuing poor relations with the press. Though he may not have known of the reporters' informal embargo on the use of his name in stories, he could see that his name was purposely omitted simply by reading newspapers. On June 25 he told his wife that he had asked their good friend Marko Bache to write the publisher of the *Philadelphia Inquirer,* William Harding, explaining to him why Meade had expelled Cropsey from the army, even to the point of sending him a copy of Cropsey's confession. Harding did not respond, nor did he take up Meade's offer to publish the letter. Meade complained, "The public are to this day ignorant of the real character of Cropsey's offense." Meade needed no more evidence of the animus of the press toward him than the attack on him in the *New York Times* on July 16 for his order to expel or deny access to two correspondents, William Swinton and William Kent. It turned out that Grant had wanted Swinton out, and Hancock wanted Kent excluded (which Grant authorized). Meade had merely been the operating authority. Meade told his wife, "Grant expressed himself very much annoyed at the injustice done me." Grant went a step further, telling Meade that "there was an evident intention to hold me [Meade] accountable for all that was condemned, and to praise him for all that was considered commendable."[75]

Hearing Grant state this truth must have pleased Meade, but other rumors he heard that came from Grant or someone close to him would be of greater concern than his usual contretemps with the press. When Hancock returned to active duty in mid-July, Meade rode over to his temporary headquarters where he found Hancock stretched out "at full length, in a covered wagon," trying to give his bad leg a rest. As Lyman fondly noted, "General Meade mounted on the front seat, put his feet on the foot-board and lighted a cigar; and we all knew he was fixed for an hour at least." What Lyman did not know at the time was the troubling information Hancock shared with Meade. Apparently, Meade was to be removed from command and replaced by Hancock. Meade told his wife, "He would not give me his authority, but said it was reliable." For once, Meade did not overreact; he wrote that the news "seemed so preposterous that I could not help laughing."[76]

Though Meade put on a brave air, writing in his usual vein, "My conscience is clear that I have done my duty to the best of my ability since this campaign commenced," he brought it up in a conversation with Grant the next day. He first asked if Grant planned to send him to Washington to take over the troops there, but Grant replied that he had no plan to do so. He then asked him "about the report that I was to be relieved," and Grant forthrightly responded that "he had never heard a word of it, and did not believe there was any foundation for it, as he would most certainly have been consulted." Grant's answer mollified Meade for a time, though Grant was being disingenuous, if not dishonest, when he feigned ignorance of such rumors, if Dana's dispatch of July 7 can be trusted. In his long letter, Dana began, "A change in the commander of the Army of the Potomac now seems probable." It went downhill from there, with Dana accusing Meade of poor leadership at Petersburg, bad temper, and injudicious temperament. "I do not think he has a friend in the whole army," he added for emphasis. Dana noted that Grant alone had "great confidence in Meade," but even Grant now feared "it would become necessary to relieve him."[77]

But Grant did not relieve Meade, nor did he immediately send him up to Washington to take command of the growing forces there. Meade vacillated on his view of this new position. On July 15 he wrote to his wife, "I do not think the position a desirable one, as the difficulty will be to get the various commands together and harmonize such conflicting elements." On July 29 Meade reported to his wife on a July 28 meeting he had with Grant at his headquarters at City Point. Grant said he had told Halleck and Stanton to send William Franklin to take charge of the new command in Washington, "but they declined to have Franklin. . . . [Grant then] suggested my name, to which he received no reply, but a message from the President asking him to meet him at Fortress Monroe." Meade now expressed an interest in the job: "So far as having an independent command, which the Army of the Potomac is not, I would like the change very well." Still, he would have to manage four new generals and "be managed by the President, Secretary, and Halleck." (Ironically, this situation would be the same as the one he had found unbearable in 1863.) Though he added that he was "quite indifferent how it turns out," that was not the sentiment he conveyed in a long conversation held with Marsena Patrick on July 26. Meade carefully detailed his view of the situation: Stanton and Halleck opposed Grant; Butler's national influence was increasing; he (Meade) was safe for the moment (protected by Grant), though most likely to be sent to command the departments "north of the Potomac"; and the politicians were looking for a "scapegoat" to answer for Grant's failure in the Overland Campaign.[78]

Meade finally got an answer after Grant met with Lincoln: Sheridan would be placed in command of the troops north of the Potomac. Grant said Lincoln would have given Meade the command but worried that Meade's "removal from the command of the Army of the Potomac might be misunderstood by the public, and be construed into a disapprobation of [Meade's] course." Hancock thought this rationale to be "political chicanery," but Meade proclaimed he was "content, as long as finding any fault with me is disclaimed."[79]

Meade was not the only commander worried about his job that July. In an effort worthy of Shakespearean drama, Baldy Smith had frequently criticized Meade and written Grant that Butler must be removed from command of the Army of the James. He then went on a short leave, and Benjamin Butler wasted no time in using his political connections and reputation to fight against Smith's proposal. The last straw for Grant was Smith's insinuation that Grant was foolish to keep Meade and Butler in command positions. On July 19, Grant removed Smith from command. When pressed for an explanation, Grant gave several, none of which satisfied Smith. According to Smith it was Grant's laconic conclusion that ended the conversation. Grant said, "You talk too much." Smith was sent to New York City and never resumed field command. The steady Maj. Gen. O. C. Ord was appointed commander of the Eighteenth Corps, and Butler retained command of the Army of the James. As Lyman wryly noted, "Thus did Smith the Bald try the Machiavelli against Butler the cross-eyed, and got floored at the first round!"[80]

With so much intrigue swirling among the generals' tents in July, it was a wonder that the primary goal—defeat Lee's army—even advanced. But advance it did, largely centered on a daring plan that grew more extensive and controversial as the hot days of July dragged on. On June 24 a Pennsylvania engineer-turned-officer, Lt. Col. Henry Pleasants of the Forty-Eighth Pennsylvania, presented to Burnside a plan to dig a tunnel between the lines at the narrowest part separating the two armies along the entire front. Pleasants would recruit miners from the Forty-Eighth Pennsylvania and supervise the construction of the tunnel and powder room. Burnside embraced the plan, and on June 25 wrote Meade of his intention to start digging. Meade endorsed the plan, and the digging of the tunnel that would lead to the infamous Battle of the Crater began that very day.[81]

At 540 feet long, it was the longest gallery built by the Union Army during the entire war. With the addition of a left branch of thirty-seven feet and a right branch of thirty-eight feet, Pleasants estimated that his men had moved eighteen thousand cubic feet of earth (using hardtack boxes and bags to haul all that dirt). When the mine was charged on July 27–28, eight thousand pounds of powder was placed in the two branches, with spliced fuses running the length of the branches and gallery.[82]

One reason Pleasants had pushed his men hard was that as early as June 30 Confederates suspected that a mine was being dug, and on July 10 they began digging their own mines. Using a smaller labor force than Pleasants had, Lt. Hugh Thomas Douglas of the First Confederate Engineers dug two shafts by the end of the month. Unfortunately, without adequate intelligence on where to dig or how deep to dig, Douglas never discovered the Union mine. In fact, Union miners were actually *under* one of the Confederate shafts. Douglas never dug deep enough.[83]

While Pleasants's men steadily dug their long gallery, Meade pursued another tactic: planning for "regular approaches" (with sapping and rollers) along the front of the Fifth Corps. Grant approved this process, but the construction of gun emplacements to protect the sapping happened too slowly for him. With authorities in Washington panicking over the closeness of Early's army, and deserters claiming that Lee would send more troops to Early or even attack the Army of the Potomac, Grant decided on a two-pronged offensive: cavalry and the Second Corps would cross the James River at Deep Bottom and destroy the railroad track for miles, either before or after Burnside's mine was exploded. After Meade thoroughly reconnoitered the area in front of Burnside, he softly questioned the plan to attack, writing to Grant, "I am compelled as a matter of judgment to state that the chances of success are not such as to make the attempt advisable." Meade enclosed a report from Maj. James C. Duane (chief engineer of the Army of the Potomac) that supported Meade's opinion, though he carefully walked the line of obedience as well: "At the same time, I do not consider it hopeless, and am prepared to make the attempt, if it is deemed of importance to do so."[84]

Meade's and Duane's advice made Grant hesitate—for a night. The next day (July 26) he sent Meade detailed instructions for the attack at Deep Bottom and a vague timetable for the explosion of the mine. Grant wanted two cavalry divisions under Sheridan's direct command, augmented by Kautz's cavalry division (also under Sheridan's command), to ride to Deep Bottom as unobtrusively as possible, cross the James River, then follow the Virginia Central Railroad "as near to the city as possible" and as far north "as the South Anna, unless driven off sooner." Two hundred "railroad men" would accompany the cavalry to aid in the destruction of the railroads. The Second Corps would also cross the river at Deep Bottom, marching to Chaffin's Bluff and farther, if possible. The infantry's main task was to protect the cavalry when it retreated to the river. Once the railroads were destroyed, "the whole expedition [would] return and resume their present place." To make the attack effective, there would not be any reconnaissance, and disinformation would be spread among the Union troops that an attack would occur on the Weldon Railroad. As for Burnside's mine, it could be "loaded" and ready to be set off when the time was right. The latest it would be exploded was two days later, on Wednesday, July 27.[85]

The first stage of the complex plan got underway on July 26. In the late afternoon, the First Division of the Second Corps moved out on another dreary night march. Almost from the beginning, however, this "northern attack" ran into problems. At a late-night meeting between Hancock, Sheridan, and Brig. Gen. Robert S. Foster (Tenth Corps general who commanded an expedition that had held a small bridgehead on the north side of the river since June 20), Foster cautioned Hancock that the Confederate works at the two pontoon bridges were stronger than he realized. Given this new information, Hancock asked Meade for permission to cross his entire corps at the lower bridge. Meade authorized this change in plans, even though it meant that Sheridan's cavalry divisions would not be crossing at a different bridge at nearly the same time, but after the Second Corps crossed over.[86] This was the first major twist in plans.

Meade played a very minor role in the Hancock-Sheridan push across the James River that became known as the First Battle of Deep Bottom. Hancock and Sheridan got their men across the river on July 27, where each encamped after meeting stiff resistance. The heaviest fighting occurred the next day, when Sheridan's cavalry fought at Darby Farm. Grant kept the bulk of the troops on the Confederate side of the river through most of July 29, hoping to draw off more Confederates before the mine explosion occurred. Though Grant admitted to Halleck that the operation "failed" to "surprise the enemy," it had prompted Lee to shift more than half of his thin army to Deep Bottom, leaving only three divisions on the Petersburg line to face four Union corps.[87]

Normally Meade would have been fuming about his secondary role in the Deep Bottom foray—he largely served as Grant's chief-of-staff—but his attention had already been diverted to the much larger operation about to commence at Petersburg. On July 26 he received an elaborate set of plans from Burnside, and on July 28 Grant gave the authorization for the assault. Meade recommended "daylight of the 30th" as the earliest time to make the assault. He wanted two days to move troops and artillery into position and remove abatis and parapets as needed. The Ninth Corps would make the attack, supported by the Second Corps, with the Eighteenth and Fifth Corps "held in readiness" to join in.[88]

The details of the assault were sent to all the commanders on July 29. Both the Ninth and Fifth Corps were supposed to have "pioneers" ready to destroy breastworks. Ord's Eighteenth Corps would line up to the rear of the Ninth Corps, and after the Ninth had seized "the crest" to the rear of the Confederate lines, the Eighteenth would move to the right of the Ninth Corps. The Fifth Corps would do the same on the left. Artillery would play a critical role, firing "upon those points of the enemy's works until fire covers the ground over which our columns must move." Though it should not have been necessary to order constant communication, Meade wisely did (and would use the failure of Burnside to follow this order against him later). The order stated, "Corps commanders will report to the commanding general when their preparations are complete, and will advise him of every step in the progress of the operation, and of everything important that occurs." Given the troubles of the last two months, Meade added, "Promptitude, rapidity of execution, and cordial cooperation, are essential to success."[89]

Meade had made two critical changes to Burnside's original plan. First, he told Burnside that the all-black regiments under Brig. Gen. Edward Ferrero would not lead the assault they had trained for. Instead, he was to use white troops as the spearhead. After the battle, Meade gave explanations for his decision. First, he felt the troops were too green. Second, if the attack failed, he did not want to be accused of recklessly sacrificing black troops. Burnside argued on behalf of his original plan, but when Meade took the matter to Grant, the commanding general agreed with him. The other major change was to send the bulk of the troops to seize the crest (cemetery), rather than send many troops to the left and right to widen the breach. As Meade saw it, if the crest was not "immediately gained, it would be impossible to remain there." He also told Burnside and his division commanders that "the troops were to be withdrawn when the assault proved unsuccessful."[90]

Though Meade made the plan, the success or failure of the operation would largely rest on Burnside's shoulders. Meade last saw Burnside late in the morning of July 29. For unknown reasons, Burnside did not make it to a conference with Meade and Grant at 4 P.M. That absence, combined with two more mistakes that evening, effectively doomed the assault long before the mine exploded the next morning. If Burnside had met with his commanders, final details could have been explained or reiterated. Burnside made matters infinitely worse when he decided that his three division commanders, Robert Potter, Orlando Willcox, and James Ledlie, would draw straws to see which division would lead the assault. Burnside later explained that he thought Potter's and Willcox's men were more fatigued owing to prior duty, and that was why he decided to cast lots. He never explained his confidence in James Ledlie, whose prior poor performances had been rumored but also covered up by sympathetic aides. Ledlie had some excellent regimental commanders who might have made up for his fear and drunkenness, but apparently Ledlie and Willcox were unsure of their exact orders after an afternoon conference with Burnside, even though his written orders were clear that evening and Potter understood what his division had to do. Tragically, Ledlie's brigade leaders thought they were to hold the breach, not push on to secure the crest.[91]

Few men on the Union side got much sleep that night. With the mine scheduled to be set off at 3:30 A.M., some troops moved into position, then dozed while waiting for the explosion. To no one's complete surprise, the mine was not blown at 3:30 A.M. Apparently the fuse had stopped burning at a splice (which was Meade's accurate guess), and after some frantic efforts to repair the splices with twine, the matches were lit again. Meanwhile, Grant had joined Meade at Burnside's old headquarters (Burnside had moved up nearly a mile to Fort Morgan, which contained a fourteen-gun battery), and together they decided the attack should occur even without an explosion. Meade sent two telegrams to Burnside in rapid succession, at 4:15 and 4:20 A.M., asking why there was a delay. In what would become an alarming and frustrating pattern throughout the long day, Burnside did not reply. So Meade sent an aide, Capt. William W. Sanders, to tell Burnside to attack anyway. Burnside still did not send a reply, as he was waiting for Pleasants and his top miners to fix the problem. Finally, at 4:44 A.M. on July 30, the largest mine explosion of the war occurred. Tens of thousands of cubic feet of dirt were flung high in the air, creating, in John Gibbon's words, "an immense mushroom-shaped column of dense smoke." The eight thousand pounds of powder carved out a crater two hundred feet long, fifty feet wide, and twenty-five feet deep, with lumps of clay ranging from fist-sized to *house-sized* scattered throughout. The Battle of the Crater had commenced.[92]

The story of the fierce fighting that day has been well told by historian Earl Hess and a growing number of other historians, not to mention the many contemporaneous accounts one can find.[93] As always, this study is focused on what Meade knew at the time, what he did, and the consequences of his actions. As often happened in battles, Meade was located just far enough from the battlefield to be safe yet within reach of couriers, though his field of vision usually extended only as far as the eye could see from his tent. For much of the morning he would be handicapped by a lack of information from Burnside.

As early as 5:40 A.M. Meade was writing to Burnside, asking, "What news from your assaulting column. Please report frequently." The time Burnside replied immediately, with the optimistic tone he often took in dispatches that morning. He wrote, "We have the enemy's first line and occupy the breach. I shall endeavor to push forward to the crest as rapidly as possible." But already Ledlie's division, followed by Brig. Gen. Simon G. Griffin's brigade, had gone into the Crater, where they soon were pinned down by Confederate rifle and artillery fire, as well as the sheer difficulty of standing upright or climbing out of the Crater. By 6 A.M. one officer estimated that two thousand Union soldiers had assembled in the Crater, many losing unit order and just standing around, waiting for orders. Col. Charles

G. Loring observed all the problems and wrote to Burnside of the situation. His courier did not know Burnside's headquarters had moved, and he delivered it to Meade instead. Meade dashed off an order to Burnside to send all of his troops "forward to the crest at once [and call] on General Ord to move forward his troops at once." He continued pressing Burnside in a dispatch sent twenty minutes later: "Our chance is now; push your men forward at all hazards (white and black) and don't lose time in making formations, but rush for the crest."[94]

Burnside followed Meade's orders, telling his division commanders "to push everything in at once." But the men could not move, and Burnside sent a plaintive update to Meade: "I am doing all in my power to push the troops forward, and, if possible, we will carry the crest. It is hard work, but we hope to accomplish it. I am fully alive to the importance of it." Perhaps prompted by the tone of the note, Meade's frustrations finally boiled over, as he showed the whiplash temper he was known for in his response: "What do you mean by hard work to take the crest? I understand not a man has advanced beyond the enemy's line which you occupied immediately after exploding the mine. Do you mean to say your officers and men will not obey your orders to advance? If not, what is the obstacle? I wish to know the truth, and desire an immediate answer." Meade's harshness and insinuation of dishonesty or lack of nerve infuriated Burnside, who replied: "I do not mean to say that my officers and men will not obey my orders to advance. I mean to say that it is very hard to advance to the crest. I have never in any report said anything different from what I conceived to be the truth." He concluded with a line that would almost end his career, "Were it not insubordinate I would say that the latter remark of your note was unofficerlike and ungentlemanly." After this exchange, Grant rode out to see for himself what was happening, but he did not talk to Burnside or get a clear view through the smoke of lingering dust of the battlefield.[95]

Meanwhile, Meade strained to salvage something from the debacle. He remained at his headquarters, receiving and sending over one hundred messages that morning. He tried to push Burnside one more time when he wrote him at 8 A.M., "Ord reports he cannot move till you get out of the way. Can't you let him pass on your right, and let him try what he can do?" An *hour* later Burnside responded, "The attack made on the right has been repulsed. A great many men are coming to the rear." That was quickly followed by a request for more troops: "Many of the Ninth and Eighteenth Corps are retiring before the enemy. I think now is the time to put in the Fifth Corps promptly." Meade had anticipated that request, ordering Warren to seize two guns on Burnside's left, then "go in" with Burnside. After observing the battlefield, Warren replied within half an hour, "[I am] no more able to take the battery now than I was at this time yesterday." Powerless to prod his young general to attack, Meade suspended the attack on the battery.[96]

Though Warren's inability to attack must have added to Meade's ire, it was probably better that his men did not assault, or they might have joined the ten

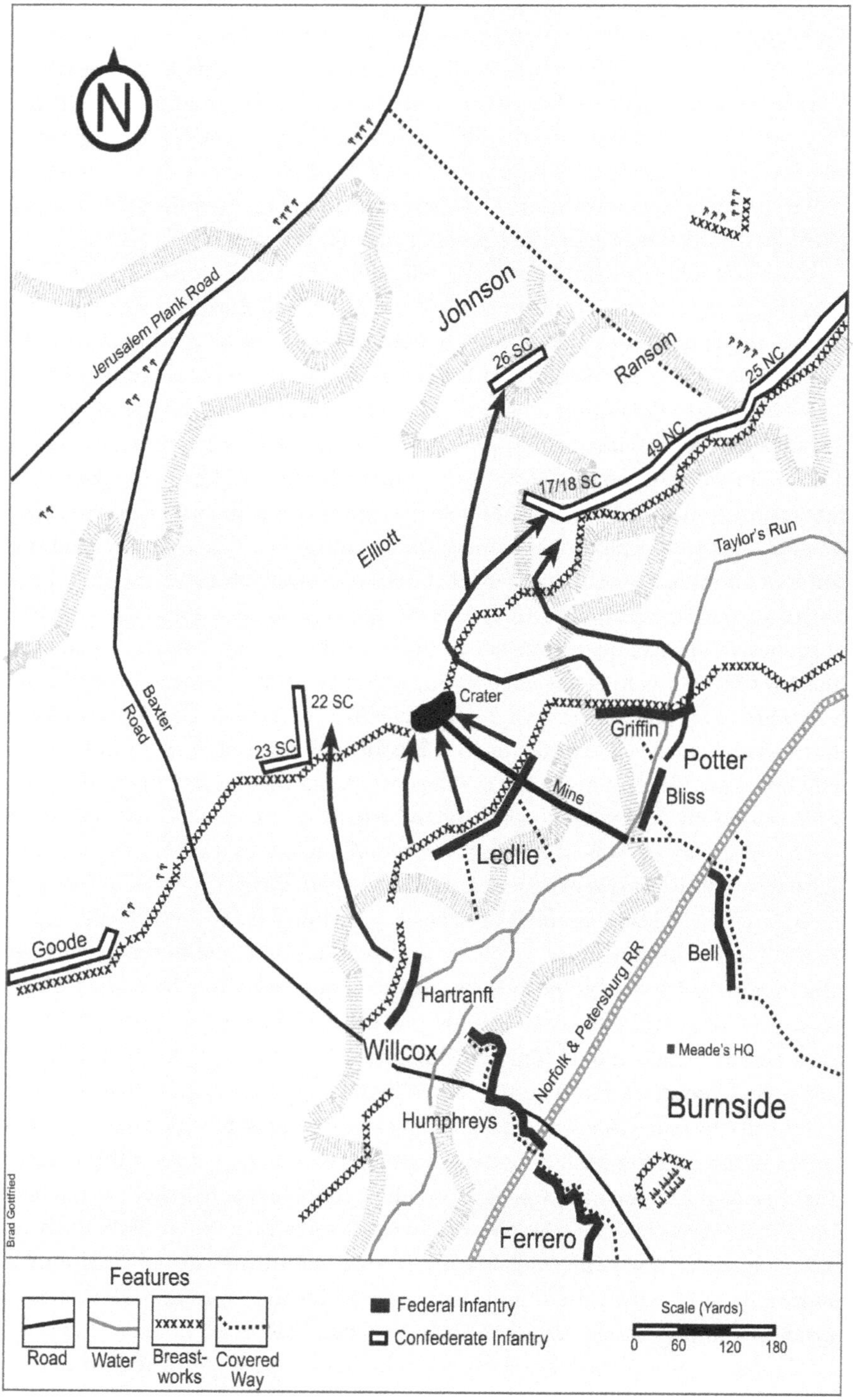

N
Jerusalem Plank Road
Johnson
26 SC
Ransom
25 NC
49 NC
17/18 SC
Elliott
Taylor's Run
Crater
22 SC
23 SC
Baxter Road
Griffin
Potter
Mine
Bliss
Ledlie
Goode
Bell
Hartranft
Willcox
Meade's HQ
Norfolk & Petersburg RR
Burnside
Humphreys
Ferrero
Brad Gottfried
Features
Road
Water
xxxxxx
Breast-works
Covered Way
Federal Infantry
Confederate Infantry
Scale (Yards)
0
60
120
180

Crater, July 30, 1864

thousand Union troops already jammed into a five-hundred-yard breach in the Confederate lines. Sometime after 9 A.M. Grant returned from his observation ride, and after talking to Meade, the generals decided to call off the attack. At 9:30 A.M. the order went out to Burnside and Ord from Meade: "If in your judgment nothing further can be effected, you withdraw to your own line, taking every precaution to get the men back safely." Fifteen minutes later, Meade specified that the men return to their "own entrenchments," followed by the restoration of some latitude to Burnside and Ord in a 10 A.M. message: "You can exercise your discretion in withdrawing your troops now or at a later period, say tonight. It is not intended to hold the enemy's line which you now occupy any longer than it is required to withdraw safely your men."[97]

This note hardly placated Burnside, who knew he had failed, smarted from Meade's criticisms, and, as he had at Fredericksburg, still clung to the hope that a fresh attack could turn the tide and save his reputation. He and Ord rode to Meade's headquarters where, according to Lyman, Burnside, "much flushed," strode up to Meade and "used extremely insubordinate language." He insisted he could attack, though he could not detail how. Ord argued the opposite, which only added to Burnside's anger. He said to Ord, "You have 15,000 men concentrated at one point. It is strange that you cannot do something with them." Returning fire, Ord replied, "You can fight if you have an opportunity; but if you are held by the throat, how can you do anything?" Meade did not change his orders, and the generals rode back to their commands. Burnside remained angry and told his division commanders to dig covered ways between their lines and the Crater, expecting to retreat at dark. Meanwhile, Meade returned to his old headquarters, while Grant was on his way to City Point.[98]

Of course the Confederates had no intention of letting up on the men in the Crater. After furious counterattacks to clear the breach in the mid-morning, they continued to fire at any men who tried to leave, and shell the Crater. As the temperature rose to 99°F and the men in the Crater begged for water, Confederates made one last push to take the Crater, which they did by mid-afternoon. With fierce hand-to-hand fighting and the murder of an unknown number of black POWs, the bloody debacle known as the Battle of the Crater came to an end. Official Union casualties stood just shy of four thousand, while Confederate losses were estimated at sixteen hundred. Though the casualties were imbalanced, they were not massive by Civil War standards, but the impact of this loss would affect the Army of the Potomac and its survivors long after the war ended.[99]

The immediate effects of the end of the battle haunted officers and men. Burnside did not contact Meade from 11 A.M. on July 30 until 9:00 A.M. the next day, pointedly ignoring two telegrams sent in the evening asking for information about the withdrawal of troops and the fate of the wounded (he later admitted he had acted wrongly). When Burnside did resume communication, he delayed reporting his losses until the evening, defended two telegraph operators in his staff who had been charged with giving him messages they were not supposed to, and finally explained that the brigade commanders in the Crater had been left to decide how to extricate their commands. In reply Meade hinted at the bombshell he was about to drop, ordering a "court" to investigate the battle. Meanwhile, the Union request for a truce was shuttled back and forth between Confederate and Union generals until the morning of August 1. When Lyman arrived at the parapet opposite the Crater, he saw "one of the most awful spectacles possible," two hundred "swollen and blackened" bodies whose "faces and hands were actually white with a moving layer of maggots!"[100]

As the stories of the battled drifted out of the camps and back home, everyone from Lincoln to the greenest private was discouraged if not depressed. Someone would have to pay for the failure, and the rumor mill said it would be Meade or Burnside. When Cyrus Comstock talked to Burnside just after the final meeting of the three generals on the morning of July 30, Burnside said "he thought he had better leave." When Comstock tried to "quiet him," Burnside turned on him, asking if Grant "had left [it to Comstock] to see that orders were obeyed." Comstock thought little of Burnside at this moment; he confided in his diary, "He is not competent to command a corps, and I have spoken freely of him—some one has repeated it." Even Grant obliquely criticized Burnside for not personally directing the assault. By July 31 Meade had made up his mind to bring up charges against Burnside, and even a late intercession by "two mutual friends," asking if Burnside could be allowed to explain the meaning of his inflammatory note on the morning of July 30, came too late to stop Meade. (Burnside also went to City Point to tell Grant he would "withdraw the letter" he had written to Meade, but when he got back to his headquarters he found charges against him lying on his table.)[101]

The Crater disaster brought swift scrutiny. On August 1, 1864, an order authorized the formation of a board of officers to examine the failed attack. On August 3 Meade formally submitted to Rawlins a letter demanding that Burnside be relieved, based on two charges: disobedience of orders and conduct prejudicial to good order and military discipline. Burnside's failure to respond to orders to keep Meade informed, and his intemperate letter of July 30, were the main points of the charges. The court, comprising officers hand-picked by Meade (Hancock, Romeyn B. Ayres, Nelson Miles, and Col. Edmund Schriver, recorder), convened on August 6 and collected testimony until August 12. Meade and Burnside gave lengthy statements, and other officers were questioned. The court took a break during August 13–28, during which time Burnside left, ostensibly on leave. The court reconvened on August 28, met off and on until September 9, then produced a summary highly critical of Burnside and three of his division commanders (Ledlie, Ferrero, and Willcox). Burnside remained in the army, but without a command. He gave his reinstatement one last shot in the winter of 1864–65, when the Joint Commission on the Conduct of the War responded to a resolution from Sen. Henry Anthony of Rhode Island (Burnside's home state) to investigate the Crater again.[102]

When the imbroglio between Meade and Burnside is looked at from the comfort of 150 years of distance, it may appear inevitable that one of the two men would have to go eventually. Grant had tried to have separate commands at the beginning of the Overland Campaign, and that had failed. He then assigned Burnside and his Ninth Corps to Meade's Army of the Potomac, and though both generals tried to make it work, it was very difficult for Burnside to take orders from a general he once commanded and outranked. Besides, many of the top officers in the Army of the Potomac had a low opinion of Burnside, stretching back to his actions at Antietam, and virtually nothing he did from April to July 1864 changed anyone's views, except for the hard fighting done by the Ninth Corps at the opening of the Petersburg Campaign. Though Meade told his wife he felt "sorry" for Burnside, he also added, "[Burnside will] never return whilst I am here."[103]

One might find three positives in the poorly managed battles of Petersburg, First Deep Bottom, and the Crater. First, and perhaps most important, Grant and Meade had tied Lee down to protecting Petersburg and Richmond, a situation Lee had struggled to avoid since assuming command in June 1862. Second, Meade would no longer have to work with Ambrose Burnside. His replacement, his chief-of-staff John Parke, was much more amenable to Meade—and had never been his superior officer. Grant and Meade had handicapped Burnside at the Battle of the Crater by forcing him to switch his assaulting columns at the eleventh hour, but Burnside had compounded his difficulty by allowing Ledlie to lead the attack. Burnside's lack of communication crippled Meade's ability to respond, and when the situation became hopeless and Meade called off the attack at 9:30 A.M., it was Burnside who dawdled in his retreat, thus wasting many lives. Ironically, it may have been the failed assault on the Crater, and not the more widely considered failed assault on Cold Harbor, that finally changed Grant's mind about the futility of attacking solid enemy fortifications. He articulated these new thoughts in a letter he wrote to Meade upon his return to City Point in the afternoon of July 30: "Our experience of today proves that fortifications come near holding themselves without troops . . . with a reasonable amount of artillery and one infantryman to six feet I am confident either party could hold their likes against a direct attack of the other."[104] These words must have brought satisfaction to Meade, who had been complaining about such assaults for months in letters to his wife.

But Grant's realization would bring little comfort to Meade in the coming weeks, as he continued to worry about his job security, Grant's true intentions in giving the new independent Middle Division to Sheridan instead of him, and, most important, how to weaken Lee's defenses.

Extending the Line

Richmond-Petersburg Operations, August 1864–March 1865

The most important tactical lesson taken from the failed Crater attack may have been the one that Grant admitted in a note to Meade: defenses could be made too strong to attack and break through. As military events heated up in other areas of the country, Grant found his attention drawn to fighting in the Shenandoah Valley and Georgia, as well as to political considerations in Washington. He kept his headquarters safely distant from Washington (remaining at City Point) but traveled more frequently in the next eight months to the capital. After sending the Sixth Corps to Washington, he left Meade with a much smaller army, limiting the moves Meade could make. For his part, Meade continued to carry out Grant's strategic wishes, chafe at his subordinate role, and grow more embittered over his treatment by the press, the government, and even Grant. He would have to endure private humiliation as other generals achieved faster promotions and public adulation—and suffer professional humiliation when called before another session of the Joint Committee on the Conduct of the War. There would be tragedy in his family and health setbacks, making the winter of 1864–65 almost as trying as the winter of 1863–64. Throughout this personal ordeal, he took heart in Union successes and allowed himself to more fully dream of the quieter days ahead when the war would be over.

In the immediate aftermath of the Crater, Meade became preoccupied with the Court of Inquiry and with the evolving situation of command in northern Virginia. Though Meade had expressed himself satisfied with Grant's explanation as to why he had sent Sheridan to command part of the new "Middle Division," on August 2 he stewed over the decision while Grant was up in Washington from August 3 through August 8. When Grant returned, he said nothing to Meade, which worried and irked the Pennsylvanian. He finally had to know the truth. On August 12 he directly asked Grant why he placed Sheridan in command, after promising him on August 2 that he (Meade) would take charge of a larger command, should that be created. Such a command *was* created by Grant, and Grant temporized by explaining that Sheridan had "not been assigned to the division" but was only "put in command of the troops in the field belonging to the different departments" (Meade's words). Meade did not accept this odd explanation, telling his wife, "[I] further remarked that I regretted it had not been deemed a simple matter of justice to me to place me in this independent command." Grant "made no remark" to Meade's comment, a response both telling and maddening to Meade. Grant did not share that *he* was the one who had recommended Sheridan and defended him when Stanton questioned his readiness for command.[1] Whether Grant preferred that Meade remain in his current position or did not believe he was aggressive enough for the northern command, he did not say at that time or even later in his memoirs. Grant's lack of response left Meade hurt and puzzled, and he wavered between thinking that either Grant opposed him or Grant did not truly think the new position was that vital. Either way, he was not given command of the new independent campaign, and when Sheridan began racking up victories, Meade's bruised feelings were further aggravated.

Sheridan's victories were in the future, however. In the first two weeks of August (while Grant was away for some of that time), Meade busied himself with the Court of Inquiry and overseeing the construction and improvement of Union fieldworks. According to Earl Hess, "most of the repair work during August centered on the Ninth Corps defenses," while the Fifth Corps did repairs and "new engineering work" on its line. Of course Confederates also reinforced their lines during the weeks and engaged in a number of countermining efforts (none led to a Crater-like explosion). There was a huge explosion within Union lines on August 9 when an ammunition box blew up at City Point. The sound of the explosion was heard for miles, and most assumed it was the work of Confederate agents. Even though fifty men were killed and nearly one hundred wounded, it did not affect the decisions of the generals, who ordered fieldwork improvement to continue. Perhaps the strangest moment of the month for Meade was the visit of Samuel Wilkeson, editor of the Washington bureau of the *New York Tribune,* to Meade's headquarters on August 6. Wilkeson called on Meade to explain that he had been given false information in the spring, and that was why he had attacked Meade so vigorously. He regretted his words and apologized to Meade. Meade wrote to his wife, "I received his apologies as if nothing had ever taken place, and he left me quite pleased."[2] Meade must have been pleased, too, to be vindicated by one of his enemies in the press. But he might have felt otherwise had he known that Wilkeson's young son was storing up critical stories of Meade to publish later.

It was good that Meade had a small triumph in early August because his next role would be the smallest part he would play in his entire time with Grant. The situation began with Grant's visit to Washington and his growing awareness of the importance of the Shenandoah Valley to the Confederacy. As Grant wrote in his memoirs, "It was the principal storehouse they now had for feeding their armies about Richmond." He knew Lee would fight hard to keep it, and Grant became determined to wrest it from him. In fact, when he learned that Lee had sent two divisions from Richmond to aid Early, he told Sheridan not to press the attack against Early just yet.

With Sheridan active in the Shenandoah Valley, Grant decided to launch another offensive at Richmond and Petersburg, the fourth since arriving at Petersburg in June. It was a complicated operation, beginning with a second assault on Deep Bottom, to be followed by either an attack on the Richmond-Petersburg line or a movement on the Union left to cut the Weldon Railroad. He outlined the entire plan to Butler in a long dispatch sent on August 12. Hoping to either "force" Lee to recall some troops to Richmond or use his "advantage" to attack Lee, Grant planned to surprise the Confederates by sending troops by steamers up the James River, then launching another march across a new pontoon bridge to assault Deep Bottom. He would use the Second Corps as the shock troops, Brig. Gen. David McM. Gregg's cavalry division as protection, and, ideally, all the troops Butler could spare.³ Grant had told Meade of the plans on the same day, though not the part about Butler's help.

By temporarily losing command of the Second Corps and Gregg's division, Meade was down to two corps (Fifth and Ninth) and one brigade of cavalry under Kautz. At least Grant gave him the Eighteenth Corps (under Ord) when he asked for it to assist him on August 14. Along with the loss (albeit for only one operation) of the Second Corps, Meade had the embarrassment of learning secondhand that Grant had granted Burnside leave when he received an update from Maj. Gen. Orlando B. Willcox at 9 P.M. on August 13 that read, "I have the honor to report myself in command of this corps." Meade promptly asked under whose "authority?" Willcox replied that it was Grant's order, which he "supposed, of course . . . was known by the major general commanding the army" (a logical supposition). Instead, Meade had to write Grant for confirmation of the order. Grant explained that it had just been ordered that evening and "directions were given to communicate that fact to you." But it had not happened instantaneously. Grant also informed him that John Parke, not Orlando Willcox, would be the new commander of the Ninth Corps.⁴

It was fortuitous that the Union army's "Fourth Offensive" began during this time of broken communication, giving Meade less time to stew over the slights. Although his role in the Second Deep Bottom operation was fundamentally supportive, he did have to be ready to respond quickly if opportunities arose. On August 13 the Second Corps set off from Deep Bottom on ships, with part of the Tenth Corps (led by David Birney) marching to the pontoon bridge at Jones's Neck and crossing the James River by 5 A.M. on the fourteenth. Hancock's corps arrived later that morning, and both corps, plus Gregg's cavalry division, soon moved forward, brushed aside some pickets, saw some forbidding breastworks, and began digging in. For the next two days, both sides shuffled positions and attempted attacks. Grant called off further attacks on August 16 but kept troops there temporarily to keep Lee guessing about his intentions.[5]

As operations at Deep Bottom sputtered out, Grant authorized Meade to try the second half of his operation, based on information that "all the cavalry" and "three brigades of infantry" had been sent "north of the river" to counteract the Deep Bottom movement. Though he did not expect "decisive results" from sending one Union corps to the left, he could send the Fifth Corps to the Weldon Railroad to "cut and destroy a few miles" of Lee's indispensable rail link to the South. Displaying his new belief in the futility of attacking when strong defenses were present, he specifically ordered that he did not want Warren "to fight any unequal battles nor to assault fortifications." He elaborated, "His movements should be more a reconnaissance in force, with instructions to take advantage of any weakness of the enemy he may discover." He recognized that the Ninth and Eighteenth Corps were stretched too thin to help Warren. Sharing his larger goals, he then wrote, "I want, if possible, to make such demonstrations as will force Lee to withdraw a portion of his troops from the Valley, so that Sheridan can strike a blow against the balance."[6]

Meade sent the order to Warren in the mid-afternoon, using some of Grant's very expressions like "reconnaissance in force." He added that if Warren found the enemy entrenched, he should not attack but "remain holding them there." The latitude given to Warren pleased him enormously, and he wrote a note to Humphreys at 4 A.M. the next morning explaining that he and the division commanders were happy with the order. He wrote, "We'll do the best we can, you may rest assured, and will never ask anyone under them to stand the responsibility of possible failure."[7]

The Fifth Corps moved out at 5 A.M. on August 18. The morning was blazing hot, and men fell out of the ranks from sunstroke. The men marched to Globe Tavern on the Weldon Railroad, then fanned out to the north and west. Rain began falling in the early afternoon, which relieved the heat but made the fighting difficult when Confederate infantry began attacking by mid-afternoon. It was a hard fight, with Brig. Gen. Romeyn Ayres's Second Division being temporarily outflanked, but Warren pulled in the lines a bit, and the men steadied. By nightfall Warren reported that he was entrenching and that his pickets connected with the Ninth Corps on his right. He said he would hold on and try to destroy rails (though the rain made it difficult to do so).[8]

Grant and Meade were already planning to reinforce Warren. Grant ordered Hancock to send a division and then asked Meade if he could send some Ninth Corps troops instead, using Mott's division as replacements. Meade agreed and

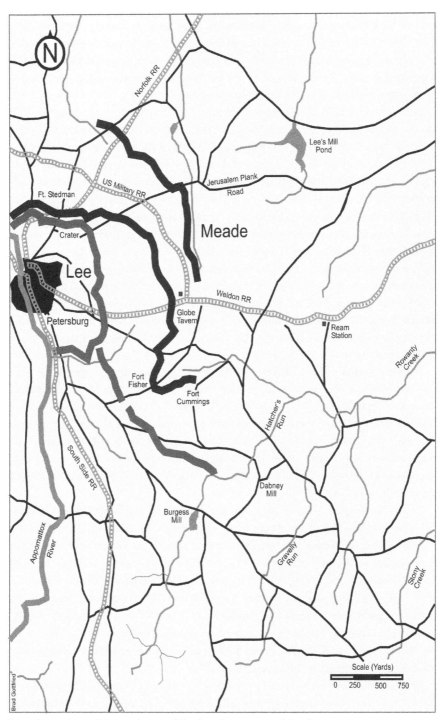

Petersburg, Area of Operations and Battles, August 1864–March 1865

ordered it done. Grant also wanted it to be made clear that Warren should repel all attacks and "follow" them up with counterattacks if possible. Because Mott's division would not arrive until morning, Meade hit on the idea to ask Ord of the Eighteenth Corps to send fifteen hundred soldiers (his reserve) to Parke's Ninth and Parke could send Willcox's and Potter's (about forty-five hundred men) divisions off to help Warren at 3 A.M.[9]

The next morning the units began moving into their new positions in a driving rain. Though it took all morning, by noon the men from the three corps had arrived at Globe Tavern and been put into position by Warren. Just after noon a nervous Meade rode out to check on Warren's situation, and Lyman noted that Warren's right "was in the air" but, he wrote, "As I am not a military critic, I thought no more of it."[10]

The Confederates, of course, thought more of it and, under the skillful direction of Mahone, pushed through the thin picket line and attacked Warren's unprotected right flank. From mid-afternoon to dusk a fierce, chaotic battle raged amidst the thick brush and patches of forest that ringed the area around Globe Tavern. In a pouring rain, advance units of Mahone's three brigades pushed all the way to Weldon Railroad, before they were stopped by Union resistance. With the aid of artillery fire, the lately employed troops of Willcox's Third Division, and the reserve force of White's First Division, the Union troops counterattacked and drove the Confederates back to their previous position.[11]

Though the final result was Union survival, the path to success was littered with "what ifs" that could have turned the sharp fight either way. As Meade and Lyman rode back to headquarters, Lyman distinctly heard "dropping shots in the woods on our left," which Meade could not hear because of his head cold. Lyman also heard that some two thousand Union soldiers had been captured. In a rare instance of criticism of his commander, Lyman blamed both Warren and Meade for the losses, noting, "The position was faulty, Warren should have corrected it, and Meade should have known it!" However, the battle came to be called a victory because the Fifth Corps had advanced to the Weldon Railroad, damaged a good chunk of it, then held on to its new position. Lyman felt otherwise about the battle; he regarded it as "an immense loss that should have been a gain."[12]

It was fortunate that Warren's losses were not official as of August 19 because it might have cost him his job. All Meade had that evening was Warren's report that he had regained all lost ground, with a "considerable" loss of men as prisoners. Meade congratulated him on his victory and asked if he could attack the next day, especially with his men in "good spirits." Warren said he would try, but by mid-morning of the next day (August 20), Warren told Meade he could not attack and would have a difficult time holding where the picket line had been the day before. This new attitude apparently bothered Grant, who by evening had read in a Richmond newspaper that Confederates had captured two thousand men and wanted to know if that number was accurate.[13]

Though Warren did not attack the Confederates on August 20, he personally supervised the construction of a defensive line. As rain poured down all day, his men worked relentlessly to construct breastworks from Globe Tavern to the plank road (to the east), and built a new line southwest alongside the railroad line. At nightfall he pulled his skirmishers back to the new line and awaited Confederate attack.[14]

Fortunately for Warren, a "strange lethargy" overcame the top Southern generals on August 20, according to historian John Horn. Lee wanted a concentrated attack on August 20, but troops did not get into position in time. Both Mahone's attack from the west and Heth's attack from the north were met with brutal artillery fire and heavy musket fire. They were both repulsed, with serious losses for the Confederates (1,400 to 302 for the Union). Confederate generals had relearned the hard lesson of attacking strong breastworks, and with these new losses, raised their total losses from Globe Tavern to just about 2,400 (versus 4,279 for the Union).[15]

Though Warren felt satisfied with his battle, Grant and Meade wanted more action. Meade wrote to Grant, "Warren, on the defensive, ought to be able not only to hold his position, but to punish the enemy severely, and undoubtedly would if we could only get our troops to act with the audacity the enemy show." For his part, Grant wondered why Warren did not go on the offensive and "either cut their force in two or get in rear of it?" To aid Warren, artillery had been firing from Ord's and Mott's positions, and Meade sent Hancock with his two divisions and one division of Parke's Ninth Corps to Warren's aid (neither got there in time to help). A peeved Warren replied to both commanders in the mid-afternoon, "I lose all the advantage of my artillery as soon as I move and get the effect of his. I believe I have fought against the army opposed to me to know pretty well what to do here on the field." He added for good measure, "General Parke is now here. He ranks me."[16]

Neither Grant nor Meade pounced on Warren's truculence. Instead, Meade rode to Warren's position, talked to him, and surveyed the lines. At 9:20 P.M. he wrote to Grant, "I find it impracticable to arrange any offensive movements for tomorrow." Hancock's men were too tired to fight, Warren's had been fighting for three days, and Parke's men had been building connecting lines. Grant submitted to the new reality—the Battle of Globe Tavern was over.[17]

The Union troops did not rest on their survival of a Confederate attack. Grant contemplated a movement by Birney's Tenth Corps north of the James for August 22 but called it off when he learned that Confederate lines had not been as depleted as he thought. Warren's Fifth Corps continued to improve its defenses around Globe Tavern, and Hancock's Second Corps was assigned the duty of helping engineers destroy the track of the Weldon Railroad to Ream's Station and farther south. Track destruction proceeded methodically for a couple of days, until Confederate infantry in large numbers were spotted moving southwest of Globe Tavern. Lee had begun pulling troops out from his thin lines to protect his supply lines, assembling eight infantry brigades and some artillery to attack the Second Corps at Ream's Station.[18]

The second Battle of Ream's Station began with cavalry skirmishes on the morning of August 25. By noon Confederate infantry had begun probing the Union picket lines and dirt works west of the Weldon Railroad, and Confederate sharpshooters were busy trying to kill every artillery horse. By 2 P.M. Hancock had grown nervous enough to write Meade, "The enemy have been feeling all around me and are now cheering in my front, advancing and driving in my skirmishers. I think they will next move across the road between Warren and myself as they press my lines."[19]

Meade did not need to know any more information. He had already ordered Mott's division to march to Hancock's aid, and upon learning of Hancock's situation, sent Willcox with his division on the "plank road," to report to Hancock. Warren was ordered to be ready to send troops if needed. Meade updated Grant on the situation (Grant was ill that day and planned to go to Fort Monroe to see a doctor). Meade also had reports from Confederate deserters that Lee had weakened his lines to gather enough troops to attack Hancock, and might even be getting Early's army back.[20]

The first Confederate assault in the early afternoon proved more feeble than ferocious. Pinned down by Union fire, Confederate infantry made very small advances. A. P. Hill considered calling off all attacks, until generals Henry Heth, John Rogers Cooke, and William MacRae convinced him to authorize one more assault. By 5 P.M. the troops were in position and ready for a classic frontal assault, preceded by an artillery barrage.[21]

The attack affected Hancock's tactical thinking. Meade had already told him he could "exercise" his "judgment about withdrawing," but after the attack, Hancock replied, "Closely engaged as I am at the present, I cannot withdraw safely at this time." He planned to withdraw at night, unless he was "forced to do so before." Adding a note of optimism, he wrote, "Everything looks promising at present."[22]

He could not have been more wrong. At 5 P.M. the Confederates launched a short, fierce artillery barrage. Then the assault began. At first the Union lines stood firm, but when MacRae's brigade and part of Cooke's brigade charged at three green New York regiments, the untested men gave way. Their retreat imperiled the troops on their flanks, and when Lane's brigade broke through another section of the line, the entire Union front looked endangered. Gibbon and Hancock sprang into action, with Hancock personally leading some troops and at times beseeching his men to either stay and fight, or counterattack. Counterattacks were made in spots, with limited success. Around 7 P.M. Hancock polled his three commanders—Miles (taking over for Barlow), Gregg (cavalry), and Gibbon—asking if they could successfully attack and retake what had been lost. Gibbon admitted his men could not, and without the reinforcements he had expected, Hancock ordered a withdrawal.[23]

With Willcox's division serving as a rearguard, Hancock's divisions were able to negotiate a retreat to the Williams house. Meade asked Hancock for a report on the attack at 9 P.M., but that message did not reach him because the telegraph operator had been captured. Meade also readied two more divisions of the Ninth

Corps to assist Hancock if he needed it. Meade received a report of the battle from Capt. John McEntee, and to salve Hancock's wounds he wrote, "No one sympathizes with you more than I do in the misfortunes of this evening." He explained the reasoning behind his earlier decisions: he kept Willcox's division in place on the plank road to protect Hancock's rear, and he held back two divisions of the Ninth Corps to be the reserve for either Hancock or Warren. He noted at the end, "Though you have met with a reverse, the honor and escutcheons of the old Second are as bright as ever."[24]

Hancock put the best spin possible on the lost battle in his initial dispatches to Meade and Grant, but as time went on, he looked for scapegoats. At 2 A.M. of August 26 he described the fight as "one of the severest and most obstinate battles the corps has ever fought." He added more detail in a mid-morning message to Meade and Grant. He noted that the enemy "broke" Miles's line and drove Gibbon's men back, but Miles's men "regained" some of their entrenchments, and Gregg's dismounted cavalry "severely checked" Confederate advancement. Repeating a theme from his first report, he continued, "A few more good troops would have given us a victory of considerable importance." Still, it had been "one of the most determined and desperate fights of the war, resembling Spotsylvania in its character."[25]

The proud Hancock could not easily accept the loss, especially when official numbers settled Union casualties at 2,727, of which 2,000 were prisoners. The Confederates also took twelve colors and nine guns, the worst loss of the war for the Second Corps. Hancock soon got into a row with Gibbon over the latter's ill-timed suggestion to reorganize the Second Corps. It led to a sharp rebuke from Hancock, a long meeting to repair the damage, and a distinct coolness in the relationship after that. Hancock's subordinates, especially his chief-of-staff and later biographer Col. Francis Walker, placed most of the blame for the loss on Meade, for not sending support troops to Hancock. But another aide, W. C. Morgan, captured the moment best when he wrote much later, "It was the first time he had felt the bitterness of defeat during the war. . . . Never before had he seen his men fail to respond to the utmost when he called upon them personally for a supreme effort." Or as Walker wrote so eloquently in his biography of Hancock, "The agony of that day never passed away from that proud soldier."[26]

In the few days following the Second Battle of Ream's Station, little was done but to move troops around. Grant pondered his next move, and casualties were officially counted. In what would come to be called the "Fourth Offensive" of the Union forces around Richmond and Petersburg, the attacking force had clearly taken a beating in casualties, losing 9,922 men to the Confederates' 4,500 men.[27] The Confederates' casualties were not lower simply because they were defending territory; when they attacked at the Second Battle of Ream's Station, for instance, they captured twice as many men as they lost. Grant had not achieved a breakthrough north of the James nor a full end sweep around Lee's southern lines, but he had secured part of the Weldon Railroad, which cut it off as a supply line for the Confederates for the rest of the war. Furthermore, Grant had managed to keep Lee too preoccupied with defending Richmond and Petersburg to send any additional troops to Early in the Shenandoah Valley or to Maj. Gen. John Bell Hood, who had suffered punishing losses around Atlanta in July and August. Overall, Grant hoped he could "win" the war of attrition.

As for Meade, he had seen his important secondary (and sometimes primary) role in the battles against Lee be diminished, as he was just one of three generals now hitting the Confederacy hard in Virginia (Butler and Sheridan had become coequal pieces in Grant's chess game). Though he may have been heartened by Grant's clarification of his authority over Ord's Eighteenth Corps on August 26 ("You are authorized at all times, until further orders, to assume command and direct the movements of all troops operating against Petersburg south of the Appomattox"[28]), other news he received concerning promotions and seniority during the Weldon Railroad expedition sent him into a funk.

Grant had asked that Sherman, Hancock, and Sheridan be immediately promoted, and that had been done. The news floored Meade because back in May he had been assured by Grant that he wanted Sherman and Meade promoted to major general at the same time. But by August he had changed his mind. When Meade asked him directly why he made a different recommendation, Grant replied that he "wished Sherman to rank me." He reassured Meade that he would be promoted, and that Lincoln and Stanton agreed. He also inserted the somewhat odd argument that the promotion would occur when he was appointed commander of the new Middle Division, but that he could not yet do that because he had placed Sheridan in temporary command. If he removed Sheridan, "it would be construed into a disapproval of his course, which was not the case." Once again Grant chose not to tell Meade that he had recommended Sheridan for the position and defended his appointment to Stanton. Clearly, Sheridan was a favorite of Grant's. Meade was shocked by the change and stunned by the logic of the new arguments, but, as he wrote to his wife, "Of course I could say nothing to this explanation." Getting to the core of his pain, he continued, "It is the same old story, an inability to appreciate the sensitiveness of a man of character and honor." He claimed that he did not "care much about the appointment," except "to prove to the ignorant public they had been imposed upon by a lying press." He recognized that Grant did *not* view his recommendations as a snub to Meade; however, he wrote, "[Grant] can't conceive why I should complain of a little delay in giving me what he tells me I am certainly to have." For a man like Meade, honor was all important, and he wanted the "vindication which the Government might give to [his] course" by conferring on him a promotion promised to him.[29]

The shock of the explanation sent Meade into one of the lowest emotional moments of the summer, if not the year. Whining to his wife that he did not have "a single friend in the army," he wrote, "[There] is not a man to whom I can and do speak freely, fully, and openly and upon whom I can depend for sympathy. Lyman is the nearest." Besides Lyman—whom Meade did not confide in completely—there was Hancock, who, he added, "[is] among officers in the main to whom I speak the most fully for I believe him honest and trustworthy." Having to hold everything in was "most trying and injurious to one's temper."[30]

He returned to this painful subject again in a letter written on August 26, insisting that despite everything that had transpired, he believed Grant to be "truthful and honest." He also updated Margaret on another lingering issue: his shunning by the press. Apparently the editor of the *Philadelphia Inquirer,* William Harding, had told Samuel Crawford that he understood why Cropsey had to be punished, though he disagreed with the method. Meade noted that he would write to Harding to express his "great gratitude" for his understanding.[31]

The other depressing matter vying for Meade's attention was the physical deterioration of his eldest son, John Sergeant. He had contracted tuberculosis in 1862, and he had to curtail his college education while he fought the disease. His condition worsened in the late summer of 1864, and Meade hurried home to spend several days with his ailing son and family in the first week of September 1864. When he left Philadelphia, the working plan was for Sergeant to go to Cuba first, then off to Europe, for rest and treatment. When he told Secretary of War Stanton of his son's condition, Stanton offered to send Sergeant to Cuba on a government steamer. Much of the correspondence between George and Margaret concerned who would accompany Sergeant, and when he would leave. By October, however, Sergeant was too sick to travel.[32]

Soon after Meade returned home, Grant left for a meeting with Sheridan at Harper's Ferry. They discussed Sheridan's plan to find and fight Early, which satisfied Grant. Grant had scarcely returned to City Point when Sheridan pulled off two strong victories over Early at Winchester (September 19) and Fisher's Hill (September 22). Meade dutifully ordered his artillery to fire for one hour in salute, and he wrote to his wife after Winchester that he was "glad for the cause and glad for Sheridan's sake." He also confessed his jealousy, writing, "This opportunity of distinction was denied me, who was, I think, from previous service and position, entitled to it." Moreover, Meade learned at the same time that Sheridan's promotion to brigadier general in the Regular Army was official, and that his assignment to command the Middle Military Division was now permanent. Trying to sound resigned to these facts, he wrote, "I must now content myself with doing my duty unnoticed," but the emotional wounds seemed fresh and raw.[33]

His "unnoticed" duties consisted of overseeing the construction of a new interior rail line, called the United States Military Railroad, from Jerusalem Plank Road to Globe Tavern (nine miles long); the building of new forts and a "Secondary Line"; and, after a daring Confederate cavalry raid behind Union lines that seized over two thousand cattle (September 14–17), digging a new line ("Micheler's Line") that protected the rear of the army strung out below Petersburg. As usual, Meade complained to his wife that he would be blamed for the "negligence" that allowed the raid to occur, though he was on solid ground when he noted that he had mentioned the vulnerability of the herd before, but his warning was ignored. For once he was not censured too heavily for the successful raid, and by September 25 he appeared to have regained some of his old spirit of optimism, though marred by a deep fatalism about his reputation, as another Gettysburg critique had come to his attention. He wrote, "I believe sincerely that someday justice will be done, though at present that period seems remote. What the future has in store no one can tell, but one thing is sure, that so long as I do my duty conscientiously, I will at least have the satisfaction of a clear conscience."[34]

While Meade fretted over his reputation and the building of new defensive lines, Grant wrestled with new offensive plans. As early as September 12 he shared some ideas for his next moves with Sherman. At that time he thought of sending a small force to capture Wilmington, while sending a much larger force southwest to capture the South Side Railroad. But Sheridan's two successes in the Valley in September pushed Grant to reconsider his initial plan. He abandoned the idea to attack Wilmington, replacing it with another two-pronged attack on Lee's Richmond-Petersburg defensive line. Based on extensive intelligence gathered by Butler's spies and interrogation of deserters, Grant decided to send the Army of the James across the James River with 26,600 men to push as far as possible into the Richmond lines, perhaps even to the capital itself. Meanwhile, Meade would send twenty-five thousand men charging toward the Boydton Plank Road, hoping to capture the vital artery and ideally push on to the South Side Railroad. At the very least, Grant hoped that Lee would be forced to weaken one section of his long line to protect the other, thus allowing either Butler or Meade to succeed with the grand goal. Even if both assaults failed to achieve their larger objectives, the attackers would force Lee to either keep all his troops currently in the area present or even call for relief from Early's men; Lee could not spare the men to aid Early.[35]

On September 27 Grant sent a long explanation of his plan to Meade. Using troops from the Tenth and Eighteenth Corps, Butler would try to "capture the works of the enemy north of the James River and between Malvern Hill and Richmond." Though Grant did not expect the force to reach Richmond, he wanted Meade's force to be ready to march at 4 A.M. on September 29 and travel light with "three or four days' rations in haversacks and sixty rounds of ammunition on the person." The principal goal of Meade's force was to "convince the enemy that the South Side road and Petersburg are the objects of our efforts." If Meade found the enemy depleted from sending troops to fight Butler, he was to move for either the South Side road or Petersburg, "without waiting for instructions, and in your own way." And if he happened to get to the road or near it, he should hold it "at all hazards," even pulling men out of the current line.[36]

It is not recorded how Meade felt about playing second fiddle to Butler, but one can assume he felt the decision to be another slight. At least he had been allowed discretion in picking his men and charting their course. On September 28 he issued his full orders. The entire Army of the Potomac would be ready to move at 4 A.M. on September 29, in case all units were needed. His strike force would consist of two divisions from the Ninth Corps. Gregg would ready his cavalry near the Weldon Railroad, prepared to move out when ordered. The strike force would be allowed to bring some ambulances, hospital wagons, and half of its ammunition wagons. The supply trains would remain behind.[37]

The men worked diligently on September 28 to be ready to move on September 29. But when 4 A.M. arrived, no order to march was issued. Thus ensued a long day of waiting on developments from Butler's unfolding two-pronged assault and analysis of intelligence that drifted into Meade's headquarters. Only Gregg's cavalry actively skirmished on September 29; the rest of Meade's strike force waited for orders.[38]

The day's fierce fighting belonged to Butler's strike force. It was a tale of two separate assaults. In the morning, Union troops in the Eighteenth Corps under Brig. Gen. George Stannard captured the lightly defended Fort Harrison, Batteries 10 and 11, and some defensive lines. In the afternoon, black and white regiments assaulted Fort Gilmer but never captured it. By evening Butler ordered his troops to hold their advances and dig in. It was good they did, because a worried Lee moved nine brigades and seven batteries from other spots on his line to attack and retake Fort Harrison on September 30. Lee reacted just as Grant hoped, creating an opportunity for Meade's strike force to make solid advances toward the Boydton Plank Road.[39]

All waited in nervous anticipation for Grant to order them to move. At 8:15 A.M. on September 30, Grant informed Meade that Butler's forces would remain in place for the time being; consequently, Meade's force could head out "to see if an advantage can be gained." Grant finished his terse three-sentence order with a glimpse of his thinking and predilection for movement: "It seems to me the enemy must be weak enough at one or the other place to let us in."[40] Ever the optimist, Grant hoped that either Richmond or Petersburg might be captured, given Lee's lack of troops to defend both in full measure from simultaneous attacks.

Meade set his strike force into motion. Warren marched down the Poplar Spring Church Road toward the intersection with Squirrel Level Road. Parke followed him, branching off to Warren's left, ideally to cross a swamp to get to Pegram's farm. Gregg's cavalry rode out on the Vaughan Road, headed toward Wilkinson's farm (on Parke's left). The cavalry and Fifth Corps got underway just after 9 A.M., but given that the two corps started on the same road, the Ninth Corps did not begin marching until 10 A.M.[41]

The day soon developed into an almost predictable Richmond-Petersburg offensive: swift gains by Union troops, followed by devastating Confederate counterattacks. The Fifth Corps marched to Squirrel Level Road, fanned out in ravines and woods, and then its First Division, led by Brig. Gen. Charles Griffin, rushed the lightly defended and poorly constructed Fort Archer, overwhelming its defenders and capturing what historian Richard Sommers calls the "key position on the entire Squirrel Level line." But with that quick success, Warren now decided to hold his gains by building a defensive perimeter around Peebles's farm (just west of Squirrel Level Road).[42]

With the way forward finally cleared by Warren's creation of a defensive line, Parke's Ninth Corps moved past the Fifth Corps through some woods onto the cleared land of Pegram's farm. Parke sent brigades to cover his flanks, before ordering Potter's Second Division to march across Jones's farm (north of Pegram's) toward Confederate works that surrounded the western and northern reaches of Jones's farm. Meade arrived at Peebles's farm around 3 P.M. and urged Parke to press on. Grant encouraged Meade to send the Ninth Corps forward, writing, "If the enemy can be broken and started, follow him closely." He even urged him to use Gregg's cavalry more aggressively (based on earlier reports on Gregg's reconnaissance): "If the enemy's cavalry has left Gregg's front, he ought to push ahead, and if he finds no obstacle turn his infantry." When he learned at 3:50 P.M. that Confederate counterattacks at Fort Harrison had been repulsed, he must have felt more sanguine about Meade's prospects than at any other time.[43]

As usual, Confederates were also preparing a response to the slow forward movement of the Ninth Corps. Around 5 P.M. two brigades under Maj. Gen. Cadmus Wilcox charged an exposed brigade (the Second) under Brig. Gen. Simon G. Griffin at the northern edge of Jones's farm, hitting the brigade from both flanks and the front, capturing hundreds of men. Soon joined by two more Confederate brigades, the hard-driving soldiers "rolled up the whole Union line from Jones's house to Arthur's Swamp in only about half an hour." Potter's division had crumbled before his eyes. The victorious Confederates pressed on to Peebles's farm, only to be stopped by a stiff line of the Fifth Corps and rearranged Ninth Corps troops. The fighting continued past dark in some places, but by the end of the day, the Confederates had thrown back the Union forces to its earlier gain, Squirrel Level Road.[44]

It had been a bad day for Meade's strike force, though it had secured the vital intersection of Poplar Church Road and Squirrel Level Road. The Union had over twenty-two hundred casualties, most from the Ninth Corps (nineteen hundred), compared to six hundred Confederate casualties. Meade summarized the day's results in an evening message to Grant, recommending that it was not "judicious to make another advance tomorrow unless reinforced or some evidence can be found of the weakening of the enemy." For once Grant accepted the recommendation, although insisting as he replied, "Hold on to what you have, and be ready to advance." Grant still hoped to find the "enemy's weak point." To that end, he planned to order Butler to "feel up the Darbytown Road" the next day.[45]

The next day (October 1) found the Confederates striving to recoup their losses with two sharp attacks on Union lines. Both attacks failed. Meanwhile, Meade was in the unusual position of pushing for a strong reconnaissance after the fighting, sensing that the Confederates were undermanned. Grant did not press him on the move, and Meade waited all day for Brig. Gen. Gershom Mott's Third Division of the Second Corps to get to Peebles's farm to augment his strike force. The last men did not arrive until dark, so Meade postponed the movement to the next day. The orders to Parke and Warren for October 2 were absolutely clear: "Move forward as soon after daylight tomorrow as practicable and attack the enemy. . . . The object being finally to effect a lodgment upon the Boydton Plank Road within reach of the South Side Railroad, or, if we prove to be strong enough, to follow the enemy closer to Petersburg."[46]

But as so often happened with Meade's plans, nothing worked as expected. The assault did not get off until after 7 A.M., and as the large force swept across Pegram's farm, they found nothing. The Confederates had abandoned the farm. The strike force went to the edge of the farm and stopped. A perplexed Meade had a decision: forge on into the unknown toward stiff Confederate defensive lines, or dig in and see if the Confederates attack. As usual, Meade chose the safest, most controlled response: he decided to set up a defensive line. Asking Grant for permission, he wrote, "Without your orders I shall not attack their entrenchments, but on being satisfied they are not outside of them I will take up the best position I can, connecting with the Weldon Railroad and extending as far left as practicable." Grant completely concurred: "Carry out what you propose in dispatch of 11 A.M.—that is, entrench and hold what you can, but make no attack against defended fortifications." He even allowed Meade to "give up" what he had gained if the troops were needed to defend other parts of the lines. Meade did not need to do that. Though some of the Union brigades exchanged fire with Confederates throughout the day, by nightfall the Union men were digging new lines around Pegram's farm.[47]

That afternoon, while inspecting the lines near Pegram's farm, Meade came the closest to death he would ever be during his entire tenure as commander of the Army of the Potomac. A stray cannon shell passed between Meade's and Humphreys's horses, grazing Meade's leg before it landed in the ground, showering the officers with dirt. Meade wrote to his wife, "A more wonderful escape I never saw." Nonplussed, Meade completed his inspection, then headed back to his headquarters. The Fifth Offensive had come to an end.[48]

Grant and Meade quickly moved on in their respective areas of responsibility. Grant began planning his next offensive against Lee, while awaiting positive developments from his other armies in the field. Meade concentrated on the construction of new lines around and south of Pegram's farm; with an engineer's love for design and construction, he watched a six-mile-long line with new forts be quickly built by October 15. For a general who coveted a strong defense, these new lines were a godsend. As for the short Fifth Offensive, Grant simply noted in his official report that in the "reconnaissance we captured and held the enemy's works near Poplar Spring Church." Meade was equally matter-of-fact in his official report, and not much more detailed in a letter to his wife, except to say, "I did extend my lines some two and a half miles, had quite a brisk affair with the enemy, but did not succeed in taking Petersburg."[49]

In its grandest goals, capturing Richmond or Petersburg, the Fifth Offensive had completely failed. A lesser goal of keeping Lee's troops in the area, however, had been achieved. Another lesser though constant goal of Grant's was to continue to stretch his lines, and thus force Lee to do the same. This goal had been admirably achieved. The loss of Fort Harrison was a blow to Lee's Richmond defense, and the western expansion of the Union line to encompass the vital intersection of Poplar Church Road and Squirrel Level Road forced Lee to place greater reliance on the Boydton Plank Road as a supply line (and thus increase its defense). Earl Hess argues that this very slow western "creep" (push to the west, grab control of an intersection or rail line, and then fortify, initiated by Gouverneur Warren back in August at Globe Tavern), when fully embraced by Grant, became the "winning tactic at Petersburg."[50]

But that view was not yet etched into strategy in early October, so the generals had to settle for other measures of performance. Grant had watched both his armies begin with initial successes, only to be stymied by fierce Confederate counterattacks. For Butler, his moment of redemption for the embarrassing failure during the Bermuda Hundred Campaign (and his initial assault on Petersburg on June 9) came and went at Chaffin's Bluff. Though he kept command of his army, he had not enhanced his military reputation. As for Meade, his collar must have felt even tighter, as he saw his role in Virginia shrink from commander of the key army to simply one of three army commanders. Though he still commanded the largest and most renowned of the three armies, the adulation of the press flowed to Sheridan, while Butler perpetually schemed for greater power, authority, and fame in Virginia and the nation. If Meade's strike force had captured the Boydton Plank Road, and if it had entered Petersburg, he would have been the new hero in the East. But when he settled for a small gain after a stinging attack from the Confederates, it seemed to be just another chapter in a familiar cycle that summer in Petersburg: attack, stop, reel from counterattack, and entrench. This tactic eventually wore down the Army of Northern Virginia, but reputations were being made that summer and fall by generals making bold and successful attacks everywhere but Richmond.

No one knew this situation better than Meade. As he astutely wrote to Margaret in mid-October, "I undoubtedly do not occupy the position I did just after the battle of Gettysburg, and no one will retain any such position in this country, unless he continues to be successful." He had not had success on the battlefield equal to Gettysburg; however, he wrote, "[My] retaining command, and the hold I have at present, is even more creditable than the exaggerated laudation immediately succeeding Gettysburg." He made a list of his predecessors to highlight his durability: "McClellan, Pope, McDowell, Burnside, Hooker, Rosecrans, Banks,

Sigel." Furthermore, he continued, "Persistent efforts have been made by influ-
ential men, politicians, and generals to destroy me, without success." So he had
survived. "[My] present status," he noted, is "not without advantages, and does
not justify my being discontented."[51]

Meade was feeling so good a few days later that he and Grant laughed "over the
ridiculous canard of [Meade] being relieved." Apparently, Grant had been asked
if this story was true when he visited authorities in Washington, and he denied it.
(Another rumor said that Grant was resigning.) Meade chalked up this round of rumors to the politicking that accompanied the presidential election. Meade even felt
magnanimous toward his rival Sheridan after hearing of his great victory at Cedar
Creek. He correctly surmised its effect on the war, the country, and Sheridan's reputation: "This certainly is very remarkable, and if not modified by later intelligence,
will prove one of the greatest feats of the war, and place Sheridan in a position that
it will be difficult for any other general to approach." For once he did not include his
familiar lament that Sheridan's command could or should have been his.[52]

However, Meade could not retain his new positive outlook in the face of a
withering attack from an old critic of his, the *New York Independent.* An anonymous writer blamed Meade not only for the failure of the Fifth Offensive but also
for stealing the "laurels which belonged to Howard and to Hancock" at Gettysburg, for the failure to capture or wound Lee's army at Williamsport and Mine
Run, and for impeding Grant throughout the Virginia Campaign, hanging "upon
the neck of Gen. Grant like an Old Man of the Sea." Why was this incompetent
general kept on? It was "in deference to a presumed, fictitious, perverted, political necessity." At first he tried to let the accusations slide, writing his wife that the
notion that he had powerful political support was "amusing," and that the article
was not "worthwhile to notice."[53]

But the more he thought about the article, the angrier he got. He wrote Grant
on October 24 (the day after he read the article for the first time) and asked him to
print something that would refute the charges that Meade had "failed to support
him" and that Grant was "anxious to get rid" of Meade. Sharing in Meade's dis-
tress, Grant wrote, "I have felt as much pained as you at the constant stabs made
at you by a portion of the public press." He then offered a bland solution: to share
with Meade every dispatch he had written in which he used Meade's name.[54]

Meade told his aide and friend Lyman that Grant's actions would be "kind"
but insufficient. He wanted Grant to publish some sort of refutation for the newspapers. Lyman tried to cheer up Meade by telling him that he "had Grant and
Stanton on his side and a good record, and history was not based on newspapers."
Meade laughed at this notion—showing a deeper understanding of how history
was formed than Lyman gave him credit for.[55]

Meade had to lay aside the issue for a few days, however, because Grant had
decided to try to lengthen Union lines and strike and destroy the South Side Railroad, Lee's last rail link to the South. A military victory, coming on the heels of

Sheridan's dramatic success at Cedar Creek, might ensure Lincoln's reelection in November. He planned a two-pronged assault with Meade's force taking the lead this time, and Butler's force to be the diversion. The main difference for this movement was timing: for the first time, he wanted both strike forces to march out on the same day, October 27.[56]

Meade suggested to Grant that the strike force be composed of three columns, with cavalry under Gregg screening the Union left. Grant agreed with Meade's idea. Parke's Ninth Corps would have the shortest distance to go, as it headed west to the Boydton Plank Road. Warren's Fifth Corps would move "simultaneously" with the Ninth Corps but march along its left and head across Hatcher's Run. The Second Corps would also cross Hatcher's Run, but below (south of) the Fifth Corps. Its destination was the South Side Railroad, though it would have to march twelve miles through woods, open fields, and creeks to get there. In total, Meade would set forty-one thousand men into operation in the early morning hours of October 27.[57]

On that same morning, Butler would put his Tenth and Eighteenth Corps into motion. The Tenth Corps would probe the Confederate defenses on the Darbytown Road. The Eighteenth Corps would strike to the north, hoping to draw defenders out of their lines. Under no instances were the troops to attack entrenched positions, according to Grant.[58]

The generals prepared their troops to move, and on an overcast, drizzly fall day, October 27, the Sixth Offensive got underway. It largely followed the pattern of earlier offensives: initial swift advances followed by fierce Confederate counterattacks and problems with reinforcement. Gregg's five thousand cavalrymen rode southwest to cover the left flank of the Army of the Potomac, while Brig. Gen. Thomas Egan's Second Division of the Second Corps led the way down Vaughan Road, followed closely by Brig. Gen. Gershom Mott's Third Division of the Second Corps. At 6:30 A.M. Egan's lead brigade fought its way across Hatcher's Run, paving the way for his division and the Third to march all the way to Boydton Plank Road and secure the intersection of the White Oak Road, which led to roads that approached the South Side Railroad. By 12:30 P.M. Hancock's entire force was in position, and a half hour later Meade ordered him to halt.[59]

Soon Meade, Grant, and their staffs rode up to Hancock's headquarters to discuss the situation with him. With over one hundred officers gathered around a large oak tree, they were an inviting target for Confederate gunners, who fired on the high-powered assembly (one shell barely missed Meade). The two senior officers confirmed all that had been communicated earlier that morning: the Fifth and Ninth Corps had run into heavy slashings and abatis, backed by steady fire, and stopped to respond; Warren had detached Brig. Gen. Samuel Crawford's division to march through the woods to connect with Hancock's right; and Hancock would hold in place until the next step could be decided.[60]

Grant wanted more information, so he rode off on one of the odd scouting missions he was known for. Grant and his aide Orville Babcock cantered down the

Boydton Plank Road to Egan's position at the intersection of White Oak Road and Boydton Plank Road, then pushed up even closer to Hatcher's Run, where they were fired upon. At one point Grant's horse got tangled in some downed telegraph wires, so Babcock extricated the horse's legs while Grant sat imperturbably in the saddle. Grant saw that Confederate defenses were longer and stronger than intelligence had predicted, and after returning to the assembly of officers, he made his decision: there would be no attack on the Confederate defenses. The movement to reach and seize the South Side Railroad would be terminated, and the Second Corps withdrawn the next day. Around 3:00 P.M. he and Meade left for their headquarters.[61]

At almost the same time that Grant and Meade were leaving Hancock, the failure of Butler's movement unfolded on the Williamsburg Road. For unknown reasons, Grant's very clear orders to Butler to *not* attempt to take strong earthworks did not filter down to Maj. Gen. Godfrey Weitzel, commanding the Eighteenth Corps strike force that marched up the Williamsburg Road. He attacked two positions, then withdrew his men in the early evening. While Butler's men had kept the Confederates busy, their futile attacks against strong defenses caused needless casualties. The Sixth Offensive was grinding to a halt.[62]

The Confederates, however, were not constrained by Union plans. Around 4:00 P.M. three brigades under the indefatigable William Mahone came in behind Hancock's troops strung out on the Boydton Plank Road and hit the regiments under Col. John Pulford especially hard. They pushed them back beyond the road, threatening to completely split Hancock's entire force. But Hancock quickly organized a counterattack, and, striking from the north and the south, Hancock's men overwhelmed the Confederate attackers, capturing over six hundred men and completely reversing the earlier breakthrough. The Second Corps had redeemed itself for Reams Station.[63]

The only thing left for the Second Corps to do was to withdraw from its position—safely. Just after 5:15 P.M., Meade asked Hancock to consider attacking if Crawford's division and Ayres's division (sent later in the day) needed him, but if a successful attack did not seem possible, he could retreat even "during the night" if he "consider[ed] it best." Faced with insufficient ammunition and no contact with Crawford as late as 9:00 P.M. that night, Hancock decided to withdraw. The retrograde movement began at 10:00 P.M., and the tired infantrymen made their way back on muddy roads in persistent rain. By 1:00 A.M. the last picket line had pulled out, and by 10:00 A.M. the next day, both divisions had recrossed Hatcher's Run to the safety of their lines.[64]

As the generals counted their losses, the interpretation of the operation began to be shaped by numerous parties. Meade's force had lost nearly eighteen hundred men, and Butler's over fifteen hundred. Neither general had any new territory to claim for the losses, so both minimized the scope of the movement. Meade took his cue from Grant, referring to the operation in his official report as a "reconnaissance." (Grant had said the same in a letter to Stanton sent in the evening of

October 27.) Grant did wonder what had happened to Crawford during the day, but Meade explained his difficulties slashing through woods. Newspapers and many soldiers critiqued the operation, with Lyman capturing the sentiment in his inimitable manner: "As the mine was to be termed an ill-conducted fizzle, so this attempt may be called a *well-conducted* fizzle." Confederate commentators celebrated the victory, though it changed nothing about the strategic balance along the Richmond-Petersburg line. As for Meade, he told his wife that the enemy was too "strongly entrenched" to capture the South Side Railroad, and the strike force had to return to Union lines. At least with Grant by his side all day he would not be the sole recipient of criticism for the movement, as Grant had been "sanctioning everything that was done." Meade could now return to the perennial issue of his tenure prior to the Sixth Offensive: criticism of his leadership.[65]

On October 29 Meade spoke bluntly to Grant about his concerns. He told him that he "did not care about his dispatches" but wanted instead "a few lines for publication that would set at rest, as far as he was concerned, the wicked and malicious falsehoods" in the article. Grant "cheerfully" agreed to produce such a statement. The ever-sensitive Meade also asked Grant to tell President Lincoln that "unless some measures were taken to satisfy the public and silent the persistent clamor against" him, he would "prefer being relieved." He even added that he was becoming "disheartened," especially when he was "ignored" in all "successful operations," yet held "wholly responsible" when anything went wrong.[66]

Perhaps just airing his grievances to Grant helped cool off Meade, as there is no record of any response from Lincoln. Instead, Meade defended Grant in a letter written to his wife two days later, highlighting some of the critical differences between the two men. He wrote, "Grant is very phlegmatic, and holds in great contempt newspaper criticism, and thinks, as long as a man is sustained by his own conscience, his superiors, and the Government, that it is not worth his while to trouble himself about the newspapers." Furthermore, he had always expressed satisfaction with Meade's services. Meade went on, "Differently constituted, with more sensitiveness in his nature, I don't doubt he would before now have taken some action, either in his official dispatches, or in some other way given publicity to such opinions of my services as would set at rest the idle stories." As usual, Meade incisively captured Grant's strengths and shortcomings (as he saw them). Now sustained by Lincoln, Stanton, and much of the Republican Party, Grant could ignore or tolerate criticism from the press or politicians (and to be fair, he had a fairly thick skin). By contrast, Meade, with his high-strung, nervous temperament, could accept criticism of his decisions but never the questioning of his honor (the basis for his reputation). Moreover, he was not paranoid or exaggerating when he wrote that "persistent efforts" had been made to destroy his career.[67]

Nor was he wrong in noticing that the press either ignored his role in operations or condemned them, a situation made intolerable after he banished the correspondent Cropsey from the army. Meade recognized the trouble he had brought on himself, so when *New York Herald* chief war correspondent Sylvanus Cadwallader decided to end the news embargo in late October and told Meade what he had done, a conciliatory Meade replied, "I am obliged to you for the trouble you have taken about the matter." He also invited Cadwallader to his headquarters and told him that "all charges of unfriendliness to correspondents as a class were absolutely and wholly untrue," and that his harsh punishment of Cropsey was "one of the greatest mistakes of his life." They parted on good terms, and this meeting may have helped Meade get over the pain of the *Independent* article.[68]

There would be no relief, however, from the anxiety caused by his son Sergeant's worsening physical condition. His health was discussed in almost every one of the sixteen letters Meade sent to his wife in October, and sometimes not mentioned because he was waiting on an update from Margaret. The major issue for the month was Sergeant's fitness for an ocean voyage to a healthier climate. Sergeant's chief physician initially opposed the trip but apparently wavered in late October when Sergeant's health temporarily improved. By the end of the month, however, the doctor had returned to his earlier position: Sergeant was not healthy enough for the trip. Trying to bolster his wife's flagging spirit, Meade wrote, "He and we must cheerfully submit to what it is not in our power to remedy, and placing our truth and reliance in the Supreme Ruler of events try to be resigned to what cannot be avoided." Whether this approach satisfied Margaret or George is not known. Regardless, Meade's worries about his oldest son added to his burdens that month.[69]

One of the few releases from stress Meade had was the steady stream of visits by foreign and domestic observers. Two French officers, Lt. Col. François De Chanal and Capt. Pierre Guzman, left headquarters in late September after a three-month stay chaperoned by Lyman. Following on their heels was the governor of Nova Scotia, Maj. Gen. Hastings Doyle, whom Meade described as a "very clever, intelligent and educated Irish gentleman." In late October Meade entertained the Mexican minister, Matias Romero, and his accompanying officer, General Doblado. There was also a host of government officials, ranging from Stanton and Treasury Secretary William P. Fessenden to an election commission from Pennsylvania. Even an artist showed up, Hans Balling, a Norwegian and former lieutenant colonel in the First New York, who was commissioned by a New York industrialist to make a "rapid water-color likeness" of Meade and other generals.[70]

When not busy entertaining visitors or complaining about his situation, Meade inspected the ever-growing Union lines. By early November, Union troops had constructed "32 miles of line that was studded with 36 forts and 50 batteries" in Meade's sector alone. In Butler's sector there were thirteen miles of earthworks north of the James River, and thirteen and a half miles of earthworks across the Bermuda Hundred peninsula. For their part, Confederates had constructed twenty miles of defense in the same sectors.[71] Every mound of earth, let alone the forts, batteries, and revetments built for these lines, made it that much harder for one side to attack the other. But for Grant, building and shelling were not enough—he had to prosecute the war. So he planned for a raid on the Weldon and Petersburg Railroad to tear up as much track as possible.

On December 5 Grant sent Meade orders for the soon-to-be-called Hicksford Raid. No fewer than twenty thousand men were ordered to destroy the railroad "as far south as Hicksford, or farther if practicable." Meade assigned the job to Warren's Fifth Corps, augmented by Gershom Mott's Third Division, Second Corps, and two brigades of cavalry under Brig. Gen. David Gregg. Warren's force left the line at daylight on December 7 in a steady rain, while Butler moved some troops north of the James River and Brig. Gen. Innis Palmer marched toward Weldon in North Carolina (to keep the Confederates guessing as to Grant's intentions). The Fifth Corps made good time despite the weather and began tearing up railroad tracks on December 8. Grant and Meade grew worried when they did not hear directly from Warren for three days, but they felt a measure of relief when his message that all was well reached Meade's headquarters on December 11. Warren's force destroyed eighteen miles of train track, all the way down to Hicksford, burning ties and twisting rails. Potter had been sent out with eight thousand men to protect Warren if necessary, but that did not prove to be the case. Warren's force safely returned to Union lines on December 12, exhausted after marching over one hundred miles and enduring rain, sleet, and ice rain. Though the Union line was not extended by this operation, for once the casualties were minimal, unless one counted the head-sore soldiers who had found "applejack" in abundance in the houses they had passed.[72]

The generals had nonmilitary issues that fall as well, including the monitoring of a presidential election while an army was in the field. Meade happily reported to his wife that the election had "passed off very quietly" on November 8, with one major exception: Republican officials accused Democratic officials of distributing "spurious or altered poll books." Meade felt compelled to have the alleged perpetrators arrested and held until an investigation could be made. Fortunately for Meade, Stanton moved quickly on the controversy, ordering Meade to send the alleged violators to Washington on November 11. Meade also informed his wife that Lincoln won the Army of Potomac's vote by eight thousand votes (two to one ratio), about what he expected. There was one last issue from the elections: a Republican official reported to his party headquarters that Meade had not voted in the election. Meade thought nothing of it; he said that "nearly all other general officers, including Grant, did the same—that is, not vote." Meade wrote his son Sergeant that, with the election over, he hoped that the government could raise enough soldiers to finally end the war.[73]

The second issue that stirred up the top leaders of the Army of the Potomac was promotions. Some news was positive: Meade's 253 recommendations for brevets had been approved. Those receiving brevets included most of Meade's aides as well as generals such as Henry Hunt (to major general). But other promotions

lagged. For several months, Hancock had chafed at his position, believing he deserved higher command and smarting under criticism of some of his decisions
during the summer and fall. He floated the idea of raising a new corps of soldiers
consisting solely of veterans, and Stanton jumped on the possibility. It languished
in Washington during election season, and by mid-November, Hancock asked
when, and if, it would be done. Meade reassured him on November 25 that the
orders would be "issued in a few days." The next day the new commander of the
Second Corps, Andrew Humphreys, had a long and friendly visit with Hancock.
Hancock then issued his departing message and left on leave, never to return to
his beloved Second Corps. Meade had lost his closest military confidant.[74]

Meade had also lost a strong right-hand man as chief of staff, Andrew Humphreys. After some deliberation he found a good replacement for Humphreys in
Alexander Webb, a hero at Gettysburg and a stalwart commander in the Second
Corps in the Overland Campaign. His appointment officially began on January 11,
1865. Of course the appointment of Humphreys to command the Second Corps
greatly miffed John Gibbon, who felt he deserved the appointment. As sensitive
as Meade to slights to his honor and reputation, Gibbon asked to be relieved from
his present command when he heard the news. Meade was disappointed in this
reaction, and Lyman thought Gibbon to be a "fool" who did not appreciate that
"Meade has done everything for him." The matter percolated up to Grant, who
temporarily mollified Gibbon with praise, then completely pleased him with a
new appointment, commander of the Twenty-Fourth Corps.[75] Now satisfied,
Gibbon maintained his friendship with Meade.

Looming over these slights and bruised feelings, however, was Meade's own
frustration with his stalled promotion. The boiling point was reached on November
15 when Meade heard news that angered but probably did not shock him: Sheridan
had been promoted to major general in the regular Army—over Meade—taking
the former position of McClellan, whose resignation had been accepted by Lincoln.
Meade fumed for a few days, then confronted Grant over the situation. Grant "disclaimed any agency in Sheridan's appointment" and told him he would fight on his
behalf to see that Meade got the promotion he had been promised and deserved—
to rank Sheridan as well. Meade told his wife, "I *believe* Grant," though still feeling
angry and sorry for himself, he continued, "*Every other officer* in this army, except
myself, who has been recommended for promotion for services in this campaign
has been promoted." Grant was as good as his word. He went up to Washington and
spoke to Lincoln about the situation. Grant suggested that Meade be appointed to
major general dating from August 18, the day the army captured the Weldon Railroad. Lincoln concurred, making Meade fourth in rank in the regular army, behind
Sherman but ahead of Sheridan. When Meade heard from Grant on November 25,
he wrote to his wife, "As justice is thus finally done, I am satisfied."[76]

But with Meade and promotion nothing was ever that simple. His appointment had to be confirmed by the Senate, and with few friends in Congress, he knew his appointment might languish (or fail to be approved). Though the Military Committee of the Senate approved his nomination in January 1865, some senators raised objections, and his nomination was temporarily put aside while other nominations were moved. Grant promised to push for Meade's confirmation while in Washington, and he sent letters to Sen. Henry Wilson and Rep. Elihu Washburne on January 23, 1865, advocating for Meade and offering to address any "objections" to Meade.[77]

Meade was hobbled in his fight by new activity from the Joint Committee on the Conduct of the War. The committee decided to investigate the Crater and in late December traveled to Petersburg to collect evidence and interview generals. Their arrival caught Meade by surprise because when called before them, he had no "official documents" on hand, except for his report on the Crater (which he read to them). He was interrogated by Sen. Benjamin Loan, then "permitted to leave." Meade recommended that the committee talk to two key aides of his, Maj. Gen. Henry Hunt and Col. James Duane. The committee complied, but "as soon as they [Hunt and Duane] began to say anything that was unfavorable to Burnside, they stopped them and said that was enough." However, the committee members listened avidly to witnesses suggested by Burnside, an indication that the entire investigation was for show. Predictably, when the committee published its report in February, it blamed Meade for the disaster because he had replaced the black troops at the last minute and had insisted that the attackers seize the crest of the line. Fortunately for Meade, Grant thought little of the report, writing to Meade that "Burnside's evidence apparently has been their only guide and to draw it mildly he has forgotten some of the facts." Meade still wanted the proceedings from the military Court of Inquiry published, and he felt "vindication" when it came out in the *Army and Navy Journal* on March 11, 1865.[78]

It is hard to say if the committee's last investigation of Meade accomplished anything. With victory in sight, the public did not hunger for scapegoats, and with Grant's political position stronger than ever, it was not likely that Meade would be miraculously dismissed. In the end, the main effect of the committee's continuing investigations into Meade and his leadership of the Army of the Potomac may have been, in the words of Bruce Tap, to add to the "destruction of Meade's reputation for generations to come."[79]

What made the efforts of the Joint Committee on the Conduct of the War particularly suspect, if not futile, was that by the time its report was published, Meade's appointment had at last been confirmed by the Senate. On February 1, 1865, by a vote of thirty-two to five, the Senate made Meade major general of the regular army. As Meade discovered, "[I had] more friends than I had any idea of."

Lyman, who was on leave in Boston, immediately sent him a note of congratulations and a box of goodies, which he said contained "books and pickles" but actually held "books and a box of champagne."[80]

As usual, any joy in Meade's life was immediately shadowed by trouble. Throughout the winter the health of his eldest son Sergeant continued to worry him. After seeing off most of his staff in December for holiday furloughs, Meade finally left for Philadelphia on December 30 and arrived home December 31. He wanted to stay for a while, but Grant called him back on January 9 to respond to a rumored evacuation of Richmond. When Meade saw Grant on January 10, he explained Sergeant's situation, and why he wanted to return to Philadelphia. Grant told him he could, once the rumor was tracked down. Meade felt bad about leaving the family at this critical time, but all he could offer his wife was his prayers to God to "have mercy on dear Sergeant and yourself, and to give you strength to bear up under the affliction you are visited with." He closed the letter poignantly, "My heart is too full to write more."[81]

For the next month, Sergeant's condition alternated between improving and declining. In the frequent letters exchanged by Meade and his wife, they always spoke of their concerns for Sergeant, as when Meade wrote on February 13, "This is the most severe affliction of my life, to be away from you and my dear child when he is such a sufferer." But he did not feel he could resign because he would lose "a great portion" of his pay, and they "could not live on what would be left." He offered to send their son George to help out.[82]

On February 21, news reached Meade (indirectly from his aide James Biddle to his son George) that Sergeant appeared to be sinking toward death. In the morning he wrote a long letter to Margaret explaining why he could not leave his command, though he so wanted to be there. Apparently, Grant gave him permission to leave, so that by noon on the same day he left his headquarters for Philadelphia. It took him two full days to get home, and while en route, he learned the sad news: his son Sergeant died on February 21 at 11 P.M. Meade reached home in time to help attend to funeral arrangements but could not stay for a long period of mourning. On February 26 he was ordered to report to Washington to see Secretary of War Stanton. He met Stanton the next day, who apologized for forgetting why Meade was even in Philadelphia. Apparently, some telegrams from Edward O. C. Ord (new commander of the Army of the James) had alarmed him, and he wanted Meade back in Petersburg as soon as possible. So with an unbearably heavy heart—"No human reasoning can afford you or myself any consolation," he wrote Margaret—Meade returned to his command.[83]

Sergeant's deteriorating condition that winter had been a constant anxiety for Meade. Somehow he disciplined himself to do his job, which sometimes meant participating in strange conferences. On February 1, 1865, he and Grant met with the three Confederate "peace commissioners," who were waiting for Lincoln to arrive at City Point. They asked Meade for his views on what the Northern public wanted to see to end the war. He replied, "The complete restoration of the Union and such a settlement of the slavery question as should be final." Meade rejected the idea that a ceasefire should precede peace talks; fighting would stop only if it "was for good." Meade also thought slavery would have to end. Whether he knew it or not, Lincoln's views were essentially the same, and the conference held on February 3 produced no results.[84]

More common than meetings with Confederate leaders were military operations. Whenever the weather cleared, Grant wanted some soldiers in motion, and during one good spell of weather during the first few days of February, Grant ordered Meade to "destroy or capture as much as possible of the enemy's wagon train." He wanted to send Gregg's cavalry south to hit the wagons, as well as portions of the Fifth and Second Corps to protect their flanks. Meade immediately made plans: Warren's Fifth Corps would march down the Vaughan Road to the Stony Creek crossing, and Humphreys's Second Corps would march toward Hatcher's Run. Meanwhile, the cavalry would ride "up and down" the Boydton Plank Road, looking for wagons. Given the history of such "reconnaissance," Meade dared to ask Grant an essential question: "Are the objects to be attained commensurate with the disappointment which the public are sure to entertain if you make any movement and return without some striking result?" Within an hour, Grant replied, "The objects to be attained are of importance. I will telegraph to Secretary Stanton in advance, showing the object of the movement, the publication of which, with the report of the operations, will satisfy the public." Meade had his answer, and he knew his next job was to ensure that the troops departed early next morning.[85]

The troops got off on the morning of February 5 as scheduled and had completely different experiences. Gregg's cavalry rode down to Dinwiddie Court House on nearly impassable roads and found few stores of supplies. He captured eighteen wagons and fifty prisoners. With these meager results, Meade ordered him to report to Warren to see how he could help the Fifth Corps. Warren marched out to Hargrave's and "met no enemy." Humphreys, however, marched to Armstrong Mills by 10 A.M., then later in the day had his right attacked. Meade called out a division from the Ninth Corps and the Sixth Corps to help him. The Battle of Hatcher's Run (also called the Seventh Offensive by modern historians) had begun.[86]

Grant was encouraged by the results because he always hoped to draw out Confederates from their lines into open battle. He told Meade to bring back the cavalry and the Fifth Corps, and if he could "follow the enemy up, do it." He added for emphasis, "Change original instructions to give all advantages you can take of the enemy's acts." Meade ordered Warren to connect with Humphreys's left and be ready to "support him" if he were attacked. He told Humphreys to "hold" his "present position" and either repulse further enemy attacks or even go on the attack, "if practicable."[87]

Warren got his Fifth Corps into position by dawn of February 6; they formed on the Vaughan Road where it crossed Hatcher's Run. Both Warren and Humphreys were then ordered to "feel the enemy in [their] front" but not attack them unless they were "outside their line of works." Warren sent Crawford's Third Division down the Dabney Mill Road toward Confederate lines outside the Boydton Plank Road. The men ran into Confederate troops that formed around Dabney's Saw Mill. Fighting raged in that area for several hours, until Confederate reinforcements pushed Crawford's division back, even as a Sixth Corps division under Brig. Gen. Frank Wheaton rushed to their aid. Neither Grant nor Meade wanted to attack entrenched lines again, and both agreed on the importance of holding on to Hatcher's Run.[88]

With the weather turning cold, neither general thought it wise to do much more than "strong reconnaissance" of the enemy's position the next day. After some initial confusion about plans, it became clear to Meade and Grant that they wanted the same things—the Hatcher's Run crossing protected for future operations, and the Union line extended to it (a distance of four miles from Fort Sampson to Armstrong Mill). Crawford's division engaged in one more firefight with Confederate troops around Dabney's Saw Mill on the afternoon of February 7, but even as they probed, Union engineers were digging trenches and putting corduroy on roads.[89]

The Seventh Offensive had ended as quietly as it began. Union losses exceeded Confederate losses again (1,539 versus 1,000), but Grant had secured another crossing and allowed his line to be extended another four miles. Just as Meade predicted, some newspapers (most noticeably the *New York Tribune*) labeled the operation "a failure" and "put the blame" on Meade. Of course Grant's telegram to Stanton (before the operation) had not been published, so the newspaper did not have the full understanding of the limited scope of the mission. Meade tried to resign himself to the constant criticism, writing, "I must make up my mind to be abused by this set, never mind what happens." At least he had the distraction of an artist measuring his head to cast a bronze to amuse him during these trying days in February.[90]

With winter weather hampering most military operations, Meade and his fellow generals spent much of March entertaining visitors. His close aide Theodore Lyman recorded visits on twelve separate days in the month. Visitors ranged from a Captain Botiano of Wallachia to Mrs. Grant to Mrs. Jay Cooke (wife of the war financier) to Edwin Stanton and even President and Mrs. Lincoln. Typically, guests visited Grant's or Meade's headquarters (or both), saw a review of a unit, and sometimes glimpsed the front lines. Meade did not seem too bothered by the steady stream of visitors ("these excursions from Washington seem to be the idea of the day"), especially when he was finally able to persuade his grieving wife to visit. She arrived in camp on March 22 with the entire family (plus the wives of most of Meade's aides, including Lyman's "Mimi"). The next few days were a whirlwind of activities: fine meals, troop reviews, observation of the enemy's lines, and even a tour of some naval vessels. Though the visit ended abruptly on March 25 with the Confederate attack on Fort Stedman, Meade clearly cherished it; waxing poetic in his letter to Margaret the day after she left, he wrote, "Your visit seems so like a dream, I can hardly realize you have been here."[91]

Though the dream was rudely disturbed by Lee's surprise attack on Fort Stedman, that assault was quickly repulsed. Though Lee hoped this daring attack might force the Union armies to retract their lines a bit (thus allowing him to send some troops south to help Johnston stop Sherman), he pinned no great hopes on it. Similarly, the attack did not alter Grant's next move: he planned to recall Sheridan's cavalry to Richmond and use them as an advancing force on his left, supported by two corps from the Army of the Potomac that would destroy the South Side and Danville Railroads, thus forcing Lee to abandon Petersburg and Richmond. He sent detailed orders to Meade, Ord, and Sheridan on March 24, 1865, with a commencement date of March 29. The final offensive would soon be underway.[92]

Before the massive operation began, details had to be hammered out. On March 28 Grant had a historic meeting with his top generals at City Point. Lyman saw Sherman for the first time, "a tall, sinewy, spare man, with a great forehead, large, thick nose, sunken gray eyes, and a wide firm mouth." The irrepressible Sheridan had finally returned to Petersburg with his tired cavalry, looking "more stubby than ever and much sun-burned." The men discussed a number of topics: Sherman's situation (he would be ready to move his full army out of Goldsboro, North Carolina, on April 10), Sherman's orders should Grant's attack fail in any manner, and Sheridan's freedom to move as he saw fit after destroying the railroads (either returning to Grant or heading into North Carolina to help Sherman). When the meeting ended, the generals departed to plan for the roles each would play in what all hoped would be the last great offensive.[93]

As Meade issued orders to his army for what might be the final battles of the war, he probably had no time to reflect on his second winter as commander of the Army of the Potomac. He had been involved in four "offensives" since August; none had greatly altered the strategic situation along the Richmond-Petersburg line, although they *had* worn down the soldiers of the Army of the Potomac even more. They had also led to testy relations with two long-standing allies of his, John Gibbon and Winfield Scott Hancock. Meade had endured continuous criticism of his performance by some in the press and Congress, and while he tried to resign himself to their complaints, he never really could. He saw two of Grant's favorites, Sherman and Sheridan, win military victories and public adulation. And he continued to feel aggrieved by Grant's inattention to his feelings and support of other generals, especially Sheridan and Sherman. Though he finally received the promotion to major general he felt he deserved, even that achievement was tainted by delays and the persistent political efforts he had to make to get it. As usual, he identified Grant as the source of his frustration, even while telling his close friend Henry Cram that Grant was "the best man the war has yet produced." The fundamental problem dated to the moment Grant announced he would make his headquarters with the Army of the Potomac. Meade knew he would always play second fiddle, but the central problem was the difference in personalities of Grant and Meade, as described by Meade: "[Grant] did no see it then, and he does not see it now; there is the difference between us." Or, put more bluntly, "I [am] oversensitive, and he deficient in sensibility." That was the heart of the matter, and it would define their relationship until Meade's death.[94]

Meade had also spent much of the fall and winter dealing with a family crisis that became a family tragedy: the slow physical deterioration and subsequent death of his oldest son, Sergeant. Though some might question his decision to place the demands of his job above attendance at his son's side in his last few months of life, none saw anything but raw grief when his son died.

The struggle to meet the demands of his position and his inability to be by his son's side were parts of the price of command George G. Meade paid in the winter of 1864–65. Almost as wearing on his psyche, however, were the steady drumbeats of criticism from the press and his "false position" of serving under Grant in the Richmond-Petersburg theater. The grand movements and major battles in the fall of 1864 happened far away from the trenches of the Richmond-Petersburg line, and the nation bestowed its gratitude upon the Union generals who led the victorious armies. For Meade it had been months of monitoring enemy activity punctuated by occasional movements into hostile territory that gained only small amounts of ground. The process wore down the enemy but never caught the fancy of the Northern public. Meade's star had indeed fallen far since the heady days of early July 1863.

The Defeat of Lee and the End of the Army of the Potomac

The end of the war in the East came faster and more abruptly than most imagined. It began with movement of Union troops on March 29 and would conclude less than two weeks later with the surrender of the Army of Northern Virginia at Appomattox on April 9. Meade was sick with a severe cold for most of that period, but he continually exerted himself to stay actively in command of his army. It was good he did, because with Sheridan given the authority to use his cavalry and some infantry to flank the Confederate army, Sheridan got the lion's share of attention for being the piston driving Grant's engine. So even with the unbridled joy and relief felt by so many Union soldiers when Lee surrendered his army, for Meade there was always the undercurrent of competition and reputation. Adding to the indignity was not only the needed dissolution of his army in the summer of 1865 but also the sudden reassignment of Halleck to be in charge of the newly reconstituted Department of Virginia.

All these momentous events lay in the future on March 28. On that day orders were issued for the Army of the Potomac to begin its concerted movement on March 29, and for three divisions of the Army of the James to relieve the Second Corps from its current line. Grant's hammer, the ten thousand cavalrymen under Sheridan, would ride out early on the twenty-ninth, go behind and then to the left of the advancing Fifth Corps, and then head for Dinwiddie Court House. Although the cavalry was not supposed to "attack the enemy in his entrenched position," they were allowed to attack or defend as dictated by circumstances. If the Confederates remained behind their lines, Sheridan was to push farther west and north, destroying as much of the South Side and Danville Railroads as possible. Once that was accomplished, Sheridan had the choice to return to the main army or ride into North Carolina to join Sherman.[1]

Sheridan had more latitude and direction than the written orders stated. According to Grant in his *Memoirs*, he had a private conversation with Sheridan about his orders, who seemed "somewhat disappointed" that he might finish the war in North Carolina (and miss defeating Lee). Grant said, "General, this portion of your instructions I have put in merely as a blind." He explained that he "intended to close the war right here, with this movement, and that he should go no farther." Sheridan joyfully responded by slapping his leg and saying, "I am glad to hear it, and we can do it." This was the confidence Grant so enjoyed and admired in Sheridan, which encouraged him to issue the private order that ultimately led to Lee's surrender and Sheridan's attendance at that event.[2]

The troops moved out on time on March 29, and in the early afternoon the lead brigade (commanded by Brig. Gen. Joshua Chamberlain) of Maj. Gen. Charles Griffin's division ran into Confederate skirmishers at the Quaker Road crossing over Gravelly Run. They forced the skirmishers back, before being counterattacked at the Lewis Farm. Griffin sent reinforcements to Chamberlain, and seeing them arrive, the Confederates pulled back. The Fifth Corps then entrenched across the Boydton Plank Road. Meade sent a note of congratulations to Warren. Meanwhile, the Second Corps marched with little opposition to a position north of Vaughn Road. Sheridan's cavalry made it to Dinwiddie Court House by 5:00 P.M., where it awaited further orders.[3]

The easy advance of the day encouraged Grant to change his plans. He instructed Sheridan *not* to "cut loose and go after the enemy's" railroads; instead, he ordered, "Push around the enemy if you can and get into his right rear." This time the forces would not simply entrench or retreat to their strong lines—they would press on. Grant told Sheridan, "I now feel like ending the matter if it is possible to do so before going back." He added, "We will act altogether as one army here until it is seen what can be done with the enemy."[4]

The grand movement, however, foundered on the second day (March 30) under heavy rains that in Lyman's words turned the roads into "sandy pudding." With Lincoln himself staying on at City Point eagerly awaiting developments, Grant and his generals felt the pressure to keep moving. But there was little they could do but push their lines out a bit more. Some of Sheridan's cavalry skirmished with Confederate cavalry near J. Boisseau's house, but then they pushed on to secure the intersection at Five Forks. That evening, the generals "began to speculate on the necessity of drawing back," according to Lyman.[5]

Such talk was merely contingency discussions because by late evening Grant had decided to ask all the corps commanders—Warren, Humphreys, Wright, and Parke—as well as Ord (Army of the James) and Sheridan to prepare to attack the next day. Sheridan had even greater authority; if he believed he could "turn the enemy's right with the assistance of a corps of infantry," Grant would send him the Fifth Corps (and it would be under his command).[6]

As had so often happened in the Eastern theater, however, the Confederates confounded Union plans by attacking first. Major General Pickett led a combined cavalry-infantry attack on Sheridan's cavalry north of Dinwiddie Court House in the afternoon of March 31. Though Union cavalry were pushed back, they managed to retain control of Dinwiddie Court House. Meanwhile, four Confederate brigades under the command of Maj. Gen. Bushrod Johnson attacked lead elements of Brig. Gen. Romeyn Ayres's division as it marched up the White Oak Road. They forced the Union troops back across Gravelly Run, where they re-formed for a counterattack a few hours later, assisted by Griffin's division and two brigades from the Second Corps. In the face of the growing numbers, the Confederate troops retreated to their trenches. Though no one could know it at the time, this was to be the Army of Northern Virginia's last offensive against Union troops at Petersburg.[7]

The day had been busy for Meade. He had ridden up to Warren's headquarters at 11:00 A.M., only to learn that Warren was with Ayres, who had been attacked. Meade then rode on to see Humphreys at the intersection of Quaker Road and Boydton Plank Road, where he ordered Brig. Gen. Nelson Miles to attack on the right of the Fifth Corps (and found that Humphreys had already given the same order). Meade then rode off to find Warren, whom he found supervising the counterattack by Union troops. Next it was off to the Butler House, where Meade and Grant conferred. When the conference ended, the two generals retired to their temporary headquarters to await news of the day.[8]

That evening, Meade and Grant had a lively exchange about the next day's movements. At first Grant had no intention of making "offensive moves" on April 1, until he heard good news from Sheridan, who thought he could "turn the enemy's left or break through his lines" if he had the assistance of the trusted Sixth Corps. Grant could not free the Sixth Corps to assist Sheridan, but he did consider sending the Second Corps. Meanwhile, Meade had ordered Warren to send a division to assist Sheridan. If Sheridan could not "overcome the force now opposed to him," Meade suggested the lines be contracted. By 9:00 P.M. Grant asked Meade to send a cavalry force to check on Sheridan. A little later, Sheridan's detailed report came to Grant, who then changed his mind. Meade had simultaneously come to a similar idea: send an entire corps to Sheridan to "smash up the force" there. Grant endorsed this new plan: "Let Warren move in the way you propose and urge him not to stop for anything." At 11:00 P.M. Ayres was ordered by Warren to march down the Boydton Plank Road and report to Sheridan at Dinwiddie Court House.[9]

Infantry from both sides were on the move the night of March 31 and the morning of April 1. Lee had ordered Pickett to hold Five Forks, so he dutifully pulled his troops back and had them improve the existing breastworks. Later that morning, Pickett and Fitzhugh Lee rode to the rear of their line and attended a shad bake. They ignored reports from Confederate cavalry that Union troops were massing near Five Forks. Those troops were the tired foot soldiers of the Fifth Corps and

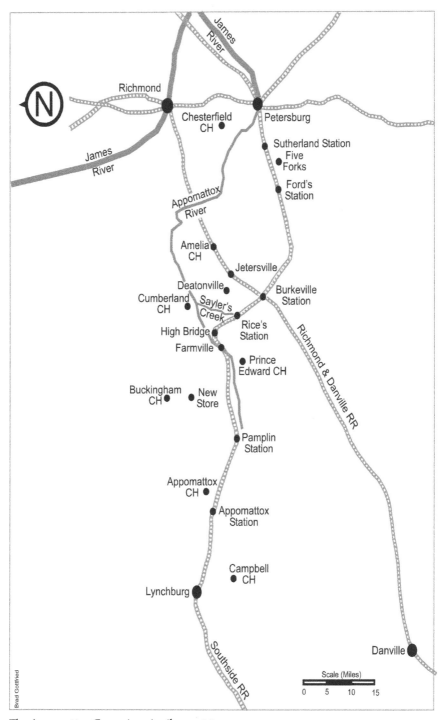

The Appomattox Campaign, April 1–9, 1865

Sheridan's cavalry. Combined, they consisted of over twenty thousand men, out-numbering Pickett's five brigades of ten thousand men by a ratio of two to one. After a long night's march (a bridge had to be built over Gravelly Run), some of Warren's weary troops reached Dinwiddie Court House by daylight. Griffin reported to Sheridan first, with Warren not appearing before him until 11:00 A.M. By this time, Warren had received Meade's very explicit order: "In the movements following your junction with General Sheridan you will be under his orders and will report to him." While this order was not surprising (Sheridan ranked him), what Warren did *not* know would have surprised him. That morning, one of Grant's staffers talked to Col. Frederick T. Locke, the Fifth Corps adjutant, about the night march. Locke had been allowed to stay behind, but this led to his conveying old information: the troops had been held up at Gravelly Run. This incensed Grant, who was fed up with Warren's dilatory ways. He told his trusted aide, Col. Orville Babcock, to give a message to Sheridan: relieve Warren if he felt that the Fifth Corps would "do better" under a different general.[10]

Babcock delivered the message to Sheridan, who allegedly told Col. Horace Porter that "he hoped such [a] step might not be necessary." Sheridan then discussed the plan of battle with Warren: the Fifth Corps would attack Pickett's left, while the cavalry feinted on Pickett's right. He left the tactical details to Warren, who drew a map before bringing up his divisions from two and a half miles away. He placed Crawford's division on the right, Griffin's division behind Crawford's, and Ayres's division on the left. It took nearly three hours for all the men to get into position, while Sheridan "fretted like a caged tiger" at Warren's perceived slowness. At 4:15 P.M. the order to attack was given: the Battle of Five Forks had begun.[11]

The attacking Union columns seemed unstoppable. At first, Ayres, then Griffin, and finally Crawford (who drifted farther to the right than anticipated) met stout resistance but rolled over it. Sheridan rode with the infantry (Ayres's division) and seemed to be everywhere, shouting encouragement as bullets whizzed around him. Warren, too, had his moment at the front when at one point, after retrieving Crawford's division, he grabbed the corps flag and had his horse jump the barricade shouting, "Now boys, follow me, this will be the last fight of the war!" The cavalry attacked soon after the infantry got rolling, and they too swooped up prisoners by the dozens. Pickett and Fitzhugh Lee raced back to see what could be done, but all they could muster was a third refused line, which held only for a brief time before Crawford's division overpowered it. It was now every soldier for himself, and the men raced to the safety of the railroad, two and a half miles away.[12]

It was one of the most lopsided Union victories against Lee's army of the entire war. Union forces captured forty-five hundred men, thirteen flags, and six guns, with fewer than one thousand casualties (Pickett had six hundred men killed or wounded). Porter rode back to Grant with the news, and as he shouted the story, "there was a bewildering state of excitement, and officers fell to grasping hands, shouting, and hugging each other like schoolboys." They all knew the victory was a turning point, the "beginning of the end." In his excitement the normally restrained Porter clapped Grant on the back. Grant kept his cool, of course, asking questions about the battle before sending out orders for a "general assault" the next day.[13]

But not every Union soldier shared the jubilation. A little after 7:00 P.M., one of Sheridan's staffers found Warren and handed him an order stating, "Major General Warren, Commanding 5th Army Corps, is relieved from duty." Shocked, Warren rode to Sheridan to see if there had been a mistake or if Sheridan would reconsider. According to Joshua Chamberlain, Sheridan's full-throated reply was, "Reconsider, hell! I never reconsider my decisions! Obey the order!" Still reeling, Warren rode in the dark to Grant's headquarters to seek salvation. He found, much to his horror, that Grant had initiated the plan. According to Warren, "[Grant said that] he thought well of my judgment but that I was too much inclined to use it in questioning orders before executing them; that I did not co-operate well with others, doubted too much the sense of my supervisors, and interfered with my subordinates." Warren argued against these points and made a case for doing nothing of the sort under Sheridan, but Grant was unmoved. Crestfallen, Warren rode to see Meade, who had learned of the dismissal in an official dispatch from Grant. Fighting the debilitating effects of a "malarial catarrh," Meade listened to his abrasive protégé, then told him he agreed with Grant's criticisms and had just been waiting for the right person to emerge as his replacement. He told Warren, "[You are] too much inclined to cavil at orders that I should have gone ahead to obey and let the consequences be where the orders originated" (as Meade himself had done). Showing he was still the same commander who refused to attack at Mine Run, Warren responded defiantly, "[It might] satisfy [your] conscience and sense of duty to see men slaughtered by order that there was a hope of modifying even at the risk of a sacrifice of position, [but] my sense of duty compelled me to act as I ever had done in these matters." With these unyielding words hanging in the air, Warren left Meade. In the end, Grant had initiated a dismissal, and Sheridan had carried it out—a decision Meade could never force himself to make. Although Grant soon assigned Warren to command the troops at Petersburg, his tenure as corps commander had ended. He would spend the rest of his life trying to clear his name and restore his reputation.[14]

The news of Warren's dismissal spread quickly through the ranks. The men of the Fifth Corps were most upset, even including one of his sharpest critics, Col. Charles Wainwright. He wrote in his diary, "To me his removal at this time, and after the victory had been won, appears wrong and very cruel." His initial theory was that "Warren might have got into one of his ugly fits and said what he ought not to." But he had seen no signs of that side of Warren in the two conversations he saw Sheridan and Warren have that day (before and after the battle). Meade did not immediately write of the matter to his wife, as he was too busy at the time. But Lyman, no strong supporter of Warren's, recorded some of his thoughts just after he saw Warren at midnight on April 1. He wrote, "He seemed unable to 'spread himself' over more than one division, and he had the incorrigible error of trying to do each thing *himself*, putting no faith in his subordinates. . . . His great strength was as a field engineer and perhaps Chief of Staff." Still, even though he was "wont to make severe criticisms on others . . . this humiliation he did not deserve." In the end, Sheridan was the hatchet man for Grant. Some assumed this, and others came to the realization later. As Grant later wrote of Warren in his *Memoirs:* "I was very much afraid that at the last moment he would fail Sheridan. . . . I had before discovered a defect which was beyond his control that was very prejudicial to his usefulness in emergencies like the one just before us. He could see every danger at a glance before he encountered it. He would not only make preparations to meet the danger which might occur, but he would inform his commanding officer what others should do while he was executing his move." Grant had tolerated this "defect" for a year, but he would not tolerate it anymore. As Stephen Sears sees it, "The Five Forks incident, abrupt as it appeared, was deeply rooted in past events on old battlefields."[15]

The dismissal of a veteran corps commander after a very successful battle did not paralyze the Army of the Potomac because events began rushing together the evening of April 1. When Grant heard the news of the victory at Five Forks, he ordered a general assault for the next morning. Initially, there was some confusion between Grant and Meade as to whether the assault would begin immediately or at 4:00 A.M., but after a series of telegraphic messages, the generals agreed that an artillery bombardment would precede an all-out attack at 4:00 A.M. Grant seemed especially pleased by the newfound confidence and enthusiasm in the normally cautious and careful Horatio Wright. He wrote of his eagerness to fight in his 11:00 P.M. dispatch to Meade, "The corps will go in solid, and I am sure will make the fur fly. . . . If the corps does half as well as I expect we will have broken through the rebel lines fifteen minutes from the word 'go.'"[16]

Meade and Grant slept little, if at all, the night of April 1–2. They exchanged messages about the disposition of troops between midnight and 4:30 A.M., when the Ninth Corps moved out first against the Confederate lines. The Ninth Corps made headway against Confederate defenses but could not break through the inner works. There would be attacks and counterattacks in their sector throughout the early morning, but by late afternoon, Confederate defenses still held.[17]

The glory of the day would fall on the battle-scarred veterans of the peripatetic Sixth Corps. Sleeping on wet ground on a cool misty night, fourteen thousand men prepared to assault a hitherto impregnable sector only one mile in length. Guarding that section of the line were only twenty-eight hundred Confederates under A. P. Hill. Wright delayed the attack until the men could at least see to their immediate front. At 4:40 A.M. the first wave set out across the field and quickly overran the first line of defenses. By 5:15 A.M. Wright wrote to Meade, "The corps has carried the woods in front and to the left of the Jones house." In the words of the historian Earl Hess, "Wright's corps completely severed the Boydton Plank Road defenses in the most decisive breakthrough of a heavily fortified line in the war." But the Sixth Corps was not finished. By 7:00 A.M. the corps had advanced to Hatcher's Run. They then turned to the north and marched up the Boydton Plank Road toward Petersburg. They drew so close to Lee at his headquarters at the Edgehill house on Cox Road that they saw him ride away. The men finally stopped around the house and began erecting breastworks. The Sixth Corps had captured almost four thousand Confederates, and another one thousand were either killed or wounded in the fighting at the breakthrough and other sectors.[18]

Other hard fighting took place that day. In the early afternoon, the Twenty-Fourth Corps captured Fort Gregg and Fort Whitworth. Meanwhile, the First Division of the Second Corps launched three attacks on Sutherland Station, and the Confederates finally abandoned the site. The South Side Railroad had finally been reached, severing Lee's last supply route into Petersburg.[19]

Of course General Lee had predicted much of this outcome by mid-morning. With the breakthrough separating his troops near Five Forks from the men still guarding Petersburg, he had no choice but to abandon Petersburg and Richmond and move his army west. Secretary of War John C. Breckenridge read Lee's message at the War Department at 10:40 A.M., and immediately sent word to President Davis, who was attending church at St. Paul's. Davis read the note and left the church. Like Lee, he now had hours, not days, or months, to evacuate. Lee hoped his army could hang on to its inner defenses until dark, when the march out would begin.[20]

Meade and Grant tried to keep up with the whirl of progress that day, meeting briefly just before 9:00 A.M. in an open field by Dabney Mill to discuss the situation. Then Meade rode off (to the sounds of cheers from the men of Mott's First Division of the Second Corps) to find Humphreys at the Rainie house. From there Meade rode "straight up the Boydton Plank Road"—a strange sensation for all those who had sought to possess the road for nine months—then on to Hatcher Run Bridge and the "wide space of open land" that surrounded Petersburg. They ran into the rear of the column of men marching east, and "the men broke into loud cheers, which men continued all along." They finally stopped at noon at the Harman house, where they found Grant again. They stayed for a few hours, before camping at Well's house on the Boydton Plank Road.[21]

Grant was in motion much of the day, too, but of course he had to keep his superiors in the loop. At 10:45 A.M. he telegraphed Lincoln the news of the morning's successes, and Lincoln sent the news to Stanton later in the day. At 4:40 P.M. Grant reported to Lincoln, "[In a] few hours we will be entrenched from the Appomattox, below Petersburg, to the river above." He expected the number of prisoners to be "no less than 12,000 men" and the captured arms to probably be "50 pieces of artillery." Lincoln gratefully replied, "Allow me to tender to you and all with you the nation's grateful thanks for this additional and magnificent success." He also accepted Grant's suggestion to meet the next day.[22]

The only note of regret that day came from Meade. As early as 10:30 A.M., he notified Grant that he had sent an officer to Sheridan encouraging him to send his cavalry along the Cox and River Roads to cut off escape routes for the Confederates at Sutherland Station. He had not heard back from Sheridan by 7:15 P.M. Sheridan *had* updated Grant, however, by early evening. Because he thought the Confederates were headed toward Burkeville Junction, he did not feel he should ride north of the Appomattox River. Grant then told Meade that Sheridan was "making dispositions to cut them off if he can." Meade replied, "It is a pity Sheridan did not move as I suggested on the Cox and River road, for had he done so these fellows would have been cut off." Grant followed up with an update: he had sent Sheridan orders to "cross the river, which he will do as soon as the enemy on this side is captured or driven off. He is marching on the Cox and River roads." Meade may have won a Pyrrhic victory, subtly showing that the favored Sheridan was not always alert to possibilities. But the reality was that many men had escaped across the river, and Lee's bedraggled army would live to fight another day.[23]

That day, of course, could occur only if the army managed to evacuate Petersburg and Richmond successfully. It did just that on the night of April 2–3, leaving burning warehouses behind as the troops marched west out of the cities. President Davis and his cabinet managed to slide out of Richmond by 11:00 P.M. on April 2, 1865, headed to Danville with the gold from the treasury and as much government paperwork as its single train could carry.[24]

Meade and Grant did not get much sleep that night, either. As early as 4:05 A.M. on April 3 Meade telegraphed Grant that Parke and Wright were sending skirmishers forward to "ascertain the condition of the enemy." About a half hour later, Meade reported that the Second Division of the Ninth Corps had occupied the enemy's old line and found no one in its front. By 5:15 A.M. Meade could send to Grant the news he had wanted to hear for at least nine months, if not four years: "The Second Brigade, 1st Division, Ninth Corps, Colonel Ely, is in possession of Petersburg." Wright soon confirmed the same information: Petersburg had been evacuated. Grant finally responded with a logical question, "Do you hear anything of the condition of the railroad and bridges in Petersburg?" Meade answered that he had not, then he set off for Petersburg.[25]

Meade and his staff rode into town on the Boydton Plank Road, passing by redoubts and breastworks. They entered the shelled city, rode out to see the Crater from the other side, then returned to the downtown, where Meade had a meeting with Grant at Thomas Wallace's house. That morning Meade learned that one of his old foes, A. P. Hill, had been shot and killed by a soldier from the Sixth Corps. Meade did not stay long enough to visit with President Lincoln, who arrived later in the morning with his two sons—Robert and Tad—and Adm. David Porter. Meade rode on to Sutherland's Station, where he set up camp for the night. Grant's camp was nearby, and someone from his camp informed Meade that Major General Weitzel had entered Richmond at 8:15 A.M. Richmond was finally in Union hands.[26]

No one rested for long that day, as both armies were in a race to get to Burkeville Junction. Lee's army had the head start, but most units had over fifty miles to march to get there. Grant wanted to intercept Lee's army before it turned south for North Carolina at Burkeville Junction, and his men had only thirty-six miles to march. In the lead of the Union force was Sheridan's cavalry and the hard-marching Fifth Corps (now under Charles Griffin). Sheridan still had the Second Corps under his temporary command, and apparently Meade wanted some of his army back. He asked Grant to return the Second Corps to him, imploring Grant to send an order to Sheridan to that effect, to prevent "confusion" that might "arise from a conflict of authority." Grant did so, although he instructed Humphreys to "follow the route designated for you by General Sheridan."[27]

Sheridan had another day of glory, with his cavalry pushing back a small cavalry force at Namozine Church and snatching twelve hundred prisoners (mainly from Hill's army), including Brig. Gen. Rufus Barringer. That evening Sheridan's cavalry went into bivouac just south of Deep Creek to Namozine Church. The Fifth Corps made camp near Deep Creek as well, with the Second Corps near Winticomack Creek and the Sixth Corps around Mount Pleasant Church. The Army of the James marched on the Cox Road three miles west of Sutherland Station, where it set up for the night. The last to arrive was the Ninth Corps (it had been held behind in Petersburg); two divisions camped near Sutherland Station, while one division stayed in Petersburg. Combining the forces of the cavalry and two armies, Grant had nearly seventy-six thousand men to pursue Lee's fifty-one thousand men.[28]

After the momentous day, Meade still found the time to write a short letter to his wife. He described some of the fighting, summarizing the results as "three glorious days." He added, "We are now moving after Lee, and if we are successful in striking him another blow before he can rally his troops, I think the Confederacy will be at an end." With that message off, he settled in for another short night, as the Sixth Corps had been ordered to move out at 5:00 A.M. the next morning.[29]

The troops got up and out at their designated times on the morning of April 4, but many found the march difficult because of the muddy roads. Meade ordered the Sixth Corps to improve the roads, where possible, especially to keep the "trains of the Fifth Corps" moving. The Second Corps (which followed the Sixth Corps) had similar duty. The Army of the James continued marching along the South Side Railroad. Sheridan's cavalry made it to Jetersville and Burkeville Junction by the afternoon. A dispatch from Sheridan spurred Grant and Meade to demand more marching from their troops; he wrote, "If we press on we will no doubt get the whole army." He reiterated this message when he wrote directly to Meade from Jetersville at 7:00 P.M., "The rebel army is in my front, three miles distant, with all its trains. If the Sixth Corps can hurry up we will have sufficient strength." Meade responded quickly and in good collaborative spirit to Sheridan's request. He ordered the Second and Sixth Corps to march at 3:00 A.M. the next day. He added for dramatic effect, "The men of this army will show that they are as willing to die of fatigue and starvation as they have ever shown themselves ready to fall by the bullets of the enemy." He sent a copy of the order to Sheridan and assured him, "Your wishes or suggestions as to any movement other than the simple one of overtaking you will be promptly acceded to by me, regardless of any other consideration than the vital one of destroying the Army of Northern Virginia."[30]

Of course it was not simply the desire to be collegial that had inspired Meade. Lyman wrote in his diary, "[Meade] suspected Sheridan of maneuvering to get to himself all the credit of success, but preparing to shift the blame, in case of failure." Meade also may have been affected by his persistent "catarrh"; he ran a high fever that night, followed by a chill so intense that his staff built a fire for him. Lyman thought that the illness "excited his nervous system greatly though it did not affect the clearness of his mind." That explained his florid language at the end of his 9:30 P.M. order to his army. Lyman referred to the "starvation" order as a result of Meade's "high fever, which made his language excited." Regardless, all plans were set to resume marching in the middle of the night.[31]

What the Union generals still did not know by the evening of April 4 was the exact location of Lee's army (or its primary destination). For that matter, even Lee might have wondered where his army was that night. Amelia Court House was the designated rendezvous, but few of his soldiers were there. Ewell's corps had not yet crossed the Appomattox River (two bridges were out), Gordon's Second Corps was camped at Scott's Shop, Mahone's division guarded Goode's Bridge, and Anderson's corps faced Union cavalry at Beaver Pond Creek. Exacerbating problems was a lack of rations; someone had slipped up, and the hoped-for rations were not there. Lee had implored the citizens of Amelia County to bring them food, but they had not. When Lee learned that the Union Army was south of the Appomattox River, he surmised that it would try to cut his route of escape. So he let his men sleep for a few hours, before some began another night march at 3:00 A.M. the next day.[32]

April 5 found most of the troops on the march and the generals evaluating a shifting situation. After experiencing a delay of over six hours caused by some of Sheridan's cavalry, the Second Corps marched on to Jetersville, where it joined the entrenched Fifth Corps. The Sixth Corps had been delayed by the Second Corps, so it did not arrive until after 6:00 P.M. The Ninth Corps initially followed the Sixth Corps, but it was diverted to guard and improve the South Side Railroad. The Twenty-Fourth Corps of the Army of the James marched twenty-eight miles on April 5 to reach Burkeville Junction after dark (after marching twenty-four miles on April 4). When the three Union corps under Meade finally arrived at Jetersville, he ordered them to prepare for an assault at 6:00 A.M. the next morning.[33]

For the Confederates, while some soldiers staggered into Amelia Court House, others (under Longstreet) headed toward Jetersville to check the strength of the enemy. They tangled with Union cavalry near the village, and as reports of Union infantry massing at Jetersville drifted in, Lee decided not to attack but to turn west and head for Farmville. He ordered another dreaded night march.[34]

With the Army of Northern Virginia within his grasp, Sheridan must have felt magnanimous because he and Meade met several times on April 5 and had genial discussions about the evolving situation. Meade was truly ailing that day, with "cough, fever, and sickness at the stomach." Still, he managed to travel in his spring wagon to Jetersville (where he met Sheridan), then out to check on troops on the Jetersville Road, then back to a temporary camp near the Childres house (where Sheridan was camped). The Fifth Corps was returned to Meade's command that day, restoring all his corps to the Army of the Potomac. Sheridan urged Grant to join him at Jetersville, writing, "I wish you were here yourself. I feel confident of capturing the Army of Northern Virginia if we exert ourselves." Catching his spirit, Grant rode twenty miles that night to get to Sheridan and Meade. Around midnight the three generals met at Sheridan's headquarters to finalize the next day's movements. With his entire army restored to him and the steady accumulation of battle field victories, Meade could feel good about his accomplishments and his status, as he was included in the conference that might be planning the end of the war in Virginia. The generals decided that the Army of the Potomac would march up the Danville Road toward Amelia Court House, while Sheridan's cavalry would ride west toward Deatonville, to flank Lee's army or perhaps get in its way if he marched due west. Ord was ordered to march to the High Bridge over the Appomattox River near Farmville.[35]

The generals got their troops out by daylight on April 6, and after some long marches, the first battle of the day occurred at the long (twenty-four hundred feet) bridge known simply as the High Bridge. Ord had sent a small force (eight hundred men) to reconnoiter the area around the bridge and if possible, destroy it. They were attacked by Confederate cavalry around noon, and after some hard fighting, the cavalry captured the entire force (and six flags). For the time being, Confederates had saved the bridge.[36]

Unfortunately for the Confederates, that small yet vital victory proved to be the apogee of their day. Union forces launched three separate attacks on different units of the retreating army, clustered around Little Sailor's Creek. The heaviest fighting occurred between Wright's Sixth Corps and Ewell's corps. Despite an initial stiff defense and even a counterattack by Confederate forces, the Sixth Corps re-formed and charged one more time, pushing in on both flanks as well. They captured thirty-four hundred men and six Confederate generals, including Ewell himself. In the second battle of the day, three divisions of cavalry under Maj. Gen. Wesley Merritt overwhelmed Anderson's corps, capturing twenty-six hundred men and two generals. Seeing this collapse from a distant high point, Lee despondently asked, "My God! Has the army been dissolved?" In the third battle of the day—between Humphreys's Second Corps and Gordon's Second Corps—the Union troops pushed the Confederates back from Lockett's farm, snaring seventeen hundred men and three hundred wagons. In just one day, General Lee had lost one fifth of his army.[37]

Meade and Grant followed developments all day from the rear. Meade had ordered the Second and Sixth Corps to change directions in the mid-morning, then rode out to observe the Fifth Corps marching on the road. Then he rode back to Jetersville to confer with Grant, who spent the bulk of the day in that tiny village. Several times that afternoon, Meade sent messages to his corps commanders to move rapidly and strike the enemy. For example, at 2:05 P.M. he told Humphreys to "push on without fear of your flanks." His generals did as instructed and had the great victory at Little Sailor's Creek.[38]

As usual, clouds appeared amidst the sunshine of victory for Meade and the Army of the Potomac. Around 8:30 P.M. one of Sheridan's staffers brought a message to Meade that Sheridan had also just sent to Grant: "I attacked them with two divisions of the Sixth Army Corps and routed them handsomely, making a connection with the cavalry." When Meade heard that the author of the message was Sheridan, not Wright, he exploded, "And so Wright *was not there!*" Lyman called Sheridan's note "pilfered glory" and complained that Wright had been in "immediate communication" with Meade, not Sheridan. Though he soon received reports from Wright and Humphreys that he sent along to Grant, Meade and his staff knew that once again, "the wide awake Sheridan had his in first and on its way to the press!"[39]

Lyman put a positive spin on the day's events, however, when he wrote in his diary, "All this did not prevent great rejoicings on our part over the news so glorious for our cause." They would not have been as pleased if they knew that the secretary of war had begun his report to Maj. Gen. John Dix and governors the next day with the sentence, "General Sheridan attacked and routed Lee's army yesterday . . . and expects to force Lee to surrender all that is left of his army." The more detailed reports of Wright and Humphreys did not reach Stanton until later that morning, and they were finally sent to Major General Dix in New York City. By that point, however, the Sheridan story had already been planted in the public's version of the battle.[40]

While Meade made camp just west of Deatonville and Grant stayed in Burkeville, Lee ordered his exhausted survivors to undertake another night march. He sent the men on muddy roads toward Farmville, where eighty thousand rations were stored. The van of Longstreet's column reached Farmville at sunrise on April 7, and rations were quickly distributed to the famished soldiers. Troops from other corps stumbled into Farmville that morning, but when the Confederate rearguard failed to torch the High Bridge, Union troops scurried across the partially damaged structure. With little time to cook the rations, Confederate troops found themselves on the march again, this time toward Cumberland Church. The first troops to arrive there dug a line of trenches to defend the area and repulsed an attack from a Second Corps brigade that afternoon. Despite this victory, Confederates knew they had to keep marching westward.[41]

Meade had spent the day in his convalescent wagon, after taking another turn for the worse. He pushed himself despite his condition, as he passed through Sailor's Creek on the way to the High Bridge. He stayed there for the rest of the day, sending Lyman out to find Wright and urge him to help Humphreys. At one point he even ordered the Twenty-Fourth Corps to attack the Confederates, but they could not because of the same difficulty of crossing the river. After learning of the Second Corps' attack at Cumberland Church, Meade and his staff rode back four miles to Rice's Station, where they spent the night. Late that night, he dashed off a short letter to his wife, summarizing the campaign so far as "brilliantly successful, beyond the most reasonable expectations." Although he was suffering from the effects of a "severe bilious catarrh," he managed to retain active command, owing to his "powerful constitution, and the good care of [his] attending physician, together with the excitement of the scenes" he had experienced. He heard that some of the captured Confederate generals "virtually admit the contest over, and say they believe Lee is prepared to surrender, or at least to disband his army."[42]

Over at the Randolph House in Farmville, Grant heard the same story and acted on it by sending a letter to Lee. Noting the "hopelessness of further resistance on the part of the Army of Northern Virginia," he asked Lee to end the "further effusion of blood" by surrendering "that portion of the C.S. Army known as the Army of Northern Virginia." According to the memoir of James Longstreet, Lee read the letter without saying a word, then handed it to Longstreet to read. Longstreet read it and tersely responded, "Not yet." He handed it back to Lee, who then replied to Grant that he did not believe in the proposition "of the hopelessness of further resistance" but did want to "avoid useless effusion of blood." He then asked Grant for the terms of his army's surrender. With that message sent, Lee ordered Longstreet to begin the fourth night march of the long flight from Richmond.[43]

As Union troops and their commanders caught a few hours of sleep the night of April 7, exhausted Confederate counterparts trudged westward on muddy roads through the night toward Appomattox Station. Union troops set into motion just after daylight on April 8, led by Humphreys's Second Corps. At 7:45 A.M. Humphreys updated Meade on the roads he traveled and noted that "the whole of Lee's army" had been "encamped" there. Meade ordered the Sixth Corps to follow the Second Corps. Meanwhile, Sheridan's cavalry used a shorter, southern route to approach Appomattox Station, riding to Prospect Station before splitting into two columns, one under Crook riding next to the railroad leading to Pamplin's Depot, the other led by Maj. Gen. George A. Custer and Brig. Gen. Thomas

Devin toward Walker's Presbyterian Church. When Sheridan learned of supply trains near Appomattox Station, he rode to Walker's Church with Merritt and sent word to Crook to rendezvous at Appomattox Station. Behind him marched the foot-sore soldiers of the Army of the James and the Fifth Corps, now attached temporarily again to Sheridan.[44]

On this day largely devoted to marching there were three moments of high drama. Grant received Lee's response to his first query in the morning and instantly replied, "There is but one condition I would insist upon, viz, that the men and officers surrendered shall be disqualified for taking up arms against the Government of the United States until properly exchanged." He added, "I will meet you, or will designate officers to meet any officers you may name for such a purpose of arranging definitely the terms upon which the surrender of the Army of the Northern Virginia will be received." He gave the message to Brig. Gen. Seth Williams (now the inspector general of the army), an old friend of Lee's, to deliver.[45]

The second moment of drama came when some of Custer's cavalrymen came upon the ration and supply trains parked at Appomattox Station. They easily captured the unguarded trains and seized 300,000 rations and boxes of clothing, medicine, and ordnance. The cavalrymen pressed on to the new camp at Appomattox Court House set up by Col. R. Lindsay Walker's artillery and Gordon's corps. After some initial skirmishes, Custer waited until his full division was up, and they attacked under moonlight around 9:00 P.M. Confederate lines held, but Custer's men captured cannons, supply wagons, and nearly one thousand soldiers. With two infantry corps headed toward the same depot, Sheridan had effectively blocked Lee's weary army from heading south or west. In an optimistic note to Grant, Sheridan wrote that night, "If General Gibbon and the Fifth Corps can get up tonight we will perhaps finish the job in the morning."[46]

Meade and Grant had been in the rear of the advancing troops during the day. In the morning, Meade and his staff rode out to High Bridge, crossed over, and caught up with Humphreys. While there, they learned of Grant's two notes sent to Lee. In the afternoon, they rode on to "Clifton," the house of Joseph Crute, at Sheppards on the Richmond-Lynchburg stage road. Grant and his staff joined them just before they got to Clifton, and Grant jubilantly called out to Meade, "How are you, old fellow?" That may have been the one and only time Grant referred to Meade so colloquially. The commanders established their headquarters at Clifton (Grant in the house, Meade outside) and waited for messages from their generals and Lee.[47]

The stay of the generals at Clifton set the stage for the third dramatic moment of the day. Lee's reply to Grant's second letter did not reach Grant until midnight. The text of the letter burst like a thunderclap amidst Grant's staff, according to the journalist Sylvanus Cadwallader. Lee wrote that he had not proposed to surrender the Army of Northern Virginia because he did not "think the emergency has arisen to call for the surrender of this army." Still, he sought the "restoration of peace" and offered to meet with Grant to discuss such ideas the following morning at 10:00 A.M. Rawlins accused Lee of trying to avoid surrender by discussing a subject Grant did not have the authority to negotiate, the entire arrangement for peace. It was, in Rawlins's words, "a positive insult." As usually happened with such outbursts, it was Grant's "soft, moderate, persuasive and apologetic voice" that calmed the situation. He told Rawlins that Lee was in a "trying position" and had to balance the wishes of his government and his generals. "But it all means precisely the same thing. If I meet Lee, he will surrender before I leave." Grant then said he needed to rest; he hoped some sleep would stop the pain from his migraine headache.[48]

While Meade and Grant attempted to grab a few hours of sleep, the thin divisions of Gordon's Second Corps woke at 2:00 A.M. to march to Appomattox Court House. They arrived around 4:00 A.M. on April 9 and soon assembled in a line of battle. At first daylight they advanced in the last attack of the Army of Northern Virginia in the Civil War. They pushed back the small cavalry forces under Brig. Gen. Charles H. Smith and Brig. Gen. Ranald S. Mackenzie. Sheridan rushed his cavalry divisions to Appomattox, and by 7:30 A.M. the first units of infantry under Ord ran up to the Union lines. As more Union cavalry and infantry arrived, Gordon saw no choice but to fall back. As his men prepared a line of defense near the town, a courier from Lee found Gordon and carried with him a request for a truce. Gordon sent him out toward Union lines.[49]

What happened faster than anticipated that morning was that Lee found his options quickly eliminated. Not only were Union cavalry and infantry now in his front, but skirmishers from Humphreys's Second Corps were firing at Longstreet's rearguard at New Hope Church. The only direction Lee's army could go was to the northwest, but it lacked major roads and was not where he wanted to go. Reluctantly, Lee and three of his aides rode out toward New Hope Church, hoping to meet Grant there.[50]

That hoped-for meeting on the picket line never happened. After a pain-filled night, Grant had sipped a cup of coffee at Meade's tent, then composed his reply to Lee's letter. Rejecting Lee's terms, he wrote, "I have no authority to treat on the subject of peace," and therefore "the proposed meeting for 10:00 A.M. today could lead to no good." He reiterated the principal requirement of the government: the Confederacy must lay down its arms. But leaving open the possibility of a meeting, he continued, "[I] sincerely hop[e] that our difficulties may be settled without the loss of another life." He then rejected his aide's offer of an ambulance and set off on a twenty-mile ride through woods and across fields to get close to Appomattox.[51]

As Grant rode west to meet Lee, Lee rode east to meet him. Stopped by pickets from the Second Corps, he waited for Grant. What he got instead was Grant's letter from the morning, to which he immediately responded with a complete change of terms. He wrote, "I now request an interview in accordance with the offer contained in your letter of yesterday for that purpose." That letter soon reached

Meade, who sent it on to Grant at 10:00 A.M. Lee also asked for "suspension of hostilities," which Meade hesitated to give, as he responded, "[without] the distinct understanding that you are prepared to accept the terms indicated in the letter of Lieutenant General Grant sent to you yesterday." However, by noon he heard from Sheridan's chief of staff that Ord and Lee had temporarily stopped fighting, so he agreed to "a suspension of hostilities till 2:00 P.M. this day" that he would be "glad to prolong" if Lee agreed to Grant's terms.[52]

It was given to Lt. Charles W. Pease to initiate one of the most joyous moments of the war for the Union army. Riding his horse hard for miles, he came across Grant and his staff having a small break over a campfire. He handed Lee's note to Rawlins, who read it first, said nothing, then handed it to Grant, who also read it without saying a word. Then Grant handed the letter back to Rawlins and asked him to read it aloud. After he was finished, the staff cheered, then cried—the war was almost over. Grant hastily wrote a reply to Lee, explaining that he was four miles west of Walker's Church and would "push forward to the front for the purpose of meeting [him]." He asked Lee to send him a note telling him where he wanted to meet, then got back on his horse Cincinnati and rode toward Appomattox Court House. As the men galloped along, Porter asked Grant about his headache. He replied, "The pain in my head seemed to leave me the moment I got Lee's letter."[53]

While Grant's aide Orville Babcock rode to Appomattox to find Lee and a place for the generals to meet, Meade and his staff spent an anxious afternoon four miles from Appomattox waiting for news. Meade had just authorized Humphreys's skirmishers to end the truce and move forward, when a top aide of Sheridan's and one of Lee's aides showed up with a note from Grant to "suspend hostilities." The skirmishers were halted, and the waiting resumed.[54]

Circumstantially, yet also symbolically, it would be "Grant men" who attended the historic signing of surrender at Appomattox. Most of the generals—Meade, Wright, Humphreys, and numerous division commanders—of the battle-scarred Army of the Potomac would be strung out on roads several miles from town, while the new men—Grant, Sheridan, Ord, and others—would be at the McLean house. There Lee signed the document that ended four years of fighting in the East. He agreed to the surrender of his men and arms, and the men were to be sent home to await parole. Officers would retain their sidearms and horses, and a separate agreement allowed artillerymen to keep their horses too. After signing the document, Lee took his leave, pausing to salute Grant before he left (Grant returned the salute). He then rode off to convey the shocking news to his troops.[55]

If Meade or his fellow soldiers felt any jealousy or bitterness over their exclusion from the surrender ceremony, few expressed it that afternoon. At 5:00 P.M. the ubiquitous Lt. Charles Pease appeared at Meade's headquarters with an eagerly awaited message: Lee had surrendered. The staff gave three cheers for victory, then three more just for Meade. The general then mounted his horse and rode through the ranks of the Second and Sixth Corps. Lyman captured the moment of jubilation: "This patient, silent old army now for once burst forth. In a frenzy of excitement, the troops rushed to the sides of the road and shouted till my very ears rung with the noise. . . . The bands and the cheering lasted late that night." The war would soon be over, and even the taciturn Meade could briefly allow himself to enjoy the moment. A reporter for the *New York Herald* wrote, "General Meade was equally excited. He seemed for the time to throw off his reserve and dignity and enter fully into the spirit of the occasion."[56]

On the next day, the generals finalized the procedures for the surrender and visited each other. Meade wanted to see Lee and Grant but only managed to find Lee. Meade went to Lee's headquarters ("consisting only of a ply, with a camp fire before it") but discovered he was gone. As they rode off, Lee suddenly appeared, and though he initially "gazed vacantly" at Meade, he quickly remembered him when Meade saluted. His first comment was a question to Meade, "What are you doing with all that gray in your beard?" Meade replied, "That *you* have a good deal to do with!" The two men talked for some time, with Lee appearing "deeply dejected" as he discussed the shortage of soldiers he had suffered in the spring, only "40,000 muskets" to hold the Richmond-Petersburg line. Lyman got to chat briefly with Lee; they had mutual acquaintances. Then the Union party left to seek Grant at Appomattox Court House.

Grant had left by the time they arrived, but the party got to meet James Longstreet and John Gordon. Lyman even saw his old Harvard classmate, "Roonie" Lee. The men also saw Brig. Gen. Henry Wise (Meade's brother-in-law), whom Lyman described as a "forlorn spectacle . . . with spectacles and a short, white beard; a stooping, sickly figure, with his legs tied round with some gray blankets." Meade was kinder in his description of Wise's condition in a letter to his wife, telling her that Wise "looked old and feeble," so he procured an ambulance and provisions for him. Wise had not lost his faculties or manners, however; he "affectionately" asked about the welfare of Mrs. Meade and her family.[57]

In the same letter to his wife, Meade commented on the "cloud" in the silver lining of victory: the unbalanced newspaper coverage of Lee's retreat. He wrote, "I have seen but few newspapers since this movement commenced, and I don't want to see anymore, for they are full of falsehood and of undue and exaggerated praise of certain individuals who take pains to be on the right side of reporters." He told her not to be angry about the biased coverage because it could not be "remedied." Nor did he have any faith in the "truth" eventually emerging; he had "a great contempt for History."[58]

Of course he could not take his own advice and "resign" himself to the situation. Two days later, he responded to Margaret's continuing criticisms of his minimal coverage in the newspapers; he believed that "if the press [was] determined to ignore" his work, all they could do was "submit and be resigned." He did not blame Grant for the situation, writing, "It is partly ignorance and partly selfishness which prevents his being aware of his acts." Not so with Sheridan: "His determination to absorb the credit of everything done is so manifest to have attracted the attention of the whole army." Moreover, Sheridan's treatment of Meade had been "beneath contempt."[59]

As Meade stewed over the latest indignity, he still had an army to manage. The Fifth and Twenty-Fourth Corps were assigned to handle the formal duties of surrender, while Grant headed off to Washington and Meade to Burkeville, where his army would be reassembled. Meade left Appomattox on April 11, spending the night in the Prince Edward Hotel in Farmville (where Fitzhugh Lee and his staff unexpectedly showed up and surrendered). The next morning, Meade rode on to Burkeville, where he set up temporary headquarters while he awaited new orders for his army.[60]

The next week was a time of limbo for Meade and the Army of the Potomac, punctuated by some shocking and depressing news. First it was personal: Col. William Sergeant of the 210th Pennsylvania Infantry, one of Margaret Meade's brothers, had died on April 11 from a gunshot wound received while fighting on March 31. Meade wrote to his wife, "My God, what misery this dreadful war has produced, and how it comes home to the doors of almost every one!" This sad news was soon followed by a national tragedy: the assassination of Abraham Lincoln. Meade got the news by telegram, and his first words to his staff were, "Bless me! This is terrible news." When notified of Lincoln's death on April 15, Meade composed an eloquent order for his army: "By this Army this announcement will be received with profound sorrow, and deep horror and indignation. . . . An honest man, a noble patriot, and sagacious statesman has fallen! No greater loss, at this particular moment, could have befallen our country."[61]

As the sorrow of the death of Lincoln sank into the hearts of the men of the Army of the Potomac, who had experienced so much loss and hardship, Meade had to say farewell to his favorite aide and closest friend, Theodore Lyman. On April 19 Lyman resigned, and in a glowing letter of tribute, Meade wrote, "[You bear] testimony to the zeal, energy and gallantry you have displayed in the discharge of your duties. Be assured I shall ever preserve the liveliest reminiscences of our intercourse." To his wife Meade wrote, "Lyman is such a good fellow, and has been so intimately connected personally with me, that I feel his separation as the loss of an old and valued friend."[62]

Meade surely missed the patient counsel of his younger friend when the next blow fell on him on April 22. On that day, he learned that the new president, Andrew Johnson (acting under Grant's advice), had formed the new Military Division of the James, which would encompass the Department of Virginia (Army of the James), the parts of the North Carolina not under Sherman's command, and the Army of the Potomac. This new division would be headed by Henry Halleck.

According to what Meade heard, Grant did not want Halleck underfoot in Washington, so he offered him command of the Army of the James (Ord to go to South Carolina). This was insufficient for Halleck, so Grant sweetened the deal by creating a new military division that oversaw Ord's and Meade's armies. A crushed and furious Meade called this action "the most cruel and humiliating indignity that has been put upon me."[63]

The decision preyed on Meade for the next week, and nothing seemed to raise his spirits. He was pleased that Lyman visited his family in Philadelphia, calling him "an honest man and a true friend." Moreover, he had a quality of constitution that Meade lacked and needed around him. He wrote to his wife, "He has a healthy mental organization, which induces him to look on all matters in the most favorable light." Without that combination of intelligent skepticism and perdurable optimism around him each day, Meade complained in every letter he sent that week about his present condition. He believed that if he had been in Washington when the discussion occurred he might have "frustrated" the plan, but by being stuck in Virginia, he could only obey the order. For a time he even entertained the possibility of asking to be relieved, but he rejected it because it would lead to a lesser position in which he would be "subjected to infinitely greater indignity and humiliation." Even the public outcry over Sherman's generous terms to General Johnston (quickly rescinded by the War Department) led him to see Sherman cast in the same unfavorable light often shined on him, leading him to write, "He is entitled to the considerations due to his past services, which should have shielded him from having his motives and loyalty impugned." He wondered whether Grant would support Sherman or "smother him as he did me."[64]

His spirits were not lifted until he received orders to march his army to Alexandria via Richmond on April 30. He thought this would be a "preliminary measure" to the disbanding of the Army of the Potomac, which also meant the elimination of the Military Division of the James. He went to Richmond to arrange for the historic march north and, while there, visited Robert E. Lee. He urged Lee to take the Oath of Allegiance, especially for "the great influence his example would have over others." Lee demurred, saying he wanted to see "what the policy of the Government was going to be towards the people of the South." Meade countered with the argument that the Northerners had to be convinced that the Rebels were now loyal before they could determine a postwar policy. Lee listened but was not persuaded. Lee also was troubled by the "status of the negro" but, in Meade's view, "did not devise any very practicable suggestions." Meade left the visit feeling "sad to think of his position, his necessities, and the difficulties which surround him."[65]

Meade also tried to fix another matter: the fate of Gouverneur Warren. On April 18 he told Grant that the Fifth Corps needed a permanent commander, and he suggested Warren be restored, assuring Grant, "Should you be disposed to reassign General Warren I shall make no objection thereto." Grant simply replied that he would send orders to Warren "in a few days." The days stretched into nearly two weeks, and on May 1, Meade wrote to Grant about Warren again. He gently prodded him, "Permit me, if you have not already acted, to call your attention to the case of General Warren." This time Grant had something specific to offer: "I have this day ordered Major General Warren to report to me in person for orders." He sent Warren to command the Department of Mississippi, keeping him very far from Washington. Warren had little to do in Mississippi and wanted no role in Reconstruction, so in late May he sent off a letter of resignation from his command. It was accepted, and Warren would soon return to his old branch, the Corps of Engineers.[66]

When not visiting people or tending to administrative matters, Meade made plans for the Army of the Potomac's march through Richmond. It was scheduled for May 4, but with a storm threatening and many men tired from marching from Burkeville, it was postponed until May 5. The day turned out to be hot, but dry. The march occurred successfully, stretching to nearly six hours. Meade rode at the head of the column, while the Twenty-Fourth Corps served as the receiving guard for the proud veterans. Then it was on to Hanover Court House, before the planned march to Alexandria.[67]

For the next week, the Army of the Potomac marched steadily up through Virginia, this time free of the dread that accompanied all the marches south. Meade arrived at Fairfax Station on May 11, with his army close behind. The next day, he went into Washington to visit the War Department and found time to write his wife. He had not yet heard where he would next be assigned, nor was he convinced there would be a "grand review" of the armies.[68]

Fortunately, he was wrong on the grand review. The top authorities definitely wanted such a review, and on May 18 Meade received formal orders for the march. It must have pleased him to find that for one moment, Sheridan would again be under his command. The order stated that on May 23, "The Army of the Potomac, General Sheridan's cavalry, and the Ninth Corps, all under the command of Maj. Gen. George G. Meade, commanding Army of the Potomac," would march through Washington. Sherman would command the two armies, the Army of the Tennessee (O. O. Howard commanding) and the Army of Georgia (H. W. Slocum commanding), that marched the following day.[69]

On a beautiful spring day, with an estimated 100,000 spectators on hand to watch the 80,000 veterans march through Washington, the review started promptly from the Capitol at 9:00 A.M., with Meade and his staff at the head of the seemingly endless column of blue-jacketed men. Meade and his staff passed the reviewing stand erected in front of the White House, where for unknown reasons both President Johnson and Lieutenant General Grant were noticeably absent (but soon appeared). Meade and his staff then dismounted and joined the large group under the covered stand that held the president, top government officials, leading military officers, and their families. For over five hours they watched as the men marched by using the classic cadence step. With his family beside him and the honor of leading the troops on May 23, even Meade must have been pleased and grateful for this memorable measure of tribute for the army and its sacrifices.[70]

The following day, May 24, Sherman's veterans made the same march, again to the ecstatic response of the large crowds. Then it was back to the camps for the soldiers to begin the rapid process of mustering out.[71]

Over the next month, Meade kept busy with the details of disbanding his army. He found time to put forward several officers for regular and brevet promotion, as the windows of opportunity for such advances (if leaving the service) were closing fast. He only had time for one visit home to Philadelphia, where he participated in the parade of returning hometown regiments.[72]

Finally, at the end of June, as his army dwindled down to the size of a corps (before ceasing to exist), Meade received new orders that helped assuage the pain of being subsumed under Halleck's temporary command for two months. He would be in charge of the Military Division of the Atlantic, with headquarters in Philadelphia, one of five divisions encompassing the whole country (Sherman, Sheridan, Thomas, and Halleck headed the other four). His command would encompass the Department of the East, the Middle Department, the Department of Virginia, the Department of North Carolina, and the Department of South Carolina. He once again had a position commensurate with his rank and experience, with an added bonus of headquarters in his hometown.[73]

Now only two tasks remained: formal disbandment of the Army of the Potomac, and a final address to his remaining troops. General Orders Number 35 took care of the process of dissolution, while Meade's letter to his army conveyed his feelings. He began by noting that he had served exactly two years as the commander of the army. Next he enunciated the key moments of his time as its leader, emphasizing two events to make his case for posterity, "the grand and decisive battle of Gettysburg, the turning point of the war, [and] the surrender of the Army of Northern Virginia at Appomattox Court-House." He offered hope that "history" would do the soldiers "justice," and that "a grateful country will honor the living, cherish and support the disabled, and sincerely mourn the dead." Revealing his affection for his men, Meade pledged, "[I will] ever bear in memory your noble devotion to your country, your patience and cheerfulness under all the privations and sacrifices you have been called upon to endure." He ended with an exhortation to thank the "Almighty God for his blessing in granting us victory and peace," and for him to give them all the "strength and light to discharge our duties as citizens, as we have endeavored to discharge them as soldiers." With these stirring words, George G. Meade closed out his tenure as Commander, Army of the Potomac.[74]

❈TWELVE❈

A Major-General in Peacetime, 1865–1872

Meade's relatively short postwar career would be neatly divided into two periods: a Reconstruction phase and a caretaker phase. Several periods in the first phase are worthy of serious attention, but it is beyond the scope of this work to do those studies. Instead, some highlights of both phases will be touched on, with the continuing effects of the war years serving as the theme connecting all of Meade's postwar activities.

In the spring and summer of 1866, Meade found himself charged with suppressing a movement to invade and conquer Canada. An Irish nationalist group, the Fenian Brotherhood, had decided the time was ripe for an invasion of Canada (they hoped to use control of Canada as leverage to obtain freedom for Ireland). A small force of over one thousand men crossed the Niagara River and marched toward Fort Erie. They were met by Canadian militia, whom they easily defeated. The Fenians had only one more brief battle before returning to America because of the inability to get reinforcements (U.S. ships stopped passage of more recruits). Meade arrived in Buffalo and ordered the men to disperse and go home (at government expense). Many did, but not all. Some traveled to northern New York and St. Albans, Vermont. Meade followed them, seized the shipment of arms headed their way, and arrested their leader, none other than the former commander of a division within the Twenty-Sixth corps, Brig. Gen. Thomas W. Sweeny. These actions broke the back of the movement, and Meade was acclaimed a hero—in Canada.[1]

Meade's next assignment would bring him little but headaches for over a year. In December 1867 he was given command of the Third Military District (Georgia, Alabama, and Florida). He then traveled to Atlanta to do the very thing he had avoided all his professional life: arbitrate between competing interests in a strictly political situation. During his tenure, the three states were restored to the Union, and Meade found that he had, in the words of his son, to perform the "duty of the civil rehabilitation of States through military agency." In his efforts to follow Army rules and then civil authority, he managed to anger all parties at one point or another, including the president, Andrew Johnson. The only group he found favor with was the parish of St. Philip's Episcopal Church in Atlanta; he helped raise money to refurbish the vandalized church. After a tumultuous fifteen months of command, Meade was thrilled and relieved to be given back his former position, Commander of the Military Division of the Atlantic in March 1869.[2]

As so often happened in Meade's life, he would again experience the sting of rejection, as another hoped-for honor was refused him. With Grant's election to the presidency in 1868 and inauguration in March 1869, it was expected that his closest military friend, William T. Sherman, would be promoted to full general (Grant's new rank created by Congress in 1866) in command of the United States Army. Meade desperately hoped that the next prize, lieutenant general of the army (Sherman's rank) would be his, even though he still lacked political allies (Halleck was in Kentucky and not in favor with Grant and Sherman). So Meade did the one thing he was usually willing to do: have a frank talk with his old commander, Grant. He met with Grant in Washington just prior to the inauguration. Meade asked Grant to dispel the rumors that Sheridan would get the promotion and then explained why he believed he deserved the promotion. According to Meade's son, Grant listened politely to Meade's arguments "but made no direct reply." Though this was almost always Grant's first response to a demand, Meade also knew from intimate experience that it signaled that Grant had already made his decision and refused to divulge so as to spare his petitioner's feelings. On March 6, 1869, he wrote to his wife, "The blow has been struck and our worst fears realized." Sherman had been promoted to general, and Sheridan to lieutenant general. Calling the decision "the cruelest and meanest act of injustice," Meade hoped that "if there is any sense of wrong or justice in this country, that the man who perpetrated it will some day be made to feel so." He closed with his usual appeal to Christian stoicism: "I cannot write all I feel; indeed it is well I should not. God has thought proper to give us grievous burden to bear, and it is our part to endeavor to be submissive."[3]

Unfortunately for Meade, God continued to add burdens to him that year. Upon returning home to Philadelphia in the spring of 1869, he fell ill with his third case of pneumonia, this time a longer and deeper bout than before. He rallied enough to attend the first meeting of the new Society of the Army of the Potomac held in New York City. He was one of three generals nominated to be president, McClellan and Sheridan being the other two. When no man won a majority on the first ballot (Meade came in third), a second vote was held, and Sheridan won. McClellan and some of his supporters then exited the building.[4] Some of the pain of rejection lessened the next year, when the Society of the Army of the Potomac met in Philadelphia. With Grant and Sherman present, Meade was elected president. With Sherman and Sheridan promoted, Grant could afford to be magnanimous toward Meade, and his presence was a desired endorsement.[5] It was not simply toil and disappointment for Meade in the years after the war. Except for his year in Atlanta, he was generally stationed in his beloved hometown of Philadelphia. There he helped found an orphanage for war orphans (Lincoln Institution) and was appointed a commissioner of Fairmount Park. In the last few years of his life, he could often be found in the park, performing surveys as it expanded into the city's green gem. In the summers his family stayed at a fine country estate just ten miles from town, "Meadow Bank." And throughout those years, honors poured in. In June 1865 he had led the parade of veterans through the streets of Philadelphia before they disbanded. The next month, he and his wife traveled to Boston, where he received an honorary doctorate of law from Harvard University. Then on to a grand dinner at the Porcellian Club, organized in his honor by his former aide and good friend, Theodore Lyman. The next year, he made the presentation address at Independence Hall on July 4 when the flags belonging to the Pennsylvania regiments were returned to Governor Curtin. And he was treated to a round of dinners and speeches in Canada in 1866 and 1867 for his role in protecting Canada from the Fenian Brotherhood.[6]

In the early 1870s, Meade seemed contented with his life. Denied the honor of a final promotion, he strove to accept his position as commander of the Military Division of the Atlantic. He had had the sad duty of being a pallbearer for the funeral of his old Army colleague, George H. Thomas, in April 1870. Thomas was the first of the renowned Union generals to pass away. Henry Halleck was next; he died in January 1872 while on duty as commander of the Division of the South. Despite these surprising deaths (Thomas was fifty-three and Halleck was fifty-six), Meade felt no premonition of his own mortality, reportedly telling his son that the summer of 1872 had been the "happiest days he had passed for many a long year."[7]

Then on October 31 his world collapsed. Complaining of pain in his side while on a daily walk with his wife Margaret, he immediately returned to his house on De Lancey Place to lie down. His physician diagnosed pneumonia, and this time, his condition did not improve. Still lucid, he took Holy Communion from his Episcopal priest in one of his periods of alertness. With the presidential election being held on November 5, few knew that Meade was seriously ill. At 6:00 P.M. on November 6, Meade spoke his last words, "I am about crossing a beautiful wide river, and the opposite shore is coming nearer and nearer."[8] George G. Meade died at age fifty-six.

The news stunned Philadelphia and the country. The *Philadelphia North American* called the news a "bolt from a clear sky." The *Somerset* (Pennsylvania) *Herald* mourned the loss of one of Pennsylvania's "noble sons." The *New York Herald* ran a long obituary on Meade's entire career, noting that Meade not only won the Battle of Gettysburg but also "directed the movements of the Army of the Potomac" through the Virginia campaigns of 1864 and "commanded the right wing of General Grant's army" that brought Lee's army to surrender at Appomattox. A contributor to a Democratic newspaper, the *Findlay Jeffersonian* of Hancock County, Ohio, stated that Meade's "cautious policy seldom made him a hero with the masses," but it led to victories.[9]

The Grant administration responded with a full military funeral, with the president, his top generals, and the cabinet in attendance. Sherman ordered Maj. Gen. Irvin McDowell to handle the funeral arrangements. On November 11 business was suspended in Philadelphia as a city draped in black watched a long funeral procession march down the same streets that the victors had trod upon not too many years before. President Grant, General Sherman, and cabinet officers took a special train from Washington to attend the procession. Generals Humphreys, Wright, and Parke, Meade's corps commanders, served as pallbearers, along with the ubiquitous Sheridan and four naval admirals. Meade's well-known horse, Old Baldy, was brought out of retirement to pace behind the caisson carrying Meade's body. A black-covered barge carried the casket up the Schuylkill River as regimental bands played dirges. On November 11, 1872, Meade's body was laid to rest on a small hill overlooking the river that runs alongside Laurel Hill Cemetery.[10]

Conclusion

George Gordon Meade was the longest-serving and most successful commander of the largest army ever assembled in North America in the nineteenth century, the Army of the Potomac. He took command of a dispirited army in June 1863, and in less than a week led it to its greatest victory of the war over the best army in the war. When he failed to capture or cripple Lee's army after the battle, whispers about his lack of resolve soon hardened into accepted fact in some quarters.

He compounded his reputational difficulties that fall when he and Lee played cat-and-mouse in northern Virginia. His great opportunity to attack Lee and boost his flagging reputation melted away when his troublesome protégé, Gouverneur Warren, refused to send twenty-eight thousand men on a suicidal assault at Mine Run.

Meade spent the winter of 1863–1864 fighting for his job. Bereft of powerful political patrons and ill-suited to play national politics, Meade bounced from one humiliation to another, as former subordinates like Daniel Sickles attacked him in the press and the Joint Committee on the Conduct of the War sought to find enough fault in his performance to have him dismissed. A combination of inadequate alternatives and the appointment of Grant saved Meade from the ignominy of dismissal.

His final fifteen months as commander often became an exercise in humility. Through punishing offensives, his army pushed Lee's Army of Northern Virginia back to Richmond and Petersburg, where it wore them down enough to complete the coup de grâce at Appomattox in April 1865. But just as Meade predicted, by standing in the shadow of Grant he was usually lost to public view. Particularly galling to Meade was the fact that Grant knew this was happening but did little to stop it. The underlying truth was that Meade served Grant's purposes: he could command a large army effectively, he knew the Army of the Potomac intimately, and he faithfully carried out Grant's orders. Together they led the army to victory in the

East—with the credit going largely to Grant and one of his favorite protégés, Philip Sheridan.

As a commander, Meade had some of the faults attributed to him, but also some faintly acknowledged strengths. Meade firmly believed in the necessity of duty, yet he gave his corps commanders considerable latitude in their decision making. He expected his generals to do their jobs, and when they did, it led to successes such as Gettysburg and the pursuit of Lee's army in April 1865. When they did not do their jobs, Meade tended to criticize, prod, and cajole, but in the end, he rarely sacked any of his generals. Ironically, Meade's greatest failing as a leader has been misread for generations. Most historians argue that his quick temper and thin skin created a tense atmosphere at headquarters that inhibited his generals. What the generals knew better than the historians was that Meade's bark was worse than his bite. In fact, some might argue that he had no bite at all when it came to his corps commanders. The problem was not an inability to suppress his temper but, rather, an unwillingness to dismiss generals who failed to perform, schemed against him, or even defied his orders. Meade, the ultimate team player, was too loyal to his subordinates.

At the same time, Meade had some decided strengths compared to his fellow commanders of the Army of the Potomac. He had more nerve than McClellan, tolerated a high casualty rate on offense or defense (something McClellan avoided), and did not openly fight with politicians (unlike McClellan). He never boasted like Pope, nor squandered enormous opportunities in battle as wantonly as Pope did at Second Manassas. His ability to manage an army of over 100,000 men—a skill praised by Grant and noticeably absent in Burnside—was superb. Though cautious in his planning and on offense, he had the moral courage to call off an assault if necessary, unlike Burnside. He worked closely with his corps commanders—too closely in the eyes of some—unlike Hooker, who thought his secrecy a plus. He also showed better tactical instincts and much more resolve than Hooker, who lost a winnable battle against Lee at Chancellorsville.

Unfortunately for Meade, he was pitted for two years against the best general on either side, Robert E. Lee. Lee had an aggressive mindset and surrounded himself with like-minded generals. Together they demonstrated a speed of maneuver, flexibility, initiative, and rapid adjustment to circumstances that the Army of the Potomac rarely matched. Furthermore, the Army of the Potomac usually had to act offensively, which raised the stakes for them in every battle. In the end, Lee's resources, manpower, and support from the people eroded, which allowed Union forces to trap and capture his army. Meade did better than his predecessors fighting Lee, but he could never amass the string of victories against Lee that Grant, Sherman, and Thomas collected fighting lesser generals in the West.

Meade had a larger role in the war than is usually noted. His army won the Battle of Gettysburg and lost the foot race to the Potomac River. After a few small battles in the fall, Meade almost had the large set-piece battle with Lee he sought, only to be thwarted by desperate (and superb) entrenching and topographic advantages (to the Confederates) at Mine Run. Meade and Grant were continually frustrated by the obstacles presented by nature and man in the tangled woods of the Wilderness. Meade's low point as a commander came not at Cold Harbor (where he played a larger role than previously thought) but at Petersburg in June 1864, when his exhausted and overwrought corps commanders failed to launch their assaults in a timely manner. When he finally told them to attack at will, it showed that he had reached the limits of his patience and confidence in them. Meade is often criticized for his role in the Crater debacle, but more responsibility rests on Burnside and his subordinates. The Petersburg offensives from August–November 1864 were more exercises in frustrating slowness of movement and limited gains. His army had some key roles in the capture of Petersburg and the last battles against Lee, but with Sheridan providing the momentum of the chase with his cavalry, more glory accrued to him than Meade.

Besides the challenges of fighting Lee and serving under Grant, Meade could often be his own worst enemy. Always cautious in operations, sometimes his caution led to paralysis. Never desirous of battle unless he felt confident he could win, Meade was reactive during most of his tenure, rather than proactive. Sarcastic, impatient with errors or mediocrity, quick tempered, and too publicly reserved to curry favor among the troops, his headquarters could be a tense place to work, and he never developed a deep reservoir of support among the foot soldiers of the army (unlike McClellan). Wary of politicians, he never learned how to play the cutthroat game of national politics (though he avoided arguments and consciously making enemies of politicians). Suspicious of the press, he did not take them into his confidence, and when he humiliated one of the popular correspondents, he became a pariah to the press. Thin skinned and overly sensitive to slights (like many of the generals in the Army of the Potomac), he spent too much time worrying about his reputation as an honorable gentleman—to little advantage. Though his complaints about his poor treatment by politicians, the press, and even other generals were warranted, he knew that he had only two options to improve his situation: do his job well, and produce military victories. He managed to succeed in the former, but not the latter.

The lack of victories lies at the heart of all assessments of Meade's leadership. His victory at Gettysburg has always been his brightest jewel, but it was a defensive victory. As Francis Walker wrote long ago in his essay on Meade at Gettysburg, "The sword is ever of higher honor than the shield."[1] Meade knew this fact only too well, writing on several occasions to his wife that "only those who produce victories" would be applauded and promoted. Grant produced victories, and for that he received accolades and promotion (and Meade was comfortable with that reality). Sherman humbled a proud South in the last year of the war, and for that he was hailed as a military genius. Sheridan had three advantages: the wisdom to cultivate his image, the powerful support of Grant, and the impeccable timing of his stunning victories over Early's army in the Shenandoah Valley just before the election of 1864. Thomas had even more decisive victories in Tennessee in the fall and winter of 1864, but his accomplishments were overshadowed by Sherman's March and Sheridan's destruction of Virginia's breadbasket, the Shenandoah Valley.

For Meade there was the victory at Gettysburg, the small gains of the Bristoe campaign, the indecisive yet strategically critical bloody slog against Lee's army in the Overland Campaign, the frustration of tightening the noose around Richmond and Petersburg in 1864, and the final victory chase with Grant and Sheridan stealing the limelight by meeting with Lee at Appomattox—while Meade sat in a tent several miles away.

Meade knew these facts only too well. Though he steadfastly did his duty as a soldier, he painfully watched as other generals grabbed the glory, both during and after the war. He largely kept his feelings private, though the pain of being passed over for promotion to lieutenant general of the army (by Sheridan) was almost too great for him to bear. He took comfort in his family, his friends, his faith, the support of his hometown community, Philadelphia, and, most of all, in his fidelity to his strong sense of duty. Still, as the meaning and the memory of the war began to be debated in the 1870s, he must have sometimes wondered if the price of command—his reputation—had been worth the responsibility. He placed little faith in the press or historians to tell his full story, and given that cynical view of historical interpretation, it is not surprising that he never began a memoir. Furthermore, his early death at age fifty-six eliminated any opportunity to set out his version of his military service.

George G. Meade was not the best general in the Union armies—that man was Ulysses S. Grant. William T. Sherman deserves the credit he gets for capturing Atlanta and using an old strategy—weaken an enemy's resolve by destroying its resources—to cripple a proud yet vulnerable Confederacy. But George G. Meade should be counted among the top three Union generals. A fierce division commander, an aggressive corps commander, and *the* commander of the largest army in the war for two years, Meade led his army to victory in the biggest battle of the war and to total victory at Appomattox. A better commander than any of his predecessors at the helm of the Army of the Potomac, he endured two years of constant criticism and one year of an awkward command relationship. Through it all he bore up well, never losing sight of who he was, his capabilities, his duty, and his goals. Though he lacked the dash and popularity of Sheridan, his steady pressure on Lee contributed more to Union victory than cavalry battles around Richmond or defeat of Early's army in the Shenandoah Valley.

For all these reasons, it is time to bring Meade back to where Grant placed him in a recommendation letter to Halleck in 1864—as one of the two fittest men in the

Union to command large armies (Sherman being the other). George G. Meade led the Army of the Potomac for two years, fought Lee's army to a standstill at Gettysburg, and in tandem with Grant's leadership and support, slowly ground down the Army of Northern Virginia to submission. For three long years, the Army of the Potomac slugged it out with the best general and the best army in the war and ultimately defeated that army. George G. Meade ably and faithfully led the Army of the Potomac for two of those three years, and under his command it won the war in the East. It is time for the longest-serving commander of the Army of the Potomac to get the credit he is due.

Notes

INTRODUCTION

1. Bache, *Life of General George Gordon Meade;* Pennypacker, *General Meade;* Meade, *Life and Letters;* Agassiz, *Meade's Headquarters.*

2. Coddington, "Strange Reputation of General Meade"; Coddington, *Gettysburg Campaign;* Cleaves, *Meade of Gettysburg;* Jones, *Civil War Command and Strategy;* Sauers, *Gettysburg;* Sauers, *Meade: Victor of Gettysburg;* Sauers, "'Rarely Has More Skill'"; Rafuse, *George Gordon Meade;* Rafuse, "'Wherever Lee Goes'"; Stowe, "Philadelphia Gentleman"; Stowe, "Certain Grave Charges"; Stowe, "'Longest and Clearest Head'"; Stowe, "George Gordon Meade"; Hattaway and Smith, "George Gordon Meade"; Huntington, *Searching for George Gordon Meade.*

3. A small sampling of modern Meade criticism: James McPherson, "The North had its McClellan and Meade who threw away chances in the East" (*Battle Cry of Freedom,* 857); Allen C. Guelzo on Meade at Gettysburg, "Apart from his single impulse to organize some strike on the morning of July 2nd, Meade's behavior was entirely reactive" (*Gettysburg,* 462); and Richard J. Sommers on Meade's leadership at Globe Tavern (and by extension, elsewhere), "Soundness, not brilliance; trustworthiness, not audacity; steadfastness, not dash characterized Meade" (*Richmond Redeemed,* 421).

4. Lieber, *Character of the Gentleman,* 18–19; Foote, *Gentlemen and the Roughs,* 6; Parker quoted in Pennypacker, *General Meade,* 7.

1. FROM CADIZ TO GETTYSBURG

1. Warner, *Generals in Blue,* 604. Edward Ferrero was the other general born in Spain. Ferrero's parents were Italian, and they moved soon after his birth in 1831 to New York. Edward would follow in his father's footsteps and become a renowned dance instructor. Warner, *Generals in Blue,* 150–51; Meade, *Life and Letters,* 1:6–7. George Meade was the son of George Gordon Meade, major general of the Army. His son, also named George Gordon Meade, edited the two volumes after his father's death; Stowe, "Philadelphia Gentleman," 24–54. Stowe's detailed and thoughtful history of Meade's early years deserves publication.

2. Stowe, "Philadelphia Gentleman," 54–58; Cleaves, *Meade of Gettysburg,* 7–9; Meade, *Life and Letters,* 1:6–7. Richard Meade died in 1828 at age fifty. The Meade family would

continue to press the federal government for payment of their claims into the twentieth century—all to no avail. See Stowe, "Philadelphia Gentleman," 60n43.

3. Cleaves, *Meade of Gettysburg,* 9–10; Meade, *Life and Letters,* 1:8–10.

4. Stowe, "Philadelphia Gentleman," 72–78; Meade, *Life and Letters,* 1:11 (quotation on Meade's desire to pursue jobs in civilian life); Cleaves, *Meade of Gettysburg,* 10–12; Haupt, *Reminiscences,* 310. A note on names: Stowe writes in his dissertation (80n17) that while at West Point Meade began signing his letters Geo. G. Meade, rather than George Meade. He would continue that practice throughout his life, signing almost all of his private letters to his wife, for example, as George G. Meade, Geo. G. Meade, or G. G. Meade. His earliest biographers usually introduced his full name at some point in their narratives, though most additional references to him used his highest military rank and last name. Later historians often refer to him by his full name, perhaps to distinguish him from his son and his grandfather. I have chosen to use his full name infrequently, preferring to use his most customary private salutation, George G. Meade.

5. Cleaves, *Meade of Gettysburg,* 11–18; Meade, *Life and Letters,* 1:12–17; Stowe, "Philadelphia Gentleman," 78–108. John Sergeant was a lawyer, state representative, and congressman from Philadelphia. He was Henry Clay's vice-presidential running mate in Clay's unsuccessful bid for the presidency in 1832. He had also helped to free Meade's father from prison in Spain.

6. Meade, *Life and Letters,* 1:16–17.

7. Cleaves, *Meade of Gettysburg,* 19.

8. Ibid., 22–36 and 44; Meade, *Life and Letters,* 1:51 and nearly two hundred pages of printed letters from Meade to his wife during the Mexican War found in the same source (19–196).

9. Cleaves, *Battle of Gettysburg,* 40–44.

10. George G. Meade to Margaret Meade: May 28, 1846; May 27, 1846; Dec. 2, 1846; June 7, 1846; July 9, 1846; Nov. 10, 1846, in George Gordon Meade Papers (henceforth Meade Papers), Historical Society of Pennsylvania (henceforth HSP); Rafuse, *McClellan's War,* 41.

11. George G. Meade to Margaret Meade, Apr. 9, 1847, in Meade Papers, HSP; Meade, *Life and Letters,* 1:200. Bache had married Meade's sister, Maria del Carmen.

12. Meade, *Life and Letters,* 1:200–208; Sauers, *Meade: Victor of Gettysburg,* 10–11; Lowe, *Meade's Army,* 5–6.

13. Meade, *Life and Letters,* 1:208–12 (quotation on p. 210); Stowe, "Philadelphia Gentleman," 205.

14. Meade, *Life and Letters,* 1:213–15.

15. Cleaves, *Meade of Gettysburg,* 52–53 (quotation from p. 52); Meade, *Life and Letters,* 1:216.

16. Cleaves, *Meade of Gettysburg,* 53–54; Stowe, "Philadelphia Gentleman," 209–10; Meade, *Life and Letters,* 1:215–16.

17. Cleaves, *Meade of Gettysburg,* 55–61; Stowe, "Philadelphia Gentleman," 210–16.

18. Cleaves, *Meade of Gettysburg,* 62–63.

19. Sears, *To the Gates of Richmond,* 346–47, 252, 296–99; Cleaves, *Meade of Gettysburg,* 67–69; Meade, *Life and Letters,* 1:290–99; George G. Meade to Margaret Meade, July 1, 1862, Meade Papers, HSP.

20. Cleaves, *Meade of Gettysburg,* 71; Meade, *Life and Letters,* 1:300–301.

21. Cleaves, *Meade of Gettysburg,* 71–72.

22. George G. Meade to Margaret Meade, Aug. 16 (on McClellan), Aug. 19, and Aug. 21 (second quotation), 1862, Meade Papers, HSP.

23. Hennessy, *Return to Bull Run,* 411–20; *War of the Rebellion* (hereafter OR), vol. 12, pt. 2, 343, McDowell report ("gallant Meade"); George G. Meade to Margaret Meade, Sept. 3, 1862, Meade Papers, HSP.

24. Burlingame, *Abraham Lincoln*, 2:376–80; Cleaves, *Meade of Gettysburg*, 75; George G. Meade to Margaret Meade: Sept. 6, 3, and 12, 1862, Meade Papers, HSP.

25. Hartwig, *To Antietam Creek*, 376–95; Cleaves, *Meade of Gettysburg*, 76–77; George G. Meade to Margaret Meade, Sept. 18, 1862, Meade Papers, HSP.

26. Hartwig, *To Antietam Creek*, 616–31; Sears, *Landscape Turned Red*, 136–39; *OR*, vol. 19, pt. 1, Meade report, 279; Cleaves, *Meade of Gettysburg*, 77–80; *OR*, vol. 19, pt. 1: A. V. Colburn, assistant adjutant general to Meade, Sept. 17, 1862, 1:25 P.M., 315 (placed Meade in command of the First Corps); R. B. Marcy to Meade, Sept. 17, 1862, 3:10 P.M., 315 (quotation); George G. Meade to Margaret Meade, Sept. 18, 1862, Meade Papers, HSP.

27. Cleaves, *Meade of Gettysburg*, 81–83; George G. Meade to Margaret Meade, Oct. 12 (quotation), Nov. 9, and Nov. 8 (quotation), 1862, Meade Papers, HSP; Sauers, *Meade: Victor of Gettysburg*, 34 (on generals who visited McClellan).

28. George G. Meade to Margaret Meade, Dec. 2 and 6, 1862, Meade Papers, HSP; Sauers, *Meade: Victor of Gettysburg*, 34–35; Stowe, "'Longest and Clearest Head,'" 115.

29. George G. Meade to Margaret Meade, Nov. 24 and 22, 1862, Meade Papers, HSP; Rafuse, *George Gordon Meade*, 168.

30. Cleaves, *Meade of Gettysburg*, 90.

31. O'Reilly, *Fredericksburg Campaign*, 138–227; Meade quoted in Cleaves, *Meade of Gettysburg*, 9. Anyone who knows Meade only from his magnificent defense at Gettysburg should read O'Reilly's detailed account of the fight for Prospect Hill; it describes a general in full attack mode.

32. Cleaves, *Meade of Gettysburg*, 95; George G. Meade to Margaret Meade, Nov. 20 and 24, Dec. 17, 23, and 26, 1862, Meade Papers, HSP. Butterfield was a brigadier general when he commanded the Fifth Corps, though his promotion to major general was later backdated to November 29, 1862.

33. Burlingame, *Abraham Lincoln*, 2:486.

34. George G. Meade to Margaret Meade, Jan. 26 and 28, 1863, Meade Papers, HSP. Apparently Halleck and Stanton suggested Meade for the job, but Lincoln decided on his own to appoint Hooker (a rising favorite among radical Republicans). See Burlingame, *Abraham Lincoln*, 2:486.

35. George G. Meade to Margaret Meade, Mar. 17 and 29 (quotation), and Apr. 9, 1862, Meade Papers, HSP.

36. George G. Meade to Margaret Meade, Apr. 9, 11, and 12, 1862, Meade Papers, HSP. Meade tried telling Lincoln some "dirty jokes" to get on his good side, but that attempt at closeness produced no results. See Stowe, "'Longest and Clearest Head,'" 128, for discussion of Lincoln's visit to the army headquarters in April 1862.

37. George G. Meade to Margaret Meade, Apr. 18 and 16 (quotation), 1862, Meade Papers, HSP.

38. Sauers, *Meade: Victor of Gettysburg*, 39; Cleaves, *Meade of Gettysburg*, 103–4.

39. Sauers, *Meade: Victor of Gettysburg*, 39–40; Cleaves, *Meade of Gettysburg*, 105–9; Stowe, "'Longest and Clearest Head,'" 134–36.

40. Furgurson, *Chancellorsville*, 240–42; Cleaves, *Meade of Gettysburg*, 111.

41. Furgurson, *Chancellorsville*, 304–5; Cleaves, *Meade of Gettysburg*, 111–12; Sauers, *Meade: Victor of Gettysburg*, 41–42. Henry W. Slocum arrived after the vote was taken and sided with those favoring attack.

42. Furgurson, *Chancellorsville*, 312–19.

43. George G. Meade to Margaret Meade, May 8, 1863, Meade Papers, HSP.

44. George G. Meade to Margaret Meade, May 10 and 8, 1863, Meade Papers, HSP; Stowe, "'Longest and Clearest Head,'" 140–41.

45. George G. Meade to Margaret Meade, May 15 and 19, 1863 (quotations from May 19 letter), Meade Papers, HSP; Stowe, "'Longest and Clearest Head,'" 142–43.

46. George G. Meade to Margaret Meade, May 20, 25, 23 (quotation), 26 (quotation), and June 11 (quotation) and 13 (quotation), 1863, Meade Papers, HSP; Sears, *Controversies and Commanders*, 162–63.

47. George G. Meade to Margaret Meade, June 25, 1863, Meade Papers, HSP.

48. Burlingame, *Abraham Lincoln*, 2:502–3 and 510–11 (Lincoln quoted in same, p. 511).

49. Stowe, "'Longest and Clearest Head,'" 145.

50. Catton, *Stillness at Appomattox*, 43.

51. George G. Meade to Margaret Meade, June 29, 1863, Meade Papers, HSP.

52. Benjamin, "Hooker's Appointment and Removal," 243; George G. Meade to Margaret Meade, June 29, 1863, Meade Papers, HSP.

53. *OR*, vol. 27, pt. 3, Hardie to General Halleck, June 28, 1863, received 5:30 A.M., 373 ("I have accomplished my mission"); Meade, *Life and letters*, 2:2.

54. Benjamin, "Hooker's Appointment and Removal," 243; Meade, *Life and Letters*, 2:2.

55. Byrne and Weaver, *Haskell of Gettysburg*, 132; Smart, *Radical View*, 52; Pennypacker, *General Meade*, 3.

56. Porter, *Campaigning with Grant*, 248 and 209; Foote, *Gentlemen and the Roughs*, 58.

57. Cadwallader, *Three Years with Grant*, 343–44; Pennypacker, *General Meade*, 6 (Devens quotation) and 7.

58. Benjamin, "Hooker's Appointment and Removal," 243; John Gibbon to Francis Gibbon, June 29, 1863, John Gibbon Papers, Historical Society of Pennsylvania.

59. *OR*, vol. 27, pt. 3, General Orders No. 194, June 27, 1863, 369; *OR*, vol. 27, pt. 1, Halleck to Meade, June 27, 1863, 61.

60. Coddington, *Gettysburg Campaign*, 225; *OR*, vol. 27, pt. 3, Orders, Headquarters, Army of the Potomac, June 28, 1863, 375–76.

61. *OR*, vol. 27, pt. 3, Meade to Halleck, June 29, 1863, 11:00 A.M., 66- 67; Couch's estimate of the number of his men under his command is found in *OR*, vol. 27, pt. 3, D. N. Couch to the Secretary of War, June 29, 1863, 407.

62. Coddington, *Gettysburg Campaign*, 228–29; *OR*, vol. 27, pt. 3, Seth Williams to Commanding Officer, Third Corps, June 30, 1863, 420.

63. Coddington, *Gettysburg Campaign*, 226–30.

64. *OR*, vol. 27, pt. 3: Couch to Secretary of War (similar letter to Meade), June 29, 1863, 407; Cameron to Lincoln, June 29, 1863, 409; Joel Parker to President Lincoln, June 29, 1863, 409.

65. *OR*, vol. 27, pt. 3, Circular, Headquarters, Army of the Potomac, June 29, 1863, 402; Coddington, *Gettysburg Campaign*, 230–31.

66. Lowe, *Meade's Army*, 34 (Sept. 13, 1863).

67. *OR, vol.* 27, pt. 1: Buford to Reynolds, June 30, 1863, 5:30 A.M., 922; Buford to General Pleasonton, June 30, 1863, 923; Buford to Reynolds, June 30, 1863, 10:30 P.M., 923–24; Buford to Pleasonton, June 30, 1863, 10:40 P.M., 924.

68. *OR*, vol. 27, pt. 3: Order, Headquarters, Army of the Potomac, June 30, 1863, 416; Haupt to General Schenck (sent by courier to Meade), June 30, 1863, midnight, 427.

69. *OR*, vol. 27, pt. 3, Williams to Commanding Officer, Eleventh Corps, June 30, 1863, 415.

70. *OR*, vol. 27, pt. 3: Orders, Headquarters, Army of the Potomac, June 30, 1863, 416; Circular, Headquarters, Army of the Potomac, June 30, 1863, 416–17.

71. Guelzo, *Gettysburg*, 119 ("withdrawal") and 459. Guelzo credits Reynolds for aggressive action that "sprang Lee's troops prematurely" (and thus brought on victory to the Union). For Meade's instructions to Reynolds on June 30, 1863, see *OR*, vol. 27, pt. 3, 419–20.

72. *OR*, vol. 27, pt. 2, Lee's report, 316–18. Coddington has an extensive discussion of Lee's choices and thinking in *Gettysburg Campaign*, 180–88.

73. *OR*, vol. 27, pt. 3, Circular, Headquarters, Army of the Potomac, July 1, 1863, 458–59.

74. Ibid. For a recent critical view of the Pipe Creek circular, see Guelzo, *Gettysburg*, 156–57.

75. *OR*, vol. 27, pt. 3, Williams (copy to Howard) to Reynolds, July 1, 1863, 460–61. His second to last paragraph in his message to Reynolds can be questioned in several ways. "The movement of your corps to Gettysburg was ordered before the positive knowledge of the enemy's withdrawal from Harrisburg and concentration was received." That is it. Was he apologizing for sending the First Corps straight into the Army of Northern Virginia? Was he merely updating Reynolds on an evolving situation? Or did he seek some cover should the First Corps be badly beaten in a battle? No further explanation comes from Meade or those around him. While the first and third questions have appeal for critics of Meade, the second question seems most revealing because he did not alter his order for Reynolds to march the First Corps into Gettysburg. He was primarily elaborating on information he conveyed in the first paragraph of his message, that intelligence "seem[s] to indicate the concentration of the enemy either at Chambersburg or at a point situated somewhere on a line drawn between Chambersburg and York, through Mummasburg and to the north of Gettysburg." In other words, be careful: Lee's army may be in force in Gettysburg; Reid, *America's Civil War*, 289.

76. George G. Meade to Margaret Meade, June 30, 1863, Meade Papers, HSP.

2. GETTYSBURG

1. *OR*, vol. 27, pt. 1, Meade to Halleck, July 1, 1863, 7 A.M., 70. Pfanz, *Gettysburg—The First Day*, 115.

2. Pfanz, *Gettysburg—The First Day*, 73–79; Sears, *Gettysburg*, 165–70.

3. Pfanz, *Gettysburg—The First Day*, 78–79; *OR*, vol. 27, pt. 1, Howard's report, 232.

4. Weld, *War Diary*, 232; *OR*, vol. 27, pt. 3: Williams to Sedgwick, July 1, 1863, 462; Butterfield to Slocum, July 1, 1863, 462; Williams to French, July 1, 1863, 462; *Report of the Joint Committee on the Conduct of the War* (henceforth *JCCW*), Hancock testimony, Mar. 22, 1864, 404–5; *OR*, vol. 27, pt. 3: Meade to Couch, July 1, 1863, 12 m., 458; Butterfield to Hancock, July 1, 1863, 12:30 P.M., 461.

5. *OR*, vol. 27, pt. 1, Hancock's report, 367; *OR*, vol. 27, pt. 3, Butterfield to Hancock (copy to General Howard), July 1, 1863, 1:10 P.M., 461.

6. Hancock, *Reminiscences*, 94–95.

7. Agassiz, *Meade's Headquarters*, 82 (Theodore Lyman to Elizabeth Lyman; all letters from this book are from Theodore to his wife, unless specifically noted otherwise, Apr. 13, 1864); Jordan, *Winfield Scott Hancock*, 57–58 and 37; Agassiz, *Meade's Headquarters*, 189 (July 12, 1864); Statement of Lt. Col. Charles H. Morgan found in Ladd and Ladd, *Bachelder Papers*, 3:1349.

8. *OR*, vol. 27, pt. 3: Butterfield to Sickles, July 1, 1863, 4:45 P.M., 466; Sickles to Gen. Seth Williams, assistant adjutant general, July 1, 1863, 3:15 P.M., 464; Sickles to Williams, July 1, 1863, 3:25 P.M., 464.

9. Morgan Statement, in Ladd and Ladd, *Bachelder Papers*, 3:1350; the most colorful story comes from Maj. E. P. Halstead, an adjutant in the First Corps, who insisted he was the only person present when Hancock and Howard met. Hancock saluted Howard, then told him he had orders from Meade to take command of the three corps. Howard told him he was the senior general on the field, and Hancock replied, "I am aware of that, General, but I have written orders in my pocket from General Meade, which I will show you if you wish to see them." Howard then stated, "No, I do not doubt your word, General Hancock, but you can give no orders here while I am here." Hancock approached the situation from

a different tack: "Very well, General Howard, I will second any order you have to give, but General Meade has also directed me to select a field on which to fight this battle. . . . I think this is the strongest position by nature upon which to fight a battle that I ever saw, and if it meets your approbation I will select this as the battlefield." Halstead, "Incidents," 285.

10. *OR*, vol. 27, pt. 1, Hancock's report, 367–69; Jerome Watrous quoted in Pfanz, *Gettysburg—The First Day*, 338; Meade, *Life and Letters*, 2:38, author's narrative on verbal note from Major Mitchell; *OR*, vol. 27, pt. 1, Hancock to Meade, July 1, 1863, 5:25 P.M., 366; *OR*, vol. 27, pt. 3, Meade to Hancock and Doubleday, July 1, 1863, 6:00 P.M., 466; Jordan, *Winfield Scott Hancock*, 86. As with so many key moments in the Civil War, there are conflicting accounts of Hancock's command in the late afternoon. Not surprisingly, Oliver Howard had a different recollection of that afternoon, remembering that the men divided the responsibility for the battlefield. While it is hard to sort out who gave each command, a preponderance of observers maintain that Hancock did issue some crucial orders on the battlefield that afternoon. See Jordan, *Winfield Scott Hancock*, 83–86, and Coddington, *Gettysburg Campaign*, 297–99.

11. *OR*, vol. 27, pt. 3: Butterfield to Sedgwick, July 1, 1863, 4:30 P.M., 465; Williams to Sedgwick, July 1, 1863, 465; Butterfield to Sickles, July 1, 1863, 4:45 P.M., 466; Meade to Hancock and Doubleday, July 1, 1863, 6:00 P.M., 466.

12. Ibid.: Butterfield to Sykes, July 1, 1863, 7:00 P.M., 467; Butterfield to Sickles, July 1, 1863, 7:30 P.M., 467; Butterfield to Sedgwick, July 1, 1863, 7:30 P.M., 467–68. In Hancock's note of 5:25 P.M. to Meade, he had a sentence, "Howard says that Doubleday's command gave way." Meade used this information to replace Doubleday with Newton, and Guelzo argues that Meade wanted the ardent abolitionist Doubleday removed (*Gettysburg*, 224). Coddington argues that the decision was not politically motivated but based on perceived impressions of incompetency (*Gettysburg Campaign*, 690n82). Without more evidence from Meade, the debate continues.

13. *OR*, vol. 27, pt. 3, Butterfield to Sedgwick, July 2, 1863, 5:30 A.M., 484–85.

14. *OR*, vol. 27, pt. 3, Butterfield to Mendell, July 2, 1863, 5:00 A.M., 484.

15. Pfanz, *Gettysburg: The Second Day*, 206–7. Sykes graduated in the same West Point class (1842) as Newton and Doubleday (and Longstreet).

16. Byrne, *Haskell of Gettysburg*, 133; Morgan Statement, in Ladd and Ladd, *Bachelder Papers*, 3:1349; *OR*, vol. 27, pt. 1: Howard to Meade, July 1, 1863, 5:00 P.M., 696; Howard to Meade, July 1, 1863, 696–97; Howard to Butterfield, July 1, 1863, 10:00 P.M., 697.

17. Meade asked Warren to become his chief of staff, but he refused, telling Meade he preferred to be chief engineer and that Butterfield was up-to-date on Army affairs. See Jordan, *"Happiness,"* 87. Meade also asked Andrew Humphreys, who declined the position but said he would consider it later. See Humphreys, *Andrew Atkinson Humphreys*, 187. Meade even asked Seth Williams if he would hold both positions, adjutant general and chief of staff, for a time, but he refused. See George G. Meade to G. G. Benedict, Mar. 16, 1870, in Meade, *Life and Letters*, 2:352.

18. Byrne, *Haskell of Gettysburg*, 133–34.

19. Meade, *Life and Letters*, 2:62–63; *OR*, vol. 27, pt. 1, Howard report, 705. One of many troubling issues of fact concerns the timing of various events at Gettysburg. For example, times for Meade's arrival at Gettysburg range from midnight to 3:00 A.M., with Meade himself stating 1:00 A.M.. With no synchronized timepieces, participants relied on memory to set times. In this instance, given the fact that the exact moment of arrival did not affect the events of that early morning, it seemed safest to land somewhere beyond midnight. For a good discussion of this issue, see Coddington, *Gettysburg Campaign*, 713n2.

20. Pfanz, *Gettysburg: The Second Day*, 58–61. Maj. Thomas W. Osborne later removed the three batteries he had placed in the gap. *OR*, vol. 27, pt. 1, Osborne Report, 749.

21. Meade, *Life and Letters*, 2:63; Gibbon, *Personal Recollections*, 140; Byrnes, *Haskell of Gettysburg*, 134.

22. Pfanz, *Gettysburg: The Second Day*, 59–64.

23. Meade, *Life and Letters*, 2:66.

24. Pfanz, *Gettysburg: The Second Day*, 83–83; Meade, *Life and Letters*, 2:66–68.

25. Hunt, "Second Day at Gettysburg," 301–2; Pfanz, *Gettysburg: The Second Day*, 90; Tremain, *Two Days*, 42–43; Historicus, "The Battle of Gettysburg," *New York Herald*, Mar. 12, 1864.

26. Hunt, "Second Day at Gettysburg," 302.

27. Ibid., 303.

28. *OR*, vol. 27, pt. 3: Butterfield to Pleasonton, two messages, July 2, 1863, and Pleasonton to Gregg, July 2, 1863, 490; Pfanz, *Gettysburg: The Second Day*, 97–102; *OR*, vol. 27, pt. 3, Circular, July 2, 1863, 11 A.M., 487.

29. *JCCW*, Sickles testimony, 299–300, and Butterfield testimony, 425; Hunt, "Second Day at Gettysburg," 297–303; *JCCW*, Gibbon testimony, 425.

30. Tremain, *Two Days*, 48–50; *JCCW*, Sickles testimony, 298.

31. *OR*, vol. 27, pt. 1: Halleck report, 16; Meade report, 116.

32. Pfanz, *Gettysburg: The Second Day*, 25–29. There are numerous articles and even books on Lee's decision on July 2. For the sake of brevity, I have made reference to one account by a modern historian. This study focuses on Meade, not Lee.

33. Pfanz, *Gettysburg: The Second Day*, 110–14; Coddington, *Gettysburg Campaign*, 373–78; Sears, *Gettysburg*, 252–57.

34. On the confusion inherent in trying to march thousands of men over country lanes *without* detection by Union signalmen, see Pfanz, *Gettysburg: The Second Day*, 119–23; in his testimony before the Joint Committee on the Conduct of the War, Meade said of his procedures during the battle, "At that time a great many orders and directions were written on little slips of paper, and no copies of them were kept," *JCCW, Report*, Meade testimony, 349; orders to Pleasonton, see note 28, this chapter; *OR*, vol. 27, pt. 3: messages from signal men, 448; Butterfield to commanding officer, Artillery Reserve, July 2, 1863, 12:50 P.M., 1086; *OR*, vol. 27, pt. 1, Meade report, 116; *OR*, vol. 27, pt. 3, Circular, 1086. Each one of the seven corps commanders was sent a copy.

35. *OR*, vol. 27, pt. 1: Meade to Halleck, July 2, 1863, 3:00 P.M. (received the next morning at 10:20 A.M.), 72.

36. *OR*, vol. 27, pt. 1, Sykes report, 592; *JCCW*, Warren testimony, 377; Meade, *Life and Letters*, 2:78–79; George Sykes to editor, *Chronicle*, Dec. 9, 1865, in Gross, *Battlefield of Gettysburg*, 26; *JCCW*, Sickles testimony, 299; Tremain, *Two Days*, 61; William Paine to George Meade, May 22, 1886, in *Gettysburg Letterbook*, Meade Papers, HSP.

37. Tremain, *Two Days*, 65; Hunt, "Second Day at Gettysburg," 307; Washington Roebling quoted in Pfanz, *Gettysburg: The Second Day*, 201; Meade quotation from Meade, *Life and Letters*, 2:79; last quotation of the paragraph from Pennypacker, "Military Historians and History," 40.

38. Tremain, *Two Days*, 70; James Starr to George Meade, Feb. 7, 1880, in *Gettysburg Letterbooks*, Meade Papers, HSP.

39. Meade, *Life and Letters*, 2:82–83; Humphreys, *Andrew Atkinson Humphreys*, 193–94.

40. Longstreet, "Mistakes at Gettysburg," *Philadelphia Weekly Times*, Feb. 23, 1878.

41. Walker, *General Hancock*, 125; *JCCW*, Hancock testimony, 406; Meade, *Life and Letters*, 2:86; Pfanz, *Gettysburg: The Second Day*, 268–70 and 333–34; *OR*, vol. 27, pt. 1: Birney report, 483; Humphreys report, 533.

42. Meade, *Life and Letters*, 2:86–88; Pfanz, *Gettysburg: The Second Day*, 391. There is controversy about Meade's original and revised orders to Slocum. See discussion in note 44; *OR*,

vol. 27, pt. 1: Hancock report, 369–71, and Meade report, 116; Hancock quoted in Pfanz, *Gettysburg: The Second Day,* 411 (there are several versions of what Hancock shouted, though all convey the same message) and page 414 for the casualty rate of the First Minnesota; *OR,* vol. 27, pt. 2, Cadmus Wilcox report, 619–20; Moe, *Last Full Measure,* 269–75.

43. Meade, *Life and Letters,* 2:89; Paul Oliver to George Meade, May 16, 1882, in *Gettysburg Letterbooks,* Meade Papers, HSP.

44. Pfanz, *Gettysburg—Culp's Hill and Cemetery Hill,* 205–83; *OR,* vol. 27, pt. 1, Newton report, 261; Meade, *Life and Letters,* 2:93. There has been a lively debate for years on the role of the Twelfth Corps—and especially the decisions of Maj. Gen. Henry W. Slocum—at Gettysburg on July 1–2, 1863. The latest participant in the debate, Brian C. Melton, defends Slocum's decisions on those days. Most historians feel that Meade dodged a bullet on July 2 when he stripped Culp's Hill of troops to help defend Cemetery Ridge. How many troops he asked for, and Slocum's response to these orders, has been a source of debate since the battle. See Melton, *Sherman's Forgotten General,* 130–40, and Pfanz, *Gettysburg—Culp's Hill and Cemetery Hill,* 194–96.

45. *OR,* vol. 27, pt. 1, Meade to Halleck, July 2, 1863, 8:00 P.M., 72. The generals killed were Gabriel L. Paul and Samuel R. Zook; the generals wounded were Francis Channing Barlow, Charles K. Graham, Daniel Sickles, and Gouverneur Warren.

46. Meade had also heard a report from two of his intelligence officers just before the conference, where they maintained that based on prisoner interviews the only fresh troops available to Lee were in Pickett's division. The precise impact this information had on Meade's decision to stay cannot be fully measured, however, because he never wrote about it. See Sauers, "'Rarely Has More Skill,'" 235; in his testimony before the Joint Committee on the Conduct of the War on March 11, 1864, Meade began his discussion of the July 2 meeting by calling it a "consultation of the corps commanders," and a bit later he referred to "the questions discussed by this council." It would appear that "council" had no special meaning in this instance. Meade testimony, *JCCW,* 350; Gibbon, "Council of War," 313.

47. *OR,* vol. 27, pt. 1, Minutes of Council, July 2, 1863, 73–74; Quaife, *From the Cannon's Mouth,* 229 (Williams to his daughters, July 6, 1863); *OR,* vol. 27, pt. 3: Ingalls to Meigs, July 1, 1863, 472, and Ingalls to Meigs, July 3, 1863, 7:00 A.M., 502; Byrne, *Haskell of Gettysburg,* 133; Gibbon, "Council of War," 313; Nevins, *Diary of Battle,* 246; *JCCW,* Meade testimony, 350–51, and Warren testimony, 378; Coddington, *Gettysburg Campaign,* 449–51.

48. *OR,* vol. 27, pt. 1, Minutes of Council, July 2, 1863, 73; Gibbon, "Council of War,"313.

49. *OR,* vol. 27, pt. 1, Minutes of Council, July 2, 1863, 73.

50. Ibid.

51. *OR,* vol. 27, pt. 1: letters from Sykes, Newton, Sedgwick, Pleasonton, and Gibbon, all dated Mar. 10, 1864 (except for Gibbon's, which was Mar. 14, 1864), in response to Meade's Circular of Mar. 10, 1864, 124–27; Gibbon quotations from his letter of Mar. 14, 1864, to General Seth Williams in *OR,* vol. 27, pt. 1, 127; *JCCW,* Meade testimony, 350; Gibbon, "Council of War,"314.

52. Meade, *Life and Letters,* 2:98; *OR,* vol. 27, pt. 1, Meade to Slocum, Feb. 25, 1864, 770.

53. Coddington, *Gettysburg Campaign,* 768n4.

54. A. J. L. Fremantle, Diary, "The Gettysburg Campaign," July 2, 1863, found in Gallagher, *Two Witnesses at Gettysburg,* 122–23; Pfanz, *Gettysburg: The Second Day,* 390 and 426–27; Coddington, *Gettysburg Campaign,* 443–48. Of course, Lee's hands-off approach to his corps commanders also allowed defenders of Lee to blame his subordinates for failures to accomplish his goals.

55. Weigley, *Great Civil War,* 254.

56. *OR,* vol. 27, pt. 1, Lt. Edward R. Muhlenberg report, 870; Pfanz, *Gettysburg—Culp's Hill and Cemetery Hill,* 291; *OR,* vol. 27, pt. 3: Pleasonton to Gregg, July 3, 1863, 6 A.M.,

502; Butterfield to French, July 3, 1863, 7 A.M., 501; Quaife, *From the Cannon's Mouth,* 285 (Henry W. Slocum to L. R. Morgan, Jan. 2, 1864); *OR,* vol. 27, pt. 3, Meade to Couch, July 3, 1863, 8:30 A.M., 499.

57. Meade, *Life and Letters,* 2:101; *OR,* vol. 51, pt. 1, Butterfield to Sedgwick, July 3, 1863, 8 A.M., 1068.

58. George G. Meade to Margaret Meade, July 3, 1863, 8:45 A.M., in Meade Papers, HSP.

59. Meade, *Life and Letters,* 2:103 (copy of the 9:15 A.M. circular reprinted); *OR,* vol. 27, pt. 3, Circular, Headquarters, Army of the Potomac, July 3, 1863, 503.

60. Byrne, *Haskell of Gettysburg,* 142–43; Meade, *Life and Letters,* 2:104.

61. Smart, *Radical View,* 51–52. Reid also noted that "in all matter of detail, Williams [Seth] or Major Barstow was referred to as an encyclopedia."

62. Meade, *Life and Letters,* 2:105; Gibbon, *Personal Recollections,* 146; Byrne, *Haskell of Gettysburg,* 145–47.

63. Meade, *Life and Letters,* 2:105.

64. Hunt, "Third Day at Gettysburg," 371–72; Hess, *Pickett's Charge,* 125 (Jacobs taught mathematics and chemistry at the college and kept daily records of the weather); Sears, *Gettysburg,* 383.

65. Gibbon, *Personal Recollections,* 146–47; Sears, *Gettysburg,* 396–97; Hunt, "Third Day at Gettysburg," 373–74; Elmore, "Meteorological and Astronomical Chronology," 13–15; Walker, *Second Army Corps,* 292; Sauers, "'Rarely Has More Skill,'" 238; Meade, *Life and Letters,* 2:106–7; Hess, *Pickett's Charge,* 134–35.

66. Meade, *Life and Letters,* 2:107. Even more detail on the movements of these units is provided by Pennypacker, *General Meade,* 193–94.

67. George G. Meade to John B. Bachelder, Dec. 4, 1869, in Ladd and Ladd, *Bachelder Papers,* 1:379; Sauers, "'Rarely Has More Skill,'" 240.

68. Walker, *General Hancock,* 145. Hancock was not the only general to ride the line; Longstreet did the same on the Confederate side. See Sears, *Gettysburg,* 404.

69. Hess, *Pickett's Charge,* 146–51; Sears, *Gettysburg,* 400–403; Meade, *Life and Letters,* 2:108. Earl Hess argues that the bombardment lasted one hour, though many contemporaries felt it lasted two hours. Hess, *Pickett's Charge,* 162. Hancock and Hunt argued over who should have control over artillery during and after the war.

70. Sears, *Gettysburg,* 419, for estimate of thirteen thousand men; Byrne, *Haskell of Gettysburg,* 158 and 160.

71. George Meade to John B. Bachelder, May 6, 1882, in Ladd and Ladd, *Bachelder Papers,* 2:1078; John Egan to George Meade, Feb. 8, 1870, in Ladd and Ladd, *Bachelder Papers,* 1:389.

72. Byrne, *Haskell of Gettysburg,* 174.

73. Ibid.

74. Byrne, *Haskell of Gettysburg,* 174–75; George G. Meade to John B. Bachelder, Dec. 4, 1869, in Ladd and Ladd, *Bachelder Papers,* 1:380.

75. Meade, *Life and Letters,* 2:109–10; George Meade to John B. Bachelder, Dec. 4, 1869, Ladd and Ladd, *Bachelder Papers,* 1:380; *JCCW,* Meade testimony, 333; *OR,* vol. 27, pt. 1, Crawford report, 654–55.

76. *OR,* vol. 27, pt. 1, Meade to Halleck, July 3, 1863, 74–75; Sears, *Gettysburg,* 459–62.

77. Sears, *Gettysburg,* 496 and 498 (using statistics drawn from John W. Busey and David G. Martin, *Regimental Strengths*).

78. Meade, *Life and Letters,* 2:112.

79. Coddington, *Gettysburg Campaign,* 573; Sauers, "'Rarely Has Such Skill,'" 243. Cleaves writes of Gettysburg in his introduction, "'Victory! Waterloo Eclipsed!!' proclaimed the *Philadelphia Inquirer.* And so it was." Cleaves, *Meade of Gettysburg,* xiii.

80. Hattaway and Jones, *How the North Won,* 416; Jones, *Civil War Command and Strategy,* 168; Weigley, *Great Civil War,* 254.

81. *OR,* vol. 27, pt. 1, Halleck to Meade, July 28, 1863, 104 (unofficial letter); Henry Hunt to Alexander Webb, Jan. 12, 1888, in Powell, *Fifth Army Corps,* 559.

82. Walker, "Meade at Gettysburg," 407.

3. THE PURSUIT OF LEE

1. *OR,* vol. 27, pt. 3, Meade to Couch, July 3, 1863, 9:57 P.M., 499. Couch confirmed the intelligence of "fortified mountain passes" in a message sent the next day to Meade: "Unquestionably the rebels have fortified the passes in South Mountain. Such information was given me a week ago from Gettysburg." Ibid., 515.

2. *OR,* vol. 27, pt. 3, Butterfield to Newton, July 4, 1863, 513; *OR,* vol. 27, pt. 1, Meade to Halleck, July 4, 1863, 78; *OR,* vol. 27, pt. 3: Meade to Lee, July 4, 1863, 514; circulars, 519–20; Meade to French, July 4, 1863, 517–18. French had been ordered to "annoy and harass" Lee's army in its retreat and cut his communications, if possible. Ibid., 501.

3. Brown, *Retreat from Gettysburg,* 93–122; Wittenberg, Petruzzi, and Nugent, *One Continuous Fight,* 30, 36–38; Coddington, *Gettysburg Campaign,* 540–41.

4. *OR,* vol. 27, pt. 1, Pleasonton report, 916; Coddington, *Gettysburg Campaign,* 543–44; *OR,* vol. 27, pt. 1, Meade to Halleck, July 4, 1863, 12 noon, 78; *OR,* vol. 27, pt. 3, General Orders No. 68, July 4, 1863, 519.

5. *OR,* vol. 27, pt. 3, Lincoln to Halleck, July 6, 1862, 567; Burlingame and Ettlinger, *Inside Lincoln's White House,* 62; *OR,* vol. 27, pt. 3: Circular, Headquarters, Army of the Potomac, June 30, 1863, 415; General Orders No. 68, July 4, 1863, 519.

6. Thomas Neill commanded the Second Brigade, Third Division, Sixth Corps. *JCCW,* Butterfield testimony, 426–27, and Meade testimony, 351. Hays took command of the Second Corps after the wounding of Gibbon and Hancock, and Birney took command of the Third Corps after the wounding of Sickles.

7. *OR,* vol. 27, pt. 3, Seth Williams to Sedgwick, July 4, 1863, 517; *OR,* vol. 27, pt. 1, Meade to Halleck, July 4, 1863, 10 P.M., 78.

8. Brown, *Retreat from Gettysburg,* 119–21, 126, 134–46.

9. *OR,* vol. 27, pt. 3: Butterfield to Sykes, July 5, 1863, 530; Sykes to Butterfield, July 5, 1863, 4:30 A.M., 530; Butterfield to Sedgwick, July 5, 1863, 530–31; three signal officer messages beginning at 5:40 A.M., July 5, 1863, 532; Butterfield to Smith, July 5, 1863, 531; Coddington, *Gettysburg Campaign,* 561; *OR,* vol. 27, pt. 3: Circular, July 5, 1863, 532–33; Meade to Sedgwick, July 5, 1863, 537.

10. *OR,* vol. 27, pt. 3, Meade to Sedgwick, July 5, 1863, 12:30 P.M., 535; *OR,* vol. 27, pt. 1, Sedgwick report, 663; *OR,* vol. 27, pt. 3: Meade to Smith, July 5, 1863, 8:00 P.M., 539; Meade to Sedgwick, July 5, 1863, 7:30 P.M., 537.

11. *OR,* vol. 27, pt. 3: Haupt to Halleck, July 4, 1863, 523; Haupt, *Reminiscences,* 220–29; *OR,* vol. 27, pt. 3, Lincoln to Halleck, July 6, 1863, 567; Stoker, *Grand Design,* 300.

12. *OR,* vol. 27, pt. 3, Couch to Meade, July 5, 1863, 9 A.M., 548; Coddington, *Gettysburg Campaign,* 549; *OR,* vol. 27, pt. 3: Circular, July 5, 1863, 533; Meade to Smith, July 5, 1863, 539.

13. Wittenberg, *One Continuous Fight,* 78; *OR,* vol. 27, pt. 3, Special Orders 181, July 5, 1863, 543; Meade, *Life and Letters,* 2:125–26; George G. Meade to Margaret Meade, July 5, 1863, Meade Papers, HSP. Meade had to know he had created an enemy in Doubleday through his dismissal; Doubleday would become one of Meade's harshest critics in years to come.

14. *OR,* vol. 27, pt. 3, Meade to Sedgwick, July 6, 1863, 2 A.M., 554.

15. George G. Meade to Margaret Meade, July 18, 1863, Meade Papers, HSP.

16. Weigley, *Great Civil War*, 62; Hattaway and Jones, *How the North Won*, 419n91.

17. *OR*, vol. 27, pt. 1, Halleck to Meade, July 5, 1863, 79; Williams, *Lincoln and His Generals*, 267; Boritt, "'Unfinished Work,'" 90. Boritt refers to Carl von Clausewitz.

18. *OR*, vol. 27, pt. 3: Sedgwick to Seth Williams, July 6, 1863, 555; Newton to Sedgwick, July 6, 1863, 3 A.M., 555; Seth Williams to Newton, July 6, 1863, 7:40 A.M., 557; Meade to Sedgwick, July 6, 1863, 9 A.M., 558; Meade to Couch, July 6, 1863, 9:50 A.M., 559; Pleasonton to French, July 6, 1863, 11 A.M., 559; McIntosh to Howard, July 6, 1863, 560; Warren to Sedgwick, July 6, 1863, 561.

19. *OR*, vol. 27, pt. 3: Meade to Couch, July 6, 1863, 4:40 P.M., 579, "the army is now in motion"; Meigs to Ingalls, July 6, 1863, 5 P.M., 569; Rucker to Ingalls, July 6, 1863, 9:30 P.M., 569; Schenck to Halleck, July 6, 1863, 7:45 A.M., 570; Schenck to Halleck, July 6, 1863, 8:30 A.M., 570–71; Meade to Couch, July 6, 1863, 8 A.M., 577; Couch to Meade, July 6, 1863, 577–78; Seth Williams to Smith, July 6, 1863, 579; Warren to Smith, July 6, 1863, 579.

20. Coddington, *Gettysburg Campaign*, 552–55; Wittenberg, *One Continuous Fight*, 107–42; Brown, *Retreat from Gettysburg*, 217–56.

21. *OR*, vol. 27, pt. 3, Warren to Smith, July 6, 1863, 10 P.M., 580–81.

22. Coddington, *Gettysburg Campaign*, 555; Brown, *Retreat from Gettysburg*, 257–87.

23. Brown, *Retreat from Gettysburg*, 274–87.

24. *OR*, vol. 27, pt. 1: Halleck to Meade, July 7, 1863, 3 P.M., 82; Halleck to Meade, July 7, 1863, 8:45 P.M., 82–83; Halleck to Meade, July 7, 1863, 83; Brown, *Retreat from Gettysburg*, has a gripping account of the bridge-destroying operation of July 4 (89–92).

25. *OR*, vol. 27, pt. 3: Lt. W. A. Roebling to General Warren, July 8, 1863, 606, "Went over both gaps on the mountain. The roads are frightful"; Howard to Warren, July 8, 1863, 6 A.M., 601; Howard to Williams, July 8, 1863, 604; Haupt to Meigs, July 8, 1863, 609; Ingalls to Rucker, July 8, 1863, 608.

26. Weigley, *Great Civil War*, 254.

27. *OR*, vol. 27, pt. 3: Halleck to Meade, July 8, 1863, 12:30 P.M., 605; Meade to Halleck, July 8, 1863, 3 P.M., 605–6; *OR*, vol. 27, pt. 1, Halleck to Meade, July 8, 1863, 85.

28. George G. Meade to Margaret Meade, July 8, 1863, Meade Papers, HSP.

29. George G. Meade to Margaret Meade, July 10, 1863, Meade Papers, HSP.

30. *OR*, vol. 27, pt. 1, Meade to Halleck, July 9, 1863, 11 A.M., 86.

31. Ibid.: Halleck to Meade, July 9, 1863, 3 P.M.; Halleck to Meade, July 9, 1863, 4:40 P.M., 88.

32. Brown, *Retreat from Gettysburg*, 298–307; Wittenberg, *One Continuous Fight*, 207–28.

33. *OR*, vol. 27, pt. 1, Halleck to Meade, July 10, 1863, 9 P.M., 89; Boritt, "'Unfinished Work,'" 99–101.

34. Brown, *Retreat from Gettysburg*, 309–18; Wittenberg, *One Continuous Fight*, 240–58. Though Brig. Gen. Henry M. Naglee had sixty-five hundred men and French another eight thousand men, it was debatable whether they would make it to Meade in time for a battle. Kelley's small army of forty-five hundred, marching east from Cumberland toward Williamsport, had received contradictory orders as it marched, and it was not close enough by July 12 to be of much help to Meade. See Wittenberg, *One Continuous Fight*, 257–58.

35. *OR*, vol. 27, pt. 3, Mackenzie to Warren, July 12, 1863, 12m, 669.

36. *OR*, vol. 27, pt. 1, Meade to Halleck, July 12, 1863, 4:30 P.M., 91.

37. *JCCW*, Meade testimony, 336; Warren testimony, 379–81; Wadsworth testimony, 415–16. Hays also opposed attack.

38. Ibid., Humphreys testimony, 396–97; Warren testimony, 379–81.

39. *OR*, vol. 27, pt. 1, Meade to Halleck, July 13, 1863, 5 P.M., 91–92; *OR*, vol. 27, pt. 3, General Kelley to the Adjutant General, July 13, 1863, 4:30 P.M., 680.

40. Nevins, *Diary of Battle*, 261; Brown, *Retreat from Gettysburg*, 310 and 312.

41. *OR*, vol. 27, pt. 1, Halleck to Meade, July 13, 1863, 9:30 P.M., 92.

42. *OR,* vol. 27, pt. 3: Circular, July 13, 1863, 9 P.M., 675; Humphreys to French, July 13, 1863, 9:30 P.M., 675–76; Pleasonton to Gregg, July 13, 1863, 9 P.M., 676. The Eleventh Corps had already done some probing that night, and the Third Corps would be the reserve for Second and Twelfth Corps the next day.

43. Brown, *Retreat from Gettysburg,* 324–29 (quotation on p. 329); Wittenberg, *One Continuous Fight,* 264.

44. Brown, *Retreat from Gettysburg,* 329–31; *OR,* vol. 27, pt. 3: Howard to Humphreys, July 14, 1863, 6:35 A.M., 683; Howard to Humphreys, July 14, 1863, 8 A.M., 683; Circular, July 14, 1863, 8:30 A.M., 686, "each corps commander will move forward with his corps to support the reconnaissance, which will be pushed until the enemy is met"; Wittenberg, *One Continuous Fight,* 286–95.

45. *OR,* vol. 27, pt. 1: Meade to Halleck, July 14, 1863, 11 A.M., 92; Halleck to Meade, July 14, 1863, 1 P.M., 92; Meade to Halleck, July 14, 1863, 2:30 P.M., 93; Halleck to Meade, July 14, 1863, 4:40 P.M., 93–94.

46. Basler, *Collected Works of Abraham Lincoln,* 6:327, letter to George G. Meade, never sent or signed. Lincoln's secretary, John Hay, wrote in his diary on July 14: "The President was deeply grieved. 'We had them within our grasp,' he said. 'We had only to stretch forth our hands and they were ours. And nothing I could say or do would make the Army move.'" Burlingame, *Inside Lincoln's White House,* 62.

47. *New York Herald,* "General Meade's New Campaign—The Rebellion Fairly within Our Grasp," July 17, 1863; *JCCW,* Pleasonton testimony, 361.

48. *JCCW,* Sedgwick testimony, 462.

49. Ibid., Warren testimony, 379–81, and Humphreys testimony, 396–98; Brown, *Retreat from Gettysburg,* 326; Wittenberg, *One Continuous Fight,* 342 (though it must be noted that the authors of *One Continuous Fight* criticize Meade for other decisions he made during the pursuit).

50. George G. Meade to Margaret Meade, July 14, 16, and 18, 1863, Meade Papers, HSP.

51. *OR,* vol. 27, pt. 1, Meade to Halleck, July 31, 1863, unofficial letter, 108–10.

52. Swinton, *Campaigns,* 371.

53. *JCCW,* Pleasonton testimony, citing from memory what he thought were the exact words of General French, 361.

54. George G. Meade to Margaret Meade, July 18, 1863, Meade Papers, HSP.

4. FALL FRUSTRATION

1. *OR,* vol. 27, pt. 1: Meade to Halleck, July 15, 1863, 94; Meade to Halleck, July 16, 1863, 95; Meade to Halleck, July 18, 1863, 96 (quotation); Meade to Halleck, July 19, 1863, 97 (quotation).

2. *OR,* vol. 27, pt. 3: Hill and Lyon to Colonel Locke, July 21, 1863, 3:20 P.M., 735; Merritt to Buford, July 21, 1863, 735; Circular, Headquarters, Army of the Potomac, July 22, 1863, 739–40; Buford to Pleasonton, July 22, 1863, 741–74; Merritt to Smith, July 22, 1863, 742.

3. Ibid., Circular, Headquarters, Army of the Potomac, July 22, 1863, 745–46 (for movement on July 23); *OR,* vol. 27, pt. 1, French report, 489–90; *OR,* vol. 27, pt. 3: Humphreys to French, July 23, 1863, 2:45 P.M., 752–53; Warren to Meade, July 23, 1863, 5:45 P.M., 753.

4. *OR,* vol. 27, pt. 1: Meade to Halleck, July 24, 1863, 98–99; Andrew Humphreys to Rebecca Humphreys, July 25, 1863, in Andrew Atkinson Humphreys Papers, Historical Society of Pennsylvania.

5. *OR,* vol. 27, pt. 3, Circular, Headquarters, Army of the Potomac, July 24, 1863, 759–60; *OR,* vol. 27, pt. 1: Meade to Halleck, July 26, 1863, 101; Halleck to Meade, July 27, 1863, 101;

Meade to Halleck, July 27, 1863, 102; Halleck to Meade, July 27, 1863, 102; Meade to Halleck, July 28, 1863, 103–4.

6. *OR,* vol. 27, pt. 1: Halleck to Meade, July 29, 1863 (Lincoln's note to Halleck enclosed), 105; Halleck to Meade, July 29, 1863, 105–6. Gideon Welles, the opinionated Secretary of the Navy, famously wrote of Halleck, "[He] originates nothing, anticipates nothing, plans nothing, suggests nothing, is good for nothing." Welles, *Diary,* 384.

7. *OR,* vol. 27, pt. 1: Meade to Halleck, July 30, 1863, 106–7; Halleck to Meade, July 29, 1863, 105.

8. Ibid., Halleck to Meade, July 30, 1863, 107–8.

9. Ibid., Meade to Halleck, Aug. 4, 1863, 113.

10. George G. Meade to Margaret Meade, Aug. 16, 1863, Meade Papers, HSP; Meade, *Life and Letters,* copy of letter, Lincoln to Howard, July 21, 1863, 2:138.

11. *OR,* vol. 27, pt. 1: Halleck to Meade, July 28, 1863, 104–5; and Meade to Halleck, July 31, 1863, 108–10 (Halleck's full comments are found at the end of chap. 2). It was fortunate that Meade had no idea what Gideon Welles thought of him. After meeting and listening to Meade for the first time at the Cabinet meeting on August 14, Welles wrote in his diary: "He has a sharp visage and a narrow head. Would do better as a second-in-command than as General-in-chief. Is doubtless a good officer, but not a great and capable commander. . . . On the whole I was as well or better pleased with him that I expected I should be." Welles, *Diary,* 404. He had been extremely critical of Meade before that, largely based on the escape of Lee's army from Pennsylvania.

12. *OR,* vol. 29, pt. 2, Meade to Halleck, Aug. 16, 1863, 53.

13. *OR,* vol. 27, pt. 1: Meade to Halleck, July 19, 1863, 96–97; Meade to Halleck, July 25, 1863, 100; Halleck to Meade, July 26, 1863, 101; Jordan, *"Happiness Is Not My Companion,"* 101–2; George G. Meade to Margaret Meade, Aug. 9, 1863, Meade Papers, HSP. Garrard had assumed command of the Third Brigade, Second Division, Fifth Corps, after the death of Brig. Gen. Stephen H. Weed at Gettysburg. He was also a friend of Meade's son George.

14. Lowe, *Meade's Army,* 29 (Sept. 6, 1863); Jordan, *"Happiness Is Not My Companion,"* 116.

15. George G. Meade to Margaret Meade, Aug. 31, 1863, Meade Papers, HSP; for example of speech coverage see *New York Herald Tribune,* Aug. 31, 1863.

16. Lowe, *Meade's Army,* 27 (Sept. 3, 1863). Meade and Lyman had stayed in touch since working together in Florida before the war, and when Lyman offered his services as a volunteer aide-de-camp in 1863, Meade accepted the offer. Commissioned as a lieutenant colonel in the Massachusetts Militia by Governor Andrew, Lyman faithfully served Meade until the end of the war. See introduction in Lowe, *Meade's Army,* 1–24.

17. Agassiz, *Meade's Headquarters,* 21 (Sept. 22, 1863); 21–22 (Sept. 24, 1863); 23 (Sept. 29, 1863); 41 (Nov. 3, 1863); 48–49 (Nov. 15, 1863); 50 (Nov. 19, 1863). All letters in this book are from Lyman to his wife, unless otherwise noted.

18. Schaff, *Battle of the Wilderness,* 40–41.

19. Lowe, *Meade's Army,* 28 (Sept. 5, 1863); Agassiz, *Meade's Headquarters,* 25 (Sept. 29, 1863).

20. Henderson, *Road to Bristoe Station,* 31–41; George G. Meade to Margaret Meade, Sept. 13, 1863, Meade Papers, HSP; *OR,* vol. 29, pt. 2, Meade to Halleck, Sept. 14, 1863, 179–80.

21. *OR,* vol. 29, pt. 2: Halleck to Meade, Sept. 15, 1863, 186–87; Lincoln to Halleck, Sept. 15, 1863, 187.

22. Henderson, *Road to Bristoe Station,* 46–63; *OR,* vol. 29, pt. 2, Meade to Halleck, Sept. 18, 1863, 201–2.

23. *OR,* vol. 29, pt. 2: Halleck to Meade, Sept. 19, 1863, 206–7; Lincoln to Halleck, Sept. 19, 1863, 207–8.

24. Ibid., Humphreys to Commanding Officer, Cavalry Corps, Sept. 20, 1863, 215–16; Humphreys to Meade, Sept. 23, 1863, 224; Henderson, *Road to Bristoe Station,* 51–63.

25. Henderson, *Road to Bristoe Station,* 64–65; Welles, *Diary,* Sept. 21, 1863, 438–40.

26. *OR,* vol. 29, pt. 2, Meade to Halleck, Sept. 22, 1863, 220; Henderson, *Road to Bristoe Station,* 66–67; Burlingame, *Abraham Lincoln,* 557; George G. Meade to Margaret Meade, Sept. 24, 1863, Meade Papers, HSP.

27. *OR,* vol. 29, pt. 1, Halleck to Meade, Sept. 24, 1863, 147.

28. Ibid.: Meade to Halleck, Sept. 24, 1863, 3 A.M., 147; Halleck to Meade, Sept. 24, 1863, 9:30 A.M., 147; Meade to Halleck, Sept. 24, 1863, 148; Williams to Howard, Sept. 24, 1863, 148; Meade to Slocum, Sept. 24, 1863, 148.

29. Henderson, *Road to Bristoe Station,* 69–72.

30. Rafuse, *George Gordon Meade,* 99; Henderson, *Road to Bristoe Station,* 74–75; *OR,* vol. 29, pt. 2, Meade to Halleck, Oct. 9, 1863, 276.

31. Henderson, *Road to Bristoe Station,* 78–119; *OR,* vol. 29, pt. 2, Meade to Halleck, Oct. 10, 1863, 279.

32. Henderson, *Road to Bristoe Station,* 120–32; *OR,* vol. 29, pt. 2: Humphreys to Sedgwick, Oct. 12, 1863, 9:15 P.M., 298–99; Meade to Halleck, Oct. 12, 1863, 293; Meade to Halleck, Oct. 12, 1863, 294; Circular, Headquarters, Army of the Potomac, Oct. 13, 1863, 12:50 A.M., 302–3.

33. Henderson, *Road to Bristoe Station,* 137–40; *OR,* vol. 29, pt. 2: Meade to Halleck, Oct. 13, 1863, 1:30 P.M., 305; Meade to Halleck, Oct. 13, 1863, 10 P.M., 305–6.

34. Henderson, *Road to Bristoe Station,* 142; George G. Meade to Margaret Meade, Sept. 16, 1863, Meade Papers, HSP; *OR,* vol. 29, pt. 2: Circular, Headquarters, Army of the Potomac, Oct. 13, 1863, 304; Circular, Headquarters, Army of the Potomac, Oct. 13, 1863, 1:00 P.M., 304–5.

35. Henderson, *Road to Bristoe Station,* 140–47; *OR,* vol. 29, pt. 2, Circular, Headquarters, Army of the Potomac, Oct. 13, 1863, 10:30 P.M., 306–7.

36. *OR,* vol. 29, pt. 1: Warren report, 237; Stuart report, 447–49; Henderson, *Road to Bristoe Station,* 150–55.

37. *OR,* vol. 29, pt. 1, Warren report, 237–41; Henderson, *Road to Bristoe Station,* 155–62.

38. *OR,* vol. 29, pt. 2, Meade to Halleck, Oct. 14, 1863, 313; *OR,* vol. 29, pt. 1, Warren report, 241.

39. *OR,* vol. 29, pt. 1: Hill report, 426; Anderson report, 428–29; Heth report, 430–31; Henderson, *Road to Bristoe Station,* 167–68.

40. *OR,* vol. 29, pt. 1: Hill report, 426–27; Heth report, 430.

41. Ibid.: Warren report, 241–42, and Webb report, 277–78; Henderson, *Road to Bristoe Station,* 169–82.

42. *OR,* vol. 29, pt. 1: Warren report, 242, 243, and 250, and Heth report, 433; Henderson, *Road to Bristoe Station,* 179–83.

43. *OR,* vol. 29, pt. 1, Robert E. Lee report, 410–11; Henderson, *Road to Bristoe Station,* 187–91.

44. *OR,* vol. 29, pt. 1, Lee report, 411; Henderson, *Road to Bristoe Station,* 192–94.

45. Henderson, *Road to Bristoe Station,* 194–201.

46. *OR,* vol. 29, pt. 2: Halleck to Meade, Oct. 15, 1863, 328; Lincoln to Halleck, Oct. 16, 1863, 332.

47. Ibid., Meade to Halleck, Oct. 16, 1863, 333.

48. Ibid.: Meade to Halleck, Oct. 17, 1863, 338–39; Halleck to Meade, Oct. 18, 1863, 345; Meade to Halleck, Oct. 18, 1863, 345; Henderson, *Road to Bristoe Station,* 199–201.

49. Henderson, *Road to Bristoe Station,* 201–5.

50. *OR,* vol. 29, pt. 2: Halleck to Meade, Oct. 18, 1863, 346; Meade to Halleck, Oct. 18, 1863, 346; Halleck to Meade, Oct. 19, 1863, 354; Meade to Halleck, Oct. 19, 1863, 361–62.

51. Ibid., Halleck to Meade, Oct. 21, 1863, 363; George Meade to Margaret Meade, Oct. 23, 1863, Meade Papers, HSP; *OR,* vol. 29, pt. 2: Halleck to Meade, Oct. 24, 1863, 375; Lincoln to Halleck, Oct. 24, 1863, 375–76; Meade to Halleck, Oct. 24, 1863, 376–77.

52. George G. Meade to Margaret Meade, Oct. 21, 1863, Meade Papers, HSP; Graham and Skoch, *Mine Run,* 8.

53. *OR,* vol. 29, pt. 2, Meade to Halleck, Nov. 2, 1863, 409–10; Rafuse, *George Gordon Meade,* 103.

54. *OR,* vol. 29, pt. 2: Halleck to Meade, Nov. 3, 1863, 412; Humphreys to Commanding Officer Cavalry Corps (Pleasonton), Nov. 3, 1863, 413.

55. George G. Meade to Margaret Meade, Nov. 3, 1863, Meade Papers, HSP.

56. *OR,* vol. 29, pt. 2: Circular, Headquarters, Army of the Potomac, Nov. 6, 1863, 425–26; Williams to French, Nov. 6, 1863, 426–27; Williams to Sedgwick, Nov. 6, 1863, 427–28.

57. Ibid.: Humphreys to Sedgwick, Nov. 7, 1863, 430; French to Humphreys, Nov. 7, 1863, 431; *OR,* vol. 29, pt. 1: 561 (Union casualties) and 632 (Confederate casualties); Graham and Skoch, *Mine Run,* 10–15.

58. Graham and Skoch, *Mine Run,* 15–20.

59. Ibid., 16–28; *OR,* vol. 29, pt. 1: 629 (Confederate casualties) and 560 (Union casualties).

60. Graham and Skoch, *Mine Run,* 27–28.

61. *OR,* vol. 29, pt. 2: Humphreys to Sedgwick, Nov. 7, 1863, 430; Humphreys to Sedgwick, Nov. 7, 1863, 431–32; Humphreys to Sedgwick, Nov. 7, 1863, 432; Humphreys to Sedgwick, Nov. 7, 1863, 433.

62. For a brief discussion of the fighting at Kelly's Ford, see Gottfried, *Maps of the Bristoe Station,* 104–9.

63. Cleaves, *Meade of Gettysburg,* 205; Leech, *Reveille in Washington,* 271; *Washington Evening Star,* Nov. 12, 1863, p. 1; *New York Herald,* Nov. 12, 1863, p. 4; George G. Meade to Margaret Meade, Nov. 9, 1863, Meade Papers, HSP; *OR,* vol. 29, pt. 2, Lincoln to Meade, Nov. 9, 1863, 443; Agassiz, *Meade's Headquarters,* 46 (Nov. 9, 1863).

64. *OR,* vol. 29, pt. 2, Meade to Halleck, Nov. 8, 1863, 435; Graham and Skoch, *Mine Run,* 30–38.

65. *New York World,* Nov. 12, 1863; McMahon, "From Gettysburg," 87–88n; *OR,* vol. 29, pt. 3: Meade to Halleck, Nov. 13, 1863, 449; Buford to Colonel Smith, Nov. 15, 1863, 461; Meade to Halleck, Nov. 20, 1863, 473–74; Graham and Skoch, *Mine Run,* 36–38.

66. *OR,* vol. 29, pt. 2: Brig. Gen. George A. Custer to Col. C. Ross Smith, Nov. 20, 1863, 474–75; Brig. Gen. Judson Kilpatrick to Col. C. Ross Smith, Nov. 21, 1863, 476; Meade to Halleck, Nov. 20, 1863, 473–74; Sparks, *Inside Lincoln's Army,* Nov. 19, 1863, 310; *OR,* vol. 29, pt. 1: Meade's report, Dec. 7, 1863, 13; Field Report of the Army of Northern Virginia, Nov. 20, 1863, 823; Returns of the Army of the Potomac, Nov. 20, 1863, 677.

67. *OR,* vol. 29, pt. 2: Circular to all corps commanders, Nov. 22, 1863, 477; Circular to all corps commanders, Nov. 23, 1863, 480–81.

68. Ibid., Williams to French, Nov. 24, 1863, 481; *OR,* vol. 29, pt. 1, Meade's report, 13.

69. *OR,* vol. 29, pt. 2: Circular, Headquarters, Army of the Potomac, Nov. 25, 1863, 488; Lee to Davis, Nov. 25, 1863, 846; Lee to Davis, Nov. 12, 1863, 832; Watson to Meade, Nov. 25, 1863, 489; Williams to Warren, Nov. 25, 1863, 488.

70. *OR,* vol. 29, pt. 1: French report, 736–38; Prince report, 760–61; Meade report, 14.

71. Ibid.: Meade report, 14; Lee report, 827–28.

72. *OR,* vol. 29, pt. 1: Samuel S. Carroll report, 730–31; Harry T. Hays report, 838–39; Rodes report, 877; Warren report, 695; Sykes report, 794; McGregg report, 806–7; Stuart report, 898–99; Prince report, 761–63; *OR,* vol. 29, pt. 2, Humphreys to French, Nov. 27, 1863, 500.

73. Graham and Skoch, *Mine Run,* 56–57; *OR,* vol. 29, pt. 1: William A. Witcher report, 856; George H. Steuart report, 863; French report, 742–43; Edward Johnson report, 847; Circular, Headquarters, Third Army Corps, Enclosure, casualty report, 746. Just one week after the battle, Meade requested that French provide an "explanation of all the facts and circumstances which in any way bear upon the causes of the delays and failures." *OR,* vol. 29, pt. 1, Humphreys to French, Dec. 3, 1863, 746.

74. Sparks, *Inside Lincoln's Army,* 314 (Nov. 27, 1863). Patrick wrote in his diary that "Meade became very greatly out of temper about it [French's performance]"; *OR,* vol. 29, pt. 1: Meade's report, 15–16; Lee's reports, 825–26 and 828–29; Warren's report, 695–96; Graham and Skoch, *Mine Run,* 59 and 69.

75. *OR,* vol. 29, pt. 1: Warren report, 696; Meade report, 16; Lowe, *Meade's Army,* 73, (Nov. 28, 1863); Hess, *Field Armies and Fortifications,* 298; Agassiz, *Meade's Headquarters,* 55 (Nov. 28, 1863).

76. *OR,* vol. 29, pt. 1: Warren report, 696; Meade report, 16.

77. Ibid.: Warren report, 696–97; J. E. B. Stuart report, 899–900; Lee report, 829; Meade report, 16–17.

78. Graham and Skoch, *Mine Run,* 73–74 (Stevens quoted in same); Lowe, *Meade's Army,* 74, (Nov. 30, 1863).

79. *OR,* vol. 29, pt. 1, Warren report, 697–98; Livermore, *Days and Events,* 304. Livermore wrote his memoir in 1867, and his children published it in 1920.

80. Agassiz, *Meade's Headquarters,* 56–57 (Nov. 30, 1863); *OR,* vol. 29, pt. 2, Warren to Meade, Nov. 30, 1863, 7:45 A.M., 517; Lowe, *Meade's Army,* 75 (Nov. 30, 1863); Walker, *Second Army Corps,* 385. When Meade stopped to give French the news on the way back from his visit with Warren, he got an earful: "You have taken all my troops away from me, an old veteran in the service, and have given them to a beardless boy, and for what? Where is your young Napoleon? Why don't we hear the sound of his guns?" Meade did not tarry to argue (ibid.).

81. *OR,* vol. 29, pt. 2: Headquarters, Army of the Potomac, To the Commanders of the First, Third, Fifth, and Sixth Army Corps, Nov. 30, 1863, 8:40 P.M., 520. All replies to Meade's questions were sent on Nov. 30, 1863; see Newton [First Corps] to Williams (520–21); Sykes [Fifth Corps] to Williams (521); French [Third Corps] to Williams. *OR,* vol. 29, pt. 1, Meade report, 18; Graham and Skoch, *Mine Run,* 80–81. Lee had ordered two divisions to march south around the Union left flank, showing the offensive spirit he was known for. *OR,* vol. 29, pt. 1, Hill report, 896.

82. Sparks, *Inside Lincoln's Army,* 317 (Nov. 30, 1863); *OR,* vol. 29, pt. 1, Meade report, 18. Hess writes that "the men of Lee's army had never built such a fieldwork as this one at Mine Run." See Hess, *Field Armies and Fortifications,* 294 and 296.

83. Hennessy, "'I Dread the Spring,'" 67.

5. WINTER'S WORRIES

1. *OR,* vol. 29, pt. 2: Circular, Headquarters, Army of the Potomac, Dec. 1, 1863, 530–32; Humphreys to Sykes, Dec. 2, 1863, 536; Circular, Headquarters, Army of the Potomac, Dec. 3, 1863, 539 (quotation); Williams to Sykes, Dec. 3, 1863, 539 (quotation); Circular, Headquarters, Army of the Potomac, Dec. 3, 1863, 540; Meade to Halleck, Dec. 4, 1863, 540; Halleck to Meade, Dec. 4, 1863, 540 (quotation).

2. George G. Meade to Margaret Meade, Dec. 7 and 2 (quotations), 1863, Meade Papers, HSP.

3. George G. Meade to Margaret Meade, Dec. 3, 1863, Meade Papers, HSP; Lowe, *Meade's Army,* 79 (Dec. 8, 1863); George G. Meade to Margaret Meade, Dec. 7, 1863, Meade

Papers, HSP. Hennessy writes that Meade "reaped a windfall of goodwill" from the soldiers for his decision at Mine Run. See "'I Dread the Spring,'" 68.

4. *OR*, vol. 29, pt. 1, Meade report, Dec. 7, 1863, 12–20.

5. Ibid.: Warren report, Dec. 3, 1863, 694–98; French's report, Dec. 4, 1863, 736–41; Henry Prince's report, Dec. 6, 1863, 760–65. Prince implied that his orders were confusing, French blamed Prince for his slowness, and Warren emphasized the correct moves of the Second Corps. For letter from George G. Meade to Margaret Meade, see Dec. 11, 1863, Meade Papers, HSP.

6. *OR*, vol. 29, pt. 2: Circular, Headquarters, Army of the Potomac, Dec. 3, 1863, 539; George A. Custer to C. Ross Smith, Dec. 4, 1863, 542; Sparks, *Inside Lincoln's Army*, 321–22 (Dec. 8, 1863), and 322 (Dec. 10, 1863). Patrick fumed in his diary on December 9, "I do not feel right towards Meade for his entire want of management, as to the interior discipline and economy of the Army." Ibid., 321. *OR*, vol. 29, pt. 2, Meade to Halleck, Dec. 12, 1863, 556–57.

7. George G. Meade to Margaret Meade, Dec. 12, 1863, Meade Papers, HSP; Lowe, *Meade's Army*, 80 (Dec. 13, 1863).

8. Williams, *Lincoln and His Generals*, 292–93; *OR*, vol. 31, pt. 3, Charles Dana to Ulysses S. Grant, Dec. 21, 1863, 457–58; George G. Meade to Margaret Meade, Dec. 28, 1863, Meade Papers, HSP.

9. Cleaves, *Meade of Gettysburg*, 218–19; George Meade to Margaret Meade, Jan. 5, 1863, Meade Papers, HSP; George Meade to John Sergeant ("Sergie") Meade, Jan. 6, 1863, Meade Papers, HSP; *OR*, vol. 33: Meade to Halleck, Jan. 5, 1864, 346–47; Sedgwick to Colonel Townsend, assistant adjutant general, Jan. 16, 1864, 384. On January 5, 1864, Meade reported to Halleck that 16,189 veteran volunteers had reenlisted, with more expected to do the same. *OR*, vol. 33, Meade to Halleck, Jan. 5, 1864, 347.

10. Cleaves, *Meade of Gettysburg*, 219; Pennypacker, *General Meade*, 257–58.

11. George G. Meade to Margaret Meade, Feb. 14, 1864, Meade Papers, HSP; on second round of meetings, George G. Meade to Margaret Meade, Feb. 21, 1864, Meade Papers, HSP; George G. Meade to Margaret Meade, Feb. 24, 1864, Meade Papers, HSP; Schultz, *Dahlgren Affair*, 83–88; Lowe, *Meade's Army*, 103 (Feb. 23, 1864, description of Kilpatrick); Schultz, *Dahlgren Affair*, 69–82; *OR*, vol. 33, 171–74, report of Meade, proposal of Kilpatrick, response to proposal from Pleasonton. Lyman wrote to his wife, "Kilpatrick is sent for by the President; oh, ah! Everybody knows it at once: he is a cavalry officer; it must be a raid. All Willard's chatters of it." Agassiz, *Meade's Headquarters*, 77 (Mar. 1, 1864).

12. George G. Meade to Margaret Meade, Feb. 24, 1864, Meade Papers, HSP; Agassiz, *Meade's Headquarters*, 73 (Feb. 22, 1864); Lowe, *Meade's Army*, 118 (Apr. 2, 1864); George G. Meade to Henry Cram, Mar. 15, 1864, Meade Papers, HSP.

13. Simpson, *Ulysses S. Grant*, 258–63.

14. Grimsley, *And Keep Moving On*, 230; Hsieh, *West Pointers and Civil War*, 241n28; Taaffe, *Commanding the Army*, 138.

15. George G. Meade to Margaret Meade, July 26, 1863, Meade Papers, HSP; Simpson, *Ulysses S. Grant*, 219–22 and 246–47; George G. Meade to Margaret Meade, Dec. 20, 1863, Meade Papers, HSP. Chapters 12 and 13 of Simpson's *Ulysses S. Grant* (216–65), covering Grant's activities and growth as a leader from July 1863 until March 1864, show in stunning detail how assiduously Grant cultivated the favor of generals and politicians alike, without overplaying his hand. His ability to handle politicians—such as Charles Dana, who he turned from enemy to ally—is particularly striking when compared to Meade's failed efforts to remain aloof from politics.

16. George G. Meade to Margaret Meade, Feb. 20 and Mar. 8, 1864, Meade Papers, HSP.

17. George G. Meade to Margaret Meade, Mar. 10, 1864, Meade Papers, HSP; Grant, *Personal Memoirs*, 405; George G. Meade to Margaret Meade, Mar. 14, 1864, Meade Papers, HSP.

18. Grant, *Personal Memoirs,* 405; Rafuse, "'Wherever Lee Goes,'" 59. Grant's full plan will be described in the next chapter. George G. Meade to Margaret Meade, Apr. 13, 1864, Meade Papers, HSP.

19. Tap, *Over Lincoln's Shoulder,* 8 (quotations), 2–9, 25–33; Stowe, "Certain Grave Charges," 21.

20. *JCCW:* Feb. 26, 1864 (Sickles testimony), 295–304; Mar. 1, 1864 (Doubleday testimony), 305–14; Mar. 3–4, 1864 (Howe testimony), 316–29; note on meeting with Lincoln, Mar. 4, 1864, xix; Tap, *Over Lincoln's Shoulder,* 182–83. Loan had been appointed to replace John Covode on the committee in January 1864. He too was considered a radical Republican. See Tap, *Over Lincoln's Shoulder,* 175–76. Howe surely knew the words the leading members of the committee wanted to hear; he accused the officer corps of the Army of the Potomac of harboring "too much copperheadism in it" (*JCCW,* 327).

21. Tap, *Over Lincoln's Shoulder,* 35; George G. Meade to Margaret Meade, Mar. 6, 1864, Meade Papers, HSP; *JCCW,* 343 and 333.

22. *JCCW,* 347.

23. *New York Tribune,* Mar. 7, 1864; George G. Meade to Margaret Meade, Mar. 9, 1864, Meade Papers, HSP.

24. *New York Herald,* Mar. 12 and Apr. 4, 1864 (Historicus); *New York Herald,* Mar. 18 (staff officer) and Mar. 21 (Barnes), 1864; *OR,* vol. 27, pt. 1, Meade to Colonel Townsend, Mar. 15, 1864, 127–28; Basler, *Collected Works of Abraham Lincoln,* Abraham Lincoln to George G. Meade, Mar. 29, 1864, 7:273.

25. George G. Meade to Margaret Meade, Mar. 14, 1864, Meade Papers, HSP; Tap, *Over Lincoln's Shoulder,* 185.

26. George G. Meade to Henry A. Cram, Mar. 15, 1864, Meade Papers, HSP; George G. Meade to Margaret Meade, Mar. 14, 1864, Meade Papers, HSP; Tap, *Over Lincoln's Shoulder,* 25–32, 176–77, 185–86; George G. Meade to Margaret Meade, Mar. 26, 1864, Meade Papers, HSP; George G. Meade to Margaret Meade, Apr. 2, 1864, Meade Papers, HSP.

27. George G. Meade to Margaret Meade, Mar. 20, 1864, Meade Papers, HSP; George G. Meade to Henry Cram, Mar. 15, 1864, Meade Papers, HSP; George G. Meade to Margaret Meade, Mar. 20, 1864, Meade Papers, HSP.

28. *JCCW,* 1865, 1:417–35 (Butterfield, Mar. 25 and 29 testimony).

29. Ibid.: 435–39 (Meade, Apr. 1 testimony), 439–47 (Gibbon, Apr. 1 testimony), 447–59 (Hunt, Apr. 4 testimony), 459–64 (Sedgwick, Apr. 8 testimony), 464–68 (Williams, Apr. 18 testimony, quotations from 466 and 468); Tap, *Over Lincoln's Shoulder,* 186–87; Simpson, *Ulysses S. Grant,* 263–73.

30. George G. Meade to Margaret Meade, Feb. 14, 1864, Meade Papers, HSP; *OR,* vol. 33: Meade to Halleck, Mar. 4, 1864, 638, and Stanton to Halleck, Mar. 5, 1864, 639; Simpson, *Ulysses S. Grant,* 283; *OR,* vol. 33: General Orders, Army of the Potomac, Mar. 24, 1864, 723; Special Orders, War Department, Mar. 24, 1864, 722; Special Orders, War Department, Mar. 25, 1864, 732; George G. Meade to Margaret Meade, Mar. 29, 1864, Meade Papers, HSP; George G. Meade to Margaret Meade, Mar. 24, 1864, Meade Papers, HSP; *OR,* vol. 33, General Orders, War Department, Apr. 4, 1864, 798. Sykes, for one, was not pleased with his removal. In orders sent to the men of the Fifth Corps he wrote, "In obeying an order so wholly unexpected, I part from you with the profoundest regret." *OR,* vol. 33, Mar. 24, 1864, 724.

31. Humphreys, *Virginia Campaign,* 3 and 12; Walker, *General Hancock,* 153; Lowe, *Meade's Army,* 117 (Mar. 30, 1864), and 119 (Apr. 7, 1864); George G. Meade to Margaret Meade, Apr. 16, 1864, Meade Papers, HSP. As often was the case, Meade presented a positive spin on events, either to reassure his wife or himself that everything would turn out all right. By contrast, Lyman observed that the "merry Excelsiors have sewed the trefoil [of the Third Corps] to the seats of their trowsers," and Humphreys wrote that the dissolution and

merger of old units into the three corps made them lose their "identity" and have "their pride and *esprit de corps* wounded." Lowe, *Meade's Army,* 119 (Apr. 7, 1864); Humphreys, *Virginia Campaign,* 3.

32. Schultz, *Dahlgren Affair,* 77–82, 94–105.

33. Ibid., 108–9; George G. Meade to Margaret Meade, Feb. 29, 1864, Meade Papers, HSP; Schultz, *Dahlgren Affair,* 119–43, 177–78; George G. Meade to Margaret Meade, Mar. 6, 1864, Meade Papers, HSP.

34. Schultz, *Dahlgren Affair,* 156 (quotation), 157, 171–79, 186, and 188–89; *OR,* vol. 33, George G. Meade to Robert E. Lee, Apr. 17, 1864, 180; George G. Meade to Margaret Meade, Apr. 18, 1864, Meade Papers, HSP.

35. *OR,* vol. 33, Ulysses S. Grant to George Meade, Apr. 9, 1864, 827–29 (quotation from 828); Grant, *Personal Memoirs,* 419; Humphreys, *Virginia Campaign,* 9–12; Simpson, *Ulysses S. Grant,* 250–53 and 269–70; Rhea, *Battle of the Wilderness,* 52–53; Rafuse, "'Wherever Lee Goes,'" 59 and 58.

36. Simpson, *Ulysses S. Grant,* 285; George G. Meade to Margaret Meade, Apr. 18 and 24, 1864, Meade Papers, HSP; Cleaves, *Meade of Gettysburg,* 60. It is unfortunate that the scope of this study does not fully include Meade's family life, for he not only was quite close to his wife but also kept in close contact with his children, extended family, and wide circle of friends. Freeman Cleaves covers some of this aspect of his life in his biography of Meade, but a new, longer biography of Meade should be written that fully develops the broader picture of Meade the soldier *and* family man.

37. George G. Meade to Margaret Meade, Apr. 26, 1864, Meade Papers, HSP.

6. NEW COMMANDER, SAME FOE

1. Rhea, *Battle of the Wilderness,* 52; *OR,* vol. 33: 1036 and 1045 (returns for the Army of the Potomac and the Ninth Corps); Grant to Meade, Apr. 9, 1864, 828; Humphreys, *Virginia Campaign,* 9–14; Rhea, *Battle of the Wilderness,* 56–57; *OR,* vol. 36, pt. 1, 133 (troops count).

2. Porter, *Campaigning with Grant,* 36; George G. Meade to Margaret Meade, May 3, 1864, Meade Papers, HSP; Schaff, *Battle of the Wilderness,* 84. Confederate troops felt confident as well. Lt. Col. William T. Poague, who was to play a critical role in the coming battle, recalled that "all were hopeful and confident as the issue of the gigantic struggle with Grant and his immense host, notwithstanding we all knew that General Lee was at a great disadvantage in numbers, equipment, and in food supplies for man and beast. Yet such was our faith in our commander, that we went into the contest cheerfully and not without some curiosity as to Grant's plan of campaign." Cockrell, *Gunner with Stonewall,* 85–86.

3. *OR,* vol. 36, pt. 2: General Orders, May 2, 1864, 331–34, and Office of the Chief Quartermaster, Gen. Rufus Ingalls, 354–55; *OR,* vol. 36, pt. 1, report of Lt. Col. Ira Spaulding, Fiftieth New York Engineers, Aug. 30, 1864, 305–6; Rhea, *Battle of the Wilderness,* 60–64; Grant, *Personal Memoirs,* 449.

4. *OR,* vol. 36, pt. 2: Wilson to Warren, May 4, 1864, 5:50 A.M., 377, and Hancock to Meade, May 4, 1864, 9:50 A.M.; Lowe, *Meade's Army,* 131 (May 4, 1864); *OR,* vol. 36, pt. 2, Circular, Headquarters, Army of the Potomac, May 2, 1864, 334; Grant, "Preparing for the Campaign," 97n; *OR,* vol. 36, pt. 3, Circular, Headquarters, Army of the Potomac, May 25, 1864, 185; *OR,* vol. 36, pt. 2, Hancock to Williams, May 4, 1864, 1:40 P.M., 375. Why Meade, normally a commander of some reserve, picked such an ostentatious flag is unknown. Why he replaced it is not known, either, though Grant himself typically had an American flag outside his headquarters.

5. *OR,* vol. 36, pt. 2: Taylor to Captain Fisher, May 4, 1864, 3:00 P.M., 372; Humphreys to Hancock, May 4, 1864, 1:00 P.M., 375; Grant to Burnside, May 4, 1864, 380; Grant to Burn-

side, May 4, 1864, 1:15 P.M., 380; Headquarters, Army of the Potomac, May 4, 1864, 6 P.M., 371 (orders); Headquarters, Army of the Potomac, Meade to troops, May 4, 1864, 370.

6. Rhea, *Battle of the Wilderness*, 74–77; Humphreys, *Virginia Campaign*, 19–20; *OR*, vol. 36, pt. 1, Grant report, 18.

7. Porter, *Campaigning with Grant*, 45–47; *OR*, vol. 36, pt. 2: Headquarters, Army of the Potomac, Orders, May 4, 1864, 6:00 P.M., 371; Grant to Burnside, May 4, 1864, 1:15 P.M., 380.

8. Catton, *Stillness at Appomattox*, 43.

9. *OR*, vol. 36, pt. 2, Walter Taylor to Richard Ewell, May 4, 1864, 8:00 P.M., 948.

10. Rhea, *Battle of the Wilderness*, 99–102; *OR*, vol. 36, pt. 2: Locke to Griffin, May 5, 1864, 6:20 A.M., 416; Meade to Grant, May 5, 1864, 7:30 A.M. (received), 403; Grant to Meade, May 5, 1864, 8:24 A.M., 403.

11. Rhea, *Battle of the Wilderness*, 104–6; *OR*, vol. 36, pt. 2: Meade to Warren, May 5, 1864, 404; Meade to Grant, May 5, 1864, 9:00 A.M., 404; Crawford to Locke (Warren's assistant adjutant general), May 5, 1864, 8 A.M., 418; Meade to Locke, May 5, 1864, 418.

12. *OR*, vol. 36, pt. 2, Orders, Headquarters, Army of the Potomac, May 4, 1864, 6:00 P.M., 371; Rhea, *Battle of the Wilderness*, 110–11; *OR*, vol. 36, pt. 2: Lieutenant Colonel Forsyth (Sheridan's chief of staff) to General Gregg, May 4, 1864, 389; Wilson to Forsyth, May 4, 1864, 7:40 P.M., 390; *OR*, vol. 36, pt. 1, Wilson's report, 876–77. Rhea puts some blame for the situation on Meade for issuing "imprecise orders" on May 3 (for May 4) to Wilson to provide "reconnaissances" on the pike "as far as Robertson's Tavern," but this hardly seems relevant when the subsequent order (May 4) is examined, which clearly orders Wilson to "keep out parties" on all the key roads. Meade may be charged with underutilizing his cavalry and choosing the wrong general to lead a key cavalry posting, but not with imprecise orders. See Rhea, *Battle of the Wilderness*, 111. The order of May 3 that Rhea refers to is found in *OR*, vol. 36, pt. 2, Forsyth to Gregg, May 3, 1864, 365–66.

13. Rhea, *Battle of the Wilderness*, 124–27 and 137 (map); *OR*, vol. 36, pt. 2: Warren to Crawford, May 5, 1864, 11:50 A.M., 419; Locke to Wadsworth, May 5, 1864, 10:30 A.M., 420; Rhea, *Battle of the Wilderness*, 131–40.

14. Rhea, *Battle of the Wilderness*, 132.

15. Ibid., 141–44 and 156–72.

16. Lowe, *Meade's Army*, 134 (May 5, 1864); Lyman, "Addenda," 167–68 (remarks read on Mar. 8, 1880); Warren to Charles Porter, Nov. 21, 1875, Gouverneur Kemble Warren Papers. Lyman added some colorful details (fastening Grant's coat) and comments on leaders in his speech that are not found in his more terse notes written during the war.

17. Swan, "Battle of the Wilderness," 129 (paper delivered on Feb. 9, 1880); Warren to Charles Porter, Nov. 21, 1875, Gouverneur Kemble Warren Papers.

18. Rhea, *Battle of the Wilderness*, 176–84.

19. Ibid., 184–87; *OR*, vol. 36, pt. 2: Grant to Burnside, May 4, 1864, 1:15 P.M., 380, and Grant to Burnside, May 5, 1864, 3 P.M., 424; Stevens, *Three Years*, 306.

20. *OR*, vol. 36, pt. 2: Humphreys to Hancock, May 5, 1864, received 11:40 A.M., 407; Hancock to Williams, May 5, 1864, 11:40 A.M., at Todd's Tavern, 407. Hancock's corps was stretched from one mile south of Todd's Tavern to the Furnace, a distance of over five miles. See ibid.: Hancock to Humphreys, May 5, 1864, 9:40 A.M., 407; Humphreys to Hancock, May 5, 1864, 12 m., 407; Humphreys to Hancock, May 5, 1864, 1:30 P.M., 409; Hancock to Humphreys, May 5, 1864, 2:40 P.M., 409–10; Humphreys to Hancock, May 5, 1864, 3:15 P.M., 410; Lowe, *Meade's Army*, 134 (May 5, 1864).

21. *OR*, vol. 36, pt. 1, Second Corps daily memoranda, Maj. W. G. Mitchell, 350; *OR*, vol. 36, pt. 2, Lyman to Meade, May 5, 1864, 5:05 P.M., 410–11.

22. Rhea, *Battle of the Wilderness*, 193–239.

23. *OR*, vol. 36, pt. 2, Humphreys to Warren, May 5, 1864, received 4:00 P.M., 414; *OR*, vol. 36, pt. 1, report of Truman Seymour, 728; Rhea, *Battle of the Wilderness*, 246; *OR*, vol.

36, pt. 2, Humphreys to Warren, May 5, 1864, 6:00 P.M., 415; Page, *Letters*, 50; *OR*, vol. 36, pt. 1, report of J. Warren Keifer, 731.

24. *OR*, vol. 36, pt. 2: Sheridan to Humphreys, May 5, 1864, 12 m., 427; Sheridan to Humphreys, May 5, 1864, 5:30 P.M., 428; Seth Williams to Sheridan, May 5, 1864, 6:00 P.M., 428; Sheridan to Humphreys, May 5, 1864, 11:10 P.M., 428; Humphreys, *Virginia Campaign*, 36; Rhea, *Battle of the Wilderness*, 253–61.

25. Porter, *Campaigning with Grant*, 53–54; *OR*, vol. 36, pt. 2, Circular, Headquarters, Army of the Potomac, May 5, 1864, 8 P.M., 406; Schaff, *Battle of the Wilderness*, 225–27; *OR*, vol. 36, pt. 2, Comstock to Burnside, May 5, 1864, 8 P.M., 425; Lowe, *Meade's Army*, 135 (May 5, 1864); *OR*, vol. 36, pt. 2: Meade to Grant, May 5, 1864, 10:30 P.M., 404–5; Lt. Col. W. R. Rowley (Grant's secretary) to Meade, May 5, 1864, 405.

26. Rhea, *Battle of the Wilderness*, 272–82.

27. Porter, *Campaigning with Grant*, 53–54.

28. *OR*, vol. 36, pt. 2: Meade to Grant, May 5, 1864, 9:20 A.M., 404, and Comstock to Burnside, May 5, 1864, 10:30 A.M., 424; Hyde, *Following the Greek Cross*, 183.

29. Porter, *Campaigning with Grant*, 54. For a brief glimpse of that night, I drew on Schaff's long and evocative section on the same in *Battle of the Wilderness*, 212–24.

30. Porter, *Campaigning with Grant*, 56; Rhea, *Battle of the Wilderness*, 284–322; *OR*, vol. 36, pt. 2: Lyman to Meade, May 6, 1864, 5:40 A.M., 439; Hancock to Humphreys, May 6, 1865, 5:40 A.M., 439; Lyman to Meade, May 6, 1864, 6:20 A.M., 440; Lyman to Meade, May 5, 1864, 6:30 A.M., 440.

31. Rhea, *Battle of the Wilderness*, 330–32; Lowe, *Meade's Army*, 136 (May 6, 1864); *OR*, vol. 36, pt. 2: Lt. Col. C. B. Comstock (Grant's aide) to Burnside, May 6, 1864, 6:20 A.M., 460; Meade to Hancock, May 6, 1864 (received 8 A.M.), 441; Humphreys to Hancock, May 6, 1864, 9 A.M. (received 9:15 A.M.), 442.

32. *OR*, vol. 36, pt. 1: Truman Seymour report, 729, and J. Warren Keifer report, 732; *OR*, vol. 36, pt. 2: Warren to Humphreys, May 6, 1864, 6:25 A.M., 450; Maj. E. R. Platt (Warren's aide) to Humphreys, May 6, 1864, 6:55 A.M., 450; Humphreys to Warren, May 6, 1864, 7:15 A.M., 450; Humphreys to Warren, May 6, 1864, 10:35 A.M., 451–52.

33. Rhea, *Battle of the Wilderness*, 331–43; Schaff, *Battle of the Wilderness*, 236; *OR*, vol. 36, pt. 2: Humphreys to Warren, May 6, 1864, 9:30 A.M., 451; Humphreys to Hancock, May 6, 1864, 9:30 A.M., 442; Lyman to Meade, May 6, 1864, 9:45 A.M., 443; Hancock to Williams, May 6, 1864, 10:30 A.M., 444.

34. *OR*, vol. 36, pt. 2: Humphreys to Hancock, May 6, 1864, 8:45 A.M., 442; Sheridan to Humphreys, May 6, 1864, 11 A.M., 466; Sheridan to Humphreys (quotation from enclosed report from Custer), May 6, 1864, 12m., 466.

35. Rhea, *Battle of the Wilderness*, 351–66; Lowe, *Meade's Army*, 138 (May 6, 1864).

36. *OR*, vol. 36, pt. 1, Hancock's report, 323; *OR*, vol. 36, pt. 2: Lyman to Meade, May 6, 1864, 11:30 A.M., 444; Meade to Warren, May 6, 1864, 12 m., 452; Sedgwick to Humphreys, May 6, 1864, 11:30 A.M., 459–60; Humphreys to Warren, May 6, 1864, 1:30 P.M., 453.

37. *OR*, vol. 36, pt. 2: Sheridan to Meade, May 6, 1864, 11:40 A.M., 466; Sheridan to Humphreys, May 6, 1864, 466; Humphreys to Sheridan, May 6, 1864, 1:00 P.M., 467; Sheridan to Humphreys, May 6, 1864, 2:35 P.M., 467; Lt. Col. James W. Forsyth (Sheridan's chief of staff) to General Gregg, May 6, 1864, 2:20 P.M., 470; Forsyth to Gregg, May 6, 1864, 2:30 P.M., 470; *OR*, vol. 36, pt. 1, 788 (Sheridan's report, submitted in 1866). For example, Sheridan's message to Humphreys sent at 2:35 P.M. was all business: "I have sent 1,300 dismounted men to Ely's Ford with it [the trains]. I have sent a regiment to scour the country to United States Ford and to watch the roads. . . . The enemy's cavalry again attacked me and were repulsed and driven, leaving their dead and wounded on the field. They are now working towards my left, and I have made new dispositions in accordance with orders received from the major-general commanding."

38. Rhea, *Battle of the Wilderness*, 366–74.

39. Ibid., 380–88; *OR*, vol. 36, pt. 2, Lyman to Meade, May 6, 1864, 2:00 P.M., 444; Lowe, *Meade's Army*, 138–39 (May 6, 1864); *OR*, vol. 36, pt. 2: Meade to Hancock, May 6, 1864, 2:15 P.M. (received 3:00 P.M.), 444–45, and Hancock to Meade, May 6, 1864, 3:00 P.M., 445.

40. Rhea, *Battle of the Wilderness*, 392–97.

41. Lowe, *Meade's Army*, 140 (May 6, 1864); *OR*, vol. 36, pt. 2: Lyman to Meade, May 6, 1864, 5:15 P.M., 445; Humphreys to Lyman, May 6, 1864, May 6, 1864, 5:15 P.M., 446; Humphreys to Warren, May 6, 1864, 5:30 P.M., 454; Hancock to Meade, May 6, 1864, 5:25 P.M., 445–46; Humphreys to Warren, May 6, 1864, 5:45 P.M., 454.

42. *OR*, vol. 36, pt. 2: Hancock to Meade, May 6, 1864, 5:30 P.M., 446; Meade to Hancock, May 6, 1864, 5:45 P.M., 447.

43. Rhea, *Battle of the Wilderness*, 398–401; *OR*, vol. 36, pt. 2, Grant to Burnside, May 6, 1864, 462; Lowe, *Meade's Army*, 140 (May 6, 1864).

44. Alexander Shaler quoted in Rhea, *Battle of the Wilderness*, 411, and further information from pp. 404–25 in same.

45. Humphreys, *Virginia Campaign*, 50–51n2; Lowe, *Meade's Army*, 140 (May 6, 1864).

46. *OR*, vol. 36, pt. 2: Humphreys to Warren, May 6, 1864, 454, and Humphreys to Warren, May 6, 1864, 455; Lowe, *Meade's Army*, 140–41 (May 6, 1864).

47. Rhea, *Battle of the Wilderness*, 422–24.

48. Porter, *Campaigning with Grant*, 70–71 (quotations) and 72.

49. Wilson, *Life of John Rawlins*, 215–17; Cadwallader, *Three Years with Grant*, 180–82; Lowe, *Meade's Army*, 141 (May 6, 1864).

50. Rhea, *Battle of the Wilderness*, 446.

51. Lowe, *Meade's Army*, 139 (May 6, 1864); Agassiz, *Meade's Headquarters*, 100 (May 18, 1864); Hess, *Trench Warfare*, 41 and 43.

52. Schaff, *Battle of the Wilderness*, 322–23.

53. Rhea, *Battle of the Wilderness*, 435 and 440; *OR*, vol. 36, pt. 2: Grant to Halleck, May 7, 1864, 10 A.M., 480, and Grant to Halleck, May 8, 1864, 11:30 A.M., 526; Grant, *Personal Memoirs*, 458.

54. Schaff, *Battle of the Wilderness*, 323; George G. Meade to Margaret Meade, Apr. 13, 1864, Meade Papers, HSP.

7. GRANT TAKES COMMAND

1. Rhea, *Battle of the Wilderness*, 439.

2. Humphreys, *Virginia Campaign*, 52; Porter, *Campaigning with Grant*, 76.

3. *OR*, vol. 36, pt. 2: Hancock to Humphreys, May 7, 1864 (received 4:30 A.M.), 486; Humphreys to Hancock, May 7, 1864, 4:40 A.M., 486; Warren to Humphreys, May 7, 1864, 5 A.M., 496; Meade to Grant, May 7, 1864, 5 A.M., 480; Grant to Meade, May 7, 1864, 481; Hancock to Meade, May 7, 1864, 6:10 A.M., 486. In that last message, Hancock also confirmed that he had the troops of Robinson and Stevenson.

4. Ibid., Grant to Meade, May 7, 1864, 6:30 A.M., 481.

5. Ibid.: Meade to Sedgwick, May 7, 1864, 8:45 A.M., 507; Humphreys to Warren, May 7, 1864, 500; Meade to Hancock, May 7, 1864, 7:45 A.M., 487; Warren to Humphreys, May 7, 1864, 10:50 A.M., 500; Hancock to Williams, May 7, 1864, 11:25 A.M., 489; Warren to Humphreys, May 7, 1864, 7:40 A.M., 499; Sedgwick to Humphreys, May 7, 1864, 508; Col. Charles E. Pease, assistant adjutant general, to Sedgwick, May 7, 1864, 11 A.M., 507; Col. John B. McIntosh to Sedgwick, May 7, 1864, 12:45 P.M., 508; Sedgwick to Humphreys, May 7, 1864, 508; Meade to Col. Samuel J. Crooks, commander, Twenty-Second New York Cavalry, May 7, 1864, 2:00 P.M., 509. Lyman recorded that when Meade appointed the second-in-command

to take over, he said, "I don't believe he's a bit better!" Lowe, *Meade's Army,* 142 (May 7, 1864). Meade apparently felt that dependable leadership would be provided by Col. John Hammond of the Fifth New York Cavalry, whom he placed in command of the Twenty-Second New York and the Second Ohio cavalry. *OR,* vol. 36, pt. 2, Meade to Hammond, May 7, 1864, 2:00 P.M., 509.

6. *OR,* vol. 36, pt. 2: Capt. Carswell McClellan (assistant adjutant general to Sheridan) to Merritt, May 7, 1864, 516; Sheridan to Humphreys, May 7, 1864, 514; James W. Forsyth (Sheridan's chief of staff) to Gen. David McM. Gregg, May 7, 1864, 7:10 A.M., 516; Pease to Sheridan, May 7, 1864, 10 A.M., 513; Sheridan to Humphreys, May 7, 1864, 12:30 P.M., 514; Sheridan to Humphreys, May 7, 1864, 515; Sheridan to Humphreys, May 7, 1864, 6:15 P.M., 515; Sheridan to Humphreys, May 7, 1864, 8 P.M., 515 (at Todd's Tavern); Orders, Headquarters, Army of the Potomac, May 7, 1864, 3 P.M., 483–84. *OR,* vol. 36, pt. 1, Sheridan's report, 788; Rhea, *Battles for Spotsylvania Court House,* 31 (map showing battles that day).

7. Rhea, *Battles for Spotsylvania Court House,* 22–23 and 27–29; *OR,* vol. 36, pt. 1, report of William N. Pendleton, 1041; *OR,* vol. 36, pt. 2, Walter H. Taylor (assistant adjutant general to Lee) to Ewell, May 7, 1864, 7 P.M., 968.

8. *OR,* vol. 36, pt. 2, Orders, Headquarters, Army of the Potomac, May 7, 1864, 3 P.M., 483–84.

9. Nevins, *Diary of Battle,* 355; Schaff, *Battle of the Wilderness,* 345.

10. Catton, *Stillness at Appomattox,* 92; Porter, *Campaigning with Grant,* 79.

11. Porter, *Campaigning with Grant,* 79; Schaff, *Battle of the Wilderness,* 345. For example, Gordon Rhea quotes from Porter, Gilbert Thompson, and even from Frank Wilkeson, the cynical private who was not even there. See Rhea, *Battle for Spotsylvania Court House,* 39. Wilkeson's battery accompanied the Sixth Corps, and he wrote of the moment when his unit turned south: "At the Chancellorsville house we turned to the right. Instantly all of us heard a sigh of relief. Our spirits rose. We marched free. The men began to sing." Wilkeson, *Turned Inside Out,* 80.

12. Porter, *Campaigning with Grant,* 80–82. See also Sparks, *Inside Lincoln's Army,* 370 (May 7, 1864), "one of the most fatiguing and disgraceful rides I ever took."

13. *OR,* vol. 36, pt. 2: Meade to Torbert or Merritt, May 8, 1864, 1 A.M., 552; Meade to Gregg, May 8, 1864, 1 A.M., 552; Meade to Sheridan, May 8, 1864, 1 A.M., 551. Torbert had fallen ill during the Wilderness fighting, and Merritt temporarily replaced him as division commander. Meade was not aware who was in command when he sent the message on May 8.

14. *OR,* vol. 36, pt. 2, Forsyth to Gregg, May 8, 1864, 1 A.M., 553; Rhea, *Battles for Spotsylvania Court House,* 41; *OR,* vol. 36, pt. 1, Sheridan's report, 788–89; Humphreys, *Virginia Campaign,* 70.

15. Nevins, *Diary of Battle,* 356 ("at Meade's headquarters I found them all asleep"); *OR,* vol. 36, pt. 2: Warren to Humphreys, May 8, 1864, 5 A.M., 538; Warren to Humphreys, May 8, 1864, 6:45 A.M., 539; Warren to Humphreys, May 8, 1864, 8 A.M., 539; Hyde, *Following the Greek Cross,* 189.

16. Rhea, *Battles for Spotsylvania Court House,* 49–55.

17. Ibid., 54–58; *OR,* vol. 36, pt. 2: Warren to Humphreys, May 8, 1864, 10:15 A.M., 539–40; endorsement from Meade, May 8, 1864, 540.

18. *OR,* vol. 36, pt. 2: Warren to Humphreys, May 8, 1864, 10:15 A.M., 539–40, and Warren to Humphreys, May 8, 1864, 12:30 P.M., 540–41; Rhea, *Battles for Spotsylvania Court House,* 62–64; *OR,* vol. 36, pt. 2, Meade to Warren, May 8, 1864, 12 m., 540.

19. *OR,* vol. 36, pt. 2, Warren to Humphries, May 8, 1864, 12:30 P.M., 540–41.

20. Rhea, *Battles for Spotsylvania Court House,* 66–68; Lowe, *Meade's Army,* 144 (May 8, 1864); Porter, *Campaigning with Grant,* 84; Sheridan, *Personal Memoirs,* 368–69; Rodenbough, "Sheridan's Richmond Raid," 189; Coffey, *Sheridan's Lieutenants,* 14. Rodenbough commanded the Second U.S. Cavalry in Merritt's Reserve Brigade in 1864.

21. Sheridan, *Personal Memoirs*, 1:368- 69; Porter, *Campaigning with Grant*, 84; *OR*, vol. 36, pt. 2, Humphreys to Sheridan, May 8, 1864, 10 P.M., 552; Sheridan, *Personal Memoirs*, 369.

22. Rhea, *Battles for Spotsylvania Court House*, 70–73; *OR*, vol. 36, pt. 2, Meade to Sedgwick, May 8, 1864, 1 P.M., 545; Wilson, *Under the Old Flag*, 395–96; Lowe, *Meade's Army*, 145 (May 8, 1864); Nevins, *Diary of Battle*, 359 (May 8, 1864).

23. Agassiz, *Meade's Headquarters*, 105 (May 19, 1864).

24. Rhea, *Battles for Spotsylvania Court House*, 83–85; Lowe, *Meade's Army*, 146 (May 8, 1864).

25. *OR*, vol. 36, pt. 1: 329 (Hancock's report) and 370 (Miles's report); Rhea, *Battles for Spotsylvania Court House*, 74–81; Swinton, *Campaigns*, 447n; Walker, *Second Army Corps*, 445.

26. Sparks, *Inside Lincoln's Army*, 370 (May 8, 1864); Lowe, *Meade's Army*, 146 (May 8, 1864).

27. *OR*, vol. 36, pt. 2, Orders, Headquarters, Army of the Potomac, May 8, 1864, 11:05 P.M., 529.

28. Ibid., Grant to Burnside, May 8, 1864, 9 P.M., 548.

29. Ibid.: Lee to Seddon, May 8, 1864, 2:30 P.M., 974, and Lee to Seddon, May 8, 1864, 9 P.M., 974; Humphreys, *Virginia Campaign*, 75–76.

30. *OR*, vol. 36, pt. 2: Meade to Hancock, May 9, 1864, 2:15 A.M., 564; Maj. A. L. Lockwood to Hancock, May 9, 1864, received 5:30 A.M., 564; Hancock to Humphreys, May 9, 1864, 6 A.M., 564–65; Hancock to Humphreys, May 9, 1864, 7 A.M., 565; Humphreys to Hancock, May 9, 1864, 6:30 A.M., 565; Humphreys to Sedgwick, May 9, 1864, 6:30 A.M., 577; Humphreys to Warren, May 9, 1864, 6:45 A.M., 574; Roebling to Warren, May 9, 1864, 7:40 A.M., 574.

31. Porter, *Campaigning with Grant*, 89; Hyde, *Following the Greek Cross*, 192–93; McMahon, "Death of General John Sedgwick," 175.

32. Agassiz, *Meade's Headquarters*, 108 (May 20, 1864).

33. *OR*, vol. 36, pt. 2, Humphreys to Wright, May 9, 1864, 10 A.M., 577; Rhea, *Battles for Spotsylvania Court House*, 96 and 101. Wright was considered a solid division commander who had been untested for corps command. See Warner, *Generals in Blue*, 575–76.

34. Walker, *Second Army Corps*, 447–48; *OR*, vol. 36, pt. 2: Rawlins to Burnside, May 9, 1864, 8:45 A.M., 580; Rawlins to Burnside, May 9, 1864, 581; Grant to Burnside, May 9, 1864, 1:15 P.M., 582. Rhea, *Battles for Spotsylvania Court House*, 108.

35. *OR*, vol. 36, pt. 2: Orders, Headquarters, Army of the Potomac, May 9, 1864, 11:15 P.M., 563, and Rawlins to Burnside, May 10, 1864, 1:30 A.M., 610; Rhea, *Battles for Spotsylvania Court House*, 97–100 and 114–21.

36. Porter, *Campaigning with Grant*, 91; Dana, *Recollections of the Civil War*, 192–93; Rhea, *Battles for Spotsylvania Court House*, 131 and 132; Matter, "Federal High Command," 38.

37. *OR*, vol. 36, pt. 2: Hancock to Humphreys, May 10, 1864, 6:40 A.M., 599, and Hancock to Humphreys, May 10, 1864, 7 A.M., 599; Walker, *Second Army Corps*, 449.

38. *OR*, vol. 36, pt. 2: Crawford to Warren, May 10, 1864, received 8:30 A.M., 606; Crawford to Warren, May 10, 1864, 9:30 A.M., 606; Warren to Crawford, May 10, 1864, 10 A.M., 607; Warren to Crawford and Cutler, May 10, 1864, 12 m., 607; Rhea, *Battles for Spotsylvania Court House*, 128–30.

39. *OR*, vol. 36, pt. 2: Grant to Halleck, May 10, 1864, 9:30 A.M., 595; Grant to Burnside, May 10, 1864, 10:30 A.M., 610.

40. Ibid.: Meade to Hancock, May 10, 1864, 10 A.M., 600; Meade to Warren, May 10, 1864, 10 A.M., 604; Meade to Wright, May 10, 1864, 10 A.M., 609.

41. *OR*, vol. 36, pt. 1, Upton report, 667–68; Rhea, *Battles for Spotsylvania Court House*, 161.

42. *OR*, vol. 36, pt. 2: Humphreys to Mott, May 10, 1864, 8:15 A.M., 602; Meade to Mott, May 10, 1864, 12:50 P.M., 602–3; Wright to Mott, May 10, 1864, received at 2 P.M., 603; Mott to Wright, May 10, 1864, 2:05 P.M., 603; Wright to Mott, May 10, 1864, 603; Rhea, *Battles for Spotsylvania Court House*, 181–85.

43. Jordan, *"Happiness Is Not My Companion,"* 147–48; *OR,* vol. 36, pt. 2: Humphreys to Hancock, May 10, 1864, 3:30 P.M., 600, and Meade to Hancock, May 10, 1864, 4 P.M., 600; Gibbon, *Personal Recollections,* 218–19 (Gibbon finished a draft of the manuscript in 1885; Rhea, *Battles for Spotsylvania Court House,* 143.

44. Rhea, *Battles for Spotsylvania Court House,* 144–49.

45. *OR,* vol. 36, pt. 1, Hancock's report, 334.

46. *OR,* vol. 36, pt. 1, Upton's report, 668; Rhea, *Battles for Spotsylvania Court House,* 166–68.

47. Rhea, *Battles for Spotsylvania Court House,* 177–81. Ward was not officially relieved until May 12, 1864.

48. Ibid., 189–97.

49. Humphreys, *Virginia Campaign,* 89; *OR,* vol. 36, pt. 1, Dana to Stanton, May 10, 1864, 66.

50. Humphreys, *Virginia Campaign,* 82; Walker, *Second Army Corps,* 463.

51. Walker, *Second Army Corps,* 463 (quotation) and 465–67.

52. Porter, *Campaigning with Grant,* 43, 97, and 98; *OR,* vol. 36, pt. 2, Grant to Halleck, May 11, 1864, 8:30 A.M., 627–28.

53. *OR,* vol. 36, pt. 2: Grant to Meade, May 11, 1864, 3 P.M., 629; Meade to Hancock, May 11, 1864, 4 P.M., 635.

54. Sparks, *Inside Lincoln's Army,* 372 (May 11, 1864); examples of Patrick's dislike of Meade will be shared in future passages.

55. Humphreys, *Virginia Campaign,* 90–91; *OR,* vol. 36, pt. 2, Humphreys to Warren, May 11, 1864, 6:30 P.M., 637–38.

56. *OR,* vol. 36, pt. 2, Grant to Burnside, May 11, 1864, 4 P.M., 643.

57. Barlow, "Capture of the Salient," 245–50.

58. Rhea, *Battles for Spotsylvania Court House,* 225–29; *OR,* vol. 36, pt. 1, Edward Johnson report, 1079–80; Sumner, *Diary of Cyrus B. Comstock,* 266 (May 11, 1864).

59. *OR,* vol. 36, pt. 1, report of Winfield S. Hancock, 335; Black, "Reminiscences," 423–24.

60. *OR,* vol. 36, pt. 1, Winfield S. Hancock report, 335; Black, "Reminiscences," 425; Porter, *Campaigning with Grant,* 101–3 (Grant quotation on p. 103). *OR,* vol. 36, pt. 2: Hancock to Meade, May 12, 1864, 5 A.M., 656; Hancock to Meade, May 12, 1864, 5:55 A.M., 656; Meade to Hancock, May 12, 1864, 6 A.M., 656; Grant to Burnside, May 12, 1864, 6 A.M., 677. Lowe, *Meade's Army:* 154 (May 12, 1864, "little hollow"), 153 (Rawlins quotation), 153–54 (Johnson and Steuart stories).

61. *OR,* vol. 36, pt. 2: Hancock to Meade, May 12, 1864, 7:15 A.M., 657, and Grant to Burnside, May 12, 1864, 8 A.M., 678; Rhea, *Battles for Spotsylvania Court House,* 246–72.

62. *OR,* vol. 36, pt. 2: Meade to Warren, May 12, 1864, 6 A.M., 661; Meade to Warren, May 12, 1864, 7:30 A.M., 662; Meade to Warren, May 12, 1864, 8 A.M., 662. Rhea, *Battles for Spotsylvania Court House,* 282–83.

63. *OR,* vol. 36, pt. 2: Warren to Humphreys, May 12, 1864, 9:10 A.M., 662; Humphreys to Warren, May 12, 1864, 9:10 A.M., 663; Warren to Humphreys, May 12, 1864, 9:10 A.M., 663.

64. Ibid., Humphreys to Warren, May 12, 1864, 9:15 A.M., 663.

65. Ibid.: Humphreys to Warren, May 12, 1864, 9:30 A.M., 663, signed, "your friend"; Humphreys to General Warren (official letter), May 12, 1864, 9:30 A.M., 663 (on Bartlett's brigade); Warren to Griffin, May 12, 1864, 9:30 A.M., 668; Warren to Crawford, May 12, 1864, 9:30 A.M., 669; Warren to Humphreys, May 12, 1864, 9:40 A.M., 664.

66. Rhea, *Battles for Spotsylvania Court House,* 285–88; *OR,* vol. 36, pt. 2, Humphreys to Warren, May 12, 1864, 10:05 A.M., 664; Humphreys, *Virginia Campaign,* 101n3; *OR,* vol. 36, pt. 2: Meade to Grant, May 12, 1864, 654; Grant to Meade, May 12, 1864, 10:40 A.M., 654.

67. Humphreys, *Virginia Campaign,* 101n3; *OR,* vol. 36, pt. 2: Meade to Humphreys, May 12, 1864, 10:30 A.M., 655; Humphreys to Meade, May 12, 1864, 655; Meade to Humphreys, May 12, 1864, 655; Meade to Humphreys, May 12, 1864, 655.

68. *OR,* vol. 36, pt. 2, Grant to Burnside, May 12, 1864, 10:20 A.M., 679; Rhea, *Battles for Spotsylvania Court House,* 294–302.

69. *OR,* vol. 36, pt. 2: Meade to Grant, May 12, 1864, 3:00 P.M., 656; Grant to Burnside, May 12, 1864, 3:15 P.M., 679.

70. Ibid.: Wright to Humphreys, May 12, 1864, 3:10 P.M., 674; Wright to Humphreys, May 12, 1864, 675.

71. Ibid., Wright to Humphreys, May 12, 1864, 5:10 P.M., 675.

72. Ibid.: Meade to Wright, May 12, 1864, 6:15 P.M., 675; Rawlins to Burnside, May 12, 1864, 6:10 P.M., 680; Grant to Burnside, May 12, 1864, 6:20 P.M., 680; Burnside to Grant, May 12, 1864, 8:00 P.M., 680.

73. Rhea, *Battles for the Spotsylvania Court House,* 305–7.

74. Ibid., 305–7; Porter, *Campaigning with Grant,* 111.

75. Rhea, *Battles for Spotsylvania Court House,* 311–12.

8. THE "HAMMERING" CONTINUES

1. *OR,* vol. 36, pt. 2: Humphreys to Wright, May 13, 1864, 12:15 A.M., 723; Wright to Humphreys, May 13, 1864, 12:20 A.M., 723–24; Humphreys to Hancock, May 13, 1864 (received 2:15 A.M.), 702; Hancock to Humphreys, May 13, 1864, 702; Grant to Burnside, May 13, 1864, 1:35 A.M., 730; Hancock to Humphreys, May 13, 1864, 5:30 A.M., 702; Hancock to Humphreys, May 13, 1864, 6:20 A.M., 703.

2. Ibid.: Humphreys to Wright, May 13, 1864, 5:30 A.M., 724; Humphreys to Wright, May 13, 1864, 8 A.M., 724; Humphreys to Warren, May 13, 1864, 5:40 A.M., 712; Warren to Humphreys, May 13, 1864 (around 7:30 A.M.), 713; Warren to Humphreys, May 13, 1864, 8 A.M., 714; Meade to Hancock, May 13, 1864, 708; Hancock to Williams, May 13, 1864, 10:55 P.M., 708 (he had given estimates earlier in the day); Meade to Warren, May 13, 1864 (received 9 A.M.), 715; Barlow to Walker (assistant adjutant general, Second Corps), May 13, 1864, 710; Meade to Warren, May 13, 1864, 5 A.M., 712; Meade to Warren, May 13, 1864, 8 A.M., 714; Warren to Meade, May 13, 1864, 8:15 A.M., 714; Warren to Meade, May 13, 1864, 714–15; Meade to Lieutenant Colonel Bowers (assistant adjutant general, Headquarters, Armies of the United States), May 13, 1864, 698 (men to be promoted); Grant to Stanton, May 13, 1864, 695. Both generals also called for Humphreys to be "confirmed" as a major general.

3. George G. Meade to Margaret Meade, May 15, 1864, Meade Papers, HSP.

4. *OR,* vol. 36, pt. 2, Stanton to Grant, May 14, 1864, 746.

5. Porter, *Campaigning with Grant,* 114–15.

6. Humphreys, *Virginia Campaign,* 83n1; Dana, *Recollections of the Civil War,* 190; James Biddle to Gertrude Biddle, May 16, 1864, James Cornell Biddle papers, HSP.

7. Grimsley, *And Keep Moving On,* 228–29. Grimsley does not mention the battle that made Meade's reputation, Gettysburg, in which he exhibited great "coping" skills as a general.

8. George G. Meade to Margaret Meade, May 23, 1864, Meade Papers, HSP.

9. See messages from the *OR* in note 2 in this chapter; *OR,* vol. 36, pt. 1: Circular, Headquarters, Army of the Potomac, May 13, 1864, 197; Stanton to Meade, May 13, 1864, 197.

10. *OR,* vol. 36, pt. 2: Grant to Meade, May 13, 1864, 8:40 A.M., 698, and Circular, Army of the Potomac Headquarters, May 13, 1864, 9:30 A.M., 705; Rhea, *To the North Anna River,* 28; *OR,* vol. 36, pt. 1, Dana to Stanton, May 13, 1864, 6:00 P.M., 69.

11. *OR,* vol. 36, pt. 2: Humphreys to Wright, May 13, 1864, 8:15 P.M., 728–29 (the plan); Grant to Burnside, May 13, 1864, 6:20 P.M., 731.

12. Ibid., Circular, Fifth Army Corps headquarters, May 13, 1864, 8:10 P.M., 721; Nevins, *Diary of Battle,* 369 (May 14, 1864); *OR,* vol. 36, pt. 2, Wright to Humphreys, May 14, 1864, 2:55 A.M., 762; Nevins, *Diary of Battle,* 369 (May 14, 1864).

13. *OR*, vol. 36, pt. 2: Meade to Grant, May 14, 1864, 6 A.M. (endorsement of Warren's earlier message), 756; Meade to Grant, May 14, 1864, 6 A.M., 747; Warren to Humphreys, May 14, 1864, 6:30 A.M., 756; Humphreys to Warren, May 14, 1864, 7:10 A.M., 756; Grant to Halleck, May 14, 1864, 7:10 A.M., 746.

14. Rhea, *To the North Anna River*, 77–90; James C. Biddle to Gertrude Biddle, May 16, 1864, in Biddle Papers, HSP; *OR*, vol. 36, pt. 2, Meade to Warren, May 14, 1864, 760.

15. *OR*, vol. 36, pt. 2: Meade to Grant, May 14, 1864, 9 P.M., 747, and Grant to Meade, May 14, 1864, 9:30 P.M., 747; Rhea, *To the North Anna River*, 97–98; *OR*, vol. 36, pt. 2, Humphreys to Hancock, May 14, 1864, 10:00 P.M., 753.

16. *OR*, vol. 36, pt. 2: Grant to Halleck, May 15, 1864, 7 A.M., 781; Meade to Warren, May 15, 1864, 3:30 P.M., 788–89 (same to Wright); Meade to Hancock, May 15, 1864, 3:30 P.M., 784; Meade to Warren, May 15, 1864, 7:45 P.M., 789 (same to Wright).

17. *OR*, vol. 36, pt. 1, Dana to Stanton, May 16, 1864, 7 A.M., 70; *OR*, vol. 36, pt. 2, Grant to Halleck, May 16, 1864, 8 A.M., 809–10.

18. *OR*, vol. 36, pt. 1, Dana to Stanton, May 16, 1864 (casualty numbers); Dana, *Recollections of the Civil War*, 199.

19. *OR*, vol. 36, pt. 1, Hunt report, 288; *OR*, vol. 36, pt. 2, Special Orders, May 16, 1864, 883; Nevins, *Diary of Battle*, May 17, 1864, 375.

20. Lowe, *Meade's Army*, 161 (May 16, 1864); George G. Meade to Margaret Meade, May 19, 1864, Meade Papers, HSP. In his letter Meade referred to Coppée's journal as the *Army Magazine*, though he meant to say the *United States Service Magazine*. Its chief competitor was the *Army and Navy Journal*.

21. Rhea, *To the North Anna River*, 14.

22. *OR*, vol. 36, pt. 2: Meade to Warren, May 16, 1864, 11 A.M., 816; Warren to Meade, May 16, 1864, 12:30 P.M., 816 (Meade's endorsement immediately follows); Warren to Meade, May 16, 1864, 12:35 P.M., 816 (Meade's and Grant's endorsements immediately follow); Meade to Warren, May 16, 1864, 1:40 P.M., 817. Rhea, *To the North Anna River*, 122–25.

23. *OR*, vol. 36, pt. 1, Dana to Stanton, May 17, 1864, 4 P.M., 72 (on road conditions); Rhea, *To the North Anna River*, 126–27 and 131–32.

24. *OR*, vol. 36, pt. 2: Meade to Hancock, May 17, 1864, 8 A.M., 844, and Grant to Burnside, May 17, 1864, 850; Rhea, *To the North Anna River*, 128–29; *OR*, vol. 36, pt. 1: Dana to Stanton, May 17, 1864, 4 P.M., 72–73, and Dana to Stanton, May 18, 1864, 5 A.M., 73; *OR*, vol. 36, pt. 2, Circular, Headquarters, Second Army Corps, May 18, 1864, 1 A.M., 870–71.

25. George G. Meade to Margaret Meade, May 17, 1864, Meade Papers, HSP; Nevins, *Diary of Battle*, 375 (May 17, 1864).

26. Rhea, *To the North Anna River*, 133–35.

27. *OR*, vol. 36, pt. 2, Grant to Burnside, May 17, 1864, 850.

28. Rhea, *To the North Anna River*, 136 and 139–48.

29. *OR*, vol. 36, pt. 2: Hancock to Humphreys, May 18, 1864, 5:40 A.M., 867; Potter to Burnside, May 18, 1864, 6:10 A.M., 881–82; Humphreys to Hancock, May 18, 1864, 6:15 A.M., 867; Wright to Hancock, May 18, 1864, 867; Hancock to Williams, May 18, 1864, 6:50 A.M., 867–68. Rhea, *To the North Anna River*, 151; *OR*, vol. 36, pt. 2: Hancock to Humphreys, May 18, 1864, 8:30 A.M., 868; Humphreys to Hancock, May 18, 1864, 8:45 A.M., 869; Grant to Burnside, May 18, 1864, 9 A.M., 880.

30. Rhea, *To the North Anna River*, 154 (casualties); Lowe, *Meade's Army*, 162–63 (May 18, 1864).

31. *OR*, vol. 36, pt. 2, Grant to Meade, May 18, 1864, 864–65; George G. Meade to Margaret Meade, May 19, 1864, in Meade Papers, HSP.

32. *OR*, vol. 36, pt. 2: Circular, Headquarters, Army of the Potomac, May 18, 1864, 866; Rawlins to Burnside, May 18, 1864, 2 P.M., 880; Wright to Humphreys, May 19, 1864, 7:15 A.M., 924; Warren to Humphreys, May 19, 1864, 9:40 A.M., 913.

33. *OR*, vol. 36, pt. 2, Lee to Seddon, May 19, 1864, 1022; Porter, *Campaigning with Grant*, 127; *OR*, vol. 36, pt. 2: Humphreys to Hancock, May 19, 1864, 911; Circular, Headquarters, Second Corps, May 19, 1864, 5:30 P.M., 912; Humphreys to Warren, May 19, 1864, 5:30 P.M., 915; Warren to Humphreys, May 19, 1864, 916. Rhea, *To the North Anna River*, 177–87; *OR*, vol. 36, pt. 1, Ewell report , 1073; *OR*, vol. 36, pt. 3, Orders, Headquarters, Army of the Potomac, May 20, 1864, 6; Wilkeson, *Turned Inside Out*, 86. *Bandbox* was a nineteenth-century term for something brand new and clean, as if taken fresh out of a "bandbox."

34. *OR*, vol. 36, pt. 2, Grant to Halleck, May 19, 1864, 10 P.M., 906.

35. *OR*, vol. 36, pt. 3, Meade to Hancock, May 20, 1864, 1:00 P.M., 8; *OR*, vol. 36, pt. 2, Humphreys to Hancock, May 19, 1864, 910; *OR*, vol. 36, pt. 3: Circular, Headquarters, Second Army Corps, May 20, 1864, 5 P.M., 10; Humphreys to Wright, May 20, 1864, 5:20 P.M., 17.

36. Rhea, *To the North Anna River*, 193–98.

37. Ibid., 212–23.

38. Ibid., 216–17 and 220–21; *OR*, vol. 36, pt. 3: Humphreys to Warren, May 21, 1864, 9:45 A.M., 55; Humphreys to Wright, May 21, 1864, 8:25 A.M., 62; Grant to Burnside, May 21, 1864, 8:25 A.M., 64; Humphreys to Hancock, May 21, 1864, 9:45 A.M., 48 (received at 3 P.M.).

39. Rhea, *To the North Anna River*, 228 (and photo); Lowe, *Meade's Army*, 167 (May 21, 1864); Rhea, *To the North Anna River*, 232–35; Sparks, *Inside Lincoln's Army*, 375 (May 21, 1864); Collis quoted in Rhea, *To the North Anna River*, 234; *OR*, vol. 36, pt. 3: Williams to Hancock, May 21, 1864, 8 P.M., 50; Hancock to Williams, May 22, 1864, 4:15 A.M., 82.

40. *OR*, vol. 36, pt. 3, Hancock to Williams, May 21, 1864, 6:15 P.M. (received 4 A.M. on May 22), 49–50.

41. Rhea, *To the North Anna River*, 241; *OR*, vol. 36, pt. 3: Humphreys to Warren, May 21, 1864, 4 P.M., 56 (includes line that reads, "Wright follows Burnside"); Grant to Burnside, May 21, 1864, 64–65. Rhea, *To the North Anna River*, 243–48.

42. Rhea, *To the North Anna River*, 248–52.

43. *OR*, vol. 36, pt. 3, Humphreys to Warren, May 22, 1864, 9:30 A.M., 90.

44. Ibid.: Orders, Headquarters, Army of the Potomac, May 22, 1864, 80–81 (two separate orders); Humphreys to Hancock, May 22, 1864, 3:30 P.M., 85; Rhea, *To the North Anna River*, 261–62.

45. Lowe, *Meade's Army*, 169 (May 22, 1864); Rhea, *To the North Anna River*, 267–70, 277, and 258–59; Sparks, *Inside Lincoln's Army*, 377 (May 22, 1864); *OR*, vol. 36, pt. 3, Orders, Headquarters, Army of the Potomac, May 22, 1864, 10 P.M. (enclosed are the orders of Grant to Meade), 81–82.

46. George G. Meade to Margaret Meade, May 23, 1864, Meade Papers, HSP (see full sentence earlier in the chapter); James Biddle to Gertrude Biddle, June 4, 1864, James Biddle Papers, HSP. Not only Meade staffers questioned Grant's decisions. Wainwright wrote in his diary, "I fear that Grant has made a botch of this move also, for Lee is certainly ahead of us now." Nevins, *Diary of Battle*, 383 (May 22, 1864).

47. Rhea, *To the North Anna River*, 280–85; Lowe, *Meade's Army*, 171 (May 23, 1864).

48. *OR*, vol. 36, pt. 3: Meade to Grant, May 23, 1864, 125; Grant to Meade, May 23, 1864, 2 P.M., 115; Humphreys to Warren, May 23, 1864, 3:20 P.M., 127.

49. Rhea, *To the North Anna River*, 286–87.

50. Ibid., 287–88.

51. *OR*, vol. 36, pt. 3: Meade to Grant, first endorsement, and Grant to Meade, second endorsement, to a report sent by Hancock to Williams, May 23, 1864, 2:35 P.M., 119; Hancock to Williams, May 23, 1864, 3:15 P.M., 120; first endorsement from Meade to the same report; Grant to Meade, May 23, 1864, 4:15 P.M., 120; Hancock to Williams, May 23, 1864, 7:50 P.M., 122; Hancock to Williams, May 23, 1864, 9:20 P.M., 122.

52. Rhea, *To the North Anna River*, 303–16.

53. *OR,* vol. 36, pt. 3, Meade to Warren, May 23, 1864, 10:30 P.M., 129; Hancock quoted in Rhea, *To the North Anna River,* 316; *OR,* vol. 36, pt. 3, Grant to Halleck, May 23, 1864, 113–14.

54. Nevins, *Diary of Battle,* 385–87 (May 23, 1864).

55. Rhea, *To the North Anna River,* 320–25.

56. Dana, *Recollections of the Civil War,* 203; *OR,* vol. 36, pt. 3: Warren to Meade, May 24, 1864, 7:30 A.M., 157; Warren to Meade, May 24, 1864, 6:00 A.M., 157.

57. Lowe, *Meade's Army,* 172 (May 24, 1864); *OR,* vol. 36, pt. 3: Hancock to Williams, May 24, 1864, 5 A.M., 148; Meade to Grant, May 24, 1864, endorsement attached to Hancock's letter to him, 149; Grant to Halleck, May 24, 1864, 8 A.M., 145.

58. *OR,* vol. 36, pt. 3, Halleck to Grant, May 23, 1864, 115.

59. Lowe, *Meade's Army,* 172 (May 24, 1864); George G. Meade to Margaret Meade, May 24, 1864, Meade Papers, HSP. The French expression means, "we shall see."

60. Agassiz, *Meade's Headquarters,* 126 (May 24, 1864); Lowe, *Meade's Army,* 173 (May 24, 1864).

61. *OR,* vol. 36, pt. 3: Meade to Grant, May 24, 1864, 9:30 A.M., 146; Burnside to Grant, May 24, 1864, 167; Rawlins to Burnside, May 24, 1864, 1 P.M., 167; Rhea, *To the North Anna River,* 331–33.

62. Rhea, *To the North Anna River,* 337–42.

63. *OR,* vol. 36, pt. 3: Meade to Hancock, May 24, 1864, 11:15 P.M., 155–56; Humphreys to Warren, May 24, 1864, 11 P.M., 160; Grant to Burnside, May 24, 1864, 8:20 P.M., 168–69.

64. Rhea, *To the North Anna River,* 344–46 and 353–54.

65. *OR,* vol. 36, pt. 3, Special Orders, Headquarters, Armies of the United States, May 24, 1864, 169; Porter, *Campaigning with Grant,* 145.

66. Lyman, *Meade's Army,* 174–75 (May 25, 1864); *OR,* vol. 36, pt. 3: Warren to Meade, May 25, 1864, 12 noon, 192–93; Cutler to Warren, May 25, 1863, 193 (enclosure to Meade); Meade to Grant, May 25, 1864, 193 (first endorsement); Grant to Meade, May 25, 1864, 193 (second endorsement); Morgan to Hancock, May 25, 1864, 6:45 A.M., 185.

67. *OR,* vol. 36, pt. 3, Grant to Halleck, May 25, 1864, 12 noon, 183.

68. Nevins, *Diary of Battle,* 388 (May 26, 1864); Sumner, *Diary of Cyrus B. Comstock,* 269 (May 26, 1864); *OR,* vol. 36, pt. 3, Grant to Halleck, May 26, 1864, 206. Mark Grimsley argues that "Union sea power" was in "many respects the Confederacy's most dangerous nemesis." More specifically, "Without the North's wealth of steamers, barges, and gunboats, Grant would have had a far more difficult time in turning Lee out of his formidable defensive positions." *And Keep Moving On,* 233.

69. George G. Meade to Margaret Meade, May 19 and 23, 1864, Meade Papers, HSP.

70. Sumner, *Diary of Cyrus B. Comstock,* 269 (May 26, 1864); Nevins, *Diary of Battle,* 388 (May 26, 1864).

71. *OR,* vol. 36, pt. 3, Grant to Meade, May 25, 1864, 183.

72. Rhea, *Cold Harbor,* 27–38; Wilkeson, *Turned Inside Out,* 122–23; *OR,* vol. 36, pt. 3, Lee to Seddon, May 27, 1864, 6:45 A.M., 836.

73. Rhea, *Cold Harbor,* 35–47.

74. Ibid., 47; Lowe, *Meade's Army,* 177 (May 27, 1864).

75. *OR,* vol. 36, pt. 3, Sheridan to Humphreys, May 27, 1864, 9 A.M., 258; Porter, *Campaigning with Grant,* 142 (Sheridan returned to headquarters on May 24); *OR,* vol. 36, pt. 1, Dana to Stanton, May 28, 1864, 80; *OR,* vol. 36, pt. 3, Sheridan to Humphreys, May 27, 1864, 5:20 P.M., 258–59.

76. Rhea, *Cold Harbor,* 57–58; *OR,* vol. 36, pt. 1, Dana to Stanton, May 27, 1864, 80.

77. Rhea, *Cold Harbor,* 59–60.

78. *OR,* vol. 36, pt. 1, Sheridan's report, 793; Rhea, *Cold Harbor,* 68–90; Wilkeson, *Turned Inside Out,* 124; *OR,* vol. 36, pt. 1, Nelson Miles report, 371. Sheridan's fight became

known as the Battle of Haw's Shop. Each side claimed victory, and each side lost approximately four hundred men.

79. Krick, *Civil War Weather,* 129; *OR,* vol. 36, pt. 1, Sheridan's report, 793; *OR,* vol. 36, pt. 3, Humphreys to Hancock, May 29, 1864, 8:45 A.M., 293–94 (same order to Warren, Wright, and Burnside); Rhea, *Cold Harbor,* 98–100.

80. *OR,* vol. 36, pt. 1, Maj. Nathaniel Micheler's report, 300; *OR,* vol. 36, pt. 3: Hancock to Meade, May 29, 1864, 5:30 P.M., 295–96, and Warren to Humphreys, May 29, 1864, 3:30 P.M., 302; Rhea, *Cold Harbor,* 100.

81. *OR,* vol. 36, pt. 3: Meade to Grant, May 29, 1864, 3 P.M., 290; Grant to Meade, May 29, 1864, 4 P.M., 290; Meade to Grant, May 29, 1864, 5:15 P.M., 290; Hancock to Williams, May 29, 1864, 9 P.M., 296–97; Humphreys to Hancock, May 29, 1864, 9:30 P.M., 297; Warren to Meade, May 29, 1864, 8 P.M., 303; Humphreys to Warren, May 29, 1864, 9:45 P.M., 303; Meade to Warren, May 29, 1864, 7 P.M., 303; Meade to Burnside, May 29, 1864, 7 P.M., 310.

82. Rhea, *Cold Harbor,* 101 and 112–13.

83. Lowe, *Meade's Army,* 180–81 (May 29, 1864).

84. Rhea, *Cold Harbor,* 132–39; *OR,* vol. 36, pt. 3, Sheridan to Humphreys, May 30, 1864, 7 P.M., 361.

85. Rhea, *Cold Harbor,* 139–41; Nevins, *Diary of Battle,* 393 (May 30, 1864); *OR,* vol. 36, pt. 3, Warren to Meade, May 30, 1864, 4 P.M., 341.

86. *OR,* vol. 36, pt. 3, Warren to Humphreys, May 30, 1864, 6:30 P.M., 343, see "endorsement" from Meade, "Hancock and Burnside ordered to attack. Wright previously ordered to push close and (if practicable) to attack"; Rhea, *Cold Harbor,* 149–51.

87. Rhea, *Cold Harbor,* 142–49 and 156. Pegram's brigade was led that day by Col. Edward Willis, who temporarily replaced the wounded John Pegram.

88. *OR,* vol. 36, pt. 3: Warren to Humphreys, May 30, 1864, 7:30 P.M., 344; Meade to Hancock, May 30, 1864, 7:30 P.M., 329 ("same to General Burnside"); Warren to Meade, May 30, 1864, 9 P.M., 345–46.

89. *OR,* vol. 36, pt. 3: Grant to Meade, May 30, 1864, 6:40 P.M., 323; Meade to Warren, May 30, 1864, 10:30 P.M., 346.

90. *OR,* vol. 36, pt. 3, Lee to Davis, May 30, 1864, 7:30 P.M., 850; Rhea, *Cold Harbor,* 159–60.

91. Krick, *Civil War Weather,* 129; *OR,* vol. 36, pt. 3: Circular, Headquarters, Army of the Potomac, May 31, 1864, 7:30 A.M., 376; Meade to Hancock, May 31, 1864, 10:20 A.M., 379; Hancock to Wright, May 31, 1864, 381–82; Warren to Humphreys, May 31, 1864, 1:00 P.M., 391; Burnside to Humphreys, May 31, 1864, 2:25 P.M., 406; Humphreys to Burnside, May 31, 1864, 6 P.M., 407.

92. *OR,* vol. 36, pt. 1: Sheridan report, 794; Wilson report, 880–81; Sheridan report, 794.

93. Rhea, *Cold Harbor,* 188–89; *OR,* vol. 36, pt. 3: Warren to Humphreys, May 31, 1864, 393; Meade to Wright, May 31, 1864, 9:45 P.M., 404.

94. Rhea, *Cold Harbor,* 191–93; *OR,* vol. 36, pt. 3, Smith to Grant, May 31, 1864, 9 A.M., 410.

95. *OR,* vol. 36, pt. 3: Meade to Hancock, June 1, 1864, 12:15 A.M., 434, and Williams to Hancock, June 1, 1864, 6:45 A.M., 434 (same to Burnside and Warren); Rhea, *Cold Harbor,* 207–9; *OR,* vol. 36, pt. 3, Special Orders, Headquarters, Armies of the United States, June 1, 1864, 466; Smith had commanded the Sixth Corps at Fredericksburg while Meade led a division there; Rhea, *Cold Harbor,* 234; *OR,* vol. 36, pt. 3, Meade to Smith, June 1, 1864, 12 m., 466.

96. Rhea, *Cold Harbor,* 198–204 and 225–26; *OR,* vol. 36, pt. 3, Wright to Humphreys, June 1, 1864, 2:10 P.M., 455; Rhea, *Cold Harbor,* 227–32.

97. Lowe, *Meade's Army,* 184 (June 1, 1864); George G. Meade to Margaret Meade, June 1, 1864, Meade Papers, HSP.

98. Lowe, *Meade's Army,* 185 (June 1, 1864); *OR,* vol. 36, pt. 3, Wright to Humphreys, June 1, 1864, 7:30 P.M., 455.

99. *OR,* vol. 36, pt. 3: Meade to Grant, June 1, 1864, 10:15 P.M., 432–33; Comstock (aide to Grant) to Meade, June 1, 1864, 10:40 P.M., 433.

100. *OR,* vol. 36, pt. 3: Meade to Hancock, June 1, 1864, 11 P.M., 441–42; Meade to Wright, June 1, 1864, 10:45 P.M., 458; Meade to Smith, June 1, 1864, 10:50 P.M., 468; Meade to Warren, June 1, 1864, 11 P.M., 452; Meade to Burnside, June 1, 1864, 11 P.M., 463.

101. Ibid., Smith to Humphreys, June 1, 1864, 10:30 P.M., 467–68; Lowe, *Meade's Army,* 185 (June 1, 1864); *OR,* vol. 36, pt. 1, Smith report, 1000.

102. Rhea, *Cold Harbor,* 266; Walker, *Second Army Corps,* 506.

103. *OR,* vol. 36, pt. 3: Warren to Meade, June 2, 1864, 5 A.M., 486–87; Hancock to Humphreys, June 2, 1864, 481; Meade to Hancock, June 2, 1864, 7:20 A.M., 481; Humphreys to Hancock, June 2, 1864, 1:30 P.M., 482.

104. Ibid., Grant to Meade, June 2, 1864, 2 P.M., 478.

105. Rhea, *Cold Harbor,* 285–306.

106. *OR,* vol. 36, pt. 3: Grant to Meade, June 2, 1864, 2 P.M., 478; Circular, Headquarters, Army of the Potomac, June 2, 1864, 2:30 P.M., 479.

107. Rhea, *Cold Harbor,* 318–19 (quotation) and 389–91; George G. Meade to Margaret Meade, June 4, 1864, Meade Papers, HSP; Agassiz, *Meade's Headquarters,* 143 (June 3, 1864); Nevins, *Diary of Battle,* 405 (June 4, 1864); Walker, *Second Army Corps,* 463.

108. Lowe, *Meade's Army,* 186–88 (June 2, 1864); *OR,* vol. 36, pt. 3, Warren to Meade, June 2, 1864, 493; Roebling report, in Warren Papers, NYSL; *OR,* vol. 36, pt. 3, Humphreys to Warren, June 2, 1864, 494; Lowe, *Meade's Army,* 188 (June 2, 1864).

109. Rhea, *Cold Harbor,* 311; Hess, *Trench Warfare,* 153.

110. Rhea, *Cold Harbor,* 359–62, quotation on p. 361.

111. *OR,* vol. 36, pt. 3: Hancock to Williams, June 3, 1864, 552; Charles Pease (assistant adjutant general) to Smith, June 3, 1864, 5:20 A.M., 552; Hancock to Meade, June 3, 1864, 6 A.M., 525; Hancock to Meade, June 3, 1864, 6:45 A.M., 530; Smith to Meade, June 3, 1864, 553; Wright to Humphreys, June 3, 1864, 7:45 A.M., 544; Warren to Meade, June 3, 1864, 6 A.M., 536; Burnside to Humphreys, June 3, 1864, 7:35 A.M., 547.

112. *OR,* vol. 36, pt. 3, Meade to Grant, June 3, 1864, 7 A.M., 525; Rhea, *Cold Harbor,* 389; *OR,* vol. 36, pt. 3, Grant to Meade, June 3, 1864, 7 A.M., 526.

113. *OR,* vol. 36, pt. 3: Meade to Hancock, June 3, 1864, 7:40 A.M., 530; Hancock to Meade, June 3, 1864, 8:25 A.M., 531.

114. *OR,* vol. 36, pt. 3, Humphreys to Warren, June 3, 1864, 539; Rhea, *Cold Harbor,* 376 and 378; *OR,* vol. 36, pt. 3: Grant to Meade, June 3, 1864, 12:30 P.M., 526; Orders, Headquarters, Army of the Potomac, June 3, 1864, 1:30 P.M., 528–29. Warren and Burnside advanced a few hundred yards that morning, then stopped. Rhea, *Cold Harbor,* 372.

115. Porter, *Campaigning with Grant,* 174–75; Rhea, *Cold Harbor,* 312; Grant, *Memoirs,* 503.

116. Rhea, *Cold Harbor,* 386; Lowe, *Meade's Army,* 191 (June 4, 1864); Agassiz, *Meade's Headquarters,* 148 (June 3, 1864).

117. George G. Meade to Margaret Meade, June 4, 1864, Meade Papers, HSP; Rhea, *Cold Harbor,* 382 (Rhea estimates Union losses for the fighting on June 3 to be over six thousand, and Confederate losses at one thousand to fifteen hundred); George G. Meade to Margaret Meade, June 4 and 5, 1864, Meade Papers, HSP.

118. *OR,* vol. 36, pt. 3, Grant to Halleck, May 26, 1864, 206; Hsieh, *West Pointers,* 178.

9. SOUTH TO PETERSBURG

1. Krick, *Civil War Weather,* 132. *OR,* vol. 36, pt. 3: Orders, Headquarters, Army of the Potomac, June 3, 1864, 1:30 P.M., 528–29; Humphreys to Hancock, June 4, 1864, 4:30 P.M.,

572; Orders, Headquarters, Army of the Potomac, June 4, 1864, 7:15 A.M., 570–71. Lowe, *Meade's Army,* 190 (June 4, 1864).

2. *OR,* vol. 36, pt. 3, Grant to Halleck, June 5, 1864, 598.

3. Ibid., Grant to Meade, June 5, 1864, 599.

4. Ibid.: Warren to Humphreys, June 5, 1864, 1 A.M., 609; Sheridan to Humphreys, June 5, 1864, 628; Humphreys (with comments from Meade) to Sheridan, June 5, 1864, 8:30 A.M., 628; Lt. Col. James Forsyth to Gen. James H. Wilson, June 6, 1864, 661.

5. Ibid.: Meade to Hancock (and Smith), June 6, 1864, 10:45 A.M., 642; Hancock to Williams, June 6, 1864, 3:20 P.M., 643; Smith to Meade, June 6, 1864, 11:25 A.M., 660; Hancock to Williams, June 5, 1864, 1 P.M., 603; Meade endorsement to Grant of Hancock request, 604; Grant endorsement to Meade, 604; Meade to Grant, June 5, 1864, 1:30 P.M., 599–600. Lowe, *Meade's Army,* 192–93 (June 5, 1864). *OR,* vol. 36, pt. 3: Grant to Lee, June 6, 1864, 638; Lee to Grant, June 6, 1864, 638; Grant to Lee, June 6, 1864, 638–39; Lee to Grant, June 6, 1864, 7:00 P.M., 639; Grant to Lee, June 7, 1864, 10:30 A.M., 666; Lee to Grant, June 7, 1864, 2:00 P.M., 667; indorsement, Grant to Meade, June 7, 1864, 667; Grant to Lee, June 7, 1864, 5:30 P.M., 667. Lowe, *Meade's Army,* 194 (June 7, 1864).

6. Daily Journal of Capt. George Meade, Meade Papers, HSP; Cleaves, *Meade of Gettysburg,* 252–53; Wilkeson, *Turned Inside Out,* 79; *Philadelphia Inquirer,* June 2, 1864.

7. George G. Meade to Margaret Meade, June 9, 1864, Meade Papers, HSP; *OR,* vol. 36, pt. 3, General Orders, Headquarters, Army of the Potomac, June 7, 1864, 670.

8. Wilkeson, *Turned Inside Out,* 146; George G. Meade to Margaret Meade, June 9, 1864, Meade Papers, HSP; Cleaves, *Meade of Gettysburg,* 254 (on Patrick's role); *OR,* vol. 36, pt. 3, Stanton to Dana, June 10, 1864, 11 P.M., 722.

9. Cadwallader, *Three Years with Grant,* 209. Sherman had *New York Herald* reporter Thomas Knox arrested and tried as a spy for his reporting on the Chickasaw Bayou operation. A military court-martial heard the evidence and found Knox guilty of disobeying orders. He was sent outside Army lines, never allowed to return. See Marszalek, *Sherman,* 211–13.

10. Lowe, *Meade's Army,* 199 (June 11, 1864, heat, photo, squabble) and 197 (June 9, 1864, visit with Hancock).

11. George G. Meade to Margaret Meade, June 12, 1864, Meade Papers, HSP; Lowe, *Meade's Army,* 200 (June 12, 1864).

12. Porter, *Campaigning with Grant,* 188–89.

13. *OR,* vol. 36, pt. 1, Sheridan to Humphreys, June 16, 1864, 2 A.M., 784–85; Chick, *Battle of Petersburg,* 62–64.

14. Chick, *Battle of Petersburg,* 84–90; Lowe, *Meade's Army,* 204 (June 14, 1864).

15. *OR,* vol. 36, pt. 1, Grant report, 25.

16. Porter, *Campaigning with Grant,* 198; *OR,* vol. 40, pt. 2, Grant to Halleck, June 14, 1864, 1:30 P.M., 18–19.

17. *OR,* vol. 40, pt. 2: Hancock to Meade, June 14, 1864, 10 P.M., 28; Meade to Hancock, June 14, 1864, 27 (placed right after a 7 P.M. letter); Meade to Hancock, June 14, 1864, 10 P.M., 29; Benham to Meade, June 14, 1864, 10:50 P.M., 23; Meade to Benham, June 14, 1864, 11:30 P.M., 24; Meade to Benham, June 14, 1864, 11:50 P.M., 24. Benham commanded the Engineering Brigade of the Army of the Potomac from the spring of 1863 to June 1865.

18. Porter, *Campaigning with Grant,* 199; Lowe, *Meade's Army,* 204–5; Porter, *Campaigning with Grant,* 199–200.

19. Chick, *Battle of Petersburg,* 101–19 and 123–35.

20. *OR,* vol. 40, pt. 2: Hancock to Butler, June 15, 1864, 60–61; Hancock to Humphreys, June 15, 1864, 3:30 P.M., 59; Butler to Hancock, June 15, 1864, 8:30 P.M., 60; Smith to Butler, June 15, 1864, midnight, 83; Chick, *Battle of Petersburg,* 136–38, on marching and weather (the moon was out in full until midnight, increasing visibility for troop movement more than Smith admitted).

21. Howe, *Petersburg Campaign*, 38–44; *OR*, vol. 40, pt. 2: Grant to Meade, June 16, 1864, 10:15 A.M., 86; Lincoln to Grant, June 15, 1864, 7 A.M. (received June 16), 47.

22. Chick, *Battle of Petersburg*, 102; Howe, *Wasted Valor*, 42; Walker, *Second Army Corps*, 532–33.

23. Agassiz, *Meade's Headquarters*, 162 (June 15, 1864); Wilkeson, *Turned Inside Out*, 160–63 (quotation on p. 161).

24. *OR*, vol. 40, pt. 2: Maj. W. G. Mitchell (Hancock's aide-de-camp) to Birney and same to Gibbon, June 16, 1864, 12:25 A.M., 93; Walker, *Second Army Corps*, 534–35; *OR*, vol. 36, pt. 1, Daily Memoranda of the Second Corps, June 16, 1864, 318, "at daybreak rode around the lines with the general."

25. *OR*, vol. 40, pt. 1, Hancock report, 305–6.

26. Chick, *Battle of Petersburg*, 163–65; *OR*, vol. 40, pt. 2, Grant to Meade, June 16, 1864, 10:15 A.M., 86; Lowe, *Meade's Army*, 207 (June 16, 1864).

27. Lowe, *Meade's Army*, 207 (June 16, 1864); Chick, *Battle of Petersburg*, 167; *OR*, vol. 40, pt. 2: Barnard to Meade, June 16, 1864, 3:45 P.M., 87; Circular, Headquarters, Second Army Corps, June 16, 1864, 4 P.M., 92.

28. Chick, *Battle of Petersburg*, 167.

29. Howe, *Wasted Valor*, 49.

30. Chick, *Battle of Petersburg*, 176–84.

31. Lowe, *Meade's Army*, 207–8 (June 16, 1864); Porter, *Campaigning with Grant*, 206.

32. Lowe, *Meade's Army*, 208; *OR*, vol. 40, pt. 2: Burnside to Williams, June 17, 1864, 3:15 A.M., 134; Meade to Burnside, June 17, 1864, 3:45 A.M., 134. Chick, *Battle of Petersburg*, 196–98; *OR*, vol. 40, pt. 2, Meade to Burnside, June 17, 1864, 7 A.M., 135.

33. *OR*, vol. 40, pt. 2, Meade to Burnside, June 17, 1864, 7 A.M., 135; Humphreys, *Virginia Campaign*, 218n1; Chick, *Battle of Petersburg*, 163–64; *OR*, vol. 40, pt. 2, Meade to Warren, June 17, 1864, 12 noon, 125.

34. Chick, *Battle of Petersburg*, 202 and 211; Howe, *Wasted Valor*, 70 and 72; George G. Meade to Margaret Meade, June 17, 1864, 12 noon, Meade Papers, HSP.

35. Sumner, *Diary of Cyrus B. Comstock*, 274 (June 17, 1864); *OR*, vol. 40, pt. 2: Meade to Warren, June 17, 1864, 8 P.M., 126; Meade to Locke, June 17, 1864, 8:30 P.M., 127; Warren to Meade, June 17, 1864, 9 P.M., 128; Meade to Warren, June 17, 1864, 8:30 P.M., 127.

36. Chick, *Battle of Petersburg*, 235–39 and 247–48.

37. *OR*, vol. 40, pt. 2: Hancock to Williams, June 18, 1864, 12:45 A.M., 163; Circular, Headquarters, Second Army Corps, June 18, 1864, 1:00 A.M., 170; Circular, Headquarters, Second Army Corps, June 18, 1864, 2:15 A.M., 170; Burnside to Meade, June 18, 1864, 3:15 A.M., 191; Meade to Burnside, June 18, 1864, 192; Circular, Headquarters, Army of the Potomac, June 17, 1864, 11 P.M., 120 (attack to commence at "4 o'clock by the whole force of the Fifth, Ninth, and Second Corps").

38. Lowe, *Meade's Army*, 214–15 (June 18, 1864).

39. Howe, *Wasted Valor*, 139–40; Chick, *Battle of Petersburg*, 249.

40. George G. Meade to Margaret Meade, June 17, 1864, Meade Papers, HSP.

41. Chick, *Battle of Petersburg*, 249–52.

42. Ibid., 254–58; *OR*, vol. 40, pt. 2: Meade to Capt. Charles E. Cadwalader (aide), June 18, 1864, 7 A.M., 203; Cadwalader to Meade, June 18, 1864, 7:50 A.M., 203; Meade to Birney, June 18, 1864, 7 A.M., 165; Meade to Birney, June 18, 1864, 10 A.M., 165; Chick, *Battle of Petersburg*, 245 (Beauregard; numbers predawn on June 18), 258–59, and 262–63.

43. *OR*, vol. 40, pt. 2, Meade to Warren (same as Burnside, Birney, and Martindale), June 18, 1864, 11:34 A.M., 176.

44. Ibid.: Warren to Meade, June 18, 1864, 11:36 A.M., 176; Meade to Warren, June 18, 1864, 11:45 A.M., 177; Lyman to Meade, June 18, 1864, 12 noon, 177; Lyman to Meade, June

18, 1864, 12:45 P.M.. Chick, *Battle of Petersburg*, 260–68; *OR*, vol. 40, pt. 2: Warren to Meade, June 18, 1864, 2 P.M., 179 (Burnside endorsement, too); Meade to Warren and Burnside, June 18, 1864, 2:20 P.M., 179.

45. *OR*, vol. 40, pt. 2, Meade to Birney, June 18, 1864, 2:30 P.M., 167.

46. Chick, *Battle of Petersburg*, 270–85; *OR*, vol. 40, pt. 2: Meade to Birney, June 18, 1864, 5 P.M., 168; Meade to Warren (same to Burnside), June 18, 1864, 6:30 P.M., 180; Meade to Martindale, June 18, 1864, 5 P.M., 206; Warren to Meade, June 18, 1864, 7 P.M., 181; Meade to Warren, June 18, 1864, 7:30 P.M., 181.

47. *OR*, vol. 40, pt. 2: Meade to Grant, June 18, 1864, 6:30 P.M., 156; Grant to Meade, June 18, 1864, 6:50 P.M., 156; Meade to Grant, June 18, 1864, 9:50 P.M., 156–57.

48. *OR*, vol. 40, pt. 2, Grant to Meade, June 18, 1864, 10 P.M., 157.

49. Nevins, *Diary of Battle*, 425 (June 18, 1864); Agassiz, *Meade's Headquarters*, 170 (June 18, 1864).

50. Wilkeson, *Turned Inside Out*, 181; Nevins, *Diary of Battle*, 425 (June 18, 1864) and 426 (June 19, 1864).

51. George G. Meade to Margaret Meade, June 21, 1864, and June 24, 1864, Meade Papers, HSP. Historian Carol Reardon argues that Meade's commander, Grant, "may not have understood the price his soldiers paid in carrying out his order, even as he insisted that they pay it." See *With a Sword*, 111.

52. Chick, *Battle of Petersburg*, 294 (battle losses) and 295 (quotation); Agassiz, *Meade's Headquarters*, 170 (June 18, 1864).

53. Hess, *In the Trenches*, 52 and 65; Lowe, *Meade's Army*, 215–17 (June 18 and 19, 1864); *OR*, vol. 40, pt. 2, Williams to Meade, June 19, 1864, 6:30 P.M., 208.

54. Krick, *Civil War Weather*, 132 (88°F in Washington, D.C., by 2:00 P.M. that day); *OR*, vol. 40, pt. 2, Meade to Grant, June 20, 1864, 10 A.M., 232.

55. OR, vol. 40, pt. 3, Meade to Warren, July 22, 1864, 393. Meade referred to the discussion occurring on June 19, but it took place on June 20.

56. G. K. Warren to Emily Warren, June 20, 1864, in Warren Papers, NYSL. Too bad Warren had not befriended Brigadier General Patrick. The provost marshal general was angry at Meade for using "his" cavalry instead of Sheridan's and wrote in his diary on June 19, "They are trying to get my Cavalry away from me and Meade is showing himself up as he really is, a very *mean* man. There is a great deal of dissatisfaction in the Army about him." Sparks, *Inside Lincoln's Army*, 386 (June 19, 1864).

57. *OR*, vol. 40, pt. 3: Meade to Warren, July 22, 1864, 393; Meade to Rawlins, June 21, 1864, Meade Papers, HSP.

58. *OR*, vol. 40, pt. 3, Meade to Warren, July 22, 1864, 393; *OR*, vol. 40, pt. 1, Dana to Stanton, June 20, 1864, 5 P.M., 26. *OR*, vol. 40, pt. 3: Warren to Meade, July 22, 1864, 393 (with clipping from the *Pittsburg Commercial*); Meade to Warren, July 22, 1864, 394. G. K. Warren to Emily Warren, July 24, 1864, Warren Papers, NYSL.

59. Meade to Rawlins, June 21, 1864, Meade Papers, HSP.

60. *OR*, vol. 40, pt. 3, Meade to Warren, July 22, 1864, 394.

61. *OR*, vol. 40, pt. 2: Grant to Meade, June 20, 1864, 232; Meade to Grant, June 20, 1864, 6:30 P.M., 233; Grant to Meade, June 20, 1864, 5:40 P.M., 233.

62. Ibid.: Meade to Grant, June 21, 1864, 9 A.M., 267; Humphreys to Wilson, June 21, 1864, 9:20 A.M., 285; Humphreys to Wilson, June 21, 1864, 12 midday, 285–86; Grant to Meade, June 21, 1864, 268.

63. Porter, *Campaigning with Grant*, 216–23; George G. Meade to Margaret Meade, June 21, 1864, Meade Papers, HSP. Lincoln saw Mrs. Meade at the Philadelphia fair where money for the war was raised, as well as money for the "sword contest" between Meade and Hancock.

64. *OR,* vol. 40, pt. 1: Birney report, 325; Morgan report, 328; Morgan to Barlow, June 22, 1864, about 10 A.M., in Birney report, 326; Morgan report, 328. Birney had taken command of the Second Corps for the incapacitated Hancock.

65. Bearss, *Battle of the Jerusalem Plank Road,* 28–36 (quotation on p. 30).

66. Ibid., 45–48; *OR,* vol. 40, pt. 2: Humphreys to Birney, June 22, 1864, 309; Meade to Grant, June 22, 1864, 9 P.M., 304.

67. Bearss, *Battle of the Jerusalem Plank Road,* 46; *OR,* vol. 40, pt. 1, Barlow report, 329.

68. *OR,* vol. 40, pt. 2: Barlow to Walker, June 23, 1864, 341; Meade to Birney, June 23, 1864, 8:30 A.M., 339; Humphreys to Wright, June 23, 1864, 12 P.M., 351; Humphreys to Wright, June 23, 1864, 12 P.M., 350.

69. Bearss, *Battle of the Jerusalem Plank Road,* 56–57; *OR,* vol. 40, pt. 2: Humphreys to Warren, June 23, 1864, 3:50 P.M., 343; Humphreys to Birney, June 23, 1864, 4 P.M., 340; Humphreys to Wright, June 23, 4 P.M., 353.

70. *OR,* vol. 40, pt. 2: Meade to Wright, June 23, 1864, 6:30 P.M., 356; Meade to Wright, June 23, 1864, 6:55 P.M., 356; Wright to Meade, June 23, 1864, 7 P.M., 357; Meade to Wright, June 23, 1864, 7:20 P.M. 357; Meade to Wright, June 23, 1864, 7:35 P.M., 358; Wright to Meade, June 23, 1864, 8:50 P.M., 358; Meade to Wright, June 23, 1864, 9 P.M., 358–59.

71. Lowe, *Meade's Army,* 223–25 (quotations from p. 225, June 24, 1864).

72. Lowe, *Meade's Army,* 225–26 (quotations from p. 226, June 25, 1864); Bearss, *Battle of the Jerusalem Plank Road,* 65.

73. *OR,* vol. 40, pt. 2, Orders, Headquarters, Sixth Corps, June 24, 1864, 1 A.M., 392; Bearss, *Battle of the Jerusalem Plank Road,* 65; *OR,* vol. 40, pt. 2: Wright to Humphreys, June 24, 1864, 10:15 A.M., 388; Humphreys to Wright, June 24, 1864, 10:30 A.M., 388; Meade to Grant, June 24, 1864, 8 A.M., 373; Meade to Grant, June 24, 1864, 11 A.M., 374.

74. Lowe, *Meade's Army,* 226 (June 24, 1864). The French officers were Lt. Col. François De Chanal and Capt. Pierre Guzman. Ibid., 452n29; *OR,* vol. 40, pt. 2, Grant to Halleck, June 25, 1864, 11:30 A.M., 402.

75. George G. Meade to Margaret Meade, June 25, 1864, and George G. Meade to Margaret Meade, July 17, 1864, Meade Papers, HSP; *New York Times,* July 16, 1864.

76. Agassiz, *Meade's Headquarters,* 189 (July 12, 1864); George G. Meade to Margaret Meade, July 12, 1864, Meade Papers, HSP.

77. George G. Meade to Margaret Meade, July 12 and 15, 1864, Meade Papers, HSP; *OR,* vol. 40, pt. 1, Dana to Stanton, July 7, 1864, 8 A.M., 35–36.

78. George G. Meade to Margaret Meade, July 15 and 29, 1864, Meade Papers, HSP; Sparks, *Inside Lincoln's Army,* 403–4 (July 27, 1864).

79. George G. Meade to Margaret Meade, Aug. 3, 1864, Meade Papers, HSP.

80. Simpson, *Ulysses S. Grant,* 349–58; *OR,* vol. 40, pt. 2, Smith to Grant, July 2, 1864, 595 (on Butler, Smith wrote, "how you can place a man in command of two army corps, who is as helpless as a child on the field of battle and as visionary as an opium eaten in council"); Smith, *From Chattanooga to Petersburg,* 116; Agassiz, *Meade's Headquarters,* 193 (July 20, 1864).

81. Hess, *Into the Crater,* 1–3, 11; *OR,* vol. 40, pt. 2: Burnside to Humphreys, June 25, 1864, 2:45 P.M., and Meade to Burnside, June 25, 1864, 3:00 P.M., 417.

82. Hess, *Into the Crater,* 11, 21–24, 50–53.

83. Ibid., 11 and 18–21.

84. Ibid., 29–30; *OR,* vol. 40, pt. 3: Grant to Meade, July 24, 1864, 424; Meade to Grant, July 24, 1864, 425; Duane to Meade, July 24, 1864, 428.

85. *OR,* vol. 40, pt. 3: Grant to Meade, July 24, 1864, 425–26; Grant to Meade, July 25, 1864 (received 8:30 A.M.), 437–38; Grant to Meade, July 25, 1864, 438.

86. Price, *Battle of First Deep Bottom,* 52, 54, 36–39; *OR,* vol. 40, pt. 3: Hancock to Meade, July 27, 1864, 1:30 A.M., 510; Meade to Hancock, July 27, 1864, 2:15 A.M., 510.

87. Price, *Battle of First Deep Bottom*, 59, 73, 81–83, 87–114, 122–23, 129; *OR*, vol. 40, pt. 3, Grant to Halleck, July 28, 1864, 9 P.M., 551; Hess, *Into the Crater*, 48–49.

88. *OR*, vol. 40, pt. 3: Burnside to Humphreys, July 26, 1864, 476–77; Grant to Meade, July 28, 1864, 12:20 P.M., 553; Meade to Grant, July 28, 1864, 1:00 P.M., 553–54.

89. Ibid., Orders, Headquarters, Army of the Potomac, July 29, 1864, 596–97.

90. *OR*, vol. 40, pt. 1, Court of Inquiry, Meade testimony, Aug. 8, 1864, 46; *RCCW*, 125; *OR*, vol. 40, pt. 1, Court of Inquiry, Aug. 10, 1864, Burnside testimony, 60–61; *OR*, vol. 40, pt. 3, Humphreys to Burnside, July 29, 1864, 10:15 A.M., 608 (Grant concurred with Meade on the use of white troops); *OR*, vol. 40, pt. 1, Court of Inquiry, Aug. 8, 1864, Meade testimony, 47.

91. Hess, *Into the Crater*, 56–57; *OR*, vol. 40, pt. 1, Court of Inquiry, Burnside testimony, Aug. 10, 1864, 61; Hess, *Into the Crater*, 58–59; Marvel, *Burnside*, 395; *OR*, vol. 40, pt. 3, Circular (orders), Headquarters, Ninth Army Corps, July 29, 1864, 611–12.

92. Hess, *Into the Crater*, 77–86; *OR*, vol. 40, pt. 3: Humphreys to Burnside, July 30, 1864, 4:15 A.M., 657; Humphreys to Burnside, July 30, 1864, 4:20 A.M., 657; Humphreys to Burnside, July 30, 1864, 4:35 A.M., 657; Gibbon, *Personal Recollections*, 253.

93. Hess, *Into the Crater*; Cavanaugh and Marvel, *Battle of the Crater*; Cannan, *Crater*; Axelrod, *Horrid Pit*; Schmutz, *Battle of the Crater*; and Levin, *Remembering the Battle*. For Confederate views, see Bernard, *War Talks of Confederate Veterans*, and selected chapters in Newsome, Horn, and Selby, *Civil War Talks*.

94. *OR*, vol. 40, pt. 3: Meade to Burnside, July 30, 1864, 5:40 A.M., 657; Burnside to Meade, July 30, 1864, 5:40 A.M., 657; Hess, *Into the Crater*, 88–99; *OR*, vol. 40, pt. 3: Meade to Burnside, July 30, 1864, 5:40 A.M., 658; Meade to Burnside, July 30, 1864, 658.

95. *OR*, vol. 40, pt. 3: Capt. William W. Sanders (aide to Burnside) to Meade, July 30, 1864, 6:10 A.M., 658; Burnside to Meade, July 30, 1864, 660; Meade to Burnside, July 30, 1864, 7:30 A.M., 660; Burnside to Meade, July 30, 1864, 660; Hess, *Into the Crater*, 101–2.

96. Hess, *Into the Crater*, 100–102; *OR*, vol. 40, pt. 3: Meade to Burnside, July 30, 1864, 8 A.M., 661; Burnside to Meade, July 30, 1864, 9 A.M. (two messages), 661; Humphreys to Warren, July 30, 1864, 8:45 A.M., 653; Warren to Humphreys, July 30, 1864, 9:15 A.M., 654; Meade to Warren, July 30, 1864, 9:25 A.M., 654.

97. Hess, *Into the Crater*, 135 and 170; *OR*, vol. 40, pt. 3: Meade to Burnside (and Ord), July 30, 1864, 9:30 A.M., 662; Meade to Burnside, July 30, 1864, 9:45 A.M., 662; Meade to Burnside (and Ord), July 30, 1864, 10 A.M., 662.

98. Lowe, *Meade's Army*, 242–43 (July 30, 1864); Hess, *Into the Crater*, 172 and 170.

99. Hess, *Into the Crater*, 150–89 and 200 (casualties).

100. *OR*, vol. 40, pt. 1, Court of Inquiry, Charge 1 (Disobedience of Orders), specification 2, 1, Aug. 3, 1864, 175; *OR*, vol. 40, pt. 3: Humphreys to Burnside, July 30, 1864, 7:40 P.M., 664; Humphreys to Burnside, July 30, 1864, 10:35 P.M., 664. *JCCW*, 24–25 (Burnside testimony); *OR*, vol. 40, pt. 3: Humphreys to Burnside, July 31, 1864, 7:20 P.M., 705–6; Burnside to Humphreys, July 31, 1864, 703; Humphreys to Burnside, July 31, 1864, 3:30 P.M., 703; Burnside to Humphreys, July 31, 1864 (received 9:10 P.M.), 706; Humphreys to Burnside, July 31, 1864, 9:30 P.M., 707; Lowe, *Meade's Army*, 224 (Aug. 1, 1864). Marvel lays the blame for Burnside's lack of communication at the feet of Brig. Gen. Julius White, a division commander under Burnside in east Tennessee who had recently arrived and been assigned the job of chief-of-staff in Maj. Gen. John Parke's absence. See Marvel, *Burnside*, 403.

101. Hess, *Into the Crater*, 220–21; Sumner, *Diary of Cyrus B. Comstock*, 285 (July 30, 1864); Porter, *Campaigning with Grant*, 269; George G. Meade to Margaret Meade, July 31, 1864, Meade Papers, HSP; *OR*, vol. 40, pt. 1, Court of Inquiry, 67 (Burnside testimony).

102. *OR*, vol. 40, pt. 1: Special Orders 205, Headquarters, Army of the Potomac, Aug. 1, 1864, 171–72; Meade to Rawlins, Aug. 3, 1864, 172–76 (letter and formal charges); Record of the Court of Inquiry, 42–164; Hess, *Into the Crater*, 221–24. Burnside asked Stanton and

Lincoln to have officers outside the Army of the Potomac on the board, but they refused. See *OR,* vol. 40, pt. 1: Burnside to Stanton, Aug. 6, 1864, 531–32; Stanton to Burnside, Aug. 8, 1864, 11 A.M., 532.

103. George G. Meade to Margaret Meade, Aug. 10 and 13, 1864, Meade Papers, HSP.

104. *OR,* vol. 40, pt. 3, Grant to Meade, July 30, 1864, 638–39.

10. EXTENDING THE LINE

1. George G. Meade to Margaret Meade, Aug. 3, 10, and 13, 1864, Meade Papers, HSP; Grant, *Personal Memoirs,* 528.

2. Hess, *In the Trenches,* 109, 110, and 111–22; Lowe, *Meade's Army,* 248 (Aug. 9, 1864); George G. Meade to Margaret Meade, Aug. 6, 1864, Meade Papers, HSP.

3. Grant, *Memoirs,* 528, 533–34; *OR,* vol. 42, pt. 2: Grant to Butler, Aug. 12, 1864, 136; Meade to Humphreys, Aug. 12, 1864, 11 A.M., 124.

4. *OR,* vol. 42, pt. 2: Meade to Grant, Aug. 14, 1864, 8:30 A.M., 168; Grant to Meade, Aug. 14, 1864, 168; Willcox to Humphreys, Aug. 13, 1864, 9 P.M., 154; Humphreys to Willcox, Aug. 13, 1864, 9:40 P.M., 155; Willcox to Humphreys, Aug. 13, 1864, 9:55 P.M., 155; Meade to Grant, Aug. 13, 1864, 10 P.M., 142; Grant to Meade, Aug. 13, 1864, 142.

5. Horn, *Siege of Petersburg,* 15–104; Hess, *In the Trenches,* 124–28.

6. *OR,* vol. 42, pt. 2, Grant to Meade, Aug. 17, 1864, 244.

7. Ibid.: Humphreys to Warren, Aug. 17, 1864, 2:30 P.M., 251; Warren to Humphreys, Aug. 18, 1864, 4 A.M., 271.

8. Horn, *Siege of Petersburg,* 122–35; *OR,* vol. 42, pt. 2: Warren to Humphreys, Aug. 18, 1864, 10 A.M., 272 (on sunstroke); Warren to Humphreys, Aug. 18, 1864, 2:30 P.M., 273 (fighting); Warren to Humphreys, Aug. 18, 1864, 7:00 P.M., 275.

9. *OR,* vol. 42, pt. 2: Grant to Hancock, Aug. 18, 1864, 10:30 A.M., 268; Hancock to Grant, Aug. 18, 1864, 268; Grant to Meade, Aug. 18, 1864, 7:40 P.M., 266; Grant to Meade, Aug. 18, 1864, 11:15 P.M., 266; Humphreys to Parke, Aug. 18, 1864, 9:45 P.M., 282; Parke to Humphreys, Aug. 18, 1864, 10 P.M., 282.

10. Horn, *Siege of Petersburg,* 140–45; Agassiz, *Meade's Headquarters,* 219 (Aug. 19, 1864).

11. Horn, *Siege of Petersburg,* 150–71. Horn provides excellent analysis and narrative of this swirling battle.

12. Lowe, *Meade's Army,* 251–53 (Aug. 19, 1864).

13. *OR,* vol. 42, pt. 2: Warren to Meade, Aug. 19, 1864, 8:15 P.M., 308–9; Meade to Warren, Aug. 19, 1864, 8:30 P.M., 309; Meade to Warren, Aug. 19, 1864, 10:30 P.M., 309–10; Warren to Meade, Aug. 19, 1864 (received 12:15 A.M. on Aug. 20, 1864), 310; Warren to Meade, Aug. 20, 1864, 10 A.M., 358–59; Grant to Meade, Aug. 20, 1864, 8:15 P.M., 328.

14. Horn, *Siege of Petersburg,* 181–82; Hess, *In the Trenches,* 132.

15. Horn, *Siege of Petersburg,* 183, 188–205.

16. *OR,* vol. 42, pt. 2: Meade to Grant, Aug. 21, 1864, 10 A.M., 354; Grant to Meade, Aug. 21, 1864, 12:45 P.M., 355; Meade to Grant, Aug. 21, 1864, 10:25 P.M., 354; Warren to Humphreys, Aug. 21, 1864, 3:00 P.M., 369.

17. Ibid.: Meade to Grant, Aug. 21, 1864, 9:20 P.M., 358; Grant to Meade, Aug. 21, 1864, 10 P.M., 358.

18. Horn, *Siege of Petersburg,* 210–26.

19. Ibid., 227–41; *OR,* vol. 42, pt. 2: Hancock to Meade, Aug. 25, 1864, 2:00 P.M., 483.

20. *OR,* vol. 42, pt. 2: Meade to Hancock, Aug. 25, 1864, 1:00 P.M., 482; Meade to Grant, Aug. 25, 1864, 2:00 P.M., 467; Grant to Meade, Aug. 25, 1864, 467. Horn, *Siege of Petersburg,* 244–45.

21. Ibid., 235–47.

22. *OR*, vol. 42, pt. 2: Meade to Hancock, Aug. 25, 1864, 1:00 P.M., 482; Hancock to Meade, Aug. 25, 1864, 2:45 P.M., 483.

23. Horn, *Siege of Petersburg*, 251–74.

24. *OR*, vol. 42, pt. 2: Humphreys to Hancock, Aug. 25, 1864, 7:30 P.M., 485; Humphreys to Hancock, Aug. 25, 1864, 9:00 P.M., 485; Humphreys to Hancock, Aug. 25, 1864, 10:30 P.M., 485; Meade to Hancock, Aug. 25, 1864, 11 P.M., 486.

25. Ibid.: Hancock to Meade, Aug. 26, 1864, 2:00 A.M., 524–25; Hancock to Meade (and Grant), Aug. 26, 1864 (received 9:45 A.M.), 525–26.

26. Horn, *Siege of Petersburg*, 27; Jordan, *Winfield Scott Hancock*, 163–64; Walker, *Second Army Corps*, 602–5; W. C. Morgan quoted in Walker, *Second Army Corps*, 598–99; Walker, *General Hancock*, 275.

27. Horn, *Siege of Petersburg*, 309–10.

28. *OR*, vol. 42, pt. 2, Grant to Meade, Aug. 26, 1864, 520.

29. George G. Meade to Margaret Meade, Aug. 24, 1864, Meade Papers, HSP.

30. Ibid.

31. George G. Meade to Margaret Meade, Aug. 26, 1864, Meade Papers, HSP.

32. Cleaves, *Meade of Gettysburg*, 60, 292; Sergeant's condition was discussed in every letter from George to Margaret Meade within Sept. 1864 (Sept. 8, 10, 12, 15, 16, 17, 19, 22, 23, 25, and 27), Meade Papers, HSP.

33. Morris, *Sheridan*, 193–94; Cleaves, *Meade of Gettysburg*, 193; George G. Meade to Margaret Meade, Sept. 22, 1864, Meade Papers, HSP.

34. Hess, *In the Trenches*, 144–49; George G. Meade to Margaret Meade, Sept. 16 and 25, 1864, Meade Papers, HSP.

35. *OR*, vol. 39, pt. 2, Grant to Sherman, Sept. 12, 1864, 364; Sommers, *Richmond Redeemed*, 3–6.

36. *OR*, vol. 42, pt. 2, Grant to Meade, Sept. 27, 1864, 1046–47.

37. Ibid.: Orders, Headquarters, Army of the Potomac, Sept. 28, 1864, 1069.

38. Sommers, *Richmond Redeemed*, 179–99.

39. Ibid., 12–101; Hess, *In the Trenches*, 160–64.

40. *OR*, vol. 42, pt. 2, Grant to Meade, Sept. 30, 1864, 8:15 A.M. (received 8:25 A.M.), 1118.

41. Ibid.: Humphreys to Parke, Sept. 30, 1864, 9:00 A.M., 1137; Humphreys to Gregg, Sept. 30, 1864, 9 A.M., 1139–40; Meade to Grant, Sept. 30, 1864, 8:30 A.M., 1118; Sommers, *Richmond Redeemed*, 235.

42. Sommers, *Richmond Redeemed*, 235–52 (quotation from p. 249).

43. Ibid., 258–68; *OR*, vol. 42, pt. 2: Grant to Meade, Sept. 30, 1864 (received 3:25 P.M.), 1119; Grant to Meade, Sept. 30, 1864, 1119 (and Gregg); Butler to Grant, Sept. 30, 1864, 3:50 P.M., 1143.

44. Sommers, *Richmond Redeemed*, 271–97 (quotation on p. 280).

45. Ibid., 300; *OR*, vol. 42, pt. 2: Meade to Grant, Sept. 30, 1864, 9:00 P.M., 1121; Grant to Meade, Sept. 30, 1864, 9:40 P.M., 1121.

46. Sommers, *Richmond Redeemed*, 326–59; *OR*, vol. 42, pt. 3: Meade to Grant, Oct. 1, 1864, 8:00 A.M. ("Parke and Warren were ordered to advance if they deemed it practicable"), 4; Grant to Meade, Oct. 1, 1864, 5; Humphreys to Parke, Oct. 1, 1864, 6:45 P.M., 26–27; Humphreys to Warren, Oct. 1, 1864, 7:00 P.M., 19.

47. Sommers, *Richmond Redeemed*, 368–73; *OR*, vol. 42, pt. 3: Meade to Grant, Oct. 2, 1864, 11 A.M., 36; Grant to Meade, Oct. 2, 1864, 11:10 A.M., 36; Grant to Meade, Oct. 2, 1864, 36; Sommers, *Richmond Redeemed*, 394–95.

48. George G. Meade to Margaret Meade, Oct. 3, 1864, Meade Papers, HSP.

49. Sommers, *Richmond Redeemed*, 376–77; Hess, *In the Trenches*, 168; *OR*, vol. 46, pt. 1,

Grant report, 30; *OR,* vol. 42, pt. 1, Meade report, 31; George G. Meade to Margaret Meade, Oct. 1, 1864, Meade Papers, HSP.

50. Hess, *In the Trenches,* 141.

51. George G. Meade to Margaret Meade, Oct. 13, 1864, Meade Papers, HSP.

52. George G. Meade to Margaret Meade, Oct. 19 and 27, 1864, Meade Papers, HSP.

53. *New York Independent,* Oct. 13, 1864; George G. Meade to Margaret Meade, Oct. 23, 1864, Meade Papers, HSP. Meade did not read the article until Oct. 23, though he knew of its existence. He did not mention the article to Grant when they met on Oct. 19.

54. George G. Meade to Margaret Meade, Oct. 25, 1864, Meade Papers, HSP; *OR,* vol. 42, pt. 3, Grant to Meade, Oct. 24, 1864, 31.

55. Lowe, *Meade's Army,* 284 (Oct. 25, 1864).

56. Newsome, *Richmond Must Fall,* 129.

57. *OR,* vol. 42, pt. 3: Grant to Meade, Oct. 24, 1864, 317; Orders, Headquarters of the Army of the Potomac, Oct. 25, 1864, 340–42; Newsome, *Richmond Must Fall,* 125 (forty-one thousand men for the strike force).

58. Newsome, *Richmond Must Fall,* 137.

59. Ibid., 183 and 197 (weather), 201, 221; *OR,* vol. 42, pt. 1, Hancock report, 231.

60. Newsome, *Richmond Must Fall,* 220–25.

61. Ibid., 225–27.

62. Ibid., 137–38, 162–77.

63. Ibid., 239–40, 245–46, 251–256, 264–68.

64. *OR,* vol. 42, pt. 3: Humphreys to Hancock, Oct. 27, 1864, 5:15 P.M., 381; Hancock to Humphreys, Oct. 27, 1864, 9:00 P.M., 382; Hancock to Humphreys, Oct. 27, 1864, 382–83; Newsome, *Richmond Must Fall,* 278–81, 287.

65. Newsome, *Richmond Must Fall,* 288–89; *OR,* vol. 42, pt. 1, Meade report, 32; *OR,* vol. 42, pt. 3: Grant to Stanton, Oct. 27, 1864, 9:00 P.M., 373; Grant to Meade, Oct. 28, 1864, 402–3; Meade to Grant, Oct. 28, 1864, 11:00 A.M., 403; Newsome, *Richmond Must Fall,* 293–95; Agassiz, *Meade's Headquarters,* 251 (Oct. 28, 1864); Newsome, *Richmond Must Fall,* 299–300; George G. Meade to Margaret Meade, Oct. 27, 1864, Meade Papers, HSP.

66. George G. Meade to Margaret Meade, Oct. 29, 1864, Meade Papers, HSP.

67. George G. Meade to Margaret Meade, Oct. 31, 1864, Meade Papers, HSP; George G. Meade to Margaret Meade, Oct. 13, 1864 ("persistent efforts have been made"), Meade Papers, HSP.

68. Cadwallader, *Three Years with Grant,* 256–57.

69. George G. Meade to Margaret Meade: Oct. 9, 23 (improved health), 31 (no to the trip), 13 (quotation), 1864, Meade Papers, HSP.

70. Lowe, *Meade's Army,* 371 (Sept. 28, 1864) and 452n29; George G. Meade to Margaret Meade, Oct. 11, 1864, Meade Papers, HSP; *OR,* vol. 42, pt. 3, Badeau to Meade, Oct. 25, 1864, 337; George G. Meade to Margaret Meade, Oct. 18 and 11, 1864, Meade Papers, HSP; Lowe, *Meade's Army,* 280 (Oct. 12, 1864) and 463n43.

71. Hess, *In the Trenches,* 174 (quotation) and 181.

72. *OR,* vol. 42, pt. 3: Grant to Meade, Dec. 5, 1864, 804–5; Williams to Warren, Dec. 6, 1864, 828–29; Meade to Grant, Dec. 7, 1864, 10:30 A.M., 842; Grant to Halleck, Dec. 7, 1864, 10 P.M., 842; Grant to Shepley, Dec. 10, 1864, 11 A.M., 950; Warren to Meade, Dec. 11, 1864, 11 A.M., 951; Grant to Halleck, Dec. 11, 1864, 4:30 P.M., 951; Meade to Grant, Dec. 11, 1864, 5:45 P.M., 953. *OR,* vol. 42, pt. 1, Warren report, 443–46. Meade had suggested an attack on Confederate lines when Warren returned, but when he did and Meade saw the exhausted condition of the men, Meade called it off (with Grant's permission). *OR,* vol. 42, pt. 3: Meade to Grant, Dec. 11, 1864, 1 P.M., 952–53; Meade to Grant, Dec. 12, 1864, 12 P.M. 972; Grant to Meade, Dec. 12, 1864, 972.

73. George G. Meade to Margaret Meade, Nov. 9, 11, and 22, 1864; George G. Meade to John Sergeant Meade, Nov. 17, 1864; Meade Papers, HSP.

74. Lowe, *Meade's Army,* 304 (Dec. 6, 1864); Jordan, *Winfield Scott Hancock,* 169–72; *OR,* vol. 42, pt. 3: Hancock to Meade, Nov. 16, 1864, 8:50 P.M., 628–29; Meade to Hancock, Nov. 16, 1864, 9 P.M., 629; Meade to Hancock, Nov. 25, 1864, 6:30 P.M., 705.

75. *OR,* vol. 46, pt. 2, Special Orders, Headquarters, Army of the Potomac, Jan. 11, 1865, 94; *OR,* vol. 42, pt. 3, Gibbon to Williams, Nov. 26, 1864, 714; Lowe, *Meade's Army,* 300 (Nov. 27, 1864); *OR,* vol. 42, pt. 3: Gibbon to Williams, Dec. 3, 1864, 788; Meade to Gibbon, Dec. 13, 1864, 10 P.M., 988.

76. George G. Meade to Margaret Meade, Nov. 15, 1864, Meade Papers, HSP; Lowe, *Meade's Army,* 296 (Nov. 16, 1864); George G. Meade to Margaret Meade, Nov. 20 and 25, 1864, Meade Papers, HSP.

77. George G. Meade to Henry A. Cram, Jan. 21, 1865, Meade Papers, HSP; *OR,* vol. 46, pt. 2: Grant to Wilson, Jan. 23, 1865, 206; Grant to Washburne, Jan. 23, 1865, reprinted in Meade, *Life and Letters,* 2:344.

78. George G. Meade to Margaret Meade, Dec. 18, 1864, Meade Papers, HSP; Tap, *Over Lincoln's Shoulder,* 189–91; Grant to Meade, Feb. 9, 1865, in Meade, *Life and Letters,* 2:344.

79. Tap, *Over Lincoln's Shoulder,* 192.

80. George G. Meade to Margaret Meade, Feb. 2, 4, and 7, 1865 (quotation from Feb. 2 letter), Meade Papers, HSP; Lowe, *Meade's Army,* 327 (Feb. 2, 1865).

81. George G. Meade to Margaret Meade, Dec. 3, 6, 16, 18, 20, 23, 24, and 26, 1864: letters mention concerns about Sergeant's health and some discuss the difficulty of leaving his post; George G. Meade to Margaret Meade, Jan. 10, 1865, Meade Papers, HSP.

82. Sergeant's health is mentioned in each of the following letters Meade sent to his wife: January 10, 12, 14, 17, and 22, and February 1, 4, 7, 9, 11, 13, 19, and 21. Unfortunately, the letters Margaret sent to George were not preserved, so her views must always be inferred. The quoted passages come from George G. Meade to Margaret Meade, Feb. 13, 1865, Meade Papers, HSP.

83. George G. Meade to Margaret Meade, Feb. 21, 27, and 28 (quotation in Feb. 27 letter), Meade Papers, HSP; Meade, *Life and Letters,* travel information in note on p. 264.

84. George G. Meade to Margaret Meade, Feb. 1, 1865, Meade Papers, HSP; McPherson, *Battle Cry of Freedom,* 822–24. The three men were Alexander Stephens, Robert M. T. Hunter, and John A. Campbell.

85. *OR,* vol. 46, pt. 2: Grant to Meade, Feb. 4, 1865, 367; Meade to Grant, Feb. 4, 1865, sent 4:30 P.M., received 5:45 P.M., 367–68; Grant to Meade, Feb. 4, 1865, 6:45 P.M., 368; Meade to Grant, Feb. 4, 1865, sent 8:15 P.M., 368.

86. Ibid.: Meade to Grant, Feb. 5, 1865, 2:30 P.M., 389; Gregg to Webb, Feb. 5, 1865, 4:20 P.M., 409; Meade to Gregg, Feb. 5, 1865, 6:25 P.M., 409; Meade to Grant, Feb. 5, 1865, 6:45 P.M., 710.

87. Ibid.: Grant to Meade, Feb. 5, 1865, 7:15 P.M., 390; Webb to Warren, Feb. 5, 1865, received 8:00 P.M., 402; Meade to Humphreys, Feb. 5, 1865, 9:00 P.M., 396.

88. Ibid.: Warren to Webb, Feb. 6, 1865, 10 A.M., 431; Webb to Warren, Feb. 6, 1865, 7:50 A.M., 423; Circular No. 8, Headquarters, Fifth Army Corps, Feb. 6, 1865, 1:15 P.M., 434; Meade to Grant, Feb. 6, 1865, 7:30 P.M., 418; Meade to Grant, Feb. 6, 1865, 1:00 P.M., 417; Grant to Meade, Feb. 6, 1865, 2:50 P.M., 417.

89. Ibid.: Meade to Grant, Feb. 7, 1865, 10:15 A.M., 447; Grant to Meade, Feb. 7, 1865, 11:30 A.M., 447; Meade to Grant, Feb. 7, 1865, 5:15 P.M., 448; Circular, Headquarters, Army of the Potomac, Feb. 7, 1865, 450.

90. Hess, *In the Trenches,* 232–33; George G. Meade to Margaret Meade, Feb. 11, 1865, Meade Papers, HSP.

91. Lowe, *Meade's Army*, 337–50 (Mar. 3–25, 1865); specific visitors noted on Mar. 3 (Boitano), Mar. 7 (Mrs. Grant), Mar. 10 (Mrs. Jay Cooke), Mar. 16 (Edwin Stanton), Mar. 25 (President and Mrs. Lincoln); George G. Meade to Margaret Meade, Mar. 10, 1865 (quotation), and Mar. 16, 1865, Meade Papers, HSP; description of activities during the visit of the Meade family from Lowe, *Meade's Army*, 348–50 (Mar. 22–25, 1865); George G. Meade to Margaret Meade, Mar. 26, 1865, Meade Papers, HSP.

92. Hess, *In the Trenches*, 245–54; *OR*, vol. 46, pt. 1, Grant to Meade, Ord, and Sheridan, Mar. 24, 1865, 50–51.

93. Lowe, *Meade's Army*, 350–51 (Mar. 28, 1865); *OR*, vol. 46, pt. 1, Grant's report, 51–52.

94. George G. Meade to Henry A. Cram, Nov. 24, 1864, Meade Papers, HSP.

11. THE DEFEAT OF LEE AND THE END OF THE ARMY OF THE POTOMAC

1. *OR*, vol. 46, pt. 3: Orders, Headquarters, Army of the Potomac, Mar. 27, 1865, 198–99, and modifications of the Orders, Mar. 28, 1865, 224; Orders, Headquarters, Department of Virginia, Mar. 27, 1865, 210–11; Grant to Sheridan, Mar. 28, 1865, 234.

2. Grant, *Personal Memoirs*, 600.

3. Calkins, *Appomattox Campaign*, 16–21; *OR*, vol. 46, pt. 3, Webb (chief of staff) to Warren, Mar. 29, 1865, 7:00 P.M., 256.

4. *OR*, vol. 46, pt. 3, Grant to Sheridan, Mar. 29, 1865, 266.

5. Lowe, *Meade's Army*, 353 (Mar. 30, 1865); *OR*, vol. 46, pt. 3: Lincoln to Stanton, Mar. 30, 1865, 7:30 P.M., 280; Grant to Lt. Col. T. S. Bowers (adjutant at City Point; Lincoln's contact man there), Mar. 30, 1865, two dispatches, 281–82.

6. *OR*, vol. 46, pt. 3: Meade to Grant, Mar. 30, 1865, 11:50 P.M., 286; Grant to Meade, Mar. 30, 1865, 286–87; Grant to Sheridan, Mar. 30, 1865, 325 (quotation).

7. Calkins, *Appomattox Campaign*, 22–27; Hess, *In the Trenches*, 258–60.

8. Lowe, *Meade's Army*, 353–54 (Mar. 31, 1865).

9. *OR*, vol. 46, pt. 3: Grant to Meade, Mar. 31, 1865, 338; Sheridan to Grant, Mar. 31, 1865, 380; Grant to Sheridan, Mar. 31, 1865, 380; Meade to Grant, Mar. 31, 1865, 5:30 P.M., 338; Meade to Grant, Mar. 31, 1865, 6:35 P.M., 338; Grant to Meade, Mar. 31, 1865, 9:10 P.M., 341; Sheridan to Grant, Mar. 31, 1865, 381; Meade to Grant, Mar. 31, 1865, 9:45 P.M., 341; Grant to Meade, Mar. 31, 1865, 10:30 P.M., 342; Locke (assistant adjutant general, Fifth Corps) to Ayres, Mar. 31, 1865, 11:00 P.M., 369.

10. Calkins, *Appomattox Campaign*, 27–28; Hess, *In the Trenches*, 260–61; Sears, *Controversies and Commanders*, 272–76; *OR*, vol. 46, pt. 3: Warren to Webb, Apr. 1, 1865, 9:30 A.M., 418; Webb to Warren, Apr. 1, 1865, 6:00 A.M., 418; *OR Supplement*, vol. 9, Babcock testimony, 901.

11. Porter, *Campaigning with Grant*, 436 and 437 ("a caged tiger"); Sears, *Controversies and Commanders*, 276–77; Calkins, *Appomattox Campaign*, 30.

12. Calkins, *Appomattox Campaign*, 30–34; Porter, *Campaigning with Grant*, 437–40; Warren quoted in Jordan, *"Happiness Is Not My Companion,"* 232; Hess, *In the Trenches*, 262–63.

13. Hess, *In the Trenches*, 262; Porter, *Campaigning with Grant*, 442–43.

14. *OR*, vol. 46, pt. 3, Field Order, Apr. 1, 1865, 420; Chamberlain, *Passing of the Armies*, 151; Warren to Stanton, Apr. 1865 (never sent), in Warren Papers, NYSL (for long quotations from Grant, Meade, and Warren); *OR*, vol. 46, pt. 3, Grant to Meade, Apr. 1, 1865, received 11:10 P.M., 399; Lowe, *Meade's Army*, 356 (on Meade's illness, Apr. 1, 1865); Jordan, *"Happiness Is Not My Companion,"* 237 and chapters 23–30 for Warren's efforts to clear his name. Stephen Sears concisely analyzes the long-building decision in chapter 10, "Gouverneur Kemble Warren and Little Phil" in *Controversies and Commanders*, 253–87.

15. Jordan, *"Happiness Is Not My Companion,"* 235–36; Nevins, *Diary of Battle*, 514 (first quotation) and 513 (second quotation); Lowe, *Meade's Army*, 356 (Apr. 1, 1865); Grant, *Personal Memoirs*, 604; Sears, *Controversies and Commanders*, 256. Joshua Chamberlain devotes the longest chapter in his memoir of the last days of the war, *Passing of the Armies*, to a dissection of what transpired at Five Forks, seeking to vindicate Warren and the Fifth Corps without castigating Sheridan and Grant.

16. *OR*, vol. 46, pt. 3: Grant to Meade, Apr. 1, 1865, 5:35 P.M., 396; Meade to Grant, Apr. 1, 1865, 8:40 P.M., 397; Grant to Meade, Apr. 1, 1865, 8:40 P.M. (received 8:56 P.M.), 397; Grant to Meade, Apr. 1, 1865, 9:05 P.M. (received 9:24 P.M.), 397–98; Meade to Grant, Apr. 1, 1865, 9:25 P.M. (received 9:45 P.M.), 398; Meade to Humphreys, Apr. 1, 1865, 9:00 P.M., 407; Meade to Grant, Apr. 1, 1865, 9:40 P.M., 407; Meade to Grant, Apr. 1, 1865, 9:40 P.M. (received 10:00 P.M.); Meade to Grant, Apr. 1, 1865, 11:05 P.M., 399; Grant to Meade, Apr. 1, 1865 (received 11:10 P.M.), 399; Wright to Webb, Apr. 1, 1865, 11:00 P.M., 423.

17. *OR*, vol. 46, pt. 3: Grant to Meade, Apr. 2, 1865, 12:15 A.M., 451; Meade to Grant, Apr. 2, 1865, 1:00 A.M., 451–52; Grant to Meade, Apr. 2, 1865, 1:25 A.M., 452; Meade to Grant, Apr. 2, 1865, 2:10 A.M., 452; Meade to Grant, Apr. 2, 1865, 4:05 A.M., 452; Calkins, *Appomattox Campaign*, 43–45 and 51–52. Meade must have been operating on pure adrenalin, because not only did he become quite ill on April 1, he had averaged only three hours of sleep per night for the past three days. George G. Meade to Margaret Meade, Apr. 1, 1865, Meade Papers, HSP.

18. Greene, *Final Battles*, 210–73, 318–19, 347–48 (casualty figures); *OR*, vol. 46, pt. 3, Wright to Webb, Apr. 2, 1865, 5:15 A.M., 478; Hess, *In the Trenches*, 273; Calkins, *Appomattox Campaign*, 52–53.

19. Calkins, *Appomattox Campaign*, 47–51; Greene, *Final Battles*, 324–31.

20. Greene, *Final Battles*, 278–79.

21. Lowe, *Meade's Army*, 357–58 (Apr. 2, 1865).

22. *OR*, vol. 46, pt. 3: Grant to Bowers, Apr. 2, 1865, 10:45 A.M., 449; Lincoln to Stanton, Apr. 2, 1865, 2:00 P.M., 447; Grant to Bowers, Apr. 2, 1865, 4:40 P.M., 449; Lincoln to Grant, Apr. 2, 1865, 449.

23. Ibid.: Meade to Grant, Apr. 2, 1865, 10:30 A.M., 456; Meade to Grant, Apr. 2, 1865, 7:15 P.M., 457; Sheridan to Grant, Apr. 2, 1865, 489; Grant to Meade, Apr. 2, 1865, 7:40 P.M., 458; Meade to Grant, Apr. 2, 1865, 8:00 P.M. (received 8:30 P.M.), 458; Grant to Meade, Apr. 2, 1865, 9:00 P.M., 458–59. Sheridan's only mention of the cavalry's role that day in his report was that his cavalry had pursued Confederate cavalry westward to Hatcher's Run, then when they would not fight, "north to the Namozine Road." *OR*, vol. 46, pt. 1, Sheridan's report on the Appomattox Campaign, 1106.

24. Marvel, *Lee's Last Retreat*, 23–26 and 31.

25. *OR*, vol. 46, pt. 3: Meade to Grant, Apr. 3, 1865, 4:05 A.M., 511; Meade to Grant, Apr. 3, 1865, 4:40 A.M., 511; Meade to Grant, Apr. 3, 1865, 5:50 A.M., 511; Grant to Meade, Apr. 3, 1865 (received 6:25 A.M.), 511; Meade to Grant, Apr. 3, 1865, 6:35 A.M., 512.

26. Lowe, *Meade's Army*, 359 (Apr. 13, 1865); Porter, *Campaigning with Grant*, 450–51. According to Porter, Lincoln never seemed happier, and he asked why Grant had not waited for Sherman and his crew to join them. Grant replied, "I had a feeling that it would be better to let Lee's old antagonists give his army the final blow, and finish up the job." Of course Lincoln, in Grant's words, had "never thought of it in that light." A beautiful story, highlighting Grant's perspicacity (and Lincoln's lack of it), but one that many members of the Army of the Potomac might have been surprised to hear, as Sheridan was leading the mobile force chasing Lee, and Warren had been relieved from command. See Porter, *Campaigning with Grant*, 450–51.

27. Calkins, *Appomattox Campaign*, 67; *OR*, vol. 46, pt. 3: Webb to Humphreys, Apr. 3,

1865, 4:30 P.M., 516; F. C. Newhall (assistant adjutant general to Sheridan) to Humphreys, Apr. 3, 1865, 8:45 P.M., 516–17; Meade to Grant, Apr. 3, 1865, 9:15 P.M., 512; Parker to Meade, Apr. 3, 1865, 513 (last quotation).

28. Calkins, *Appomattox Campaign*, 70–74; Marvel, *Lee's Last Retreat*, 202 (on Lee's numbers). Marvel devotes an entire appendix to a discussion of the controversial issue of Lee's troop strength. He estimates that Lee had 77,400 men as of mid-March, and somewhere between 51,200 and 57,200 men who began the retreat. He further estimates that Lee had 45,000 men who finally gathered in Amelia County. I chose the lower retreat figure as an estimate, given the huge amount of desertions and straggling on April 3.

29. George G. Meade to Margaret Meade, Apr. 3, 1865, Meade Papers, HSP; *OR*, vol. 46, pt. 3, Orders, Sixth Corps, Apr. 3, 1865, 522. The Fifth Corps would depart at 5:00 A.M. (*OR*, vol. 46, pt. 3, 517).

30. *OR*, vol. 46, pt. 3, Meade to Grant, Apr. 4, 1865, 1:30 P.M., 545–46; Marvel, *Lee's Last Retreat*, 44–47; *OR*, vol. 46, pt. 3: Sheridan to Grant, Apr. 4, 1865, 556; Sheridan to Meade, Apr. 4, 1865, 7:00 P.M., 557; Orders, Headquarters, Army of the Potomac, Apr. 4, 1865, 9:30 P.M., 549; Meade to Sheridan, Apr. 4, 1865, 11:00 P.M., 558.

31. Lowe, *Meade's Army*, 360–61 (Apr. 4, 1865).

32. Marvel, *Lee's Last Retreat*, 49–53.

33. Lowe, *Meade's Army*, 361–62 (Apr. 5, 1865); Calkins, *Appomattox Campaign*, 78, 79, and 89.

34. Marvel, *Lee's Last Retreat*, 53, 62–65; Calkins, *Appomattox Campaign*, 90–91.

35. Lowe, *Meade's Army*, 362 (Apr. 5, 1865); Calkins, *Appomattox Campaign*, 93; *OR*, vol. 46, pt. 3: Sheridan to Grant, Apr. 5, 1865, 3:00 P.M. (received 1:30 P.M.), 582; Orders, Army of the Potomac, Apr. 5, 1865, 7:00 P.M., 577–78; Orders, Cavalry Headquarters, Apr. 5, 1865, 583; Grant to Ord, Apr. 5, 1865, 10:10 P.M., 583.

36. Calkins, *Appomattox Campaign*, 101–4.

37. Ibid., 106–15 (Lee quoted on p. 115); Marvel, *Lee's Last Retreat*, 78–97.

38. Lowe, *Meade's Army*, 363–64 (Apr. 6, 1865); *OR*, vol. 46, pt. 3: Webb to Humphreys, Apr. 6, 1865, 12:40 P.M., 599 (same to Wright and Griffin); Webb to Humphreys, Apr. 6, 1865, 2:05 P.M., 599; Webb to Wright, Apr. 6, 1865, 4:00 P.M., 604 (same to Humphreys).

39. *OR*, vol. 46, pt. 3, Sheridan to Grant, Apr. 6, 1865, 610; Lowe, *Meade's Army*, 364 (Apr. 6, 1865).

40. Lowe, *Meade's Army*, 364 (Apr. 6, 1865); *OR*, vol. 46, pt. 3: Stanton to Dix, Apr. 7, 1865, 10:00 A.M., 640; Stanton to Dix, Apr. 7, 1865, 11:30 A.M., 640; Meade to Grant, Apr. 6, 1865, 10:00 P.M. (received 3:20 A.M. on the seventh), 596; Humphreys to Webb, Apr. 6, 1865, 7:30 P.M., 600; Wright to Webb, Apr. 6, 1865, 9:10 P.M., 604–5.

41. Marvel, *Lee's Last Retreat*, 92–93 and 119–32; Calkins, *Appomattox Campaign*, 115–35.

42. Lowe, *Meade's Army*, 365–67 (Apr. 7, 1865); George G. Meade to Margaret Meade, Apr. 7, 1865, Meade Papers, HSP.

43. Calkins, *Appomattox Campaign*, 130; *OR*, vol. 46, pt. 3: Grant to Lee, Apr. 7, 1865, 5:00 P.M., 619; Grant to Lee, Apr. 7, 1865, 5 P.M., 619; Longstreet, *From Manassas to Appomattox*, 617, 618–19; *OR*, vol. 46, pt. 3, Lee to Grant, Apr. 7, 1865, 619; Marvel, *Lee's Last Retreat*, 133.

44. Marvel, *Lee's Last Retreat*, 134–40; *OR*, vol. 46, pt. 3: Humphreys to Webb, Apr. 8, 1865, 6:00 A.M., 642; Humphreys to Webb, Apr. 8, 1865, 7:45 A.M., 643; Meade to Grant, Apr. 8, 1865, 8:45 A.M., 642; Forsyth (Sheridan's chief of staff) to Crook, Apr. 8, 1865, 653; Sheridan to Crook, Apr. 8, 1865, 654; John Gibbon (commander of the Twenty-Fourth Corps) to Grant, Apr. 8, 1865, 7:15 P.M., 654; Calkins, *Appomattox Campaign*, 150–51.

45. *OR*, vol. 46, pt. 3, Grant to Lee, Apr. 8, 1865, 641; Marvel, *Lee's Last Retreat*, 140–41.

46. Calkins, *Appomattox Campaign*, 152–55; *OR*, vol. 46, pt. 3, Sheridan to Grant, Apr. 8, 1865, 9:20 P.M., 653.

47. Lowe, *Meade's Army,* 367 (Apr. 8, 1865); Calkins, *Appomattox Campaign,* 156–57.

48. Cadwallader, *Three Years with Grant,* 317–19 (Rawlins's and Grant's quotations on p. 319); *OR,* vol. 46, pt. 3, Lee to Grant, Apr. 8, 1865, 641; Porter, *Campaigning with Grant,* 462–63.

49. Marvel, *Lee's Last Retreat,* 161–74.

50. Calkins, *Appomattox Campaign,* 164–67.

51. Simpson, *Ulysses S. Grant,* 432; *OR,* vol. 46, pt. 3, Grant to Lee, Apr. 9, 1865, 664; Porter, *Campaigning with Grant,* 466.

52. Marvel, *Lee's Last Retreat,* 173; *OR,* vol. 46, pt. 3: Lee to Grant, Apr. 9, 1865, 664; Meade to Grant, Apr. 9, 1865, 10:00 A.M., 667; Lee to Grant, Apr. 9, 1865, 664; Meade to Lee, Apr. 9, 1865, 12:00 P.M., 666.

53. Porter, *Campaigning with Grant,* 466–68 (headache quotation on p. 468); Cadwallader, *Three Years with Grant,* 321–22; *OR,* vol. 46, pt. 3, Grant to Lee, Apr. 9, 1865, 11:50 A.M., 665.

54. Marvel, *Lee's Last Retreat,* 177 and 179; Lowe, *Meade's Army,* 369 (Apr. 9, 1865).

55. Calkins, *Appomattox Campaign,* 171–76; Marvel, *Lee's Last Retreat,* 180–81.

56. Lowe, *Meade's Army,* 369 (Apr. 9, 1865); *New York Herald,* Apr. 14, 1865.

57. Lowe, *Meade's Army,* 369–71 (Apr. 10, 1865); George G. Meade to Margaret Meade, Apr. 10, 1865, Meade Papers, HSP.

58. George G. Meade to Margaret Meade, Apr. 10, 1865, Meade Papers, HSP.

59. George G. Meade to Margaret Meade, Apr. 12, 1865, Meade Papers, HSP. A quick word search of historic newspapers found in the Library of Congress database entitled "Chronicling America" confirms Meade's view of limited coverage of his leadership in the Appomattox Campaign: one finds that Meade's name is buried deep in stories, if found at all in dispatches, while Sheridan and Grant get headlines and more mention.

60. Lowe, *Meade's Army,* 372–73 (Apr. 11–12, 1865); Calkins, *Appomattox Campaign,* 187–92.

61. George G. Meade to Margaret Meade, Apr. 13, 1865, and Apr. 1, 1865, Meade Papers, HSP; Lowe, *Meade's Army,* 372–73 (Apr. 15, 1865); *OR,* vol. 46, pt. 3, General Orders No. 15, Headquarters, Army of the Potomac, Apr. 16, 1865, 789.

62. Lowe, *Meade's Army,* 375 (Apr. 19, 1865); George G. Meade to Margaret Meade, Apr. 20, 1865, Meade Papers, HSP.

63. George G. Meade to Margaret Meade, Apr. 23, 1865, Meade Papers, HSP; *OR,* vol. 46, pt. 3: General Orders No. 1, Headquarters, Military Division of the James, Apr. 22, 1865, 891; General Orders No. 71, War Department, Apr. 19, 1865, 833.

64. George G. Meade to Margaret Meade: Apr. 23, 29, 27, and 24, 1865, Meade Papers, HSP.

65. *OR,* vol. 46, pt. 3, Halleck to Meade, Apr. 30, 1865, 4:00 P.M., 1016; George G. Meade to Margaret Meade, May 1 and 5, 1865, Meade Papers, HSP.

66. *OR,* vol. 46, pt. 3: Meade to Grant, Apr. 18, 1865, 10:00 A.M., 822; Bowers to Meade, Apr. 18, 1865, 823; Meade to Grant, May 1, 1865, 1:00 P.M., 1055; Grant to Meade, May 1, 1865, 9:10 P.M., 1056; Jordan, *"Happiness Is Not My Companion,"* 238–42.

67. *OR,* vol. 46, pt. 3: Special Orders No. 114, Headquarters, Army of the Potomac, May 4, 1865, 1084; Special Orders, Headquarters, Army of the Potomac, May 5, 1865, 9:30 A.M., 1092 (march postponed); Special Orders No. 115, Headquarters, Army of the Potomac, May 5, 1865, 1092–93; Sparks, *Inside Lincoln's Army,* 504–5 (May 6, 1865). Sherman's Army marched through Richmond on May 11 (see Sparks, *Inside Lincoln's Army,* 506).

68. *OR,* vol. 46, pt. 2, Meade to Grant, May 11, 1865, 8:45 A.M., 1134; George G. Meade to Margaret Meade, May 12, 1865, Meade Papers, HSP.

69. *OR,* vol. 46, pt. 3, Special Orders 239, Headquarters of the Army, May 18, 1865, 1171.

70. *New York Times,* May 24, 1865; *OR,* vol. 46, pt. 3, Special Orders 239, Headquarters of the Army, May 18, 1865, 1171 (cadence step ordered).

71. *New York Times,* May 25, 1865.

72. *OR*, vol. 46, pt. 3: Meade to Col. Thomas Vincent, assistant adjutant general, War Department, May 25, 1865, 1211; Meade to adjutant general of the Army, May 31, 1865, 1241; Meade to Stanton, June 6, 1865, 1259; Meade to Col. Theodore Bowers, June 6, 1865, 1259; Meade, *Life and Letters*, 2:282 (on Meade's trip to Philadelphia).

73. *OR*, vol. 46, pt. 3: Special Orders No. 339, Headquarters of the Army, June 28, 1856, 1301; General Orders No. 118, War Department, June 27, 1865, 1298–99.

74. Ibid.: General Orders No. 35, Headquarters, Army of the Potomac, June 28, 1865, 1302; Meade's letter to the soldiers of the Army of the Potomac, June 28, 1865, 1301–2.

12. A MAJOR-GENERAL IN PEACETIME, 1865–1872

1. Senior, *Last Invasion of Canada*; Cleaves, *Meade of Gettysburg*, 341–43; Meade, *Life and Letters*, 2:285–87. Sweeny had plenty of friends in the right places. He was released from custody later that year, was restored to the U.S. Army in November 1866, and retired from the Army in 1870. He lived quietly on Long Island for another twenty-two years. See Warner, *Generals in Blue*, 482.

2. Cleaves, *Meade of Gettysburg*, 344–46; Meade, *Life and Letters*, 2:290–96 (quotation on pp. 293–94).

3. Cleaves, *Meade of Gettysburg*, 347–48; Meade, *Life and Letters*, 2:296–300 (quotation from George Meade on p. 298; quotations found in letter from George G. Meade to Margaret Meade, Mar. 6, 1869, 299–300).

4. Cleaves, *Meade of Gettysburg*, 348.

5. Ibid., 348–49.

6. Meade, *Life and Letters*, 2:301–2, 283, 288–89; Lowe, *Meade's Army*, 388–92 (July 17–25, 1865); Cleaves, *Meade of Gettysburg*, 340 and 349.

7. Wills, *George Henry Thomas; New York Times*, Jan. 10, 1872; Meade, *Life and Letters*, 2:302.

8. Cleaves, *Meade of Gettysburg*, 350; Meade, *Life and Letters*, 2:302–3 (quotation on p. 303).

9. *Philadelphia North American*, Nov. 7, 1872; *Somerset Herald*, Nov. 13, 1872; *New York Herald*, Nov. 7, 1872; *Findlay Jeffersonian*, Nov. 22, 1872.

10. Cleaves, *Meade of Gettysburg*, 350–51; Meade, *Life and Letters*, 2:303–5.

CONCLUSION

1. Walker, "Meade at Gettysburg," 406.

Bibliography

PRIMARY SOURCES

GOVERNMENT DOCUMENTS

The War of the Rebellion: A Compilation of the Official Records of the Union and Confederate Armies, Series 1. 53 vols. Washington, D.C.: Government Printing Office (cited as *OR*).

Report of the Committee on the Conduct of the War on the Attack on Petersburg on the Thirtieth Day of July, 1864. Washington, D.C.: Government Printing Office, 1865 (cited as *RCCW*).

Report of the Joint Committee on the Conduct of the War. Vol. 1. Washington, D.C.: Government Printing Office, 1865 (cited as *JCCW*).

MANUSCRIPT COLLECTIONS

John B. Bachelder Papers, copies of selected letters, in Gettysburg National Military Park Archival Box Collection.

James Cornell Biddle Papers, Historical Society of Pennsylvania (HSP), Philadelphia, Pa.

C. B. Comstock Papers, Library of Congress.

Civil War Biographies—Union: Abner Doubleday, Winfield S. Hancock, Alexander Hays, Andrew A. Humphreys, George G. Meade, John F. Reynolds—U. S. Army Military History Institute, Carlisle Barracks, Pa.

John Gibbon Papers, Historical Society of Pennsylvania (HSP), Philadelphia, Pa.

Andrew Atkinson Humphreys Papers, Historical Society of Pennsylvania (HSP), Philadelphia, Pa.

Henry Jackson Hunt Papers, Library of Congress.

George Gordon Meade Papers, Historical Society of Pennsylvania (HSP), Philadelphia, Pa.

George Gordon Meade Papers, The Heritage Center of the Union League of Philadelphia.

Selected Papers, Western Reserve Historical Society, copies found in Gettysburg National Military Park Archival Box Collection.

Gouverneur Kemble Warren Papers, New York State Library, Manuscripts and Special Collections, Albany, N.Y.

NEWSPAPERS

Findlay Jeffersonian (Ohio)

New York Herald

New York Independent

New York Times
New York Tribune
New York World
Philadelphia North American
Philadelphia Weekly Times
Somerset Herald (Pa.)
Washington Evening Star

BIOGRAPHIES, MEMOIRS, PERSONAL NARRATIVES, AND ARTICLES

Agassiz, George R., ed. *Meade's Headquarters, 1863–1865: Letters of Colonel Theodore Lyman from the Wilderness to Appomattox.* Boston: Atlantic Monthly, 1922.

Bache, Richard Meade. *Life of General George Gordon Meade, Commander of the Army of the Potomac.* Philadelphia: Henry T. Coates, 1897.

Barlow, Francis Channing. "Capture of the Salient, May 12, 1864." In *Papers of the Military Historical Society of Massachusetts,* 4:245–50. Boston: Military Historical Society of Massachusetts, 1905 (read before the Society on Jan. 13, 1879).

Basler, Roy P., ed. *The Collected Works of Abraham Lincoln.* 9 vols. New Brunswick, N.J.: Rutgers Univ. Press, 1953–55.

Benjamin, Charles F. "Hooker's Appointment and Removal." In Johnson and Buel, *Battles and Leaders,* 3:239–43.

Bernard, George, ed. and comp. *War Talks of Confederate Veterans.* 1892. Reprint, Dayton, Ohio: Morningside, 1981.

Black, John D. "Reminiscences of the Bloody Angle." In *Glimpses of the Nation's Struggle: Fourth Series. Papers Read before the Minnesota Commandery of the Military Order of the Loyal Legion of the United Sates, 1892–1897,* 423–24. St. Paul, Minn.: H. L. Collins, 1898.

Burlingame, Michael, and John R. Ettlinger, eds. *Inside Lincoln's White House: The Complete Civil War Diary of John Hay.* Carbondale: Southern Illinois Press, 1997.

Byrne, Frank L., and Andrew T. Weaver. *Haskell of Gettysburg: His Life and Civil War Papers.* Kent, Ohio: Kent State Univ. Press, 1989.

Cadwallader, Sylvanus. *Three Years with Grant.* Edited by Benjamin P. Thomas. New York: Alfred A. Knopf, 1961.

Chamberlain, Joshua. *The Passing of the Armies.* 1915. Reprint, Dayton: Morningside, 1974.

Cockrell, Monroe F., ed. *Gunner with Stonewall: Reminiscences of William Thomas Poague.* 1957. Reprint, Wilmington: Broadfoot, 1987.

Dana, Charles A. *Recollections of the Civil War.* 1898. Reprint, Lincoln: Univ. of Nebraska Press, 1996.

Gallagher, Gary, ed. *Two Witnesses at Gettysburg: The Personal Accounts of Whitelaw Reid and A. J. L. Fremantle.* St. James, N.Y.: Brandywine, 1994.

Gibbon, John. "The Council of War on the Second Day." In Johnson and Buel, *Battles and Leaders,* 3:313–14.

———. *Personal Recollections of the Civil War.* 1928. Reprint, Dayton, Ohio: Morningside House, 1988.

Grant, Ulysses S. *Personal Memoirs of U. S. Grant.* Lincoln: Univ. of Nebraska Press, 1996.

———. "Preparing for the Campaign of '64." In Johnson and Buel, *Battles and Leaders,* 4:97–117.

Gross, George G. *The Battlefield of Gettysburg.* Philadelphia: Collins, Printer, 1866.

Halstead, E. P. "Incidents of the First Day at Gettysburg." In Johnson and Buel, *Battles and Leaders,* 3:284–89.

Hancock, Almira R. *Reminiscences of Winfield Scott Hancock.* New York: Charles L. Webster, 1887.

Haupt, Herman. *Reminiscences of General Herman Haupt.* Milwaukee: Wright and Joys, 1901.

Humphreys, Andrew A. *The Virginia Campaign: 1864 and 1865.* 1883. Reprint, New York: Da Capo, 1995.

Humphreys, Henry H. *Andrew Atkinson Humphreys: A Biography.* 1924. Reprint, Gaithersburg, Md.: Ron R. Van Sickle Military Books, 1988.

Hunt, Henry J. "The Second Day at Gettysburg." In Johnson and Buel, *Battles and Leaders,* 3:290–313.

Hyde, Thomas W. *Following the Greek Cross; or, Memories of the Sixth Army Corps.* 1894. Reprint, Columbia: Univ. of South Carolina Press, 2005.

Johnson, Robert Underwood, and Clarence Clough Buel, eds. *Battles and Leaders.* Vols. 3 and 4. Secaucus, N.J.: Castle, 1982.

Ladd, David L., and Audrey J. Ladd, eds. *The Bachelder Papers: Gettysburg in Their Own Words.* 3 vols. Dayton: Morningside House, 1995.

Lieber, Francis. *The Character of the Gentleman.* 3rd ed. Philadelphia: J. B. Lippincott, 1864.

Livermore, Thomas L. *Days and Events: 1860–1866.* Boston: Houghton Mifflin, 1920.

Longstreet, James. *From Manassas to Appomattox.* Philadelphia: J. B. Lippincott, 1896.

Lowe, David W., ed. *Meade's Army: The Private Notebooks of Lt. Col. Theodore Lyman.* Kent, Ohio: Kent State Univ. Press, 2007.

Lyman, Theodore. "Addenda to the Paper by Brevet Lieutenant Colonel W. W. Swan, USA, on the Battle of the Wilderness." In *Papers of the Military Historical Society of Massachusetts, The Wilderness Campaign,* 4:167–68. Boston: Military Historical Society of Massachusetts, 1905 (remarks read on Mar. 8, 1880).

McMahon, Martin T. "The Death of General John Sedgwick." In Johnson and Buel, *Battles and Leaders,* 4:175.

———. "From Gettysburg to the Coming of Grant." In Johnson and Buel, *Battles and Leaders,* 4:81–94.

Meade, George. *The Life and Letters of George Gordon Meade, Major-General United States Army.* 2 vols. New York: Charles Scribner's Sons, 1913.

Nevins, Allan, ed. *A Diary of Battle: The Personal Journals of Colonel Charles S. Wainwright, 1861–1865.* 1962. Reprint, Gettysburg: Stan Clark Books, 1993.

Page, Charles A. *Letters of a War Correspondent.* Boston: L. C. Page, 1899.

Pennypacker, Isaac R. *General Meade.* New York: D. Appleton, 1901.

Porter, Horace. *Campaigning with Grant.* Edited with notes by Wayne C. Temple. New York: Bonanza Books, 1961.

Powell, William H. *The Fifth Army Corps (Army of the Potomac): A Record of Operations during the Civil War in the United States of America, 1861–1865.* New York: Putnam's, 1896.

Quaife, Milo M., ed. *From the Cannon's Mouth: The Civil War Letters of General Alpheus Williams.* Detroit: Wayne State Univ. Press, 1959.

Rodenbough, Theodore. "Sheridan's Richmond Raid." In Johnson and Buel, *Battles and Leaders,* 4:188–93.

Schaff, Morris. *The Battle of the Wilderness.* Boston: Houghton Mifflin, 1910.

Sheridan, Philip H. *Personal Memoirs.* Vol. 1. New York: Charles L. Webster, 1888.

Smart, James G., ed. *A Radical View: The "Agate" Dispatches of Whitelaw Reid, 1861–1865.* Vol. 2. Memphis, Tenn.: Memphis State Univ. Press, 1976.

Smith, William Farrar. *From Chattanooga to Petersburg under Generals Grant and Butler: A Contribution to the History of the War and a Personal Vindication.* New York: Houghton Mifflin, 1893.

Sparks, David S. *Inside Lincoln's Army: The Diary of General Marsena Rudolph Patrick, Provost Marshal General, Army of the Potomac.* New York: A. S. Barnes, 1964.

Stevens, George T. *Three Years in the Sixth Corps.* Albany, N.Y.: S. R. Gray, 1866.

Sumner, Merlin E., ed. *The Diary of Cyrus B. Comstock.* Dayton, Ohio: Morningside House, 1987.

Swan, William. "The Battle of the Wilderness." In *Papers of the Military Historical Society of Massachusetts,* 4:129. Boston: Military Historical Society of Massachusetts, 1905 (paper delivered on Feb. 9, 1880).

Swinton, William. *Campaigns of the Army of the Potomac.* 1866. Secaucus, N.J.: Blue and Grey, 1998.

Tremain, Henry Edward. *Two Days of War: A Gettysburg Narrative and Other Excursions.* New York: Bonnell, Silver and Bowers, 1905.

Walker, Francis A. *General Hancock.* New York: D. A. Appleton, 1894.

———. *History of the Second Army Corps in the Army of the Potomac.* New York: Charles Scribner's Sons, 1887.

———. "Meade at Gettysburg." In Johnson and Buel, *Battles and Leaders,* 3:406–12.

Weld, Stephen Minot. *War Diary and Letters of Stephen Minot Weld.* 1912. Reprint, Boston: Massachusetts Historical Society, 1979.

Welles, Gideon. *Diary of Gideon Welles: Secretary of the Navy under Lincoln and Johnson.* Vol. 1, *1861–March 30, 1864.* Boston: Houghton Mifflin, 1911.

Wilkeson, Frank. *Turned Inside Out: Recollections of a Private Soldier in the Army of the Potomac.* Lincoln: Univ. of Nebraska Press, 1997.

Wilson, James H. *A Life of John Rawlins.* New York: Neale, 1916.

———. *Under the Old Flag: Recollections of Military Operations in the War for the Union, the Spanish War, the Boxer Rebellion, Etc.* New York: D. Appleton, 1912.

SECONDARY SOURCES

BOOKS AND ARTICLES

Axelrod, Alan. *The Horrid Pit: The Battle of the Crater, the Civil War's Cruelest Mission.* New York: Carroll and Graf, 2007.

Bearss, Edwin C. *The Battle of the Jerusalem Plank Road, June 21–24, 1864.* U.S. Department of the Interior, National Park Service, 1966.

Boritt, Gabor S. "'Unfinished Work': Lincoln, Meade, and Gettysburg." In *Lincoln's Generals,* edited by Gabor S. Boritt, 79–120. New York: Oxford Univ. Press, 1995.

Brown, Kent Masterson. *Retreat from Gettysburg: Lee, Logistics, and the Pennsylvania Campaign.* Chapel Hill: Univ. of North Carolina Press, 2005.

Burlingame, Michael. *Abraham Lincoln: A Life.* Baltimore: John Hopkins Univ. Press, 2008.

Busey, John W., and David G. Martin. *Regimental Strengths and Losses at Gettysburg.* Highstown, N.J.: Longstreet House, 1994.

Calkins, Chris M. *The Appomattox Campaign: March 29–April 9, 1865.* Lynchburg: Schroeder, 2015.

Cannan, John. *The Crater: Burnside's Assault on the Confederate Trenches, July 30, 1864.* Cambridge, Mass.: Da Capo, 2002.

Catton, Bruce. *A Stillness at Appomattox.* New York: Doubleday, 1953.

Cavanaugh, Michael A., and Andrew Marvel. *The Battle of the Crater: "The Horrid Pit," June 25–August 6, 1864.* Lynchburg: H. E. Howard, 1989.

Chick, Sean Michael. *The Battle of Petersburg, June 15–18, 1864.* Lincoln: Potomac Books, an imprint of the Univ. of Nebraska Press, 2015.

Cleaves, Freeman. *Meade of Gettysburg.* Norman: Univ. of Oklahoma Press, 1960.

Coddington, Edward. *The Gettysburg Campaign: A Study in Command.* New York: Charles Scribner's Sons, 1968.

———. "The Strange Reputation of General Meade: A Lesson in Historiography." *Historian* 23, no. 2 (1961): 145–66.

Coffey, David. *Sheridan's Lieutenants: Phil Sheridan, His Generals, and the Final Year of the Civil War*. Lanham, Md.: Rowman and Littlefield, 2005.

Elmore, Thomas L. "Torrid Heat and Blinding Rain: A Meteorological and Astronomical Chronology of the Gettysburg Campaign." *Gettysburg Magazine*, no. 13, July 1995.

Foote, Lorien. *The Gentlemen and the Roughs: Manhood, Honor, and Violence in the Union Army*. New York: New York Univ. Press, 2010.

Furgurson, Ernest B. *Chancellorsville, 1863: The Souls of the Brave*. New York: Alfred A. Knopf, 1992.

Gottfried, Bradley M. *The Maps of the Bristoe Station and Mine Run Campaigns*. El Dorado, Calif.: Savas Beatie, 2013.

Graham, Martin F., and George F. Skoch, *Mine Run: A Campaign of Lost Opportunities, October 21, 1863–May 1, 1864*. Lynchburg: H. E. Howard, 1987.

Greene, A. Wilson. *The Final Battles of the Petersburg Campaign: Breaking the Backbone of the Rebellion*. 2nd ed. Knoxville: Univ. of Tennessee Press, 2012.

Grimsley, Mark. *And Keep Moving On: The Virginia Campaign, May–June 1864*. Lincoln: Univ. of Nebraska Press, 2002.

Guelzo, Allen C. *Gettysburg: The Last Invasion*. New York: Alfred A. Knopf, 2013.

Hartwig, D. Scott. *To Antietam Creek: The Maryland Campaign of September 1862*. Baltimore: Johns Hopkins Univ. Press, 2012.

Hattaway, Herman, and Michael D. Smith. "Meade, George Gordon." In *American National Biography*. Oxford Univ. Press, 2010. Accessed Feb. 5, 2018. doi.org/10.1093/anb/9780198606697.article.0400697.

Hattaway, Herman, and Archer Jones. *How the North Won: A Military History of the Civil War*. Urbana: Univ. of Illinois Press, 1991.

Henderson, William D. *The Road to Bristoe Station: Campaigning with Lee and Meade, August 1–October 20, 1863*. Lynchburg: H. E. Howard, 1987.

Hennessy, John J. "'I Dread the Spring': The Army of the Potomac Prepares for the Overland Campaign." In *The Wilderness Campaign*, edited by Gary Gallagher, 66–105. Chapel Hill: Univ. of North Carolina Press, 1997.

———. *Return to Bull Run: The Campaign and Battle of Second Manassas*. New York: Simon and Schuster, 1993.

Hess, Earl J. *Field Armies and Fortifications in the Civil War: The Eastern Campaigns, 1861–1864*. Chapel Hill: Univ. of North Carolina Press, 2005.

———. *In the Trenches at Petersburg: Field Fortifications and Confederate Defeat*. Chapel Hill: Univ. of North Carolina Press, 2009.

———. *Into the Crater: The Mine Attack at Petersburg*. Columbia: Univ. of South Carolina Press, 2010.

———. *Pickett's Charge—The Last Attack at Gettysburg*. Chapel Hill: Univ. of North Carolina Press, 2001.

———. *Trench Warfare under Grant and Lee: Field Fortifications in the Overland Campaign*. Chapel Hill: Univ. of North Carolina Press, 2007.

Horn, John. *The Siege of Petersburg: The Battles for the Weldon Railroad, August 1864*. El Dorado Hills, Calif.: Savas Beatie, 2015.

Howe, Thomas J. *The Petersburg Campaign: Wasted Valor, June 15–18, 1864*. Lynchburg: H. E. Howard, 1988.

Hsieh, Wayne Wei-siang. *West Pointers and the Civil War: The Old Army in War and Peace*. Chapel Hill: Univ. of North Carolina Press, 2009.

Huntington, Tom. *Searching for George Gordon Meade: The Forgotten Victor of Gettysburg.* Mechanicsburg, Pa.: Stackpole Books, 2013.

Jones, Archer. *Civil War Command and Strategy: The Process of Victory and Defeat.* New York: Free Press, 1992.

Jordan, David M. *"Happiness Is Not My Companion": The Life of General G. K. Warren.* Bloomington: Indiana Univ. Press, 2001.

————. *Winfield Scott Hancock: A Soldier's Life.* 1988. Reprint, Bloomington: Indiana Univ. Press, 1996.

Krick, Robert K. *Civil War Weather in Virginia.* Tuscaloosa: Univ. of Alabama Press, 2007.

Leech, Margaret. *Reveille in Washington: 1860–1865.* New York: Grosset and Dunlap, 1941.

Levin, Kevin. *Remembering the Battle of the Crater: War as Murder.* Lexington: Univ. Press of Kentucky, 2012.

Marszalek, John F. *Sherman: A Soldier's Passion for Order.* New York: Free Press, 1993.

Marvel, William. *Burnside.* Chapel Hill: Univ. of North Carolina Press, 1991.

————. *Lee's Last Retreat: The Flight to Appomattox.* Chapel Hill: Univ. of North Carolina Press, 2002.

Matter, William D. "The Federal High Command at Spotsylvania." In *The Spotsylvania Campaign,* edited by Gary Gallagher, 29–60. Chapel Hill: Univ. of North Carolina Press, 1998.

McPherson, James. *The Battle Cry of Freedom: The Civil War Era.* New York: Oxford Univ. Press, 1988.

Melton, Brian. *Sherman's Forgotten General: Henry W. Slocum.* Columbia: Univ. of Missouri Press, 2007.

Moe, Richard. *The Last Full Measure: The Life and Death of the First Minnesota Volunteers.* New York: Henry Holt, 1993.

Morris, Roy, Jr. *Sheridan: The Life and Wars of General Phil Sheridan.* New York: Crown, 1992.

Newsome, Hampton. *Richmond Must Fall: The Richmond-Petersburg Campaign, October, 1864.* Kent, Ohio: Kent State Univ. Press, 2013.

Newsome, Hampton, John Horn, and John G. Selby, eds. *Civil War Talks: Further Reminiscences of George S. Bernard and His Fellow Veterans.* Charlottesville: Univ. of Virginia Press, 2012.

O'Reilly, Francis Augustin. *The Fredericksburg Campaign: Winter War on the Rappahannock.* Baton Rouge: Louisiana State Univ. Press, 2003.

Pennypacker, Isaac. "Military Historians and History." *Pennsylvania Magazine of History and Biography* 53, no. 1 (1929): 28–50.

Pfanz, Harry W. *Gettysburg—Culp's Hill and Cemetery Hill.* Chapel Hill: Univ. of North Carolina Press, 1993.

————. *Gettysburg—The First Day.* Chapel Hill: Univ. of North Carolina Press, 2001.

————. *Gettysburg: The Second Day.* Chapel Hill: Univ. of North Carolina Press, 1987.

Price, James S. *The Battle of First Deep Bottom.* Charleston, S.C.: History, 2014.

Rafuse, Ethan S. *George Gordon Meade and the War in the East.* Abilene, TX: McWhiney Foundation, 2003.

————. *McClellan's War: The Failure of Moderation in the Struggle for Union.* Bloomington: Indiana Univ. Press, 2005.

————. "'Wherever Lee Goes' . . . : George Meade." In *Grant's Lieutenants: From Chattanooga to Appomattox,* edited by Steven E. Woodworth, 47–84. Lawrence: Univ. Press of Kansas, 2008.

Reardon, Carol. *With a Sword in One Hand and Jomini in the Other: The Problem of Military Thought in the Civil War North.* Chapel Hill: Univ. of North Carolina Press, 2012.

Reid, Brian Holden. *America's Civil War: The Operational Battlefield, 1861–1863*. Amherst, N.Y.: Prometheus Books, 2008.

Rhea, Gordon C. *The Battle of the Wilderness: May 5–6, 1864*. 1994. Reprint, Baton Rouge: Louisiana State Univ. Press, 2004.

———. *The Battles for Spotsylvania Court House and the Road to Yellow Tavern, May 7–12, 1864*. Baton Rouge: Louisiana State Univ. Press, 1997.

———. *Cold Harbor: Grant and Lee, May 26–June 3, 1864*. Baton Rouge: Louisiana State Univ. Press, 2002.

———. *To the North Anna River: Grant and Lee, May 13–25, 1864*. 2000. Reprint, Baton Rouge: Louisiana State Univ. Press, 2005.

Sauers, Richard A. *Gettysburg: The Meade-Sickles Controversy*. Dulles, Va.: Potomac Books, 2003.

———. *Meade: Victor of Gettysburg*. Dulles, Va.: Brassey's, 2003.

———. "'Rarely Has More Skill, Vigor, or Wisdom Been Shown': George G. Meade on July 3 at Gettysburg." In *Three Days at Gettysburg: Essays on Confederate and Union Leadership at Gettysburg*, edited by Gary Gallagher, 231–44. Kent, Ohio: Kent State Univ. Press, 1999.

Schmutz, John F. *The Battle of the Crater: A Complete History*. Jefferson, N.C.: McFarland, 2008.

Schultz, Duane. *The Dahlgren Affair: Terror and Conspiracy in the Civil War*. New York: W. W. Norton, 1998.

Sears, Stephen W. *Controversies and Commanders: Dispatches from the Army of the Potomac*. Boston: Houghton Mifflin, 1990.

———. *Gettysburg*. 2003. Reprint, Boston: Mariner Books, 2004.

———. *Landscape Turned Red: The Battle of Antietam*. New York: Ticknor and Fields, 1983.

———. *To the Gates of Richmond: The Peninsula Campaign*. New York: Ticknor and Fields, 1992.

Senior, Hereward. *The Last Invasion of Canada: The Fenian Raids, 1866–1870*. Toronto: Dundurn, 1991.

Simpson, Brooks D. *Ulysses S. Grant: Triumph over Adversity, 1822–1865*. Boston: Houghton Mifflin, 2000.

Sommers, Richard J. *Richmond Redeemed: The Siege at Petersburg—The Battle of Chaffin's Bluff and Poplar Spring Church, September 29–October 2, 1864*. Rev. sesquicentennial ed. El Dorado, Calif.: Savas Beatie, 2014.

Stoker, Donald. *The Grand Design: Strategy and the U. S. Civil War*. Oxford: Oxford Univ. Press, 2010.

Stowe, Christopher. "Certain Grave Charges." *Columbiad* 3, no. 1 (1999): 19–46.

———. "George Gordon Meade and the Boundaries of Nineteenth-Century Military Masculinity." *Civil War History* 61, no. 4 (2015): 362–99.

———. "'The Longest and Clearest Head of Any General Officer': George Gordon Meade as Corps Commander, December 1862–June 1863." In *Corps Commanders in Blue: Union Major Generals in the Civil War*, edited by Ethan S. Rafuse, 112–55. Baton Rouge: Louisiana State Univ. Press, 2014.

Taaffe, Stephen R. *Commanding the Army of the Potomac*. Lawrence: Univ. Press of Kansas, 2006.

Tap, Bruce. *Over Lincoln's Shoulder: The Committee on the Conduct of the War*. Lawrence: Univ. Press of Kansas, 1998.

Warner, Ezra J. *Generals in Blue: Lives of the Union Commanders*. Baton Rouge: Louisiana State Univ. Press, 1964.

Weigley, Russell E. *A Great Civil War: A Military and Political History, 1861–1865*. Bloomington: Indiana Univ. Press, 2000.

Williams, T. Harry. *Lincoln and His Generals.* New York: Alfred A. Knopf, 1952.

Wills, Brian Steel. *George Henry Thomas: As True as Steel.* Lawrence: Univ. Press of Kansas, 2012.

Wittenberg, Eric J., J. David Petruzzi, and Michael F. Nugent. *One Continuous Fight: The Retreat from Gettysburg and the Pursuit of Lee's Army of Northern Virginia, July 4–14, 1863.* 2008. Reprint, New York: Savas Beatie, 2011.

UNPUBLISHED DISSERTATIONS

Stowe, Christopher. "A Philadelphia Gentleman: The Cultural, Institutional, and Political Socialization of George Gordon Meade." Ph.D. diss., University of Toledo, 2005.

Index

Halleck, Henry (cont.)
57, 84–85; promotes Warren to major general, 85; promotions of Meade and Sherman, 189–90; rejects Meade's proposed maneuvers, Fall 1863, 83–84, 87–88, 97–98; supports Meade's plan to attack Williamsport, 72; tells French to ignore Hooker, 14; testimony to Joint Commission on Sickles, 40; urges Meade to pursue Lee, 68, 75, 95–96; vague orders to Meade, September 1863, 87–88

Hamlin, Hannibal, 73, 112

Hammill, John S., 162

Hampton, Wade, 159

Hancock, Winfield Scott, 18, 19, 180, 248, 269; Bloody Angle, May 17–18, 181–82; ceremonial sword contest, 211; Cold Harbor, 199, 200, 201, 203, 205, 209; considered for command of Army, 14, 111; Deep Bottom, first battle, 234; Deep Bottom, second battle, 244–45; Guiney Bridge, 184; Henagan's Redoubt, 187–88; leaves command, 264; Meade on, 252; Milford Station, 185; North Anna River, 189, 190, 191–92; Petersburg, 213, 214–15, 217, 218; promotion of, 174, 251; Ream's Station, second battle, 248–50; and rumor of Meade's dismissal, 231; South Side Railroad offensive, 259, 260; support of Meade, 110; temperament and appearance of, 29–30; the Wilderness, 127, 129–30, 133, 140–44, 141, 147, 150–51; the Wilderness, extended battles, 177, 179, 181, 182, 183, 184, 185

Hancock, Winfield Scott, Gettysburg: assumes command, 29; Cemetery Ridge, 42; "council" of generals, 45; Meade's support, 33; orders, 30–31; performance, 47; reaction to Confederate shelling, 53

Hancock, Winfield Scott, Spotsylvania Court House, 151, 159, 160, 161, 162, 173; attempted assault on salient, 168, 171, 172; crossing the Po River, 166; Laurel Hill, 163, 164, 165

Hanover Court House, 195, 198, 291

Hanover Junction, 184, 188

Hanovertown, 193

Hardie, James A., 15, 16, 18

Hardin, Martin D., 196

Harding, Benjamin, 119

Harding, William, 211, 230, 252

Hare House, 221

Harman, John Alexander, 62

Harman house, 278

Harper's Ferry, 81, 252

Harrison farm, 164

Harris's farm, 183

Harris's store, 186

Haskell, Frank: death of, 203; on Meade's temperament and appearance, 16, 49, 54–55; on

officers lunching, Gettysburg, 51; on Pickett's Charge, 53–54; on Pleasonton, 34

Hatcher's Run, 259, 260, 278

Hatcher's Run, Battle of, 267–68

Hattaway, Herman, 56, 57, 66

Haupt, Herman: Gettysburg, 34; on Lee's movements, eve of Gettysburg, 21–22; on Meade, 2; on Meade's decision not to pursue Lee, 63–64

Haw's Shop, 194–95

Hay, John, 77

Hays, Alexander, 43, 51

Hays, William, 54, 62, 74

Henagan, John, 187

Henagan's Redoubt, 187–88

Hennessy, John J., 106

Hess, Earl, 103, 106, 147, 202, 236, 243, 257, 278

Heth, Henry, 27, 249; Bristoe Station, 93; Globe Tavern, 248; Spotsylvania Court House, 162; the Wilderness, 130, 133

Hewson, Addinell, 6

Hickory Hill, 216–17

Hicksford Raid, 263

High Bridge, 282, 283–84, 285

Hill, A. P., 21, 181, 229; Amissville, 91; Appomattox Campaign, 277; Bristoe Station, 93, 95; death of, 279; Gettysburg, 27, 40; Mine Run, 102, 104; New Hope Church, 102; Petersburg, 220; Ream's Station, second battle, 249; Weldon Railroad, 228; the Wilderness, 129, 130, 131, 136, 140, 147

"Historicus," 118

Hoffman, John S., 195

Holland, Henry, 86

Hood, John Bell, 8, 251

Hooker, Joseph: appointment to command Army, 10, 11; corps commanders meeting, 12–14; management style of, 11; Meade on, 11; plan for Chancellorsville, 12; proposed replacement for Meade, 116–17; secrecy of, 11, 298; Sickles's and Butterfield's influence over, 34; transfers command to Meade, 16, 18; troubled command of, 13–14; woundings of, 8, 12

Horn, John, 248

Howard, Oliver O., 19, 291; Gettysburg, 27, 28, 30, 31, 34–35, 44, 46; on lack of supplies, 70; performance at Gettysburg, 33–34; post-Chancellorsville commanders' meeting, 12–13; post-Gettysburg commanders' meetings, 61, 62, 73–74

Howe, Albion Parris, 116

Howe, Thomas, 219

Hsieh, Wayne Wei-siang, 114, 207

Hughes Crossroads, 194

Humphreys, Andrew: appointed commander of 2nd Corps, 264; Appomattox Campaign, 273, 278, 280, 283, 284, 285, 286, 287; assigned